Foundations
of Marketing

Foundations of Marketing

SIXTH CANADIAN EDITION

M. DALE Beckman
UNIVERSITY OF VICTORIA

DAVID L. Kurtz
UNIVERSITY OF ARKANSAS

LOUIS E. Boone
UNIVERSITY OF SOUTH ALABAMA

DRYDEN

Harcourt Brace & Company, Canada

Toronto Montreal Fort Worth New York Orlando
Philadelphia San Diego London Sydney Tokyo

Canadian Cataloguing in Publication Data

Beckman, M. Dale, 1934–
    Foundations of marketing

6th Canadian ed.
Includes bibliographical references and index.
ISBN 0-03-923107-0

1. Marketing.   I. Kurtz, David L.   II. Boone, Louis E.
III. Title.

HF5415.B56 1997   658.8   C95-932932-3

Director of Product Development: Heather McWhinney
Acquisitions Editor: Ken Nauss
Projects Manager: Liz Radojkovic
Developmental Editor: Su Mei Ku
Editorial Assistant: Martina van de Velde
Director of Publishing Services: Jean Davies
Editorial Manager: Marcel Chiera
Supervising Editor: Semareh Al-Hillal
Editorial Assistant: Stacey Roderick
Production Manager: Sue-Ann Becker
Production Co-ordinator: Sheila Barry
Copy Editor: Claudia Kutchukian
Photo Research: Patricia Buckley
Cover Design: Sonya V. Thursby/Opus House
Interior Design: Sonya V. Thursby/Opus House (based on interior design of fifth edition by Robert Garbutt Productions)
Typesetting and Assembly: Compeer Typographic Services Limited
Technical Art: Matthew Beck
Printing and Binding: Metropole Litho Inc.

Cover Art and Detail on Part Openers: Jay Belmore, *Man Making Bridge With Puzzle Pieces.* © Jay Belmore/The Image Bank. Reproduced with permission.

This book was printed in Canada.

1 2 3 4 5   01 00 99 98 97

To Bobby, Wendy, and Terry — the original support group

Preface

The goal of this sixth Canadian edition of *Foundations of Marketing* is to provide a contemporary, comprehensive, and readable perspective on marketing. It builds on the strengths of the past five editions, which have been acclaimed by instructors and students for the interesting and relevant way in which the topic of marketing is described.

The spirit of contemporary realism has been applied throughout. The book deals with current marketing practices and provides an up-to-date perspective on the literature of marketing. Text references and bibliographical information reflect current marketing thinking. For example, contemporary marketing applications such as large-format specialty stores, multilevel marketing, and retailing through the Internet are discussed. As another example, Chapter 18, "Marketing Communications Applications," has been increased substantially and includes new material on such topics as message themes, direct marketing, publicity, celebrity marketing, and role model marketing. These are but a few examples of the way in which each chapter presents germane theory and practice.

Foundations of Marketing, Sixth Canadian Edition, is comprehensive. It covers all aspects of marketing as thoroughly as the past editions. Through careful editing of nontextual material and supplying cases separately in a *Case Supplement*, it has been possible to produce an attractive four-colour, slimmer volume at a price advantage to the student. Users will find *Foundations* easier to read and to study because of the revamped layout and organization of the material.

Readability has been a hallmark of the previous five editions of *Foundations of Marketing*. The same lively, readable style can be found in this edition. Past students have often commented that the reading/study experience has been facilitated by the engaging writing style. Interest is maintained through the use of many topical business illustrations related to the theoretical discussion. These are often found in "Applying the Concepts" boxes that appear in most chapters. Moreover, at the end of each box, a question is posed to the students as a way of ensuring that the ideas discussed up to that point, and which are being illustrated in the box, have been understood.

This edition continues to pay special attention to the topics of marketing strategy, marketing planning, and the marketing mix in a manner that is consistent, clear, and pedagogically appropriate. It uses the terms *strategy, marketing planning*, and *marketing mix* in such a way that their meaning is consistent and unclouded. We avoid using these terms until they can be introduced and developed properly. The strategy of a firm, of which marketing strategy is an essential component, is shown to be paramount. A marketing plan is required to implement the marketing strategy, and the marketing mix is part of the marketing plan.

The marketing mix becomes a more powerful concept if taught after students have become familiar with the various introductory concepts. Too often, it is introduced very early, and simplified so that students miss its importance. By tying its exposition to the concepts of strategy and marketing planning, it can be made much more meaningful. This edition not only introduces the concept of synergy between the elements of the mix, but expands this to show that customer sensitivity, convenience, and service have taken a very important role in the development of marketing planning and the marketing mix.

Chapter 21 has been substantially rewritten under the new title "Total Customer Satisfaction in Marketing." Starting with the marketing planning process introduced in Chapter 3, Chapter 21 shows the importance of establishing a process of reviewing the results of the marketing effort and the importance of striving for total customer satisfaction in marketing planning. The concept of benchmarking and its application in producing customer satisfaction and company competitiveness is also developed.

Most business decisions occur in an international context. Consistent with this idea, the various chapters of the text include international considerations as a regular part of the textual discussion. For example, in Part Five: Pricing, the discussion is extended from the traditional considerations in the domestic market to the special considerations required when setting prices internationally. In addition to this coverage, an entire chapter — Chapter 19 — has been included that discusses the important topic of international marketing.

Another new feature of the sixth edition of *Foundations of Marketing* is the section "Interactive Summary and Discussion Questions" that concludes each chapter. This section is based on the process of reviewing material to be learned, and then answering questions based on the review to ensure understanding. Chapter material is summarized, and then the student is asked to answer one or more thought-provoking questions that go beyond the summary. The questions challenge the student to demonstrate mastery of the concepts of the chapter.

A complete educational package is also available. It includes:

- **Case Supplement** Cases are now provided separately in a *Case Supplement* to meet the needs of instructors and students. By providing them in this way, cases can be more readily kept current and fresh.

- **Computerized Test Bank** Prepared by Scott Fraser and Mike LeRoy, the new *Computerized Test Bank* has been extensively rewritten with an increased number of challenging multiple-choice questions that instructors can select from.

- **Thinking Like a Marketer: A Canadian Learning Guide** This is a new learning tool that helps to bring marketing concepts and theories to life for students. Containing real-life marketing issues and events, with exercises and working spaces, this workbook is designed to enhance students' understanding. Packaged with the workbook is a disk containing interactive multiple-choice questions that give students a fun and enjoyable way of learning marketing.

- **Instructor's Manual** Formatted on disk and easy to use, the new *Instructor's Manual* has been completely rewritten with learning outcomes, teaching tips, computer applications problems, and video cases.

- **Video Cases** These high-quality and relevant real-life videos are an outstanding enhancement to the teaching/learning process. Matching video cases are included in each chapter of the *Instructor's Manual*. They show students how professional marketers actually meet the changes of the marketplace. The twenty videos, in half-inch VHS format, are available to adopters at no cost.

- **Full-Colour Overhead Transparencies** This innovative component consists of 250 full-colour transparency acetates. All of the transparencies are described in detail in accompanying transparency notes.

- **Marketing Disk** This contains complete programs for the computer applications problems in the *Instructor's Manual*. It is available free to adopters for use with any IBM-compatible computer.

ACKNOWLEDGEMENTS

There are many people who have made a significant contribution to the development of this book. Special thanks go to the authors and researchers of the cases. Case writing makes an invaluable contribution to the teaching and learning process.

    Reviewers also added greatly to the substance of the book. Many colleagues have offered suggestions for improvements. Our thanks go to:

Harold Baerthel	Centennial College
Jack Brown	Georgian College of Applied Art and Technology
Ted Brown	Mount Royal College
Wayne Carlson	Southern Alberta Institute of Technology
Fred Crane	Dalhousie University
Simon Curwen	Ryerson Polytechnic University
Jack Dart	University of Saskatchewan
Dwight Dyson	Centennial College
Jim Forbes	University of British Columbia
Mary Foster	Ryerson Polytechnic University
Scott Fraser	University of British Columbia
Dan Gardiner	University of British Columbia
Ted Goddard	Conestoga College
James Graham	University of Calgary
Clark Green	Lethbridge University
Kristi Harrison	Centennial College
George Jacob	British Columbia Institute of Technology
Rob Jakes	Saskatchewan Institute of Applied Science and Technology
Knud Jensen	Ryerson Polytechnic University
Robert Kelly	University of British Columbia
Gordon Kennedy	Centennial College
Paul Larson	University of Alberta
Gordon Lee	Kwantlen College
Mike LeRoy	University of British Columbia
John Lille	Centennial College
Paulette Padanyi	Ryerson Polytechnic University
Mike Pearl	Centennial College
Art Pierce	Ryerson Polytechnic University
John Rigby	University of Saskatchewan
Marvin Ryder	McMaster University
Terry Seawright	McMaster University

Jerry Smith	Humber College
Ravi Tangri	Saint Mary's University
Vivian Vaupshas	McGill University
Lynn Voss	Kwantlen College
Ann Walker	Ryerson Polytechnic University
Keith Wallace	Kwantlen College
Peter Yannopoulos	Brock University

Many people work very diligently to bring a book to the marketplace and to keep it there. Special appreciation goes to the marketing representatives of Harcourt Brace for their strong support and representation over the numerous editions of the book. We also acknowledge the hard work of professionals at Harcourt Brace for their efforts in the book's development and production. In particular, our thanks to Su Mei Ku, who competently handled the development with patience, good spirit, and diplomacy. We also recognize the contributions of Ken Nauss, Marcel Chiera, Semareh Al-Hillal, and Martina van de Velde.

M. Dale Beckman	David L. Kurtz	Louis E. Boone
Professor and Head,	Department Head and	Professor of Business
International Programs	R.A. and Vivian Young	Administration
Faculty of Business	Chairholder	University of South
University of Victoria	University of Arkansas	Alabama
Victoria, British Columbia	Fayetteville, Arkansas	Mobile, Alabama

A Note from the Publisher

Thank you for selecting *Foundations of Marketing*, Sixth Canadian Edition, by M. Dale Beckman, David L. Kurtz, and Louis E. Boone. The authors and publisher have devoted considerable time and care to the development of this book. We appreciate your recognition of this effort and accomplishment.

We want to hear what you think about *Foundations of Marketing*. Please take a few minutes to fill in the stamped reader reply card at the back of the book. Your comments and suggestions will be valuable to us as we prepare new editions and other books.

Brief Contents

Contents

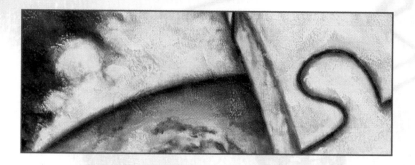

The fundamental philosophy of marketing is that an organization should orient itself to serve the customer's needs. Part One of *Foundations of Marketing* shows why marketing must identify and respond to these needs. These chapters also provide essential definitions and explain some of the basic concepts on which marketing is based. As well, the relationship of marketing to society at large is explored.

CHAPTER 1

The Nature of Marketing

CHAPTER OBJECTIVES

1. To define marketing and describe its primary nature.
2. To show how marketing bridges the gap between producer and consumer.
3. To outline the functions of marketing.
4. To demonstrate the scope of marketing.
5. To contrast activities in each of the three orientations of business in the marketing domain.
6. To position marketing as one of the basic business functions.

INTRODUCTION

All business organizations, whether a farmer's roadside vegetable stand, a student-run painting business, or a software manufacturer, must do marketing to survive. This also pertains to not-for-profit organizations such as a church or the United Way. This book shows why marketing is so essential and provides an understanding of the basic marketing concepts.

Marketing has to do with matching producers' output to consumers' activities. As a consumer, you know that sometimes this is done very well, and other times not. Generally, this matching process results in a continuous flow of goods and services for consumers, and the economic activity that maintains profitable business and employment.

The idea of matching producers' output to consumers' activities sounds less complicated than it really is. There are many product and even company failures, and often people cannot seem to find the product that really satisfies their needs. Poor marketing frequently causes these problems. The cause of poor marketing is usually a lack of focus on customers. Peter Drucker, an expert on business management, says

> If we want to know what a business is we have to start with its purpose. And its purpose must lie outside the business itself. In fact, it must lie in society since a business enterprise is an organ of society. *There is one valid definition of business purpose: to create a customer.*[1]

Serving the needs of customers is what business should be all about. A good example is the well-known philosophy of Federal Express, which is to strive for 100 percent customer satisfaction and on-time delivery. This philosophy has made Federal Express the leader in its field. Marketing is the business function that interprets customer needs to the rest of the organization and brings the resulting offerings of the firm to the consumer.

There is a gap between producer and consumer that marketing bridges. The components of this gap are possession, wants or needs, perspective, space, and time. Consider the gap between a producer of a car stereo system and a university student whose car stereo works but is not especially good:

- *Possession.* The producer has specific goods and services to sell. The consumer has some money to spend, and there are a great variety of alternatives.
- *Wants/needs.* The producer needs to make sales to fulfil the purposes of the business. The consumer has functional needs (e.g., to listen to music) and symbolic needs (e.g., a system that fulfils the need for prestige.)
- *Perspective.* The producer believes that the features of its products are good. Various consumers have their own criteria for the characteristics of a good car stereo. These two perspectives may not match.
- *Space.* Products are often produced thousands of kilometres from the point of purchase. Consumers expect to find them where they shop.
- *Time.* Business must plan production cycles so that the system will be ready and available whenever the customer decides to buy.

A careful study of customer needs marketing and the rest of the organization can bridge the gap between producer and consumer. This is done through eight **marketing functions**: *buying, selling, transporting, storing, grading, financing, risk taking,* and *information collection and dissemination.* These are inherent to a greater or lesser degree in all marketing transactions. They may be shifted to various members of the channel, or to the customer, but they cannot be eliminated.

> **marketing functions**
> Buying, selling, transporting, storing, grading, financing, risk taking, and information collection and dissemination.

Figuratively speaking, management asks itself the following questions:

1. What problems do our customers or potential customers have that our products or services can solve better than those of other suppliers?
2. Who has these problems?
3. What are the particular circumstances, actual or potential, that would suggest modifications in our products, prices, distribution, or communication?

The idea of thinking in terms of providing *solutions to problems* is a very useful one in marketing. It helps considerably in identifying new markets, finding new products for existing customers, finding new customers for existing products, and, very importantly, discovering potential and possibly unsuspected competition.[2] These concepts provide the basis for marketing planning.

THE ESSENCE OF MARKETING

The essence of marketing is the **exchange process**. This is the means by which two or more parties give something of value to one another to satisfy felt needs.[3] In many cases, the item is a tangible good, such as a newspaper, a calculator, or a pair of shoes. In other cases, intangible services, such as a car wash, transportation, or a concert performance, are exchanged for money. In still other instances, funds or time donations may be offered to political candidates, a Red Cross office, or a church or synagogue.

> **exchange process**
> The means by which two or more parties give something of value to one another to satisfy felt needs.

The marketing function is both simple and direct in subsistence-level economies. For example, assume that a primitive society consists solely of Person A and Person B. Assume also that the only elements of their standard of living are food, clothing, and shelter. The two live in adjoining caves on a mountainside. They

■ **Be Sure to Know Your Market**

weave their own clothes and tend their own fields independently. They are able to subsist even though their standard of living is minimal.

Person A is an excellent weaver but a poor farmer, while Person B is an excellent farmer but a poor weaver. In this situation, it would be wise for each to specialize in the line of work that he or she does best. The net result would then be a greater total production of both clothing and food. In other words, specialization and division of labour will lead to a production surplus. But neither A nor B is any better off until they *trade* the products of their individual labour, thereby creating the exchange process.

Exchange is the origin of marketing activity. In fact, marketing has been described as "the process of creating and resolving exchange relationships."[4] When there is a need to exchange goods, the natural result is marketing effort on the part of the people involved.

As Wroe Alderson, a leading marketing theorist, has said, "It seems altogether reasonable to describe the development of exchange as a great invention which helped to start primitive man on the road to civilization."[5]

While the cave-dweller example is simplistic, it does point up the essence of the marketing function. Today's complex society may have a more complicated exchange process, but the basic concept is the same: production is not meaningful until a system of marketing has been established. Perhaps the adage "Nothing happens until somebody sells something"[6] sums it up best.

Marketing Defined

Ask five people to define marketing and you will likely get five different definitions. Most of them will be too limited, and wrong. Because of the visibility of personal selling and advertising, many respondents will say that marketing is selling or that marketing is advertising. But marketing is much more comprehensive than these narrow perspectives.

Marketing can be defined at a micro (or organizational) level, or from a macro (or societal) perspective. At a micro level, we can think of marketing as "the sum total of activities that keep a company focussed on its customers and, with good management and a little luck, ensure that the company's offerings are valued by its customers."[7] More formally, the definition of **marketing** is "*the process of planning and executing the conception, pricing, promotion, and distribution of ideas, goods, and services to create exchanges that satisfy individual and organizational objectives.*"[8]

This definition implies much more than you may at first think. The rest of this book is required to elaborate it. The definition applies to not-for-profit as well as business organizations. Note also that the definition is specific in pointing out that exchanges created by marketing activities must satisfy individual (consumer) objectives and organizational objectives. Professional marketers have found that success comes about much more easily when planning starts with a thorough analysis of customers and their needs. This is such an important idea, with so many ramifications, that we will spend the next section elaborating it.

On the macro level, marketing is defined as *the development of systems that direct an economy's flow of goods and services from producers to consumers*. This definition shows that, when added up, all marketing activities produce a flow of goods and services that are distributed throughout society. Thus, at a macro level, marketing makes the economy tick.

> **marketing**
> The process of planning and executing the conception, pricing, promotion, and distribution of ideas, goods, and services to create exchanges that satisfy individual and organizational objectives.

Three Types of Business Organization

Most companies have an orientation that fits one of the following three categories: *product-oriented*, *sales-oriented*, or *market-oriented*.[9]

PRODUCT AND/OR PRODUCTION ORIENTATION

In firms with a **product orientation**, the emphasis is on the product itself rather than on the consumer's needs. For the production-oriented firm, the dominant considerations in product design are those of ease or cheapness of production. In either case, market considerations are ignored or de-emphasized. Firms stress production of goods or services,[10] then look for people to purchase them. The prevailing attitude of this type of firm is that a good product will sell itself. Such a strategy is very limiting, for it assumes that the producer's tastes and values are the same as those of the market. Often a firm does not consider changing from this narrow approach until it runs into trouble.

> **product orientation**
> A focus on the product itself rather than the consumer's needs.

SALES ORIENTATION

A **sales orientation** is an improvement on a product orientation. The firm is still quite product-oriented, but it recognizes that the world will not beat a path to its door to purchase its products. Therefore, the firm focusses its marketing efforts on developing a strong sales force to convince consumers to buy. "Get the customer to fit the company's offerings" could be a motto of such a sales-oriented strategy. Thus, to be successful, what you really need is an aggressive, high-powered sales organization and advertising program. Clearly, good, persuasive communication is an important part of a marketing plan. However, selling is only one component of marketing. As marketing expert Theodore Levitt has pointed out, "Marketing is as different from selling as chemistry is from alchemy, astronomy from astrology, chess from checkers."[11]

> **sales orientation**
> Focussing on developing a strong sales force to convince consumers to buy whatever the firm produces.

MARKET ORIENTATION

Many firms have discovered that the product and sales orientations are quite limiting. They have found that it makes a great deal of sense to *pay careful attention to understanding customer needs and objectives and then make the business serve the interests of the customer rather than trying to make the customer buy what the business wants to produce.* A primary task under a **market orientation**, then, is to develop ways to research and understand various aspects of the market.

A market-oriented strategy can produce any of the good effects of the other two orientations, but it avoids their drawbacks. In addition, it can identify new opportunities and avoid nasty surprises as changes occur in the market.

In a market-oriented firm, the marketing function is not something that is tagged on at the end of the process. It takes a primary role right from the beginning of the planning process. A marketing orientation represents a set of processes touching on all aspects of the company.[12] It involves much more than just understanding the customer. Three characteristics make a company market-driven:

1. Information on all important buying influences permeates every corporate function. This means that detailed market knowledge is not the domain of the marketing department alone. A company can be market-oriented only if it completely understands its markets and the people who decide whether to buy its products or services. Customer information must reach all aspects of the organization, including R & D, engineering, manufacturing, and accounting.
2. Strategic and tactical decisions are made interfunctionally and interdivisionally. Functions and divisions of an organization will inevitably have conflicting objectives that mirror distinctions in cultures and modes of operation. The customer-oriented company possesses mechanisms for discovering these differences, encouraging candid discussion, and finding trade-offs that reconcile the various points of view. A good understanding of market needs serves as the basis for final decisions.
3. Divisions and functions make well–co-ordinated decisions and execute them with a sense of commitment. Marketing should not send a set of specifications to R & D, which then sends finished blueprints and designs to manufacturing, and so on. Joint discussion between functions makes the final company strategy much more relevant to the needs of the market.

The Marketing Concept: A Guiding Philosophy for Marketing

The foregoing discussion provides a guiding philosophy for the marketing aspects of organization strategy. This market orientation, commonly known as the **marketing concept**, may be succinctly defined as *an organization-wide focus on providing chosen groups of customers with products that bring optimal satisfaction so as to achieve long-run profits.*

The words "long-run profits" differentiate the marketing concept from policies aimed at short-run profit maximization. The marketing concept, as a philosophy, provides the best chance for success in today's environment. The authors contend that marketing efforts should reflect ethical business practices and be congruent with the needs of society. The focus on consumer needs and the longer-run perspective encourages this.

The marketing concept also requires careful analysis and monitoring of competitors' actions. A company practising the marketing concept holds basic assumptions in relation to its competitors. Management believes that the firm has the capability to compete, that it is not at the mercy of its competitors and is a force of its own. At the same time, it recognizes that the firm has to be up-to-date on its competitors' actions to make sure that it does not lose its competitive edge. An organi-

---

market orientation
Paying careful attention to understanding customer needs and objectives, then making the business serve the interests of the customer rather than trying to make the customer buy what the business wants to produce.

marketing concept
An organization-wide focus on providing chosen groups of customers with products that bring optimal satisfaction so as to achieve long-run profits.

APPLYING THE CONCEPTS

Thinking Globally

A principle tenet of this book is that business is best viewed as an international activity. The principles of marketing outlined in the following chapters should be applied to Canadian *and* global markets. Peter Drucker says it well:

> Increased participation in the world economy has become the key to domestic growth and prosperity.
>
> The experience of four decades teaches that protection does not protect. In fact, it shows that protection hastens decline.
>
> That it breeds complacency, inefficiency and cartels has been known since the days of Adam Smith. The counter argument has always been that it protects jobs. The evidence strongly suggests it does not even do that.
>
> The world economy has become too vital for a country not to have a world-economy policy. Managed trade is a delusion of grandeur. Outright protectionism can do only harm. But simply trying to thwart protectionism is not enough.
>
> What is needed is an active, indeed aggressive, policy that gives the demands, opportunities and dynamics of the global economy priority over those of the domestic scene.
>
> Will a proposed domestic move advance competitiveness and participation in the world economy? The answer to this question determines the right economic policy and business decisions.

Source: Peter Drucker, quoted in John Raymond, "Worth Repeating," *The Globe and Mail* (February 7, 1994).

Explain how this idea is congruent with the philosophy of market orientation.

zation that views itself as dominated by others is incapable of taking new initiatives even if it identifies major unsatisfied customer needs.[13]

The Importance of Marketing

This discussion shows that marketing is a core business discipline. It is important to people, companies, and the economy.

• *Importance to people.* Each of us responds to marketing every time we buy a product. Marketing efforts attempt to match goods and services to our needs. An infinite variety of offerings is available, and marketers try to tell us about these offerings. Marketing communications permeate the media and, sometimes, our consciousness. Marketing costs amount to between 40 and 60 percent of everything we buy.

Jobs in marketing are also numerous. Marketing-related occupations account for 25 to 33 percent of the jobs in our country — a good reason to study marketing. Starting salaries rank high, and marketing positions often lead to the most senior company posts.

■ **How Not to Attract Customers**

"I don't know if I agree with your method of bringing customers into the store!"

Source: PA Graphics. Reprinted by permission of Arnoldo DeAlmeida.

- *Importance to companies.* As the main revenue-producing function, marketing is essential to the continuation of a firm. Without sales, the firm dies. As sales increase, fixed costs are spread over more units. This increases profitability, and enables firms to compete through lower prices.
- *Importance to the economy.* The benefits brought to people and firms make marketing a vital component of the economy. The more efficient the marketing process, the higher a nation's standard of living.

The study of marketing is therefore truly relevant for students. Furthermore, working in marketing is fascinating because it requires considerable initiative and creativity. Many find great satisfaction in such work. It is little wonder that marketing is now a popular field of academic study.

Marketing Is for Not-for-Profit Organizations, Too

Nonbusiness organizations like art galleries, churches, and charities have also found that they can benefit from applying marketing principles. For instance, the Canadian government is one of Canada's leading advertisers, spending approximately $44 million annually on advertising. World Vision and other charitable groups have developed considerable marketing expertise, some police departments have used marketing-inspired strategies to improve their image with the public, and we are all familiar with the marketing efforts employed in political campaigns. Most arts organizations now employ a director of marketing. Chapter 20 discusses marketing in not-for-profit settings more fully.

APPLYING THE CONCEPTS

Quality in Marketing Comes from Knowing Customers

Darrel Rhea is president of Cheskin & Masten, a design research consulting firm in California. These excerpts are from a speech at a design forum organized by Spencer Francy Peters Inc. of Toronto.

The focus in marketing now is knowing customers — not thinking about them as data, but really knowing them as actual people. That means knowing what they think, feel, and do, and recognizing in your gut what they will and will not like.

One technique that tries to get at this is what we [in the product research business] call an "identity audit." I'll describe how it works in the context of the teenage market.

With an identity audit, we use a variety of techniques. We read a lot about people who have written about teens. We review all the advertising that goes to teens; we tear it out of papers and put it up on walls, and try to look for patterns.

We do expert interviews; every year, twice a year, we're interviewing 50 experts on the teen markets. So we're talking to the owners of Viacom and MTV. We're talking to people who are making millions of dollars successfully aiming at teenagers and observing teenagers, and seeing what they say is going on.

Then we go out and we talk to teens; we bring a teenager in and we bring in his best friend with him, which encourages honesty and more openness. We know a lot about those teenagers now because their friends have been interviewed. They have brought in high-school year books and identified where they fit within the teen hierarchy: the dweebs, the nerds, the geeks or the cool kids.

Finally, we do what we call visual research. We actually take cameras and film — four rolls of film and a camera — and we send it to hundreds of teenagers. When we given them the cameras, we just say: "Take pictures of your lives." That's the only direction; send us the undeveloped film back. We get tens of thousands of images several times a year, put it on the computer database, put it on a CD-ROM and analyze it, and look for the patterns.

By getting this visual database, we can see kids from their own perspective. We get into their lives in a very, very powerful way.

Teenagers are always either eating or talking on the phone. You don't really get the impact of that until you see 10,000 pictures of kids eating or talking on the phone. Their bedrooms represent their aspirations. This represents who they want to be. To be able to see that and understand how the teen segments show up in that setting is very interesting.

Source: Darrel Rhea, "The Nosy Art of Knowing Customers," *The Globe and Mail* (April 26, 1994), p. B28.

How is the marketing concept illustrated in this methodology?

■ KEY TERMS

marketing functions	product orientation	market orientation
exchange process	sales orientation	marketing concept
marketing		

Here, human human human...

cat O Rama 94 ● metro toronto zoo

Most people in the Toronto area know about the existence of the not-for-profit Metropolitan Toronto Zoo. However, for the zoo to continue to educate people about animals and help preserve species, it must continue to attract former patrons and create interest in those who have never been to the zoo. Advertisements for new exhibits such as "Cat O Rama" let former patrons know there is something new to see and attempt to draw new zoo patrons.

■ INTERACTIVE SUMMARY AND DISCUSSION QUESTIONS

1. The gap between producer and consumer has the following components: possession, wants/needs, perspective, space, and time. Choose a product and explain how marketing could be said to be "the actualizing force that bridges the gap between producer and consumer."

2. The marketing gap components are satisfied by one or more of the marketing functions. Match functions with gap components in the columns that follow.

possession	buying
wants/needs	selling
perspective	transporting
space	storing
time	grading
	financing
	risk taking
	information collection and dissemination

3. The exchange process is the means by which two or more parties give something of value to one another to satisfy felt needs. Explain how this is the core of all marketing activity.

4. Marketing is *"the process of planning and executing the conception, pricing, promotion, and distribution of ideas, goods, and services to create exchanges that satisfy individual and organizational objectives."*[14] Explain why the definition mentions ideas, goods, and services.

5. In a product-oriented firm, the emphasis is on the product itself rather than on the consumer's needs. Give an example of such a firm, and explain the limitations of this approach.

6. A sales-oriented firm is still quite product-oriented, but it focusses its marketing efforts on developing a strong sales force to convince consumers to buy. Is this not what most companies need?

7. A market-oriented firm tries to understand customer needs, and then makes the business serve the interests of the customer. How can such an approach be a practical way of making money?

8. Relate the definition of marketing to the concept of the exchange process.

9. Identify the product and the consumer market in the following:
   a. Local cable television firm
   b. Vancouver Canucks hockey team
   c. Planned Parenthood
   d. Annual boat and sports equipment show in local city auditorium
   e. Regional shopping mall
10. Explain the effect of a market orientation on products offered to the market, and on marketing planning.

CHAPTER 2

The Environment for Marketing Decisions

CHAPTER OBJECTIVES

1. To identify the environmental factors that affect marketing decisions.
2. To explain the major legislative framework that regulates marketing activities.
3. To introduce three categories of competition faced by marketers and outline the issues to consider in developing a competitive strategy.
4. To show how the economic environment has a bearing on marketing planning.
5. To illustrate the association between marketing plans and the technological environment.
6. To demonstrate how the socio-cultural environment influences marketing decisions.

Bowing to pressure from Greenpeace, the British-based unit of Scott Paper Co. has cancelled all contracts for pulp from companies operating in British Columbia's Clayoquot Sound.

MacMillan Bloedel Ltd., the forest company with the largest operation in that controversial region, said it sells about 3 percent of its market pulp production to Scott Ltd., Britain's largest manufacturer of disposable tissue products, for about $4.6 million to $5.5 million (U.S.) a year at current prices.

Clayoquot logging — and clear-cutting in particular — has been the primary target of environmental activists' protests since the B.C. government decided last spring to allow logging in about 45 percent of the Sound, a still largely pristine area of old-growth forest on the west coast of Vancouver Island.

More than 800 protesters have been arrested at Clayoquot since that decision, most of them for blocking a MacMillan Bloedel logging road.

The groups have taken their high-profile, save-Clayoquot campaign to Europe, and Greenpeace, which released news of the Scott Ltd. contract cancellation, said it was about to launch an advertising campaign in Britain "linking Scott tissue with Canadian rain forest destruction."

Greenpeace was jubilant over Scott's decision. "Clear-cutting in Clayoquot Sound isn't good business," said Karen Mahon, a forest campaigner for Greenpeace Canada.

Scott Paper Ltd., the Vancouver-based Canadian arm of Scott Paper Co., says it has no need to follow the example of its British cousin. The Canadian company makes much of its own pulp from cottonwood trees grown on plantations, said president Robert Stewart, and what pulp it buys comes mainly from Fletcher Challenge Canada Ltd., which is not involved in Clayoquot Sound.

Scott of Britain said it is assessing the operations of all of its pulp suppliers and is "giving priority to those which demonstrate the best environmental practices overall."

The company said it began its assessments in 1991, setting standards for emissions from suppliers' mills. The current study, focussing on forestry practices, should be completed in the fall of 1995, it said.

MacMillan Bloedel says it expects the study to exonerate it of accusations of environmentally unfriendly logging practices. Consequently, "we don't view this as a cancellation," spokesman Scott Alexander said. Rather, "it is a suspension or a postponement until Scott can assure itself that our practices in Clayoquot Sound are up to world standard."[1]

INTRODUCTION

The changing environment is constantly creating and destroying business opportunities. MacMillan Bloedel has found that long-standing practices have now come under fire from a significant segment of the population. Values in the socio-cultural milieu have changed. MacMillan Bloedel's competitive position has weakened. Furthermore, political/legal decisions have also forced the company and the forestry industry to operate in a restricted manner. These are three of the environmental forces we will discuss in this chapter. Environmental forces cannot be controlled by the marketing decision-maker. However, it is essential that they be identified and analyzed, and that their bearing on marketing plans be carefully considered.

The environment for marketing decisions may be classified into five components: the *competitive* environment, the *political and legal* climate, the *economic* environment, the *technological* environment, and the *social and cultural* milieu. This is the structure upon which marketing decisions are made, as well as the frame of reference for marketing planning. Skilful environmental analysis is one of the major criteria for success in marketing planning. Figure 2.1 portrays this relationship.

The dynamic nature of the environment means that management at every level must continually re-evaluate marketing decisions and prepare for change. Even modest shifts in one or more of the environmental elements can alter the results of marketing decisions. For example, political/legal changes are now permitting the mass marketing of digital audio tape recorders, a relatively new technological advance. This situation could have profound effects on the marketing of compact disc players, as people will be able to play and record CD-quality music.

■ Figure 2.1 **Components of the Marketing Environment**

THE COMPETITIVE ENVIRONMENT

competitive environment
The interactive process that
occurs in the marketplace in which
competing organizations seek to
satisfy markets.

The interactive process that occurs in the marketplace in which competing organizations seek to satisfy markets is known as the **competitive environment**. Marketing decisions by an individual firm influence consumer responses in the marketplace; they also affect the marketing strategies of competitors. As a consequence, marketers must continually monitor and adjust to the marketing activities of competitors — their products, channels of distribution, prices, and communication efforts.

In a few instances, organizations enjoy a monopoly position in the marketplace. Utilities, such as natural gas, electricity, water, and cable television service, accept considerable regulation from government in such marketing-related activities as rates, service levels, and geographic coverage in exchange for exclusive rights to serve a particular group of consumers. However, such instances are relatively rare. In addition, portions of such traditional monopoly industries as telephone service have been deregulated in recent years, and telephone companies currently face competition in such areas as the sale of telephone receivers, some long-distance services, and installation and maintenance of telephone systems in larger commercial and industrial firms.

In many industries, the competition among firms is fierce. For example, consider the retail food industry. For supermarkets, the profit margin on most items is quite low. Therefore, to make an adequate return on investment a store must generate a high volume of sales. Supermarkets are thus very sensitive to fluctuations in sales caused by the actions of competitors. If one competitor advertises a sale on certain products, another will be inclined to match those sale prices. Or if a new store format (such as Loblaws superstores) is developed, it will be countered (as was done with Safeway's Food for Less outlets).

Types of Competition

Marketers face three types of competition. The most direct form of competition is inter-product competition, which is among marketers of similar products. Xerox photocopiers compete with models offered by Canon, Sharp, and Olivetti. Estée Lauder cosmetics face competition from Lancôme and Revlon. Competitors are as likely to be from abroad as from the local market.

A second type of competition is product-substitute competition, which is among products that can be substituted for one another. In the construction industry and in manufacturing, steel products by Stelco may compete with similar products made of aluminum by Alcan. Paper bags compete with bags made of plastic. In circumstances where a change such as a price increase or an improvement in the quality of a product occurs, demand for substitute products is directly affected.

The final type of competition is alternative-gratification competition. This involves all organizations that compete for the consumer's purchases. Traditional economic analysis views competition as a battle among companies in the same industry or among substitutable products and services. Marketers, however, accept the argument that *all* firms are competing for a limited amount of discretionary buying power. The Ford Festiva competes with a vacation in the Bahamas; the local live theatre centre competes with pay television and the Leafs, Blue Bombers, or Expos for the consumer's entertainment dollars.

Changes in the competitive environment can wipe out a product, or an entire business, in short order. Marketers must therefore continually assess the marketing strategies of competitors, as well as monitor international business developments. New product offerings with technological advances, price reductions, special promotions, or other competitive actions must be monitored in order to adjust the firm's marketing program in the light of such changes. Among the first purchasers of any new product are the product's competitors. Careful analysis of the product — its physical components, performance attributes, packaging, retail price, service requirements, and estimated production and marketing costs — allows competitors to forecast its likely competitive impact. If necessary, adjustments to current marketing procedures may take place as a result of the new market entry. The competitive environment is a fact of life for most marketers. They ignore it at their peril!

THE POLITICAL AND LEGAL CLIMATE

Before you play the game, learn the rules! It would be absurd to start playing a new game without first understanding the rules, yet some businesspeople exhibit a remarkable lack of knowledge about marketing's **political and legal climate** — *the laws and interpretation of laws that require firms to operate under competitive conditions and to protect consumer rights.* Ignorance of laws, ordinances, and regulations could result in fines, embarrassing negative publicity, and possibly civil damage suits.

It requires considerable diligence to develop an understanding of the legal framework of marketing. Numerous laws, often vague and legislated by a multitude of different authorities, characterize the legal environment for marketing decisions. Regulations affecting marketing have been enacted at the federal, provincial, and local levels as well as by independent regulatory agencies. Our existing legal framework was constructed on a piecemeal basis, often in response to a concern over current issues.

Canada has tended to follow a public policy of promoting a competitive marketing system. To maintain such a system, competitive practices within the system have been regulated. Traditionally, pricing and promotion have received the most legislative attention.

political and legal climate
The laws and interpretation of laws that require firms to operate under competitive conditions and to protect consumer rights.

Society's Expectations Create the Framework

We live in and desire a "free-enterprise society" — or do we? The concept of free enterprise is not clear, and has been gradually changing. At the turn of the century, the prevalent attitude was to let business act quite freely. As a result, it was expected that new products and jobs would be created and the economy would develop and prosper. Currently, the former communist countries are chaotically trying to make free enterprise develop their economies.

In North America, an uncontrolled approach provided great freedom for the scrupulous and the unscrupulous. Although many businesses sought to serve their target markets in an equitable fashion, abuses did occur. Figure 2.2 shows an example of dishonest marketing practices. Such advertisements were not unusual in the late 1800s and early 1900s. Advancing technology led to the creation of a multitude of products in many fields. Often the buying public did not have the expertise needed to choose among them.

With the increasing complexity of products, the growth of big, impersonal business, and the unfair or careless treatment of consumers by some firms, society's values changed. "Government should regulate business more closely," we said. Over

■ Figure 2.2 **An Example of Dishonest Advertising**

I CURE FITS!

When I say cure I do not mean merely to stop them for a time and then have them return again. I mean a radical cure. I have made the disease of FITS, EPILEPSY or FALLING SICKNESS a life-long study. I warrant my remedy to cure the worst cases. Because others have failed is no reason for not now receiving a cure. Send at once for a treatise and a Free Bottle of my infallible remedy. Give Express and Post Office.

H. G. ROOT, M.C., 183 PEARL ST., NEW YORK.

Source: S. Watson Dunn and Arnold M. Barban, *Advertising: Its Role in Modern Marketing*, 5th ed. (Hinsdale, IL: Dryden, 1986), p. 84. Reproduced with permission.

time, governments at the federal and provincial levels have responded to this shift: many laws have been passed to protect consumers, and to attempt to maintain a competitive environment for business. Large bureaucracies have grown with this increase in market regulation.

A significant development in the legal environment at the federal level was the consolidation in 1967 of consumer and business regulation programs into Consumer and Corporate Affairs Canada (now called Consumer and Commercial Relations Canada), and the appointment of a cabinet minister to represent these interests at the highest level. Previously these functions had been scattered among several different government departments. Following the lead of the federal government, most provinces have established consumer and corporate affairs branches and have generally streamlined the regulation of these sectors. Table 2.1 lists some of the significant federal legislation that affects business today. The list shows that regulation is quite comprehensive. A detailed study of provincial laws and regulations is beyond the scope of this text.

The Competition Act Sets the Standards

Of all the legislation mentioned in Table 2.1, the Competition Act (formerly the Combines Investigation Act) has the most significance in the legal environment for marketing decisions. The Act dates back to 1889, when it was enacted to protect the public interest in free competition. Since then, various revisions have occurred in response to changes in social values and in business practices (see Table 2.2).

The Act prohibits rather than regulates. That is, it does not spell out in detail the activities that industry may undertake, but greatly discourages certain activities through the threat of penal consequences.

The provisions of the Act fall into three main classes. Generally, they prohibit the following:

1. Combinations that prevent, or lessen unduly, competition in the production, purchase, sale, storage, rental, transportation, or supply of commodities, or in the price of insurance.

■ Table 2.1 **Legislation Administered by Consumer and Commercial Relations**

1. **Fully Administered by CCR**
   - Bankruptcy Act and Bankruptcy Rules
   - Boards of Trade Act
   - Canada Business Corporations Act
   - Canada Cooperative Associations Act
   - Canada Corporations Act
   - Competition Act
   - Companies' Creditors Arrangement Act
   - Consumer Packaging and Labelling Act
   - Copyright Act
   - Department of Consumer and Corporate Affairs Act
   - Electricity and Gas Inspection Act
   - Government Corporations Operation Act
   - Hazardous Products Act
   - Industrial Design Act
   - National Trade Mark and True Labelling Act
   - Patent Act
   - Pension Fund Societies Act
   - Precious Metals Marking Act
   - Public Servants Invention Act
   - Tax Rebate Discounting Act
   - Textile Labelling Act
   - Timber Marking Act
   - Trade Marks Act
   - Weights and Measures Act

2. **Administered Jointly with Other Departments**
   - Bills of Exchange Act (with Finance)
   - Canada Agricultural Products Standards Act (with Agriculture)
   - Canada Dairy Products Act (with Agriculture)
   - Fish Inspection Act (with Fisheries and Oceans)
   - Food and Drugs Act (with Health and Welfare)
   - Maple Products Industry Act (with Agriculture)
   - Shipping Conferences Exemption Act (with Transport)
   - Winding-up Act (with Finance)

2. Mergers, monopolies, or abuses of dominant market position that may operate to the detriment of the public.
3. Deceptive trade practices, including
   - Price discrimination
   - Predatory pricing
   - Certain promotional allowances
   - False or misleading representations, by any means, to promote the sale of a product or to promote a business
   - Unsubstantiated claims of performance
   - Misleading warranties or guarantees
   - Misrepresentation of the ordinary price
   - Misleading testimonials for a product or service
   - Double ticketing
   - Pyramid sales
   - Referral selling
   - Nonavailability of advertised specials

■ Table 2.2 **Evolution of Major Combines Legislation**

Date	Legislation	Reason for Legislation
1888	Combines Investigation Commission	To protect small businesses that suffered from monopolistic and collusive practices in restraint of trade by large manufacturers.
1889	Act for the Prevention and Suppression of Combinations Formed in Restraint of Trade	To declare illegal monopolies and combinations in restraint of trade.
1892	Above Act incorporated into the Criminal Code as Section 502	To make the above a criminal offence.
1900	Above Act amended	To make the Act effective, because as it stood, an individual would first have to commit an illegal act within the meaning of common law. Now, any undue restriction of competition became a criminal offence.
1910	Additional legislation passed to complement the Criminal Code and assist in the application of the Act	To stop a recent rush of mergers that had involved some 58 firms.
1919	The Combines and Fair Prices Act	To prohibit undue stockpiling of the "necessities of life" and prohibit the realization of exaggerated profits through "unreasonable prices."
1923	Combines Investigation Act	To consolidate combines legislation.
1952, 1960	Amendments to the above	
1976	Bill C-2; amendments	To include the service industry within the Act; to prohibit additional deceptive practices; to give persons the right to recover damages; to protect the rights of small businesses.
1986	Competition Act replaces Combines Investigation Act	To facilitate prosecutions of illegal combinations, mergers, and monopolies.

- Sale above advertised price
- Promotional contests

Despite the long history of the Combines Investigation Act, it proved remarkably powerless for prosecuting those who appeared to contravene either of the first two categories. The passage of the Competition Act to replace the Combines Investigation Act in June 1986 was an important change. Being classified as civil law, it corrected many problems in the strictly criminal, proof-beyond-a-reasonable-doubt approach of the old Combines Act. The new Competition Act also created a quasi-judicial body, known as the Competition Tribunal, to deal with matters via the civil route, and to make certain rules.

The first antimonopoly case after the new Competition Act was passed in 1986 was laid in 1989. NutraSweet Co., a subsidiary of U.S. chemical giant Monsanto, was charged with "abuse of dominance" (monopoly) in the Canadian market for aspartame, an artificial sweetener. The Bureau of Competition Policy said in a statement that NutraSweet, the sole supplier of aspartame in the United States, had captured more than 95 percent of the Canadian market. It claimed that NutraSweet demanded contracts with customers that precluded them from buying aspartame from anyone other than NutraSweet. Where exclusive contracts were not made, it claimed, NutraSweet insisted that customers give the company a chance to match the lowest prices charged by a competitor. The Bureau also charged NutraSweet with selling aspartame in Canada at a price below its acquisition cost or below its long-run average cost, with the result of substantially lessening competition.

NutraSweet issued a statement disagreeing with the Bureau's charges and believed that the issue would be decided in its favour.[2] However, a few months later, in a precedent-setting decision, the Competition Tribunal ruled that NutraSweet had effectively maintained monopolistic powers over the $25-million domestic aspartame market at the expense of potential competitors.

NutraSweet invented aspartame in the 1960s, but health testing delayed its introduction in many countries, including Canada, until the early 1980s. Soon afterward, NutraSweet's patents on the product began running out. In Canada, that took place in 1987. But in preparation, NutraSweet tied up its customers in exclusive contracts. Under the Tribunal's order, NutraSweet can no longer enforce existing contracts or sign new ones that make it the exclusive aspartame supplier. Nor can NutraSweet sign contracts that give it the right to match, in the future, a competing bid from another aspartame producer. As well, it has been prohibited from giving financial inducements on the sale of aspartame to companies that display NutraSweet's swirl insignia on their products. The director of the Bureau of Competition Policy called the Tribunal's ruling a significant sign that anticompetitive behaviour by companies will not be tolerated.[3]

Combines and Restraint of Trade

It is an offence to conspire, combine, agree, or arrange with another person to prevent or lessen competition unduly. The most common types of combination relate to price fixing, bid rigging, market sharing, and group boycotting of competitors, suppliers, or customers.

While this list covers much territory, it should be noted that in the following circumstances agreements between businesspersons are *not* unlawful:

1. Exchanging statistics
2. Defining product standards
3. Exchanging credit information
4. Defining trade terms
5. Co-operating in research and development
6. Restricting advertising

Consequently, it is permissible to report statistics centrally for the purpose of analyzing factors relating to industrial operation and marketing, as long as competition is not lessened unduly.

Mergers

Until the passage of the Competition Act in 1986, the law regarding mergers was largely ineffective. Important provisions in the new Act changed the situation. The Competition Tribunal has the power to stop mergers that substantially lessen competition without offering offsetting efficiency gains. Furthermore, the Tribunal must be notified in advance of large mergers (transactions larger than $35 million in sales or assets, and/or companies with combined revenues or assets of more than $400 million). This enables the review and modification of large, complex mergers that are difficult to reverse once consummated.

Deceptive Trade Practices

This is an extremely important section for marketing decision-makers, as it contains a number of directly related provisions. There are real teeth in the legislation, which the marketer should be aware of. Many successful prosecutions have been made under this section.

MISLEADING ADVERTISING

False statements of every kind (even in the picture on a package) made to the public about products or services are prohibited. For example, on November 15, 1986, First Choice Canadian Communications Corporation was convicted of making statements designed to mislead the public.[4] The company, in promoting the sale of subscriptions to its pay television service, claimed in newspaper advertisements that it would offer "all new movies every month." It was established that all new movies were provided for only the first three months of the service. The company was convicted and fined $15 000.

Often carelessness has been seen as responsible for the offence, and over the years, numerous advertisers have been prosecuted under the misleading-advertising provisions of the Combines Investigation Act. The fines meted out have been surprisingly small.

A greater level of determination to discourage deceptive advertising was signalled in 1983, when a fine levied against Simpsons-Sears sent shock waves through the entire advertising industry. Simpsons-Sears had been found guilty of advertising (through its catalogues and through newspapers, between 1975 and 1978) diamond rings that it claimed had been appraised at values significantly higher than those given by bona fide diamond appraisers consulted by Consumer and Corporate Affairs Canada. The fine imposed was $1 million — the highest ever levied under the Act. This set a precedent for vigorous prosecution of violaters of the Act.[5]

It is an offence to make unsubstantiated claims. Therefore, claims for a product are expected to be based on an adequate and proper test. Significantly, the onus is on whoever is making the claim to prove its efficacy, rather than on someone else to prove that the product is not as claimed. This reverse onus has been challenged before the courts under the Charter of Rights as being unconstitutional because it purports to put the onus on the accused to prove innocence, but the section was upheld. One example, and there are many, concerns Professional Technology of Canada, which was convicted in Edmonton on May 27, 1986, for promoting a gas-saving device that purported to offer 10 to 35 percent better mileage for cars. The company was fined $12 500.[6]

Another important facet of the misleading-advertising legislation concerns pricing. Many businesses seem to be unaware that much care needs to be taken when advertising comparative prices. It is, for example, considered misleading for a retailer to advertise a television set as follows:

Manufacturer's suggested list price	$680
On sale for	$500

if the manufacturer's suggested list price is not normally followed in this area of activity, and the usual price is around $600. Although the retailer *is* offering a bargain, the magnitude of the saving is not indicated accurately.

Retailers may try to get around this provision by choosing different comparative expressions, such as "regular price," "ordinarily $ . . . ," "list price," "hundreds sold at," "compare with," "regular value," and the like. But such tactics may nevertheless be problematic. For example, in Moncton, Best for Less (a division of Dominion Stores Ltd.) compared its price to a "why pay up to" price on in-store signs, and depicted the savings. It was established that items were available from competitors at lower prices than the "why pay up to" prices, and the firm was convicted and fined $7650.[7]

The businessperson who genuinely seeks to comply with this provision should ask two questions:

1. Would a reasonable shopper draw the conclusion from the expression used that the figure named by way of comparison is a price at which goods have been, are, or will ordinarily be sold?
2. If the answer is yes, would such a representation be true?

PRICING PRACTICES

It is an offence for a supplier to make a practice of discriminating in price among purchasers who are in competition with one another and who are purchasing like quantities of goods. Selling above the advertised price is also prohibited. Furthermore, the lowest of two or more prices must be used in the case of double-ticketed products. This latter provision has led to the development of easy-tear-off, two-price stickers, so that the sale price can readily be removed after a sale.

If you are a ski manufacturer and wish all ski shops to sell your skis at your suggested list price, can you force them to do so? No; it is an offence under the Act to deny supplies to an outlet that refuses to maintain the resale price. Thus, resale price maintenance is illegal, and a reseller is generally free to set whatever price is considered appropriate.

The Competition Act includes several other prohibitions, including ones against bait-and-switch selling, pyramid selling, and some types of referral selling and promotional contests.

Other Provisions of the Competition Act

PROTECTION AGAINST FOREIGN LAWS AND DIRECTIVES

Foreign companies doing business in Canada have sometimes been constrained by laws or judgements in their home country to the detriment of competition in Canada, or of opportunities for Canadian international trade. For example, Canadian subsidiaries of American companies have felt constrained by American law against doing business with countries the United States is having disputes with. This is theoretically no longer the case, because the Restrictive Trade Practices Commission (established under the anticombines provisions of the Competition Act) has been given power to rule against such interference in Canadian affairs. Practically, companies can still face strong external government pressures. For example, in 1996 the United States demanded that any foreign company that wished to do business with the United States must stop trading with Cuba.

CIVIL DAMAGES

In some situations, persons have the right to recover damages incurred as a result of a violation by others. This has profound implications. In some jurisdictions, not only can an individual sue for damages, but if he or she wins, that judgement will apparently serve as evidence for anyone else who has experienced a similar loss. Would this mean that a company could face the possibility of virtually every purchaser of a product claiming damages? Consider the millions of dollars involved for an automobile manufacturer, for example. To our knowledge, there have been no such cases in Canada.

Regulation, Regulation, and . . . More Regulation

So far, only some of the provisions from the most important federal Act have been cited. Table 2.1 shows that the federal government has a virtual sea of regulations that marketers must be aware of. Provincial governments are also very active in this area. Fortunately, each marketer need not be aware of all provisions, for many are specific to situation, time, place, and products.

In addition, provincial and municipal governments have other laws and by-laws that must be considered when developing marketing plans. For example, regulations vary from province to province concerning the amount and nature of advertising directed at children. Some other significant laws or regulations relate to bilingual specifications for packaging and labelling; there are special language requirements in Quebec.

From a broad point of view, the legal framework for relations between business and consumers is designed to encourage a competitive marketing system employing fair business practices. In many respects, various laws have resulted in more effective competition, although there are many who feel business is overregulated and others who think that more regulations are needed. There is little doubt that consumers in Canada are protected as well as or better than consumers in any other country in their dealings with sellers, especially regarding truth in advertising. It is clear that governments will continue to act in response to society's expectations of a fair and honest marketplace.

ECONOMIC CONDITIONS

economic environment
The factors in a region or country that affect the production, distribution, and consumption of its wealth. Key elements are monetary resources, inflation, employment, and productive capacity.

In addition to the competition and the political and legal climate, marketers must understand economic conditions and their impact on the organization. An economy with growing monetary resources, high employment, and productive power is likely to create strong demand for goods and services.

In a deteriorating **economic environment**, on the other hand, many firms experience a decline. However, such conditions may represent good news for other com-

Bilingualism on packages and labels is a legal requirement in Canada. Although an expensive mandate for companies, both English and French must appear. A&P Master Choice's attractive award-winning packages creatively integrate the two languages into the designs.

panies. As inflation and unemployment go up and production declines, consumer buying patterns shift. Flour millers note that flour sales go up. Automobile repairs and home improvements also increase. Greeting card firms report that consumers buy fewer gifts, but more expensive cards. Hardware stores show higher sales. The economic environment will considerably affect the way marketers operate.

Stages of the Business Cycle

Within the economic environment, there are fluctuations that tend to follow a cyclical pattern comprising three or four stages:

1. Recession (sometimes involves such factors as inflation and unemployment)
2. Depression[8]
3. Recovery
4. Prosperity

No marketer can disregard the economic climate in which a business functions, for the type, direction, and intensity of a firm's marketing strategy depend on it. In addition, the marketer must be aware of the economy's relative position in the business cycle and how it will affect the position of the particular firm. This requires the marketer to study forecasts of future economic activity.

Of necessity, marketing activity differs with each stage of the business cycle. During prosperous times, consumers are usually more willing to buy than when they feel economically threatened. For example, during a recent recession, personal savings climbed to high levels as consumers (fearing possible layoffs and other workforce reductions) cut back their expenditures for many products they considered nonessential. Marketers must pay close attention to the consumer's relative willingness to buy. The aggressiveness of one's marketing strategy and tactics often depends on current buying intentions. More aggressive marketing may be called for in periods of lessened buying interest, as when auto makers use cash rebate schemes to move inventories. Such activities, however, are unlikely to fully counteract cyclical periods of low demand.

While sales figures may experience cyclical variations, the successful firm has a rising sales trend line. Achieving this depends on management's ability to foresee, correctly define, and reach new market opportunities. Effective forecasting and research is only a partial solution. Marketers must also develop an intuitive awareness of potential markets. This requires that one be able to correctly delineate opportunities.[9]

Besides recession, two other economic subjects have been of major concern to marketers in recent years: inflation and unemployment.

Inflation

inflation
A rising price level resulting in reduced purchasing power for the consumer.

Inflation, which can occur during any stage in the business cycle, critically influences marketing strategy. Inflation is *a rising price level resulting in reduced purchasing power for the consumer.* A person's money is devalued (in terms of what it can buy). Traditionally, this circumstance has been more prevalent in countries outside North America. However, in the late 1970s and early 1980s, Canada experienced "double-digit inflation" (an inflation rate higher than 10 percent a year). Although the rate of inflation has declined considerably since then, experiences of inflation's effects have led to widespread concern over political approaches to controlling interest rates and stabilizing price levels, and over ways in which the individual can adjust to such reductions in the spending power of the dollar.

stagflation
High unemployment and a rising price level at the same time.

Stagflation is a word that has been coined to describe a peculiar brand of inflation that Canada experienced in the 1970s. It applies to a situation where an economy has *high unemployment and a rising price level at the same time.* Formulating effective strategies is particularly difficult under these circumstances.

Unemployment

Another significant economic problem that has affected the marketing environment in recent years is unemployment. The ranks of the unemployed — officially defined as people actively looking for work who do not have jobs — fluctuate as a result of the business cycle. Since 1966, the unemployment rate in Canada has ranged from 4.4 percent to 12.4 percent.

In the severe recession of the early 1980s, numerous businesses failed, production slowed, many factories ceased operation entirely, and thousands of workers found themselves out of work. The consequences of reduced income and uncertainty about future income were reflected in the marketplace in many ways. Similar conditions have been experienced in Canada during some of the 1990s. This is in sharp contrast to some Asian countries such as Korea, China, Malaysia, and Singapore. Canadian companies with an international outlook have benefited by concentrating on such prosperous markets while things have been slow at home.

GOVERNMENT TOOLS FOR COMBATTING INFLATION AND UNEMPLOYMENT

The government can attempt to deal with the twin economic problems of inflation and unemployment by using two basic approaches: fiscal policy and monetary policy. **Fiscal policy** concerns *the receipts and expenditures of government.* To combat inflation, an economy could reduce government expenditures, raise its revenue (primarily taxes), or do a combination of both. It could also use direct controls such as wage and price controls. **Monetary policy** refers to *the manipulation of the money supply and market rates of interest.* In periods of rising prices, monetary policy may dictate that the government take actions to decrease the money supply and raise interest rates, thus restraining purchasing power.

Both fiscal and monetary policy have been used in our battles against inflation and unemployment. Their marketing implications are numerous and varied. Higher taxes mean less consumer purchasing power, which usually results in declining sales for nonessential goods and services. However, some taxes that have been collected may find their way into various job-creation programs. Income earned from these will tend to be spent on basic goods and services. Lower federal expenditure levels make the government a less attractive customer for many industries. A lowered money supply means that less liquidity is available for potential conversion to purchasing power. High interest rates often lead to a significant slump in the construction and housing industries.

Both unemployment and inflation affect marketing by modifying consumer behaviour. Unless unemployment insurance, personal savings, and union supplementary unemployment benefits are sufficient to offset lost earnings, the unemployed individual has less income to spend in the marketplace. Even if the individual is completely compensated for lost earnings, his or her buying behaviour is likely to be affected. As consumers become more conscious of inflation, they are likely to become more price-conscious in general. This can lead to three possible outcomes, all important to marketers. Consumers can (1) elect to buy now in the belief that prices will be higher later (automobile dealers have often used this argument in their commercial messages); (2) decide to alter their purchasing patterns; or (3) postpone certain purchases.

Demarketing — Dealing with Shortages

Shortages — temporary or permanent — can be caused by several factors. A brisk demand may exceed manufacturing capacity or outpace the response time required to gear up a production line. Shortages may also be caused by a lack of raw materials, component parts, energy, or labour. Regardless of the cause, shortages require marketers to reorient their thinking.[10]

Demarketing, a term that has come into general use in recent years, refers to *the process of cutting consumer demand for a product, because the demand exceeds the level that can reasonably be supplied by the firm or because doing so will create a more favourable corporate image.* Some oil companies, for example, have publicized tips on how to cut gasoline consumption as a result of the gradual depletion of oil reserves. Utility companies have encouraged homeowners to install more insulation to lower heating bills. And growing environmental concerns have resulted in companies' discouraging demand for plastic packaging for their products.

Shortages sometimes force marketers to be allocators of limited supplies. This is in sharp contrast to marketing's traditional objective of expanding sales volume. Shortages require marketers to decide whether to spread a limited supply over all customers so that none are satisfied, or to back-order some customers so that others may be completely supplied. Shortages certainly present marketers with a unique set of marketing problems.

fiscal policy
The receipts and expenditures of government.

monetary policy
The manipulation of the money supply and market rates of interest.

demarketing
The process of cutting consumer demand for a product, because the demand exceeds the level that can reasonably be supplied by the firm or because doing so will create a more favourable corporate image.

TECHNOLOGY

technological environment
The applications of knowledge based on scientific discoveries, inventions, and innovations.

The **technological environment** consists of *the applications of knowledge based on scientific discoveries, inventions, and innovations.* It results in new products for consumers and improves existing products. It is a frequent source of price reductions through the development of new production methods or new materials. It also can make existing products obsolete virtually overnight — as purchasers of computer products would attest.

Marketing decision-makers must closely monitor the technological environment for a number of reasons. New technology may be the means by which they remain competitive in their industries. It may also be the vehicle for the creation of entirely new industries. For example, the development of biotechnology and genetic engineering is resulting in the development of new industries that will revolutionize current practices in fields such as agriculture and medicine.

In the case of high-technology products such as computers and related items, marketers face real challenges in keeping up with the pace of change. They not only must maintain an understanding of the industry, but also must somehow try to communicate totally new concepts and ways of solving problems to potential customers. As Francis McInerney, president of Northern Business Information, says, "The time it takes to explain a product may be longer than the time it takes to introduce a whole new generation of products."[11]

In addition, marketers must anticipate the effect such technological innovations are likely to have on the lifestyles of consumers, the products of competitors, the demands of industrial users, and the regulatory actions of government. The development of the Internet and the "information highway" has made communication of ideas and new approaches to business available at any computer.

THE SOCIO-CULTURAL MILIEU

A probation officer and his wife have found a novel way of marrying people who do not belong to an organized religion or who prefer not to get married in a church. Edward and Ruth Simmons have formed a company called Weddings and have opened chapels in Hamilton and Burlington, Ontario. Weddings offers five different ceremonies: four religious and one secular. The rituals are open to change, at clients' request.

Edward Simmons says that he came up with the idea when he saw couples being married in the courts. "They would go in happy and come out with a stunned look on their faces. I don't think they realized the abruptness of the proceedings. That really bothered me," he said. "Religion doesn't always meet the needs of a secular society," he added. "In many cases, a place of worship won't marry couples who don't belong to it, people who have been divorced, couples that have been living together, and those who have crossed religious barriers."[12]

A few years ago, the success of the Simmons' company would have been doubtful. However, changes in the socio-cultural fabric of Canada now make this type of business quite viable. This example illustrates the importance of understanding and assessing the relevant social and cultural components when making marketing decisions. The **socio-cultural environment** is *the mosaic of societal and cultural components that are relevant to the organization's business decisions.* Obviously, there are many different aspects of significance. One important category is the general readiness of society to accept a marketing idea; this aspect was important in the Simmons' decision.

socio-cultural environment
The mosaic of societal and cultural components that are relevant to the organization's business decisions.

APPLYING THE CONCEPTS

Providing Customer Satisfaction in Marketing: Technology Scorecard

Before you invest in new technology to improve your customer service, consult your peers: 272 small to midsize companies recently rated the effectiveness of various technologies designed to expedite orders, track sales, and log customer comments. They ranked each gadget "not effective at all," "so-so," or "highly effective." Many had mixed feelings. This survey is based upon their satisfaction and usage levels.

GOOD BETS

Fax/modem for order taking	87%
Cellular phones for salespeople	71%
Pagers for salespeople	67%

COULD BE BETTER

Customer-contact software	56%
Automated phone system for handling customer calls	53%
Data base to log client complaints	49%

WORTH CHECKING OUT

Bar coding to track orders and deliveries	80%
On-line computer system for order taking	72%

BUYER BEWARE

Interactive video disks for customers	13%

Note: December '93 survey, 66% of companies had sales of $25-million or less. Source: *The Executive Committee/Inc.* magazine.

Source: "Technology Scorecard," *The Globe and Mail* (August 8, 1994), p. B4. Reprinted by permission of *The Globe and Mail.*

The technological environment provides many opportunities. What has to go along with these technological innovations to truly provide total customer satisfaction?

Another important category is the trust and confidence of the public in business as a whole. Such relationships have been on the decline since the mid-1960s. Opinion polls suggest that people have lost confidence in major companies (although they maintain faith in the private-enterprise system). These declines should, however, be viewed in perspective. All institutions have lost public confidence to some degree. In fact, some would argue that governments and labour unions are even less popular than business.

The socio-cultural environment for marketing decisions has both expanded in scope and increased in importance. Today, no marketer can initiate a strategy without taking the social context into account. Marketers must develop an awareness of the manner in which this context affects their decisions. The constant flux of social issues requires that marketing managers place more emphasis on solving these questions as part of the marketing decision process. Some firms have created a new position — manager of public policy research — to study the changing social environment's future impact on the company.

One question facing contemporary marketing is how to measure the accomplishment of socially oriented objectives. A firm that is attuned to its social environment must develop new ways of evaluating its performance. Traditional income statements and balance sheets are no longer adequate. This issue is one of the most important problems facing contemporary marketing.

Many marketers recognize societal differences between countries, but assume that a homogeneous social environment exists domestically. Nothing could be further from the truth! Canada is a mixed society composed of varied submarkets. These submarkets can be classified by age, place of residence, gender, ethnic background, and numerous other determinants. For example, the Quebec market segment has enough distinctive characteristics that separate marketing programs are sometimes developed for that province.

Gender is another increasingly important social factor. The feminist movement has had a decided effect on marketing, particularly promotion. Television commercials now feature women in less stereotyped roles than in previous years.

Since social variables change constantly, marketers must continually evaluate this dynamic environment. What appears to be out-of-bounds today may be tomorrow's greatest market opportunity. Consider the way that previously taboo subjects, such as feminine hygiene products, are now commonly advertised.

The social variables must be recognized by modern business executives since they affect the way consumers react to different products and marketing practices. One of the most tragic — and avoidable — of all marketing mistakes is the failure to appreciate social differences within our own domestic market.

The rise of consumerism can be partly traced to the growing public concern with making business more responsible to its constituents. Consumerism is an evolving aspect of marketing's social environment. Certainly the advent of this movement has influenced the move toward more direct protection of consumer rights in such areas as product safety and false and misleading advertising. These concerns will undoubtedly be amplified and expanded in the years ahead.

■ KEY TERMS

competitive environment	misleading advertising	monetary policy
political and legal climate	resale price maintenance	demarketing
Competition Act	economic environment	technological
Combines Investigation	business cycle	environment
Act	recession	socio-cultural
combine	inflation	environment
restraint of trade	stagflation	
merger	fiscal policy	

■ INTERACTIVE SUMMARY AND DISCUSSION QUESTIONS

1. The competitive environment is the interactive process that occurs in the marketplace in which competing organizations seek to satisfy markets. Give an example of how the competitive environment might be viewed for the following firms:

   a. McCain Foods
   b. Local aerobics exercise centre
   c. Swiss Chalet franchise
   d. Avon products
   e. Sears catalogue department
   f. Local television station

2. Marketers face three types of competition: similar products, products that can be substituted for one another, and all organizations that compete for the consumers' purchases. Give an example of each for three different organizations that you are familiar with.

3. The political and legal climate consists of the laws and the interpretation of laws that require firms to operate under competitive conditions and to protect consumer rights. Give examples of how the political and legal climate might apply to the five firms listed in question 1.

4. Explain how the expectations of society can be said to create the legal framework for business practice.

5. Can the consumerism movement be viewed as a rejection of the competitive marketing system? Defend your answer.

6. The Competition Act has the most significance in the legal environment for marketing decisions. In which areas has the Act had little effect, and for what types of business practices has it been productive?

7. Would a gas station that sold gasoline to a city's police department for one cent a litre less than its price for other customers be in violation of the Competition Act? Why? Explain your answer.

8. The economic environment is the third variable that sets the framework for developing marketing plans. Where are we now in the business cycle? Give examples of how the economic environment currently could be affecting the marketing practices of the firms listed in question 1.

9. The technological environment consists of the applications of knowledge based on scientific discoveries, inventions, and innovations. Discuss the relevance of the technological environment for the firms listed in question 1.

10. The socio-cultural milieu is the fifth component of the environment that must be carefully considered when establishing marketing plans. Identify some aspects of the socio-cultural milieu that would likely be of specific relevance to the firms listed in question 1.

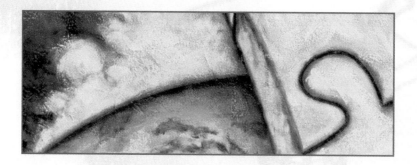

PART TWO

Foundations of the Marketing Plan

The focus of the four chapters in Part Two is planning — *anticipating the future and determining the courses of action designed to achieve organizational objectives*. The chapters follow a logical sequence, commencing with the establishment of a basis for the orientation of the marketing plan through market segmentation. The market segmentation process is then outlined, followed by marketing research and sales forecasting. Part Two culminates with a chapter on developing the marketing plan.

CHAPTER 3

Marketing Segmentation: Finding a Base to Start

CHAPTER OBJECTIVES

1. To introduce the concept of the marketing plan.
2. To define market segmentation.
3. To present four types of market segmentation in consumer markets.
4. To illustrate some aspects of the Canadian market in terms of the four types of consumer market segmentation.
5. To show the main types of segmentation in industrial markets.

Restaurateurs have watched baby boomers grow up — and out.

Now they are trying to appeal to this health-conscious postwar generation with ambitious plans for chains of restaurants featuring low-calorie, rotisserie-cooked chicken.

Coming soon to a lot of neighbourhoods are Swiss Chalet's Blazin Grill Rotisserie, Golden Griddle's Didgeridoos, or maybe a Kenny Rogers Roasters restaurant.

"Chicken is on the ascendancy," says Bill Hood, president of Didgeridoos. Didgeridoos opened its first restaurant in Newmarket, Ontario, in May 1994, and had plans to open 100 within two years.

Hood says the company was born by marrying the rotisserie chicken concept with the Australian flavour of a U.S. steakhouse chain called Outbacks. "We took a look around for something unique," Hood says. "We followed the success of the Outback steakhouse in the U.S. and married the concept to rotisserie chicken."

For 40 years, Swiss Chalet has offered customers rotisserie chicken in a full-service eatery. Now it is branching out with its first Blazin Grill restaurant to grab the customers its traditional restaurants weren't catching. Blazin Grill is supposed to offer speedy counter service and a buffet where customers create their own meals.

"We saw the increase in the popularity of chicken and the success [of the rotisserie concept] in the U.S.," says Cara marketing manager Joanne Macgrath. "And we expected some competitors to come into Canada, so we went ahead. We talked to customers, watched trends in people's habits, and found out where people liked to go. Then we came up with the concept."

It seems like everyone in the chicken business is looking at demographics and drooling with pleasure. Baby boomers are going grey and worrying about their health. They are turning toward chicken and away from beef.

Chicken is certainly gaining a more prominent spot in Canadian cuisine. Today, chicken accounts for about 26 percent of meat and poultry consumption in the country, up from 14.3 percent 20 years ago.

In 1993, per capita consumption of chicken was 23.2 kilograms; beef consumption was 31.8 kilograms. In 1974, the average Canadian was eating 13.6 kilograms of chicken and 42.7 kilograms of beef.[1]

These restaurant chains have found that market segment analysis can be a sound basis for developing a marketing plan. Markets are usually not homogeneous. They comprise many different groups of people from many different locations with a multitude of differing lifestyles and needs. These restaurant chains are responding to changes that they have seen in the market. They hope that the market segments that they have identified will be of significant size, and that they will be able to capture a significant portion of it. Companies must plan constantly, and the plan must be based on an understanding of market trends and market segments.

INTRODUCTION

The marketing plan involves many factors, two of which are consumer and environmental analysis, the topics introduced in Chapters 1 and 2. They provide an important base for the rest of this book. Now we turn to the question of developing plans for marketing a product.

If you have a product to market, a decision must be made about the *target market* — that is, to whom will the product be marketed? In most cases, greater success can be achieved by focussing on part of the entire market. Therefore, an analysis of appropriate target market segments is necessary. Other aspects of marketing planning include taking a careful look at what competitors are doing and at your own firm's situation and resources. Marketing research is also required. A marketing manager and his or her staff take all these elements into consideration in forecasting sales and developing a unique marketing plan that will enable the organization to compete successfully in the marketplace.

Table 3.1 shows a model of the marketing planning process. It will provide a preliminary perspective on the role each of Part Two's chapter topics plays in the marketing planning process. An expanded discussion of the model is included in Chapter 6. We will start the discussion of marketing planning with the topic of market segmentation.

FUNDAMENTAL TASKS IN DEVELOPING A MARKETING PLAN

Although marketers may face hundreds of decisions in developing an effective plan for achieving organization objectives, these decisions may be summarized as two fundamental tasks:

1. They must identify, evaluate, and ultimately select a target market.
2. Once the target market has been selected, they must develop and implement a marketing program designed to satisfy the chosen target group.

These two tasks reflect the philosophy of consumer orientation in action. The choice of a target market is based on recognizing differences among consumers and organizations within a heterogeneous market. The starting point is to understand what is meant by a *market*.

■ Table 3.1 **The Marketing Planning Process**

I. Situation Analysis: Where Are We Now?
  A. Historical background
  B. Consumer analysis
    • Who are the customers we are trying to serve?
    • What market segments exist?
    • How many consumers are there?
    • How much do they buy and why?
  C. Competitive analysis

II. Marketing Objectives: Where Do We Want to Go?
  A. Sales objectives
  B. Profit objectives
  C. Consumer objectives

III. Strategy: How Can We Get There?
  A. Product/service decisions
  B. Pricing decisions
  C. Distribution decisions
  D. Communication decisions
  E. Financial considerations
  F. Control aspects

Source: Adapted from Thomas O'Connor, Stephen K. Keiser, Robert E. Stevens, and Lynn J. Loudenback, *Contemporary Marketing*, 6th ed., Study Guide (Fort Worth, TX: Dryden, 1989), p. 482.

What Is a Market?

A market is *people*. It is also business, not-for-profit organizations, and government — local, provincial, and federal purchasing agents who buy for their "firms." But people alone do not make a market. The local dealer for foreign automobiles is unimpressed by news that 60 percent of the marketing class raise their hands in response to the question "Who wants to buy a new BMW?" The next question is, "How many of them are waving cheques in their outstretched hands?" A **market** *requires not only people and willingness to buy, but also purchasing power and the authority to buy.*

One of the first rules that the successful salesperson learns is to determine who in the organization or household has the authority to make particular purchasing decisions. Much time can be wasted convincing the wrong person that a product or service should be bought.

market
Requires not only people and willingness to buy, but also purchasing power and the authority to buy.

Types of Markets

Products may be classified as consumer or industrial goods. **Consumer goods** are *those products and services purchased by the ultimate consumer for personal use.* **Industrial goods** are *those products purchased to be used, either directly or indirectly, in the production of other goods or for resale.* Most of the products you buy — books, clothes, milk — are consumer goods. Refined nickel is an industrial good for the mint; rubber is a raw material for Michelin. It is important to make the distinction because often the motivations and buying process in each case are quite different.

Sometimes the same product is destined for different uses. The new set of tires purchased by your neighbour are clearly consumer goods, yet when they are

consumer goods
Those products and services purchased by the ultimate consumer for personal use.

industrial goods
Those products purchased to be used, either directly or indirectly, in the production of other goods or for resale.

bought by Chrysler Corporation to become part of a new Neon, they are classified as industrial goods, since they become part of another good destined for resale. The key to the proper classification of goods lies in the purchaser and in *the reasons for buying the good.*

Market Segmentation

A country is too large and filled with too many diverse people and firms for any single marketing plan to satisfy everyone. Unless the product is an item such as an unbranded commodity, an attempt to satisfy everyone may doom the marketer to failure. Even a seemingly functional product like toothpaste is aimed at a specific market segment. Stripe was developed for children; Crest focusses on tooth-decay prevention; Ultra Brite hints at enhanced sex appeal; and Aquafresh promises both protection and teeth whiteners.

The auto manufacturer who decides to produce and market a single car model to satisfy everyone will encounter seemingly endless decisions to be made about such variables as the number of doors, type of transmission, colour, styling, and engine size. In its attempt to satisfy everyone, the firm may be forced to compromise in each of these areas and, as a result, may discover that it does not satisfy anyone very well. Other firms appealing to particular segments — the youth market, the high-fuel-economy market, the large-family market, and so on — may capture most of the total market by satisfying the specific needs of these smaller, more homogeneous target markets. Although all people are different, we can group them according to their similarity in one or more dimensions related to a particular product category. This aggregation process is called **market segmentation**.

Once a specific market segment has been identified, the marketer can design an appropriate marketing approach to match its needs, improving the chance of sales to that segment. Market segmentation can be used by both profit-oriented and not-for-profit organizations.[2]

market segmentation
Grouping people according to their similarity in one or more dimensions related to a particular product category.

SEGMENTING CONSUMER MARKETS

Market segmentation results from a determination of factors that distinguish a certain group of consumers from the overall market. These characteristics — such as age, gender, geographic location, income and expenditure patterns, and population size and mobility, among others — are vital factors in the success of the overall marketing strategy. Toy manufacturers such as Fisher Price and Mattel study not only birthrate trends, but also shifts in income and expenditure patterns. Colleges and universities are affected by such factors as the number of high-school graduates, changing attitudes toward the value of college educations, and increasing enrollment of older adults. Figure 3.1 identifies four commonly used bases for segmenting consumer markets. The first two are descriptive, while the next two are behavioural approaches.

Geographic segmentation, the dividing of an overall market into homogeneous groups based on population location, has been used for hundreds of years. The second basis for segmenting markets is *demographic segmentation* — dividing an overall market on the basis of characteristics such as age, gender, and income level. Demographic segmentation is the most easily used method of subdividing total markets, and is therefore often implemented.

■ Figure 3.1 **Bases for Market Segmentation**

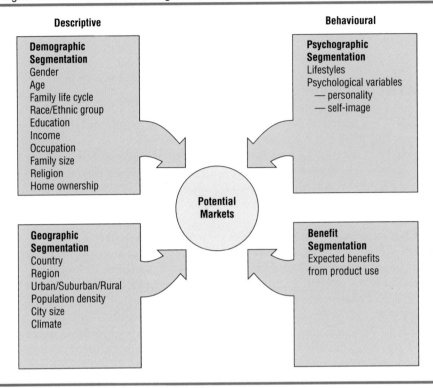

The third and fourth bases require more sophisticated techniques to implement. *Psychographic segmentation* uses behavioural profiles developed from analyses of the activities, opinions, interests, and lifestyles of consumers in identifying market segments. *Benefit segmentation* depends on advanced marketing research techniques that focus on benefits the consumer expects to derive from a product. Product attributes can then be designed to provide desired benefits. These segmentation bases can be important to marketing strategies provided they are significantly related to differences in buying behaviour.

GEOGRAPHIC SEGMENTATION

A logical starting point in market segmentation is to find out where buyers are. It is not surprising, therefore, that one of the first bases for segmentation to be considered is geographic. Country and regional variations in consumer tastes often exist. In Japan, for example, consumers are much more particular about the type of rice used and the way it is cooked than most Canadians. In Canada, per capita consumption of seafood is higher in the Maritimes than in Alberta. Brick and stone construction, a mainstay in many homes in Ontario, is much less common in the West.

Geographic Location of the Canadian Population

Canada's population has grown from 3 million in 1867 to about 30 million in 1996. The Canadian population, like that of the rest of the world, is not distributed evenly. In fact, it is extremely uneven; large portions of this country are uninhabited.[3]

In Canada, less than 8 percent of the land surface is occupied farmland. The inhabited space in Canada is depicted in Figure 3.2. This map shows dramatically that a relatively small strip lying adjacent to the American border is the land area most heavily settled and utilized. Business and social activities therefore must operate in an east–west manner, over tremendous distances. It is thus not surprising to see the emergence of various distinct market segments, such as Central Canada (Ontario and/or Quebec), the Maritimes, the Prairies, and British Columbia.

Not only do provinces vary widely in total population (see Figure 3.3 and Table 3.2), but pronounced shifts also occur. People tend to move where work and opportunities exist. Thus, Ontario and British Columbia have been continuously attractive to those on the move. In the late 1970s, Alberta experienced large population influxes because of the oil-induced prosperity there. Many left during the recession of the early 1980s.

Natural factors and immigration also influence population. Growth has occurred as a result of natural increase (births minus deaths) and net migration (immigration minus emigration). Overall, the rate of natural increase has been considerably higher than that of net migration. In fact, the Atlantic provinces and Saskatchewan

■ Figure 3.2 **Main Inhabited Areas in Canada**

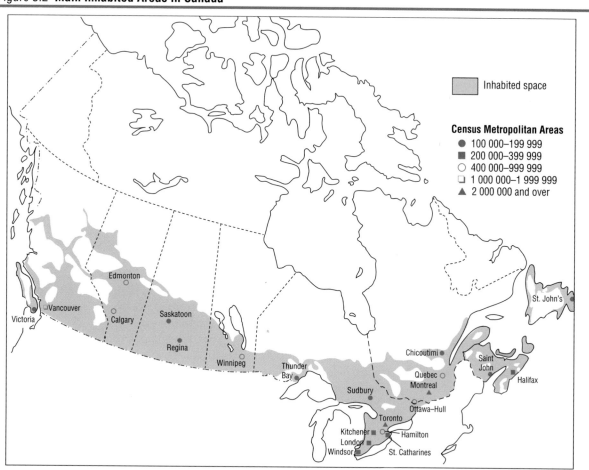

■ Figure 3.3 **Percentage Distribution of the Population of Canada by Province**

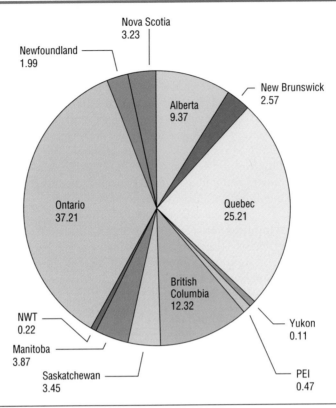

Source: Adapted from Statistics Canada, *Annual Demographics Statistics, 1994*, Catalogue No. 91-213, p. 64. Used by permission of the Minister of Supply and Services Canada.

depend on natural increase to restore population levels lost by emigration. On the other hand, Ontario, British Columbia, and Alberta have shown significant total population increases because they have received migration flows plus a natural increase. In recent years natural increases have been declining.

Immigration has had a tremendous impact on Canadian society. The injection of a steady stream of British immigrants and short bursts of Central, Eastern, and Southern Europeans and Southeast Asians into the Canadian population have created social pressures in assimilation and citizenship. Some areas have attracted much more immigration. In fact, Ontario contains 51.8 percent of Canada's living foreign-born people. The western provinces contain the greatest percentages of foreign-born "old-timers" (people who immigrated before 1946).

Postwar immigration tended to be from European urban centres to Canadian cities, whereas immigration before World War II was largely from European rural areas to Canadian rural areas.

A remarkable influence has been the immigration–emigration flow in Canada. Despite the fact that 8 million people entered the country through immigration between 1851 and 1961, it is estimated that more than 6 million *left*. From Confederation to 1967, Canada's growth was due largely to natural increase (14.5 million), whereas net migration produced only a 2.4-million increase.[4]

It is estimated that emigration has decreased in recent years. However, the tremendous immigration and emigration in proportion to the size of Canada's pop-

■ Table 3.2 **Provincial and Territorial Populations, 1976, 1985, 1994**

	1976	1985 (thousands)	1994
Newfoundland	563.9	580.9	582.4
Prince Edward Island	118.8	128.1	134.5
Nova Scotia	836.6	887.7	936.7
New Brunswick	691.5	726.1	759.3
Quebec	6 420.5	6 690.3	7 281.1
Ontario	8 432.1	9 334.4	10 927.8
Manitoba	1 033.7	1 084.6	1 131.1
Saskatchewan	933.8	1 028.8	1 016.2
Alberta	1 874.3	2 311.1	2 716.2
British Columbia	2 545.0	2 990.0	3 668.4
Yukon	22.6	24.6	30.1
Northwest Territories	44.6	55.0	63.3
Total	**23 517.4**	**25 841.6**	**29 247.1**

Source: Statistics Canada, *Annual Demographics Statistics, 1994*, Catalogue No. 91-213, p. 64. Reproduced by permission of the Minister of Supply and Services Canada.

ulation has resulted in a somewhat unstable set of common goals and ends for Canadian society. The character of Canadian society has continually been pulled in various directions through the infusion of different ethnic groups at varying periods of history via immigration.

These factors have traditionally affected the political outlook of Canada's geographic regions. Marketers also recognize that they must take geographic market segments into account.

PEOPLE ARE IN THE CITIES

Canada's population is predominantly urban. People have been migrating to the cities for many years. Figure 3.4 shows that by 1991, the percentage of rural dwellers had dropped to 26 percent, whereas 74 percent of the population was urban. Table 3.3 shows populations and growth rates for Canada's 25 largest metropolitan areas. The 3 largest — Toronto, Montreal, and Vancouver — already contained approximately 31.3 percent of Canada's total population by 1994, and approximately 61 percent of Canada's population lived in cities of 100 000 and over.

The Canadian population, along with the American and the Australian, is one of the most mobile in the world. The average Canadian moves twelve times in a lifetime, as compared with eight times for the average English citizen and five for the typical Japanese.[5] However, this trend may be waning. The slowdown may be due to a number of factors: poor job prospects elsewhere, the tendency of wage earners in two-income families to refuse transfers, an aging population, and a heightened concern for the quality of one's life.

Using Geographic Segmentation

There are many instances where markets for goods and services may be segmented on a geographic basis. Country and regional variations in taste often exist. Breakfast

■ Figure 3.4 **Urban–Rural Population Distribution, 1871–1991**

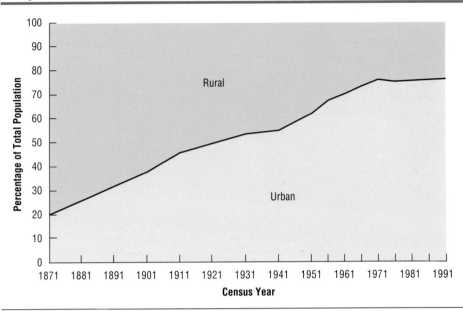

Source: Censuses of Canada, 1871 to 1986. Statistics Canada, *Focus on Canada*, Catalogue No. 98-120, p. 22. Data for 1991 were obtained from Statistics Canada, the 1986 and 1991 *Census of Population: Urban Areas, Population and Dwelling Counts*, Catalogue No. 93-305, as appearing in *Market Research Handbook*, 1995, Catalogue No. 63-224, p. 152.

in Germany normally includes bread, cheese, and cold meat. In countries with large Chinese populations, this segment will eat rice porridge and other "non-breakfast" items (by Canadian standards). Quebec has long been known for its interest in fine and varied foods.

Residence location within a geographic area is another important geographic variable. Urban dwellers may eat more meals in restaurants than their suburban and rural counterparts, while suburban dwellers spend proportionally more on lawn and garden care than do people in rural or urban areas. Both rural and suburban dwellers may spend more of their household income on gasoline and automobile needs than do urban households.

Climate is another important factor. Snow blowers, snowmobiles, and sleds are popular products in many parts of Canada. Residents of southwestern British Columbia may spend proportionately less of their total income on heating and heating equipment than other Canadians. Climate also affects patterns of clothing purchases.

Geographic segmentation is useful only when true differences in preference and purchase patterns for a product emerge along regional lines. Geographic subdivisions of the overall market tend to be rather large and often too heterogeneous for effective segmentation for many products without careful consideration of additional factors. In such cases, it may be necessary to use other segmentation variables as well.

DEMOGRAPHIC SEGMENTATION

The most common approach to market segmentation is to group consumers according to demographic variables. These variables — age, gender, income, occu-

■ Table 3.3 **The 25 Largest Metropolitan Areas in 1994**

Rank	Area	1994 Population (thousands)	Average Annual Growth Rate (percent)
1	Toronto	4128	2.3
2	Montreal	3280	1.5
3	Vancouver	1714	2.7
4	Ottawa–Hull	981	2.3
5	Edmonton	897	1.9
6	Calgary	814	2.4
7	Quebec	679	1.5
8	Winnipeg	662	0.7
9	Hamilton	618	1.3
10	London	401	2.0
11	Kitchener	380	2.5
12	St. Catharines–Niagara	376	1.2
13	Halifax	339	1.7
14	Victoria	304	2.2
15	Windsor	264	0.5
16	Oshawa	259	3.1
17	Saskatoon	217	1.0
18	Regina	194	0.5
19	St. John's	178	1.2
20	Chicoutimi–Jonquière	164	0.4
21	Sudbury	162	1.0
22	Sherbrooke	147	1.6
23	Trois-Rivières	143	1.3
24	Kingston	142	1.9
25	Saint John	127	0.6

Source: *Canadian Markets* (The Financial Post Information Service, 1994), p. 15. Reprinted by permission of *The Financial Post*.

pation, education, household size, and others — are typically used to identify market segments and to develop appropriate market mixes. Demographic variables are often used in market segmentation for three reasons:

1. They are easy to identify and measure.
2. They are associated with the sale of many products and services.
3. They are typically referred to in describing the audiences of advertising media, so that media buyers and others can easily pinpoint the desired target market.[6]

Vast quantities of data are available to assist the marketing planner in segmenting potential markets on a demographic basis. Gender is an obvious variable for segmenting many markets, since many products are gender-specific. Electric-razor manufacturers have used gender as a variable in the successful marketing of such brands as Lady Remington. Diet soft drinks have often been aimed at female markets. Even deodorants are targeted at males or females.

Age, household size, stage in the family life cycle, and income and expenditure patterns are important factors in determining buying decisions. The often distinct differences in purchase patterns based on such demographic factors justify their frequent use as a basis for segmentation.

Age — An Important Demographic Segmentation Variable

The population of Canada is expected to grow by 10 percent between 1995 and 2006, but this growth will be concentrated in persons aged 45 and older. This group represents two potentially profitable target markets.

The older and senior middle-aged adult segment (45–64) includes households where the children have grown up and most have left home. For many, housing costs are lower because mortgages are paid off. In general, this group finds itself with substantial disposable income because it is in a peak earning period, and many basic purchases for everyday living have been completed. This disposable income is often used for luxury goods, new furniture, and travel. While this segment currently represents 20.8 percent of the Canadian population, it will account for 65 percent of the growth in population between 1995 and 2006.

Not so many years ago, there was no such thing as a senior-citizen market, since few people reached old age. Now, however, some 11.8 percent of the total population is 65 or older. Not only is it comforting for this year's retiree to learn that at age 65 his or her average life expectancy is at least another 11.4 years, but the trend also creates a unique and potentially profitable segment for the marketing manager. The manager of course will not ignore the youth segment, which will decline in proportion to the whole population, but remain large. Figure 3.5 shows the changing profile of the Canadian population.

Each of the age groups in Figure 3.5 represents different consumption patterns and each serves as the target market for particular firms. For instance, Gerber

Recent years have seen more advertising targeted at senior consumers. Most of these campaigns are for products ranging from tourism to life insurance to medical remedies. In a series of television commercials and newspaper advertisements, Nestlé takes a humorous approach to marketing its Nescafé Cappuccino to older consumers. The campaign clearly sets aside traditional views of senior citizens.

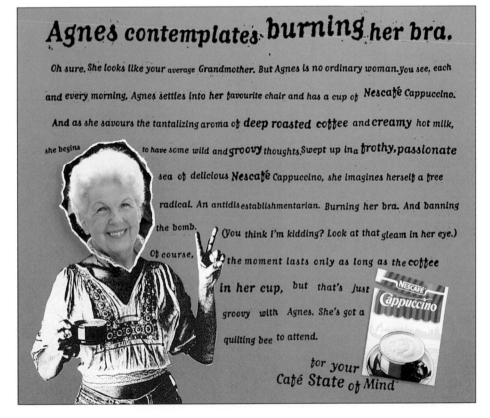

■ Figure 3.5 **Population Projections by Age Group**

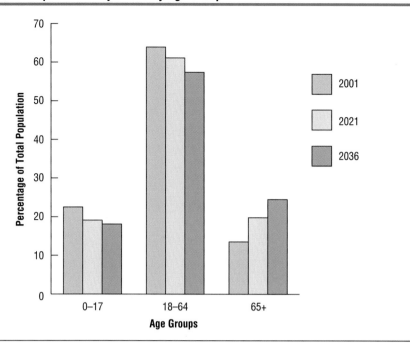

Source: Statistics Canada, *Population Projections for Canada, Provinces and Territories, 1981–2036*, Catalogue No. 91-520. Reproduced by authority of the Minister of Industry, 1995.

Products Company has been extremely successful in aiming at the parents-of-infants market, and prepackaged tours appeal to older consumers. Table 3.4 lists some of the types of merchandise often purchased by the various age groups.

Segmenting by Family Life Cycle

The **family life cycle** is *the process of family formation, development, and dissolution.* Using this concept, the marketing planner combines the family characteristics of age, marital status, presence or absence of children, and ages of children in developing the marketing strategy. Patrick E. Murphy and William A. Staples have proposed a six-stage family life cycle with several subcategories. The stages of the family life cycle are shown in Table 3.5.

The behavioural characteristics and buying patterns of people in each life cycle stage often vary considerably. Young singles have relatively few financial burdens; tend to be early purchasers of new fashion items; are recreation-oriented; and make purchases of basic kitchen equipment, cars, and vacations. By contrast, young marrieds with young children tend to be heavy purchasers of baby products, homes, television sets, toys, and washers and dryers. Their liquid assets tend to be relatively low, and they are more likely to watch television than young singles or young marrieds without children. The empty-nest households in the middle-aged and older categories with no dependent children are more likely to have more disposable income; more time for recreation, self-education, and travel; and more than one

family life cycle
The process of family formation, development, and dissolution.

■ **Table 3.4 Buying Patterns for Different Age Groups**

Age	Name of Age Group	Merchandise
0–5	Young children	Baby food, toys, nursery furniture, children's wear
6–19	School children (including teenagers)	Clothing, sports equipment, records, school supplies, food, cosmetics, used cars
20–34	Young adults	Cars, furniture, houses, clothing, recreational equipment, purchases for younger age groups
35–49	Younger middle-aged	Larger homes, better cars, second cars, new furniture, recreational equipment
50–64	Older middle-aged	Recreational items, purchases for young marrieds and infants
65+	Senior adults	Medical services, travel, drugs, purchases for younger age groups

APPLYING THE CONCEPTS

The Over-50s

Fifty-five percent of disposable income is in the hands of Canadians 50 and over. They have 80 percent of the savings-account dollars. They buy a third of all new cars, a third of the groceries sold. They switch brands and try new products.

WHAT DO OVER-50S BUY?
New cars: They like them big and comfortable
Travel: 82 percent last year; 65 percent used a travel agent
Microwaves, dishwashers, computers, VCRs
Clothes: Over-50s women spend more than over-30s

WHAT ELSE DO THEY DO WITH THEIR MONEY?
Canadian Over-50s control around 75 percent of all household financial holdings: stocks, bonds, savings.

Sixty-four percent own their own homes, and don't plan to move. They don't pay mortgages, don't have to support kids. They're *loaded* and they want to enjoy that money. They eat out more than yuppies, buy creature comforts, pay extra for quality because they feel that means value.

This is obviously a market well worth considering. It could be segmented and marketing plans developed for each segment, with significant profit potential from each.

Source: Adapted from an advertisement for *Today's Seniors* in *Marketing Magazine* (April 10, 1989), p. 5. Used with permission.

Which types of business would be most interested in this market segment? Is it fair to call it a segment?

member in the labour force than their full-nest counterparts with younger children. Similar differences in behavioural and buying patterns are evident in the other stages of the family life cycle.[7]

Analysis of life-cycle stages often gives better results than reliance on single variables, such as age. The buying patterns of a 25-year-old bachelor are very different from those of a father of the same age. The family of five headed by parents in their 40s is a more likely prospect for the *World Book Encyclopedia* than the childless 40-year-old divorced person.

Marketing planners can use published data such as census reports to divide their markets into more homogeneous segments than would be possible if they were analyzing single variables. Such data are available for each classification of the family life cycle.

The Changing Household

Half the households in Canada are composed of only one or two persons, and the average household size is three persons. This development is in marked contrast to households that averaged more than four persons before World War II. Married couples still form the largest segment of households, but in relative terms their numbers are decreasing.

There are several reasons for the trend toward smaller households. Among them are lower fertility rates, the tendency of young people to postpone marriage, the increasing desire among younger couples to limit the number of children, the ease and frequency of divorce, and the ability and desire of many young single adults and elderly people to live alone.

■ Table 3.5 **Family-Life Cycle Stages**

1. Young Single

2. Young Married without Children

3. Other Young
   a. Young divorced without children
   b. Young married with children
   c. Young divorced with children

4. Middle-Aged
   a. Middle-aged married without children
   b. Middle-aged divorced without children
   c. Middle-aged married with children
   d. Middle-aged divorced with children
   e. Middle-aged married without dependent children
   f. Middle-aged divorced without dependent children

5. Older
   a. Older married
   b. Older unmarried (divorced, widowed)

6. Other
   All adults and children not accounted for by family life-cycle stages

---

Source: Adapted from Patrick E. Murphy and William A. Staples, "A Modernized Family Life," *Journal of Consumer Research* (June 1979), p. 16. Used by permission of the University of Chicago Press.

SSWDs
Single, separated, widowed, or
divorced people.

Over 1.6 million people live alone today. The single-person household has emerged as an important market segment with a special title: **SSWD** (*single, separated, widowed, or divorced*). SSWDs buy approximately 25 percent of all passenger cars, but a much higher proportion of specialty cars. They are also customers for single-serving food products, such as Campbell's Soup-for-One and Green Giant's single-serving casseroles.

Segmenting Markets on the Basis of Income and Expenditure Patterns

Earlier, markets were defined as people and purchasing power. A very common method of segmenting consumer markets is on the basis of income. Fashionable specialty shops that stock designer-label clothing obtain most of their sales from high-income shoppers.

Income statistics can be analyzed by family structure. Families can be divided into two groups: husband–wife families and lone-parent families. The latter can be further subdivided by sex of the parent. Significant changes have occurred in the structure of families over time, as Table 3.6 shows. Between 1985 and 1994, the number of husband–wife families increased by 16.3 percent, while that of male lone-parent families increased by 1.3 percent. However, the number of female lone-parent families increased by 12.8 percent. The three groups fared differently with respect to their incomes over the five-year period. Each group experienced a significant increase in real income. The average income in the husband–wife families increased more than twice that in female lone-parent families. In 1985, the average income in male lone-parent families was 63 percent higher than in female lone-parent families but lowered to 46 percent in 1994.[8]

■ Table 3.6 **Percentage Distribution by 1985 and 1994 Family Income Groups by Family Structure, Canada**

Family Income Group (1993 dollars)	Husband–Wife Families		Male Lone-Parent Families		Female Lone-Parent Families	
	1985	1994	1985	1994	1985	1994
Under $10 000	5.2	0.9	15.3	5.1	33.6	7.9
$10 000–14 999	7.1	1.5	10.0	7.9	16.4	18.8
15 000–19 999	8.7	3.1	9.9	10.0	11.9	17.0
20 000–24 999	8.5	4.9	9.8	8.0	10.5	11.0
25 000–34 999	19.0	11.1	20.4	18.6	14.0	18.1
35 000–49 999	25.2	20.1	19.8	19.8	9.2	14.9
50 000 and over	26.2	58.4	14.8	30.6	4.4	12.3
Total	99.9	100.0	100.0	100.0	100.0	100.0
Number (in thousands)	5 881	6 838	151	153	702	792
Average income (in dollars)	40 222	63 753	31 252	41 228	19 177	28 301
Median income (in dollars)	35 758	56 682	27 405	35 294	15 005	22 824

Source: The 1985 data have been obtained from Statistics Canada, *Family Income: Census Families*, 1986 Census, Catalogue No. 63-005. Reproduced by authority of the Minister of Industry, 1995. The 1994 data have been obtained from Statistics Canada, *Income Distributions by Size in Canada*, 1994, Catalogue No. 13-207, p. 88. Reproduced by permission of the Minister of Supply and Services Canada.

A household's expenditures may be divided into two categories: (1) basic purchases of essential household needs, and (2) other purchases that can be made at the discretion of the household members once the necessities have been purchased (disposable income). Total Canadian disposable income is estimated to have tripled in constant dollars since 1961.[9] This is a substantial increase.

Engel's Laws

How do expenditure patterns vary with increased income? More than 100 years ago a German statistician named Ernst Engel published three general statements — **Engel's Laws** — based on his studies of spending behaviour. According to Engel, *as family income increases:*

1. A smaller *percentage* of expenditures goes for food.
2. The *percentage* spent on housing and household operations and clothing will remain constant.
3. The *percentage* spent on other items (such as recreation, education, etc.) will increase.

Are Engel's Laws still valid today? Figure 3.6 supplies the answers. A small decline in the percentage of total income spent for food occurs from low to high incomes. Note the emphasis on the word *percentage*. The high-income families will spend a greater absolute amount on food purchases, but their purchases will represent a smaller percentage of their total expenditures than will be true of low-income households.

With respect to Engel's second law, expenditures for shelter decline rather than remain constant. However, as predicted, there is relatively little change in the percentage of income spent on household operations and in household furnishings and equipment, as well as on clothing.

The third law is also true with respect to recreation and education. However, there are notable exceptions to the original generalization, such as transportation. It has become a much greater part of family expenditures than Engel might have dreamed.

Engel's Laws provide the marketing manager with useful generalizations about types of consumer demand that will evolve with increased income. They may also be useful when evaluating a foreign country as a potential target market. Other countries may well have different expenditure patterns, however. For example, in countries with high population densities, such as Hong Kong and parts of England, housing that is equivalent to North American size and quality is available only to the rich. The marketer cannot assume that Engel's conclusions apply without checking carefully.

PSYCHOGRAPHIC SEGMENTATION

Although geographic and demographic segmentation traditionally have been the primary bases for grouping customers and industries into segments to serve as target markets, marketers have long recognized the need for richer, more in-depth representations of consumers for use in developing marketing programs.

Even though traditionally used variables such as age, gender, family life cycle, income, and population size and location are important in segmentation, lifestyles

Engel's Laws
As family income increases, (1) a smaller percentage goes for food, (2) the percentage spent on housing and household operations and clothing will remain constant, and (3) the percentage spent on other items will increase.

■ Figure 3.6 **Percentage Annual Family Expenditures by Income Groups, 1992**

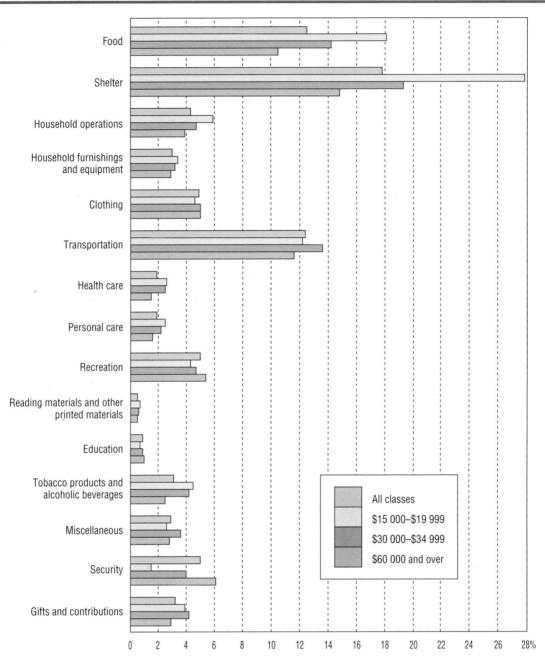

Legend:
- All classes
- $15 000–$19 999
- $30 000–$34 999
- $60 000 and over

Source: Data from Statistics Canada, *Family Expenditure in Canada*, 1992, Catalogue No. 62-555, as appearing in *Market Research Handbook*, 1995, Catalogue No. 63-224, pp. 204–205. Used by permission of the Minister of Supply and Services Canada.

of potential consumers often prove much more important. Demographically, a truck driver and a college professor may be the same age and have the same income. Yet their purchasing behaviour will likely be very different.

lifestyle
The mode of living.

Lifestyle refers to *the mode of living* of consumers. Consumers' lifestyles are regarded as a composite of their individual behaviour patterns and psychological

■ Table 3.7 **Lifestyle Dimensions**

Activities	Interests	Opinions	Demographics
Work	Family	Themselves	Age
Hobbies	Home	Social issues	Education
Social events	Job	Politics	Income
Vacation	Community	Business	Occupation
Entertainment	Recreation	Economics	Family size
Club membership	Fashion	Education	Dwelling
Community	Food	Products	Geography
Shopping	Media	Future	City size
Sports	Achievements	Culture	Stage in life cycle

Source: Joseph T. Plummer, "The Concept and Application of Lifestyle Segmentation," *Journal of Marketing* (January 1974), p. 34. Reprinted by permission of the American Marketing Association.

make-up — their needs, motives, perceptions, and attitudes. A lifestyle also bears the mark of many other influences — those of reference groups, culture, social class, and family members. Thus, segmentation by lifestyles provides a much more comprehensive picture of customer needs and wants. A frequently used classification system for lifestyle variables is shown in Table 3.7.

Psychographics

A technique more comprehensive than lifestyle segmentation is **psychographics**. Psychographics is *the use of psychological attributes, lifestyles, and attitudes in determining the behavioural profiles of different consumers.* These profiles are usually developed through market research that asks for agreement or disagreement with several hundred statements dealing with activities, interests, and opinions, such as those listed in Table 3.7. Because of the basis of the statements (*activities, interests,* and *opinions*), they are sometimes referred to as **AIO statements**. Table 3.8 contains a sample list of such statements. Market segments are identified on the basis of similar psychographic characteristics.

The Print Measurement Bureau, along with two market research organizations, Goldfarb and Thompson Lightstone, jointly surveyed the Canadian market using the methodology outlined above.[10] Each research organization analyzed the data somewhat differently, and developed some interesting psychographic groupings (see Figure 3.7).

THE GOLDFARB SEGMENTS

There are six Goldfarb segments, divided neatly into *more* or *less* traditional, with 56 percent of the population falling into the *more* traditional segment. The Goldfarb segments are as follows:

- *Day-to-Day Watchers* are quite satisfied with what life has to offer. They are early followers, rather than leaders, but they keep a close eye on the world around them.
- *Old-Fashioned Puritans* are conservative to the point of being defensive, traditional to the point of inflexibility, and indifferent to the point of apathy. This is not the best group for new-product advertising.
- *Responsible Survivors* are a cautious group; they are very brand-loyal and are heavy TV viewers.

psychographics
The use of psychological attributes, lifestyles, and attitudes in determining the behavioural profiles of different consumers.

AIO statements
Statements about activities, interests, and opinions that are used in developing psychographic profiles.

■ Table 3.8 **Lifestyle Profiles: Target Segment (TS) Compared with the Rest of the Population (ROP)**

	Percent Agreeing		Significances of Differences by Dimension
	TS (%)	ROP (%)	
Innovativeness			
I often try new brands before my friends and neighbours do	40*	22	(0.00)
I like to try new and different things	95	69	
When I see a new brand on the shelf I often buy it just to see what it is like	40	20	
Opinion Leaders			
My friends or neighbours often come to me for advice	60	46	(0.44)
I often seek out the advice of my friends regarding which brand to buy	20	21	
I sometimes influence what my friends buy	30	32	
I spend a lot of time talking to my friends about products and brands	20	06	
Home Cleaners			
I am uncomfortable when my home is not completely clean	60	67	(0.11)
I must admit I really don't like household chores	15	51	
My home is usually very neat and clean	70	65	
I don't like to see clothes lying about	85	84	
Physical Fitness			
Maintaining my physical fitness is important to me	90	89	(0.63)
I think that most people should try to stay physically fit	100	94	
Bargain Hunters			
I shop a lot for specials	70	63	(0.27)
I usually watch for advertisements of announcements of sales	75	65	
I find myself checking the prices in the grocery store even for small items	70	64	
Enjoy Outdoors			
I enjoy hiking	55	49	(0.05)
I would rather see a movie than go camping	20	38	
I enjoy visiting state and national parks	95	84	
Home Centred			
I would rather spend a quiet evening at home than go out to a party	80	67	(0.13)
I am a homebody	75	67	
I like parties where there are lots of music and talk	20	48	
Like Cooking			
I love to cook	70	57	(0.15)
I am a good cook	65	60	

* Forty percent of the target segment agreed that they often try new brands before their friends and neighbours do, compared with 22 percent in the rest of the population.

Source: T.K. Clarke, D.A. Schellinck, and Thomas L. Leonard, "Developing an Effective Communication Strategy to Modify Environment-Related Consumer Behaviour," *International Journal of Advertising* 4 (1985), p. 112.

- *Joiner–Activists* are leading-edge thinkers, but tend to be nonconformists.
- *Aggressive Achievers* are confident, success-oriented people. They want to be leaders, love status-signalling goods, and need to have their psyches stroked regularly.
- *Disinterested Self-Indulgents'* TV viewing is not dissimilar from the previous group. Their music tastes are a little more conservative, leaning to pop rock and oldies. They are also above-average pay TV viewers and VCR users (see Figure 3.8).

THE THOMPSON LIGHTSTONE SEGMENTS

Thompson Lightstone isolated the traditional lifestyles' values based on needs, interests, and aspirations, and merged them with views toward pricing and advertising, buying behaviours, and preferences for products and services. Here are their market segments (see Figure 3.8):

■ Figure 3.7 **Psychographic Analysis**

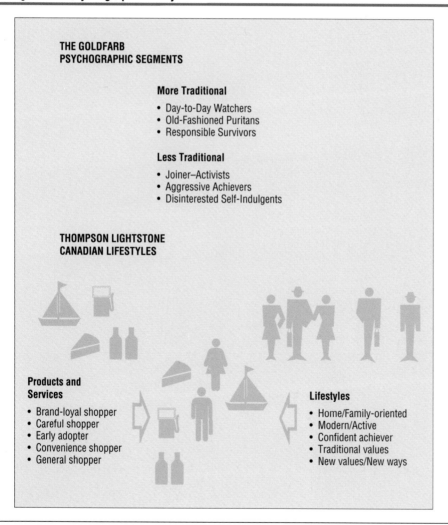

THE GOLDFARB PSYCHOGRAPHIC SEGMENTS

More Traditional
- Day-to-Day Watchers
- Old-Fashioned Puritans
- Responsible Survivors

Less Traditional
- Joiner–Activists
- Aggressive Achievers
- Disinterested Self-Indulgents

THOMPSON LIGHTSTONE CANADIAN LIFESTYLES

Products and Services
- Brand-loyal shopper
- Careful shopper
- Early adopter
- Convenience shopper
- General shopper

Lifestyles
- Home/Family-oriented
- Modern/Active
- Confident achiever
- Traditional values
- New values/New ways

Source: John Chaplin, "Pigeonholes for Consumers," *Marketing Magazine* (October 16, 1989), p. 1.

- The *Passive/Uncertain* segment exhibits low levels of involvement in the process of shopping, and a generally negative sentiment toward advertising.
- The *Mature* market segment is a mix of secondary shoppers and empty-nesters. They tend to be older, with less financial clout. They buy a lot of lottery tickets.
- *Home Economists* are the true bargain hunters. They include many homemakers. They spend a lot of time shopping.
- The *Active/Convenience* segment is the typical "yuppie" (young upwardly mobile professional) in attitudes and purchase habits. They are the buyers of the premium products.
- *Modern Shoppers* enjoy shopping for shopping's sake. They usually buy well, even if it is on impulse.
- People in the *Traditional Home/Family-Oriented* segment tend to be very cautious in all their dealings and their attitudes. They shop for value, are brand-loyal, and are preoccupied with family life and their children.

■ Figure 3.8 **Application of Psychographic Analysis**

Old-Fashioned Puritan

- Heavy TV viewers—preference for game shows, soaps, family dramas, mini-series, and children's cartoons
- Light radio listeners—preference for country and "oldies"
- Low pay TV/VCR use

Disinterested Self-Indulgent

- Medium/heavy TV viewing—preference for sitcoms, variety, suspense/crime drama, and sports
- Heavy radio listening—preference for top 40, hard rock, "oldies," and hockey and football broadcasts
- Above-average pay TV use—Nashville Network, TSN, First Choice/Super Channel
- Above-average VCR use
- Never delete commercials

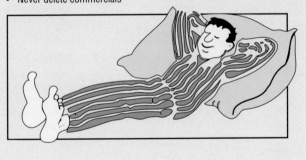

Source: John Chaplin, "Pigeonholes for Consumers," *Marketing Magazine* (October 16, 1989), p. 1.

What can be done with such segment analyses? Each segment can be related to product preference and use. There are many possibilities. For example, the Print Measurement Bureau cross-tabulated the two different sets of lifestyle clusters against questions they had asked about radio or TV listening/watching. Old-Fashioned Puritans were found to be heavy TV viewers and light radio listeners. They have a preference for game shows, soaps, family dramas, mini-series, and children's cartoons. In radio listening, they have a preference for country music and "oldies." They have low ownership of VCRs and low pay TV usage. Such information is extremely useful to broadcasters and advertisers because they know what types of messages and products to feature on different shows. The procedure used for broadcasting could be applied to many other goods and services as well. The insights developed by such a process go far beyond demographic segmentation.

Psychographic segmentation often serves as a component of an overall segmentation strategy in which markets are also segmented on the basis of demographic/geographic variables. These more traditional bases provide the marketer with accessibility to consumer segments through orthodox communications channels such as newspapers, radio and television advertising, and other promotional outlets. Psychographic studies may then be implemented to develop lifelike, three-dimensional profiles of the lifestyles of the firm's target market. When combined with demographic/geographic characteristics, psychographics emerges as an important tool in understanding the behaviour of present and potential target markets.[11]

BENEFIT SEGMENTATION

Benefit segmentation is based on the attributes of products as seen by the customer. Segments are developed by asking consumers about the benefits they perceive in a good or service. Since many people perceive and use the same product differently, those who perceive benefits that are similar are clustered into groups. Each group then constitutes a market segment.

Many marketers now consider benefit segmentation one of the most useful methods of classifying markets. One analysis of 34 segmentation studies indicated that benefit analysis provided the best predictor of brand use, level of consumption, and product type selected in 51 percent of the cases. In a pioneering benefit segmentation investigation, Daniel Yankelovich revealed that much of the watch industry operated with little understanding of the benefits watch buyers expect in their purchases. At the time of the study, most watch companies were marketing relatively expensive models through jewellery stores and using prestige appeals. However, Yankelovich's research revealed that less than one-third of the market was purchasing a watch as a symbol. In fact, 23 percent of his respondents reported they purchased the lowest-price watch and another 46 percent focussed on durability and overall product quality. The Timex Company decided to focus its product benefits on those two categories and market its watches in drugstores, variety stores, and discount houses. The rest is history. Within a few years of adopting the new segmentation approach, it became the largest watch company in the world.[12]

Table 3.9 illustrates how benefit segmentation might be applied to the toothpaste market. The table reveals that some consumers are primarily concerned with price, some with preventing tooth decay, some with taste, and others with brightness

■ Table 3.9 **Benefit Segmentation of the Toothpaste Market**

	Segment Name			
	The Sensory Segment	The Sociables	The Worriers	The Independent Segment
Principal benefit sought	Flavour, product appearance	Brightness of teeth	Decay prevention	Price
Demographic strengths	Children	Teens, young people	Large families	Men
Special behavioural characteristics	Users of spearmint-flavoured toothpaste	Smokers	Heavy users	Heavy users
Brands disproportionately favoured	Colgate, Stripe	MacLean's, Plus White, Ultra Brite	Crest	Brands on sale
Personality characteristics	High self-involvement	High sociability	High hypochondriasis	High autonomy
Lifestyle characteristics	Hedonistic	Active	Conservative	Value-oriented

Source: Russell I. Haley, "Benefit Segmentation: A Decision-Oriented Research Tool," *Journal of Marketing* (July 1968), p. 33. Reprinted by permission of the American Marketing Association.

"benefits." Also included are the demographic and other characteristics used in focussing on each subgrouping.[13] Although this table was first published in 1968 and some of the information in it seems dated by today's standards, it is still a classic example of how benefit segmentation can be used.

SEGMENTING INDUSTRIAL MARKETS

While the bulk of market segmentation research has concentrated on consumer markets, the concept can also be applied to the industrial sector. The overall process is similar. Three industrial market segmentation approaches have been identified: geographic segmentation, product segmentation, and segmentation by end-use applications (see Figure 3.9).

Geographic Segmentation

Geographic segmentation is useful in industries where the bulk of the customers are concentrated in specific geographical locations. This approach can be used in such instances as the automobile industry, concentrated in the central Ontario area, or the lumber industry, centred in British Columbia and Quebec. It might also be used in cases where the markets are limited to just a few locations. The oil-field equipment market, for example, is largely concentrated in cities like Calgary and Edmonton.

■ Figure 3.9 **Segmentation Bases for Industrial Markets**

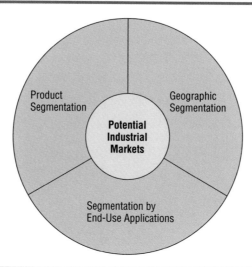

Product Segmentation

It is possible to segment some industrial markets in terms of their need for special-ized products. Industrial users tend to have much more precise product specifica-tions than do ultimate consumers, and such products often fit very narrow market segments. For example, special rivets for bridge-building might be a market seg-ment. Therefore, the design of an industrial good or service and the development of an associated marketing plan to meet specific buyer requirements is a form of market segmentation.

Segmentation by End-Use Applications

A third segmentation base is end-use applications — that is, precisely how the industrial purchaser will use the product. (This is similar to benefit segmentation in consumer markets.) A manufacturer of, say, printing equipment may serve markets ranging from a local utility to a bicycle manufacturer to Agriculture Canada. Each end use may dictate unique specifications of performance, design, and price. The market for desktop computers provides a good example: IBM has several comput-ers for different market sizes. Caterpillar has equipment designed for road con-struction, as well as for other industrial applications. Regardless of how it is done, market segmentation is as vital to industrial marketing as it is in consumer markets.

This chapter has introduced the concept of market segmentation, and has shown the main bases for segmenting both consumer and industrial markets. Some seg-mentation procedures are quite uncomplicated. Others require the use of advanced research techniques. The next chapter examines how segmentation concepts may be applied to market segmentation strategies.

A unique family-owned business founded in 1968, Grenville Management and Printing Ltd. began as a small instant-print operation. Since then, it has grown into a vast, diversified company that offers commercial printing, facilities management, warehousing, and distribution. From Imperial Oil to IBM to Pepsi-Cola Canada, Grenville's customer base is large and varied. The firm must, therefore, cater to specific and differing needs, and customize its goods and services to the end-use applications of each client.

■ KEY TERMS

market	demographics	lifestyle
consumer goods	family life cycle	psychographics
industrial goods	SSWD	AIO statements
market segmentation	Engel's Laws	benefit segmentation

■ INTERACTIVE SUMMARY AND DISCUSSION QUESTIONS

1. In developing a marketing plan, managers must select a target market, then develop and implement a marketing program for that segment. Show how these tasks reflect the philosophy of consumer orientation in action.

2. A market consists of people with the willingness, purchasing power, and authority to buy. Illustrate the application of this concept in the case of a salesperson for a photocopier company who is trying to make a sale to the Royal Bank.

3. Illustrate how some products can be classified as both consumer and industrial products. Why is it important to make a distinction between the two?

4. Market segmentation is the grouping of people according to their similarity in one or more dimensions related to a particular product category. Show how segmentation might be advantageous in developing a marketing plan for the following products:
   a. Textbooks
   b. Women's clothing
   c. Chain saws
   d. Life insurance

5. Four commonly used bases for segmenting consumer markets are geographic, demographic, psychographic, and benefit. Suggest one descriptive segmentation approach and one behavioural segmentation approach for each item in the list in question 4. Give as detailed an example as possible.

6. Suggest two *different* types of geographic segmentation approaches that could be used in each of the following markets:
   a. Canada
   b. United States
   c. Mexico
   d. Germany
   e. Japan
   f. Italy
   g. Hong Kong

7. Canadian census data reveal that a significant number of Canadians have a mother tongue other than English or French (mother tongue is defined as the language first learned and still understood). Some of the larger language groups are Italian, German, and Chinese (approximately 500 000 people each) and Ukrainian (approximately 200 000 people). How could a marketer use this demographic information? How could a behavioural segmentation approach enhance the demographic segmentation?

8. Industrial market segmentation methods are geographic segmentation, product segmentation, and segmentation by end-use applications. Give an example of how Xerox Corporation might use each segmentation method.

9. Explain and describe the use of AIO questions.

10. How might a fast-food marketer such as Harvey's respond to the changing age-group projections shown in Figure 3.5?

CHAPTER 4

The Market Segmentation Process

CHAPTER OBJECTIVES

1. To show the factors underlying market segmentation strategy choices.
2. To outline the stages in the market segmentation process.
3. To explain the concept of positioning within market segments.
4. To show how target market decision analysis can be used in market segmentation.
5. To show how target market decision analysis can be used to assess the assortment of products offered to the market.

When *Live at the BBC*, the album of early Beatles performances, was released it hit the stores as a double cassette, double CD, and double long-playing vinyl record.

Vinyl? The dinosaur of the recording industry? The technology squashed as flat as, well, a record, by the roaring compact-disc express? Weren't our personal music libraries supposed to disappear altogether thanks to cable companies providing songs on demand, rather than revert to a nearly century-old format?

Yes, yes, and yes. Still, vinyl is back, if not bigger than ever. Record companies, which stopped having anything to do with vinyl as the eighties became the nineties, are bringing out some of their hottest acts on vinyl (as well as CD and cassette). Pearl Jam's album was released on vinyl two weeks before it appeared on cassette or CD; Nirvana, Liz Phair, The Tragically Hip and the Black Crowes are other acts who have released their later works in that flat, familiar sleeve.

The LP never disappeared altogether, of course. Some jazz and classical aficionados will listen to nothing else, swearing that vinyl sounds "warmer," although warmth is a difficult quality to define. Hip-hop also relies on vinyl — DJs, whether recording or playing in clubs, manipulate LPs to achieve desired mixes and effects.

Ten years ago, the special thing about a record was that it was coming out on CD, says David Corr, import buyer at Sam's in Toronto. "Now we know it's special if it's coming out on vinyl."

Record companies have noticed the same thing, and being in business, are looking to cash in. "There's been a resurgence in the interest in vinyl recently," says Ron Morse, who's in charge of import marketing for Warner Music Canada. "With the alternative crowd and the cool crowd, it's become cool to collect vinyl again." Morse says that "the demand has come from the street. It's not something we're trying to create."

Take the introduction of the Pearl Jam record, *Vitalogy*, which was one of the most anticipated rock titles of the year. It was scheduled to arrive in vinyl form on November 22, but it was not available on CD or cassette until December 6. "For a band like Pearl Jam, the other musicians they hang out with in Seattle are vinyl people. It's a gesture to them and what they consider to be their core fan base," says Faye Perkins, product manager with Sony/Epic, which carries Pearl Jam.

This is not to say that vinyl is coming back in numbers that threaten the CD, or that the battered milk box in the basement filled with BeeGees records is now worth a fortune. Vinyl is being produced in small quantities, with specialty collectors and fanatics — who must have every object a particular band puts out — making up a large part of the market. To enhance collectibility, most records are now pressed on vinyl that is any colour but black.

Pierre Hallett has owned a store named Rotate This for three years. He says the market for vinyl has always been out there, even if major labels are only realizing it now. "The [record] companies wanted to lead people to believe vinyl was dead — now they realize people still want it. The sound is just more pure."

But there's definitely a less tangible aspect to vinyl's appeal; one record-store buyer calls it "street credibility." If everyone at your high school has the corporation-approved CD, it's more cool, more "indie," more fringe, to have it on vinyl.[1]

There are clearly many market segments in this industry. The return of the vinyl record introduces another significant dimension to this market. If you are a marketer of music and entertainment, you not only have to think about market segments with different music tastes, but also about the medium that carries that music. Market segmentation strategy must be carefully planned and implemented.

INTRODUCTION

This chapter continues the discussion of market segmentation. Chapter 3 discussed the role of market segmentation in developing a marketing strategy, and the bases for segmenting the consumer market (geographic, demographic, psychographic, and benefit segmentation). In this chapter, the emphasis shifts to the process of market segmentation.

We will consider the rationale for and process of matching product offerings to specific market segments. As we will see, selecting an appropriate strategy depends on a variety of internal and external variables facing the firm.

ALTERNATIVE MARKET MATCHING STRATEGIES

Market segmentation may take many forms, theoretically ranging from treating the entire market as a single homogeneous entity to subdividing it into several segments and providing a separate marketing plan for each segment.

The very core of the firm's strategies is to match product offerings with the needs of particular market segments. To do so successfully, the firm must take the following factors into consideration:

1. *Company resources.* These must be adequate to cover product development and other marketing costs.
2. *Differentiability of products.* Some products can be easily differentiated from others. Some can be produced in versions designed specially for individual segments.
3. *Stage in the product life cycle.* As a product matures, different marketing emphases are required to fit market needs.

4. *Competitors' strategies.* Strategies and product offerings must be continually adjusted in order to be competitive.
5. *Size of segment.* The potential segment must be large enough to make it worthwhile to develop.

Essentially, the firm makes a number of goods/service offerings to the market in view of these determinants. One firm may decide on a **single-offer strategy**. This is defined as *the attempt to satisfy a large or a small market with one product and a single marketing program.* Such a strategy may be adopted for different reasons. A small manufacturer of wheelbarrows might concentrate on marketing one product to retailers in one city only because it does not have the resources to serve a mass market. A large producer of drafting equipment might offer a single product line with a marketing program aimed at draftspersons because it believes that only this limited segment would be interested in the product. A single-offer strategy aimed at one segment is often called *concentrated marketing*; when aimed at mass markets it is often call *undifferentiated* or *mass marketing*. The marketing of Coca-Cola® is an example of the latter.

On the other hand, another company with greater resources may recognize that there are several segments of the market that would respond well to specifically designed products and marketing programs. It adopts a **multi-offer strategy**. This is defined as *the attempt to satisfy several segments of the market very well with specialized products and unique marketing programs aimed at each segment.* A bank designs particular services to fit the unique needs of different consumer and commercial market segments. A multi-offer strategy is also called *differentiated marketing*.

When these determinants are combined with markets segmented on the dimensions discussed in Chapter 3, the firm is able to develop a market matching strategy. A successful match of products to segments through the development of a market-

single-offer strategy
The attempt to satisfy a large or a small market with one product and a single marketing program.

multi-offer strategy
The attempt to satisfy several segments of the market very well with specialized products and unique marketing programs aimed at each segment.

Levi's uses a single-offer strategy to aim its products mainly at a younger market segment. However, as is evident in these advertisements of its jeans, Levi's tries to fulfil the different needs and tastes of consumers within the segment.

ing program with the appropriate product design, pricing strategy, distribution strategy, and communication strategy is vital to the market success of the firm.

Many firms, large and small, practise a multi-offer strategy in today's environment. Procter & Gamble markets Tide, Dash, Duz, Cheer, Bold, Gain, Oxydol, and Bonus, among other detergents, to meet the desires of specific groups of detergent buyers. IBM offers huge mainframe computers, mid-range sizes tailored for medium-sized organizations, and computers designed for the home market.

Generally speaking, the company with a multi-offer marketing strategy should produce more sales by providing higher satisfaction for each of several target

APPLYING THE CONCEPTS

Single- versus Multi-Offer Strategies

A SINGLE-OFFER STRATEGY — FORD MOTOR COMPANY IN 1908

In 1908, Henry Ford introduced the Model T and revolutionized the automobile business around the world. Until the late 1920s, he sold only the Model T car and Model T truck. Ford's strategy was based on the belief that if he could get the price of a serviceable, utilitarian automobile low enough, he could develop a large mass market. His competitors were several hundred manufacturers who were producing vehicles that were virtually custom-built, with short production runs and high costs. Ford's strategy generated unprecedented sales. A dealership organization evolved that carried spare parts and service facilities to users across North America and through much of Europe. The marketing program, including an excellent service network, quickly made Henry Ford a multimillionaire and contributed to economic development through improving the transportation system.

There are some dangers inherent in a single-offer strategy, however. A firm that attempts to satisfy a very wide market with a single product or service *fairly well* is vulnerable to competition from those who choose to develop more specialized products that appeal to and serve segments of the larger market very well. Over time, General Motors and Chrysler developed a wider variety of models, price ranges, styles, and colour options. What worked superbly in 1908 faltered in the 1920s, and Ford had to move to a multi-offer strategy. The firm developed the Model A and the Model B, offering them with various options. The company differentiated the product line further in the 1930s by introducing the first mass-produced V-8 engine, which was a company hallmark for years.

AN EXTENSIVE MULTI-OFFER STRATEGY — FORD MOTOR COMPANY IN THE EARLY 1990S

The market matching strategy of the Ford Motor Company in the 1990s is quite different from that of 1908. It has evolved with the changing environment that faces the automobile industry. Ford's product line is much expanded from the Model T days, but the company still does not produce products for all markets. Instead, it serves those markets where its resources, marketing skills, product strengths, and competitive offerings can be best exploited. Table 4.1 compares the product lines then and now.

1. *Can a firm use a single-offer strategy today?*
2. *Using one or more of the four segmentation approaches discussed in Chapter 3, write a short description of the segment served by each of the Ford cars listed in Table 4.1.*

■ Table 4.1 **Market Matching Strategies**

Market Segment	Product Offerings			
	Ford Motor Company		Audi/Volkswagen/Porsche	
	1908 Single-Offer Strategy	Early 1990s Multi-Offer Strategy	1955 Single-Offer Strategy	Early 1990s Multi-Offer Strategy
General-Purpose Cars				
Small	Model T	Festiva Escort Mercury Tracer	Beetle	Fox Golf
Medium	Model T	Tempo Topaz		Jetta
Large		Taurus Crown Victoria		
Sporty Cars				
Low-priced		EXP		
Medium-priced		Mustang/Probe Capri		Scirocco
High-priced		Thunderbird Cougar		Porsche 911, 928, 944
Luxury Cars				
Medium-priced		Lincoln		Audi Quattro Audi Avant
High-priced		Continental Mark series		Audi 5000
Vans		Aerostar Clubwagon Ford Explorer/ Villager/Quest		Vanagon
Trucks				
Small	Model T (truck)	Ford Ranger Ford "B" series		
Medium		Ford "F" series Bronco		

markets than would be possible with only a single-offer strategy. However, whether a firm should choose a single- or a multi-offer strategy depends on management's goals, as well as on the economics of the situation — whether the company has the resources, and whether greater profits can be expected from the additional expense of a multi-offer strategy.

THE STAGES OF MARKET SEGMENTATION

The marketer has a number of potential bases for determining the most appropriate market matching strategy. Geographic, demographic, and psychographic bases, as well as product attributes, are often used in converting heterogeneous markets into specific segments that serve as target markets for the consumer-oriented mar-

APPLYING THE CONCEPTS

Segmentation Strategies Reflect Other Competitive Considerations

A SINGLE-OFFER STRATEGY FOR DIFFERENT REASONS — AUDI/VOLKSWAGEN/PORSCHE IN 1955

When Volkswagen decided to enter the North American market, it chose to do so with only the "Beetle" for a variety of reasons. First, the company was strapped for funds and could not expand its production facilities, which were stretched to the limit in trying to supply automobile-short postwar Europe. It also recognized that a dealer-support system and spare-parts inventory had to be developed from scratch if it was to compete successfully in North America. With these constraints in mind, Volkswagen marketers determined that the serviceable Beetle was the answer. The Beetle was relatively low-priced, was supported by an imaginative promotional campaign, and become an immediate success with those who wanted a small, relatively basic car. Volkswagen sold a much wider variety of products in Europe (and continued to introduce new products in that market much earlier than in North America). It deliberately chose to make a single offer to the North American market.

A STRATEGIC MOVE TO A MULTI-OFFER STRATEGY — AUDI/VOLKSWAGEN/PORSCHE IN THE EARLY 1990S

Today, products under the Volkswagen parent company's control compete for a much broader number of market segments than did the Beetle. The changes are indicative of a major change in the segmentation strategies. The company has not only the products but also the resources and the marketing infrastructure to serve more segments.

keter. The industrial marketer segments geographically, by product, or by end-use application. In either case, a systematic five-stage decision process is followed. This framework for market segmentation is shown in Figure 4.1.

No single base for segmentation is necessarily the best, so the firm should segment the market in a way that most suits the situation. For example, demographic segmentation may be used in planning an advertising campaign using print media because magazines are normally aimed at specific demographic segments. The marketer thus often experiments with segmenting markets in several ways in the process of discovering which of the marketing elements can be changed for greatest effect. (Similarly, marketing opportunities are sometimes discovered by rating how well competitors have served segments differentiated on a particular dimension.) This is part of the interactive process of analysis. The systematic five-stage decision process shown in Figure 4.1 lends form to what are otherwise often complex and unstructured problems.[2]

Stage I: Identify Market Segmentation Bases

The decision process begins when a firm identifies characteristics of potential buyers as bases that will allow the marketer to classify them into market segments. For example, IBM might segment on the basis of computer usage (accounting firms) or by company size. Segmentation bases should be selected so that each

■ Figure 4.1 **Market Segmentation Decision Process**

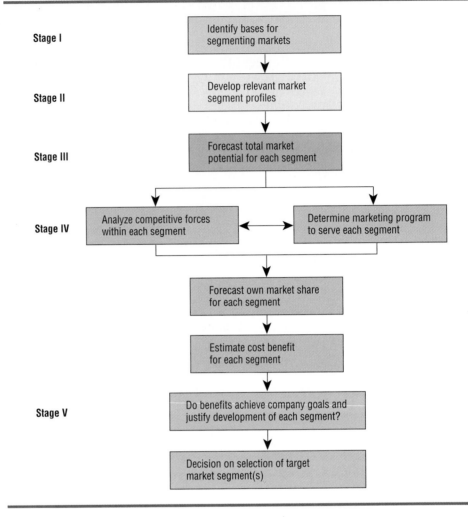

segment contains customers who have similar needs, so that specific marketing programs can be designed to satisfy those needs. For example, before Procter & Gamble decides to market Crest to a segment made up of large families, management should be confident that most large families are interested in preventing tooth decay and thus receptive to the Crest marketing offer. In some cases, this objective is difficult to achieve. Consider the marketer seeking to reach the consumer segment that is over 50 years of age. Saturday-evening television commercials can reach this group, but much of the expenditure may be wasted since the other major viewer group at that time consists of teenagers.

Stage II: Develop Relevant Profiles for Each Segment

Once segments have been identified, marketers should develop a profile of the relevant customer needs and behaviours in each segment.

Segmentation bases provide some insight into the nature of customers, but typically not enough for the kinds of decisions that marketing managers must make.

Managers need precise descriptions of customers in order to match marketing offers to their needs. In other words, the task at this stage is to develop profiles of the typical customer in each segment with regard to lifestyle patterns, attitudes toward product attributes and brands, brand preferences, product-use habits, geographic location, demographic characteristics, and so on. For example, one regional retail chain surveyed female customers and identified the following profile: age 25–55, 147–160 cm tall, 38–55 kg, career-oriented, and having a household income of $20 000 or higher. The retailer used this profile to set up separate "petites" sections, one of the fastest-growing segments in the women's fashion industry.[3]

Stage III: Forecast Market Potentials

In the third stage, market segmentation and market opportunity analysis are used together to produce a forecast of market potential within each segment. Market potential is the upper limit on the demand that can be expected from a segment and, combined with data on the firm's market share, sales potential.

This stage is management's preliminary go or no-go decision point as to whether the sales potential in a segment is sufficient to justify further analysis. Some segments will be screened out because they represent insufficient potential demand; others will be sufficiently attractive for the analysis to continue.

Consider the segments of the CD market. A producer must think carefully as to whether it will be profitable to enter the reggae segment, given the existing competition.

Stage IV: Forecast Probable Market Share

Even when the segment is large enough, a firm may not be able to compete in it successfully. Therefore, once market potential has been estimated, the share of that market that can be captured by the firm must be determined. This requires an analysis of competitors' positions in target segments. At the same time, the specific marketing strategy and tactics should be designed for these segments. These two activities should lead to an analysis of the costs of tapping the potential demand in each segment.

Procter & Gamble once outsold Colgate nearly two to one in dishwashing liquids. Colgate also ran behind in heavy-duty detergents and soaps. A realistic assessment indicated that for most directly competitive products, Colgate had little chance of overtaking P&G. So Colgate diversified its product line. Today, 75 percent of the firm's offerings do not face a directly competitive Procter & Gamble product, and those that do compete effectively.[4]

Stage V: Select Specific Market Segments (Target Markets)

Finally, the accumulated information, analyses, and forecasts allow management to assess the potential for the achievement of company goals and justify the development of one or more market segments. These are known as **target markets**. Demand forecasts combined with cost projections are used to determine the profit and return on investment that can be expected from each segment. Analyses of marketing strategy and tactics will determine the degree of consistency with

target market
A market segment that a company chooses to serve.

corporate image and reputation goals, as well as with unique corporate capabilities that may be achieved by serving a segment. These assessments will, in turn, determine management's selection of specific segments as target markets.

At this point of the analysis, the costs and benefits to be weighed are not just monetary, but also include many difficult-to-measure but critical organizational and environmental factors. For example, the firm may not have enough experienced personnel to launch a successful attack on a segment that has the potential to be an almost certain monetary success. Similarly, a firm with a product suitable for export may choose one country over another because management likes that country better. A public utility may decide not to encourage higher electricity consumption because of environmental and political repercussions. Assessing both financial and nonfinancial factors is a vital and final stage in the decision process.

There is not, and should not be, any simple answer to the market segmentation decision. The marketing concept's prescription to serve the customer's needs and to earn a profit while doing so implies that the marketer has to evaluate each possible marketing program on how it achieves this goal in the marketplace. By performing the detailed analysis outlined in Figure 4.1, the marketing manager can increase the probability of success in profitably serving consumers' needs.

Delta Hotels & Resorts has started to offer the Delta In-Room Business Zone service to travelling businesspeople in some of its hotels. With this plan, the hotel chain is trying to accommodate the office needs of its target market. In a highly competitive market, Delta recognizes that it must be innovative in identifying niches within its larger clientele.

TARGET MARKET DECISION ANALYSIS

Identifying specific target markets is an important aspect of overall marketing strategy. Clearly delineated target markets allow management to effectively employ marketing efforts like product development, distribution, pricing, and advertising to serve these markets.

Target market decision analysis, *the evaluation of potential market segments*, is a useful tool in the market segmentation process. Targets are chosen by segmenting the total market on the basis of any given characteristics (as described in Chapter 3). The example that follows illustrates how target market decision analysis can be applied.[5]

target market decision analysis
The evaluation of potential market segments.

A Useful Method of Identifying Target Markets

Sometimes marketers fail to take all potential market segments into consideration. A useful process is the "divide-the-box" procedure. Visualize the entire market for the product category as a single box. Then divide this total market box into realistic boxes or cells, with each cell representing a potential target segment (see Figure 4.2). How the cells are defined is up to you. They can be based on consumer benefits desired; on geographic, demographic, and psychographic characteristics; or on some combination of these. While this concept is simple, it can be extremely complex in practice, and creativity is required.

Consider the decisions of an airline company's marketing manager who wishes to analyze the market potential for various levels of passenger service. The company wants to delineate all possible target markets and to assess the most profitable multi-offer strategy.

As a tool for outlining the scope of the market, the marketing manager devises a grid like the one in Figure 4.3. This enables the company to match the possible types of service offerings with various customer classifications. The process of developing the target market grid forces the decision-maker to consider the entire range of possible market matching strategies. New or previously underserved segments

■ Figure 4.2 **The Divide-the-Box Procedure**

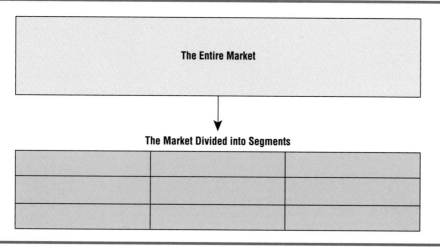

■ Figure 4.3 **Market for Airline Passenger Travel**

Market	First-Class	Extra-Service Business Class	Regular Tourist Class	Seat-Sale Class	Age Specials	Charter
Senior executives	X	X	?			X
Employees of large firms		X	X	?		X
Employees of small businesses		X	X	X		
Wealthy individuals	X	X				?
Other individuals			X	X		X
Senior citizens			?	X	X	X
Youth			X	X	X	X

X = Probable demand for service   ? = Uncertain or limited demand

may be uncovered. The framework also encourages an assessment of the sales potential in each of the possible segments, and aids in the proper allocation of marketing efforts to areas of greatest potential.

Once the cells of the grid have been identified, the marketer can then evaluate the wants, needs, and motivations of each market segment. For example, it appears that senior executives would be the appropriate targets for the first-class service and extra-service categories. Further research could confirm or modify these evaluations and enable the marketer to determine whether the market segment's size makes it worth developing a special offering for. Apparently, airlines have analyzed the needs and motivations for this segment. They provide roomier seating, improved food, and check-in service to satisfy the needs thus identified. *Market segmentation thus enables appropriate marketing plan design.*

The cross-classification in Figure 4.4 shows that the matrix can be further subdivided to gather more specific data about the characteristics of the proposed target market and to accurately develop a suitable marketing mix. The potential bases for segmenting markets are virtually limitless. For example, the segments might have been based on psychographic data or on the benefits sought. In the latter instance, prestige, comfort, and basic transportation might be some benefits that would assist in designing market offerings. Such divisions are sometimes made intuitively in the first place, but the final decisions are usually supported by concrete data.

Using Target Market Decision Analysis in Assessing a Product Mix

product mix
The assortment of product lines and individual offerings available from a marketer.

Product mix, a concept we will take a detailed look at in Chapter 10, refers to *the assortment of product lines and individual offerings available from a marketer.* Target market decision analysis can be used to assess a firm's product mix and to point up

■ Figure 4.4 **Employees of Large Firms, Extra-Service Class**

Service Benefit Desired	Heavy-Traffic Regions	Southern Canada	Northern Canada
Schedules	X		
Food			
Attendant service			
Leg room			

needed modifications. For example, one telephone company has used the concept to evaluate its product offerings.[6] The company segments the total market by psychographic categories as shown in Figure 4.5. Two of these categories are "belongers" and "achievers." Belongers were defined in this instance as those who are motivated by emotional and group influences. Achievers were defined as those whose dominant characteristic is the need to get ahead.

The telephone company's rule is to offer two and only two types of telephone sets in a given market segment in order not to have too complicated a market offering. Belongers were thus offered a regular phone and a romantic-type telephone to appeal to their sentiments. Achievers were offered the regular phone plus one designed to suggest the idea of efficiency and character. This analysis helped to select a product from the assortment shown in Figure 4.5.

Target market decision analysis can go beyond merely identifying target markets. It can play a crucial role in actually developing marketing strategies such as product mixes.

PRODUCT POSITIONING

After a target market has been selected, the task has just begun. Your firm will naturally find others competing in that segment. The challenge is to develop a marketing

■ Figure 4.5 **Using Target Market Decision Analysis to Evaluate a Product Mix**

Product Offering	Psychographic Category		
	Belongers	Achievers	Etc.
Romantic	Phone M Phone A Phone C		
Character		Phone R Phone Y	
Contemporary			

Source: "Properly Applied Psychographics Add Marketing Luster," *Marketing News* (November 12, 1982), p. 10.

positioning
Shaping the product and developing a marketing program in such a way that the product is perceived to be (and actually is) different from competitors' products.

plan that will enable your product to compete effectively against them. It is unlikely that success will be achieved with a marketing program that is virtually identical to competitors', for they already have attained a place in the minds of individuals in the target market and have developed brand loyalty. Since people have a variety of needs and tastes, market acceptance is more easily achieved by **positioning** — *shaping the product and developing a marketing program in such a way that the product is perceived to be (and actually is) different from competitors' products.*

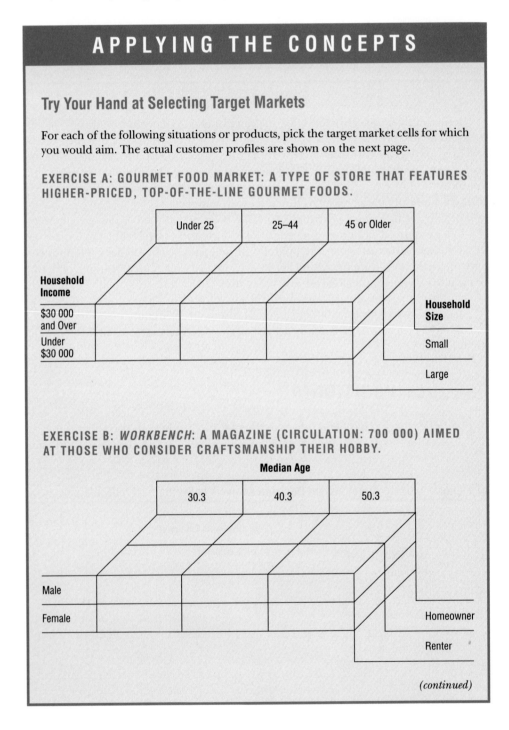

APPLYING THE CONCEPTS

Try Your Hand at Selecting Target Markets

For each of the following situations or products, pick the target market cells for which you would aim. The actual customer profiles are shown on the next page.

EXERCISE A: GOURMET FOOD MARKET: A TYPE OF STORE THAT FEATURES HIGHER-PRICED, TOP-OF-THE-LINE GOURMET FOODS.

EXERCISE B: *WORKBENCH*: A MAGAZINE (CIRCULATION: 700 000) AIMED AT THOSE WHO CONSIDER CRAFTSMANSHIP THEIR HOBBY.

(continued)

EXERCISE C: MERCEDES-BENZ: SOME MODELS RUN IN THE $50 000 RANGE. THIS EXERCISE REFERS TO NORTH AMERICAN BUYERS ONLY.

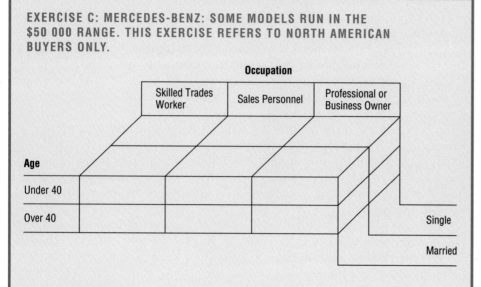

THE SOLUTIONS

The actual customer profiles for these items are as follows:

EXERCISE A: GOURMET FOOD MARKET

EXERCISE B: *WORKBENCH* MAGAZINE

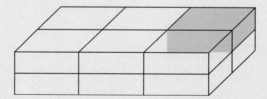

EXERCISE C: MERCEDES-BENZ

Source: Janet Guyon, "Gourmet-Food Market Grows as Affluent Shoppers Indulge," *Wall Street Journal* (May 6, 1982), p. 31; "Magazine Publisher Advertisers' Target Growing, 'Overlooked' Empty Nest Market," *Marketing News* (October 2, 1981), pp. 1, 10; and "Rolling Along," *Fortune* (December 14, 1981), p. 13.

Consider, for example, a simple positioning map of the cola market (see Figure 4.6). By plotting brands on a price-reputation/quality matrix the relative positions of the brands listed can be determined. At the time of writing, the positions of Pepsi and Coca-Cola® were being threatened by brands such as Cott and President's Choice. Many consumers were positioning the quality of the newer brands near Pepsi and Coca-Cola®, and were quite aware that they cost less. If you were a potential newcomer to the cola market segment, a positioning analysis such as this would be essential. Where would you position a new brand of cola?

The positioning process requires a careful analysis of the features and strengths of competitive offerings, as well as a good understanding of the needs and wants of the target market. From comparing the two, the marketer tries to find a niche of significant size that is currently poorly served, and to develop an offering to fit that opportunity. Positioning can sometimes be accomplished by using advertising to differentiate a product.

7-Up used promotion as the sole element in positioning. The firm discovered that its product was missing the primary market for soft drinks — children, teenagers, and young adults — because 7-Up's image was as a mixer for older people's drinks. The firm used its now well-known "uncola" campaign to first identify the product as a soft drink and then position it as an alternative to colas in the soft-drink market. Since then the company has continued its focus on advertising that emphasizes youth and action.

Another classic positioning campaign was that used by Avis to position itself against Hertz with the theme "Avis is only number two, why go with us? Because we try harder." In this case, the service was also adjusted to make the claim true.

A total marketing program is often dictated to secure position. An example is the establishment of CFM Inc. In 1987, Colin Adamson and Heinz Rieger were senior managers for a wood-burning fireplace maker. In the fireplace market, they saw an opportunity to develop a product to position against wood-burning and gas fireplaces, so they formed their own company and began to develop a product. They positioned their product away from the more traditional style of gas fireplace — a row of uniform, nonflickering blue flames coming from a steel pipe decorated, per-

■ Figure 4.6 **Positioning Map of Cola Market**

haps, with a poor imitation of a log. Instead, Adamson and Rieger developed a way to produce dancing yellow flames that simulate a wood fire, and surrounded them with natural-looking logs. The product could then be positioned as a realistic-looking alternative to wood.

CFM has now developed a range of products to enhance its gas fireplace position. Colin Adamson says, "A lot of people make things and then try to sell the market on them, [but] success comes from making what people want."[7] The firm has developed a loyal group of dealers, and therefore has the distribution system necessary to move its products from manufacturer to consumer. In product development, CFM pays much attention to regional tastes in materials, trims, and sizes. CFM's positioning strategy enabled the company to focus on developing product and marketing plans that led to achieving a sales volume of over $13 million by 1994.

Using product positioning to evaluate and develop marketing strategies in the light of competitive offerings in the market is a valuable and basic concept. It should follow naturally from the market segmentation decision.

■ KEY TERMS

single-offer strategy	multi-offer strategy	target market decision
concentrated marketing	differentiated marketing	analysis
undifferentiated	market segmentation	product mix
marketing	process	positioning
mass marketing	target market	

■ INTERACTIVE SUMMARY AND DISCUSSION QUESTIONS

1. Market segmentation ranges from treating the market as one to subdividing it into a number of portions. Give examples of firms that have adopted each of the two alternatives. In your opinion, have these firms made the correct decision?

2. A single-offer strategy is an attempt to satisfy a large or a small market with one product and a single marketing program. Give an example of where this seems to be working out well for a company, as well as an example of where this strategy may not be so beneficial to the company.

3. A multi-offer strategy is a bid to satisfy several segments of the market very well with specialized products and unique marketing programs aimed at each segment. Illustrate how a company marketing in Canada and Europe might manage this.

4. A firm may choose to adopt a single-offer strategy in a market that has several obvious market segments. Explain why.

5. Give an example of how a not-for-profit organization might apply a multi-offer segmentation strategy.

6. "No single base for segmentation is necessarily the best, therefore the firm should segment the market in a way that most suits the situation." Explain.

7. The stages of the market segmentation process are (1) identify segmentation bases, (2) develop relevant profiles for each segment, (3) forecast market potentials, (4) forecast probable market share, and (5) select specific target markets. Explain how each of these steps would apply to a marina and to a radio station.

8. Assume you are a manufacturer of computers and associated hardware. Using the divide-the-box procedure, identify the various target markets among college students.

9. Positioning is shaping the product and developing a marketing program in such a way that the product is perceived to be different from competitors' products. Draw a positioning matrix for a product category that you are familiar with.

10. Positioning can sometimes be accomplished through advertising alone, and sometimes requires a total marketing program to accomplish. Give an example of each situation.

CHAPTER 5

Obtaining Data for Marketing Decisions

CHAPTER OBJECTIVES

1. To describe the development and current status of the marketing research function.
2. To present the steps of the marketing research process.
3. To discuss the nature and sources of primary and secondary data.
4. To outline the methods of collecting survey data.
5. To discuss the nature of marketing information systems, and relate them to the marketing research function.

The need for business information has always existed. However, companies with extra information have a good chance of establishing leadership. The process of developing information through marketing research is being greatly enhanced through advanced telecommunications.

Businesses struggling to deal with the fast pace of change in telecommunications can get to feeling a little overwhelmed. "How do you handle change before it takes you over?" asks John Jung, director of planning and development for the Toronto Harbour Commission.

It's a question for which Jung is attempting to offer an answer. With his urban planning background, Jung has mounted a self-styled crusade to convince all major Canadian cities that what they need are "teleports," if their locally based business and employees are to stay globally competitive into the next century.

A teleport is like an airport or seaport but transports a new economy of weightless cargo: voice, data, text, and video. The basic teleports that now exist in Toronto, Montreal, and Calgary need to be enlarged beyond their current levels involving a mere couple of dozen firms, says Jung, who is also a director of the World Teleport Association based in New York.

"This is the way of the future for cities," says Jung. "The technology is moving so fast that we have to bring all the elements together." The next step up from the basic teleport is what is known as a "smart park" where many businesses come together to share facilities. The top rung is the "intelligent city" approach like the 1000-acre Teleport City in Tokyo or the 12 000-acre Las Colinas site near Dallas where thousands of people can be interconnected to each other and the world beyond.

Businesses occupying space in such integrated surroundings can transport information over short or long distances through seamless access to satellites, fibre-optic networks, and microwave hubs. Because everything is shared, including security, it is also more affordable. There is no need to worry about new technology; updates are continuously being done for you.

Jung argues that Canada needs to evolve similar new tools and techniques. The traditional means of planning how we live and how we structure our communities

WASHINGTON INTERNATIONAL TELEPORT
"Communications Gateway to the World."

no longer works. Just as the cities of the past needed electricity, water, gas, and sewers, teleports are as essential to the future. "The difference could mean life or death for our cities," he says.[1]

This urgency applies to businesses as well as to cities. Business information has always been important. Today, marketing research–generated information helps to define target markets. It also aids managers to understand consumer needs and responses to product offerings in those target markets. The process of generating, analyzing, and transmitting that information must continually become more sophisticated.

INTRODUCTION

The quality of all marketing planning decisions depends on the quality of the information on which they are based. A variety of sources of marketing information are available to the marketing decision-maker. Some involve the regular information flow that occurs in a company — for example, sales-force reports, accounting data, and other internal statistics. Sophisticated firms apply the power of computers to analyze such internal data, and to simulate the effects of changes in strategy.

Another important source of information is **marketing research**. Marketing research is *the systematic gathering, recording, and analyzing of data about problems relating to the marketing of goods and services.* This is the function that links the consumer to the company through information — information that is used to identify and define marketing opportunities and problems; to generate, refine, and evaluate marketing actions; to monitor marketing performance; and to improve understanding of marketing as a process.

Marketing research specifies the information required to address these issues, designs the method for collecting information, manages and implements the data

marketing research
The systematic gathering, recording, and analyzing of data about problems relating to the marketing of goods and services.

collection process, analyzes the results, and communicates the findings and their implications.[2]

The critical task of the marketing manager is decision making. Managers earn their salaries by making effective decisions that enable their firms to solve problems as they arise, and by anticipating and preventing the occurrence of future problems. Many times, though, they must make decisions with limited information of uncertain accuracy. If the decision-maker undertakes some marketing research, much valuable additional information can be gained to help with the decision. Although the marketing research does not *make* the decision, it does make it easier for the manager to do so.

Most of the market segmentation procedures outlined in Chapters 3 and 4 are based on information collected through marketing research. There is a growing use of marketing research for the development of marketing plans. Its regular use is now considered indispensable by most successful companies.

Marketing research in Canada may be said to have existed since there first were buyers and sellers. However, the day on which marketing research became a full-time profession was January 2, 1929. On that day, Henry King became the first full-time marketing researcher in Canada. His employer was an advertising agency, Cockfield Brown.[3]

In 1932, through the encouragement of Cockfield Brown, the first independent research company — Ethel Fulford and Associates — was founded in Toronto. In 1937, the Fulford company became known as Canadian Facts. Marketing research firms are now found in most major centres.

Marketing research studies generate data that may serve many purposes, for example, developing sales forecasts, determining market and sales potential, designing new products and packages, analyzing sales and marketing costs, evaluating the effectiveness of a firm's advertising, and determining consumer motives for buying products.

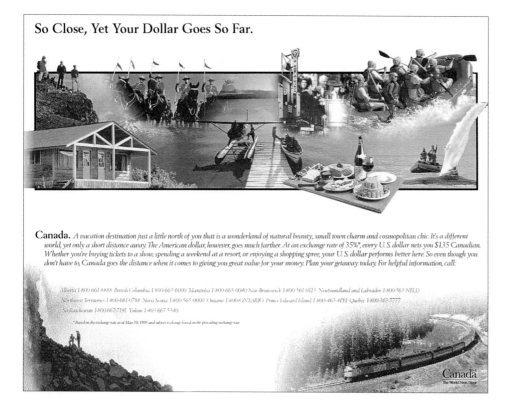

So Close, Yet Your Dollar Goes So Far.

Canada. *A vacation destination just a little north of you that is a wonderland of natural beauty, small town charm and cosmopolitan chic. It's a different world, yet only a short distance away. The American dollar, however, goes much farther. At an exchange rate of 35%*, every U.S. dollar nets you $135 Canadian. Whether you're buying tickets to a show, spending a weekend at a resort, or enjoying a shopping spree, your U.S. dollar performs better here. So even though you don't have to, Canada goes the distance when it comes to giving you great value for your money. Plan your getaway today. For helpful information, call:*

Alberta 1-800-661-8888 British Columbia 1-800-663-6000 Manitoba 1-800-665-0040 New Brunswick 1-800-561-0123 Newfoundland and Labrador 1-800-563-NFLD Northwest Territories 1-800-661-0788 Nova Scotia 1-800-565-0000 Ontario 1-800-ONTARIO Prince Edward Island 1-800-463-4PEI Quebec 1-800-363-7777 Saskatchewan 1-800-667-7191 Yukon 1-403-667-5340

* Based on the exchange rate as of May 30, 1995 and subject to change based on the prevailing exchange rate

Canada
The World Next Door

One of the Canadian Tourism Commission's goals is to attract the lucrative American tourist market to Canada. To this end, the commission researched and collected data. By the end of this process, the commission knew that Americans had a low awareness of Canada as a tourist destination and that the stiffest competition for the U.S. travel business came from the United States itself. Knowing this, the commission then developed a market strategy. One of the resulting advertisements, shown here, targets Americans in the northern states who, research showed, had a greater understanding of currency values than did their southern counterparts.

Many companies do not have their own marketing research departments. The function is often at least partly contracted out to specialists, because the research skill and activity levels are quite variable for different projects. Even large firms typically rely on outside agencies to conduct interviews. Such agencies have a large number of trained interviewers and have the appropriate systems in place to conduct the studies.

There are two basic types of marketing research organizations that a firm may use. The first can be categorized as a *full-* or *partial-service research supplier*. Full-service firms will handle all aspects of the research and provide a final report to management, whereas those offering partial service specialize in some activity, such as conducting field interviews.

The second type of external research organization is known as a *syndicated service*. A syndicated service provides a standardized set of data on a regular basis to all who wish to buy it. Normally, such research firms specialize in providing information on a small number of industries. For example, the Consumer Panel of Canada regularly gathers information on consumer purchases of food and other household items from 3400 households. These data inform marketers about brand preferences, brand-switching, and the effects of various promotional activities. Since all major products in the category are reported, a purchaser of this information can see how competitors are doing as well.

Research is likely to be contracted to outside groups when

1. Problem areas can be defined in terms of specific research projects that can easily be delegated.
2. There is a need for specialized know-how or equipment.
3. Intellectual detachment is important.[4]

THE MARKETING RESEARCH PROCESS

Infotech, a provincially based organization, was intrigued by the possibilities of stimulating in the province a computer software industry that would specialize in producing software for use in schools (known as "courseware"). Such an industry could be on the leading edge in the rapidly growing computer sector and thus could stimulate much economic growth in the province. In order to know whether such a strategy was worthwhile, Infotech commissioned a marketing research study. It wanted to know (a) the size of the courseware market in North America, (b) the trends in courseware for education usage, (c) what channels of distribution exist in the courseware industry and what it costs to use them, and (d) the marketing and financial aspects of courseware development.

Given the need for information, how is marketing research actually conducted? Normally, there are six steps involved in the marketing research process: (1) defining the problem, (2) exploratory research, (3) formulating a hypothesis, (4) research design, (5) collecting data, and (6) interpretation and presentation.

Figure 5.1 diagrams the marketing research process from information need to the research-based decision.

Problem Definition

Problems are barriers that prevent the accomplishment of organizational goals. A clearly defined problem helps the researcher to focus the research process on securing data that are necessary to solve the problem. Someone once remarked that well-defined problems are half solved.

■ Figure 5.1 **The Marketing Research Process**

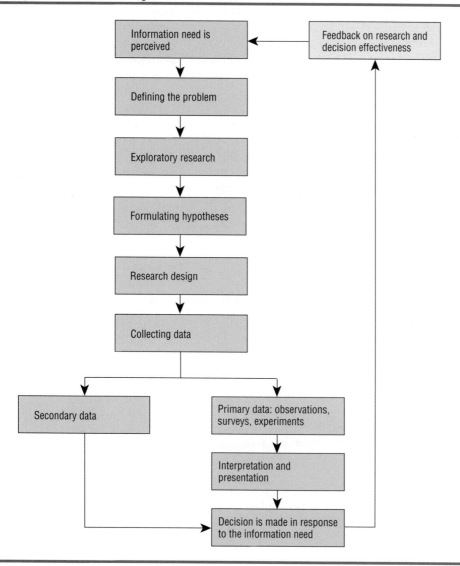

Problem definition is not always simple. Suppose a tennis player with a sore knee and other symptoms goes to the doctor for treatment. His "problem," he tells the doctor, is a sore knee. However, on further investigation, it is discovered that the knee pain is merely a symptom of the real problem: damage to an Achilles tendon. Business problems are much the same. Sometimes it is easy to pinpoint the problem that requires research information to solve. However, it is often difficult to determine the specific problem since what the researcher is confronted with may be only symptoms of the real underlying problem. To focus research properly, the research must look *beyond* the symptoms. This is done through exploratory research.

Exploratory Research

In searching for the cause of a problem, the researcher will learn about the problem area and begin to focus on specific areas for study. This search, often called **exploratory research**,

exploratory research
Learning about the problem area and beginning to focus on specific areas of study by discussing the problem with informed sources within the firm (a process often called *situation analysis*) and with knowledgeable others outside the firm (the *informal investigation*).

consists of discussing the problem with informed sources within the firm and with wholesalers, retailers, customers, and others outside the firm, and examining secondary sources of information. Marketing researchers often refer to internal data collection as the *situation analysis* and to exploratory interviews with informed persons outside the firm as the *informal investigation*. Exploratory research also involves evaluating company records, such as sales and profit analyses of its own and its competitors' products. Table 5.1 provides a checklist of topics that might be considered in an exploratory analysis.

In the Infotech case, exploratory research was done through a review of the literature about courseware; then a series of in-person and telephone interviews was undertaken with knowledgeable people in departments of education and the

■ Table 5.1 Topics for the Exploratory Analysis

The Company and Industry	1. Company objectives
	2. The companies in the industry (size, financial power) and industry trends
	3. Geographic locations of the industry
	4. The company's market share as compared with competitors'
	5. Marketing policies of competitors
The Market	1. Geographic location
	2. Demographic characteristics of the market
	3. Purchase motivations
	4. Product-use patterns
	5. Nature of demand
Products	1. Physical characteristics
	2. Consumer acceptance — strengths and weaknesses
	3. Package as a container and as a promotional device
	4. Manufacturing processes, production capacity
	5. Closeness and availability of substitute products
Marketing Channels	1. Channels employed and recent trends
	2. Channel policy
	3. Margins for resellers
Sales Organization	1. Market coverage
	2. Sales analysis by number of accounts per salesperson, size of account, type of account, etc.
	3. Expense ratios for various territories, types of product, size of accounts, etc.
	4. Control procedures
	5. Compensation methods
Pricing	1. Elasticity
	2. Season or special promotional price cuts
	3. Profit margins of resellers
	4. Legal restrictions
	5. Price lines
Advertising and Sales Promotion	1. Media employed
	2. Dollar expenditures as compared with competitors'
	3. Timing of advertising
	4. Sales promotional materials provided for resellers
	5. Results from previous advertising and sales promotional campaigns

school systems. Before a specific research plan could be designed, the researchers needed to know more about the subject and about the existing trends in the industry. Only then was it possible to begin planning a more complete research program. It was determined that the next steps should be (1) to systemically explore every current article written on the subject, and (2) to develop a plan to obtain information directly from different market groups. In some research projects, the next step might have been formulating hypotheses, but this did not seem appropriate in the Infotech situation.

Formulating Hypotheses

After the problem has been defined and an exploratory investigation conducted, the marketer should be able to formulate a **hypothesis**, *a tentative explanation about the relationship between variables as a starting point for further testing.* In effect, the hypothesis is an educated guess.

A marketer of industrial products might formulate the following hypothesis: "Failure to provide 36-hour delivery service will reduce our sales by 20 percent." Such a statement may prove correct or incorrect. Formulating a hypothesis does, however, provide a basis for investigation and an eventual determination of its accuracy. It also allows the researcher to move to the next step: developing the research design.

hypothesis
A tentative explanation about the relationship between variables as a starting point for further testing.

Research Design

The research design should be a comprehensive plan for testing the hypotheses formulated about the problem. **Research design** refers to *a series of advance decisions that, taken together, make up a master plan or model for conducting the investigation.* Developing such a plan allows the researcher to control each step of the research process. Table 5.2 lists the steps involved in the research design.

The research design for Infotech was quite complicated. No fewer than five individual data-collection procedures were planned. These included surveys of (1) departments of education across Canada and in selected American states, (2) principal textbook and software publishers, (3) key hardware and software manufacturers in Canada, and (4) a sampling of the teacher population.

research design
A series of advance decisions that, taken together, make up a master plan or model for conducting the investigation.

DATA COLLECTION

After the research design has determined what data are needed, the data must then be collected. Data collection is a major part of the marketing research project. Two type of data are typically obtained: primary data and secondary data. **Primary data** refer to *data being collected for the first time* during a study. Primary data are normally the *last* to be collected.

Secondary data are *previously published matter.* They serve as an extremely important source of information for the marketing researcher.

primary data
Data being collected for the first time.

secondary data
Previously published matter.

Collecting Secondary Data

Not only are secondary data important, they are also abundant in many areas that the marketing researcher may need to investigate. In fact, the overwhelming

■ Table 5.2 **Questions Typically Addressed at the Various Stages of the Research Process**

Stage in the Process	Typical Questions
Formulate problem	What is the purpose of the study — to solve a problem? identify an opportunity? Is additional background information necessary? What information is needed to make the decision at hand? How will the information be utilized? Should research be conducted?
Determine research design	How much is already known? Can a hypothesis be formulated? What types of questions need to be answered? What type of study will best address the research questions?
Determine data-collection method	Can existing data be used to advantage? What is to be measured? How? What is the source of the data to be collected? Can objective answers be obtained by asking people? How should people be questioned? Should the questionnaires be administered in person, over the phone, or through the mail? Should electronic or mechanical means be used to make the observations?
Design data-collection forms	Should structured or unstructured items be used to collect the data? Should the purpose of the study be made known to the respondents? Should rating scales be used in the questionnaires? What specific behaviours should the observers record?
Design sample and collect data	Who is the target population? Is a list of population elements available? Is a sample necessary? Is a probability sample desirable? How large should the sample be? How should the sample be selected? Who will gather the data? How long will the data gathering take? How much supervision is needed? What operational procedures will be followed? What methods will be used to ensure the quality of the data collected?
Analyze and interpret the data	Who will handle the editing of the data? How will the data be coded? Who will supervise the coding? Will computer or hand tabulation be utilized? What tabulations are called for? What analysis techniques will be used?
Prepare the research report	Who will read the report? What is their technical level of sophistication? What is their involvement with the project? Are managerial recommendations called for? What will be the format of the written report? Is an oral report necessary? How should the oral report be structured?

Source: Gilbert A. Churchill, Jr., *Basic Marketing Research*, 2nd ed. (Fort Worth, TX: Dryden, 1992), p. 52. Reprinted by permission of the publisher.

quantity of secondary data available at little or no cost often challenges the researcher who wants to select only pertinent information.

Secondary data consist of two types: internal and external. *Internal secondary data* include company records of sales, product performances, sales-force activities, and marketing costs. *External data* are obtained from a variety of sources. Governments — local, provincial, and federal — provide a wide variety of secondary data. Private sources also supply secondary data for the marketing decision-maker. An appendix at the end of this chapter describes a wide range of secondary data sources.

GOVERNMENT SOURCES

The federal government provides the country's most important sources of marketing data, the most frequently used being census data. Although the government spends millions of dollars in conducting the various censuses of Canada, the information obtained thereby is available at no charge at local libraries and Statistics Canada offices, or it can be purchased at a nominal charge on computer tapes or in various other electronic forms for instant access. In fact, Statistics Canada produces several different censuses. Table 5.3 briefly describes the main ones.

The current data are so detailed for large cities that breakdowns of population characteristics are available for areas comprising only a few city blocks (census tracts) or by postal code. Thus local retailers or shopping-centre developers can easily gather detailed information about the immediate neighbourhoods that will constitute their customer bases without spending time or money to conduct a comprehensive survey.

So much data are produced by the federal government that the marketing researcher often purchases summaries such as the *Canada Year Book* or *Market Research Handbook* or subscribes to *Statistics Canada Daily*. It is also possible to receive *Infomat Weekly*, which provides a listing of new releases by Statistics Canada. A further source of Statistics Canada data is the *Statistics Canada Catalogue*, which lists

■ Table 5.3 **Census Data Collected by Statistics Canada**

Census of Canada
Conducted once each decade, with certain categories checked every five years. It provides a count of all residents of Canada by province, city or town, county, or other suitable division, and, in large cities, by census tract. Particularly useful to marketers are the data provided by economic rather than political boundaries, such as greater metropolitan areas. Data are also gathered on age, gender, race, citizenship, education level, occupation, employment status, income, and family status of inhabitants. A less detailed census is conducted at the halfway point in the decade.

Census of Housing
Provides information regarding the housing conditions of Canadians, such as value of the dwelling, number of rooms, type of structure, ethnic origin of occupants, and year built.

Census of Manufacturers
Annual coverage of major industries revealing the value of products produced by industry, cost of materials and equipment, number of establishments, and wages paid.

Census of Agriculture
Conducted every five years. Data regarding the number of farms, number of persons residing on farms (by age and gender), value of farm products sold, area of each major crop, number of tractors, number of livestock, and presence of electricity and running water.

Census of Minerals
Data on employees, wages, quantities produced, cost of materials and supplies, types of equipment used, and hours worked.

major data published by the agency. Furthermore, the researcher can gain access to unpublished data through on-line terminals at Statistics Canada User Local Reference Centres. Many statistics are also available on CD-ROM.

Provincial and city governments are other important sources of information on employment, production, and sales activities within a particular province.

PRIVATE SOURCES

Numerous private organizations provide information for the marketing executive. In the *Handbook of Canadian Consumer Markets*, published by the Conference Board of Canada, the marketer will find a wide range of illuminating and valuable data. Another excellent source is *Canadian Markets*, published by the *Financial Post*. Other good summary data can be found in the annual survey of buying power published by *Sales and Marketing Management* magazine. For activities in a particular industry, trade associations are excellent resources. Advertising agencies continually collect information on the audiences reached by various media.

Several national firms offer information to business on a subscription basis. The largest of these, A.C. Nielsen Company, collects data that are reported weekly on product sales, retail prices, and promotional activities. The company also reports on consumer purchase behaviour, which is sourced from its 7250-member Home Scan panel, Canada's only electronic consumer-based household panel. The Consumer Panel of Canada (International Surveys) also gathers information on consumer purchases.

Advantages and Limitations of Secondary Data

The use of secondary data offers two important advantages over that of primary data:

1. Assembling previously collected data is almost always less expensive than collecting primary data.
2. Less time is involved in locating and using secondary data. Table 5.4 shows the estimated time involved in completing a research study requiring primary data.

■ Table 5.4 **Time Requirements for a Primary-Data Research Project**

Step	Estimated Time Required for Completion
Problem definition	Several days
Development of methodology	1 week
Questionnaire design	1 week
Questionnaire pretest and evaluation of pretest results	2 weeks
Field interviews	1–6 weeks
Coding of returned questionnaires	1 week
Data transfer to computer	1 week
Data processing and statistical analysis	7–10 days
Interpretation of output	1 week
Written report and presentation of findings	2 weeks
Total elapsed time	**12–17 weeks**

Source: Estimates by Alfred S. Boote, Corporate Director of Market Research, The Singer Company, quoted in "Everyone Benefits from Closer Planning, Research Ties," *Marketing News* (January 9, 1981), p. 30. Used by permission of the American Marketing Association.

The time involved will naturally vary considerably depending on such factors as the research subject and the scope of the study.

The researcher must be aware of two potential limitations to the use of secondary data: (1) the data may be obsolete, and (2) the classifications of the secondary data may not fit the information needs of the study. Published information has an unfortunate habit of rapidly going out of date. A marketing researcher analyzing the population of the Calgary metropolitan market in 1998, for example, may well discover that much of the 1996 census data are already obsolete due to an upturn or downturn in the economy or new developments in the oil and gas industry.

Data may also have been collected previously on such bases as county or city boundaries, when the marketing manager requires it to be broken down by city blocks or census tracts. In such cases, the marketing researcher may not be able to rearrange the secondary data in a usable form and must therefore collect primary data.

Secondary information proved very valuable in the Infotech study. A wide range of information sources was found. For example, relevant articles were found in such magazines as *Maclean's, Popular Computing,* and *Businessweek.* An especially valuable publication was *Electronic Learning,* which had no fewer than eight articles relating to the topic.

In addition to such periodicals, the researchers found eleven different special reports on various aspects of the educational use of computers. Report titles included "School Uses of Computers" (from Johns Hopkins University, in the United States) and "Phase Two: A Periodical Reporting on Education Computing in Scotland."

Studying such secondary sources gave the researchers immense insight into the fundamental issues involved in using courseware in the educational system. But some important information was still needed before a decision could be made about proceeding with the courseware project. Thus, it was time to plan a primary-data collection process.

Survey Design and Execution

Since secondary data are incomplete or do not fully relate to the problem at hand, the necessary information must then be obtained through one of several primary research methods. If hypotheses have been stated, facts should be gathered in such a way as to allow direct testing of the hypotheses.

Collecting primary data requires a considerable amount of technical expertise. Companies have found that they get the best information when specially trained individuals handle the design and execution of the research.

Collecting Primary Data

The marketing researcher has three alternative methods for collecting primary data: observation, survey, or controlled experiment. No one method is best in all circumstances.

THE OBSERVATION METHOD

Observational studies are conducted by actually viewing (either directly or through mechanical means such as hidden cameras) the overt actions of the respondent.

Examples of this approach include conducting traffic counts at a potential location for a fast-food franchise, checking licence plates at a shopping centre to determine the area from which shoppers are attracted, or using supermarket scanners to record sales of certain products.

The observation method has both advantages and drawbacks. The advantages are that observation is often more accurate than questioning techniques like surveys and interviews, and that it may be the only way to get information about such things as actual shopping behaviour in a supermarket. Observation may also be the easiest way to get specific data. The drawbacks include observer subjectivity and errors in interpretation. For instance, researchers might incorrectly classify people's economic status because of the way they were dressed at the time of observation.

Sometimes firms use the observation method in evaluating advertisements. A specialist research service is hired to study patterns of viewer eye movements when looking at advertisements. This is done under laboratory conditions. The results from one such eye-tracking test led the advertiser to move the headline from the bottom of the ad to the top, since a majority of eye movements flowed to the top. Observation could also be used to determine the route shoppers take once inside a supermarket. From this information, positioning of items might be determined.

THE SURVEY METHOD

The amount and type of information that can be obtained through mere observation of overt consumer acts is limited; to obtain information on attitudes, motives, and opinions, the researcher must ask questions. The survey method is the most widely used approach to collecting primary data. There are three kinds of surveys: telephone interviews, mail surveys, and personal interviews.

Telephone interviews are inexpensive and fast ways to obtain limited quantities of relatively impersonal information. Many firms have leased WATS[5] services, which considerably reduce the cost of long-distance calls.

Telephone interviews account for the majority of all primary marketing research. They are limited to a small number of simple, clearly worded questions. Such interviews have two drawbacks: it is extremely difficult to obtain information about the personal characteristics of the respondent, and the survey may be prejudiced since two groups will be omitted — those households without telephones and those with unlisted numbers. One survey reported that alphabetical listings in telephone directories excluded one-quarter of large-city dwellers, and that they underrepresented service workers and separated and divorced persons. In addition, the mobility of the population creates problems in choosing names from telephone directories. As a result, a number of telephone interviewers have resorted to using digits selected at random and matched to telephone prefixes in the geographic area to be sampled. This technique is designed to correct the problem of sampling those with new telephone listings and those with unlisted numbers.

Mail surveys allow the marketing researcher to conduct national studies at a reasonable cost. While personal interviews with a national sample may be prohibitively expensive, by using the mail, the researcher can reach each potential respondent for the price of a postage stamp. Costs may be misleading, however, since *returned* questionnaires for such a study range between 10 and 80 percent, depending on the length of the questionnaire and respondent interest (a 20 percent return is not uncommon). When returns are low, the question arises as to the opinions of the majority (who did not respond). Some surveys use a coin or other incentive to gain the reader's attention, an approach that can increase returns, but also increases

APPLYING THE CONCEPTS

Using Unobtrusive Marketing Research

Sometimes it is better to use unobtrusive methods of marketing research than to ask people direct questions about their attitudes or behaviour. "Garbology" — a technique whereby the researcher monitors consumption behaviour by rummaging through selected garbage — is a good example of such a method.

The *Saturday Evening Post* used this technique during the early 1900s to convince Campbell Soup that working-class, not upper-class, families were the appropriate target market for canned soups. Empty soup cans were widely documented in trash found in working-class neighbourhoods but not upper-class neighbourhoods. The success of this project resulted in Campbell becoming a regular advertiser in the *Saturday Evening Post.*

Restaurant managers have used garbology for years to monitor customer satisfaction. Patrons throw away what they don't want to eat, or don't have room for. Thus, quality or quantity of food can be flagged by this method.

A marketing director for a large regional hospital was able to calculate the actual bed count of other area hospitals. Her unobtrusive measure involved the laundry. Her hospital happened to wash the bed sheets for all the other hospitals. A simple tally gave her daily bed counts for each competing community hospital.

Source: William T. Neese, "Don't Be So Direct When Assessing Customer Satisfaction," *Marketing News* (February 4, 1991), p. 8; Leonard M. Fuld, "Did You Hear the One about the Oil Spots?" *Marketing News* (September 3, 1990), p. 30.

Can you think of other applications of this methodology?

costs. Unless additional information is obtained from nonrespondents, the results of the study are likely to be biased, since there may be important differences between the characteristics of these people and the characteristics of those who took the time to complete and return the questionnaire. For this reason, a follow-up questionnaire is sometimes mailed to nonrespondents, or telephone interviews may be used to gather additional information. These extra steps naturally add to the survey's cost. In spite of these difficulties, mail surveys are widely used.

Mail questionnaires must be carefully worded and pretested to eliminate any potential misunderstanding by respondents. But misunderstandings can occur with even the most clearly worded questions. When a truck operated by a government agency accidently killed a cow, an official responded with an apology and a form to be filled out. It included a space for "disposition of the dead cow." The farmer responded "kind and gentle."[6]

Personal interviews are typically the best means of obtaining more detailed information, since the interviewer has the opportunity to establish rapport with the respondent. The interviewer can also explain questions that might be confusing or vague to the respondent.

Personal interviews are slow and are the most expensive method of collecting data. However, their flexibility — coupled with the detailed information that can be collected — often offset these limitations. Marketing research firms sometimes rent locations in shopping centres, where they have greater access to potential buyers of

APPLYING THE CONCEPTS

Telephone Interviewing with a Personal Computer

It is now possible to design a questionnaire on a personal computer and then have the machine guide the researcher through each interview. This is done by using readily available software packages. After the questionnaire is developed, interviewers can sit at computers and start calling respondents. As questions are answered, a single keystroke records the response. Answers can be easily corrected, removed, or restored. The software program does the rest. It automatically pages to the next question and simultaneously tabulates answers.

When the survey is finished, the researcher can select how to analyze the data. If he or she wants to know the number of people between the ages of 25 and 45 who prefer Product X, the program will display the answer on the screen or on a printer. Various other tabulations are also available.

Systems like this expedite marketing research, and make it possible for even the smallest businesses and organizations to do the marketing research that is necessary for sound decision-making.

Suggest an application of this process for a company you are familiar with.

the products in which they are interested. Downtown retail districts and airports are other on-site locations for marketing research.

A special type of personal interview is the focus group interview. *Focus group interviews* are widely used as a means of gathering preliminary research information. In a focus group interview, eight to twelve people are brought together to discuss a subject of interest. Although the moderator typically explains the purpose of the meeting and suggests an opening discussion topic, he or she is interested in stimulating interaction among group members in order to develop the discussion of numerous points about the subject. Focus group sessions, which are often one to two hours long, are usually taped so that the moderator can devote full attention to the discussion.[7] This process gives the researcher an idea of how consumers view a problem. Often it uncovers points of view that the researcher had not thought of.

THE CONTROLLED EXPERIMENT METHOD

The final and least-used method of collecting marketing information involves using *controlled experiments*. An experiment is a scientific investigation in which the researcher controls or manipulates a test group and observes this group as well as another group that did not receive the controls or manipulations. Such experiments can be conducted in the field or in a laboratory setting.

Although a number of marketing-related experiments have been conducted in the controlled environment of a laboratory, most have been conducted in the field. To date, the most common use of this method has been in *test marketing*.

Marketers face great risks in introducing new products. They often attempt to reduce this risk by **test marketing**: *the selection of areas considered reasonably typical of the total market, and introducing a new product to these areas with a total marketing campaign to determine consumer response before marketing the product nationally.* Frequently used

test marketing
The selection of areas considered reasonably typical of the total market, and introducing a new product to these areas with a total marketing campaign to determine consumer response before marketing the product nationally.

cities include Calgary, Lethbridge, and Winnipeg. Consumers in the test-market city view the product as they do any other new product, since it is available in retail outlets and is advertised in the local media. The test-market city becomes a small replica of the total market. The marketing manager can then compare actual sales with expected sales and can project them on a nationwide basis. If the test results are favourable, the risks of a large-scale failure are reduced. Many products fail at the test-market stage; thus, consumers who live in these cities may purchase products that no one else will ever be able to buy.

The major problem with controlled experiments is the difficult task of controlling all the variables in a real-life situation. The laboratory scientist can rigidly control temperature and humidity, but how can the marketing manager determine the effect of varying the retail price through refundable coupons when the competition decides to retaliate against or deliberately confuse the experiment by issuing its own coupons?

In the future, experimentation will become more frequent as firms develop more sophisticated simulated competitive models requiring computer analysis. Simulation of market activities promises to be one of the great new developments in marketing.

In the Infotech market study, primary data were collected through four different research methods: (1) telephone surveys of departments of education across Canada and in selected American states, (2) personal and telephone interviews of principal Canadian textbook suppliers, (3) personal and telephone interviews of key hardware and software manufacturers and distributors, and (4) in-class surveys of teachers taking summer-school courses.

The Data-Collection Instrument

Most of the data-collection methods depend on the use of a good questionnaire. Developing a good questionnaire requires considerable skill and attention. It should be done with reference to specified objectives concerning information needed to complete the study. With this list as a foundation, specific questions are written for the questionnaire. The questionnaire must then be pretested; a small sample of persons similar to those who will be surveyed are asked to complete it. Discussions with these sample respondents help uncover points that are unclear. The nature, style, and length of the questionnaire will vary depending on the type of data-collection technique chosen. After pretesting and revising until the questionnaire works well, the researcher plans the necessary computer-coding set-up on the questionnaire to facilitate later data analysis.

The actual execution of the survey is beyond the scope of this book. Other important issues that need to be dealt with in planning the study are selecting, training, and controlling the field interviewers: editing, coding, tabulating, and interpreting the data; presenting the results; and following up on the survey. It is crucial that marketing researchers and research users co-operate at every stage in the research design. Too many studies go unused because marketing management views the results as not meaningful to them.

For the Infotech study, a team of four researchers worked almost full-time for approximately three months to collect the secondary data, design and pretest questionnaires, and gather the primary data. The data were analyzed and presented in a 195-page report to the client.

The report highlighted the size and growth of the market. It also showed that despite the favourable market size, the idea as originally conceived would be extremely difficult to implement. As a result of the study, the sponsor was able to make an informed decision about whether or not to go ahead. The marketing research presented information that could save the sponsor a great deal of time and money.

Sampling Techniques

Sampling[8] is one of the most important aspects of marketing research. *The total group that the researcher wants to study* is called the **population** or **universe.** For a political campaign, the population would be all eligible voters. For a new cosmetic line, it might be all women in a certain age bracket. If this total group is contacted, the results are known as a **census.** Unless the group is small, the cost of such a survey will be overwhelming. Even the federal government attempts a full census only once every ten years.

Information, therefore, is rarely gathered from the total population during a survey. Instead, researchers select a representative group called a sample. Samples can be classified either as probability samples or as nonprobability samples. A **probability sample** is *a sample in which every member of the population has a known chance of being selected.* Because **nonprobability samples** are *arbitrary,* standard statistical tests cannot be applied to them. Marketing researchers usually base their studies on probability samples, but it is important to be able to identify all types of samples.[9] Some of the best-known sampling plans are outlined below.

A **convenience sample** is *a nonprobability sample based on the selection of readily available respondents.* Broadcasting's "on-the-street" interviews are a good example. Marketing researchers sometimes use such samples in exploratory research, but not in definitive studies, because of the weakness of this method.

A nonprobability sample of people with a specific attribute is called a **judgement sample**. Election-night predictions are usually based on polls of "swing voters" and are a type of judgement sample.

A **quota sample** is *a nonprobability sample that is divided so that different segments or groups are represented in the total sample.* An example would be a survey of imported-auto owners that included 33 Nissan owners, 31 Toyota owners, 7 BMW owners, and so on.

A **cluster sample** is *a probability sample that is generated by randomly choosing one or more areas or population clusters and then surveying all members in the chosen cluster(s).* This approach can be helpful in a situation where it is difficult to obtain a complete list of all members of the population, but where there is good information on certain *areas* (such as census tracts).

The basic type of probability sample is the **simple random sample**, *a sample in which every item in the relevant universe has an equal opportunity of being selected.* Provincial lotteries are an example. Each number that appears on a ticket has an equal opportunity of being selected, and each ticket holder has an equal opportunity of winning. Using a computer to select 200 respondents randomly from a mailing list of 1000 would give every name on the list an equal opportunity of being selected.

A probability sample that takes every nth item on a list, after a random start, is called a **systematic sample**. Sampling from a telephone directory is a common example. This is a frequently used sampling procedure.

---

population or **universe**
The total group that the researcher wants to study.

census
A collection of marketing data from all possible sources.

probability sample
A sample in which every member of the population has a known chance of being selected.

nonprobability sample
A sample chosen in an arbitrary fashion so that each member of the population does not have a representative chance of being selected.

convenience sample
A nonprobability sample based on the selection of readily available respondents.

judgement sample
A nonprobability sample of people with a specific attribute.

quota sample
A nonprobability sample that is divided so that different segments or groups are represented in the total sample.

cluster sample
A probability sample that is generated by randomly choosing one or more areas or population clusters and then surveying all members in the chosen cluster(s).

simple random sample
A probability sample in which every item in the relevant universe has an equal opportunity of being selected.

systematic sample
A probability sample that takes every nth item on a list, after a random start.

MARKETING INFORMATION SYSTEMS

For all companies, some market data flow in on a regular basis from sales and other marketing activities. And companies that undertake marketing research gain other periodic bursts of facts from such studies.

The value of such material can vary significantly. Data and information are not necessarily synonymous terms. *Data* refer to statistics, opinions, facts, or predictions categorized on some basis for storage and retrieval. *Information* is data relevant to the marketing manager in making decisions. Often, the right information does not seem to be available when a marketing decision has to be made. This can be because the company simply does not have it, or because the information is not readily available in the firm's system.

The solution to the problem of obtaining relevant information appears simple — establish a systematic approach to information management by installing a planned marketing information system (MIS). Establishing an effective information system is, however, much easier said than done, as evidenced by the large number of firms that have attempted to develop an MIS and have succeeded only in increasing the amounts of irrelevant data available to them.

A **marketing information system** is *a set of routine procedures to continuously collect, monitor, and present internal and external information on company performance and opportunities in the marketplace.* Properly constructed, the MIS can serve as the nerve centre for the company, providing instantaneous information suitable for each level of management. It can act like a thermostat, monitoring the marketplace continuously so that management can adjust its actions as conditions change.

The analogy of an automatic heating system illustrates the role of marketing information in a firm's marketing system. Once the objective of a temperature setting (perhaps 20°C) has been established, information about the actual temperature in the house is collected and compared with the objective, and a decision is made based on this comparison. If the temperature drops below an established figure, the decision is made to activate the furnace until the temperature reaches some established level. On the other hand, a high temperature may require a decision to turn off the furnace.

Deviation from the firm's goals of profitability, return on investment, or market share may necessitate changes in price structures, promotional expenditures, package design, or numerous marketing alternatives. The firm's MIS should be capable of revealing such deviations and possibly suggesting tactical changes that will result in attaining the established goals.

Some marketing executives feel that their company does not need a marketing information system, for various reasons. Two arguments are most often given: (1) the size of the company's operations does not warrant such a complete system, and (2) the information provided by an MIS is already being supplied by the marketing research department.

These contentions arise from a misconception regarding the services and functions performed by the marketing research department. Marketing research has already been described as typically focussing on a specific problem or project; the investigations involved have a definite beginning, middle, and end.

Marketing information systems, on the other hand, are much wider in scope and involve the continual collection and analysis of marketing information. Figure 5.2 indicates the various information inputs — including marketing research studies — that serve as components of a firm's MIS.

marketing information system
A set of routine procedures to continuously collect, monitor, and present internal and external information on company performance and opportunities in the marketplace.

■ Figure 5.2 **Information Components of a Firm's MIS**

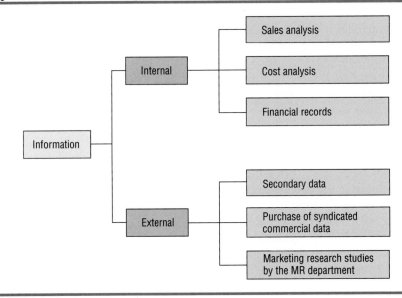

Robert J. Williams, creator of the first and still one of the most notable marketing information systems in 1961 at the Mead Johnson division of Edward Dalton Company, explains the difference this way:

> The difference between marketing research and marketing intelligence is like the difference between a flash bulb and a candle. Let's say you are dancing in the dark. Every 90 seconds you're allowed to set off a flash bulb. You can use those brief intervals of intense light to chart a course, but remember everybody is moving, too. Hopefully, they'll accommodate themselves roughly to your predictions. You may get bumped and you may stumble every so often, but you can along.
>
> On the other hand, you can light a candle. It doesn't yield as much light, but it's a steady light. You are continually aware of the movements of the other bodies. You can adjust your own course to the courses of the others. The intelligence system is a kind of candle. It's no great flash on the immediate state of things, but it provides continuous light as situations shift and change.[10]

By focussing daily on the marketplace, the MIS provides a continuous, systematic, and comprehensive study of areas that indicate deviations from established goals. The up-to-the-minute data allow problems to be corrected before they adversely affect company operations.

Successful Marketing Information Systems

The Monsanto Company and General Mills Incorporated are examples of firms with a successful MIS in operation.

Monsanto has designed one of the most advanced marketing information systems in operation. The system provides detailed sales analyses by product, sales, district, type of mill, and end use. Computer analyses are obtained from a continuing panel of households that represent a cross section of the national market. Information is collected on purchase patterns by socio-economic group and is then analyzed to determine current buying trends.

Monsanto also collects survey data to record the actions of competitors. In addition, the system generates short-, medium-, and long-range forecasts for the company and industry. Short-term forecasts are developed for each of 400 individual products.

The General Mills computer supplies each zone, regional, and district manager with a daily report on the previous day's orders by brand and a comparison of current projects of monthly sales with the monthly total projected the week before. Each of 1700 individual products is analyzed in terms of current profitability and projected annual profitability as compared with target projections made at the beginning of the year. The "problem" products requiring management attention are then printed out on the daily reports. A similar report looks for problem areas in each region and breaks down the nature of the problem according to cause (i.e., profit margins, over- or underspending on advertising and sales promotion.)[11]

As marketing research becomes increasingly scientific and is combined by a growing number of organizations into fully functional information systems, decision-makers benefit by making informed decisions about problems and opportunities. Sophisticated computer simulations make it possible to consider alternative courses of action by posing a number of "what if?" situations.

This chapter has shown that information is vital for marketing decision-making. No firm should operate without detailed information on consumers, competitors, and conditions in its market. Marketing research information enables the company to identify market segments and serves as a base for developing the marketing plan.

The first five chapters of this book have been designed to serve as building blocks for marketing planning. The next chapter will show how a marketing plan is developed.

■ KEY TERMS

marketing research	primary data	judgement sample
full-service research supplier	secondary data	quota sample
partial-service research supplier	focus group interview	cluster sample
	test marketing	simple random sample
syndicated service	population or universe	systematic sample
exploratory research	census	marketing information system
hypothesis	probability sample	
research design	nonprobability sample	
	convenience sample	

■ INTERACTIVE SUMMARY AND DISCUSSION QUESTIONS

1. Marketing research is the systematic gathering, recording, and analyzing of data about problems relating to the marketing of goods and services. Does information collected in such a scientific manner reduce the scope of management decision-making? Explain.

2. Full- and partial-service research suppliers handle various amounts of specific research needed by a firm. Syndicated service organizations collect and sell regularly collected information. Give examples of when each of these types of service would be used by a company.

3. The six steps of the marketing research process are (1) defining the problem, (2) exploratory research, (3) formulating a hypothesis, (4) research design, (5) collecting data, and (6) interpretation and presentation. A small firm recognizes that it has the abilities to develop high-quality air-monitoring equipment. Illustrate how the marketing research process might be applied to help management decide whether or not to enter this market.

4. Explain how problem definition in marketing research can sometimes be confused with symptoms.

5. Research design is a master plan or model for conducting the investigation. Differentiate between research design and the steps of the marketing research process.

6. Secondary data are previously published matter. Give examples of sources of external secondary data.

7. Discuss the advantages and limitations of secondary data.

8. Primary data are those collected for the first time. Primary data may be collected by observation, survey, or controlled experiment. Give examples of each of these data-collection methods.

9. The three kinds of surveys are telephone interviews, personal interviews, and mail surveys. Discuss the advantages and disadvantages of each.

10. Test marketing is one of the experimental designs used for collecting information. Why would a firm undertake test marketing? Why don't all firms do so?

11. In drawing a sample to research, firms can choose between probability and nonprobability samples. Why are nonprobability samples generally considered to be unreliable?

12. A marketing information system is a set of routine procedures to continuously collect, monitor, and present internal and external information on company performance and opportunities in the marketplace. Explain how a marketing information system could provide better information for management decisions than periodic marketing research surveys.

Locating Secondary Data

The publications listed and described in this appendix refer mainly to the Canadian market. Some international marketing sources are covered in the final section.

These are by no means all the sources of secondary data available for Canada or for international markets. However, it is hoped that these sources will serve as a representative list and as a starting part in the search for secondary sources of marketing data.

CANADIAN GOVERNMENT PUBLICATIONS

The federal government generates a vast array of publications through its various departments and agencies. Two publications or finding aids are useful in keeping track of these publications. The *Weekly Checklist of Canadian Government Publications* put out by Canada Communication Group, Publishing Division lists departmental and parliamentary priced and nonpriced monographs and serials that have been released during the week. These materials are available free of charge to libraries that have negotiated a depository status agreement with the federal government. Check on the status of a library when using its federal government publications.

The second finding aid, *Special List of Canadian Government Publications*, includes reprints of publications that have already appeared in the above-mentioned *Weekly Checklist*, scientific and technical publications that have a limited print run, and Crown Corporation publications. Both publications make it clear whether the issuing agency or the Canada Communication Group itself is responsible for distribution of a particular publication.

Due to the diversity and sheer quantity of these materials, library users are advised to consult with library staff when using federal government publications.

Statistics Canada

Statistics Canada publishes extensive statistical information gathered through various sources. In addition to standard print publications, data are disseminated on computer printouts, microform, and in electronic format. Maps and other geographic reference materials are also available for some types of data. With over 900 titles available, it is not practical to describe all the publications and services. However, detailed information can be obtained in several ways. There are Statistics Canada regional centres in the following locations:

- Halifax, Nova Scotia
- Montreal, Quebec
- Ottawa, Ontario
- Toronto, Ontario

- Winnipeg, Manitoba
- Regina, Saskatchewan
- Edmonton, Alberta
- Calgary, Alberta
- Vancouver, British Columbia

Each centre has a collection of current Statistics Canada publications and reference materials that can be consulted or purchased. Copying facilities for printed materials and microform are also available, as is access to CANSIM (Statistics Canada's computerized database)

STATISTICS CANADA CATALOGUE

This catalogue, published on an annual basis, provides a comprehensive description of the print publications, electronic products, and services available from Statistics Canada. Each entry contains a brief summary of the publication as well as technical details and pricing information.

A special section entitled "Finding and Using Statistics" has been added to the catalogue to help users in locating what they are after and how to use it once they find it. This section is particularly useful for first-time users of Statistics Canada's services.

CANSIM

CANSIM (Canadian Socio-economic Information Management System) is Statistics Canada's computerized database network and information retrieval service. It provides public access at cost to current and historical statistics, specialized analysis packages, graphics capabilities, and a bibliographic search service.

CANADIAN ECONOMIC OBSERVER

Generally, the most readily available Statistics Canada publication is likely to be the *Canadian Economic Observer*. It was titled the *Canadian Statistical Review* up to 1988. It is published monthly and as of September 1993 has been split into two parts, a journal with feature articles and economic analysis, and a statistical summary. The journal part provides authoritative commentary on Canadian and international economic trends, analysis of current economic conditions including the composite leading indicator, and a monthly feature article. The statistical summary provides the complete range of hard data on critical market indicators, prices, markets, trade, and demographics. Data on the provinces and the G7 international scene are also compiled. An annual historical statistical supplement that compiles monthly data is also available individually or as part of the subscription to the *Canadian Economic Observer*.

PROVINCIAL GOVERNMENT PUBLICATIONS

The provincial governments publish thousands of documents through their various department and agencies. These publications cover a variety of topics, reflecting the nature of the department from which the document originated. They range across the entire information spectrum, from agriculture to urban affairs.

As the available documents are too numerous to describe individually, one can only offer direction to the major sources that list and describe the documents published by the provincial governments. As an illustration, here is the way one would find publications generated by the province of Manitoba. Documents published by other provincial jurisdictions can be identified and obtained in a similar fashion.

The Province of Manitoba

Like a number of provinces, Manitoba makes its publications available through a department or agency of the government. It publishes a *Monthly Checklist of Manitoba Government Publications* that lists the publications. The publications are listed by their issuing department, and this means by department, their branches and subdivisions, as well as boards, committees, and other agencies or bodies of the government. The publications can be obtained from their issuing body or from Statutory Publications, a government department, as indicated in the Monthly Checklist.

The *Monthly Checklist* itself is arranged alphabetically by issuing department. Each entry provides bibliographic specifics and notes when required. An annual cumulation is also arranged alphabetically by issuing department, but has an index that provides access by name, title, and keyword.

CHAMBERS OF COMMERCE

Most major cities and towns have a Chamber of Commerce. A Chamber of Commerce is an association established to further the business interests of its community. The Chambers in most metropolitan cities publish information about their cities for promotional reasons. The types of information one can expect to find at most Chambers of Commerce include economic facts, employment figures, government descriptions, demographic data, and quality of life statistics.

As an illustration, the Winnipeg Chamber of Commerce publishes an annual *Membership Directory and Buyer's Guide*. This publication provides a description of Chamber services, individual and corporate member listings, and a buyer's guide arranged by service and product.

OTHER BUSINESS ORGANIZATIONS

Municipalities, cities, and towns, in their promotional efforts to stimulate business development, often create special agencies to act as a catalyst for economic development. As part of their efforts, such agencies create resource material that can be of great value to the researcher when gathering secondary material at the local level.

An example of such an agency is Winnipeg 2000, established in 1990 by the City of Winnipeg. It is composed of influential community leaders in the city. Winnipeg 2000's mandate is to use its leadership to ensure implementation of new economic development initiatives. Consequently, the agency has generated publications like *Winnipeg 2000 Profile* that highlight and focus on the strengths of Winnipeg through an analysis of its existing industry, workforce, energy costs, assistance programs and services, taxes, and quality of life indicators.

Most of the information contained in the Profile is available elsewhere but when packaged as one entity as it is, the research process is made easier. Similar organizations to Winnipeg 2000 exist in other jurisdictions across the country. The researcher seeking marketing data must be aware of their possible existence.

MARKET REPORTS, SURVEYS, DIRECTORIES, SPECIAL ISSUES, MAGAZINES, AND NEWSLETTERS

Many of the publications listed in the remained of this appendix are available through university, public, and special business libraries. As many of them can be either fairly expensive or difficult to locate, consult with a librarian as to cost and possible locations where they may be held.

Once again the annotated lists are not meant to be comprehensive, but rather a sampling of some of the more significant publications in each of the fields.

The publications are listed under major headings that describe the industry, trade, or sector to which they pertain. Remember that the headings are not clear-cut: there may be overlap and therefore a need to consult more than one heading.

Some "special issues" may appear in libraries under the title of the magazine with which they are associated. Furthermore, some of the "annual" publications may not always be published on a regular basis, and some special issues may appear with little or no prepublication announcement.

Advertising

Canadian Advertising Rates and Data
Published monthly. Known by its acronym *CARD*. Advertises itself as Canada's media authority for both print and broadcast media. Provides addresses, advertising rates, circulation, mechanical requirements, and personnel and branch office information for radio and TV stations, newspapers, and magazines for all of Canada. (Maclean Hunter Publishing)

Canadian Media Directors' Council Media Digest
Published annually as a supplement to *Marketing Magazine*, formerly called *Marketing*. Profiles the advertising industry in a statistical format. Provides net advertising revenues by medium as well as analysis of each medium, including television, radio, newspapers, business publications, and consumer magazines. Also contains a useful media terminology dictionary. (Maclean Hunter Publishing)

National List of Advertisers
Published annually in December. Provides the addresses, telephone numbers, brand names, and personnel for over 3000 major advertisers in Canada. In a special section, the companies are arranged by their Standard Industrial Classification Code. Advertising agencies are also listed. (Maclean Hunter Publishing)

Publication Profiles
An annual publication that is a supplement to the above-described *Canadian Advertising Rates and Data*. Describes the editorial profile of all the major consumer, farm, and business publications published on an ongoing basis in Canada. (Maclean Hunter Publishing)

Canadian Market, General

Bank of Canada Review
Now published quarterly, with monthly statistical supplements, as opposed to its former monthly schedule. Combines short articles and news items on monetary policy with extensive charts and tables on the major financial and economic statistical indicators collected and analyzed by the Bank. (Bank of Canada)

Canada Year Book

Published every two years. Records in narrative and statistical format the developments in Canada's economic, social, and political life. Useful for determining "where Canada is at" on general topics. (Statistics Canada)

Canadian Economic Observer

Published monthly but now in two parts, a journal with feature articles and economic analysis and a statistical summary. The data in both parts are retrieved from CANSIM, Statistics Canada's computerized data bank. An annual historical statistical supplement that compiles monthly data is also available. All three combine to become the definitive source for Canadian statistical information. For a more complete description of the *Canadian Economic Observer*, see above under Statistics Canada. (Statistics Canada)

Canadian Markets

Published annually. One of the most extensive sources for demographics on Canadian urban markets. Provides data and projections for population, households, retail sales, and personal income for markets nationwide. The markets are defined by the census divisions. Buying power indices are developed, allowing for market comparisons. Municipal and provincial profiles are also provided. (Financial Post Company)

Canadian Outlook: Economic Forecast

Published quarterly. Features forecasts on the major components of the Canadian economy, including consumer expenditures, housing, government, business, international trade, energy, employment, labour force, costs and prices, and the financial markets. Statistical tables covering the same range of topics follow. An *Executive Summary* of *Canadian Outlook* is also available on a quarterly basis. (Conference Board of Canada)

Editor and Publisher Market Guide

Published annually. A compilation of marketing data on all Canadian and U.S. markets where daily newspapers are published. The main sections survey each of the cities or communities supporting a daily. Another section provides a nationwide summary of population income, households, and farm products. Market ranking tables are shown for population, disposable income, income per household, and total retail sales. Retail sales are in turn broken into nine categories. (Editor and Publisher Company)

Market Research Handbook

Published annually. Provides a convenient source of data for analyzing Canadian markets. It is based on the latest census data and estimates of that data. Divided into sections, the first six cover national and international markets, the next two cover metropolitan markets, and the final one covers projections that are of particular interest to researchers and marketers. (Statistics Canada)

Provincial Outlook: Economic Forecast

Published quarterly. Similar in format to *Canadian Outlook*, but with individual sections for each of the Canadian provinces. Statistics tables of key economic indicators for each province follow the forecasts. An *Executive Summary* of *Provincial Outlook* is also available on a quarterly basis. (Conference Board of Canada)

Sales and Marketing Management

Published monthly. An American journal that features articles on sales and marketing management. Of particular note are its annual issues of various types of market survey data. These include *Survey of Buying Power, Survey of Media Markets, Sales Manager's Budget Planner*, and *Survey of Selling Costs*. These surveys can be invaluable when analysis of the North American market is required. However, Canadian data are represented in only some of the survey analysis. (Bill Communications Inc.)

Clothing

Canadian Apparel Manufacturer: Buyer's Guide
Published annually as a special issue of *Canadian Apparel Manufacturer*. Lists apparel associations, educational institutions, suppliers, manufacturers, products, and trade names for the apparel industry. (Canadian Textile Journal Inc.)

Canadian Textile Journal Manual
Published annually in July/August as a special issue of *Canadian Textile Journal*. A comprehensive source of information that provides access to textiles, chemical specialties, yarn sources (importers and domestic producers), Canadian machinery agents, and textile mills. The largest section is a buyer's guide listing products and services, with the companies paying a fee for a listing. Other information sources cover business opportunities, associations, and conferences. (Canadian Textile Journal Inc.)

Style: Buyer's Guide
Published annually in August as a special issue of *Style*. A valuable source of information for manufacturers and retailers of women's apparel in Canada. (Style Communications)

Computers

Computing in Canada
Published every two weeks in newspaper format. Provides news on current developments for information technology management in Canada. Normally contains a special report featuring some aspect of the field. Companies are indexed for each issue, and articles providing statistics for the industry are common. Special, supplementary issues published irregularly are devoted to major trends. (Plesman Publications)

Construction, Public Works, and Hardware

Civic Public Works: Municipal Reference Manual and Buyers Guide
Published annually as a special issue of *Civic Public Works*. Lists suppliers and products in the field of public works, including water supply, sewage, highway construction, and waste management. The intended audience is government officials at all levels. (Maclean Hunter Publishing)

Construction Equipment Buyer's Guide
Published annually as a special issue of *Heavy Construction News*. Focusses on manufacturers, distributors, products, and accessories for the construction industry in Canada. (Maclean Hunter Publishing)

Hardware Merchandising: Buyer's Guide and Annual Sources Directory
Published annually as a special issue of *Hardware Merchandising*. Provides informa-

tion on suppliers, agents, and products in the hardware and home improvement industry. (Maclean Hunter Publishing)

Electronics

Canadian Electronics: Buyer's Guide
Published annually in August as a special issue of *Canadian Electronics*. Provides information on manufacturers of electronic equipment, systems and components, and end users of the equipment. (Action Communications)

Electronic Bluebook
Published annually. Lists the names, products, and companies of the electrical equipment industry. (Kerrwil Publications)

Electronic Products and Technology: Electrosource Product Reference Guide and Telephone Directory
Intended audience are the buyers and engineers in Canada's electronics industry. Lists companies, products and their suppliers, U.S. and foreign manufacturers, and manufacturers' representatives and distributors. (Lakeview Publications)

Financial and Insurance

Canadian Insurance, Annual Review of Statistics
Published annually in May as a special issue of *Canadian Insurance*. Reviews the Canadian insurance industry in a largely statistical format. The major portion of the publication is taken up by the company exhibits, which provide five years of underwriting experience for insurers in Canada. Five-year data are also provided for the various lines of insurance, such as liability, aircraft, accident and sickness, and marine insurance. Recent developments and trends in the industry are also highlighted in narrative form. (Stone and Cox Ltd. Publishers)

Canadian Underwriter: Annual Statistical Issue
Published annually in June as a special issue of *Canadian Underwriter*. Five years of underwriting experience by individual company makes up the core of this issue. Statistical tables by type of insurance and by type of company are also provided. Leading companies are ranked by type of insurance and also by their rank within their provincial jurisdiction. (Southam Magazine Group)

Directory of Employee Benefits Consultants
Published annually in August as a special section of *Benefits Canada*. The 1994 *Directory* contains 174 firms, with their branch offices, listed geographically by province. (Maclean Hunter Publishing)

Directory of Group Insurance
Published annually in August as a special section of *Benefits Canada*. The companies are arranged alphabetically, with address, contact, telephone number, and branch office information provided. (Maclean Hunter Publishing)

Directory of Pension Fund Investment Services
Published annually in November as a special section of *Benefits Canada*. The 1993 *Directory* lists 125 money management firms and 42 consulting houses that manage Canadian pension fund assets. The primary purpose is to identify the managers,

although asset managed information and fees are provided. (Maclean Hunter Publishing)

Food and Restaurants

Directory of Restaurant and Fast Food Chains in Canada
Published annually. Provides coverage for more than 600 companies, listing head and regional office information, personnel, financial and advertising data, and expansion plans. (Maclean Hunter Publishing)

Food in Canada
Published nine times a year. Special issues or features within an issue that focus on the entire food and beverage industry in Canada. Special issues may include an annual economic review that provides forecasts and reviews historical performance, a buyer's directory, and reports on sectors within the industry, such as beverages, snacks, and fruits/vegetables. (Maclean Hunter Publishing)

Forestry

Madison's Canadian Lumber Directory
Published annually. Provides products and services listings, addresses, phone and fax numbers, key contacts, and names for all sectors of the Canadian forest industry. Also provides statistics and five-year price graphs for the industry. (Madison's Canadian Lumber Reporter)

Pulp and Paper Canada: Annual and Directory
Published annually in November for professionals in the pulp and paper industry. Lists information on products, personnel, mills and their equipment, suppliers, and other sources required for purchasing. (Southam Business Communications)

Industrial

Heating-Plumbing-Air Conditioning: Buyer's Guide
Published annually in July/August as a special issue of *Heating-Plumbing-Air Conditioning*. A directory of manufacturers, wholesalers, distributors, and agents that supply products and services in the heating, plumbing, and air-conditioning industry. (Cowgate Communications)

PE&M Sourcebook
Published twice a year in conjunction with *Plant Engineering and Maintenance*. A directory for plant engineers and industrial and purchasing managers. It provides address and name information for companies, organizations, and associations in the industry. (Clifford/Elliot Ltd.)

Materials Handling

MM&D's Handling Directory of Buying Sources
Published annually in June as the directory issue of *Materials Management and Distribution*. The companies are arranged in a classified-ad format and cover all

aspects of the materials handling sector, from computers to conveyor belts. (Maclean Hunter Publishing)

Metalworking

Canadian Machinery and Metalworking: Census
Published annually as a special issue of *Canadian Machinery and Metalworking*. Focusses on already installed machine tools, providing user name, location, and other specifics. Includes robotic installations. (Maclean Hunter Publishing)

Canadian Machinery and Metalworking: Directory and Buying Guide
Published annually in the summer as a special issue of *Canadian Machinery and Metalworking*. Acts as a guide to worldwide sources of tooling, components, and supplies for the metalwork manufacturing industry. This is a significant directory — the 1994/95 edition numbers 176 pages. (Maclean Hunter Publishing)

Office Equipment and Supplies

Office Products Sourcing Guide
Published several times a year as a special section of *Modern Purchasing*. The intent is to give potential retailers and buyers a visual opportunity to see what is new and innovative in the office supplies sector. (Maclean Hunter Publishing)

Purchasing Profile and Salary Survey
Published annually as a special section of *Modern Purchasing* in conjunction with the Purchasing Management Association of Canada. Profiles the purchasing industry, looking at job titles, location within industry, education, salary levels, and trends. (Maclean Hunter Publishing)

Packaging

Canadian Packaging: Buyer's Guide
Published annually in July as a special issue of *Canadian Packaging*. This is a significant publication providing access to companies involved in packaging materials and components, containers, machinery, and services in the packaging industry. Associations connected to the industry are also listed. (Maclean Hunter Publishing)

Canadian Packaging: Machinery Specifications Manual
Published annually as the January issue of *Canadian Packaging*. Presents in chart form performance and machinery information from machinery manufacturing to the packaging industry. (Maclean Hunter Publishing)

Petroleum and Mining

Canadian Mines Handbook
Published annually. Features publicly traded mining companies. Also provides five-year stock exchange data, maps of mining areas, industry associations, and statistical data for the mining industry. (Southam Mining Group)

Canadian Mining Journal: Mining Sourcebook
Published annually as a special issue of *Canadian Mining Journal*. Provides operating and cost data for the mining and mineral-processing industry. Also, as a source-book, it details sources of supply for materials, equipment, and services. (Southam Mining Group)

Canadian Oil Register
Published annually. Coverage of over 4000 companies in the oil- and gas-related industry. Contains a 17 000-entry Who's Who of management and technical personnel, and sections on companies, products, and services. (C.O. Nickle/Southam Information Group)

Mining Review: Directory and Buyer's Guide
Published annually early in the year as a special issue of *Mining Review*. Focus is on the Western Canadian mining industry and the equipment and services used in this geographic area. (Naylor Communications)

Mining Review: Exploration and Development Review
Published annually as a special issue of *Mining Review*. Focusses on exploration and new developments in the Western Canadian mining industry over the past twelve months. (Naylor Communications)

Survey of Mines and Energy Resources
Published annually. A comprehensive review of over 3000 mining and energy companies in Canada. The financial statistical tables and ratios are useful for comparative investment analysis. (Financial Post Datagroup)

Photography

Professional Photographers of Canada
Published annually. Contains member listings broken down by province. Also contains an awards section, provincial associations listing, and advertising by major photography suppliers. (Craig Kelman and Associates)

Printing, Publishing, and Graphic Arts

Canadian Printer: Buyer's Guide and Directory
Published annually as the March issue of *Canadian Printer*. Provides information on equipment, supplies, and suppliers, as well as statistical information on the printing industry. (Maclean Hunter Publishing)

Estimator's and Buyer's Guide
An annual guide for the graphics industry published by the publisher of *Graphic Monthly*. Lists companies and services of relevance to the graphics industry. (North Island Sound Ltd.)

Product Design and Engineering

Design Engineering: Fluid Power Buyer's Guide
Published annually as a special issue of *Design Engineering*. Lists information on suppliers, systems, and products in the engineering/fluid power sector. (Maclean Hunter Publishing)

Design Engineering: Mechanical Power Transmission Buyer's Guide
Published annually as a special issue of *Design Engineering*. Lists information on products, suppliers, and manufacturers in the mechanical power transmission industry. (Maclean Hunter Publishing)

Retailing

Canadian Directory of Shopping Centres
Published annually. Provides information on major shopping centres across the country. Lists include tenants and managers/owners. Statistical data includes rent costs, traffic, sales, and market population. (Maclean Hunter Publishing)

Franchise Annual
Published annually. Covers Canadian, American, and international business franchise opportunities. Specific information about each product or service is provided along with general information on franchising. (Info Franchise News)

Monday Report on Retailers
Published weekly as a newsletter. Provides articles on the expansion plans of the major chain retailers in North America. Contains no advertising. (Maclean Hunter Publishing)

Source Book of Franchise Opportunities
Published annually. Presents relatively detailed profiles of over 3000 companies that offer franchise opportunities in North America. A How to Use the Data section is particularly useful for potential franchisees. (Business One Irwin)

Transportation

Canadian Transportation Logistics: Buyer's Guide and Directory
Published annually as a special issue of *Canadian Transportation Logistics*. Arranged by transportation mode: air cargo, marine lines, motor carriers, and rail lines. Other transport-related companies are listed under services such as customs brokers, logistic providers, and consultants. (Southam Magazine Group)

Transportation Industry Directory
Published annually by the publisher of *Cargo Express* magazine. Classifies companies in the broad transportation industry by sector, such as air carriers, freight forwarders, rail transportation, and warehousing. Each company entry has address information, branch offices, and number of employees. A cross-index provides a sector and geographic breakdown. (Baxter Publications)

Regional and City Business Magazines

There are a number of regional and city business magazines published in Canada that devote themselves to a restricted geographic area. They often provide a wealth of information and analysis on the local scene that is available nowhere else. Some examples follow, with their respective publishers also indicated.

BC Business Magazine
Has a top 100 listing and profiles local entrepreneurs in a separate issue. (Canada Wide Magazines)

Manitoba Business
Has special issues focussing on the top 100 companies and the 50 fastest growing companies in the province. (Canada Wide Magazines)

Northern Ontario Business
Has a newspaper format that reports on all aspects of business and industry that relate to Northern Ontario. (Laurentian Publishing)

City business magazines like *Toronto Business Magazine* (Zanny Ltd.) and *Montreal Business Magazine* (Mark R. Weller) focus on the current business events of their respective city. *Victoria's Business Report* (Monday Publications) focusses not only on Victoria, but on business matters on South Vancouver Island.

BUSINESS GUIDES, DIRECTORIES, AND INDEXES

BOSS — Business Opportunities Sourcing System
A comprehensive multivolume set of directories that covers a broad range of products and services in Canada. A separate directory is devoted to each of the following: manufacturers/products, trading houses, customs brokers/freight forwarders, construction companies, computer services, consulting agrologists, management consultants, architects, surveyors/mappers, and consulting engineers. The information contained in the directories is also available online from Industry, Science and Technology's database. (Industry, Science and Technology Canada)

Canadian Trade Index
Published annually. A two-volume directory that provides a classified list of some 10 000 Canadian products and an alphabetical list of some 15 000 Canadian companies. Also includes sections on distributors and export businesses and their areas of trade, as well as a trademark section with some 27 000 trade names. (Canadian Manufacturers Association)

Fraser's Canadian Trade Directory
Published annually in four volumes. Provides a comprehensive listing of manufacturers by product classification, as well as an alphabetical listing. Trade names and their manufacturers and foreign firms who have agents or distributors in Canada also have their own specific listings. (Maclean Hunter Publishing)

Moody's International Manual
Published annually, with an updating service. One of eight Moody's manuals, this one provides coverage of major international, including Canadian, corporations in over 100 countries. Each entry contains a company history, business and product description, subsidiary and personnel listings, and financial statements. (Moody's Investors Service)

Scott's Industrial Directories
There are four Scott's Directories: Atlantic, Quebec, Ontario, and Western. They have identical formats, with three main sections. The first is a list of Canadian manufacturers in alphabetical order. The second is alphabetical by geographic location of the company, with addresses, products, and number of employees. The third section lists companies by their product arranged by Standard Industrial Classification Code. (Scott's Directories/Southam Information Group)

Survey of Industrials
Published annually. Covers all major Canadian, public, listed, and unlisted industrial corporations. Provides details of operations, personnel and subsidiary listings,

financial tables and ratios. Recently added is a listing by Standard Industrial Classification Code. (Financial Post Datagroup)

INTERNATIONAL MARKETING PUBLICATIONS

European Marketing Data and Statistics
Published annually. A compendium of statistical information on the countries of Western and Eastern Europe that can be very useful to market planning. Some 24 principal subject areas are broken down into subcategories over 420 pages. Some representative subject areas are demographic trends/forecasts, economic indicators, labour force indicators, and advertising patterns. Within the subject of labour force indicators, for example, there are twelve subcategories ranging from employment level to average working week in manufacturing. The data compilation normally is provided over a ten- to fifteen-year time span, which allows for trend analysis. The data for Eastern Europe are not quite as extensive and as complete as those for Western Europe due to the former communist bloc. There is also a special chapter that identifies the major information sources for further researching the European market. (Euromonitor)

International Marketing Data and Statistics
Published annually. A publication similar in format to the above-described *European Marketing Data and Statistics* except that the 24 principal subjects deal with the Americas, Asia, Africa, and Oceania. The country coverage includes over 150 countries and is particularly useful for smaller countries for which it is difficult to find statistical information. Also includes a chapter dealing with other major information sources that can be consulted. (Euromonitor)

Statistical Yearbook
Published annually. Provides information on some 200 countries and territories that are members of the United Nations. The data are presented mainly in table format. Some of the specific areas covered include education, science and technology, libraries, book publication, cultural information, and radio and television broadcasting. (UNESCO)

World Economic Survey
Published annually. Provides access to current trends and policies in the world economy, allowing analysis of their implications for regions of the world and in particular their effect on the progress of developing countries. (United Nations, Department of Economic and Social Development)

World Tables
Published annually. A collection of tables dealing with social and economic data from World Bank members. Specifically, the tables show basic economic data for individual countries, indicators suitable for comparative purposes, and demographic/social data. (World Bank/Johns Hopkins University Press)

Year Book of Labour Statistics
Published annually. Summarizes the principal labour statistics for some 180 countries, usually covering the most recent ten-year period. Data are drawn from national statistical services and are presented in nine chapters on such topics as wages, unemployment, and hours of work. A companion volume to the annual is the *Retrospective Edition on Labour Statistics, 1945–1989*. This volume pulls together data for the period and thus offers an opportunity to analyze participation rates of the population in the labour force over a 25-year period. (International Labour Organization)

BIBLIOGRAPHIC DATABASES

ABI/INFORM

This CD-ROM database contains thorough indexing and summaries of significant articles from more than 800 business and management journals. This includes all the major marketing journals. Although the majority of the journals originate in the United States, over 200 of the titles are non–U.S. English-language publications. ABI has company and subject indexes that make it easy to search for articles on a specific industry or company. The service is updated on a monthly basis, and coverage dates back to 1981. ABI is user-friendly and its users require only a few minutes of instruction to feel comfortable with the system. It is available in many university and business libraries. (University Microfilms International)

Canadian Business and Current Affairs (CBCA)

This CD-ROM product provides indexing to over 220 000 articles per year that have appeared in 200 Canadian business periodicals, 300 popular magazines, and 10 newspapers. Many of the special issues described in previous sections of this appendix are indexed in this database. As of 1991, the majority of the business articles come with an abstract or summary. Company, product, and industry information are readily searchable. The service is updated every two months, and the coverage goes back to 1981. A few minutes of instruction will allow a new user to quickly feel at ease with the system. It is available in many public, university, and business libraries. (Micromedia Ltd.)

CHAPTER 6

Marketing Strategy and the Marketing Plan

CHAPTER OBJECTIVES

1. To show the importance of a strategic orientation for marketing.
2. To show the connection between organization strategy and marketing strategy.
3. To show the connection between marketing strategy and the marketing plan.
4. To show that a marketing plan should be based on a good analysis of the character of the external environment.
5. To discuss in detail the steps in the marketing planning process.
6. To show the connection between the marketing plan and the marketing mix.
7. To show how the elements of the marketing mix can be combined to produce synergistic effects.

It didn't take long for Harvey's Restaurants to find itself in a food fight with McDonald's Corp. in the Canadian chain's first international foray.

What has angered McDonald's Czech Republic is that Harvey's, a unit of Toronto-based Cara Operations Ltd., is using McDonald's bun and meat suppliers for the hamburger and chicken sandwiches at its new Prague location.

"They have our products, which we don't like," said Thomas Hubner, managing director of McDonald's Czech Republic. He added that Harvey's staff of 65 are "all McDonald's people nearly."

McDonald's cracked open the Czech fast food market when it began laying the groundwork for its restaurants four years ago. Harvey's defends its business ties with McDonald's suppliers and says it is not looking for a fight.

The chain's first restaurant outside of Canada, the result of Cara's $4-million first-phase investment in the Czech Republic, sits directly across the street from McDonald's on Wenceslas Square, in the heart of Prague's shopping and tourism hub. Food prices at the two outlets are comparable, but Harvey's hopes to pull in additional business with a larger menu featuring hamburgers, chicken, and breakfast.

As for staff, Robert Levy, special counsel in Central Europe to the restaurant's Canadian parent, said: "We have a terrific team in place. We went out into the market and hired only people that we thought were . . . customer-oriented."

Harvey's has ambitious expansion plans. Within five years, the company hopes to open as many as 30 restaurants in the Czech Republic at a cost of about $1 million each.

In comparison, McDonald's has nine locations there and plans to open up to eight more by the end of the year. "The Czech Republic is Europe for us," said Gunter Otto, Cara president and chief operating officer. "Cara's approach is to use the Czech Republic as a springboard — not only for other central and eastern European countries — but for its expansion into western Europe."

Unlike McDonald's, which opened its first company-owned restaurant in 1992, Cara entered the Czech market in a joint venture partnership with Czech food company Koospol. Cara and Koospol each control 50 percent of Harvey's Czech operations. Koospol is the Czech Republic's second largest food importer and exporter, with revenue last year of $545 million.[1]

Developing an appropriate strategy is challenging at any time. However, the task is greater for Cara in that it also faces the uncertainties of operating in another part of the world. Matching competition is clearly a factor in the development of a marketing plan. Furthermore, a sensitive understanding of customer needs and expectations takes on greater importance as Cara is not familiar with the Czech environment. The strategic alliance with Koospol should help greatly in this regard.

INTRODUCTION

Success and excellence are temporary phenomena. Once achieved, they must be pursued continuously or they will erode.[2] The situation in which McDonald's and Harvey's have found themselves is commonplace. Firms often — suddenly or gradually — find that they need to reorient the direction of their efforts. A new strategy is called for.

On the basis of what we learned in the foregoing chapters, we can now consider the development of marketing strategy and the consequent marketing plan. In Chapter 1, we saw that marketing efforts will be more successful if a company has a market orientation. Chapter 2 showed that marketing activities are bounded by five components of the environment. Any strategy should explicitly take them into consideration.

As we discovered in Chapters 3 and 4, markets are not homogeneous. There are normally several different segments to any market. In accordance with the marketing concept, marketing strategy must start with segmentation because it is almost impossible to plan effectively based on a diffuse set of customer needs.

Theodore Levitt has said that there are four simple requisites for the success of a business.[3]

1. The purpose of an enterprise is to create and keep a customer.
2. To do that you have to produce and deliver goods and services that people want and value, at prices and under conditions that are reasonably attractive relative to those offered by others to a proportion of customers large enough to make those prices and conditions possible.
3. No enterprise, no matter how small, can do any of this by mere instinct or accident. It has to clarify its purposes, strategies, and plans, and the larger the enterprise the greater the necessity that these be clearly written down, clearly communicated, and frequently reviewed by the senior members of the enterprise.
4. In all cases, there must be an appropriate system of rewards, audits, and controls to assure that what's intended gets properly done, and when not, that it gets rectified quickly.

With respect to Levitt's third point, let us now consider how strategies are formulated. Two main aspects of strategy formulation will be discussed: strategy for

■ Figure 6.1 **An Overview of the Strategy and Marketing Planning Process**

the organization as a whole (corporate strategy), and marketing strategy. After marketing strategy has been established, the marketing plan can be developed (see Figure 6.1). You will find that discussing these concepts is relatively simple. But practitioners know that implementing them is extremely difficult.

STRATEGY FOR THE ORGANIZATION AS A WHOLE

Strategy is *the overall purpose and direction of the organization that is established in the light of the challenges and opportunities found in the environment, as well as available organizational resources.* This is often referred to as **corporate strategy**. The process of developing a corporate strategy starts with an analysis of market and environmental opportunities and threats facing the company as a whole. Simultaneously, the company undertakes an analysis of its own strengths and weaknesses. From this external and internal examination, the organization generates a list of *possible* alternative courses of action and objectives that could be followed. The next step involves evaluating and selecting the *most appropriate* alternative options for the organization. Finally, implementation and control programs must be planned for the strategy that has been developed. Figure 6.2 shows all five stages of the corporate strategy process.

The development of corporate strategy is the responsibility of the head of the organization, and requires input from all the functional areas of the company (for example, finance, production, and marketing).

The strategy chosen is often expressed in a *mission statement*. This formal statement channels all of the organization's activities. From the mission statement, all individuals can determine which activities are appropriate to engage in, and which are not. This keeps activities within the scope considered most suitable for the company. An example of a mission statement — this one from Medical Devices of Canada (MEDEC), an industry association — can be found in Table 6.1.

corporate strategy
The overall purpose and direction of the organization that is established in the light of the challenges and opportunities found in the environment, as well as available organizational resources.

MARKETING STRATEGY

Marketing strategy, which is based on the strategy set for the company as a whole, *focusses on developing a unique long-run competitive position in the market by assessing consumer needs and the firm's potential for gaining competitive advantage.*[4] Day and Wensley add that "[marketing] strategy is about seeking new edges in a market while slowing the erosion of present advantages."[5]

Knowing everything there is to know about the customer is not enough. To succeed, marketers must know the customer in a context that includes the competition; government policy and regulation; and the broader economic, social, and political macroforces that shape the evolution of markets. In other words, a strategic approach is necessary.

Figure 6.3 illustrates a marketing-oriented approach to strategy formulation and evaluation.[6] This model extends the corporate strategy model depicted in Figure 6.2 and shows the important components of marketing strategy. It incorporates

marketing strategy
A strategy that focusses on developing a unique long-run competitive position in the market by assessing consumer needs and the firm's potential for gaining competitive advantage.

■ Figure 6.2 **Stages in Formulating a Strategy for the Company as a Whole**

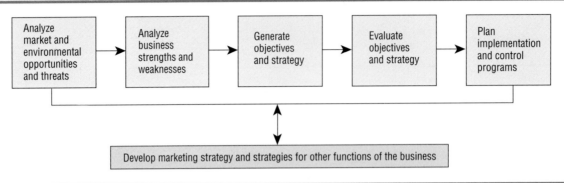

three main interrelated sections: market opportunities and business strength analysis, the strategic marketing considerations, and objectives and strategy generation.

Marketing strategy is based on a thorough understanding of the company's strengths and weaknesses and of the opportunities and threats that it faces. Thus, Section I of Figure 6.3 shows the assessment of the firm from the perspective of *market opportunities and business strength analysis*. As we have seen, planners also take this perspective when developing an overall corporate strategy. Marketing strategy analysis pays special attention to consumers and competitors.

The development of marketing strategy then turns to an examination of market segments, and the relative positionings within these segments. Five strategic marketing evaluations must be undertaken: (1) a segment and positioning analysis, (2) an examination of the opportunities and strengths of each segment or positioning, (3) a synergy analysis, (4) a functional requirement analysis, and (5) a portfolio analysis. Together, they constitute the *strategic marketing considerations*. Let's look at each of the five strategic marketing components in a little more detail.

Segment and positioning analysis Each segment must first be subjected to an analysis by positioning. This means that the competing companies and brands in each segment are identified, and their positioning in the segment is indicated. For example, in the business microcomputer segment, Compaq, IBM, Apple, and a number of other manufacturers compete. IBM positions itself as the firm with leading-edge technology and high quality. Apple might be positioned as providing the most user-friendly and versatile quality computer. Several clones also compete in this seg-

■ Table 6.1 **Example of a Company Mission Statement**

MEDEC, a key participant in the Canadian health-care delivery system, actively meets the needs and promotes the common interests of the industry which manufactures/distributes medical devices in the Canadian market. MEDEC is chief spokesman for the industry and undertakes:	• to assist the industry in delivering safe, effective, best-technology medical devices to all Canadians; and • to seek a business environment that encourages the growth of the industry and maximizes the value added to products and services in Canada.

Source: Medical Devices of Canada, Annual Report, 1988 [inside front cover; no page number].

■ Figure 6.3 **A Marketing-Oriented Approach to Strategy Formulation and Evaluation**

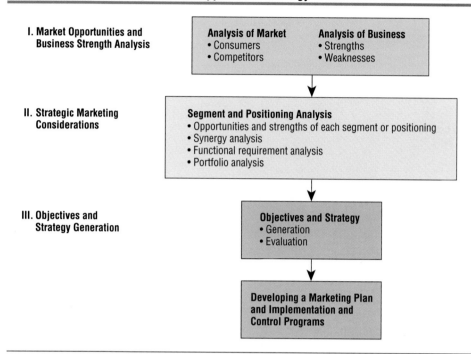

Source: Adapted from Yoram Wind and Thomas S. Robertson, "Marketing Strategy: New Directions for Theory and Research," *Journal of Marketing* (Spring 1983), p. 12. Reprinted by permission of the American Marketing Association.

ment, and will be positioned as providing various combinations of features at a low price (see Figure 6.4).

The result of this analysis is the identification of certain segments and positions that are deemed worthy of further consideration. Many different reasons could lead to the decision to consider a segment further — for example, size of market, an opportunity to position a product where there is little competition, or evidence that existing competition can be overcome.

Opportunities/strengths analysis Next, a more thorough analysis of the selected segments is undertaken. One method of doing this is by using a **SWOT analysis**. SWOT stands for *strengths, weaknesses, opportunities, and threats.* SWOT analysis helps to develop a picture of the situation faced by a business. For example, within the above-mentioned microcomputer segment, it is important to identify what are the firm's strengths, and what are the firm's weaknesses. A firm might have a unique product (a strength), but limited additional funds for advertising (a weakness). This strongly affects the type of marketing program that can be developed.

Following this, the positioning analysis shown in Figure 6.4 makes it possible to clearly identify areas of opportunity. In our example, the upper left quadrant has no other direct competitors. If the size of that market is of significance, the company might design a product to match that segment.

It is also necessary to have a realistic assessment of the current or potential threats faced within the market segment. For example, companies with two closely positioned products, such as Compaq and IBM, can see that there are threats posed

SWOT analysis
A method used for analyzing a firm's chances for success in a market under the headings of *strengths, weaknesses, opportunities, and threats.*

■ Figure 6.4 **Positioning Map for Business Microcomputer Segment**

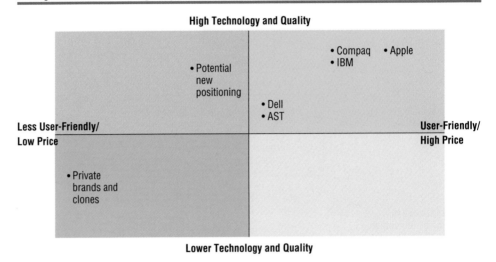

by each other, as well as by other companies that might be trying to move in for a share of their position. Management should carefully select the most desirable bases for segmentation and positioning to encompass all of the firm's current and potential offerings. In addition, the size and characteristics of each selected segment are identified as input into the next steps.

Synergy analysis Synergy is the result of two or more variables working together so that their total effect is greater than normally would be expected by summing them (a sort of "2 + 2 = 5" effect). The development of a marketing plan should explicitly analyze synergistic effects. For example, advertising, distribution, and price could be combined in such a way as to result in positive *or* negative synergy.

Functional requirement analysis Each segment and the positioning within it must then be considered in terms of the requirements for success in each functional area. These requirements are compared with the company's strengths in each area. It may well be, for example, that the low-price segment requires manufacturing expertise as the key to success, whereas the high-technology/quality segment requires technology (R & D) as the key to success. If the company's strengths lie in manufacturing rather than in R & D (or vice versa), there may be implications for segment/positioning selection.

Portfolio analysis The final marketing consideration is a portfolio analysis. Each organization normally has a range of goods or services. Some are new, with great potential, and the market for them is just being developed. Developing new markets often requires considerable resources. Other products are well established, and produce a strong positive cash flow. Still others are producing very little. This mix of products constitutes the product "portfolio." It is important to manage the portfolio in such a way that resources are allocated to the profitable and promising products. Decisions must be made about whether to delete those that are "over the hill."

Section III of the model in Figure 6.3 outlines the *objectives and strategy generation and evaluation process*, which is common to most strategic planning models. Its central focus is the generation of objectives and strategies, and, for the marketer, the development of the *marketing plan* (which we will discuss next). The final stage is

For learning at home, working at home and playing at home, one computer is all you really need to take home.
Introducing Macintosh Performa.
With Macintosh Performa, everything you need (and want) — twenty software and CD titles, hardware, colour monitor, CD-ROM drive, modem, keyboard, mouse — comes in one box. All you have to do is plug it in. It's that easy. Easy to set up, to learn, and most important, to use.
A computer for the classroom.
The way we see it, wherever there's an eager

mind, there's a classroom. And, wherever there's a classroom, there's often a Macintosh. One reason is because Apple has always led other computer makers in multimedia. And when you stimulate their eyes and ears — can their minds be far behind?
Open your future and theirs.
So open a Macintosh Performa box and open the door — to learning, to the future, to the power to be your best. Visit your Authorized Apple Canada Dealer today. For the dealer nearest you, call **1 800 665-2775**, ext **500**

Opening their minds is as simple as opening one box.

It's everything you need in one box.

 Apple

Apple computers have always been positioned as user-friendly. Accordingly, in advertisements of its new Macintosh Performa, Apple depicts children working on the computer to reinforce the message of versatility and friendliness.

the necessary condition for all planning: devising the necessary implementation and control programs.

THE MARKETING PLAN

The **marketing plan** — defined as *a program of activities that lead to the accomplishment of the marketing strategy* — is a tool of marketing strategy. Sometimes the marketing plan is referred to as the *marketing program*. In marketing planning, the first question to be addressed is "What should be included in the plan?" How can the planner have confidence that the marketing plan developed accomplishes the strategy that has been set out and includes the appropriate planning elements? The criterion for a marketing plan should be that it leads to organization effectiveness.

How does a manager know whether the plans made will be effective or not? Contingency theory, which originated in the organization behaviour literature, provides some excellent guidance. It argues that managerial decisions are not right or wrong per se. They must be made and assessed in the light of the circumstances surrounding the decisions. For example, if profits are falling because of declining sales, a decision to reduce or increase advertising might depend on whether the drop is caused by lack of awareness of the product, or adverse economic conditions (people know about the product but have no money). Therefore, a marketing plan

marketing plan
A program of activities that lead to the accomplishment of the marketing strategy.

should be based on a careful analysis of the key factors in the business environment. In a generic sense, most firms face the following conditions. Since the importance of each condition varies according to the individual firm's situation, it is impossible to present an exhaustive set.

1. Increasing competition The current environment is characterized by intense and increasing competitiveness. Some authors have argued that marketing strategy should be based on a competitive rather than a marketing orientation.[7] This is an extreme position. However, increased competition can be observed in several ways:

a. Intertype competition. Firms readily cross industry lines to compete if they think they can apply their technology to another field (for example, agricultural companies may begin producing recreational vehicles, or computer software firms may play a leading role in the production of machine tools and industrial robots).

b. International competition. A fundamental strategy of most countries today is to increase exports. Alert companies are responding. Consequently, domestic firms are finding aggressive new competitors facing them in traditional domestic markets.

c. More demanding economic conditions. As a result of the economic decline in the early 1980s, virtually all firms had to become more efficient and aggressive in order to survive. Many have continued this posture as the economy turned around. Through the business cycles of the 1990s, it has been clear that a prolonged period of intense domestic and worldwide competition has turned into the norm for businesses.

To take account of these conditions, a marketing plan should have a realistic assessment of the competitive domestic and worldwide industry environment. It should also include a statement of current market share, and a recognition of the shares and strategies of leading competitors. The plan should include an analysis of competitive strengths and weaknesses, and a forecast of market demand.

2. Dynamic consumer society Today's marketplace is characterized by fragmented, rapidly changing, sophisticated consumers. More products have emerged to more precisely meet tastes and higher consumer expectations. International travel and world communication have added to this sophistication. A marketing plan must include a thorough analysis of current customer motivations and trends.

3. Hi-tech environment Computers have revolutionized products and services. The inherent nature of many products, as well as their design and production, has changed. For example, the microchips now commonly built into such products as telephones and tools enable functions unheard of a few years ago. Many services are similarly affected.

4. Social consciousness An acute sensitivity to ecological issues continues to grow. The marketplace is showing evidence of the desire for a clean environment, as well as environmentally friendly products. In a related development, the requirements for socially responsible business behaviour continue to increase. If changes do not happen voluntarily, governmental regulation and legislation may be expected.

A comprehensive marketing plan should explicitly take such factors into consideration. Failing this, contingency theory suggests that it would be more difficult for the organization to be effective and competitive, and that the firm will sooner or later fall out of phase with its competitors and the environment.

Benetton is a global apparel manufacturer with 7000 licensed retail stores in over 110 countries on 6 continents. Its colourful knitwear and sportswear have become its signature around the world. Through innovative and provocative — and sometimes controversial — advertising campaigns, the Benetton name has become synonymous with multicultural diversity, corporate involvement in social issues, and an upscale approach to fashion retailing.

5. Other requirements for a marketing plan: Planning process requirements For every marketing plan statement, a system for expeditiously developing a complete plan is necessary. Possible elements of such a system include identifying problems and opportunities, conducting a post-mortem of previous plans, stating alternative strategies considered, identifying risk factors, stating objectives, stating an action plan, and developing contingency plans.

6. Other requirements for a marketing plan: Operational organizational requirements In order to make it operational, each plan should also include a statement of objectives, a budget statement, a section identifying those responsible for executing the plan, and specific timetables and controls for the new plan.

Table 6.2 presents a model that demonstrates how these important environmental features might be identified. It also shows the corresponding marketing planning activities required to operate effectively in the environment. This can serve as a comprehensive guide for marketing planning.

When this model is used as a base for developing a marketing plan, decisions about whether to include a component of the plan are *contingent on the conditions found in the environment.* Following a contingency approach enables a firm to be more relevant in its planning. Because the process begins with a careful analysis of the environment, current conditions that are of direct significance as well as long-term trends can be identified and responded to. This process should also lead to a more comprehensive plan, as outlined in the right-hand column of the table.

What, then, should be included in a marketing plan? The answer can be determined from Table 6.2. The left-hand column shows the environmental conditions that must be addressed. The marketing plan should meet these conditions. The right-hand column outlines the marketing plan components that are required to meet the conditions in the illustration. Obviously, as conditions change, different marketing plan components will be included, excluded, or emphasized.

■ Table 6.2 A Marketing Planning Model Based on Environmental Antecedents

Environmental Antecedents	Marketing Plan Requirements

1. Increasing Competition
  a. Intertype competition
  b. Increasing complexity of economic conditions
  c. International competition
	• Statement of market share
	• Recognition of shares and strengths of leading competitors
	• Analysis of competitive strengths and weaknesses
	• Forecast of market demand

2. Dynamic Consumer/Buyer Society
  a. Rapid changes in tastes and behaviours
  b. High customer expectations
  c. Exposure to varied domestic and international mass media
  d. Highly fragmented customer groups
  e. Increasing customer sophistication
	• Consideration of the changing needs of customers
	• Product life-cycle analysis
	• Market segmentation analysis
	• Product portfolio position analysis

3. Hi-tech Environment
  a. Effect of technology on
    • product design
    • product performance
    • price
  b. Automation of production
	• Technological trends statement

4. Social Consciousness
  a. Health and safety issues
  b. Clean/pure environment issues
  c. Increasing expectations for responsible business behaviour
  d. Expectations for proactive governmental regulation/legislation
	• Environmental issues statement
	• Consideration of government regulatory issues

5. Planning Process Requirements a. Existence of a system for expeditiously developing a complete plan	• Identification of problems and opportunities • Post-mortem of previous plans • Statement of alternative strategies considered • Identification of risk factors • Statement of objectives • Statement of action plan • Development of contingency plans

6. Operational Organizational Requirements
  a. Guidance
  b. Control
  c. Financial responsibility
  d. Efficiency
	• Statement of objectives
	• Budget statement of proposed plan
	• Responsibility for execution pinpointed
	• Timetables and controls for the new plan specified

APPLYING THE CONCEPTS

An Innovative Way to Speed Strategic Planning

David Talbot has pioneered a way of conducting brain storming and strategic planning sessions that speeds the process considerably. It is called the Business Huddle.

Mr. Talbot goes into planning sessions with a game plan, starting with a "visualization" exercise. The client group is asked to pretend that it is a year from today, and the organization has become very successful. Each individual visualizes this success and describes it — whether it amounts to sitting on the beach with $1-million in the bank, or saving the environment from pollution. Each is then asked to describe the steps that were taken to get there.

While it sounds simplistic, the process allows an unencumbered stream of ideas to pour out. That's in contrast to many traditional strategic planning sessions where few ideas are aired. Participants tend to spend more time criticizing old concepts than putting new ones on the table.

The process can be summarized in six steps:

- Start by visualizing future success in "pictures."
- No abstract talk about "mission statements."
- Group then lists hurdles and how to leap over them.
- Action plan developed with assigned tasks and deadlines.
- Each person's ideas are typed into a computer, projected on a screen and discussed. NO flip charts.
- At the end of the day, the computer prints out ideas.

"In three to four hours, we can accomplish what normally takes 30 to 40 hours for traditional strategic planners," Mr. Talbot says. And instead of the $25,000 charged for a typical strategic planning session, the Business Huddle costs about $5,000.

Source: Excerpted from Jerry Zeidenberg, "A Break from the Huddle," *The Globe and Mail* (August 6, 1994), p. B20. Reprinted by permission of *The Globe and Mail.*

Try the process yourself. Visualize success for yourself one year from today. Then describe the necessary steps to get there.

Identifying key elements of the environment that must be responded to ensures that the marketing plan is focussed on the right things. A further important advantage of this approach is that the marketing plan is not focussed solely on current conditions. To properly understand the environment requires taking long-term trends into consideration. Providing that the organization's reward structure is not excessively focussed on short-term results, a marketing plan based on current environmental conditions, as well as the forces behind them, will have a longer-term perspective. This should help to eliminate the excessively short and narrow vision that such critics as Hayes and Abernathy[8] decry. A more common description of a process for developing a marketing plan is shown in Table 6.3. (It should in fact look familiar: we saw a less detailed version early in Chapter 3.)

▪ Table 6.3 **The Marketing Planning Process**

I. Situation Analysis: Where Are We Now?

A. Historical Background
- Nature of the firm, its sales and profit history, and current situation

B. Consumer Analysis
- Who are the customers we are trying to serve?
- What market segments exist?
- How many consumers are there?
- How much do they buy and why?
- Are there significant international market segments?

C. Competitive Analysis
- Given the nature of the markets — size, characteristics, competitive activities, and strategies — what marketing opportunities exist for this firm?

II. Marketing Objectives: Where Do We Want to Go?

A. Sales Objectives
- What level of sales volume can we achieve during the next year?

B. Profit Objectives
- Given the sales level and the cost structure of the firm, what level of profits should be achieved?

C. Consumer Objectives
- How will we serve our target market customers?
- What do we want consumers to think about our firm?

III. Developing A Marketing Mix: What Should We Do with Each of the Marketing Mix Elements?

A. Product/Service Decisions
- What products should we offer to meet consumers' needs?
- What is the exact nature of these products?

B. Pricing Decisions
- What level of prices should be used?
- What specific prices and price concessions are appropriate?

C. Distribution Decisions
- What channel(s) will be used in distributing our product offerings?
- Where should they be located?
- What should be their major characteristics?

D. Communication Decisions
- What mix of personal selling, advertising, and sales promotional activities is needed?
- How much should be spent, using what themes and what media?

E. Financial Considerations
- What will be the financial impact of this plan on a one-year pro-forma (projected) income statement?
- How does this income statement compare with our objectives?

F. Control Aspects

Source: Adapted from Thomas O'Connor, Stephen K. Keiser, Robert E. Stevens, and Lynn J. Loudenback, *Contemporary Marketing*, 6th ed., Study Guide (Fort Worth, TX: Dryden, 1989), p. 482.

IMPLEMENTING THE PLAN: THE MARKETING MIX

Marketing plans are implemented through four main elements: *products, pricing, distribution,* and *communication.* Each is an essential part of the marketing plan.

Product management includes *decisions about what kind of product is needed, its uses, package design, branding, trademarks, warranties, guarantees, product life cycles, and new-product development.* The marketer's concept of product involves much more than just the physical product. It takes into account the satisfaction of all consumer needs in relation to a good or service.

Pricing involves decisions concerning *the methods of setting competitive, profitable, and justified prices.* Most prices are freely set in Canada. However, some prices, such as those for public utilities and housing rentals, are regulated to some degree, and are therefore subject to public scrutiny.

Distribution decisions involve *the selection and management of marketing channels and the physical distribution of goods.* **Marketing channels** are *the steps or handling organizations that a good or service goes through from producer to final consumer.* Channel decision-making entails selecting and working with the institutional structure that handles the firm's goods or services. This includes wholesalers, retailers, and other intermediaries.

Communication includes *personal selling, advertising, sales promotion, and publicity.* The marketing manager has many decisions to make concerning when, where, and how to use these elements of communication so that potential buyers will learn about and be persuaded to try the company's products.

The marketing mix is sometimes called the "four P's" for ease of remembering: product, price, place, promotion. The rest of this book will be devoted largely to explaining these four marketing elements. The elements of the marketing mix are shown in Figure 6.5.

Starting with a careful evaluation of the market — using market segmentation — every marketing plan must take into consideration the appropriate product for a particular segment, the price that should be charged for it, and the appropriate outlet in which it ought to be sold; and all of this information must be effectively communicated to the target market.

product management
Decisions about what kind of product is needed, its uses, package design, branding, trademarks, warranties, guarantees, product life cycles, and new-product development.

pricing
The methods of setting competitive, profitable, and justified prices.

distribution
The selection and management of marketing channels and the physical distribution of goods.

marketing channels
The steps or handling organizations that a good or service goes through from producer to consumer.

communication
Personal selling, advertising, sales promotion, and publicity.

■ Figure 6.5 **The Marketing Mix**

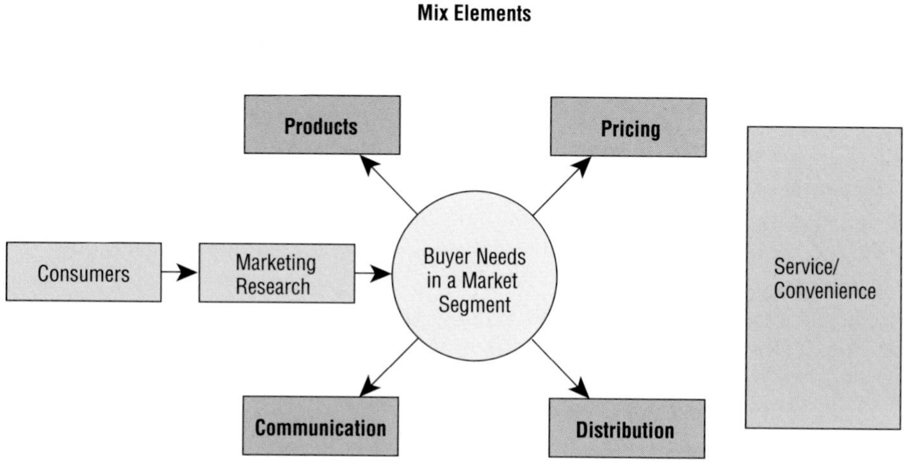

A quick examination of various companies' marketing programs shows that, even though they each have all the marketing variables, no two programs use them in exactly the same way. The *emphasis* and *use* of each can vary markedly. For example, the target market for McDonald's might be families with children. Its products are standardized and reliable, but not considered to match the same calibre as those of Dubrovnik's, a famous Winnipeg restaurant that one might visit on an evening out. Dubrovnik's target market would be couples celebrating a special event or businesspeople entertaining their clients. Prices at McDonald's are low compared with those at the fine restaurant. In terms of distribution, it is important for McDonald's to have outlets at many locations, because consumers are not prepared to drive great distances to visit them. In contrast, people are fully prepared to drive downtown to the one Dubrovnik's location. McDonald's employs a communication program that involves extensive television advertising. Dubrovnik's counts on favourable word-of-mouth publicity, and purchases only a limited number of advertisements in local magazines and theatre guides.

marketing mix
The blending of the four elements of marketing to satisfy chosen consumer segments.

The point is that each firm uses the elements of marketing differently — the marketing elements are *harmonized* in a unique way to form the main aspects of the marketing plan. This *blending of the four elements of marketing to satisfy chosen consumer segments* is known as the **marketing mix**. The marketing mix concept is one of the most powerful ever developed for marketers. It is now the main organizing concept for countless marketing plans. It gives executives a way to ensure that all elements of their program are considered in a simple yet disciplined fashion.[9]

The marketing planner must actually make wise decisions about *many* subelements of the marketing mix. This takes much skill and attention. While we normally talk of the four main categories of the mix, it should be clearly understood that each of the mix elements can, and should, be divided into many subcategories when developing a marketing plan. For example, *communication* includes decisions about advertising, selling, and point-of-purchase promotion, to name a few. Neil Borden, who first coined the term "marketing mix," used to use a much more extensive list in his teaching and consulting. It is reproduced in Table 6.4.

Quality Emphasis for the Marketing Mix in the 1990s

In 1990, Dick Berry surveyed a sample of executives concerning which marketing mix variables they consider to be most important. He broadened the list of options from the traditional four discussed earlier, and asked the managers to rank them by importance. They are listed below from most to least important.

1. *Customer sensitivity.* Employee attitude, customer treatment, and response to customers.
2. *Product.* Product quality, reliability, and features.
3. *Customer convenience.* Availability to the customer, customer convenience, and selling.
4. *Service.* Postsale service, presale service, and customer convenience.
5. *Price.* Price charged, pricing terms, and pricing offers.
6. *Place [distribution].* Provider accessibility, provider facilities, pricing terms, and availability to customer.
7. *Promotion [communication].* Advertising, publicity, selling, presale service, and pricing offers.[10]

■ Table 6.4 **The First Marketing Mix List**

Elements of the Marketing Mix of Manufacturers

1. Product Planning

Policies and procedures relating to:

a. Product lines to be offered — qualities, design, etc.

b. Markets to sell — whom, where, when, and in what quantity.

c. New-product policy — R & D program.

2. Pricing

Policies and procedures relating to:

a. Price level to adopt.

b. Specific prices to adopt — odd–even, etc.

c. Price policy — one price or varying price, price maintenance, use of list prices, etc.

d. Margins to adopt — for company, for the trade.

3. Branding

Policies and procedures relating to:

a. Selection of trademarks.

b. Brand policy — individualized or family brand.

c. Sale under private label or unbranded.

4. Channels of Distribution

Policies and procedures relating to:

a. Channels to use between plant and consumer.

b. Degree of selectivity among wholesalers and retailers.

c. Efforts to gain co-operation of the trade.

5. Personal Selling

Policies and procedures relating to:

a. Burden to be placed on personal selling and the methods to be employed in:
- Manufacturer's organization.
- Wholesale segment of the trade.
- Retail segment of the trade.

6. Advertising

Policies and procedures relating to:

a. Amount to spend — i.e., burden to be placed on advertising.

b. Copy platform to adopt:
- Product image desired.
- Corporate image desired.

c. Mix of advertising — to the trade, through the trade, to consumers.

7. Promotions

Policies and procedures relating to:

a. Burden to be placed on special selling plans or devices directed at or through the trade.

b. Form of these devices for consumer promotions, for trade promotions.

8. Packaging

Policies and procedures relating to:

a. Formulation of package and label.

9. Display

Policies and procedures relating to:

a. Burden to be put on display to help effect sale.

b. Methods to adopt to secure display.

10. Servicing

Policies and procedures relating to:

a. Providing service needed.

11. Physical Handling

Policies and procedures relating to:

a. Warehousing.

b. Transportation.

c. Inventories.

12. Fact-Finding and Analysis

Policies and procedures relating to:

a. Securing, analyzing, and using facts in marketing operations.

Source: Neil H. Borden, "The Concept of the Marketing Mix," *Journal of Advertising Research* (June 1964), pp. 2–7. Reprinted by permission of the Advertising Research Foundation.

It is clear from this list that customer sensitivity, convenience, and service have taken a very important role in the development and implementation of marketing plans. This is associated with the TQM (total quality management) movement in business. In one way this is new; in another, it reinforces the philosophy of the marketing concept. Regardless, it is clear that managers find that this type of orientation is essential and that it works.

APPLYING THE CONCEPTS

Interaction within the Mix

The marketing mix concept emphasizes the fit of the various pieces and the quality and size of their interaction. There are three degrees of interaction. The least demanding is *consistency* — a logical and useful fit between two or more elements. It would seem generally inconsistent, for example, to sell a high-quality product through a low-quality retailer. It can be done, but the consumer must understand the reason for the inconsistency and respond favourably to it. Even more difficult is maintaining such an apparent inconsistency for a long time.

The second level of positive relationship among elements of the mix is *integration*. While consistency involves only a coherent fit, integration requires an active, harmonious interaction among the elements of the mix. For example, heavy advertising is sometimes harmonious with a high selling price because the added margin from the premium price pays for the advertising, and the heavy advertising creates the brand differentiation that justifies the high price. National brands of consumer packaged goods such as Tide laundry detergent, Campbell soup, and Colgate toothpaste use this approach. This does *not* mean, however, that heavy advertising and high product pricing are always harmonious.

The third — and most sophisticated — form of relationship is *synergy*, whereby each element is used to the best advantage in support of the total mix and results in effects greater than the sum of the parts.

Source: Adapted from Benson P. Shapiro, "Getting Things Done," *Harvard Business Review* (September–October 1985), p. 29. Used with permission.

Explain how an intelligent application of these concepts will provide customer satisfaction.

DEVELOPING A COMPETITIVE STRATEGY

A major objective in strategic planning is to create and sustain competitive advantage. Therefore, along with customer analysis, competitor analysis is fundamental. In addition to identifying the relative positions of competitors, an effective strategy for dealing with competitors is essential. For example, if you should develop a new soft drink that is as good as or better than Pepsi, you would be foolish to develop a plan for marketing it without taking into consideration the competitive response of Pepsi if that company thought you might threaten its market share.

Competitor assessment will lead some firms to specialize in particular market segments. Others with greater resources will compete in a broad range of product markets in several areas of the world. Essentially, determining a competitive strategy involves answering five questions:

1. Who are our competitors, and what are their strengths and weaknesses?
2. What is their strategy, and what will be their likely response to our competitive moves?
3. Should we compete?
4. If so, in what markets should we compete?
5. How should we compete?

The first question, "Who are our competitors?" focusses attention on the various potential challenges to be faced to gain a share of the market. Firms sometimes enter a market with an inadequate understanding of the extent of the competition. Or, if they are already established, firms sometimes respond poorly to the entrance of a new and powerful competitor. In Canadian retailing, the responses of various firms to the entrance of the powerful Wal-Mart chain is a good example. Zellers and Canadian Tire anticipated that they would be some of the most affected retailers. Each studied the Wal-Mart operation carefully and made adjustments to their pricing and advertising to compete. As discussed in Chapter 2, two types of competition must be clearly identified: inter-product, and product-substitute competition.

How to Assess Competitive Advantage

Peter Chandler suggests two steps for thinking strategically about gaining competitive advantage:

1. Think through your own organization's strategic capabilities, and also how you can link these business processes to serve customer needs in a way that is superior to your competitors.
2. Read everything you can about how other organizations in other industries and countries are gaining competitive advantage. "To be ignorant of how others are succeeding is a bit like fighting set piece trench warfare as occurred in World War I. The smart commander will be looking outside the square to see what new forces or approaches can be brought to bear."[11]

The second question, "What is our competitors' strategy?" points out that a marketing strategy cannot be developed in a vacuum. It must be at least as good as, more effective than, or different from that of competitors. Often a great deal of creativity is required to come up with a winning plan.

The third question, "Should we compete?" should be answered based on the resources and objectives of the firm and the expected profit potential for the firm. In some instances, potentially successful ventures are not considered due to a lack of a match between the venture and the overall organizational objectives. For example, a clothing manufacturer may reject an opportunity to diversify through the purchase of a profitable chain of retail clothing stores. Or a producer of industrial chemicals might refrain from entering the consumer market and instead sell chemicals to another firm familiar with serving consumers at the retail level.

In other cases, a critical issue is expected profit potential. If the expected profits are insufficient to pay an adequate return on the required investment, then the firm should consider other lines of business. Many organizations have switched from less profitable ventures quite efficiently. This decision should be subject to continual re-evaluation so that the firm avoids being tied to traditional markets with declining profit margins. It is also important to anticipate competitive responses.

"In what markets should we compete?" Whatever decision is made acknowledges that the firm has limited resources (engineering and productive capabilities, sales personnel, advertising budgets, research and development, and the like) and that these resources must be allocated to the areas of greatest opportunity. Too many firms have taken a "shotgun" approach to market selection and thus do an ineffective job in many markets rather than a good one in selected markets.

"How should we compete?" is the fifth question. It requires the firm's marketers to make the tactical decisions involved in setting up a comprehensive marketing strategy. Product, pricing, distribution, and communication decisions are the major elements of this strategy.

THE ROLE OF THE MARKETING MANAGER

To conclude our examination of marketing strategy and the marketing plan, Figure 6.6 illustrates some aspects of the role of the marketing manager in the process of developing a marketing plan. In the light of the opportunities and constraints perceived in the environmental framework, appropriate market segments are selected.

Based on the strategy, objectives, and resources of the firm, the manager and his or her team establishes marketing strategy and then develops a competitive marketing plan. Products, pricing, distribution, and communication are blended in a unique manner to make up the marketing mix. The result wins customers, sales, and profits for the firm.

This is the essence of the first six chapters of this text. The rest of the book will elaborate on the many considerations involved in formulating and implementing marketing strategy and subsequent marketing plans, as well as managing the elements of the marketing mix.

■ Figure 6.6 **The Role of the Marketing Manager**

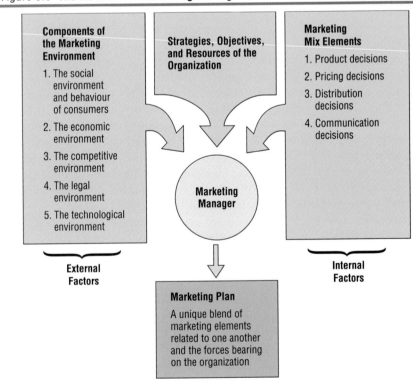

■ KEY TERMS

corporate strategy	contingency approach	distribution
mission statement	marketing planning	communication
marketing strategy	process	marketing channels
SWOT analysis	product management	marketing mix
marketing plan	pricing	competitive strategy

■ INTERACTIVE SUMMARY AND DISCUSSION QUESTIONS

1. Corporate strategy is the overall purpose and direction of the organization that is established in the light of the challenges and opportunities found in the environment, as well as available organizational resources. Using a small firm that you are familiar with as an example, write a hypothetical statement of strategy for the organization using the above definition. Make your statement as comprehensive as possible.

2. Marketing strategy is based on the strategy set for the company as a whole, and focusses on developing a unique long-run competitive position in the market by assessing consumer needs and the firm's potential for gaining competitive advantage. Explain, using an example, the relation between corporate strategy and marketing strategy.

3. Part of the process of developing marketing strategy is the undertaking of a segment and positioning analysis. Using the computer industry illustration given in the text discussion, construct a positioning map.

4. The marketing plan is a program of activities that lead to the accomplishment of the marketing strategy. Using the text discussion as a base, explain how the manager can make sure that the plan includes the appropriate elements for the conditions facing the enterprise.

5. A marketing plan must take into consideration six major factors: increasing competition, dynamic consumer society, hi-tech environment, social consciousness, planning process requirements, and operational organizational requirements. Using the following organizations as examples, specify key elements that a marketing plan should include under each of the above headings:
    a. Canadian Tire store
    b. Exporter of apples to Japan

6. Marketing plans are implemented through four main elements: product, pricing, distribution, and communication. Describe the marketing mix for the following:
    a. Canadian Tire store
    b. Clearly Canadian mineral water
    c. Royal Bank mortgage service
    d. Tide detergent

7. "The 'mix' concept is very important in marketing." Discuss.

8. In marketing planning, it is helpful to think of a broader list of subelements of the marketing mix. Explain.

9. Illustrate why it is important for the marketing planner to base the plan on a competitive analysis as well as on a consumer analysis.

10. Figure 6.6 illustrates some aspects of the role of the marketing manager in the process of developing a marketing plan. Translate this into an example based on the job of the marketing manager of a city transit system.

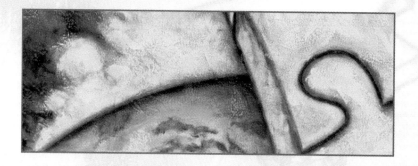

PART THREE

Consumer Behaviour

CHAPTER 7
Consumer Behaviour

CHAPTER 8
Industrial Buyer Behaviour

The foundation of the marketing concept involves developing an understanding of the needs and desires of the customer, and then striving to serve those needs. Market segmentation provides a way to identify groupings of customers. After identification, a deeper understanding of the consumer helps establish successful marketing plans. Part Three discusses some of the many concepts that marketers bring to bear in analyzing consumer behaviour. Both the internal factors and the external influences that affect decision making in consumers and industrial buyers are explored.

CHAPTER 7

Consumer Behaviour

CHAPTER OBJECTIVES

1. To show how consumer behaviour is affected by two main categories of influence: personal and interpersonal influences.
2. To distinguish between needs and motives.
3. To explain perception.
4. To define attitudes and show how they influence behaviour.
5. To demonstrate how learning theory can be applied to marketing strategy.
6. To explain the role of culture in consumer behaviour.
7. To consider the effect of reference groups on consumer behaviour.
8. To differentiate among routinized response behaviour, limited problem solving, and extended problem solving.

A new battle is shaping up on the video games front — and child's play has little to do with it.

The industry's two major rivals, Nintendo of Canada Ltd. and Sega of Canada Inc., are marshalling forces for the kind of showdown only Sonic the Hedgehog and Super Mario could imagine.

At stake is dominance of a market estimated to be worth at least $350 million. Nintendo claims the crown, but Sega is an impatient pretender.

Both firms are planning to blitz the airwaves with a barrage of new commercials. Their combined media budgets were estimated to top $20 million in 1994. But Sega has another weapon waiting in the wings. It wants to put its games on cable TV and charge parents for the privilege, a strategy Nintendo dismisses as premature.

"For a number of years Nintendo has had the capability of doing networking between systems and tested it in several places, particularly in Japan," says marketing manager Kirsty Henderson. "At this stage we don't feel that it's proven technology."

That's not how Jon Gill, Sega's director of business development, sees it. He believes it would be an ideal showcase for Sega's back catalogue. "We have built up over the last number of years a library of almost 700 titles," he says. "Those titles have a lifespan of, say, anywhere from two to six months, depending on their popularity with the consumer. There's a lot of people who haven't played the games in that library.

"Providing a cost-effective way for consumers to go back and take a look at that library, and receive it in their homes through a cable service, is very appealing to a lot of people."

A chip in the channel adaptor cartridge that makes a game console compatible with the service will allow parents to program suitable subjects, and avoid materials unfit for a young audience. The cost has yet to be determined, but it will be about $15 a month — a bargain when you consider some games can cost up to $70, Gill says.

Henderson is not convinced the demand is there. "All these services, whether it's the video game channel or home-buying services, are really attractive when you first hear about them," she says. "But whether there is actually going to be that usage that's going to make it worthwhile remains to be seen."[1]

Who will be correct? The answer depends on consumer behaviour. Marketers can win or lose big, depending on how consumers respond to their offerings. That is why great efforts have been made to try to understand the processes that affect customer decisions.

This book has made a point of emphasizing the importance of understanding the consumer before developing a marketing plan. Consumer behaviour studies try to apply a microscope to the basic understanding of people and their purchase behaviour. This chapter and the next chapter provide an introduction to the extensive marketing literature concerning consumer behaviour.

INTRODUCTION

Consumer behaviour consists of *the activities of individuals in obtaining, using, and disposing of goods and services, including the decision processes that precede and follow these actions.*[2] This definition includes both the ultimate consumer and the purchaser of industrial products. However, in the case of industrial consumers, a major difference

consumer behaviour
The activities of individuals in obtaining, using, and disposing of goods and services, including the decision processes that precede and follow these actions.

■ Consumers Often Do Not See Things as We Expect Them To

Source: PA Graphics. Reprinted by permission of Arnoldo DeAlmeida.

is that additional influences from within the organization may be exerted on the industrial purchasing agent. This will be discussed in more detail in the next chapter.

The basic premise of marketing is to understand the consumer in order for sound marketing planning to occur. We can categorize people into various segments, but it is essential to go deeper than that. Marketing planners must consider *what* motivates potential consumers, and *why*. The study of consumer behaviour has become a well-established discipline within the field of marketing.

Much marketing research into consumer behaviour has been undertaken. In addition, the field of consumer behaviour borrows extensively from other areas, like psychology and sociology. The work of Kurt Lewin, for instance, provides an excellent classification of influences on buying behaviour. Lewin's proposition was that

$$B = f(P,E),$$

where behaviour (B) is a function (f) of the interactions of personal influences (P) and the pressures exerted on them by outside forces in the environment (E).[3]

This statement is usually rewritten for consumer behaviour as follows:

$$B = f(I,P),$$

where consumer behaviour (B) is a function (f) of the interaction of interpersonal influences (I), such as reference groups and culture, and personal determinants (P), such as attitudes, on the consumer. Understanding consumer behaviour, as Figure 7.1 illustrates, requires understanding both the individual's psychological make-up and the influences of others.

PERSONAL DETERMINANTS OF CONSUMER BEHAVIOUR

Consumer behaviour is a function of both interpersonal and personal influences. The personal determinants of consumer behaviour include the individual's needs, motives, perceptions, attitudes, and learning. Figure 7.2 shows these personal determinants.

■ Figure 7.1 **Determinants of Consumer Behaviour**

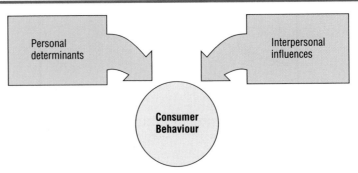

■ Figure 7.2 **Personal Determinants of Consumer Behaviour**

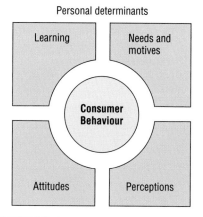

Source: Adapted from C. Glenn Walters and Gordon W. Paul, *Consumer Behavior: An Integrated Framework* (Homewood, IL: Irwin, 1970), p. 14. Copyright © 1970 by Richard D. Irwin, Inc. Used by permission of the publisher.

Needs and Motives

The starting point in the purchase decision process is the recognition of a felt need. A **need** is *the perceived difference between the current state and a desired state*. The consumer is typically confronted with numerous unsatisfied needs. It is important to note that a need must be sufficiently aroused before it may serve as a motive.

Motives are *inner states that direct us toward the goal of satisfying a felt need*. The individual is *moved* (the root word of motive) to take action to reduce a state of tension and to return to a condition of equilibrium.

need
The perceived difference between the current state and a desired state.

motive
An inner state that directs us toward the goal of satisfying a felt need.

HIERARCHY OF NEEDS

Although psychologists disagree on specific classifications of needs, a useful theory that may apply to consumers in general was developed by A.H. Maslow.[4] He proposed a classification of needs (sometimes referred to as a hierarchy), as shown in Figure 7.3. It is important to recognize that Maslow's hierarchy *may not apply to each individual*, but seems to be true of groups in general. His list is based on two important assumptions:

1. People are wanting animals, whose needs depend on what they already possess. A satisfied need is not a motivator; only those needs that have not been satisfied can influence behaviour.
2. Once one need has been largely satisfied, another emerges and demands satisfaction.

Physiological needs The primary needs for food, shelter, and clothing normally must be satisfied before the higher-order needs are considered. A hungry person is possessed by the need to obtain food. Other needs are ignored. Once the physiological needs are at least partly satisfied, other needs come into the picture.

Safety needs Safety needs include protection from physical harm, the need for security, and avoidance of the unexpected. Gratification of these needs may take

■ Figure 7.3 **Need Classification Structure**

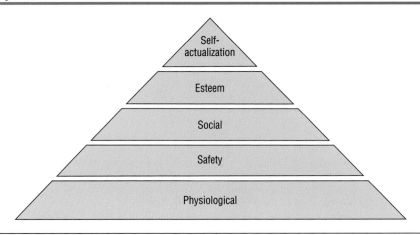

Source: Adapted from "A Theory of Human Motivation," in Abraham H. Maslow, *Motivation and Personality*, 3rd ed. Revised by Robert Frager, James Fadiman, Cynthia McReynolds, and Ruth Cox. Copyright 1954. © 1987 by Harper & Row Publishers, Inc. Copyright © 1970 by Abraham H. Maslow. Reprinted by permission of HarperCollins Publishers, Inc.

the form of a savings account, life insurance, the purchase of radial tires, or membership in the local health club. Michelin Tire advertisements target this need.

Social needs Satisfaction of physiological and safety needs may be followed by the desire to be accepted by members of the family and other individuals and groups — that is, the social needs. Individuals may be motivated to join various groups and to conform to their standards of dress, purchases, and behaviour, and may become interested in obtaining status as a means of fulfilling these social needs. Social needs seem to be becoming a more important cultural value. Many "lifestyle" advertisements, such as those often used by Coca-Cola and Pepsi, appeal to social needs.

Esteem needs The higher-order needs are prevalent in all societies. In developed countries with high per capita income, most families have been able to satisfy the basic needs. Therefore, one would expect such consumers to concentrate more on the desire for status, esteem, and self-actualization. These needs are more difficult to satisfy. At the esteem level is the need to feel a sense of accomplishment, achievement, and respect from others. The competitive need to excel — to better the performance of others and "stand out" from the crowd — is an almost universal human trait.

Esteem needs are closely related to social needs. At this level, however, the individual desires not just acceptance but also recognition and respect in some way.

Self-actualization needs Self-actualization needs are the desire for fulfilment, for realizing one's own potential, for using one's talents and capabilities totally. Maslow defines self-actualization this way: "The healthy man is primarily motivated by his needs to develop and actualize his fullest potentialities and capacities. What man can be, he must be."[5] The author Robert Louis Stevenson was describing self-actualization when he wrote, "To be what we are, and to become what we are capable of becoming, is the only end in life."

As already noted, Maslow argues that a satisfied need is no longer a motivator. Once the physiological needs are satiated, the individual moves on to the higher-

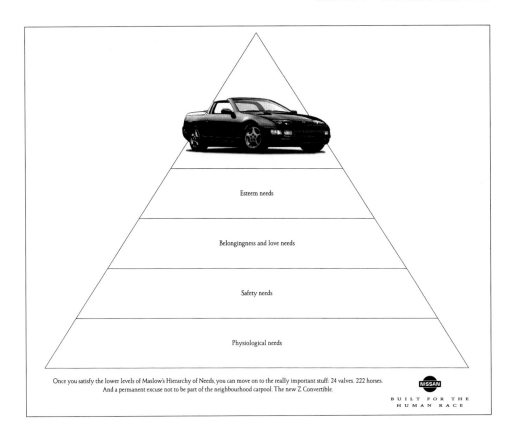

Esteem needs

Belongingness and love needs

Safety needs

Physiological needs

Once you satisfy the lower levels of Maslow's Hierarchy of Needs, you can move on to the really important stuff: 24 valves. 222 horses. And a permanent excuse not to be part of the neighbourhood carpool. The new Z Convertible.

NISSAN

BUILT FOR THE HUMAN RACE

This award-winning newspaper advertisement by Chiat/Day for Nissan Canada Inc. effectively uses the concept of Maslow's hierarchy of needs to sell its new product. The Z Convertible is depicted to be the ultimate in cars — one that has become the best that cars can become. For buyers, the Z convertible will satisfy all levels of their needs in the hierarchy.

order needs. Consumers are periodically motivated by the need to relieve thirst or hunger, but their interests are most often directed toward the satisfaction of safety, social, and other needs.

Caution must be used in applying Maslow's theory. Empirical research shows little support for a universal hierarchical ordering of needs in *specific individuals.*[6] It would therefore be unsafe to use the theory to explain a particular purchase. The needs hierarchy and motive strength concept may be useful in considering the behaviour of consumers *in general,* however. It has been verified that in consumer buying, previously ignored desires often surface only after a purchase has satisfied a predominant (and *perhaps* lower-order) motive.[7] The Nissan advertisement for its new Z convertible makes an interesting use of Maslow's hierarchy.

Perceptions

In some Asian countries, a prized product is ginseng root. This is used as a key ingredient in certain drinks and medications. The product is not cheap, but demand is huge, because many Asians perceive that it has positive medicinal benefits for a number of conditions. In the West, however, the vast majority see no value in ginseng, and are not at all interested in buying or using it.

Individual behaviour resulting from motivation is affected by how we perceive stimuli. **Perception** is *the meaning that each person attributes to incoming stimuli received through the five senses.*

perception
The meaning that each person attributes to incoming stimuli received through the five senses.

Asians perceive ginseng as beneficial, while North Americans have little experience of ginseng and do not see a need for it. In recent years, however, many North Americans have started to look for alternative medicines. Ginseng companies like Chai-Na-Ta, the largest grower of North American ginseng, based in Langley, BC, have jumped on this trend. Multiple vitamins, which are perceived by North Americans to be beneficial, are now being combined with ginseng to stimulate interest in the herb.

Psychologists once assumed that perception was an objective phenomenon — that is, that the individual perceived what was there to be perceived. It is now recognized that what we perceive is as much a result of what we *want* to perceive as of what is actually there. This does not mean that people view dogs as pigeons. We can distinguish shopping centres from churches, and a retail store stocked with well-known brand names and staffed with helpful, knowledgeable sales personnel is perceived differently from a largely self-serve discount store. Kmart and Birks are both important retailers, but they carry quite different images.

Our perception of an object or event is the result of the interaction of two types of factors:

1. Stimulus factors, which are characteristics of the physical object, such as size, colour, weight, or shape.
2. Individual factors, which are characteristics of the perceiver. These factors include not only sensory processes but also past experiences with similar items and basic motivations and expectations.

PERCEPTUAL SCREENS

The individual is continually bombarded with a myriad of stimuli, but most are ignored. In order to have time to function, each of us must respond selectively to stimuli. What stimuli we respond to, then, is the problem of all marketers. How can they gain the attention of the individual so that he or she will read the advertisement, listen to the sales representative, react to a point-of-purchase display?

Even though studies have shown that the average consumer is exposed to more than 1000 ads daily, most of them never break through our **perceptual screen**, *the filter through which messages must pass*. Sometimes breakthroughs may be accomplished in the printed media through larger ads, since doubling the size of an ad increases its attention value by approximately 50 percent. Black-and-white TV ads with selective use of one colour, in contrast with the usual colour ads, are another device to break the reader's perceptual screen. Another method of using contrast in print advertising is to include a large amount of white space to draw attention to

perceptual screen
The filter through which messages must pass.

the ad, or to use white type on a black background. In general, the marketer seeks to make the message stand out, to make it sufficiently different from other messages that it gains the attention of the prospective customer. Piercing the perceptual screen is a difficult task.

With such selectivity at work, it is easy to see the importance of the marketer's efforts to develop brand loyalty to a product. Satisfied customers are less likely to seek or pay attention to information about competing products. They simply tune out information that is not in accord with their existing beliefs and expectations.

WEBER'S LAW

Our understanding of what it takes to get attention may be added by considering Weber's Law. The relationship between the actual physical stimulus (such as size, loudness, or texture) and the corresponding sensation produced in the individual is known as *psychophysics*, which can be expressed as a mathematical equation:

$$\frac{\Delta I}{I} = k$$

where ΔI = the smallest increase in stimulus that will be noticeably different from
the previous intensity
I = the intensity of the stimulus at the point where the increase takes place
k = a constant (that varies from one sense to the next)

In other words, *the higher the initial intensity of a stimulus, the greater the amount of the change in intensity that is necessary in order for a difference to be noticed.*

This relationship, known as **Weber's Law**, has some obvious implications in marketing. A price increase of $300 for an Achieva is readily apparent for prospective buyers; the same $300 increase on a $45 000 Mercedes seems insignificant. A large package requires a much greater increase in size to be noticeable than a smaller-sized package requires. People perceive *by exception*, and the change in a stimulus must be sufficiently great to gain the individual's attention.[8]

Weber's Law
The higher the initial intensity of a stimulus, the greater the amount of the change in intensity that is necessary in order for a difference to be noticed.

SUBLIMINAL PERCEPTION

Is it possible to communicate with persons without their being aware of the communication? In other words, does **subliminal perception** — *a subconscious level of awareness* — really exist? In 1957, the phrases "Eat popcorn" and "Drink Coca-Cola®" were flashed on the screen of a New Jersey movie theatre every 5 seconds for 1/300th of a second. Researchers then reported that these messages, although too short to be recognizable at the conscious level, resulted in a 58 percent increase in popcorn sales and an 18 percent increase in Coca-Cola® sales. After the publication of these findings, advertising agencies and consumer protection groups became intensely interested in subliminal perception.[9] Subsequent attempts to duplicate the test findings have, however, invariably been unsuccessful.

subliminal perception
A subconscious level of awareness.

If used, subliminal advertising would be aimed at the subconscious level of awareness to avoid the perceptual screens of viewers. The goal of the original research was to induce consumers to purchase products without being aware of the source of the motivation. Although subliminal advertising has been universally condemned (and declared illegal in Canada and California), experts believe that it is in fact unlikely that such advertising can induce purchases anyway. There are several reasons for this: (1) strong stimulus factors are typically required even to gain attention, as discussed earlier; (2) only a very short message can be transmitted subliminally; (3) individuals vary greatly in their thresholds of consciousness[10] (a message transmitted at the threshold of consciousness for one person will not be perceived at all by some people and will be all too apparent for others; when exposed subliminally, the message "Drink Coca-Cola®" might go unseen by some viewers, while others read it as "Drink Pepsi-Cola," "Drink Cocoa," or even "Drive Slowly");[11] and (4) perceptual defences *also* work at the subconscious level.

Contrary to earlier fears, research has shown that subliminal messages cannot force the receiver to purchase goods that he or she would not consciously want.[12]

Attitudes

Perception of incoming stimuli is greatly affected by attitudes regarding these stimuli. In fact, decisions to purchase products are based on currently held attitudes about the product, the store, or the salesperson.

attitudes
A person's enduring favourable or unfavourable evaluations of some object or idea.

Attitudes may be defined as *a person's enduring favourable or unfavourable evaluations of some object or idea.* Attitudes are formed over a period of time through individual experiences and group contacts, and are highly resistant to change.

COMPONENTS OF AN ATTITUDE

Attitudes consist of three related components: affective, cognitive, and behavioural. The *affective* component is one's feelings or emotional reactions. The *cognitive* component is the information and knowledge one has about an object or concept. The *behavioural* component is the way one tends to act or to behave. In considering the decision to shop at a warehouse-type food store, a person obtains information from advertising, trial visits, and input from family, friends, and associates (cognitive). A consumer also receives inputs from others about their acceptance of shopping at this new type of store, as well as impressions about the type of people who shop there (affective). The shopper may ultimately decide to make some purchases of canned goods, cereal, and bakery products there, but continue to rely on a regular supermarket for major food purchases (behavioural).

As Figure 7.4 illustrates, the three components exist in a relatively stable and balanced relationship to one another and combine to form an overall attitude about an object or idea.

PRODUCING ATTITUDE CHANGE

Given that a favourable consumer attitude is a prerequisite to market success, how can a firm lead prospective buyers to adopt a more favourable attitude toward its products? The marketer has two choices: either attempt to change attitudes to bring them into accord with the product, or determine consumer attitudes and then change the product to match them.[13]

If consumers view the product unfavourably, the firm may choose to redesign the product to better conform with their desires. To accommodate the consumer, the firm may make styling changes, variations in ingredients, changes in package size, and changes in retail stores handling the product. The other course of action — changing consumer attitudes toward the product without changing the product — is much more difficult.

AFFECTING ATTITUDE THROUGH THE MODIFICATION OF ONE ATTITUDINAL COMPONENT

Attitude change may occur when inconsistencies are introduced among the three attitudinal components. If one component can be influenced, the other two may be

■ Figure 7.4 **Three Components of an Attitude**

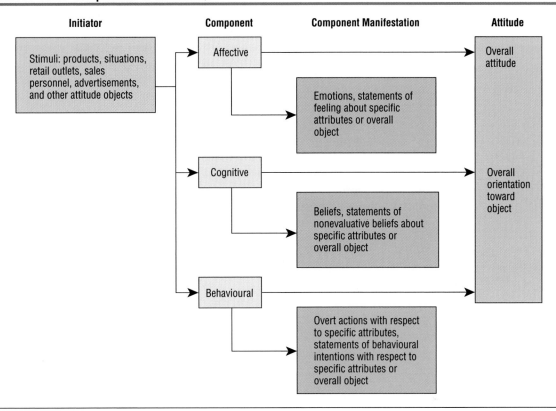

Source: Adapted from M.J. Rosenberg and C.I. Hovland, *Attitude Organization and Change* (New Haven, CT: Yale University Press, 1960), p. 3. Reprinted with permission.

brought into congruence with the changed component, and the attitude will be modified.

Affective component The affective component of attitude may be altered by relating the use of the product to desirable consequences for the user. This is a common appeal for health and beauty-aid products. Advertisements for a new perfume or cologne may imply that it will make one more attractive to the opposite sex.

Cognitive component One way to create an inconsistency in the cognitive component involves providing new information. In the early 1990s, General Motors mounted a huge advertising program showing that its cars were more fuel-efficient and reliable than Japanese-produced cars. This information was expected to counteract "common knowledge" that Japanese-produced cars were superior on these characteristics. In another instance, beef producers first modified their product, then undertook comparative advertising to show the low amount of fat now contained in beef.

Behavioural component The third alternative in attempting to change attitudes is to focus on the behavioural component by inducing someone to engage in behaviour that is contradictory to the person's currently held attitudes. Attitude-discrepant behaviour of this type may occur if the consumer is given a free sample of a product. Such trials may lead to attitude change.

Learning

Consumers *learn* about the values and uses of products. Since marketing is as concerned with the process by which consumer decisions change over time as with describing those decisions at one point in time, the study of how learning takes place is important. A useful definition of **learning** is *changes in knowledge, attitudes, and/or behaviour, as a result of experience.*[14]

The learning process includes several components. The first component, **drive**, refers to *any strong stimulus that impels action.* Examples of drives include fear, pride, the desire for money, thirst, pain avoidance, and rivalry.

Cues, the second component of the learning process, are *any objects existing in the environment that determine the nature of the response to a drive.* Cues might include a newspaper advertisement for a new French restaurant, an in-store display, or a Petro-Canada sign on a major highway. For the hungry person, the shopper seeking a particular item, or the motorist needing gasoline, these cues may result in a specific response to satisfy a drive.

A **response** is *the individual's reaction to the cues and drives,* such as purchasing a bottle of Pert Plus shampoo, dining at Harvey's, or deciding to enrol at a particular university or community college.

Reinforcement is *the reduction in drive that results from a proper response.* The more rewarding the response, the stronger the bond between the drive and the purchase of that particular item becomes. Should Pert Plus result in shiny, manageable hair through repeated use, the likelihood of its purchase in the future is increased.

APPLYING LEARNING THEORY TO MARKETING DECISIONS

Learning theory has some important implications for marketing strategists.[15] A desired outcome such as repeat purchase behaviour may have to be developed gradually. **Shaping** is *the process of applying a series of rewards and reinforcement so that more complex behaviour* (such as the development of a brand preference) *can evolve over time.* Both promotional strategy and the product itself play a role in the shaping process.

Figure 7.5 shows the application of learning theory and shaping procedures to a typical marketing scenario, in which marketers attempt to motivate consumers to become regular buyers of a certain product. An initial product trial is induced by a free sample package that includes a coupon offering a substantial discount on a subsequent purchase. This illustrates the use of a cue as a shaping procedure. The purchase response is reinforced by satisfactory product performance and a coupon for the next purchase.

The second stage is to entice the consumer to buy the product with little financial risk. The large discount coupon enclosed with the free sample prompts such an action. The package that is purchased has a smaller discount enclosed. Again, the reinforcement is satisfactory product performance and the second coupon.

The third step would be to motivate the person to buy the item again at a moderate cost. The discount coupon accomplishes this objective, but this time there is no additional coupon in the package. The only reinforcement is satisfactory product performance.

The final test comes when the consumer is asked to buy the product at its true price, without a discount coupon. Satisfaction with product performance is the only continuing reinforcement. Thus, repeat purchase behaviour has literally been shaped.

---

learning
Changes in knowledge, attitudes, and/or behaviour, as a result of experience.

drive
Any strong stimulus that impels action.

cue
Any object existing in the environment that determines the nature of the response to a drive.

response
The individual's reaction to the cues and drives.

reinforcement
The reduction in drive that results from a proper response.

shaping
The process of applying a series of rewards and reinforcement so that more complex behaviour can evolve over time.

■ Figure 7.5 **Application of Learning Theory and Shaping Procedure to Marketing**

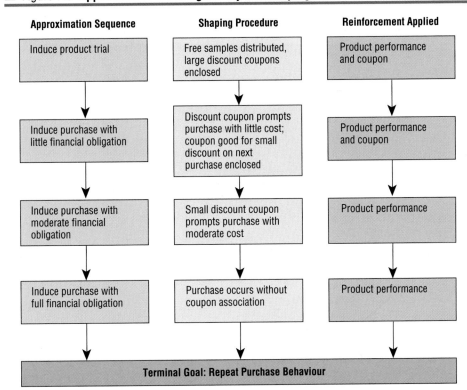

Source: Adapted from Michael L. Rothschild and William C. Gaidis, "Behavioral Learning Theory: Its Relevance to Marketing and Promotion," *Journal of Marketing* (Spring 1981), p. 72. Reprinted by permission of the American Marketing Association.

Kellogg used learning theory and shaping when it introduced its Nutri-Grain brand sugarless whole-grain cereal. Coupons worth 40 cents off — about a third of the product's cost — were distributed to elicit trial purchases by consumers. Inside boxes of the new cereal were additional cents-off coupons of lesser value.[16] Kellogg was clearly trying to shape future purchase behaviour by effectively applying learning theory within a marketing strategy context.

INTERPERSONAL DETERMINANTS OF CONSUMER BEHAVIOUR

People are social animals. They often buy products and services that will enable them to project a favourable image to others. The cultural environment, membership in reference groups, and family may influence such purchase decisions. A general model of the interpersonal (or group) determinants of consumer behaviour is shown in Figure 7.6. It indicates that there are three categories of interpersonal determinants of consumer behaviour: cultural influences, social influences, and family influences. The figure also shows the involvement of personal determinants.

◼ Figure 7.6 **Interpersonal Determinants of Consumer Behaviour**

Source: Adapted from C. Glenn Walters and Gordon W. Paul, *Consumer Behavior: An Integrated Framework* (Homewood, IL: Irwin, 1970), p. 16. Copyright © 1970 by Richard D. Irwin, Inc. Used by permission of the publisher.

Cultural Influences

Culture is the broadest environmental determinant of consumer behaviour. Sometimes it is a very elusive concept for marketers to handle. General Mills knew that few Japanese homes had ovens, so it designed a Betty Crocker cake mix that could be made in the electric rice-cookers widely used in that country. The product failed because of a cultural factor. Japanese homemakers regard the purity of their rice as very important, so they were afraid that a cake flavour might be left in their cookers.[17]

culture
The complex of values, ideas, attitudes, institutions, and other meaningful symbols created by people that shape human behaviour, and the artifacts of that behaviour, transmitted from one generation to the next.

Culture can be defined as *the complex of values, ideas, attitudes, institutions, and other meaningful symbols created by people that shape human behaviour, and the artifacts of that behaviour, transmitted from one generation to the next.*[18] It is the way of life learned and handed down through generations that gives each society its own peculiar characteristics and values.

CORE VALUES IN THE CANADIAN CULTURE

The list in Table 7.1 provides a useful summary of characteristics significant to the Canadian culture today. There are trends and shifts in cultural values, yet traditionally these changes have been gradual. Nevertheless, marketers must constantly assess cultural norms. One of the most recent cultural trends is the search for more interpersonal relationships, rather than the self-centred orientation that characterized value structures in the recent past. In other words, many people want greater

◼ Table 7.1 **Summary of Significant Canadian Characteristics**

As a Function of Being a Part of the North American Reality
- Modern orientation
- Openness to new ideas
- Egalitarianism
- A rich, developing society with many needs and high materialistic expectations
- Growing, more diffuse middle class

In Relation to the United States
- Conservative tendencies
- Traditional bias
- Greater confidence in bureaucratic institutions
- Collectivity orientation — reliance on institutions such as state, big business, and the church as vs. personal risk-taking
- Less achievement-oriented
- Lower optimism — less willing to take risks
- Greater acceptance of hierarchical order and stratification
- Tolerance for diversity — acceptance of cultural mosaic
- Family stability
- Selective emulation of the United States — resistance to some American characteristics and dominance, yet willingness to emulate
- Elitist and ascriptive tendencies

friendship.[19] This trend has been noted by marketers, who now feature more family and friendship groups in their commercials.

CULTURAL INFLUENCES: AN INTERNATIONAL PERSPECTIVE

An awareness of cultural differences is particularly important for international marketers. Different attitudes, mores, and folkways all affect marketing strategy. Examples of cultural influences on marketing strategy are abundant in the international environment. Look at the marketing implications of the following situations:

- In Malaysia and Indonesia, the left hand is considered unclean. Therefore, it is insulting to hand an object to someone using the left hand.
- In Japan, as well as some other Asian countries, it is much easier to get things done, or to get to see a prospective client, if you have been recommended or introduced by a mutual acquaintance.
- In Ethiopia, the time required to make a decision is directly proportional to its importance. This is so much the case that lower-level bureaucrats there attempt to elevate the prestige of their work by taking a long time to make decisions. North Americans there are innocently prone to downgrade their work in the local people's eyes by trying to speed things up.[20]

Often a marketing program that has been proven successful in Canada cannot be applied directly in international markets because of cultural differences. Real differences exist among different countries, and the differences must be known and evaluated by the international firm. When Helene Curtis introduced its Every Night shampoo line in Sweden, it renamed the product Every Day, since Swedes usually wash their hair in the morning.[21]

World marketers must become familiar with many aspects of the local population — including their cultural heritage. The local market segments in each country must be thoroughly analyzed prior to developing a marketing plan, just as they are at home. The topic of cultural influences in international marketing is explored more fully in Chapter 19.

SUBCULTURES

microculture
A subgroup with its own distinguishing modes of behaviour.

Within each culture are numerous **microcultures** — *subgroups with their own distinguishing modes of behaviour.* Any culture as heterogeneous as that existing in Canada is composed of significant microcultures based on such factors as race, nationality, age, rural–urban location, religion, and geographic distribution. The size of such microculture groups can be very significant. For example, the Italian population in the Toronto area is about 500 000 — larger than the entire population of most Canadian cities.

Many people on the West Coast display a lifestyle emphasizing casual dress, outdoor entertaining, and water recreation. Mormons refrain from purchasing tobacco and liquor; orthodox Jews purchase kosher or other traditional foods; Chinese people may exhibit more interest in products and symbols that reflect their Chinese heritage.

The French-Canadian market Although Canada has many microcultures, the two founding cultures — English and French — are the most influential, through sheer force of numbers. The francophone population is a significant market in Canada.[22] Twenty-five percent of the Canadian population identify French as their mother tongue. While most of this population resides in Quebec, there are significant French-speaking segments in other provinces. Proportionately, the largest is in New Brunswick, where 33.6 percent of the population (or 224 000 people) have French as their mother tongue.[23] Numerically, Ontario has the largest group, with 462 000.

The Quebec market is large enough and different enough to create an entire advertising industry of its own. Quebec constitutes about 27 percent of the total Canadian market for goods and services, and is the second-largest market in Canada.[24]

While there is no doubt that the Quebec market is substantially different from the rest of Canada, it is difficult to define those differences precisely. Considerable research over the years has pointed out many characteristics specific to the area — French-Canadians, for example, are said to be fonder of sweets than other Canadians. However, other data can usually be found to contest any such find, or at least to show that it is no longer true.

Such statements reflect measurement of traits in the Quebec culture at only one particular period. These measurements may be legitimate and necessary for a firm wishing to market a product in that segment at a particular point in time. However, similar differences can probably be detected between consumers in Nova Scotia and consumers in British Columbia, if you look for them.

Attention should not be concentrated on *specific* differences between the Quebec market and the rest of Canada, but rather on the fact that there is a basic cultural difference between the two markets. "Culture is a way of being, thinking, and feeling. It is a driving force animating a significant group of individuals united by a common tongue, and sharing the same customs, habits and experiences."[25] Because of this cultural difference, some marketing programs may be distinctly different in Quebec than in the rest of Canada. In the French-Canadian market, it is not the products that are different, but the state of mind.[26] For example, Renault achieved a Quebec market penetration ten times greater than in the rest of Canada. Since the product and price were the same, the difference must have lain in the marketing program attuned to the Quebec market.

Michel Cloutier argues that many differences between the French- and English-Canadian cultures are the result of education and income.[27] As the gap between these factors narrows, and as cultures are affected by similar political and technological influences, the differences in values and consumption patterns will also narrow. Nevertheless, it appears that frames of reference and significant cues will continue to be different, requiring the marketer to be astute in dealing with these market segments.

The key to success in this important Canadian market is having marketing specialists who understand people and who understand how to deal in that specific market. Sophisticated marketers now realize this. That is why there are so many Quebec advertising agencies.

Social Influences

The earliest awareness of children confirms that they are members of a very important group — the family — from which they seek total satisfaction of their physiological and social needs. As they grow older, they join other groups — neighbourhood play groups, school groups, the Cub Scouts, Brownies, minor league hockey teams — as well as groups of friends. From these groups they acquire both status and role. **Status** refers to their *relative position in a group*. **Role** refers to *the rights and duties expected of an individual in a group by other members of the group*. Some of these are

status
Relative position in a group.

role
The rights and duties expected of an individual in a group by other members of the group.

APPLYING THE CONCEPTS

The Right Words for the Right Market

In advertising, language plays a key role. Misuse of language can be, and often is, a source of confusion and misunderstanding. Since language is more than just a sequence of words without reference to cultural context, the problem of translation is never as simple as the mere mechanical use of a dictionary. Occasionally, a literal translation may be acceptable. However, there are serious pitfalls. The following "gems" illustrate the point:

1. Car wash: Lavement d'auto (car enema).
2. Fresh milk used: Lait frais usagé (used fresh milk).
3. They are terrific: Elles sont terrifiantes (they are terrifying).
4. Big John: Gros Jos (large breast).
5. Chicken to take out: Poulet pour sortir (chicken to go out with).

The same observation applies to literal translations from French to English. Here are the literal English translations of a few extremely successful French-Canadian slogans:

1. He there knows that: Lui y connaît ça (he really knows what he's talking about)!
2. There is in it: Y en a dedans (there's a lot to it)!
3. That — that walks: Ça, ça marche (that really works)!
4. One chance out of thirteen: Une chance sur treize (thirteen to one)!
5. That's all a number: C'est tout un numéro (He's a [terrific] guy)!

Source: Eleine Saint-Jacques and Bruce Mallen, "The French Market Under the Microscope," *Marketing Magazine* (May 11, 1981), p. 14. Reprinted by permission of the publisher.

How should firms avoid such errors?

formal groups (for example, Cub Scouts) and others are informal (friendship groups). But both types supply their members with status and roles and, in doing so, influence the activities, including the consumer behaviour, of each member.

THE ASCH PHENOMENON: GROUP INFLUENCE EFFECTS ON CONFORMITY

Although most people view themselves as individuals, groups are often highly influential in purchase decisions. In situations where individuals feel that a particular group or groups are important, they tend to adhere in varying degrees to the general expectations of that group.

The surprising *impact that groups and group norms can exhibit on individual behaviour* has been called the **Asch phenomenon**. The phenomenon was first documented in the following study conducted by the psychologist S.E. Asch:

> Eight subjects are brought into a room and asked to determine which of a set of three unequal lines is closest to the length of a fourth line shown some distance from the other three. The subjects are to announce their judgements publicly. Seven of the subjects are working for the experimenter, and they announce incorrect matches. The order of announcement is arranged such that the naive subject responds last. In a control situation, 37 naive subjects performed the task 18 times each without any information about others' choices. Two of the 37 subjects made a total of 3 mistakes. However, when another group of 50 naive subjects responded *after* hearing the unanimous but *incorrect* judgement of the other group members, 37 made a total of 194 errors, all of which were in agreement with the mistake made by the group.[28]

This widely replicated study illustrates the influence of groups on individual choice-making. Marketing applications range from the choice of automobile models and residential locations to the decision to purchase at least one item at a Tupperware party.

REFERENCE GROUPS

In order for groups to exert such influence on individuals, they must be categorized as **reference groups**, or *groups whose value structures and standards influence a person's behaviour*. Consumers usually try to keep their purchase behaviour in line with what they perceive to be the values of their reference group.

The status of the individual within the reference group produces three subcategories: **membership groups**, in which *the person actually belongs* (as is the case with, say, a country club); **aspirational groups**, a situation where *a person desires to associate with a group*; and **disassociative groups**, ones *with which the individual does not want to be identified*. For example, teenagers are unlikely to enjoy the middle-of-the-road music played on radio stations catering to their parents' generation.

It is obviously not essential that the individual be a member in order for the group to serve as a point of reference. This partly explains the use of famous athletes and celebrities in advertisements. Even though few possess the skills necessary to pilot a racing car, all racing fans can identify with the Mosport winner by injecting their engines with STP.

The extent of reference-group influence varies widely among purchases. For reference-group influence to be great, two factors must be present:

1. The item purchased must be one that can be seen and identified by others.
2. The item purchased must also be conspicuous in the sense that it stands out, is unusual, and is a brand or product that not everyone owns.

Asch phenomenon
The impact that groups and group norms can exhibit on individual behaviour.

reference group
A group whose value structures and standards influence a person's behaviour.

membership group
A type of reference group to which individuals actually belong, as with, say, a country club.

aspirational group
A type of reference group with which individuals desire to associate.

disassociative group
A type of reference group with which an individual does not want to be identified.

Based in Winnipeg, Mondetta Clothing was founded by four young entrepreneurs who have already won numerous business awards in a very short time. Their clothes are very popular with young people. Using a unique concept of sewing the Mondetta label and international flags on sweatshirts, the founders hope to create recognition for the need for global unity. What role do you think the label plays with regard to reference groups?

Figure 7.7 shows the influence of reference groups on both the basic decision to purchase a product and the decision to purchase a particular brand. The figure shows that reference groups had a significant impact on both the decision to purchase an automobile *and* the type of brand that was actually selected. By contrast, reference groups had little impact on the decision to purchase canned peaches or the brand that was chosen.

SOCIAL CLASSES

Consumer behaviour is affected by **social class**, *the relatively permanent divisions in a society into which individuals or families are categorized based on prestige and community status*. Research by Lloyd Warner in the United States in the 1940s and by John Porter in Canada in the late 1950s identified a six-class system within the social structure of both small and large cities. Families were divided into two categories each of lower, middle, and upper classes on the basis of occupation, source of income (not amount), education, family background, and dwelling area. It was discovered that activities, interests, opinions, and buying behaviour were significantly affected by social class.

Income is not the main determinant of social-class behaviour, and the view that "a rich person is just a poor person with more money" is incorrect. Pipe-fitters paid at union scale will earn more money than many university professors, but their purchase behaviour may be quite different. For example, a professor may be more interested in expenditures related to the arts and similar entertainment, whereas a pipe-fitter may have quite different tastes and interests in satisfying esthetic and entertainment needs.

Marketers have found that it is more meaningful to think about such differences in terms of variations in *lifestyle*. Market segmentation by lifestyle is described in the next section.

social class
The relatively permanent divisions in a society into which individuals or families are categorized based on prestige and community status.

■ Figure 7.7 **Extent of Reference-Group Influence on Product and Brand Decision**

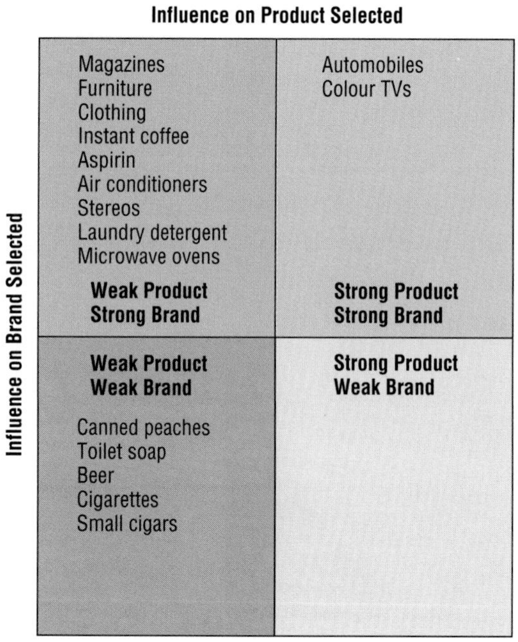

Influence on Product Selected

Magazines Furniture Clothing Instant coffee Aspirin Air conditioners Stereos Laundry detergent Microwave ovens **Weak Product** **Strong Brand**	Automobiles Colour TVs **Strong Product** **Strong Brand**
Weak Product **Weak Brand** Canned peaches Toilet soap Beer Cigarettes Small cigars	**Strong Product** **Weak Brand**

(vertical axis label: **Influence on Brand Selected**)

Source: Donald W. Hendon, "A New and Empirical Look at the Influence of Reference Groups on Generic Product Category and Brand Choice: Evidence from Two Nations," *Proceedings of the Academy of International Business: Asia–Pacific Dimensions of International Business* (Honolulu: College of Business Administration, University of Hawaii, December 18–20, 1979), pp. 752–76, based on Francis S. Bourne, *Group Influence in Marketing and Public Relations* (Foundation for Research on Human Behavior, 1956), p. 8.

RELATING SOCIAL-CLASS HIERARCHY AND LIFESTYLES

Analysis of people's lifestyle can be a revealing thing. It can tell you where they live, how they live, where they travel, what motivates them. More important, it can tell you the kinds of things they purchase. Because it is lifestyle, not just income, that determines what a person buys!

Without knowledge of a person's lifestyle you cannot intelligently target a product or service. With that knowledge you have the means to accurately profile your consumer base. You will know where to market a new product, where to best locate a new store, where to promote with direct mail, where to spend your advertising budget wisely. In fact, you will have the answers to most important marketing questions!

In order to meet marketers' needs for better information, Compusearch has developed a system that groups all the neighbourhoods in Canada into unique clusters. A total of 70 different lifestyles has been identified (48 in urban centres and 22 in rural or nonurban areas). Following is a description of the major categories and a sample target market profile. (See Tables 7.2 and 7.3).

Who can use these new insights?

• Direct-response advertisers can profile test mailings, target unaddressed mail, or boost name-list response.
• Publishers can profile their subscription lists, know who their readers are, and acquire more.

■ Table 7.2 **Major Categories — Lifestyles™**

Code	Lifestyle Category	No. of Lifestyles	Percentage of All Households
	Urban		
A	Affluent	4	1.29
U	Upscale	4	6.95
M	Middle and Upper-Middle Class	7	17.68
W	Working (Lower-Middle) Class	6	15.34
L	Lower Class	5	7.01
L	Young Singles	5	4.25
C	Young Couples	3	3.46
N	Empty Nesters	5	8.58
O	Old and Retired	5	3.92
E	Ethnic	4	3.32
	Nonurban		
X	Upscale and Middle Class	8	10.38
Y	Working and Lower Class	9	15.14
Z	Farming	5	2.70

"Lifestyles" is a trademark of Compusearch Micromarketing Data and Systems.

Source: Reprinted by permission of Compusearch Micromarketing Data and Systems, 1995.

- Banks, credit card companies, retailers — anyone with a list of customers who buy more than one product or service — can attach the codes to each customer record, find their own areas of strength, and cross-sell products to those most likely to buy.
- Manufacturers can put their products in the right hands or test new products in the right place.
- Retailers can find the best areas to expand into, or they can better customize merchandise mix in existing locations.[29]

OPINION LEADERS

Each group usually contains a few members who can be considered **opinion leaders** or trend setters. These individuals are *more likely to purchase new products early and to serve as information sources for others in a given group.*[30] Their opinions are respected, and they are often sought out for advice.

Generalized opinion leaders are rare. Individuals tend to be opinion leaders in specific areas. Their considerable knowledge about and interest in a particular product or service motivates them to seek out further information from mass media, manufacturers, and other sources, and, in turn, they transmit this information to their associates through interpersonal communications. Opinion leaders are found within all segments of the population.

APPLYING THE OPINION LEADERSHIP CONCEPT

Opinion leaders play a crucial role in interpersonal communication. The fact that they distribute information and advice to others indicates their potential importance to marketing strategy. Opinion leaders can be particularly useful in the launching of new products.

General Motors once provided a popular small car to college marketing classes as a basis for a course project. Rock stations have painted teenagers' cars for them;

opinion leaders
Trend setters; individuals who are more likely to purchase new products early and to serve as information sources for others in a given group.

■ Table 7.3 **Elaboration of Two Lifestyle Categories in One Market Segment**

		Lifestyle Descriptor	No. of Clients	Percentage of Clients
A F F L U E N T	A1	Wealthiest, highest education, large families in very expensive houses, age 45–54	2 539	1.03
	A2	Wealthy, well-educated families in expensive houses, age 45–64	6 732	2.73
	A3	Older, wealthy, well-educated couples and widow(er)s in apartments and condominiums	1 388	0.56
	A4	Younger, wealthy, well-educated, larger families with young teenagers in high-value houses	3 651	1.48
	Total	**Affluent**	**14 310**	**5.80**
U P S C A L E	U1	High-income, older families with teenagers in higher-value houses; stable neighbourhoods	12 665	5.13
	U2	High-income, very well-educated, small mixed and older households in old, expensive mixed housing	7 648	3.10
	U3	Younger professional families with young children in new houses; both spouses work	12 797	5.18
	U4	Middle-aged to older families with older children in modest housing	11 741	4.76
	Total	**Upscale**	**44 851**	**18.17**

Source: Reprinted by permission of Compusearch Micromarketing Data and Systems, 1995.

of course, the paint job included the stations' call letters and slogans. Politicians sometimes hold issues forums for community leaders. All these efforts are directed at the opinion leaders in a particular marketplace. These people play an important role in how successfully a new or established product, idea, or political candidacy is communicated to consumers.

Family Influences

The family is an important interpersonal determinant of consumer behaviour. The close, continuing interactions among family members are the strongest group influences for the individual consumer.

Most people in our society are members of two families during their lifetime: the family into which they are born, and the family they eventually form as they marry and have children. With divorce an increasingly common phenomenon, many people become involved with three or more families.

The establishment of a new household upon marriage produces marketing opportunities. A new household means a new home and accompanying furniture. The need for refrigerators, vacuum cleaners, and an original oil painting for the living room depends not on the number of people in each household but on the number of *households* themselves.

As children are added to the household, sizes of some products purchased naturally increase. Two litres of milk will be purchased instead of one. Some larger families will purchase larger vehicles. Many other child-related purchases will be made over the period of time the youngsters remain in the home. Marketers find many opportunities in this market segment. For example, Chrysler achieved great success with its Magic Wagon, a vehicle with ample capacity for families that nevertheless handled as easily as a car.

Another market evolves as parents are left alone when the children move away from home. These parents may find themselves with a four-bedroom "empty nest" and a sizable lawn to maintain each week. Lacking assistance from their children and no longer needing the extra space, they become customers for townhouses, condominiums, and high-rise luxury apartments in the larger cities. This market segment also eventually purchases bifocals, and is a good target for organized tour packages.

MARITAL ROLES IN PURCHASE DECISIONS

Although an infinite variety of roles are played in household decision-making, four role categories are often used: (1) *autonomic* — situations in which an equal number of decisions is made by each partner, but each decision is made individually by one partner or the other; (2) *male-dominant*; (3) *female-dominant*; and (4) *syncratic* — situations in which decisions are made jointly by male and female.[31] Figure 7.8 shows the roles commonly played by household members in the purchase of a number of products.

CHANGING FAMILY ROLES

Two forces have changed the female's role as sole purchasing agent for most household items. First, a shorter work week provides each wage-earning household member with more time for shopping. Second, a large number of women are now in the workforce. In 1950, only about a quarter of married women were also employed outside the home; by 1981, that figure had doubled. Currently, over half of all married women with school-age children hold jobs outside the home. Studies of family decision-making have shown that wives who work outside the home tend to exert more influence than wives who work in the home only. Households with two wage earners also exhibit a large number of joint decisions and an increase in night and weekend shopping.

These changing roles of household members have led many marketers to adjust their marketing programs. Men's clothing stores, such as Stollery's in Toronto, now offer suits and accessories for the career woman. Although demand for men's suits has been sluggish in recent years, sales of women's suits increased 70 percent in 1980. Meanwhile, a survey of 1000 married men revealed that 77 percent participate in grocery shopping and 70 percent cook. A Del Monte promotional campaign recognized these changes and de-emphasized women as the sole meal preparer. Its theme, "Good things happen when you bring Del Monte home," is applicable to both male and female food shoppers.[32]

CHILDREN'S ROLES IN HOUSEHOLD PURCHASING

The role of the children evolves as they grow older. Their early influence is generally centred on toys to be recommended to Santa Claus and the choice of brands of cereals. Younger children are important to marketers of fast-food restaurants. Even though the parents may decide when to eat out, the children often select the restaurant.[33] As they gain maturity, they increasingly influence their clothing purchases.

One study revealed that 13- to 15-year-old teenage boys spend most of their money on food, snacks, movies, and entertainment. Girls in this same age group

■ Figure 7.8 **Marital Roles in 25 Decisions**

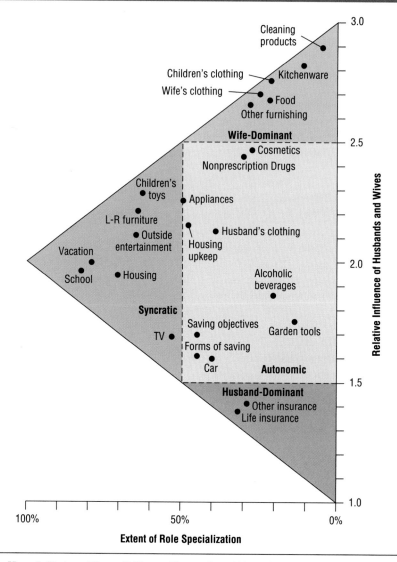

Source: Harry L. Davis and Benny P. Rigaux, "Perception of Marital Roles in Decision Processes," *Journal of Consumer Research* (June 1974), p. 57. Reprinted by permission of the *Journal of Consumer Research*, published by The University of Chicago Press.

buy clothing, food, snacks, movies, entertainment, cosmetics, and fragrances. Sixteen- to 19-year-old boys spend most of their money on entertainment, dating, movies, automobiles and gasoline, clothing, food, and snacks, while girls of the same age buy clothing, cosmetics, fragrances, automobiles and gasoline, movies, and entertainment.[34]

THE CONSUMER DECISION PROCESS

This chapter has shown that consumer behaviour is the result of two main types of influences: personal determinants and interpersonal determinants. The purchase

APPLYING THE CONCEPTS

Identifying Target Markets by Lifestage

The latest word in marketing is, it's not the age, it's the stage. J. Walter Thompson, a major international advertising agency, has developed a whole new way of classifying buyer behaviour called *lifestages*. They are: *At Home Singles, Starting Out Singles, Young Couples, Young Parents, Single Parents, Mature Singles, Empty Nesters,* and *Left Alone Singles*. The lifestage model is research-based, and looks at the consumer and his/her stage in life rather than the stage in the family. It also takes into account some of the modern trends such as young singles who live with their parents and the increase in single parents in the market.

From the nine categories defined, JWT determined what products each group was buying and how much they had to spend on those products. For example, Starting Out Singles are buying furniture and living in multiple-person households. Mature singles are insecure and pessimistic; they travel and tend to drink heavily.

Armed with the information that the lifestage research provides, marketers can identify the ideal consumer for their product, profile that consumer, and design a campaign to appeal to that consumer's needs based on this lifestage.

Source: Excerpted from Gillian Rice, "Lifestages," *Academy of Marketing Science News*, Vol. 2 (October 1990), p. 4. © Academy of Marketing Science.

Can you think of other ways to categorize consumers?

of all goods and services will be affected by some or all of the many variables discussed.

In the light of all this information, researchers have spent considerable effort trying to identify the process that a consumer goes through in making a purchase decision. One commonly accepted hypothesis suggests that the consumer decision process consists of six stages: (1) problem recognition, (2) search, (3) evaluation of alternatives, (4) purchase decision, (5) purchase act, and (6) postpurchase evaluation. Figure 7.9 is a model of this process. Each step of the model is covered in the discussion that follows.

Problem Recognition

This first stage in the decision process occurs when the consumer becomes aware of a discrepancy of sufficient magnitude between the existing state of affairs and a desired state of affairs. Once the problem has been recognized, it must be defined in order that the consumer may seek out methods to solve it. Having recognized the problem, the individual is motivated to achieve the desired state.

What sort of problems might a person recognize? Perhaps the most common is a routine depletion of the stock of products. A large number of consumer purchases involve replenishing items ranging from gasoline to groceries. In other instances, the consumer may possess an inadequate assortment of products. The individual whose hobby is gardening may make regular purchases of different kinds of fertilizers, seeds, or gardening tools as the size of the garden grows.

■ Figure 7.9 **Steps in the Consumer Decision Process**

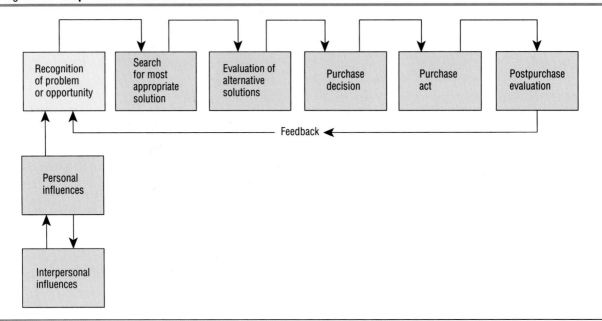

Source: Adapted from C. Glenn Walters and Gordon W. Paul, *Consumer Behavior: An Integrated Framework* (Homewood, IL: Irwin, 1970), p. 18; and John Dewey, *How We Think* (Boston: D.C. Heath, 1910), pp. 101–105.

A consumer may also be dissatisfied with a present brand or product type. This situation is a common factor in the purchase of a new car, new furniture, or a new fall wardrobe. In many instances, boredom with current products and a desire for novelty may be the underlying rationale for the decision process leading to new-product purchases.

Another important factor is changed financial status. The infusion of added financial resources from such sources as a salary increase, a second job, or an inheritance may permit the consumer to recognize desires and make purchases that previously had been postponed due to their cost.[35]

Search

Search, the second stage in the decision process, is the gathering of information related to the attainment of a desired state of affairs. This stage involves identifying alternative means of solving the problem.

An *internal search* is a mental review of the information that a person already knows that is relevant to the problem. This includes actual experiences and observations, plus remembered reading or conversations, and exposures to various persuasive marketing efforts.

An *external search* is the gathering of information from outside sources. These may include family members, friends and associates, store displays, sales representatives, brochures, and such product-testing publications as *Consumer Reports*.

In many instances, the consumer does not go beyond an internal search but merely relies on stored information in making a purchase decision. Achieving a favourable experience flying with Canadian Airlines may sufficiently motivate a consumer to purchase another ticket from Canadian rather than consider possible alternatives. Since an external search involves both time and effort, the consumer will rely on it only in instances in which, for some reason, the information remembered is inadequate.

The search process will identify alternative brands for consideration and possible purchase. *The number of brands that a consumer actually considers in making a purchase decision* is known as the **evoked set**. In some instances, the consumer will already be aware of the brands worthy of further consideration; in others, the external search process will permit the consumer to identify those brands. Not all brands will be included in the evoked set. The consumer may remain unaware of certain brands, and others will be rejected as too costly or as having been tried previously and considered unsatisfactory. In other instances, unfavourable word-of-mouth communication or negative reactions to advertising or other marketing efforts will lead to the elimination of some brands from the evoked set. While the number of brands in the evoked set will vary by product categories, research indicates that the number is likely to be as few as four or five brands.[36]

evoked set
The number of brands that a consumer actually considers in making a purchase decision.

Evaluation of Alternatives

The third step in the consumer decision process involves evaluating the alternatives identified during the search process. Actually, it is difficult to completely separate the second and third steps, since some evaluation takes place simultaneously with the search process as consumers accept, discount, distort, or reject some incoming information as they receive it.

Since the outcome of the evaluation stage is the choice of a brand or product in the evoked set (or, possibly, the search for additional alternatives, should all those identified during the search process prove unsatisfactory), the consumer must develop a set of **evaluative criteria**, *features the consumer considers in making a choice among alternatives.* These criteria can be either *objective* (comparison of gas mileage figures for cars, or comparison of retail prices) or *subjective* (favourable image of Calvin Klein sportswear). Commonly used evaluative criteria include price, reputation of the brand, perceived quality, packaging, size, performance, durability, and colour. Most research studies indicate that consumers seldom use more than six criteria in the evaluation process. Evaluative criteria for detergents include suds level and smell as indicators of cleaning power. High quality and potential for long wear were the underlying criteria in the choice of nylon stockings, according to one research study.[37]

evaluative criteria
Features the consumer considers in making a choice among alternatives.

Purchase Decision and Purchase Act

When the consumer has evaluated each of the alternatives in the evoked set, using his or her personal set of evaluative criteria, and narrowed the alternatives to one, the result is the purchase decision and the act of making the purchase.

The consumer must decide not only to purchase a product but also where to buy it. Consumers tend to choose the purchase location by considering such factors as ease of access, prices, assortment, store personnel, store image, physical design, and services provided. The product category will also influence the store selected. Some consumers will choose the convenience of in-home shopping by telephone, mail order, or through the Internet by modem rather than complete the transaction in a retail store.[38]

Postpurchase Evaluation

The purchase act results in the removal of the discrepancy between the existing state and the desired state. Logically, it should result in satisfaction to the buyer. However, even in many purchase decisions where the buyer is ultimately satisfied, it is common for that person to experience some initial postpurchase anxieties. He or she often wonders if the right decision has been made. Leon Festinger refers to this postpurchase doubt as cognitive dissonance.[39]

cognitive dissonance
The postpurchase anxiety that occurs when there exists a discrepancy between a person's knowledge and beliefs (cognitions).

Cognitive dissonance is the postpurchase anxiety that occurs *when there exists a discrepancy between a person's knowledge and beliefs (cognitions)* about certain attributes of the final products under consideration. This occurs because several of the final product-choice candidates have desirable characteristics, making the final decision difficult. Consumers may, for example, experience dissonance after choosing a particular car over several alternative models, when one or more of the rejected models have some desired features that the purchased car lacks.

Dissonance is likely to increase (1) as the dollar value of the purchase increases, (2) when the rejected alternatives have desirable features not present in the chosen alternative, and (3) when the decision is a major one. The consumer may attempt to reduce dissonance in a variety of ways. He or she may seek out advertisements and other information supporting the chosen alternative or seek reassurance from acquaintances who are satisfied purchasers of the product. At the same time, the individual will avoid information favouring unchosen alternatives. The Toyota purchaser is more likely to read Toyota ads and to avoid Honda and Ford ads. The cigarette smoker may ignore magazine articles reporting links between smoking and cancer.

Marketers should try to reduce cognitive dissonance by providing informational support for the chosen alternative. Automobile dealers recognize "buyer's remorse" and often follow up purchases with a warm letter from the president of the dealership, offering personal handling of any customer problems and including a description of the quality of the product and the availability of convenient, top-quality service.

The consumer may ultimately deal with cognitive dissonance by concentrating on positive aspects of the purchase, changing opinions, deciding that one of the rejected alternatives would have been the best choice, and forming the intention of purchasing it in the future.[40]

Should the purchase prove unsatisfactory, the consumer will revise his or her purchase strategy to obtain need satisfaction. Feedback from the results of the decision process, whether satisfactory or not, will be called upon in the search and evaluation stages of similar buying situations.

Classifying Consumer Problem-Solving Processes

The consumer decision process depends on the type of problem-solving effort required. Problem-solving behaviour has been divided into three categories: routinized response, limited problem solving, and extended problem solving.[41]

Routinized response Many purchases are made as a routine response to a need. The selection is a preferred brand or is made from a limited group of acceptable brands. The consumer has set the evaluative criteria and identified the available options. The routine purchase of a particular newspaper or regular brands of soft drinks or toilet soap would be examples.

Limited problem solving Consider the situation in which the consumer has set evaluative criteria but encounters a new, unknown brand. The introduction of a new fragrance line might create a situation calling for limited problem solving. The consumer knows the evaluative criteria but has not assessed the new brand on the basis of these criteria. A certain amount of time and external search will be required. Limited problem solving is affected by the multitude of evaluative criteria and brands, the extent of external search, and the process by which preferences are determined. Some products — *those with little significance, either materially or emotionally — a consumer may purchase first and evaluate later (while using them).* These are known as **low-involvement products**.

Extended problem solving Extended problem solving occurs with important purchase decisions when evaluative criteria have not been established for a product category or when the individual wishes to review such criteria. Today, many individuals are in the process of purchasing personal computers. Since many have never owned one before, they generally engage in an extensive search process. The main aspect of this process is determining appropriate evaluative criteria that are relevant to the needs of the decision-maker. How much computing power is required? Is portability important? What will be the machine's main uses? What special features are required? As the criteria are being set, an evoked set of brands is also established. Most extended problem-solving efforts are lengthy, involving considerable external search. *Products for which the purchaser is highly involved in making the purchase decision* are known as **high-involvement products**.

low-involvement products
Products with little significance, either materially or emotionally, which a consumer may purchase first and evaluate later (while using them).

high-involvement products
Products for which the purchaser is highly involved in making the purchase decision.

■ KEY TERMS

consumer behaviour	cue	membership group
need	response	aspirational group
motive	reinforcement	disassociative group
perception	shaping	social class
perceptual screen	culture	opinion leader
Weber's Law	microculture	evoked set
subliminal perception	status	evaluative criteria
attitudes	role	cognitive dissonance
learning	Asch phenomenon	low-involvement product
drive	reference group	high-involvement product

■ INTERACTIVE SUMMARY AND DISCUSSION QUESTIONS

1. The work of Kurt Lewin provides a summarization of influences on buying behaviour: $B = f(P,E)$. Explain this equation and apply it to the purchase of a service.

2. A major factor affecting consumer behaviour is personal determinants, which include needs, motives, perceptions, attitudes, and learning.

   A need is the perceived difference between the current state and a desired state. Maslow established a need classification system with the following categories: physiological needs, safety needs, social needs, esteem needs, and self-actualization needs. Which needs are being referred to in the following slogans?
   • No caffeine. Never had it. Never will. (7-Up)
   • Swedish engineering. Depend on it. (SAAB)

- The best bed a body can buy. (Simmons)
- Don't leave home without it. (American Express Card)

3. Motives are inner states that direct us toward the goal of satisfying a felt need. Explain this statement using one of Maslow's need categories.

4. Perception is the meaning that each person attributes to incoming stimuli received through the five senses. There are so many stimuli that individuals establish a perceptual screen to filter out undesired stimuli. Name some methods that a marketer might use to break through such a screen. Consider selective perception and Weber's Law in your answer.

5. Attitudes consist of three related components: cognitive, affective, and behavioural.
   a. Explain each component.
   b. How do attitudes influence consumer behaviour?
   c. How can negative attitudes be changed?

6. Another major category of determinants of consumer behaviour is interpersonal determinants: cultural influences, social influences, and family influences.

   Based on Figure 7.7, for which of the following products is reference-group influence likely to be strong?
   - Rolex watch
   - Skis
   - Shaving foam
   - Ten-speed bicycle
   - Deodorant
   - Portable radio
   - Personal computer
   - Contact lenses

7. Compare and contrast influences on product use that you are aware of between two cultural groups. Outline the implications for marketing the product(s) specified.

8. The impact that groups and group norms can exhibit on individual behaviour has been called the Asch phenomenon. Its effect can be seen in the influence of membership, aspirational, and disassociative reference groups. Give an example of each type of group, and how such influence might influence product usage.

9. Opinion leaders are individuals who are more likely to purchase new products early and to serve as information sources for others in the group. Give an example of how a salesperson might make use of the phenomenon of opinion leadership in promoting her or his product.

10. Marital roles vary in purchase decisions. They have been categorized as autonomic, male-dominant, female-dominant, and syncratic. List a number of products whose purchase would be influenced more by a female. Explain how this knowledge could be used in developing an advertising program for a product in this category.

11. The consumer decision process is outlined in Figure 7.9. Relate a recent purchase you made to this consumer decision process model.

12. Cognitive dissonance is the postpurchase anxiety that occurs after a purchase when there exists a discrepancy between a person's knowledge and beliefs (cognitions) about certain attributes of the final products under consideration. Describe a purchase situation in which you or someone you know experienced

cognitive dissonance. Explain how the company that produced the good or service helped or could have helped to reduce that dissonance.

13. Low-involvement products are those with little significance that a consumer might purchase first and evaluate later. High-involvement products are those for which the purchaser is highly involved in making the purchase decision. Explain the type of distribution and advertising messages that would be appropriate for each category.

CHAPTER 8

Industrial Buyer Behaviour

CHAPTER OBJECTIVES

1. To provide an overview of the industrial buying process.
2. To differentiate among the three types of industrial markets.
3. To identify the three distinctive features of industrial markets.
4. To explain the characteristics of industrial market demand.
5. To identify the basic categories of industrial products.
6. To show the nature and importance of government markets.

Two new airplanes, aimed at the most elite market in the world, will soar through the skies before the decade is out. They are the first ultra long-range corporate jets, and the fastest of them will be able to fly eight passengers and a crew of four from New York to Tokyo in 13 hours without refuelling. Over the next 15 to 20 years, between 350 and 800 such planes will be sold, at a price of about US $30 million each. This is the ultimate in niche marketing. The potential buyers are *Fortune 500*-type companies with deep pockets, a handful of Asian and Middle Eastern entrepreneurs, and, perhaps, a few heads of state. Only two companies in the world have the

combination of resources, know-how, and the nerve to think they can make a profit by purveying such an expensive item to such an absurdly small group of customers.

One of them is an established U.S. aerospace leader, Gulfstream Aerospace Corp. The other is Bombardier Inc. of Montreal, an outfit that only entered the aviation business in 1986 and whose main claims to fame, until recently, were snowmobiles and subway cars. Bombardier has purchased four aircraft manufacturers and become the sixth-largest civil aviation company in the world.

In entering the complex and risky aerospace industry, Bombardier executives developed a twofold strategy. Part 1 was to minimize dependence on defence contracts — a shrinking segment of the industry — and to stay out of the large passenger-jet business, which has been weakened by recession and deregulation. Part 2 was to specialize in two growing segments of the aviation business — regional passenger aircraft that feed the major airline hubs, and business jet aircraft.

The strategy and its implementation have been successful. Employment is up and, at Bombardier's aerospace division, four former money-losers made $136.5 million for the year ended January 31, 1994, on revenues of $2.2 billion.

Good management practices have much to do with this success. A significant part is a clear understanding of the buying behaviour of the business market which the company has concentrated on.[1]

INTRODUCTION

The marketing activities of a company that, like Bombardier, operates in the industrial market are obviously quite different from those of consumer product companies such as Chanel or Procter & Gamble. Many companies having products that might cross over into the other market have found that marketing practices that have proven successful in one will not necessarily produce success in the other.

The consumer market consists of individuals who purchase goods and services for *personal* use. The **industrial market** consists of *individuals and organizations that acquire goods and services to be used, directly or indirectly, in the production of other goods and services or to be resold.*

Important differences from the consumer market exist in the motivations and buying process followed by industrial buyers. As a result, marketing planning and the resulting marketing mix often take a considerably different nature from consumer marketing.

industrial market
Individuals and organizations that acquire goods and services to be used, directly or indirectly, in the production of other goods and services or to be resold.

TYPES OF INDUSTRIAL MARKETS

In assessing industrial buyer behaviour, it is helpful to think about it in terms of the types of industrial markets. The industrial market can be divided into three categories: producers, trade industries (wholesalers and retailers), and governments. **Producers** are *those who transform goods and services through production into other goods and services.* Producers include manufacturing firms, farms and other resource industries, construction contractors, and providers of services (such as transportation, public utilities, and banks). In the production process, some products aid in producing another product or service (for example, an airplane provides transportation); others are physically used up in the production of a product (wheat

producers
Those who transform goods and services through production into other goods and services.

becomes part of cereal); and still others are routinely used in the day-to-day operations of a firm (light bulbs and cleaning materials are maintenance items).

Trade industries are *organizations, such as retailers and wholesalers, that purchase for resale to others.* In most instances, resale products (for example, clothing, appliances, sports equipment, and automobile parts) are finished goods that are marketed to customers. In other instances, some processing or repackaging may take place. Retail meat markets may make bulk purchases of sides of beef and convert them into individual cuts for their customers. Lumber dealers and carpet retailers may purchase in bulk, then provide quantities and sizes to meet customers' specifications. In addition to resale products, trade industries also buy cash registers, computers, display equipment, and other products required to operate their business. These products (as well as maintenance items and the purchase of such specialized services as marketing research studies, accounting services, and consulting) all represent industrial purchases. Retailing and wholesaling activities are discussed in separate chapters later in the text.

Governments at the federal, provincial, and local level represent the final category of industrial purchasers. This important component of the industrial market purchases a wide variety of products, ranging from highways to education to F-16 fighter aircraft. The primary motivation of government purchasing is to provide some form of public benefit such as transportation infrastructure, education, or health services. Buying behaviour in government markets is discussed separately in this chapter because of its immense size and importance.

trade industries
Organizations, such as retailers and wholesalers, that purchase for resale to others.

SCOPE OF THE INDUSTRIAL MARKET

The industrial market is vast. As Table 8.1 shows, in the manufacturing sector alone there are over 34 000 establishments, and they employ more than 1.6 million people. The significance of this market is dramatized in the amount of materials and supplies used in their operations — over $201 billion worth! In total, the industrial market accounts for some 50 percent of purchases of manufactured goods in Canada.

One measure of industrial output is the **value added** by manufacturing: *the increase in value of input material when transformed into semi-finished or finished goods.* For example, value is added to a tonne of iron ore when it is made into steel plate, and more value is added when the plate is stamped into refrigerator bodies. As shown in Table 8.1, the value added by manufacturing in Canada totalled approximately $124.3 billion in 1992.

value added
The increase in value of input material when transformed into semi-finished or finished goods.

DISTINCTIVE FEATURES OF THE INDUSTRIAL MARKET

The industrial market has three distinctive features: geographic market concentration, a relatively small number of buyers, and systematic buying procedures.

Geographic Market Concentration

The market for industrial goods in Canada is much more concentrated geographically than that for consumer goods. The largest markets are in Ontario and Quebec. However, industrial markets for specific items often do not follow the general pattern. As an example, the market for marine engines and fishing gear is con-

■ Table 8.1 **Summary of Manufacturers by Province, 1992**

Province	Number of Establishments	Total Employees	Materials and Supplies Used (millions)	Total Value Added (millions)
All Canada*	34 511	1 673 740	201 367.0	124 342.3
Newfoundland	288	12 323	864.4	668.8
Prince Edward Island	135	3 910	320.7	218.2
Nova Scotia	708	37 168	3 537.4	2 040.6
New Brunswick	643	31 550	3 956.0	1 879.5
Quebec	11 129	454 767	42 201.3	31 896.3
Ontario	13 491	828 384	116 704.9	65 881.3
Manitoba	1 047	48 263	3 667.5	2 945.0
Saskatchewan	750	19 588	2 300.0	1 301.2
Alberta	2 512	88 330	12 606.2	7 107.0
British Columbia	3 761	148 979	15 167.3	10 380.3
NWT & Yukon	47	478	41.2	24.2

* There may be a discrepancy between figures for Canada the total of all provinces due to varying sources of information.

Source: Statistics Canada, *Manufacturing Industries of Canada, National and Provincial Areas*, Catalogue No. 31-203, as cited in *Market Research Handbook*, 1995, Catalogue No. 63-224, p. 97. Reproduced by permission of the Minister of Supply and Services Canada.

centrated on the Atlantic and Pacific coasts, while that for oil-drilling equipment centres on Alberta, British Columbia, and to a lesser extent Saskatchewan. The latter market is now expanding into Newfoundland.

Small Number of Buyers

The industrial market is concentrated not only on a geographical basis, but also by a limited number of buyers. Although there are approximately 34 000 manufacturing firms in Canada, a small proportion of firms — those with 500 or more employees — are typically responsible for approximately half the total value added by manufacturing.

The concentration of industrial market greatly influences the strategy used in serving this market. The industrial marketer can usually make more profitable use of a sales force to provide regular personal contacts with a small, geographically concentrated market than consumer goods companies can provide with ultimate consumers. Wholesalers are less frequently used, and the marketing channel for industrial goods is typically much shorter than that for consumer goods. Advertising plays a much smaller role in the industrial-goods market, as funds may be more effectively spent on the sales force and other means of promotion than with consumer goods.

STANDARD INDUSTRIAL CLASSIFICATIONS

The marketer focussing on the industrial market is aided by a wealth of information collected by the federal government, including data on the number of firms, their

Standard Industrial Classification (SIC) codes
A series of industrial classifications developed by the federal government for use in collecting detailed statistics for each industry.

sales volumes, and the number of employees by category for firms in each industry. The data are broken down using a system known as **Standard Industrial Classification (SIC) codes**. The SIC codes begin with eighteen divisions; under each division is a list of major groups into which all types of businesses are divided. Table 8.2 lists the main divisions.

Each major division within these broad groups is further divided into three subcategories (known as "major group," "group," and "class"). For example, Division A (the full name of which is Agricultural and Related Service Industries) is divided as follows:

DIVISION A — AGRICULTURAL AND RELATED SERVICE INDUSTRIES
Major Group 01 — Agricultural Industries
Group — 011 Livestock Farms
Class —   0111 Dairy Farms
          0112 Cattle Farms
          0113 Hog Farms
          etc.
Group — 012 Other Animal Specialty Farms
          0121 Honey and Other Apiary Product Farms
          0122 Horse and Other Equine Farms
          etc.

Statistics Canada collects statistics for each of the subcategories. The SIC code system can thus aid greatly in analyzing the industrial market.

Beyond the SIC data, trade associations and business publications provide additional information on the industrial market. Many such publications are listed in

◼ Table 8.2 **Industrial Classifications**

Division	Industry	Groups	Number of Groups
A	Agriculture	011–023	10
B	Fishing and trapping	031–033	3
C	Logging and forestry	041–051	2
D	Mines, quarries, and oil wells	061–092	8
E	Manufacturing industries	101–399	110
F	Construction industries	401–449	14
G	Transportation and storage	451–479	12
H	Communications and other utilities	481–499	8
I	Wholesale trade industries	501–599	30
J	Retail trade industries	601–692	29
K	Finance and insurance industries	701–749	18
L	Real estate operator and insurance agent industries	751–761	3
M	Business service industries	771–779	8
N	Government service industries	811–841	17
O	Educational service industries	851–859	6
P	Health and social service industries	861–869	9
Q	Accommodation, food, and beverage service industries	911–922	6
R	Other service industries	961–999	25

Source: Adapted from Statistics Canada, *Standard Industrial Classification*, 1980, Catalogue No. 12-501, pp. 29–47. Used by authority of the Minister of Industry, 1994.

Appendix A (which follows Chapter 5). Such secondary sources often serve as useful starting points for analyzing industrial markets.

INDUSTRIAL MARKET DEMAND

Demand for goods and services is affected by many factors. Beyond the strength or weakness of the general economic environment, four primary characteristics distinguish industrial market demand: derived demand, joint demand, inventory adjustments, and demand variability.

Derived Demand

The demand for an industrial product is typically **derived demand** — that is, *demand derived from (or linked to) demand for a consumer good*. The demand for cash registers (an industrial good) is partly derived from demand at the retail level (consumer products). Lower retail sales may ultimately result in lower demand for cash registers.

The "downsizing" of automobile engines by auto manufacturers in an attempt to develop smaller, fuel-efficient cars adversely affects spark-plug manufacturers like Champion. Since four-cylinder engines use half as many plugs as V-8s, Champion's total sales may decline drastically unless total auto sales increase dramatically, or unless Champion can increase its share of the total market. On the other hand, booming personal computer sales, along with advances in computing power, have boosted shipments of CD-ROM disk drives.

derived demand
In the industrial market, demand for an industrial product derived from (or linked to) demand for a consumer good.

Joint Demand

The demand for some industrial products is *related to the demand for other industrial goods*. There is a **joint demand** for paper and printing ink in the manufacture of newspapers, for example. If the paper supply is reduced, there will be an accompanying reduction in the demand for printing ink.

joint demand
In the industrial market, demand for an industrial product that is related to the demand for other industrial goods.

Inventory Adjustments

Changes in the amounts of materials a manufacturer keeps on hand can have an impact on industrial demand. Suppose a two-month supply of raw materials is considered the optimal inventory in some manufacturing industries. But suppose economic conditions or other factors dictate that this level be increased to a 90-day supply. The raw materials supplier would then be bombarded with a tremendous increase in new orders. Thus, **inventory adjustments** can be a major determinant of industrial demand.

inventory adjustments
In the industrial market, changes in the amounts of materials a manufacturer keeps on hand.

Demand Variability

Derived demand in the industrial market is related to and often creates immense variability in industrial demand. Assume the demand for industrial product A is derived from the demand for consumer product B — an item whose sales volume has been growing at an annual rate of 10 percent. Now suppose that the demand for product B slowed to a 5 percent annual increase. Management might decide to delay further purchases of product A, using existing inventory until the market conditions were clarified. Therefore, product A's **demand variability** becomes significantly affected by even modest shifts in the demand for product B. *The disproportionate impact that changes in consumer demand have on industrial market demand* is called the **accelerator principle**.

An example of shifting demand is in the market for coal. Several countries, including Canada, the United States, South Africa, and Australia, have the potential to produce and sell great quantities of coal, but the market is extremely volatile. Demand of late has been declining, which has led to significant price falls. One of the reasons for the decline in demand has been technological change. Demand for steel has levelled off, and electric-arc furnaces are being used to make steel from scrap. Also, pulverized coal injection, which allows steel makers to replace half their coking coal with cheaper steam coal is eroding the value of sales in the market that remains. Another effect on demand is the availability of substitutes such as gas and oil. As gas supplies have increased, its clean-burning properties have made it the fuel of choice in some applications.

Is there any hope for coal? Over the next few years, new materials and technologies for generating electricity from coal are expected to become available. This will increase the percentage of energy in coal that can be converted into electricity. In addition, rapidly developing nations such as China are expected to buy more coal. Demand will fluctuate, but the prospects are not all bad.

BASIC CATEGORIES OF INDUSTRIAL PRODUCTS

There are two general categories of industrial products: capital items and expense items. **Capital items** are *long-lived business assets that must be depreciated over time.* **Depreciation** is *the accounting concept of charging a portion of the cost of a capital item as a deduction against the company's annual revenue for purposes of determining its net income.* Examples of capital items include major installations like new plants and office buildings as well as equipment.

Expense items, by contrast, are *products and services that are used within a short period of time.* For the most part, they are charged against income in the year of purchase. Examples of expense items include the supplies that are used in operating the business, ranging from raw materials and fabricated parts to paper clips and machine lubricants.

Chapter 9 presents a comprehensive classification of industrial products. This initial breakdown into capital and expense items is useful because buying behaviour varies significantly depending on how a purchase is treated from an accounting viewpoint. Expense items may be bought routinely and with minimal delay, while capital items involve major fund commitments and are thus subject to considerable review by the purchaser's personnel. Differences in industrial purchasing behaviour are discussed in the sections that follow.

THE NATURE OF THE INDUSTRIAL PURCHASE: SYSTEMATIC AND COMPLEX

Industrial purchasing behaviour tends to be more complex than the consumer decision process described in Chapter 7. There are several reasons for this increased complexity:

demand variability
In the industrial market, the impact of derived demand on the demand for interrelated products used in producing consumer goods.

accelerator principle
The disproportionate impact that changes in consumer demand have on industrial market demand.

capital items
Long-lived business assets that must be depreciated over time.

depreciation
The accounting concept of charging a portion of the cost of a capital item against the company's annual revenue for purposes of determining its net income.

expense items
Products and services that are used within a short period of time.

1. Many people may exert influence in industrial purchases, and considerable time may be spent obtaining the input and approval of various organizational members.
2. Organizational purchasing may be handled by committees with greater time requirements for majority or unanimous approval.
3. Many organizations attempt to use several sources of supply as a type of insurance against shortages.

Most industrial firms have attempted to systematize their purchases by employing a professional buyer — the industrial *purchasing manager* — who is responsible for handling most of the organization's purchases and for securing needed products at the best possible price. Unlike the ultimate consumer (who makes periodic purchase decisions), a firm's purchasing department devotes all of its time and effort to determining needs, locating and evaluating alternative sources of supply, and making purchase decisions.

The Complexity of Industrial Purchases

Where major purchases are involved, negotiations may take several weeks or months, and the buying decisions may rest with a number of people in the organization. The choice of a supplier for industrial drill presses, for example, may be made jointly by the purchasing manager and the company's production, engineering, and maintenance departments. Each of these principals has a different point of view, and they must all be reconciled in making a purchase decision. As a result, representatives of the selling firm must be well versed in all aspects of the product or service and be capable of interacting with the managers of the various departments involved. In the industrial instruments industry, for instance, it takes an average of 5.3 face-to-face presentations to make a sale. The average cost of closing the sale — including salesperson compensation and travel and entertainment expenses — is $1197.80. Table 8.3 shows the average number of sales calls required to complete a sale in several industries and the average cost of each sale.

Many industrial goods are purchased over long periods of time on a contractual basis. A manufacturing operation requires a continual supply of materials, and a one- or two-year contract with a supplier ensures a steady supply of raw materials as they are needed. Other industrial goods, such as conveyors, typewriters, and forklifts, generally last several years before they will need to be replaced.

Purchase decisions are frequently made on the basis of service, certainty of supply, and efficiency of the products. These factors may be even more important than the prices quoted for the products. Automobile manufacturers purchase steel, glass windows, spark plugs, and batteries as ingredients for their output. Since demand for these parts is derived entirely from the demand for consumer goods, price changes do not substantially affect their sale. Price increases for paint will have little effect on auto sales at General Motors, since paint represents a minute portion of the total costs of the automobile.

Purchase of a Capital Item

A utility company that was considering buying a reinforced Fiberglas utility pole faced a complicated decision process. The sales representative dealt with the members of several departments of the utility company and went through months of

■ Table 8.3 Sales Call Statistics and Operating Expenses

Industry Group	Cost per Call	Number of Calls Needed to Close a Sale	Sales Force Cost as a Percentage of Total Sales
Business services	$ 46.00	4.6	19.3
Chemicals	165.80	2.8	3.0
Communications	40.60	4.0	21.6
Construction	111.20	2.8	3.2
Electronics	133.30	3.9	12.0
Fabricated metals	80.80	3.3	6.4
Food products	131.60	4.8	9.6
Instruments	226.00	5.3	10.3
Insurance	53.00	3.4	15.6
Machinery	68.50	3.0	13.0
Miscellaneous manufacturing	85.90	2.8	13.2
Office equipment	25.00	3.7	15.0
Printing/Publishing	70.10	4.5	8.3
Retail	25.00	3.3	23.5
Rubber/Plastics	248.20	4.7	2.8
Utilities	89.90	4.8	17.3
Wholesale (consumer)	84.10	3.0	7.0
Wholesale (industrial)	50.00	3.3	12.6
Average	**96.39**	**3.8**	**11.9**

Note: Industry groups reflect categories selected and reported by Dartnell Corporation. The overall average has been calculated based on data from the 18 industries listed.

Source: Dartnell Corporation, *25th Survey of Sales Force Compensation*, © 1989, Dartnell Corporation.

negotiations before a purchase was made. The new pole had several advantages over the traditional steel, wood, or aluminum post: it was lightweight, had nonelectrical-conducting and noncorrosive properties, never needed painting, and met all strength requirements. Its major disadvantage, other than its unfamiliarity to the purchaser, was its high initial purchase price compared with the alternatives. The decision process began when the manager of the utility consulted the engineering head, who in turn brought in the purchasing manager. Purchasing then prepared a list of alternative suppliers and materials, which was approved by engineering. The purchasing manager then discussed the organization's needs in detail with the sales representatives of three suppliers. The salespeople met with the managers of the stores department, the marketing department, and the engineering department. After a series of meetings with the salespeople and numerous discussions among the utility's department heads, the utility company decided to submit the new Fiberglas pole to a test conducted by the engineering department. The results of the test were reported to the various department heads, and bids were then requested from suppliers A, B, and C. These bids were reviewed by the department heads, who ultimately decided to select the Fiberglas pole offered by supplier B. This complex decision process is diagrammed in Figure 8.1.[2]

Figure 8.1 The Decision to Purchase a New Type of Utility Pole

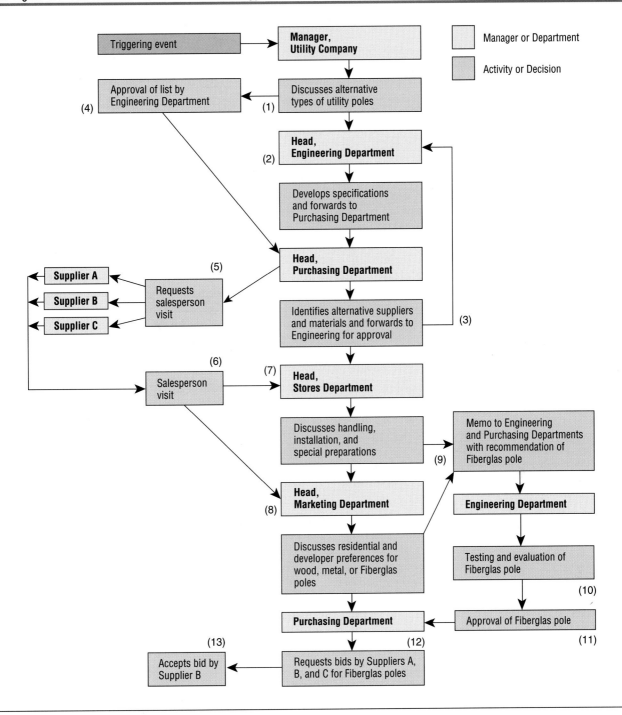

Source: Adapted from Arch G. Woodside, "Marketing Anatomy of Buying Process Can Help Improve Industrial Strategy," *Marketing News* (May 1, 1981), Section 2, p. 11. Used by permission of the American Marketing Association.

CLASSIFYING INDUSTRIAL PURCHASING SITUATIONS

Industrial buying behaviour is affected by the degree of effort and involvement by different levels within the organization. There are three generally recognized industrial purchasing situations: straight rebuy, modified rebuy, and new task buying.[3]

Straight Rebuy

straight rebuy
A recurring purchase decision involving an item that has performed satisfactorily and is therefore purchased again by a customer.

A **straight rebuy** is *a recurring purchase decision involving an item that has performed satisfactorily and is therefore purchased again by a customer.* This industrial buying situation occurs when a purchaser is pleased with the good or service and the terms of sale are acceptable. Seeing little reason to assess other options, the purchaser follows some routine buying format.

Low-cost items like paper clips and pencils are typically rebought. If the purchaser is pleased with the products, their prices, and their terms, future purchases will probably be treated as a straight rebuy from the current vendor. Even expensive items specially designed for a customer's needs can be treated as a straight rebuy in some cases. For example, a manufacturer might be virtually committed to buying additional lathes from a certain company because it purchased them before and wants to keep a standardized production process.

Marketers facing straight rebuy situations should concentrate on maintaining good relations with the buyer through prompt attention and adequate service. Competitors are faced with the difficult task of presenting a unique sales proposal that will break this chain of repurchases.

Modified Rebuy

modified rebuy
A situation in which purchasers are willing to re-evaluate their available options.

A **modified rebuy** is *a situation in which purchasers are willing to re-evaluate their available options.* The decision-makers feel that it is to their advantage to look at alternative product offerings using established purchasing guidelines. A modified rebuy situation may occur if a marketer allows a straight rebuy situation to deteriorate because of poor service or delivery or if quality, cost, and service differences are perceived by the customer.

Industrial marketers want to move purchasers into a straight rebuy position by responding to all their product and service needs. Competitors, on the other hand, try to move buyers into a modified rebuy situation by correctly assessing the factors that would make buyers reconsider their decisions.

New Task Buying

new task buying
First-time or unique purchase situations that require considerable effort on the part of the decision-makers.

New task buying refers to *first-time or unique purchase situations that require considerable effort on the part of the decision-makers.* Once a need has been identified, evaluative criteria can be established and an extensive search for a product launched. Alternative product and service offerings and vendors are considered. A new task buying situation may arise when a firm enters a new field and has to seek out suppliers of component parts that have not previously been purchased.

Industrial marketers should work closely with the purchaser in the case of new task buying situations. This will allow them to study the factors the purchaser considers important and to design their marketing proposal to match the needs of the purchaser.

THE BUYING CENTRE CONCEPT

The buying centre concept is an important key to understanding industrial purchase behaviour.[4] The **buying centre** simply refers to *everyone who participates in some fashion in an industrial buying action.* For example, a buying centre may include the architect who designs a new research laboratory, the scientist who will use the facility, the purchasing manager who screens contractor proposals, the chief executive officer who makes the final decision, and the vice-president for research who signs the formal contracts for the project.

Buying centres are not part of a firm's formal organizational structure. They are informal groups whose composition will vary from one purchase situation to another and from one firm to the next. Buying centres typically include anywhere from four to twenty participants, and tend to evolve as the purchasing process moves through its various stages.

Buying centre participants play the roles of users, gatekeepers, influencers, deciders, and buyers in the purchasing decision process. Each of these roles is described in Table 8.4.

A critical task for the industrial marketer is to determine the specific role and the relative buying influence of each buying centre participant. Sales presentations and information can then be tailored to the role that the individual plays at each step in the purchase process. Industrial marketers have also found that while their initial, and in many cases most extensive, contacts are with the purchasing department, the buying centre participants having the greatest influence are often elsewhere in the company.[5]

buying centre
Everyone who participates in some fashion in an industrial buying action.

THE PROCESS OF BUYING INDUSTRIAL GOODS AND SERVICES

The exact procedures that are used in buying industrial goods and services vary according to the buying situation confronted — straight rebuy, modified rebuy, or new task buying.[6] Most industrial purchases follow the same general process. Research by Agarwal, Burger, and Venkatesh suggested the model presented in Figure 8.2. While this model was formulated for industrial machinery purchases, it has general application to the industrial buying process.

Dissecting the Model

The specific steps shown in Figure 8.2 are outlined below.

Need recognition A triggering event such as an equipment failure stimulates recognition of a perceived need for an industrial purchase.

Information search Buying centre members begin to collect information on potential suppliers from sales personnel, advertisements, word of mouth, pamphlets, and other sources. The net result is to delineate the technical nature of the purchase.

■ Table 8.4 **Definitions of Buying Centre Roles**

Role	Description
Users	As the role name implies, these are the personnel who will be using the product in question. Users may have anywhere from an inconsequential to an extremely important influence on the purchase decision. In some cases, the users initiate the purchase action by requesting the product. They may even develop the product specifications.
Gatekeepers	Gatekeepers control information to be reviewed by other members of the buying centre, either by the ways they disseminate printed information or advertisements or by controlling which salesperson will speak to which individuals in the buying centre. The purchasing manager might perform this screening role by opening the gate to the buying centre for some sales personnel and closing it to others.
Influencers	These individuals affect the purchasing decision by supplying information for the evaluation of alternatives or by setting buying specifications. Typically, technical personnel such as engineers, quality control personnel, and research and development personnel are significant influences to the purchase decision. Sometimes individuals outside the buying organization can assume this role (e.g., an engineering consultant or an architect who writes very tight building specifications).
Deciders	Deciders are the individuals who actually make the buying decision, whether or not they have the formal authority to do so. The identity of the decider is the most difficult role to determine: buyers may have formal authority to buy, but the president of the firm may actually make the decision. A decider could be a design engineer who develops a set of specifications that only one vendor can meet.
Buyers	The buyer has *formal* authority for selecting a supplier and implementing all procedures connected with securing the product. The power of the buyer is often usurped by more powerful members of the organization. Often the buyer's role is assumed by the purchasing manager, who executes the clerical functions associated with a purchase order.

Source: Adapted from Frederick E. Webster, Jr., and Yoram Wind, *Organizational Buying Behavior* (Englewood Cliffs, NJ: Prentice Hall, 1972), pp. 77–80. Used by permission of Prentice Hall. This adaptation is reprinted from Michael D. Hutt and Thomas W. Speh, *Industrial Marketing Management* (Hinsdale, IL: Dryden, 1981), p. 83. Copyright © 1981 by The Dryden Press. Reproduced by permission of the publisher.

Delineation of suppliers Given the specifications established in the previous step, potential suppliers are then determined. Budget considerations may also be a factor in this step.

Sales demonstration/proposal Vendor sales representatives are then invited to provide demonstrations and sales proposals. These proposals typically include technical and economic options as well as prices.

Advertisements Advertisements have the effect of informing and persuading. Often, industrial advertising will invite a reader response requesting further information to be supplied.

Technical articles The buying group examines technical articles for an in-depth analysis of the product, its features, and its performance.

■ Figure 8.2 **A Model of the Industrial Buying Process**

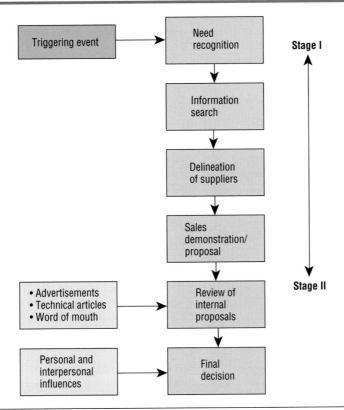

Source: Adapted from Manoj K. Agarwal, Philip C. Burger, and Alladi Venkatesh, "Industrial Consumer Behavior: Toward an Improved Model," in *Developments in Marketing Science*, Venkatakrishna V. Bellur, et al., eds. (Miami Beach: Academy of Marketing Science, 1981), p. 72.

Word of mouth Buying centre members may then contact current users of the product for their evaluation of its performance. Reliability, costs, and operational abilities are explored. Some vendors are eliminated because of negative information.

Personal and interpersonal influences Despite the fact that the industrial buying process is generally more deliberate and involves more people in the decision, personal and interpersonal influences as discussed in the previous chapter also play a significant role in the final decision. Some salespeople are *liked* more than others. In other cases, a product will be purchased because it is popular, trendy, or adds a degree of prestige to the buyer or buying organization. The purchase decision may favour a known brand, despite the better promise of an unknown product, as a risk-reducing measure.

Review of internal proposals In some industrial purchase decisions, more than one group within the organization may have an interest in the purchase. For example, accounting, production scheduling, and research and forecasting departments would be interested in the purchase of a new computer system. After all of the information on various systems has been generated, such interest groups should each be asked to recommend a system. These proposals would be taken into consideration in the process of coming to a final decision.

Final decision Eventually a purchase decision is made. In many cases, this extensive process leads to a consensus decision, but some buying centre members have more influence than others in this final decision stage.

Reciprocity

reciprocity
The extension of purchasing preference to suppliers who are also customers.

A controversial practice in a number of industrial purchasing situations is **reciprocity**, *the extension of purchasing preference to suppliers who are also customers*. For example, an office equipment manufacturer may favour a particular supplier of component parts if the supplier has recently made a major purchase of the manufacturer's office equipment. Reciprocal arrangements have traditionally been used in industries with homogeneous products with similar prices, such as the chemical, paint, petroleum, rubber, and steel industries.

Two other forms of reciprocity have been used. *Reverse reciprocity* is the practice of supplying parts and raw materials that are in short supply to firms who can provide other needed supplies in return. In times of shortages, reverse reciprocity occasionally emerges as firms attempt to obtain raw materials and parts to continue operations. A more recent reciprocity spinoff is the *voluntary price roll-back*, in which purchasers request vendors to agree to temporary price cuts or freezes. While no threats are made, it is difficult for a supplier to refuse a request from a major purchaser. This sometimes forces the vendor to ask for concessions from its own workforce and/or suppliers.[7] The various forms of reciprocity are evidence of the close links that exist between the different elements of the industrial marketplace.[8]

GOVERNMENT MARKETS

The various levels of government make up a sizable segment of the market for industrial products. There are many similarities between the government market and other industrial markets, for they seek to purchase many similar goods and services. However, the numerous regulations that affect government purchases create differences in the way items are procured.

Government expenditures represent nearly 52 percent of Canada's gross domestic product. More than 60 000 firms supply close to 20 000 items and services to the various levels of government, whose total spending in 1993–94 amounted to over $340 billion. The federal government accounted for about 49.5 percent of that total. Table 8.5 indicates the major categories of government expenditures.

How Governments Buy

bids
Price quotations from potential suppliers.

specifications
Specific descriptions of needed items for prospective bidders.

Since most government purchases must, by law, be made on the basis of **bids** (*price quotations from potential suppliers*), the government buyer must develop **specifications** — *specific descriptions of needed items for prospective bidders* (this is often done in the industrial market also). For the federal government most of the branded items, such as general-purpose supplies, are purchased by the Department of Supply and Services. Each province generally has a comparable office for such items.

■ Table 8.5 **Gross General Expenditures, All Levels of Government, 1993/94**

Function	$ (millions)
General services	19 603
Protection of persons and property	26 248
Transportation and communications	16 317
Health	47 820
Social services	85 616
Education	44 420
Resource conservation and industrial development	14 573
Environment	8 049
Recreation and culture	7 328
Foreign affairs and international assistance	3 910
Regional planning and development	1 706
Debt charges	64 739
Other expenditures	374
Total gross general expenditure	**340 703**

Source: Statistics Canada, *Consolidated Federal, Provincial, Territorial and Local Government Expenditure,* Fiscal Years 1988/89 to 1993/94 from Public Sector Finance, 1994–1995, Catalogue No. 68-212, p. 166. Reproduced by permission of the Minister of Supply and Services Canada.

Bidding on Government Contracts

All Canadian business and industrial operations are eligible to bid on federal government contracts.[9] The only requirement is that a firm must indicate interest and be prepared to provide evidence that it can supply needed goods or services in accordance with the specified time, cost, quality, performance, and other terms and conditions.

There are three way of obtaining bids:

1. An *invitation to tender* is normally used for all purchases of more than $5000. Two or more bids are requested, and the contract award is based on the lowest responsive bid. To ensure fairness, unclassified tenders are opened publicly.
2. *Requests for quotations* may be used for all purchases of less than $5000. They are not opened publicly.
3. *Requests for proposals* are used for all noncompetitive purchases valued at more than $5000, and for competitive purchases where the selection of the supplier cannot be made solely on the basis of the lowest-priced responsive bid. The evaluation of proposals is based on schedule, price, and relevant technical, scientific, financial, managerial, and socio-economic factors identified in the solicitation. Requests for proposals are not opened publicly.

In addition to the Department of Supply and Services' head office (in Hull, Quebec), there are regional or district suboffices throughout the country that also purchase for the federal government. Although the details are not exactly the same, similar types of procedures are used by provincial and municipal governments.

Source Lists

The Department of Supply and Services keeps extensive records of thousands of commodity groupings purchased. Matched against these are the names of companies that have indicated they want to be considered as suppliers, and that the department considers capable of carrying out a contract. These records are referred to when requirements arise. A firm wishing to be listed should write to the Executive Secretary for Supply Administration in Hull, or to the regional or district office in its area. Separate lists are maintained at head office and in each regional or district office.

Selling to Government Markets

Sometimes it is difficult for government to obtain bidders, even for relatively large contracts. Despite its immense size, the government market is often viewed as too complex and unprofitable by many suppliers. A survey conducted by *Sales and Marketing Management* reported that industrial marketers registered a variety of complaints about government purchasing procedures. These included excessive paperwork, bureaucracy, needless regulations, emphasis on low bid prices, decision-making delays, frequent shifts in procurement personnel, and excessive policy changes.[10]

On the other hand, marketers generally credit the government with being a relatively stable market. Once an item is purchased from a firm by the government, the probability of more sales is good. Other marketers cite such advantages as the instant credibility established by sales to the federal government, timely payment, excise and sales tax exemptions, acceptance of new ideas, and reduced competition.

Only a few industrial firms maintain a separate government sales manager or sales force. But many firms have experienced success with specialized government marketing efforts. It is expected that a growing number of large companies will organize to deal with government purchasers. This is especially true since the North American Free Trade Agreement opened the possibility of selling to U.S. and Mexican governments.

■ KEY TERMS

industrial market	joint demand	modified rebuy
producers	inventory adjustments	new task buying
trade industries	demand variability	buying centre
value added	accelerator principle	reciprocity
Standard Industrial	capital items	bids
Classification (SIC)	depreciation	specifications
codes	expense items	
derived demand	straight rebuy	

■ INTERACTIVE SUMMARY AND DISCUSSION QUESTIONS

1. Categorization of industrial buyers is important for assessing buyer behaviour. The three categories are producers, trade industries, and governments. Why is this categorization useful?

2. The industrial market accounts for approximately 50 percent of purchases of manufactured goods. What significance does this have for jobs for business graduates?

3. The industrial market has three distinctive features: geographic market concentration, a relatively small number of buyers, and systematic buying procedures. Give an example, and discuss some of the implications for a marketing program targeted at that market.

4. Illustrate how a marketing planner can use the Standard Industrial Classification (SIC) system.

5. Industrial market demand is distinguished by four characteristics: derived demand, joint demand, inventory adjustments, and demand variability. Explain and give examples of each.

6. The two general categories of industrial products are capital items and expense items. Distinguish between the two.

7. The nature of the industrial purchase is generally characterized by being systematic and complex. Explain and illustrate with an example.

8. There are three generally recognized industrial purchasing situations: straight rebuy, modified rebuy, and new task buying. Describe each type, and discuss the marketing task in each.

9. A model of the industrial buying process is shown in Figure 8.2. Compare and contrast salesperson influence, advertising influence, and word-of-mouth influence. In which type of buying situations might each be more influential?

10. Prepare a report on a recent purchase by a local organizational buyer. What can be learned from this exercise?

11. Prepare a brief report on the market opportunity that exists in a specific government market. Identify all the information sources that are available for such an assessment.

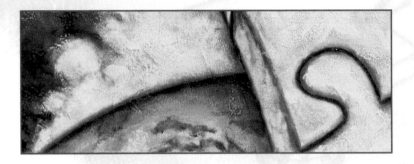

The concept of a product is more complex than it may seem at first. The chapters in this section point out the many important attributes that comprise a product. The development and management of products over time is also discussed. The last chapter is devoted to considering one important category of products known as services. A large and growing portion of economic activity is accounted for by services.

CHAPTER 9

Product Strategy

CHAPTER OBJECTIVES

1. To introduce the concept of a product and of product management.
2. To explain the concept of the product life cycle, as well as its uses and limitations.
3. To relate product strategy to the other variables of the marketing mix.
4. To identify the determinants of the speed of the adoption process.
5. To explain the methods for accelerating the speed of adoption.
6. To identify the classifications for consumer products and to briefly describe each category.
7. To classify the types of industrial products.

When Seiko Corp. marketed the world's first quartz wristwatch back in 1969, not everyone saw the revolution coming.

The first models were made by hand and cost about 500 000 yen (about $1 400 at that time). The watch was 100 times more accurate than a fine mechanical watch, but it also cost more than 12 times as much. Seiko had to shrink the quartz technology itself, because initial sales projections were not high enough to interest partners.

Even its own retailers were sceptical. Some refused to handle any of the fewer than 200 quartz watches produced that year. In 1993, Seiko alone churned out more than 30 million watches.

Today, the company badly needs another breakthrough product. The world watch market is all but saturated and tough new competitors are springing up around Asia. The average consumer is reluctant to shell out for a fancy timepiece when stylish, dependable ones are readily available.

"Total demand for watches is increasing very modestly," says Yutaka Sugiyama, a precision instruments and electronics analyst at UBS Securities, Japan. In 1993, Seiko's watch sales slipped from 160.3 billion yen to 147.5 billion yen, and Seiko projected another 21 percent drop in 1994. The soaring yen did most of the damage. At the beginning of the 1994 fiscal year, there were 114 yen to the US dollar, and at the end there were about 102.

The company is fighting back by jazzing up its product lineup, a strategy that Sugiyama at UBS Securities sees as essential for watchmakers in the 1990s.

A "kinetic" quartz wristwatch, revamped and put back on the market is selling "very well." The energy generated by the movement of the wearer's arm creates the electric power to run the watch. Titanium casings, designed for allergy-sensitive wrists, also look promising.

And Seiko officials are excited about a pager watch the company is testing on 10 000 subscribers in Seattle and Portland, Oregon. A network transmitting digital signals on unused FM frequencies can send messages, traffic reports, and other data to wearers.

Seiko is also looking at international expansion to boost sales. Seiko expects to see the booming economies of Southeast Asia and China provide the biggest boost to sales in the years to come.[1]

You can never rest on your laurels. After a difficult product launch, Seiko electronic watches swept the market. Nevertheless, some years later the watch division found itself in a loss position. Management of existing products is essential, as is the development of a continuous stream of new ones.

Marketing managers not only face many decisions about designing and positioning new products, but also must manage existing ones. Over the life of each product, they have to determine whether prices should be lowered or raised, whether money should be spent on redeveloping older products, and how such products should be promoted and distributed. Finding and introducing new products and managing older ones are major aspects of marketing management.

INTRODUCTION

This is the first of three chapters dealing with the "product" component of the marketing mix. Here the basic concepts and definitions of this marketing element are laid out.

Marketing planning efforts begin with the choice of products to offer the target market. Pricing, marketing channels, and marketing communication (the other variables of the marketing mix) are all based on the nature of the product.

Everyone knows what a product is — or do they? We must first make sure we understand what a product really is.

Product: A Definition

A narrow definition of the word *product* might focus on the physical or functional characteristics of a good that is offered to consumers. For example, a Sony videocassette recorder is a rectangular container of metal and plastic wires connecting it to a television set, accompanied by a series of special tapes for recording and viewing. This is the core product. But purchasers have a much broader view of the VCR. They have bought the convenience of viewing television programs at their leisure; the warranty and service that Sony, the manufacturer, provides; the prestige of owning this fine product; and the ability to rent or purchase recently released movies for home viewing. Thus, the brand image, warranty, and service are also all parts of the product as seen by the consumer.

Marketing decision-makers must have this broader concept in mind and realize that people purchase more than just the physical features of products. *They are buying want satisfaction.* Most drivers know very little about the gasoline they regularly purchase. If they bother to analyze it, they discover that it is almost colourless and emits a peculiar odour. However, most drivers do not think of gasoline as a product at all — to them, gasoline is a tax. It is a payment that they must make periodically for the privilege of driving their cars on the streets and highways, and the friendly service-station attendant is a tax collector. Petroleum retailers should be aware of this image in the minds of many customers before spending huge sums to promote dozens of secret ingredients designed to please the motorist.

The shopper's conception of a product may be altered by such features as packaging, labelling, or the retail outlets in which the product may be purchased. An image of high quality has been created for Maytag appliances, whose television commercials describe the Maytag repairer as "the loneliest person in town." More than 30 years ago, the firm's president set a standard of "10 years of trouble-free operation" for automatic clothes washers. The company's success in achieving a reputation for high product quality is evident in Maytag's continued sales growth record, even though the washer's retail price is higher than the nearest competitor's.

Some products have no physical ingredients. A haircut and blow-dry at the local hairstylist produces only well-groomed hair. A tax counsellor produces only advice. Thus, a broader view of product must also include services.

product
A total bundle of physical, service, and symbolic characteristics designed to produce consumer want satisfaction.

A **product**, then, may be defined as *a total bundle of physical, service, and symbolic characteristics designed to produce consumer want satisfaction.* Figure 9.1 reflects this broader definition — known as the total product concept — by identifying the various components of the total product.

warranty
A guarantee to the buyer that the supplier will replace a defective product (or part of a product) or refund its purchase price during a specified period of time.

An important feature of many products is a product **warranty**. The warranty is *a guarantee to the buyer that the supplier will replace a defective product (or part of a product) or refund its purchase price during a specified period of time.* Such warranties serve to increase consumer purchase confidence and can prove to be an important means of stimulating demand. Midas Muffler uses a warranty as an important feature of the firm's marketing strategy. The manufacturer offers a lifetime guarantee, promising to repair or replace any damaged or defective muffler regardless of age. Many retailers have a broad, unwritten, but frequently honoured warranty of satisfaction or your money back.

THE PRODUCT LIFE CYCLE

Product *types*, like individuals, pass through a series of stages. The life cycle for humans is quite specific: infancy to childhood to adulthood to retirement to death. Product types also progress through stages, although a product's progress through

■ Figure 9.1 **The Total Product Concept**

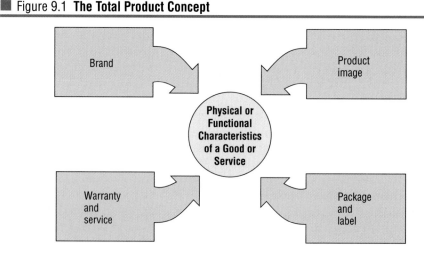

the stages is sometimes not very clear-cut. This progression of *introduction, growth, maturity, and decline* is known as the **product life cycle**. An idealized model of the cycle is depicted in Figure 9.2, with examples of products currently at each stage of development.[2] The length of time in each stage varies widely, as represented by the broken line on the bottom axis. The model is representative of many, but not all, situations. For example, there is little evidence that refrigerators enter a decline or death stage.

At each stage of the life cycle, the emphasis and focus of the marketing program should change to fit the requirements at that phase. For example, at the introductory stage, communication efforts should emphasize information. At the growth stage, with competitors entering the market, communication should emphasize comparative features and advantages. Taking into consideration this need to change the marketing mix emphasis, particularly in the introduction and growth stages, can be useful in guiding marketing planning.

product life cycle
A product's progress through introduction, growth, maturity, and decline stages.

Stages of the Cycle

INTRODUCTORY STAGE

The firm's objective in the early stages of the product life cycle is to stimulate demand for the new market entry. Since the product is not known to the public, promotional campaigns stress information about its features. Promotion may also be directed toward channels of distribution to induce them to carry the product. In this initial phase, the public is being acquainted with the merits of the new product and acceptance is being gained.

As Figure 9.2 indicates, losses are common during the introductory stage due to heavy promotion as well as extensive research and development expenditures. But the groundwork is being laid for future profits. Firms expect to recover their costs and to begin earning profits when the new product moves into the second phase of the cycle — the growth stage.

■ Figure 9.2 **Stages in the Product Life Cycle**

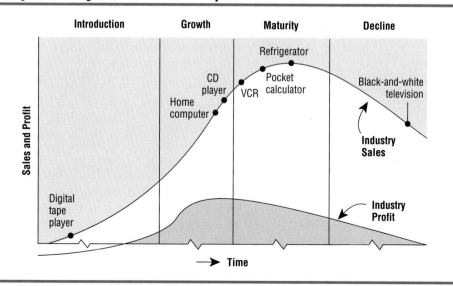

The costs of development and promotion at this stage are very high. New small business innovators often badly underestimate the costs of even a simple product launch. Big electronics companies such as Philips have spent more than $200 million in this stage of the product life cycle.

GROWTH STAGE

Sales volume rises rapidly during the growth stage as new adopters make initial purchases and as repurchases are made by the early users of the product. Word-of-mouth and mass advertising induce hesitant buyers to make trial purchases. Home computers are now in this phase of the cycle.

As the firm begins to realize substantial profits from its investment during the growth stage, it attracts competitors. Success breeds imitation, and firms rush into the market with competitive products in search of profit during the growth stage. As soon as the dramatic market acceptance of mountain bikes was realized, for instance, many manufacturers jumped into the market with their versions of the product.

MATURITY STAGE

Industry sales continue to grow during the early portion of the maturity stage, but eventually reach a plateau as the backlog of potential customers is exhausted. By this time a large number of competitors have entered the market, and profits decline as competition intensifies.

In the maturity stage, differences among competing products have diminished as competitors have discovered the product and promotional characteristics most desired by the market. Heavy promotional outlays emphasize subtle differences among competing products, and brand competition intensifies.

Available products now exceed demand. Companies attempting to increase sales and market share must do so at the expense of competitors. As competition inten-

Used by Canadian women for over 85 years, Pond's cold cream has had a very long life cycle. In the early stages of its cycle, Pond's relied on testimonials from recognized beauties of the day. Recently, Pond's kindled new interest in its original product by introducing a line of cleansers, moisturizers, and anti-aging products. The new advertising gave women information on how to care for their skin using Pond's products. As a result, dollar sales for 1994 increased over 250 percent from 1992, with the original Pond's cold cream still performing consistently well.

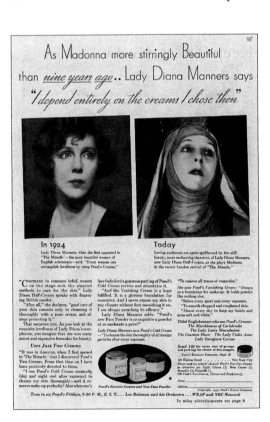

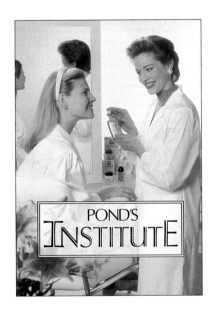

sifies, the tendency grows among competitors to cut prices in a bid to attract new buyers. Even though a price reduction may be the easiest method of inducing additional purchases, it is also one of the simplest moves for competitors to duplicate. Reduced prices will result in decreased revenues for all firms in the industry unless the price cuts produce enough increased purchases to offset the loss in revenue on each product sold.

DECLINE STAGE

In the final stage of the product's life, new innovations or shifting consumer preferences bring about an absolute decline in total industry sales. The safety razor and electric shavers replace the straight razor, a new Nintendo game replaces an earlier version as the latest fad, and the slower personal computer is replaced by a faster, more powerful model. As Figure 9.3 indicates, the decline stage of the old product is often also the growth stage for the new market entry.

Industry profits decline and in some cases actually become negative as sales fall and firms cut prices in a bid for the dwindling market. Manufacturers gradually begin to leave the industry in search of more profitable products.

DEPARTURES FROM THE TRADITIONAL PRODUCT LIFE-CYCLE MODEL

The preceding discussion has examined what is considered the traditional product life cycle, with its four clearly delineated stages. Some marketing theorists divide the life cycle into additional stages, but these four, identified in Figure 9.2, are generally accepted within the marketing discipline.

Yet despite the vast body of material written on the subject, considerable controversy surrounds the format and usefulness of product life-cycle theory. On the one hand, the concept has an enduring appeal because of the intuitive logic of the birth-to-decline biological analogy.[3] As such, it has considerable descriptive value when used as a systematic framework for explaining market dynamics.

However, the simplicity of the concept has led to simplistic uses and expectations for the model, and this has called the concept itself into question. Part of the prob-

■ Figure 9.3 **Overlap of Life Cycle for Products A and B**

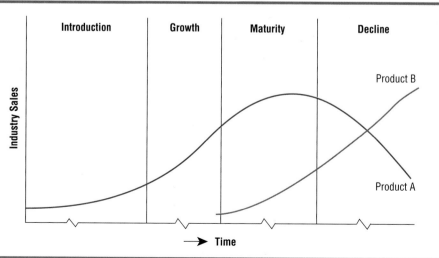

lem lies in failing to distinguish between the life cycle of a *product type* and that of an *individual brand* within that generic product category. Life-cycle theory is most applicable to product types. A truly new brand is obviously also the generic category for a while, but as competing brands are introduced, it becomes one of several brands within that category. The greatest misuse of produce life-cycle theory is to consider it a *predictive* model for anticipating when changes will occur and to presume that one stage will always succeed another. Managers can make grave errors if they naïvely interpret a particular rise or fall in sales as a sign that a product has moved from one stage to another. Such an interpretation could lead to serious errors in strategy, such as concluding that a product is in decline and removing it from the market.

A second criticism involves the use of the life cycle as a *normative* model, which *prescribes* the alternative strategies that should be considered at each stage. As will be shown later, there are strategies that are generally appropriate at various stages of the life cycle of a product *category*. In the case of an individual brand *within* a product category, however, as Enis, LaGrace, and Prell argue, "the product life cycle [of a brand] is a *dependent* variable. . . . That is, the brand's stage in the product life cycle depends primarily upon the marketing strategy implemented for that product at a particular time."[4]

A more realistic view is that life-cycle analysis serves several different roles in the formulation of strategy. In the case of both generic product type and individual brand, the life cycle serves as an *enabling condition* in the sense that the underlying forces that inhibit or facilitate growth create opportunities and threats with strategic implications. The stage of the life cycle also acts as a *moderating variable* through its influence on the value of market-share position and the profitability consequences of strategic decisions. In the case of an individual brand, a stage in the life cycle is partly a *consequence* of managerial decisions. Its position is not necessarily a *fait accompli*, which can only be reacted to, but instead is only one of several scenarios that are conditional on the life cycle of the product category, on competitive actions, and on managerial decisions.

Other Life-Cycle Issues

Three other issues that modify the original life-cycle concept are (1) the length of each product life-cycle stage, (2) the existence of product life-cycle variants, and (3) the current role of product and service fashions and fads.

LENGTH OF CYCLE STAGES

Professor John O. King has argued that product life-cycle models should reflect the reality that goods and services move through the cycle at varying speeds. He suggests that the model should be drawn to show a broken horizontal axis to reflect the fact that the stages may be of varying lengths, as we did in Figures 9.2 and 9.3. Research now suggests that product life cycles may be getting shorter, especially in the introductory and growth stages.[5] While definitive conclusions are not yet available, most marketers do accept the fact that product life cycles and their stages show considerable variation in length.

ALTERNATIVE PRODUCT LIFE CYCLES

Thus far, an idealized product life-cycle model has been presented. Because of the realities of the marketplace, the actual resulting life cycle can take on several other shapes. Some common variants to the traditional model are shown in Figure 9.4.

As shown in Figure 9.4, some products simply do not make it. These can be labelled the "instant busts" — failures that simply do not go through the four steps of the traditional model. Still other products are introduced but information derived from test-market situations indicates that changes will be necessary if the product launch is to be successful (test markets are described in Chapter 10). The products then have to be modified in some way —such as in design, packaging, or promotional strategy — before they are reintroduced. This type of start-up, start-again launch is labelled the "aborted introduction" in Figure 9.4.

Still other products become market specialty items (discussed later in this chapter) and provide long and stable maturity stages. A common variant is the "pyramid cycle," where the product is adapted through new technology or a revised marketing strategy. The pyramid cycle (also discussed later in the chapter under "Extending the Product Life Cycle") is characterized by a series of regrowth periods.

FASHIONS AND FADS

Fashions and fads are also important to marketers. **Fashions** are *currently popular products that tend to follow recurring life cycles.*[6] Women's apparel fashions provide the best examples. The miniskirt was reintroduced in 1982 after being out of fashion for over a decade. In 1990 it appeared again.

In contrast, **fads** are *fashions with abbreviated life cycles.* Consider the case of popular music for teenagers. Disco gave way to punk and new wave, which was replaced by the "new music," a take-off on rock and roll. Rap music is another example of the many music fads that come and go. Most fads experience short-lived popularity and

fashions
Currently popular products that tend to follow recurring life cycles.

fads
Fashions with abbreviated life cycles.

◼ Figure 9.4 **Alternative Product Life Cycles**

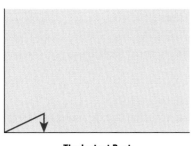

The Instant Bust

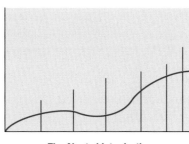

The Aborted Introduction

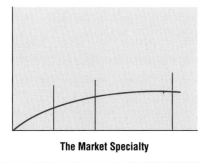

The Market Specialty

Regrowth periods

The Extended Life Cycle

Source: Chester R. Wasson, *Dynamic Competitive Strategy and Product Life Cycle*, 3rd ed. (Austin, TX: Austin Press, 1978), p. 13.

■ Figure 9.5 **Fad Cycles**

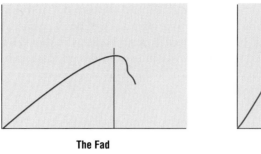
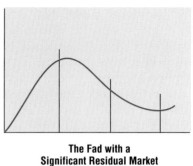

The Fad

The Fad with a Significant Residual Market

Source: Chester R. Wasson, *Dynamic Competitive Strategy and Product Life Cycle*, 3rd ed. (Austin, TX: Austin Press, 1978), p. 13.

then fade quickly. However, some maintain a residual market among certain market segments. Both of these fad cycles are shown in Figure 9.5.

PRODUCT LIFE-CYCLE CONSIDERATIONS IN MARKETING STRATEGY

Marketing strategy related to the product life cycle is most useful when carried out on an individual *brand* basis rather than a generic product category basis.[7] There are too many uncontrollable variables at the generic level.

The product life cycle — with all its variants — is a useful tool in marketing strategy decision making. The knowledge that profits assume a predictable pattern through the stages and that promotional emphasis must shift from product information in the early stages to brand promotion in the later ones allows the marketing decision-maker to take advantage of conditions that often exist in each stage of the product life cycle through appropriate marketing efforts.

A firm's marketing efforts should emphasize stimulating demand at the introductory stage. The emphasis shifts to cultivating selective demand in the growth period. Market segmentation should be used extensively in the maturity period. During the decline, the emphasis again shifts to increasing primary demand. Table 9.1 suggests possibilities for appropriate pricing, distribution, product development, and service and warranty strategies for each life-cycle stage. The reader is again cautioned that the life cycle does not determine the strategy.

Extending the Product Life Cycle

The life cycle of a *brand* can often be affected by managerial strategy. One example is the practice of extending the cycle as long as possible. Marketing managers can accomplish this objective if they take action early in the maturity stage. Product life cycles can sometimes be extended indefinitely by actions designed to accomplish one or more of the following:

1. Increase the frequency of use by present customers.
2. Add new users.

■ Table 9.1 **Organizational Conditions, Marketing Efforts, and Environmental Conditions at Each Stage of the Product Life Cycle**

| Introduction | Growth | Maturity | | Decline |
		Early Maturity	Late Maturity	
Organizational Conditions				
High costs	Smoothing production	Efficient scale of operation	Low profits	
Inefficient production levels	Lowering costs	Product modification work	Standardized production	
Cash demands	Operation efficiencies	Decreasing profits		
	Product improvement work			
Environmental Conditions				
Few or no competitors	Expanding markets	Slowing growth / Strong competition	Faltering demand / Fierce competition	Permanently declining demand
Limited product awareness and knowledge	Expanded distribution	Expanded market	Shrinking number of competitors	Reduction of competitors
Limited demand	Competition strengthens	Heightened competition	Established distribution patterns	Limited product offerings
	Prices soften a bit			Price stabilization
Marketing Efforts				
Stimulate demand	Cultivate selective demand	Emphasize market segmentation	Ultimate in market segmentation	Increase primary demand
Establish high price	Product improvement	Improve service and warranty	Competitive pricing	Profit opportunity pricing
Offer limited product variety	Strengthen distribution	Reduce prices	Retain distribution	Prune and strengthen distribution
Increase distribution	Price flexibility			

Source: Adapted from Burton H. Marcus and Edward M. Tauber, *Marketing Analysis and Decision Making* (Boston: Little, Brown, 1979), pp. 115–16. Copyright © 1979 by Burton H. Marcus and Edward M. Tauber.

3. Find new uses for the product.
4. Change product quality or packaging.

Examples of such actions follow.

INCREASE THE FREQUENCY OF USE

Noxzema was originally intended as an occasional-use skin medicine, but it was repositioned as a routine-use beauty-care item. This substantially increased the rate of use — and amount purchased.

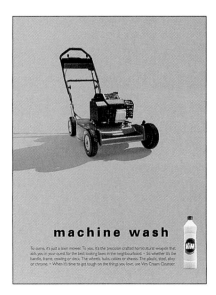

Vim, a cleaning product from Lever Canada, has traditionally been used for pots and pans and other common household cleaning chores. Recently, Lever advertised Vim as not just a cleaning solution for the usual household items, but also for such things as motorcycles and lawnmowers. By advertising in this way, Lever hopes to extend the product's life cycle.

ADD NEW USERS

Cadillac introduced its Cimarron, a more sporty model, to attract non-Cadillac buyers who usually purchased cars like BMWs. In 1994, the company announced its intention to move downscale with what was called the LSE, a sedan made in Europe by GM's Opel division. New variations of Crest and Colgate were introduced as sweeter-tasting gels to appeal to younger consumers, further extending the life cycles of these well-known brands.[8] Finding new users is often difficult, however. Gerber, for example, failed in attempts to sell its products to the 15-to-22 age group as desserts and snacks. Many still regarded Gerber products as baby food.[9]

FIND NEW USES

Q-tips cotton swabs were originally sold as a baby-care item, but Cheseborough-Pond's Inc.'s marketers found a new use for them as make-up applicators. Cow Brand baking soda was used primarily in cooking until its product life cycle was extended by finding new uses for it as a denture cleaner, swimming-pool pH adjuster, cleaning agent, flame extinguisher, first-aid remedy, and refrigerator freshener.[10]

CHANGE THE PRODUCT QUALITY OR PACKAGING

One of the best examples of a product that has been managed well and has avoided the decline stage is Tide. This synthetic detergent, introduced in 1947, continues to sell well in the 1990s. But more than 50 modifications of packaging, cleaning performance, sudsing characteristics, aesthetics, and physical properties have been made during its lifetime.

CONSUMER ADOPTION PROCESS

adoption process
A series of stages consumers go through, from learning of a new product to trying it and deciding to purchase it regularly or to reject it.

Once the product is launched, consumers begin a process of evaluating the new item. This evaluation is known as the **adoption process** — the process whereby potential consumers go through *a series of stages from learning of the new product to trying it and deciding to purchase it regularly or to reject it.* The process has some similarities to the consumer decision process discussed in Chapter 7. The stages in the consumer adoption process can be classified as follows:

1. *Awareness.* Individuals first learn of the new product but lack information about it.
2. *Interest.* They begin to seek out information about it.
3. *Evaluation.* They consider whether the product is beneficial.
4. *Trial.* They make a trial purchase, test it, or mentally visualize its use, in order to determine its usefulness.
5. *Adoption/Rejection.* If the trial purchase is satisfactory, they decide to make regular use of the product.[11] Of course, rejection may take place at any stage of the process.

Marketing managers need to understand the adoption process so that they can move potential consumers to the adoption stage. Once the manager is aware of a large number of consumers at the interest stage, steps can be taken to stimulate sales. For example, when consumer interest in buying a combined shampoo/conditioner began to grow, Procter & Gamble introduced Pert Plus with samples sent to homes in addition to its regular advertising campaign. Sampling, if it is successful, is a technique that reduces the risk of evaluation and trial, moving the consumer quickly to the adoption stage.

Adopter Categories

Some people will purchase a new product almost as soon as it is placed on the market. Others wait for additional information and rely on the experiences of the first purchasers before making trial purchases. **Consumer innovators** are *the first purchasers at the beginning of a product's life cycle.* They are found to be the first in the community to buy CD players. Some doctors are the first to prescribe new drugs,[12] and some farmers will use new hybrid seeds much earlier than their neighbours do.[13] Some people are quick to adopt new fashions,[14] while some drivers are early users of automobile diagnostic centres.[15]

consumer innovators
The first purchasers — those who buy a product at the beginning of its life cycle.

A number of investigations analyzing the adoption of new products have resulted in the identification of five categories of purchasers based on relative time of adoption: innovators, early adopters, early majority, late majority, and laggards. These categories are shown in Figure 9.6, as well as the proportion of the population in each category.

The **diffusion process** refers to *the filtering and acceptance of new products and services by the members of a community or social system.* Figure 9.6 shows this process as following a normal distribution. A few people adopt at first, and then the number of adopters increases rapidly as the value of the innovation becomes apparent. The rate finally diminishes as fewer potential consumers remain in the nonadopter category.

diffusion process
The filtering and acceptance of new products and services by the members of a community or social system.

Since the categories are based on the normal distribution, standard deviations are used to partition each category. Innovators are defined as the first 2.5 percent of those individuals who adopt the new product; laggards are the final 16 percent to adopt. Excluded from the figure are the nonadopters — people who never adopt the new product.

Identifying the First Adopters

Locating first buyers of new products represents a challenge for the marketing manager. If the right people can be reached early in the product's development or introduction, they may serve as a test market, evaluating the product and possibly

■ Figure 9.6 **Categories of Adopters on the Basis of Relative Time of Adoption**

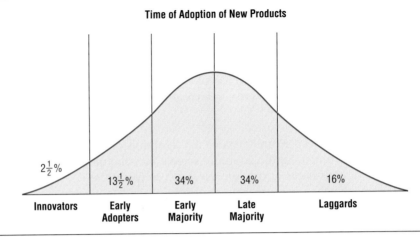

Time of Adoption of New Products

$2\frac{1}{2}$%	$13\frac{1}{2}$%	34%	34%	16%
Innovators	Early Adopters	Early Majority	Late Majority	Laggards

Source: Everett M. Rogers, *Diffusion of Innovations,* 3rd ed. (New York: The Free Press, 1983). Copyright © 1962, 1971, 1983 by The Free Press. Reprinted with the permission of The Free Press, a Division of Simon & Schuster.

making suggestions for modifications. Since early purchasers are frequently opinion leaders from whom others seek advice, their attitudes toward new products are communicated in their neighbourhoods, clubs, and organizations. Acceptance or rejection of the innovation by these purchasers may serve as a kind of signal for the marketing manager, indicating the probable success or failure of the new product.[16]

Unfortunately, people who are first adopters of one new product may not necessarily be innovators for other products or services. A large number of studies have, however, established some general characteristics possessed by most first adopters.

In general, first adopters tend to be younger, have a high social status, be better educated, and enjoy a higher income. They are more mobile than later adopters, and change both their jobs and their home addresses more often. They are more likely to rely on impersonal information sources than are later adopters, who depend more on promotional information from the company and word-of-mouth communication.[17]

What Determines the Rate of Adoption?

The electronic calculator replaced the slide rule as the engineering student's friend as soon as prices came within range of the student budget. On the other hand, it took thirteen years to convince most corn farmers to use hybrid seed corn — an innovation capable of doubling corn yields — even though some progressive farmers adopted it at once. The adoption rate is influenced by five characteristics of the innovation.[18]

1. *Relative advantage.* The degree to which the innovation appears superior to previous ideas. The greater the relative advantage — whether manifested in lower price, physical improvements, or ease of use — the faster the adoption rate.
2. *Compatibility.* The degree to which the innovation is compatible with existing facilities or consistent with the values and experiences of potential adopters.

The business student who purchases a personal computer will likely buy one that is compatible with those at the school he or she attends or with those of his or her friends.

3. *Complexity.* The more difficult it is to understand or use the new product, the longer it will take to be generally accepted in most cases.

4. *Divisibility.* The degree to which the innovation may be used on a limited basis. First adopters face two types of risk — financial losses and the risk of ridicule by others — if the new product proves unsatisfactory. The option of sampling the innovation on a limited basis allows these risks to be reduced and, in general, should accelerate the rate of adoption.[19]

5. *Communicability.* The degree to which the results of the product may be observable by or communicated to others. If the superiority of the innovation can be displayed in a tangible form, this will increase the adoption rate.

These five characteristics can be used, to some extent, by the marketing manager in accelerating the rate of adoption. First, will consumers perceive the product as complex, or will its use necessitate a significant change in typical behavioural patterns? Product complexity must be overcome with promotional messages of an informational nature. Products should be designed to emphasize their relative advantages and, whenever possible, be divisible for sample purchases. If divisibility is physically impossible, in-home demonstrations or trial placements in the home may be used. Positive attempts must also be made to ensure compatibility of the innovation with the adopters' value systems.

These actions are based on extensive research studies of innovators in agriculture, medicine, and consumer goods. They should pay off in increased sales by accelerating the rate of adoption in each of the adopter categories.

CONSUMER PRODUCTS AND INDUSTRIAL PRODUCTS: A DEFINITION

How a firm markets its products depends largely on the product itself. For example, a perfume manufacturer stresses subtle promotions in prestige media such as *Chatelaine* and *Vogue* magazines, and markets the firm's products through exclusive department stores and specialty shops. Cadbury Schweppes Powell Ltd. markets its candy products through candy wholesalers to thousands of supermarkets, variety stores, discount houses, and vending machines. Its marketing objective is to saturate the market and make buying its candy as convenient as possible for potential buyers. A firm that manufactures and markets fork-lifts may use sales representatives to call on purchasing managers, and ship its product either directly from the factory or from regional warehouses.

Marketing strategy differs for consumer products and industrial products. As defined earlier, consumer products are those destined for use by the ultimate consumer, and industrial products are those used directly or indirectly in producing other goods for resale. These two major categories can be broken down further.

Characteristics of Consumer Products

The consumer assesses satisfaction by calculating benefits expected minus costs incurred. Costs involve *effort* and *risk.*[20] Effort is the amount of money, time, and energy the buyer is willing to expend to acquire a given product. In addition, there are risks that the product will not deliver the benefits sought. There are five types of such possible risk: financial, psychological, physical, functional, and social.

There are four categories of products: convenience, preference, shopping, and specialty. Each category can be defined according to the buyer's evaluation of the effort and risk required to obtain the product. Figure 9.7 illustrates the classification system. Two points shown in the figure should be especially noted. First, increasing risk and effort permits the marketer to broaden the scope of marketing strategy (shown by the widening arrow). That is, a wider variety of marketing-mix combinations can be used to gain a differential advantage for shopping and specialty products than can be used for convenience and preference products. Second, the concept of high and low product involvement is incorporated into this classification. The green area represents low involvement.

convenience products
Products that are lowest in terms of both effort and risk.

Convenience products As shown in Figure 9.7, **convenience products** are defined as *lowest in terms of both effort and risk*. That is, the consumer will not spend much money or time in purchasing these products, nor does he or she perceive significant levels of risk in making a selection. These are the products the consumer wants to pur-

■ Figure 9.7 **A Strategic Classification of Products**

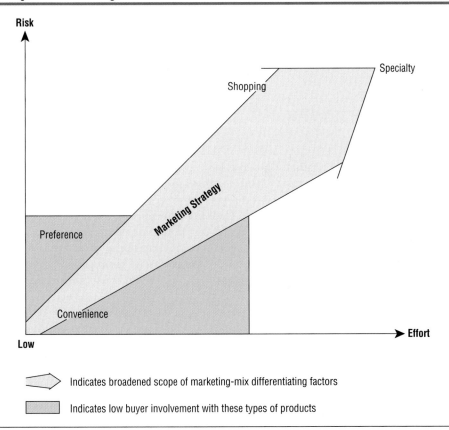

Indicates broadened scope of marketing-mix differentiating factors

Indicates low buyer involvement with these types of products

Source: Patrick Murphy and Ben M. Enis, "Classifying Products Strategically," *Journal of Marketing* (July 1986), p. 25. Reprinted by permission of the American Marketing Association.

chase frequently, immediately, and with a minimum of effort; common illustrations are commodities, "unsought" (emergency) items, and impulse products.

Examples of consumer goods that fall into the convenience category include fresh produce and grocery staples, umbrellas, gum, and batteries. Convenience services include taxis and mass transit.

Preference products
The second category shown in Figure 9.7 is termed **preference products**. Such products are *slightly higher on the effort dimension and much higher on risk than convenience products*. In fact, the distinction between convenience and preference products is primarily one of buyer-perceived risk. Often the consumer perceives a higher level of risk chiefly due to the marketer's efforts, particularly in branding and advertising. Some companies, for example, have successfully convinced consumers that their brand of a low-priced product conveys greater benefits than competing ones — as, for example, with Bayer aspirin.

The most prominent examples of preference products are in the consumer packaged goods industry (for example, toothpaste and soft drinks). Consumers may "prefer" the taste and image of Diet Coca-Cola®, based on advertising appeals or brand preference. However, they are likely to substitute Diet Pepsi or perhaps a low-calorie brand of iced tea if the monetary or time effort involved in acquiring the preferred product is too large.

Since the consumer is unwilling to expend much effort in purchasing convenience or preference goods, the manufacturer must strive to make obtaining them as convenient as possible. Newspapers, soft drinks, and candy are sold in almost every supermarket, variety store, service station, and restaurant. Where retail outlets are physically separated from a large number of consumers, the manufacturers may use vending machines for their customers' convenience. They must protect fragile brand loyalty by ensuring that their product is easily available.

Retailers usually carry several competing brands of preference products and are unlikely to promote any particular brand. The promotional burden therefore falls on the manufacturer. Firms must advertise extensively to develop consumer acceptance for their products.

Shopping products
In contrast with convenience goods, **shopping products** are usually purchased only *after the consumer has compared competing products* on such bases as price, quality, style, and colour in competing stores. The consumer is willing to forgo consumption for a period in order to evaluate product offerings because he or she anticipates gaining monetary savings and/or greater satisfaction of needs by evaluating alternatives.

The purchaser of shopping products lacks complete information prior to the actual purchase and gathers additional information during the shopping trip. A woman intent on adding a new dress to her wardrobe may visit many stores, try on perhaps 30 dresses, and spend days making the final decision. She may follow a regular route from store to store in surveying competing offerings and will ultimately select the dress that most appeals to her. New stores carrying assortments of shopping products must ensure that they are located near other shopping-product stores so that they will be included in shopping expeditions.

Shopping products are typically more expensive than convenience or preference products and are most often purchased by women. In addition to women's apparel, shopping products include such items as jewellery, furniture, appliances, shoes, and used cars.

Some shopping products, such as children's shoes, may be classified as *homogeneous* — that is, the consumer views them as essentially the same — while others,

preference products
Products that are slightly higher on the effort dimension and much higher on risk than convenience products.

shopping products
Products that are usually purchased only after the consumer has compared competing products.

such as furniture and clothing are, *heterogeneous* — essentially different. Price is a more important factor in the purchase of homogeneous shopping products, while quality and styling are more important in the purchase of heterogeneous products.

Brands are often less important for shopping than for convenience products. Although some furniture brands may come to mind, they are typically less important than the physical attributes of the product, its price, styling, and even the retail store that handles the brand. And although apparel companies have spent large amounts of money in promoting their brands, the dress buyer knows that the brand is (usually) inside the dress, and is generally more impressed with how the dress looks on her and with its fit than with the hidden label.

Manufacturers of shopping products use fewer retail stores than is common for convenience or preference products, since purchasers can be expected to expend some effort in finding what they want to buy and retailers will expend more effort in selling an exclusively distributed product. Thinness of the market may also affect the number of outlets. Retailers often purchase directly from the manufacturer or its representative rather than going through the wholesalers. Fashion merchandise buyers for department stores and specialty shops make regular visits to Toronto, Montreal, New York, and Winnipeg on buying trips. Manufacturers often visit regional centres such as Vancouver, Edmonton, or Moncton to meet retailers there. Buyers for furniture retailers often go directly to the factories of furniture manufacturers or visit major furniture trade shows.

Specialty products As the arrowhead in Figure 9.7 shows, marketing managers may attempt to move their shopping products into the specialty category. This means that consumers will no longer "shop" for alternatives but will accept only one brand. The major distinction between shopping products and specialty products revolves around effort rather than risk. The specialty-products purchaser is well aware of what he or she wants and is willing to make a special effort to obtain it. The nearest Leica camera dealer may be 20 km away, but the camera enthusiast will go

Entrepreneur Alex Tilley and his wife, Susan, wear two models of the popular Tilley hat. Customers who have been introduced to Tilley's hard-wearing, good-looking hats and clothing are unwilling to accept substitutes and will either make a special visit to Tilley Endurables stores or request a mail-order catalogue. Tilley Endurables has positioned its clothing as specialty items in the travel and recreation market by ensuring excellent quality and special features, such as secret pockets that discourage pickpockets and wrinkle-resistant fabrics.

to that store to obtain what he or she may consider to be the ultimate in cameras. The Campbell River, BC, collector who longs for a $2500 *objet d'art* of Steuben glassware is willing to journey to Vancouver to find the nearest Steuben dealer.

Specialty products are the *highest in both effort and risk, due to some unique characteristics that cause the buyer to prize that particular brand.* The buyer possesses relatively complete information about the product prior to the shopping trip and is unwilling to accept substitutes.

Specialty products are typically high-priced and are frequently branded. Since consumers are willing to exert a considerable effort in obtaining such goods, fewer retail outlets are needed. Mercury outboard motors and Porsche sports cars may be handled by only one or two retailers for each 100 000 population.

Unsought products Some products are not sought by consumers. They are products that people know about but normally do not think of buying. Products that are usually thought of in this category are funerals and life insurance.

specialty products
Products that are highest in both effort and risk, due to some unique characteristics that cause the buyer to prize that particular brand.

Applying the Consumer Goods Classification System

The four-way classification system described above gives the marketing manager additional information for use in developing a marketing strategy. For example, if a new food product sells well in a test market as a preference good, this provides insights about marketing needs in branding, promotion, pricing, and distribution methods. The impact of the product classifications on their associated consumer factors and to marketing-mix variables is shown in Table 9.2.

But the classification system also poses problems of which the marketing manager must be aware. One pitfall is that it suggests a neat, four-way series of demarcations into which all products can easily be fitted. Some products do fit neatly into one of the classifications, but others fall into grey areas between categories.

How, for instance, should a new car be classified? It is expensive, is branded, and is handled by a few exclusive dealers in each city. But before it is classified as a specialty good, other characteristics must be considered. Most new-car buyers shop extensively among competing models and auto dealers before deciding on the best deal. A more effective method of using the classification system, therefore, is to consider it a continuum representing degrees of effort expended by the consumer. The new-car purchase can then be located between the categories of shopping and specialty products, but nearer the specialty-products end of the continuum.

A second problem with the classification system is that consumers differ in their buying patterns. One person will make an unplanned purchase of a new Toyota Corolla, while others will shop extensively before purchasing a car. One buyer's impulse purchase does not make the Corolla a convenience product. Products are classified by the purchase patterns of the *majority* of buyers.

Classifying Industrial Products

The foregoing classification system can also be used for industrial products. But a more common system categorizes industrial products into five categories: installations, accessory equipment, fabricated parts and materials, raw materials, and industrial supplies. Industrial buyers are professional customers; their job is to make effective purchase decisions. Although details may vary, the purchase decision process involved in buying supplies of flour for General Mills, for example, is much

■ Table 9.2 **Managerial Implications of Classifying Products Strategically**

	Product Category			
Managerial Focus	Convenience	Preference	Shopping	Specialty
Buyer's perception of price	Low effort, low risk	Low effort, medium risk	High effort, medium risk	High effort, high risk
Buyer behaviour	Impulse or habit (auto reorder)	Routine (straight rebuy)	Limited (modified rebuy)	Extensive (new task)
Marketer's objective	Move to preference or shopping category, or dominate via low cost	Brand loyalty	Source or store loyalty	Absolute (source *and* brand) loyalty
Marketer's basic strategy	High volume, cost minimized, or move product	High volume, brand identity, differentiation	High volume or high margin, segmentation	High margin, limited volume, market "niche"
Product strategy	Standard grades and quantities, quality control, innovations copied quickly	Standard grades and quantities, quality control, some R & D	Standard base, many options, much R & D, warranties	Custom design, much R & D, warranties, personalized service
Price strategy	Market	Market	Bundled or negotiated	Negotiated
Monetary, nonmonetary	Minimize time and risk	Minimize time, warrant risk	Accommodate time, warrant risk	Pamper for time and risk
Place strategy	Saturation distribution	Intensive distribution	Selective distribution	Exclusive distribution
Promotion	Point-of-purchase, some sales promotion	Mass advertising, sales promotion, some personal selling	Personal selling, some advertising,	Publicity, personal selling, testimony

Source: Patrick Murphy and Ben M. Enis, "Classifying Products Strategically," *Journal of Marketing* (July 1986), p. 35. Reprinted by permission of the American Marketing Association.

the same as that used in buying the same commodity for Robin Hood. Thus this classification system for industrial goods is based on product uses rather than on consumer buying patterns.

installations
Major capital assets that are used to produce products and services.

Installations Installations are *major capital assets (like factories and heavy machinery) that are used to produce products and services.* Installations are the specialty products of the industrial market. New aircraft for Canadian Airlines International, locomotives for Canadian National, or a new pulp mill for MacMillan Bloedel are examples of installations.

Since installations are relatively long-lived and involve large sums of money, their purchase represents a major decision for an organization. Sales negotiations often extend over a period of several months and involve the participation of numerous decision-makers. In many cases, the selling company must provide technical expertise. When custom-made equipment is involved, representatives of the selling firm work closely with the buyer's engineers and production personnel to design the most feasible product.

Price is almost never the deciding factor in the purchase of installations. The purchasing firm is interested in the product's efficiency and performance over its useful life. The firm also wants a minimum of breakdowns. "Down time" is expensive because employees are nonproductive (but must still be paid) while the machinery is being repaired.

Since most of the factories of firms that purchase installations are geographically concentrated, the selling firm places its promotional emphasis on well-trained salespeople, who often have a technical background. Most installations are marketed directly on a manufacturer-to-user basis. Even though a sale may be a one-time transaction, contracts often call for regular product servicing. In the case of extremely expensive installations, such as computers and electronic equipment, some firms lease the installations rather than sell them outright and assign personnel directly to the lessee to operate or to maintain the equipment.

Accessory equipment Fewer decision-makers are usually involved in purchasing **accessory equipment** — *second-level capital items that are used in the production of products and services but are usually less expensive and shorter-lived than installations.* Although quality and service remain important criteria in purchasing accessory equipment, the firm is likely to be much more price-conscious. Accessory equipment includes such products as desktop calculators, hand tools, portable drills, small lathes, and typewriters. Although these goods are considered capital items and are depreciated over several years, their useful life is generally much shorter than that of an installation.

Because of the need for continuous representation and the more widespread geographic dispersion of accessory equipment purchasers, a *wholesaler*, often called an **industrial distributor**, may be used to contact potential customers in each geographic area. Technical assistance is usually not necessary, and the manufacturer of accessory equipment can often use such wholesalers quite effectively in marketing the firm's products. Advertising is more important for accessory manufacturers than it is for installation procedures.

Component parts and materials While installations and accessory equipment are used in producing the final product, **component parts and materials** are the *finished industrial goods that actually become part of the final product.* Champion spark plugs make a new Chevrolet complete; nuts and bolts are part of a Peugeot bicycle; tires are included with a Dodge pickup truck. Some materials, such as flour, undergo further processing before producing a finished product.

Purchasers of component parts and materials need a regular, continuous supply of uniform-quality goods. These goods are generally purchased on contract for a period of one year or more. Direct sale is common, and satisfied customers often become permanent buyers. Wholesalers are sometimes used for fill-in purchases and in handling sales to smaller purchasers.

Raw materials *Farm products (such as cattle, wool, eggs, milk, pigs, and canola) and natural products (such as coal, copper, iron ore, and lumber)* constitute **raw materials**. They are similar to component parts and materials in that they become part of the final products.

Since most raw materials are graded, the purchaser is assured of standardized products with uniform quality. As with component parts and materials, direct sale of raw materials is common, and sales are typically made on a contractual basis.

---

accessory equipment
Second-level capital items that are used in the production of products and services but are usually less expensive and shorter-lived than installations.

industrial distributor
A wholesaler who operates in the industrial goods market and typically handles small accessory equipment and operating supplies.

component parts and materials
Finished industrial goods that actually become part of the final product.

raw materials
Farm products (such as cattle, wool, eggs, milk, pigs, and canola) and natural products (such as coal, copper, iron ore, and lumber).

Wholesalers are increasingly involved in the purchase of raw materials from foreign suppliers.

Price is seldom a controllable factor in the purchase of raw materials, since it is often quoted at a central market and is virtually identical among competing sellers. Purchasers buy raw materials from the firms they consider most able to deliver in the quantity and the quality required.

Supplies If installations represent the specialty products of the industrial market, then operating supplies are the convenience products. **Supplies** are *regular expense items necessary in the daily operation of a firm, but not part of its final product.*

Supplies are sometimes called **MRO items**, because they can be divided into three categories: (1) *maintenance items*, such as brooms, floor-cleaning compounds, and light bulbs; (2) *repair items*, such as nuts and bolts used in repairing equipment; and (3) *operating supplies*, such as heating fuel, lubricating oil, and office stationery.

The regular purchase of operating supplies is a routine aspect of the purchasing manager's job. Wholesalers are very often used in the sale of supplies due to the items' low unit prices, small sales, and large number of potential buyers. Since supplies are relatively standardized, price competition is frequently heavy. However, the purchasing manager spends little time in making purchase decisions about such products. He or she frequently places telephone orders or mail orders, or makes regular purchases from the sales representative of the local office-supply wholesale.

This brings to an end the discussion of products, their classification, and broad management principles that apply in the product life cycle. Product classification analysis also has shown many different strategic needs and opportunities. The next chapter continues with a more detailed look at the numerous considerations required in the management of products.

supplies
Regular expense items necessary in the daily operation of a firm, but not part of its final product.

MRO items
Industrial supplies, so called because they can be categorized as maintenance items, repair items, and operating supplies.

■ KEY TERMS

product	diffusion process	industrial distributor
warranty	convenience products	component parts and
product life cycle	preference products	materials
fashions	shopping products	raw materials
fads	specialty products	supplies
adoption process	installations	MRO items
consumer innovators	accessory equipment	

■ INTERACTIVE SUMMARY AND DISCUSSION QUESTIONS

1. A product is a total bundle of physical, service, and symbolic characteristics designed to produce consumer want satisfaction. Explain how this definition applies to
   a. A lawyer's service in drafting a will
   b. A pail of chemical fertilizer used by a farmer
   c. Alfred Sung perfume
2. The product life-cycle stages are introduction, growth, maturity, and decline. Draw the typical life-cycle model, and then the way the model would appear for a fad, a fashion item, and an aborted (re)introduction.

3. At different stages in the product life cycle, the emphasis differs for the elements of the marketing mix. Discuss and give examples.

4. Fashions are currently popular products that tend to follow recurring life cycles. For some marketers, it would be desirable to speed up the cycle so there would be a revived demand for the new fashion. Is this possible?

5. The life-cycle concept is most applicable to a product category, not to individual brands. Discuss, using examples.

6. The product life cycle may be extended by increasing the frequency of use by present customers, adding new users, finding new uses for the product, or changing product quality or packaging. Discuss the pros and cons of such efforts in comparison with introducing a completely new product.

7. Consumers go through a process from first learning about a product to deciding whether to purchase or not. This adoption process has the following stages: awareness, interest, evaluation, trial, and adoption/rejection. Discuss how a marketer can use this information.

8. The rate of adoption is influenced by the five characteristics of the innovation: relative advantage, compatibility, complexity, divisibility, and communicability. Using these characteristics, give an example of a product that would be adopted relatively quickly, and one that would be adopted more slowly.

9. Consumer products can be categorized as convenience products, preference products, shopping products, and specialty products. Describe how the marketing mix varies for products in each category.

10. Industrial products are categorized as installations, accessory equipment, component parts and materials, raw materials, and supplies. Explain how the marketing mix varies for products in each category.

CHAPTER 10

Product Management

CHAPTER OBJECTIVES

1. To explain the concept of the product mix, and indicate various mix decisions that can be made.
2. To show the importance of developing a line of related products.
3. To outline new-product strategies and the determinants of their success.
4. To describe various organizational arrangements for new-product development.
5. To examine the stages in the product development process.
6. To discuss the role of brands, brand names, and trademarks.
7. To show the importance, role, and functions of packaging.

What happened when the Pillsbury doughboy took a liking to Nabisco Oreos? You got Oreo Bars Baking Mix and Frosting. And when Betty Crocker joined hands with Mars Inc., they gave birth to M&M's Cookie Bars baking mix.

Welcome to the world of "co-branding," where two companies join to create a new product carrying both their brands. Two brands, the theory goes, means double recognition, double endorsement power, and double consumer confidence.

"This craze is about to explode," predicts Bryan Mattimore, president of Mattimore Group consultants. "Marketers have line-extended to death. Co-branding is the next cheap way to get new products out there, to leverage psychological shares of mind."

Co-branding is almost mandatory in today's marketplace, says Elinor Selame, president of Brand Equity International. "Sharing expenses is the least expensive way to develop new products. And it's a way to unload excess product . . . and not at the commodity level."

Co-branding is typically done through licensing as Nabisco Brands does, or via a separate company such as Johnson & Johnson–Merck Consumer Pharmaceutical Co. Inc.

There are pitfalls to this kind of marketing. "If one product isn't good, it can hurt both guest and host," Ms. Selame warns. "If the guest has a stronger trademark than the host, it can hold up the host as hostage." For example, a baker of cookies teamed up with Chiquita Brands. "If Chiquita leaves the baker, what does the baker have left?" Mr. Mattimore adds that co-brands fizzle if the combination doesn't offer a real consumer benefit.[1]

Co-branding is one example of the many facets involved in product management. Having appropriate products and brand names that are attractive and memorable are fundamental tasks of the business.

INTRODUCTION

Product management requires continual diligence in assessing the changing needs of the market. Normally it is important to have products that provide a range of opportunities for the company. This range of products is described as a product mix. A **product mix** is *the assortment of product lines and individual offerings available from a company.* Its two components are the **product line**, *a series of related products,* and the **individual offerings**, or *single products within those lines.*

Product mixes are typically measured by width and depth of assortment. Width of assortment refers to the number of different product lines that the firm offers, while depth of assortment refers to the extension or variety within a particular product line. Canada Packers offers an assortment of consumer product lines — meats, and several unrelated grocery items such as peanut butter (see Table 10.1). These product lines would be considered the width of the Canada Packers product mix. The depth is determined by the number of individual offerings within each product line. For example, the company's meat line consists of fresh meats, smoked meats, and processed meats, while the grocery line is represented by York peanut butter and several types of canned vegetables. The company also sells a nonedible line of by-products.

product mix
The assortment of product lines and individual offerings available from a company.

product line
A series of related products.

individual offering
Single product within a product line.

THE EXISTING PRODUCT MIX

The starting point in any product-planning effort is to assess the firm's current product mix. What product line does it now offer? How deep are the offerings

■ Table 10.1 **The Canada Packers Product Mix**

	Width of Assortment		
	Meats	**Groceries**	**Nonedible**
Depth of Assortment	Fresh meats Bacon Pepperoni Wieners Bologna Canned ham Poultry Kolbassa Garlic sausage	Peanut butter Mincemeat Canned pumpkin Cheese Lard Shortening	By-products Soap Hides Pharmaceutical raw materials

within each of the product lines? The marketer normally looks for gaps in the assortment that can be filled by new products or by modified versions of existing products. Expansion or redevelopment of existing product lines is usually the easiest approach for a firm to take, since the market requirements for these lines are generally well known.

Cannibalization

cannibalizing
Situation involving one product taking sales from another offering in a product line.

The firm wants to avoid a costly new-product introduction that will adversely affect sales of one of its existing products. A *product that takes sales from another offering in a product line* is said to be **cannibalizing** the line. Marketing research should ensure that cannibalization effects are minimized or at least anticipated. When Clearly Canadian introduced new flavours, its marketers were resigned to the fact that sales of their existing brand would be negatively affected.

Line Extension

line extension
The development of individual offerings that appeal to different market segments but are closely related to the existing product line.

An important rationale for assessing the current product mix is to determine whether line extension is feasible. A **line extension** refers to *the development of individual offerings that appeal to different market segments but are closely related to the existing product line.* If cannibalization can be minimized, line extension provides a relatively cheap way of increasing sales revenues at minimal risk. Oh Henry chocolate bars can be purchased in an ice-cream-bar format, in addition to their traditional form. This illustrates the line extension of an existing product.

Once the assessment of the existing product mix has been made and the appropriate line extensions considered, marketing decision-makers must turn their attention to product-line planning and the development of new products.

THE IMPORTANCE OF PRODUCT LINES

Firms that market only one product are rare today. Most offer their customers a product line — a series of related products. Polaroid Corporation, for example, began operations with a single product, a polarized screen for sunglasses and other products. Then, in 1948, it introduced the world's first instant camera. For the next

Baby Dove or 'baby' soap.
What difference does it make?

A new baby comes wrapped in more questions than answers. What's the best way to treat delicate baby skin? What kind of soap should you use? Does it matter? You may not realize it, but like adult soap, baby soap is drying. Dry skin is more sensitive, therefore more easily irritated.

Baby Dove is not a soap. It's a cleansing bar specially formulated

to be milder than soap. So it cleans your baby's skin without drying the way soaps can.

Baby Dove is softly-scented; it's just the right size and shape to caress baby curves.

So while you can't see the difference between Baby Dove and baby soap, your baby can certainly feel the difference.

Try Baby Dove.

Baby Dove capitalizes on consumers' perceptions of the original Dove cleansing bar as a mild alternative to soap. As well, consumers trust the Dove brand and believe its claims. Developing Baby Dove as a line extension of Dove has paid off for Lever Canada, as Baby Dove is the price leader in its market segment.

30 years, these products proved sufficient for annual sales and profit growth. By 1983, however, instant cameras accounted for only about two-thirds of Polaroid's sales. The company has now added hundreds of products in both industrial and consumer markets, ranging from nearly 40 different types of instant films (for various industrial, medical, and other technical operations) to batteries, sonar devices, and machine tools. Several factors account for the inclination of firms such as Polaroid to develop a complete line rather than concentrate on a single product.

Desire to Grow

A company places definite limitations on its growth potential when it concentrates on a single product. In a single twelve-month period, Lever Brothers once introduced 21 new products in its search for market growth and increased profits. A study by a group of management consultants revealed that firms expect newly developed products to account for 37 percent of their sales and 51 percent of their profits over the five years following the products' introduction.[2]

Firms often introduce new products to offset seasonal variations in the sales of their current products. Since the majority of soup purchases are made during the winter months, Campbell Soup Company has made attempts to tap the warm-weather soup market. A line of fruit soups to be served chilled was test-marketed, but results showed that consumers were not yet ready for fruit soups. The firm continued to search for warm-weather soups, however, and in some markets it has added gazpacho (and other varieties meant to be served chilled) to its product line.

Making Optimal Use of Company Resources

By spreading the costs of operations over a series of products, a company may find it possible to reduce the average costs of all products. Texize Chemicals Company started with a single household cleaner and learned painful lessons about marketing costs when a firm has only one major product. Management rapidly added the products K2r and Fantastik to the line. The company's sales representatives can now call on middlemen with a series of products at little more than the cost of marketing a single product. In addition, Texize's advertising produces benefits for all products in the line. Similarly, production facilities can be used economically in producing related products. For example, auto companies regularly produce a range of products, from convertibles to vans to sports cars, from a basic car design. Finally, the expertise of all the firm's personnel can be applied more widely to a line of products than to a single one.

Increasing Company Importance in the Market

Consumers and middlemen often expect a firm that manufacturers and markets small appliances to also offer related products under its brand name. The Maytag Company offers not only washing machines but also dryers, since consumers often demand matching appliances. Gillette markets not only razors and blades but also a full range of grooming aids, including Foamy shaving cream, Right Guard deodorant, Gillette Dry Look hair spray, and Super Max hair dryers.

The company with a line of products is often more important to both the consumer and the retailer than is the company with only one product. Shoppers who purchase a tent often buy related items, such as tent heaters, sleeping bags, air mattresses, camp stoves, and special cookware. Recognizing this tendency, the Coleman Company now includes in its product line dozens of items associated with camping. The firm would be little known if its only product were lanterns. Similarly, new cameras from Eastman Kodak help the firm sell more film — a product that carries a significant profit margin.

Exploiting the Product Life Cycle

As its output enters the maturity and decline stages of the life cycle of a product category, the firm must add new products if it is to prosper. The regular addition of new products to the firm's line helps ensure that it will not become a victim of product obsolescence. The automobile industry continually adds new products, deletes those that are not doing so well, and upgrades popular models.

NEW-PRODUCT PLANNING

The product development effort requires considerable advance planning. New products are the lifeblood of many business firms, and a steady flow of new entries must be available if such firms are to survive. Some new products represent major technological breakthroughs: for instance, biotechnology, which permits the transfer of genes from any living organism to another, has the potential to spur the invention of many new pharmaceutical products. Other new products are simple product-line extensions — that is, the "new" product is new only to the company or to the customer. One survey found that for products introduced in one five-year period, about 85 percent were line extensions, and only 15 percent were truly new products.[3]

The Product Decay Curve

New-product development is risky and expensive. In 1989, despite the continuing potential of biotechnology, only 1 of 400 North American start-ups, Geneutech, had made a sustained profit.[4] A Conference Board study of 148 medium and large North American manufacturing companies revealed that one out of three new industrial and consumer products introduced within the previous five years had failed. The leading cause of new-product failure was insufficient or poor marketing research.[5]

Dozens of new-product ideas are required to produce even one successful product. Figure 10.1 depicts the product decay curve from a 1968 survey of 51 companies. Of every 58 ideas produced in these firms, only 12 passed the preliminary screening test designed to determine whether they were compatible with company resources and objectives. Of these 12, only 7 showed sufficient profit potential in the business analysis phase. Three survived the development phase, two made it through the test-marketing stage, and only one, on the average, was commercially successful. Thus, less than 2 percent of new ideas resulted in a successful product.

A 1981 follow-up study reported that while the success rate had not improved, new-product development was becoming more cost-effective. According to the new data, some 54 percent of total new-product expenditures were made on products that became successes, compared with 30 percent in 1968. Capital investment in new products had fallen from 46 percent to 26 percent of total new-product spending.[6] These figures suggest that new-product development has become more efficient.

Determinants of Success for New Products

What determines the success or failure of a new product? A research effort known as Project New Product suggests the following six categories as determinants of new-product outcomes:

■ Figure 10.1 **Decay Curve of New-Product Ideas**

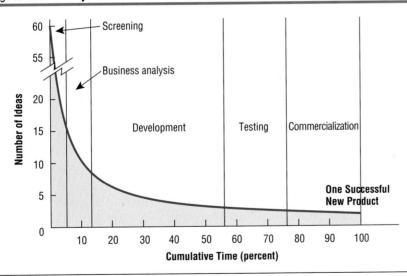

Source: *New Products Management for the 1980s* (New York: Booz, Allen & Hamilton, 1982), p. 3. Reprinted by permission of the publisher.

1. The relative strengths of the new product and its marketplace launch
2. The nature and quality of the information available during the product development process
3. The relative proficiency of new-product development efforts
4. The characteristics of the marketplace at which the new product is aimed
5. The fit or compatibility of the new product and the firm's resource base
6. The specific characteristics of the new-product effort[7]

These hypothetical variables allowed Robert Cooper of McMaster University to classify types of new products. Cooper contends that the most important key to new-product success lies in the product strategy itself. In his research, he found that in the cases he studied, the best 20 percent of the products had an astounding success rate of 82 percent. In contrast, 20 percent at the other end of the scale (the "me-too" products) suffered a *failure* rate of 78 percent.

CHARACTERISTICS OF THE SUPERIOR PRODUCT

What, then, *is* a superior product? Cooper found that a number of characteristics constituted the superior-product dimension. In descending order of importance, these critical characteristics are as follows:

1. A product that meets customers' needs better than competing products
2. A product that offers features or attributes to the customer that competing products do not
3. A product of higher quality than competitive products (one that has tighter specifications, is stronger, lasts longer, or is more reliable)
4. A product that does a special task or job for the customer — something that cannot be done with existing products
5. A product that is highly innovative, totally new to the market
6. A product that permits the customer to reduce costs[8]

Products with these characteristics supported by creative marketing strategies will greatly contribute to a profitable product line.

Product Development Strategies

The firm's strategy for new-product development should vary according to the existing product mix and the determinants cited above. Marketing decision-makers also need to look at the firm's current market position. Figure 10.2 provides a means for looking at overall product development strategy. Four forms of product development are suggested: product improvement, market development, product development, and product diversification.

product improvement strategy
A modification in existing products.

A **product improvement strategy** refers to *a modification in existing products.* Tide is an example of a product that has undergone constant product improvement over the years. Because of such improvements, it continues to be a leading product. Another example is the "Quality Is Job One" program established by Ford. And this was more than just a slogan: Ford's products are now more competitive with Japanese cars. Currently, Daewoo Electronics is seeking to break into the North American electronics market with more consumer-friendly products such as VCRs.

■ Figure 10.2 **Forms of Product Development**

	Old Product	**New Product**
Old Market	Product improvement	Product development
New Market	Market development	Product diversification

Source: Charles E. Meisch, "Marketers, Engineers Should Work Together in 'New Product' Development Departments," *Marketing News* (November 13, 1981), p. 10. Used by permission of the American Marketing Association. Earlier discussion of these strategies is credited to H. Igor Ansoff, "Strategies for Diversification," *Harvard Business Review* (September–October 1957), pp. 113–24; see also Philip Kotler, *Principles of Marketing*, 2nd ed. (Englewood Cliffs, NJ: Prentice Hall, 1983), pp. 34, 52.

A **market development strategy** concentrates on *finding new markets for existing products.* Market segmentation (discussed in Chapters 3 and 4) is a useful tool in such an effort. Penetrating the home market with the fax machine — a product already established in the office — illustrates such a strategy. In another classic example, the sales of baking soda were greatly increased when it was found that the product could be marketed as an air freshener in refrigerators and for other applications.

market development strategy
Finding new markets for existing products.

A **product development strategy** refers to *introducing new products into identifiable or established markets.* Chrysler's Magic Wagon, for example, was a tremendous success because it provided consumers with a spacious vehicle that was as easy to drive, and as comfortable, as a car. This is a major strategy of the computer industry. A continuous flow of products makes the computer you just bought somewhat obsolete within a few months of purchase.

product development strategy
Introducing new products into identifiable or established markets.

Sometimes the new product is the firm's first entry in a particular market. In other cases, firms choose to introduce new products into markets in which they have already established positions, in an attempt to increase overall market share. These new offerings are called *flanker brands.*

Product diversification strategy refers to *the development of new products for new markets;* the introduction of the CD-ROM is an example. In some cases, the new target markets complement existing markets; in others, they do not. For example, a computer company might develop a range of products for the home security market.

product diversification strategy
The development of new products for new markets.

Each of these strategies has advantages and disadvantages and must carefully be considered in the light of consumer needs and behaviour, competitors' strengths, and the strengths and abilities of the company. New products should be consistent with the firm's overall strategic orientation. Assume that a beverage firm has set four strategic requirements for a new product:

1. It must appeal to the under-21 age segment.
2. It must use off-season or excess capacity.
3. It must successfully penetrate a new product category for the firm.
4. It could simply be a "cash cow" that funds other new products.[9]

Each of these criteria would fit in well with the orientation, skills, and resources of the firm.

THE ORGANIZATIONAL STRUCTURE FOR NEW-PRODUCT DEVELOPMENT

As the above section indicates, new-product planning is a complex area. The critical nature of product-planning decisions requires an effective organizational structure to make them. A prerequisite for efficient product innovation is an organizational structure designed to stimulate and co-ordinate new-product development. New-product development is a specialized task that requires the expertise of many departments. A company that delegates new-product development responsibility to the engineering department often discovers that engineers sometimes design products that are good from a structural standpoint but poor in terms of consumer needs. Many successful medium and large companies assign new-product development to one or more of the following: (1) new-product committees, (2) new-product departments, (3) product managers, or (4) venture teams.

New-Product Committees

The most common organizational arrangement for new-product development is the *new-product committee*. Such a committee typically comprises representatives of top management in such areas as marketing, finance, manufacturing, engineering, research, and accounting. Committee members are less concerned with conceiving and developing new-product ideas than with reviewing and approving new-product plans.

Since key executives in the functional areas are committee members, their support for a new-product plan is likely to result in its approval for further development. However, new-product committees tend to be slow, are generally conservative, and sometimes compromise in order to expedite decisions so that members may get back to their regular company responsibilities.

New-Product Departments

To overcome the limitations of the new-product committee, a number of firms have established a separate, formally organized department responsible for all phases of a product's development within the firm, including making screening decisions, developing product specifications, and co-ordinating product testing. The head of the department is given substantial authority and usually reports to the president or to the top marketing officer.

Product Managers

product managers (brand managers)
Individuals assigned one product or product line and given responsibility for determining its objectives and marketing strategies.

Product managers (also called **brand managers**) are *individuals assigned one product or product line and given responsibility for determining its objectives and marketing strategies.* Procter & Gamble assigned the first product manager back in 1927 when it made one person responsible for Camay soap.[10] The role of product manager is now widely accepted by marketers. Johnson & Johnson, Canada Packers, and General Mills are examples of firms that employ product managers.

Product managers are deeply involved in setting prices, developing advertising and sales promotion programs, and working to provide assistance to sales representatives in the field. Although product managers have no line authority over the field sales force, they share the objective of increasing sales for the brand, and managers try to help salespeople accomplish this task. In multiproduct companies, product managers are key people in the marketing department. They provide individual attention to each product, while the firm as a whole has a single sales force, a marketing research department, and an advertising department that all product managers can use.

In addition to performing product analysis and planning, the product manager must use interpersonal skills and sales skills to gain the co-operation of people over whom he or she has no authority. This occurs with levels above the manager, as well as with those in sales and advertising.

Besides having primary responsibility for marketing a particular product or product line, the product manager often is also responsible for new-product development, creating new-product ideas, and making recommendations for improving existing products. These suggestions become the basis for proposals submitted to top management.

The product manager system is open to one of the same criticisms as the new-product committee: new-product development may get secondary treatment because of the manager's time commitments for existing products. Although a number of extremely successful new products have resulted from ideas submitted by product managers, it cannot be assumed that the skills required for marketing an existing product line are the same as those required for successfully developing new products.[11]

Venture Teams

Many companies have found that new venture teams have provided a good method of bringing new products to the market.

The **venture-team concept** *develops new products through combining the management resources of marketing, technology, capital, and management expertise in a team.* Like new-product committees, venture teams are composed of specialists from different functions in the organization: engineering representatives for expertise in product design and the development of prototypes; marketing staff members for development of product-concept tests, test marketing, sales forecasts, pricing, and promotion; and financial accounting representatives for detailed cost analyses and decisions concerning the concept's probable return on investment.

venture-team concept
An organizational strategy for developing new products through combining the management resources of marketing, technology, capital, and management expertise.

Unlike new-product committees, venture teams do not disband after every product developed. Members are assigned to the project as a major responsibility, and the team possesses the necessary authority to both plan and carry out a course of action.

As a means of stimulating product innovation, the team is typically separated from the permanent organization and is also linked directly with top management. One company moved its three-member venture team from its divisional headquarters to the corporate head office. Since the venture-team manager reports to the division head or to the chief administrative officer, communications problems are minimized and high-level support is assured.

The venture team usually begins as a loosely organized group of members with a common interest in a new-product idea. Team members are frequently given released time during the workday to devote to the venture. If viable product proposals are developed, the venture team is formally organized as a task force within a venture department or as a task force reporting to a vice-president or to the chief executive officer. When the commercial potential of new products has been demonstrated, the products may be assigned to an existing division, may become a division within the company, or may serve as the nucleus of a new company. The flexibility and authority of the venture team allows the large firm to operate with the manoeuvrability of smaller companies.

STAGES IN THE NEW-PRODUCT DEVELOPMENT PROCESS

New-product development strategy should be built upon the existing business strategy of the company. Companies that have successfully launched new products are more likely to have had a formal new-product process in place for some time. They are also more likely to have a strategic plan, and be committed to growth through internally developed new products.[12]

Once the firms is organized for new-product development, it can establish procedures for evaluating new-product ideas. The product development process may be thought of as involving seven stages: (1) development of overall new-product strategy, (2) new-product idea generation, (3) screening, (4) business analysis, (5) final product development, (6) test marketing, and (7) commercialization. At each stage, management faces the decision to abandon the project, continue to the next stage, or seek additional information before proceeding further.[13] The process is illustrated in Figure 10.3.

New-Product Strategy

New-product strategy links corporate objectives to the new-product effort, provides direction for the new-product process, and identifies the strategic roles in the product line that the new products should play. It also helps set the formal financial criteria to be used in measuring new-product performance and in screening and evaluating new-product ideas.[14]

Figure 10.3 Seven Stages of the New-Product Development Process

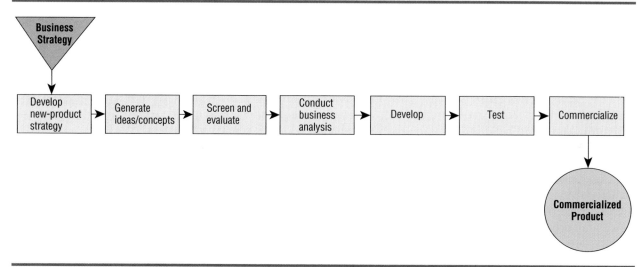

Idea Generation

New-product development begins with an idea. Ideas emanate from many sources: the sales force, marketing employees, research and development (R & D) specialists, competitive products, retailers, inventors outside the company, and customers who write letters asking, "Why don't you . . . ?" It is extremely important for the firm to develop a system of stimulating new ideas and rewarding people who develop them.

Screening

This crucial stage involves separating ideas with potential from those incapable of meeting company objectives. Some organizations use checklists to determine whether product ideas should be eliminated or subjected to further consideration. These checklists typically include such factors as product uniqueness; availability of raw materials; and compatibility of the proposed product with current product offerings, existing facilities, and capabilities. In other instances, the screening stage consists of open discussions of new-product ideas among representatives of different functional areas in the organization. This is an important point in the product development process, since any product ideas that go beyond this point will cost the firm considerable time and money. Table 10.2 presents some basic criteria used in the screening process.

Business Analysis

Product ideas that survive the initial screening are then subjected to a thorough business analysis. This involves assessing the potential market, its growth rate, and the likely competitive strength of the new product. Decisions must be made in determining the compatibility of the proposed product with such company

■ Table 10.2 **Basic Criteria for Preliminary Screening**

1. The item should be in a field of activity in which the corporation is engaged.

2. If the idea involves a companion product to others already being manufactured, it should be made from materials to which the corporation is accustomed.

3. The item should be capable of being produced on the type and kind of equipment that the corporation normally operates.

4. The item should be easily handled by the corporation's existing sales force through the established distribution pattern.

5. The potential market for the product should be at least $_____.

6. The market over the next five years should be expected to grow at a faster rate than the GNP.

7. Return on investment, after taxes, must reach a minimum level of _____ percent.

Source: William S. Sachs and George Benson, *Product Planning and Management* (Tulsa, OK: Penn Well Books, 1981), p. 231.

resources as financial support for necessary promotion, production capabilities, and distribution facilities.

Concept testing, or the consideration of the product idea prior to its actual development, is an important aspect of the business analysis stage. **Concept testing** is *a marketing research project that attempts to measure consumer attitudes and perceptions relevant to the new-product idea.* Focus groups (see Chapter 5) and in-store polling can be effective methods for assessing a new-product concept.

concept testing
A marketing research project that attempts to measure consumer attitudes and perceptions relevant to a new-product idea.

Product Development

Those product ideas with profit potential are then converted into a physical product. The conversion process becomes the joint responsibility of development engineering, which is responsible for developing the original concept into a product, and the marketing department, which provides feedback on consumer reactions to alternative product designs, packages, features, colours, and other physical appeals. Numerous changes may be necessary before the original mock-up is converted into the final product.

Even after basic production processes have been solved, there is often a considerable amount of testing with potential consumers. Such testing is done in many ways. Sometimes employees are given the product and asked to report on performance on a regular, structured basis. As a textbook such as this one is written, it is subject to review by faculty members across the country. In other cases, limited market tests are undertaken under carefully monitored conditions, as discussed in Chapter 5. The series of revisions, tests, and refinements should result in the ultimate introduction of a product with a greater likelihood of success.

Despite such careful testing, further problems are often uncovered in daily use. For example, the first edition of computer software often has some "bugs" that have to be corrected. And the first printing of this book will also likely have some typographical or other errors that will be corrected with the next printing a few months later. Cars are sometimes recalled to dealers to replace a part that does not work out as expected.

Test Marketing

To determine consumer reactions to their products *and* to the proposed marketing plan under normal shopping conditions, a number of firms test-market their new offerings. Up to this point, consumer information has been obtained by giving free products to consumers, who then gave their reactions. Other information may have been gathered by asking shoppers to evaluate competitive products, but test marketing is the first point at which the product must perform in a "real-life" environment.

Test marketing involves *selecting usually one to three cities or television-coverage areas considered reasonably typical of the total market, and introducing a new product to these areas with a total marketing campaign.* A carefully designed and controlled test allows management to develop estimates of the effectiveness of marketing-mix decisions and projections of sales following full-scale introduction.

test marketing
The selection of areas considered reasonably typical of the total market, and introducing a new product to these areas with a total marketing campaign to determine consumer response before marketing the product nationally.

Some firms omit the test-marketing stage and move directly from product development to full-scale production. They cite three problems with test marketing:

1. Test marketing is expensive. As one marketing executive pointed out,

   > It's very difficult to run a little [test market] for six months or a year in three or four markets across the [country] and then project what your sales volume is going to be two or three years in the future, mainly because you're testing in such small localities, generally to keep your costs down.
   >
   > You simply can't afford to test your products in markets like [Toronto or Montreal]. So you run your test in [smaller cities]. And your test costs are over $1 million even in places like that.[15]

2. Competitors who learn about the test market may disrupt the findings by reducing the price of their products in the test area, distributing cents-off coupons, installing attractive in-store displays, or giving additional discounts to retailers to induce them to display more of their products.

   Test marketing a new product also communicates company plans to competitors before the product's introduction. The Kellogg Company discovered a new product with suspected sales potential by learning of the test marketing of a new fruit-filled tart designed to be heated in the toaster and served hot for breakfast. Kellogg rushed a similar product into full-scale production and became the first national marketer of the product they named Pop Tarts.

3. Long-lived durable goods (such as dishwashers, hair dryers, and VCRs) are seldom test-marketed due to the major financial investment required for the development, the need to develop a network of dealers to distribute the products, and the parts and servicing required. A company such as Whirlpool invests from $1 million to $33 million in the development of a new refrigerator. To develop each silicon chip in an Apple microcomputer costs approximately $1 million and takes from one to fifteen months. Producing a prototype for a test market is simply too expensive, so the "go/no-go" decision for the new durable product is typically made without the benefit of test-market results.[16]

A decision to skip the test-marketing stage should be based on there being a very high likelihood of the product's success. The cost of developing a new detergent from idea generation to national marketing has been estimated at *$10 million*. Even though a firm will experience losses on any product that passes the initial screening process but is not introduced, it will still be much better off if it stops as soon as it discovers that the product cannot succeed. Otherwise, it may be faced with a failure like Corfam, an artificial leather that Du Pont introduced; the company suffered losses of more than *$100 million* over the lengthy period it tried to make Corfam a success.

Commercialization

The few product ideas that have survived all the steps in the development process are now ready for full-scale marketing. Marketing programs must be established, outlays for production facilities may be necessary, and the sales force, middlemen, and potential customers must become acquainted with the new product.

New-product development should follow the step-by-step approach outlined in Figure 10.3. Systematic planning and control of all phases of development and introduction can be accomplished through the use of such scheduling methods as the Program Evaluation and Review Technique (PERT) and the Critical Path Method (CPM). These techniques map out the sequence in which each step must be taken and show the time allotments for each activity. Detailed PERT and CPM flow charts not only will assist in co-ordinating all activities in the development and introduction of new products, but can also highlight the sequence of events that will be the most critical in scheduling.

PRODUCT DELETION DECISIONS

While many firms devote a great deal of time and resources to the development of new products, the thought of eliminating old products from the firm's line is painful for many executives. Often sentimental attachments to marginal products prevent objective decisions to drop products with declining sales. Management finds it difficult to bury an old friend.

If waste is to be avoided, product lines must be pruned, and old unprofitable products must eventually be eliminated from the firm's line. This decision is typically faced in the late-maturity and early-decline stages of the product life cycle. Periodic reviews of all products should be conducted in order to prune weak products or to justify their retention.

In some instances, a firm will continue to carry an unprofitable product so as to provide a complete line of goods for its customers. Even though most supermarkets may not make much money on low-unit-value items such as salt, they continue to carry it to meet shopper demands.

Other cases arise in which profitable products are dropped because of failure to fit into the firm's existing product line. IBM found that its marketing system, including the training of representatives, was so focussed on computers that it was difficult to do an adequate job in marketing printers. Therefore, it removed printers from the main product line and turned them over to a subsidiary company, Lexmark.

PRODUCT IDENTIFICATION

Manufacturers identify their products through the use of brand names, symbols, and distinctive packaging. So also do large retailers such as Canadian Tire, with its line of Mastercraft products, and The Bay with its Beaumark brand. Almost every product that is distinguishable from another contains a means of identification for the buyer. Even a 5-year-old can distinguish a Chiquita banana from other ones. And the California Fruit Growers Exchange literally brands its oranges with the name Sunkist. The purchasing manager for a construction firm can turn over an ordinary sheet of roofing and find the name and symbol for Domtar. Choosing the means of identification for the firm's output often represents a major decision area for the marketing manager.

Brands, Brand Names, and Trademarks

brand
A name, term, sign, symbols, or design (or some combination thereof) used to identify the products of one firm and to differentiate them from competitive offerings.

brand name
Words, letters, or symbols that make up a name used to identify and distinguish the firm's offerings from those of its competitors.

trademark
A brand that has been given legal protection and has been granted solely to its owner.

A **brand** is *a name, term, sign, symbol, or design (or some combination thereof) used to identify the products of one firm and to differentiate them from competitive offerings.* A **brand name** is that part of the brand consisting of *words, letters, or symbols making up a name used to identify and distinguish its firm's offerings from those of its competitors.*[17] The brand name is, therefore, that part of the brand that may be vocalized. A **trademark** is *a brand that has been given legal protection and has been granted solely to its owner.* Thus, the term trademark includes not only pictorial design but also the brand name. Many thousands of trademarks are currently registered in Canada. Today, virtually all trademarks are developed with careful consideration of the visual and emotional impact of the name. Some other common trademarks have emerged through various iterations over the years. The Procter & Gamble "moon and stars" trademark that was used until recently is one example (see the box on the next page).

For the consumer, brands facilitate repeat purchases of products that have been found satisfactory. The brand assures a uniform quality and identifies the firm producing the product. The purchaser associates the satisfaction derived from a carbonated soft drink with the brand name Pepsi-Cola.

For the marketing manager, the brand serves as the cornerstone around which the product's image is developed. Once consumers have been made aware of a particular brand, its appearance becomes further advertising for the firm. The Shell Oil Company symbol is instant advertising to motorists who view it while driving. Well-known brands also allow the firm to escape some of the rigours of price competition. Although any chemist will confirm that all ASA tablets contain the same amount of the chemical acetylsalicylic acid, Bayer has developed so strong a reputation that it can successfully market its Aspirin at a higher price than competitive products. Similarly, McDonald's "golden arches" attract customers to its outlets.

What Constitutes a Good Brand Name?

Good brand names are easy to pronounce, recognize, and remember. Short names like Vim, Gleem, Dash, and Kodak meet these requirements. Multinational marketing firms face a particularly acute problem in selecting brand names: a brand name that works terrifically well in one country may prove disastrous in another due to language problems.

For 21 years, Nissan Motor Corporation marketers struggled with an easily mispronounced brand name — "Datsun" — for its cars and trucks. Nissan found that in English-speaking nations some people pronounced the *a* like the *a* in *hat*, while others pronounced it like the *o* in *got*, and the difference hindered brand recognition. Finally, Nissan marketers decided to change the name of all its automobile products to "Nissan" beginning with its Stanza model in 1982. Total cost of the change — effected in more than 135 countries — is estimated to have been as high as $150 million.[18]

Every language has "O" and "K" sounds, and "okay" has become an international word. Every language also has a short "a," so that Coca-Cola® and Texaco are good in any tongue. An American advertising campaign for E-Z washing machines failed in the United Kingdom because the British pronounced "Z" as "zed," as we do in Canada.

The brand name should give the buyer the right connotation. Mercury Marine presents favourable images of boating pleasures. The Craftsman name used on the Sears line of quality tools also produces the correct image. Accutron suggests the quality of the high-priced and accurate timepiece made by the Bulova Watch Company. But what can the marketing manager do if the brand name is based on a strange-sounding company name? Sometimes the decision may be to poke fun at this improbable name, as in a promotional campaign built around the theme "With a name like Koogle, it has to be good!"

APPLYING THE CONCEPTS.

Development and Defence of a Trademark

PROCTER & GAMBLE'S SYMBOL OF QUALITY

The Moon and Stars has been used as P&G's corporate trademark for over 100 years and remains an important Company identification.

False Rumors

Unfortunately, this familiar trademark has been subjected to preposterous, unfounded rumors since 1980–81. The rumors falsely allege that the trademark is a symbol of satanism. Typically, the story reports that a P&G executive discussed satanism on a nationally televised talk show.

The rumors are, of course, totally false. The P&G trademark originated about 1851 as a symbol for Star brand candles. Later it was designed to show a "man-in-the-moon" looking over a field of thirteen stars commemorating the original American colonies. It represents *only* P&G.

The stories about an executive appearing on a talk show are totally false. Producers for the programs mentioned in connection with the rumor have confirmed that no one from P&G has *ever* appeared on their shows.

Religious Leaders Offer Support

Several nationally prominent religious leaders also have called for an end to the false stories. These leaders include Reverend Jerry Falwell; Evangelist Billy Graham; Reverend Jimmy Draper, former president of the Southern Baptist Convention; His Eminence Joseph Cardinal Bernardin, Catholic Archbishop of Chicago; and Reverend Donald E. Wildmon, a Methodist minister and Executive Director of American Family Association. These and other prominent religious leaders have asked people to stop the rumors, calling the stories "vicious" and "ludicrous."

Legal Victories

P&G is taking this problem seriously and has filed and won over a dozen lawsuits against individuals who spread the rumors.

History of the Moon and Stars Trademark

P&G's trademark originated around 1851, when many products did not carry a visible brand name. Even people who could not read could see P&G's trademark and know they would get consistent quality.

The original trademark was refined into a star which multiplied into thirteen stars for the 13 original colonies and a man-in-the-moon, a popular decorative fancy of the 1800's.

P&G management recognized the importance of the man-in-the-moon element when they eliminated it from the trademark in the 1860's. A merchant "down river" rejected a shipment of Star Candles, an early P&G product, which carried the modified trademark. He chided the Company by letter for sending imitations. The moon promptly went back into service, and the trademark was officially registered with the U.S. Patent Office in 1882.

Evolution of the Moon and Stars Trademark

The oldest documented use of the Moon and Stars in P&G's Archives is this crude rendering on a price list from the late 1860's.

(continued)

The Moon and Stars had been refined to this point by 1882, and registered in the U.S. Patent Office.

By the late 1890's, the trademark was still basically the same, but displayed some of the decorations typical of the turn-of-the-century.

In 1930, a sculptor was commissioned by P&G to refine the Moon and Stars trademark.

In 1991, the Moon and Stars trademark continued to evolve, with minor refinements to simplify its look.

Procter & Gamble's Corporate Biography

Established in 1837, Procter & Gamble (P&G) began as a small, family operated soap and candle company in Cincinnati, Ohio. From that modest beginning, P&G has grown into a global company which today has sales in over 140 countries and on the ground operations in over 50 countries.

P&G is a recognized leader in the development, manufacture and marketing of a broad range of superior quality products including Crest toothpaste, Tide laundry detergent, Ivory soap and Pampers diapers to name just a few.

P&G's corporate tradition, spanning over 150 years, is rooted in the principles of personal integrity; doing what's right for the long-term; respect for the individual; and being the best at what it does.

Source: Procter & Gamble. Reprinted with permission.

Do you think P&G should have dropped the trademark?

The Brand Name Should Be Legally Protectable

S.C. Johnson and Son, makers of OFF, lost a court case against Bug Off since it was held that OFF was an improper trademark because it was not unusual enough to distinguish it from other, similar products.

When all offerings in a class of products become generally known by the brand name of the first or leading brand in that product class, the brand name may be ruled a descriptive or **generic name**, after which the original owner loses all right to the exclusive use of it. Generic names like nylon, zipper, kerosene, linoleum, escalator, and shredded wheat were once brand names.

Bayer's Aspirin is the only ASA tablet permitted to carry that protected trademark in Canada. All other acetylsalicylic acid tablets are called ASA. In the United States, because Bayer did not protect its trade name, the generic name "aspirin" is given to all acetylsalicylic acid tablets. Most drug purchasers there would not know what an ASA tablet is.

generic name
A brand name over which the original owner has lost exclusive claim because all offerings in the associated class of products have become generally known by the brand name (usually that of the first or leading brand in that product class).

There is a difference between brand names that are legally generic and those that could be perceived to be generic in the eyes of many consumers. Jell-O is a brand name owned exclusively by General Foods. But to most grocery purchasers the name Jell-O is the descriptive generic name for gelatin dessert. Legal brand names — such as Formica, Xerox, Frigidaire, Kodak, Frisbee, Styrofoam, Coke®, Kleenex, Scotch Tape, Fiberglas, Band-Aid, and Jeep — are often used by consumers in a descriptive manner. Xerox is such a well-known brand name that it is frequently used as a verb. British and Australian consumers often use the brand name Hoover as a verb for vacuuming.

To prevent their brand names from being ruled descriptive and available for general use, companies must take deliberate steps to inform the public of their exclusive ownership of brand names. They may resort to legal action in cases of infringement. The Eastman Kodak Company developed a series of advertisements around the theme "If it isn't an Eastman, it isn't a Kodak." Coca-Cola Ltd. and many other companies use the ® symbol for registration immediately after their brand names. Coca-Cola sends letters to newspapers, novelists, and other writers who use the name Coke® with a lowercase first letter, informing them that the trademark is owned by Coca-Cola. Walt Disney Co. actively protects its brand names and is prepared to sue if necessary. West Edmonton Mall learned this the hard way when it lost a ten-year court battle with Disney over its indoor amusement park named Fantasyland. It lost an estimated $5 million in replacing all the Fantasyland signs and paraphernalia associated with the name. Thus, companies may face the ironic dilemma of attempting to retain the exclusive rights to a brand name that, chiefly due to the success of their own marketing efforts, could become generic to a large market segment if they do not take appropriate steps to protect their trademarks.

Since any dictionary word may eventually be ruled to be a generic name, some companies create new words to use for brand names. Such brand names as Keds, Rinso, and Kodak have obviously been created by their owners.

Brand Loyalty Categories

Brand vary widely in consumer familiarity and acceptance.[19] While a boating enthusiast may insist on a Mercury outboard motor, one study revealed that 40 percent of homemakers could not identify the brands of furniture in their own homes.[20]

Brand loyalty may be measured in three stages: brand recognition, brand preference, and brand insistence.

Brand recognition is a company's first objective for newly introduced products — *to make them familiar to consumers.* Often the company achieves this goal through advertising. Sometimes it uses free samples or coupons offering discounts for purchases. Several new brands of toothpaste have been introduced on college campuses through free samples contained in Campus Pacs. Once the consumer has used the product, it moves from the "unknown" to the "known" category, and provided the consumer was satisfied with the trial sample, he or she is more likely to repurchase it.

brand recognition
The first stage of brand loyalty; situation in which a firm has developed enough publicity for a brand that its name is familiar to consumers.

Brand preference is the second stage of brand loyalty. Because of previous experience with the product, *consumers will choose it rather than one of its competitors — if it is available.* Even if students in a classroom prefer Coca-Cola® as a means of quenching their thirst, almost all of them will quickly switch to Pepsi-Cola or 7-Up when they discover that the vending machine has no Coca-Cola® and the nearest supply is two buildings away. Companies with products at the brand-preference stage are in a favourable position with respect to competing in their industries.

brand preference
The second stage of brand loyalty; situation in which, based on previous experience, consumers will choose a product rather than one of its competitors — if it is available.

The ultimate stage in brand loyalty is **brand insistence**, which occurs when *consumers will accept no alternatives and will search extensively for the product*. Such a product has achieved a monopoly position with this group of consumers. Even though brand insistence may be the goal of many firms, it is seldom achieved. Only the most exclusive specialty goods attain this position with a large segment of the total market.

brand insistence
The ultimate stage of brand loyalty; occurs when consumers will accept no alternatives and will search extensively for the product.

The importance of brand loyalty A study of twelve patented drugs (including well-known drugs like Librium and Darvon) illustrates the importance of brand loyalty. The research indicated that patent expiration had a minimal effect on the drugs' market shares or price levels, a resiliency credited to the brand loyalty for the pioneer product in the field.[21] Another measure of the importance of brand loyalty is found in the Brand Utility Yardstick used by the J. Walter Thompson advertising agency. These ratings measure the percentage of buyers who remain brand-loyal even if a 50 percent cost savings is available from generic products. Beer consumers were very loyal, with 48 percent refusing to switch. Sinus-remedy buyers were also brand-loyal, with a 44 percent rating. By contrast, only 13 percent of the aluminum-foil buyers would not switch to the generic product.[22]

Some brands are so popular that they are carried over to unrelated products because of their marketing advantages. *The decision to use a popular brand name for a new product entry in an unrelated product category* is known as **brand extension**. This should not be confused with line extension (discussed earlier in this chapter), which refers to adding new sizes, styles, or related products. Brand extension, by contrast, refers only to carrying over the brand name.

brand extension
The decision to use a popular brand name for a new product entry in an unrelated product category.

Examples of brand extension are abundant in contemporary marketing. Pears soap has been extended to the Pears shampoo line. Bic used the brand name developed for its pens and applied it to disposable razors. Similarly, General Foods is extending its Jell-O brand: in some markets the company now has Jell-O Pudding Pops, Jell-O Slice Creme, and Jell-O Gelatin Pops.

Choosing a Brand Strategy

Brands may be classified as family brands or individual brands. A **family brand** is *one brand name used for several related products*. E.D. Smith markets dozens of food products under the E.D. Smith brand. Black & Decker has a complete line of power tools under the Black and Decker name. Johnson & Johnson offers parents a line of baby powder, lotions, plastic pants, and baby shampoo under one name.

family brand
Brand name used for several related products.

On the other hand, such manufacturers as Procter & Gamble market hundreds of products with **individual brands** (for example, Tide, Cheer, Crest, Gleem, Oxydol, and Dash). Each such item is *known by its own brand name rather than by the name of the company producing it or an umbrella name covering similar items*. Individual brands are more expensive to market, since a new promotional program must be developed to introduce each new product to its target market.

individual brand
Brand that is known by its own brand name rather than by the name of the company producing it or an umbrella name covering similar items.

Using family brands allows promotional outlays to benefit all products in the line. The effect of the promotion is spread over each of the products. A new addition to the products marketed by the H.J. Heinz Company gains immediate recognition due to the well-known family brand. Family brands also facilitate the task of introducing the product — for both the customer and the retailer. Since supermarkets carry an average of nearly 10 000 items in stock, they are reluctant to add new products unless they are convinced of potential demand. A marketer of a new brand of turtle soup would have to promise the supermarket-chain buyer huge advertising outlays for promotion and evidence of consumer buying intent before getting the product into the stores. The Campbell Soup Company, with approximately 85 percent of the market, would merely add the new flavour to its existing line and could secure store placements much more easily than could a company using individual brand names.

Family brands should be used only when the associated products are of similar quality — or the firm risks the danger of harming its product image. Using the Mercedes brand name on a new, less expensive auto model might severely tarnish the image of the other models in the Mercedes product line.

Individual brand names should be used for dissimilar products. Campbell Soup once marketed a line of dry soups under the brand name Red Kettle. Large marketers of grocery products (such as Procter & Gamble, General Foods, and Lever Brothers) employ individual brands to appeal to unique market segments. Unique brands also allow the firm to stimulate competition within the organization and to increase total company sales. Product managers are also freer to try different merchandising techniques with individual brands. Consumers who do not prefer Tide may choose Dash or Oxydol rather than purchase a competitor's brand.

National Brands or Private Brands?

national brand (manufacturer's brand)
A brand promoted and distributed by a manufacturer.

private brand
A brand promoted and distributed by a wholesaler or retailer.

Most of the brands mentioned in this chapter have been **manufacturers' brands**, also commonly termed **national brands**. But, to an increasing extent, large wholesalers and retailers operating over a regional or national market are placing their own brands on the products that they market. These *brands offered by wholesalers and retailers* are usually called **private brands**. Loblaws' popular President's Choice line is one example. Eaton's carries its own brands, such as Viking, Birkdale, Haddon Hall, Eatonia, and Teco. Safeway store shelves are filled with such company brands as Edwards, Town House, Empress, and Taste Tells. Safeway brands represent a large percentage of all products in an average Safeway supermarket.

For a large retailer such as Eaton's, Loblaws, or Canadian Tire, private brands allow the firm to establish an image and to attain greater control over the products that it handles. Quality levels, prices, and availability of the products become the responsibility of the retailer or wholesaler who develops a line of private brands.

Even though the manufacturers' brands are largely presold through national promotional efforts, the wholesaler and retailer may easily lose customers, since the same products may be available in competing stores. But only Eaton's handles the Viking line of appliances. By eliminating the promotional costs of the manufacturers' brands, the dealer may be able to offer a private brand at a lower price than the competing national brands — or make higher margins. Both consumers and the company benefit. As private brands achieve increasing brand loyalty they may even enable a retailer to avoid some price competition, since the brand can be sold only by the brand owner.

BATTLE OF THE BRANDS

Competition among manufacturers' brands and the private brands offered by wholesalers and large retailers has been called the "battle of the brands." Although the battle appears to be intensifying, the marketing impact varies widely among industries. One survey showed that private brands represented 36 percent of the market in replacement tires but only 7 percent in portable appliances. A full 52 percent of shoe sales involve private brands. For example, Sears and Bata stores distribute their own private brands. Department stores capture about 53 percent of heavy-appliance sales, most of which are private brands.[23]

Retailers with their own brands become customers of the manufacturer, who place the chains' private brands on the products that the firm produces. Such leading corporations as Westinghouse, Armstrong Rubber, and Heinz obtain an increasingly larger percentage of total sales through private labels.

Manufacturers often debate whether they should serve the private brand market. On the one hand, potential orders are large, so marketing efforts can be reduced. On the other hand, the manufacturer can become dependent on one or two retailers rather than remaining independent by serving a broad range of customers.

Generic Products

Food and household staples characterized by plain labels, little or no advertising, and no brand names are called **generic products**. Generic products were first sold in Europe, where their prices were as much as 30 percent below brand-name products. By 1979, they had captured 40 percent of total volume in European supermarkets.

This new version of private brands has received significant acceptance in Canada. Surveys indicate that both professional, college-educated consumers and lower-income, blue-collar consumers are heavy purchasers of generics. Most shoppers have experimented with generic products and formed opinions about those that are acceptable to them.

In the retail food industry there are thus three types of brands. Manufacturers promote their own national brands. Retailers promote, to a limited degree, private brands (for example, Canadian Tire and President's Choice), and generic brands are available at the low end for those who are prepared to accept a wider variation in quality and little information about the product.

generic products
Food and household staples characterized by plain labels, little or no advertising, and no brand names.

PACKAGING

In a very real sense, the package is a vital part of the total product. Indeed, in an overcrowded supermarket, packaging very often *is* the significant difference between one product and another. Take Nabob, for example. Nabob coffee was packaged in a new type of tough, vacuum-seal package that gave the coffee greater freshness. "Five years ago our market share [of the ground coffee market] was 5 percent" says John Bell, vice-president of marketing. "Today we have 26 percent."[24]

Packaging represents a vital component of the total product concept. Its importance can be inferred from the size of the packaging industry. Approximately $9.1 billion is spent annually on packaging in Canada.[25] Packaging costs in the food industry as a percentage of net processed food sales range from 4 to 59 percent, averaging about 22 percent. In cases where packaging costs seem to be disproportionately high, cost of ingredients (e.g., salt) have been found to be very low.

The package has several objectives, which can be grouped into three general categories: (1) protection against damage, spoilage, and pilferage; (2) assistance in marketing the product; and (3) cost-effectiveness.

Protection against Damage, Spoilage, and Pilferage

The original purpose of packaging was to offer physical protection. The typical product is handled several times between manufacture and consumer purchase, and its package must protect the contents against damage. Perishable products must also be protected against spoilage in transit, in storage, or while awaiting selection by the consumer.

Another important role provided by many packages is in preventing pilferage, which at the retail level is very costly (even "sampling" from bulk food displays has become a major cost concern for retailers). Many products are packaged with over-sized cardboard backings too large to fit into a shoplifter's pocket or purse. Large plastic bags are used in a similar manner on such products as cassette tapes.

Assisting to Market the Product

Package designers frequently use marketing research in testing alternative designs. Increasingly scientific approaches are used in designing a package that is attractive, safe, and aesthetically appealing. Kellogg, for instance, has been known to test the package for a new product as well as the product itself.[26]

In a grocery store containing as many as 15 000 different items, a product must capture the shopper's attention. Walter Margulies, chairman of Lippincott & Margulies advertising agency, summarizes the importance of first impressions in the retail store: "Consumers are more intelligent [these days], but they don't read as much. They relate to pictures." Margulies also cites another factor: one of every six shoppers who needs eyeglasses does not wear them while shopping. Consequently, many marketers offering product lines are adopting similar package designs throughout the line in order to create more visual impact in the store. The adoption of common package designs by such product lines as Weight Watchers foods and Planter's nuts represents attempts to dominate larger sections of retail stores the way Campbell does.[27]

Packages can also offer the consumer convenience. Pump-type dispensers facilitate the use of products ranging from mustard to insect repellent. Pop-top cans provide added convenience for soft drinks and for other food products. The six-pack carton, first introduced by Coca-Cola® in the 1930s, can be carried with minimal effort by the food shopper.

A growing number of firms provide increasing consumer utility with packages designed for reuse. Peanut butter jars and jelly jars have long been used as drinking glasses. Bubble bath can be purchased in plastic bottles shaped like animals and suitable for bathtub play. Packaging is a major component in Avon's overall marketing strategy. The firm's decorative reusable bottles have even become collectibles.

Hershey Canada launched its Life Savers Sours in January 1993 to capitalize on changing taste trends and revitalize its core Life Savers business. Thanks to aggressive marketing and a vibrant brand identity design created by Flight Path Design (which won a Design Effective Award), sales of Life Savers Sours were double initial forecasts. At the same time, awareness and approval of the 80-year-old Life Savers brand among the all-important teen market has measurably increased.

Cost-Effective Packaging

Although packaging must perform a number of functions for the producer, marketer, and consumer, it must accomplish them at a reasonable cost. Packaging currently represents the single largest item in the cost of producing numerous products. For example, it accounts for 70 percent of the total cost of the single-serving packets of sugar found in restaurants. However, restaurants continue to use the packets because of the saving in wastage and in washing and refilling sugar containers.

Environmentally safer packaging has become a concern in recent years, as evidenced by this example:

Procter & Gamble has introduced a new, less expensive, more environmentally compatible package for eight of its liquid products. The company estimates that 15 to 25 percent of consumers who use those products will choose to buy them in the new format. That would mean five million fewer plastic bottles — about 700 fewer dump trucks — going to Canadian dumps annually.[28]

An excellent illustration of how packaging can be cost-effective is provided by the large Swedish firm Tetra-Pak, which pioneered aseptic packaging for products like milk and juice. Aseptic packaging wraps a laminated paper around a sterilized product and seals it off. The big advantage of this packaging technology is that products so treated can be kept unrefrigerated for months. Aseptically packaged sterilized milk, for instance, will keep its nutritional qualities and flavour for six months. With 60 percent of a supermarket's energy bill going for refrigeration, aseptic packaging is certainly cost-effective. The paper packaging is also cheaper and lighter than the cans and bottles used for unrefrigerated fruit juices. Handling costs can also be reduced in many cases.[29] These containers have recently been criticized because of ecological concerns over recycling. Tetra-Pak has responded aggressively, showing that its containers can be recycled into such items as picnic furniture.

Labelling

Sometimes the label is a separate item applied to the package, but most of today's plastic packages contain the label as an integral part of the package. Labels perform both a promotional and an informational function. A **label** in most instances *contains (1) the brand name or symbol, (2) the name and address of the manufacturer or distributor, (3) information about product composition and size, and (4) information about recommended uses of the product.*

Government-set and voluntary packaging and label standards have been developed in most industries. The law requires a listing of food ingredients, in descending order of the amounts used, and the labels of such companies as the Del Monte Corporation now show specific food values and include a calorie count and a list of vitamins and minerals. In other industries (such as drugs, fur, and clothing), federal legislation requires the provision of various information and prevents false branding. The marketing manager in such industries must be fully acquainted with these laws and must design the package and label in compliance with these requirements.

The informational aspect of a label is particularly noteworthy. People who condemn all types of elaborate or fancy packaging fail to realize that the information on the label and the nature of the container enhance the product itself. In some

label
The part of a package that contains (1) the brand name or symbol, (2) the name and address of the manufacturer or distributor, (3) information about product composition and size, and (4) information about recommended uses of the product.

cases, the dispenser is almost as important as the contents and is really an integral part of the total "product." Furthermore, with the advent of self-service nearly everywhere, the information on the label takes the place of a salesperson. Self-service improves marketing efficiency and lowers costs.

Universal Product Code (UPC)

The Universal Product Code (UPC) designation is another very important part of a label or package. Most grocery items display the zebra-stripe UPC on the label or package. The **Universal Product Code**, which was introduced to cut expenses in the supermarket industry, is *a code readable by optical scanners that can print the name of the item and the price on the cash register receipt.*

The advantages of optical scanning include

1. Labour saving (because products are no longer individually priced)
2. Faster customer check-out
3. Better inventory control, since the scanner can be tied to inventory records
4. Easier marketing research for the industries involved with it
5. Fewer errors in entering purchases at the check-out counter

PRODUCT SAFETY

If the product is to fulfil its mission of satisfying consumer needs, it must above all be safe. Manufacturers must design their products in such a way as to protect not only children but all consumers who use them. Packaging can play an important role in product safety. The law requires that bottle tops on dangerous products such as pharmaceuticals be child-proof (some are virtually parent-proof). This safety feature has reduced by two-thirds the number of children under 5 years of age who swallow dangerous doses of ASA. Prominent safety warnings on the labels of such potentially hazardous products as cleaning fluids and drain cleaners inform users about the dangers of these products and urge purchasers to store them out of the reach of children. Changes in product design have reduced the dangers involved in the use of such products as lawn mowers, hedge trimmers, and toys.

The need for fire-retardant fabrics for children's sleepwear was recognized long before federal regulations were established. While fire-retardant fabrics were available, the problems lay in how to produce them to meet consumer requirements for softness, colour, texture, durability, and reasonable cost. Today, government flame-retardancy standards are strictly enforced.

Federal and provincial legislation has long played a major role in promoting product safety. The **Hazardous Products Act**, passed in 1969, was *a major piece of legislation that consolidated previous legislation and set significant new standards for product safety.* The Act defines a hazardous product as any product that is included in a list (called a schedule) compiled by Consumer and Corporate Affairs Canada or Health and Welfare Canada. Any consumer product considered to be a hazard to public health or safety may be listed in the schedule. Table 10.3 lists some of the main items and outlines the regulations that affect them.

The Act itself comprises just fifteen clauses. Those relating to criminal penalties and seizure put sharp teeth in the law. Inspectors designated under the Act have powers of search and seizure. Hazardous products inspectors may enter, at any rea-

Universal Product Code
A code readable by optical scanners that can print the name of the item and the price on the cash register receipt.

Hazardous Products Act
A major piece of legislation that consolidated previous legislation and set significant new standards for product safety; defines a hazardous product as any product that is included in a list (called a schedule) compiled by Consumer and Corporate Affairs Canada or Health and Welfare Canada.

■ Table 10.3 **Some Hazardous Products Act Regulations**

Bedding may not be highly flammable.

Children's sleepwear, dressing gowns, and robes must meet flammability standards.

Children's toys or equipment may not contain toxic substances (such as lead pigments) beyond a prescribed limit.

Certain household chemical products must be labelled with appropriate symbols to alert consumers to their hazards.

Hockey helmets must meet safety standards to protect young hockey players.

Pencils and artists' brushes are regulated to limit lead in their decorative coating.

Matches must meet safety standards for strength and packaging.

Safety glass is mandatory in domestic doors and shower enclosures.

Liquid drain cleaners and furniture polishes containing petroleum-based solvents must be sold in child-proof packaging.

Toys and children's playthings must comply with safety standards.

Crib regulations provide for increased child safety.

sonable time, any place where they reasonably believe a hazardous product is manufactured, prepared, packaged, sold, or stored for sale. They may examine the product, take samples, and examine any records believed to contain information relevant to enforcement of the Act. Products that an inspector has reasonable grounds to believe are in contravention of the Act may be seized.

These regulatory activities have prompted companies to voluntarily improve safety standards for their products. For many companies, safety has become a very important ingredient in the broader definition of product.

In conclusion, the management of products is a many-faceted affair. It can involve the way that the organization is structured, both in the development of new products and the management of them. Product management also includes an analysis of the product mix, as well as the appropriate branding and packaging of each product. And, as always, such decisions must be made in the light of the marketing strategy, and in harmony with the rest of the elements of the marketing mix.

■ KEY TERMS

product mix
product line
individual offering
cannibalizing
line extension
product improvement strategy
market development strategy
product development strategy
product diversification strategy

product managers (brand managers)
venture-team concept
concept testing
test marketing
brand
brand name
trademark
generic name
brand recognition
brand preference
brand insistence
brand extension

family brand
individual brand
national brand (manufacturer's brand)
private brand
generic products
label
Universal Product Code
Hazardous Products Act

■ INTERACTIVE SUMMARY AND DISCUSSION QUESTIONS

1. A product mix is the assortment of product lines and individual offerings available from a company. Product mixes are typically measured by width and depth of assortment.
   a. Describe the product mix by depth and width for a company having ten or more products.
   b. Indicate where each product type is in the life cycle for that product category.
2. A line extension is the development of individual offerings that appeal to different market segments but are closely related to the existing product line. Explain this using the photocopier market as an example.
3. In product development, many initial ideas fall by the wayside. This is known as the product decay curve. Draw a typical decay curve of new-product ideas, indicating the related phases: screening, business analysis, development, testing, and commercialization.
4. Assume you work for the product manager of a company in the consumer electronics business. You have been asked to write your manager a memo on determinants of success for new products. Base your memo on the chapter material.
5. There are four product development strategies: product improvement, market development, product development, and product diversification. In what instances would each strategy be appropriate?
6. Organizational structures used to make product-planning decisions are new-product committees, new-product departments, product managers, and venture teams. Explain and discuss the advantages of each.
7. Product managers are individuals assigned one product or product line and given responsibility for determining its objectives and marketing strategies. Do you think they would do as good a job at suggesting and initiating new products as they do at managing existing products? Why or why not?
8. The stages of the new-product development process are outlined in Figure 10.3. With two or three classmates, develop a product strategy for a product category of your choice. Then brainstorm an extensive list of product ideas. Following this, look more closely at the list and screen it into those that seem to have the most potential. Finally, suggest some ways of performing a business analysis for the remaining candidates.
9. In parallel with product introduction decisions, there will normally be product deletion decisions. Give some examples of products that have been (or should be) deleted.
10. A brand is a name, term, sign, symbols, or design (or some combination of these) used to identify and differentiate the products of a firm. What constitutes a good brand name?
11. Three brand loyalty categories are brand recognition, brand preference, and brand insistence. Explain and discuss the importance of these categories to the marketer.
12. Companies choose different types of branding strategy: family brands, individual brands, national brands, and private brands. Explain and discuss each.
13. Packaging has the following main objectives: protection against damage, spoilage, and pilferage; assistance in marketing the product; and cost-effectiveness. Find examples of products that fulfil all of these objectives.

CHAPTER 11

Services

1. To elaborate on the discussion of products by exploring the "service product."
2. To discuss the similarities and differences between goods and services.
3. To explain the four main characteristics of services.
4. To outline the major issues that must be addressed by marketers for each of the characteristics.
5. To show the main methods marketers use to address these issues.

Letters, documents, computer parts: they're routine cargo for courier companies. But the world's most expensive teddy? That's what DHL Worldwide Express once handled — an $86 350 antique teddy. It was sent to Southern California from London. The bear, purchased anonymously, was intended as a 25th anniversary gift.

The shipment, of course, required special handling. The bear was put aboard a regular commercial flight and given a DHL employee as an escort. The bruin was even assigned a separate seat.

The teddy bear isn't the only unusual item DHL has moved. The company once flew medical supplies and baby diapers from London to a gorilla orphanage in Brazzaville, Congo. DHL has also airlifted six quarts of ice cream from Minneapolis to a sheik in Saudi Arabia who wanted to go into the ice cream business, but who first wanted to sample the product.

Federal Express Canada has moved deer from Canada to China, as well as race horses, parrots, and rare budgies.[1]

Since the typical goods moved by courier services are envelopes and packages, the above-mentioned deliveries might be called oddities. On the other hand, another way of looking at them is as an indication of the lengths to which a company specializing in services will go for its customers. These are examples of what an effective service organization can do. Customers' needs can be better addressed with services tailored to meet them. Customers are willing to buy such a service, provided that they view it as good value and they have confidence in the service firm. People have to trust the service well enough to buy it *before* they try it.

INTRODUCTION

As Chapter 1 states, a service is a type of product. For the most part, discussions about the marketing of goods apply to services as well. Some, in fact, would argue that since they *are* products, services should not be treated in a separate chapter. But services have a number of important special characteristics that differentiate them from goods.

Figure 11.1 clarifies the relationships among these concepts. General marketing notions, approaches, and theories apply to both goods and services. However, some techniques and ideas are relatively exclusive to services marketing; others, to goods marketing. And within either type of marketing, distinctions may also be made among various industries or various marketing situations.[2]

The service sector today is so large that a good understanding of it is necessary. In Canada, services account for more than 47 percent of consumer expenditures (compared with 15.6 percent for durable goods, 10.2 percent for semi-durables, and 27.1 percent for nondurable goods). A recent report published by the General Agreement on Tariffs and Trade (GATT) estimates that total trade in services among that organization's 96 nations has reached $560 billion (U.S.).[3]

service
A product without physical characteristics; a bundle of performance and symbolic attributes designed to produce consumer want satisfaction.

tangible attributes
Those attributes that can be experienced by the physical senses, such as sight, touch, and smell.

intangible attributes
Those attributes that cannot be experienced by the physical senses.

SERVICES VERSUS GOODS

A **service** is *a product without physical characteristics — a bundle of performance and symbolic attributes designed to produce consumer want satisfaction.* Leonard Berry states that "the pivotal difference between goods businesses and services businesses is that goods businesses sell *things* and service businesses sell *performances*."[4] In other words, goods are produced, whereas services are performed.

Despite the relatively clear-cut definition of a service, many products have *both* **tangible and intangible attributes**. For example, a pail of fertilizer sold by a farm-

■ Figure 11.1 **Services Marketing in Context**

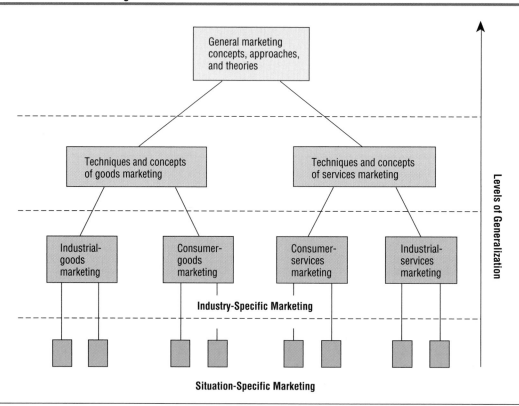

Source: A. Rushton and D. Carson, "The Marketing of Services: Managing the Intangibles," *European Journal of Marketing* (1989), p. 25. Reprinted by permission of M.C.B. University Press Ltd.

If you really want to be certain, look into UPS.

1-800-PICK-UPS

Customers who want to send parcels safely and quickly look to courier companies for such a service. What they are buying is the peace of mind that comes from knowing their package will reach its destination on time. Recognizing these customer needs, United Parcel Service's advertisement promises safe and on-time delivery.

supply dealer to a farmer seems like a pure good. However, if that dealer also provides expertise — for example, counselling about its application — a service is added. Consequently, it is more accurate to consider products as falling on a spectrum between "tangible elements dominant" and "intangible elements dominant" (see Figure 11.2).

Buying Promises

As mentioned earlier, potential customers often have difficulties conceptualizing the service product, because it has no physical properties. Basically, they are buying promises. No product trial or return is possible. Three types of product properties are attached to every good or service: **search qualities**, **experience qualities**, and **credence qualities**.[5] Products that can be physically examined and compared are high in *search* qualities. Others are primarily assessed on the basis of the *experience* of using them. They include a large proportion of both tangible and intangible attributes. Products with *credence* qualities are those for which, even after purchasing, the buyer must simply trust that the supplier has performed the correct service. Figure 11.3 shows this range of product properties. In intangibles, credence (buying a promise) and experience qualities dominate, while search qualities are central for tangible products.

search qualities
Physical qualities that enable products to be examined and compared. This eases the task of choosing between them.

experience qualities
Characteristics of products that can be assessed mainly through using them.

credence qualities
Qualities for which, even after purchasing, the buyer must simply trust that the supplier has performed the correct service.

CHARACTERISTICS OF SERVICES

Four unique characteristics of services distinguish them from goods: *intangibility, inseparability of production and consumption, heterogeneity,* and *perishability.*

■ Figure 11.2 **Goods and Services: Scale of Elemental Dominance**

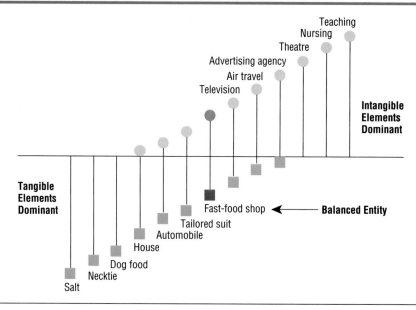

Source: A. Rushton and D. Carson, "The Marketing of Services: Managing the Intangibles," *European Journal of Marketing* (1989), p. 29. Reprinted by permission of M.C.B. University Press Ltd.

APPLYING THE CONCEPTS

Why the Service Segment Is So Important

A question for businessman's Trivial Pursuit: what is the world's biggest civilian industry? The answer, it seems, is travel and tourism. It has worldwide sales of some $2 trillion. Quite staggering — that is 5% of all global sales of goods and services.

In a recent study of some 200 developed and developing countries by Wharton Econometric Forecasting Associates on behalf of American Express, a charge card to travel agency business whose commercial interest is self-evident, travel and tourism was found to be the biggest industry by almost any measure. Its definition of the industry is broad (including such things as railways, sightseeing buses, taxicabs, hotels, restaurants, theatres and museums), but the figures remain impressive — however they are added up.

If travel and tourism were a country, its GNP would rank fifth in the world after the United States, the Soviet Union, Japan and West Germany. Value added, the industry's direct contribution to GNP, is worth nearly $950 billion: $516 billion in employee wages; $268 billion in cash available for investment and dividends; and a whopping $166 billion in tax payments — more than the GNP of Austria or Belgium. In most of the 200 countries studies by the Wharton group this is also more than the added value of agriculture, steel, electronics, and other more-familiar industries whose grandees are frequently consulted by governments when trying to decide economic and social policy.

(continued)

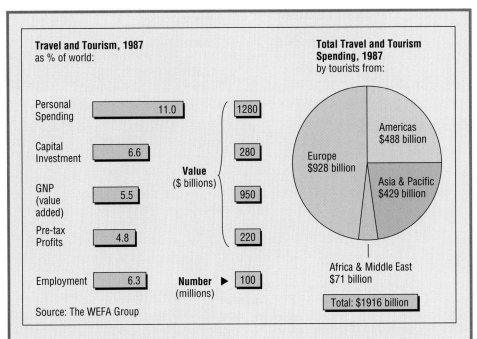

Travel and Tourism, 1987 as % of world:

Personal Spending	11.0
Capital Investment	6.6
GNP (value added)	5.5
Pre-tax Profits	4.8
Employment	6.3

Value ($ billions)

	1280
	280
	950
	220

Number ▶ 100 (millions)

Source: The WEFA Group

Total Travel and Tourism Spending, 1987 by tourists from:

Americas $488 billion

Europe $928 billion

Asia & Pacific $429 billion

Africa & Middle East $71 billion

Total: $1916 billion

The industry is also the largest employer in almost every country, accounting for one out of every 16 jobs worldwide. It purchases some $1 trillion worth of goods and services each year. And its new capital expenditure of $280 billion, 7% of the world total, is larger than many key manufacturing industries, such as cars and textiles.

Where do the industry's raw materials, travellers and tourists, come from? Businesses and governments spend some $600 billion a year on travel and associated "tourist" costs such as accommodation and food. That is about 2% of their total costs. The rest, nearly $1.3 trillion, is spent by people travelling at their own expense. Time for another holiday to do your bit for the world economy?

Source: "The Business of Going Away," *The Economist* (April 15, 1989), p. 73. © 1989 The Economist Newspaper Ltd. Reprinted with permission.

What local businesses in your area might benefit more from this tourism trade if they should choose to make the effort?

Intangibility

Unlike goods, which can be displayed before the sale, services cannot be seen, smelled, or touched. The student who goes to a counsellor for assistance in deciding what kind of a career to choose cannot foretell the result of that counselling service. J. Bateson believes that besides being physically intangible, services can also be mentally intangible, because it is sometimes hard for the human mind to grasp them.[6]

The intangibility of services creates a number of marketing problems:

Services cannot be stored. A Canadian Airlines plane provides a transportation service for 90 people to fly from Montreal to Vancouver. Revenue from empty seats is lost forever.

Services cannot be protected through patents. Patents apply to physical objects. Thus, because they are intangible, services are ineligible for patents. This can create a real problem for a services marketer, since the service can easily be copied.

■ Figure 11.3 **Intangibility and Customer Evaluation**

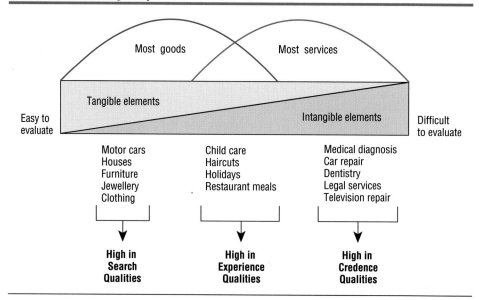

Source: A. Rushton and D. Carson, "The Marketing of Services: Managing the Intangibles," *European Journal of Marketing* (1989), p. 31. Reprinted by permission of M.C.B. University Press Ltd.

It is hard to readily display or communicate services. It is easy to show a good, allowing potential customers to hold, handle, or try it out before purchase. That way, they can get a good idea of whether or not the good will satisfy their needs. In the case of a service, a purchaser must purchase in order to experience it.

Prices are difficult to set. At the best of times, pricing is complex. In the case of a good, each of its components can be costed out, which helps in determining what it is worth. Costing out, say, an accountant's services proves to be much more complex.

MARKETING STRATEGIES TO SOLVE THE PROBLEMS OF INTANGIBILITY

Some of the above-mentioned problems cannot be avoided. But certain marketing strategies can help resolve others, particularly the problem of marketing communication. Because services are so intangible, many marketers *stress tangible cues* in advertising and selling. For example, advertisements for long-distance phone calling dramatize the pleasure on the face of a loved one receiving a call. Marketing messages should also *use personal sources more than nonpersonal sources.* Thus a recommendation for life insurance would likely be more persuasive if it came from John Hanchuck, rather than the more impersonal Life Insurance Council. The personal source adds tangibility to the service.

Services marketers also have found that it is helpful to *stimulate word-of-mouth communications.* If a purchaser can be induced — through the superior service received or by other incentives — to speak to friends and acquaintances positively about a service, that service will tend to be purchased by those people. *Engaging in postpurchase communications* is a related useful strategy. For example, a provider of financial counselling services might write a letter to a new client assuring the client of the wise choices she or he made.

Services marketers also try to *create a strong image* of their organization. This is a very important approach affecting the choice of a service. Since potential pur-

chasers cannot physically evaluate the product offered, they may be reassured that they are purchasing a service from a well-known organization.

Finally, with respect to the difficulty of setting prices, it has been found useful to *develop a strong cost accounting system.* Such a system enables an accurate and realistic analysis of various costs involved in the operation. This information provides a strong foundation for setting the ultimate price of the service.

Inseparability of Production and Consumption

Whereas goods are first produced, then sold, and then consumed, services are first sold, then produced and consumed simultaneously.[7] The *customer* therefore *has an active role during production* of the service. For instance, professional legal counselling is consumed at the same time as the service of providing legal advice is performed. The client raises questions, seeks opinions, and responds with the details required by the lawyer.

The **inseparability** of production and consumption also results in marketing problems: (1) consumers are involved in production, so performance depends on the quality of input from the customer, as well as on the relationship between the customer and the provider; (2) other consumers are involved in production; and (3) centralized mass production of services is difficult.

Other consumers are involved in production. Many services are offered in a setting with other people present. For example, the service provided by a restaurant server is performed not just for one customer, but for many simultaneously. This fact can have a number of positive and negative influences on the service actually experienced by an individual buyer. For instance, the presence of others can distract a server, or create so much pressure that service is negatively affected.

Centralized mass production of services is difficult. Services are normally provided where the people are. Whereas Honda might have one or two factories to serve the entire country, Royal Bank must have many "little factories" (branches) in each city.

Air Canada recognizes the intangibility of services and, therefore, tries to solve the marketing problems created by this. By positioning itself with the new Toronto Raptors basketball team, Air Canada is marketing its service as being of such quality that it is sought even by basketball celebrities. Moreover, the ever-increasing popularity and recognition of the Raptors' name and logo provides a good marketing tool for selling Air Canada's service.

inseparability
A characteristic of services in which the product is produced and consumed simultaneously.

Cost efficiencies and standardization are therefore difficult to achieve because there are so many producers (people) involved.

MARKETING STRATEGIES TO SOLVE THE PROBLEMS OF INSEPARABILITY

With services, since production and consumption occur simultaneously and in the same place, production personnel have a tremendous impact on consumers' perceptions of product acceptability. It is therefore essential to *emphasize the selection and training of public-contact personnel.* Personnel not only have to perform the service well, but must be able to interact in a positive manner with the customer. The famous Avis "We Try Harder" program was based on this principle.

Multi-site locations may help offset the fact that services cannot be "sent" from a warehouse to a retail outlet. Banking, travel counselling, and other such services must be produced and consumed where consumers shop. Developing, managing, and maintaining so many locations is a major task for the marketer. This is one of the reasons why employment in the service sector is so high.

Managing customer flows also helps to make the "inseparability" condition positive for both buyer and seller. Customer flows can be facilitated by guiding, directing, and expediting their movements and interactions in the service situation. For example, banks channel the flow of customers to tellers through specially laid-out channels. Restaurants provide chairs for or seat waiting customers in lounges while they wait for a table to become available.

Heterogeneity

Services are highly variable. Because they are performed by a provider, who is a fallible human being, they are difficult to standardize. Service providers can vary in skill and training, and individual performance can vary from day to day. Furthermore, performance varies from individual to individual. A customer may pay the same price for a hair styling at the same shop on subsequent dates from two different people, with far from similar outcomes.

The main marketing problem arising from heterogeneity is that *standardization and quality control are difficult to achieve.* Services marketers try to overcome this problem by *industrializing the service or customizing it.* To industrialize a service, Levitt has suggested substituting organized, preplanned systems for individual service operations. For example, a travel agency could offer prepackaged vacation tours to remove the need for the selling, tailoring, and haggling involved in customization.[8] Customization — the opposite of industrialization — is another possible solution. If each service is produced for an individual customer, the problem of standardization disappears.

Perishability

A service cannot be stored. No service can be produced before required, and then stocked up to meet future demand. Whatever is not used when available is wasted. Motel rooms not occupied, airline seats not purchased, and telephone line capacity not used cannot be reclaimed. Because of this, service businesses frequently find it difficult to balance supply and demand. The fact that *services cannot be inventoried* is a major problem with services.

The problem of perishability can be solved to some degree by *using strategies to cope with fluctuating demand.* Restaurants, airlines, and other service businesses often give special discounts to those who use the service in periods of low demand. This

I see leather bucket seats, four on the floor, and wide performance tires that shine in the sun.

I see cruising downtown, then heading over to the beach, and then doing it all over again. Just driving for the sake of driving.

I see myself shifting into overdrive, and it's like that car has been waiting for this moment as long as I have. And I hear that hungry purr turn into an angry roar.

And if that car had a set of wings, man, it would fly."

Personalvision™
Car Ownership

If you have a goal that you would like to see fulfilled, your CIBC personal banker would like to help. We can show you how to realize your goals and become loan free faster. We offer:

- custom tailored loans
- competitive rates on all loans

At CIBC we're working hard to help you get from where you are today to where you want to be tomorrow.

Call 1-800-465-CIBC

CIBC
We see what *you* see.™

"I see a classic cherry red convertible, purring along like a hungry cat. With me behind the wheel.

An important part of a bank's services is providing loans for its customers. The interaction between customer and bank representative is something that cannot be standardized, since each person's needs are different, as is each representative's way of meeting those needs. For this reason, the CIBC emphasizes custom-tailored loans and loan officers who provide a service suited to a particular customer.

shifts some demand from high to low periods. A second approach to the perishability problem is to *make simultaneous adjustments in demand and capacity to achieve a closer match between the two.* Capacity can often be increased by adding staff or equipment at peak times. This approach may be used simultaneously with the previous solution.

Table 11.1 summarizes the foregoing discussion of features that are unique to services, the resulting marketing problems, and suggested marketing solutions. Ziethaml, et al. (from whose important study Table 11.1 is adapted) found that service firms did not view most of the problems as especially serious. The authors speculated that this viewpoint may be founded on the providers' being used to facing these problems. Or, the problems may not in fact be as significant as they first seem.

OTHER STRATEGIES IN SERVICES MARKETING

Internal Marketing

Traditionally, the marketing mix is thought to be oriented toward the external market. While services do face a competitive external environment, they must also contend with an internal market — those who provide the service. Since service producers interact so directly with consumers, the way they feel about their task within the marketing strategy is extremely important. In fact, their feelings directly influence the quality of the service they perform. Leonard Berry has suggested that "internal marketing means applying the philosophy and practices of marketing to

■ Table 11.1 **Unique Service Features and Resulting Marketing Problems and Solutions**

Unique Service Features	Resulting Marketing Problems	Marketing Strategies to Solve Problems
Intangibility	1. Service cannot be stored. 2. Cannot protect services through patents. 3. Cannot readily display or communicate services. 4. Prices are difficult to set.	1. Stress tangible cues. 2. Use personal sources more than nonpersonal sources. 3. Simulate or stimulate word-of-mouth communications. 4. Create strong organizational image. 5. Use cost accounting to help set prices. 6. Engage in postpurchase communications.
Inseparability	1. Consumer involved in production. 2. Other consumers involved in production. 3. Centralized mass production of services difficult.	1. Emphasize selection and training of public-contact personnel. 2. Manage consumers. 3. Use multisite locations.
Heterogeneity	1. Standardization and quality control difficult to achieve.	1. Industrialize service. 2. Customize service.
Perishability	1. Services cannot be inventoried.	1. Use strategies to cope with fluctuating demand. 2. Make simultaneous adjustments in demand and capacity to achieve a closer match between the two.

Source: Adapted from Valarie A. Zeithaml, A. Parasuraman, and Leonard L. Berry, "Problems and Strategies in Services Marketing," *Journal of Marketing* (Spring 1985), p. 35. Reprinted by permission of the American Marketing Association.

the people that serve the external customer so that (1) the best possible people can be employed and retained, and (2) they will do the best possible work."[9]

internal marketing
A marketing effort aimed at those who provide the service so that they will feel better about their task and therefore produce a better product.

The objective of the **internal marketing** function is to develop motivated, customer-conscious, market-oriented, and sales-minded employees. The successful service company must first sell the job to its employees before it can sell its services to customers.[10]

Managing Evidence

As discussed earlier, prospective customers like to associate tangibles with a service for cues as to its quality. Marketers, therefore, must try to manage tangibles to convince customers about the service.

Goods marketing tends to give prime emphasis to creating abstract associations with the product. Services marketers, on the other hand, should focus on enhancing and differentiating the "realities" through manipulation of tangible cues. The management of evidence comes first for services marketers.[11] There are several ways that the evidence can be managed.

The environment Services are totally integrated with their environment. The physical setting — where the service is performed — has a great influence on the customer's mentality. The physical milieu should be intentionally created so as to provide the appropriate situation-specific atmosphere to impress the customer. For example, even though two lawyers might provide identical services, customers still differentiate between the two by the environmental differences. If one decorates her office with leather and subdued carpeting, and the other has a plain painted office with steel-and-formica furniture, customers will judge them accordingly.

Appearance of service providers The appearance of service providers also affects customers' perception of the product. Salespeople in an optical shop wearing white lab coats will look more "professional" than those with ordinary attire.

Service pricing Research confirms that there is a high tendency for customers to perceive a direct relationship between price and quality for service.[12] Price is seen as an index of quality. Professional practitioners may charge an unusually high price for their services in order to assure clients. Setting the right price can be critical in differentiating one service from the crowd.

Organizational Responsibility for Marketing

In many service firms, the organizational responsibility for marketing may be considerably different than in manufacturing companies. In any company there may be confusion about what marketing is. It is frequently considered to be what the marketing department does. Marketing is, however, often carried out by others in the company to some degree. This confusion may be much more acute for service firms than for manufacturing firms and may in fact constitute an organizational dilemma. In many professional service organizations, the marketing department's role may be limited to handling advertising, sales promotion, and some public relations. The "sales force" comprises those people who are in direct contact with customers (for example, the branch managers and tellers in a bank). Except for the people in the marketing department, however, staff members are not hired for their marketing know-how but for their ability to produce services. *Yet the person who produces a service must also be able to market that service.* In most cases, what is needed is not professional salespeople but service workers who sell — in effect, producer-sellers.

The dilemma arises when service firms are insufficiently aware of the need to have personnel who are able to adequately perform both marketing and service-production functions. Furthermore, when the workload is high, too little time may be spent on marketing — an imbalance that will likely have very serious long-term consequences for the organization.

This overview of services concludes our discussion of products. The reader should remember that the term "product" includes services, as well as goods. Life-cycle analysis, as well as product classification systems and other product management processes, can be applied to all products. The next two chapters consider issues concerning price, another element of the marketing mix.

■ KEY TERMS

service	experience qualities	perishability
tangible attributes	credence qualities	internal marketing
intangible attributes	inseparability	managing the evidence
search qualities	heterogeneity	producer-seller

■ INTERACTIVE SUMMARY AND DISCUSSION QUESTIONS

1. A service is a product without physical characteristics — a bundle of performance and symbolic attributes designed to produce consumer want satisfaction. Use banking services to explain this definition.

2. Many products have both tangible and intangible attributes. Select three products not discussed in this chapter and identify for each both types of attributes.

3. Buyers of services are often buying promises. Explain this statement.

4. Four characteristics of services distinguish them from goods: intangibility, inseparability of production and consumption, heterogeneity, and perishability. Explain each of these characteristics.

5. Suggest some marketing strategies to take account of each of the characteristics listed in question 4.

6. In addition to marketing to target market customers, services often have to be marketed internally. Why?

7. Marketers of services must try to manage tangibles to convince customers about the services. Give some examples.

8. Organizational responsibility for marketing services goes beyond those people charged with marketing planning. The person who produces a service must also be able to market that service. Why is this so? How can this requirement be implemented?

9. Describe the last transportation service you purchased. What was your impression of the way it was marketed? How could the firm's marketing effort have been improved?

10. Identify three or four service firms and propose methods by which they could overcome problems with the perishability of their respective services.

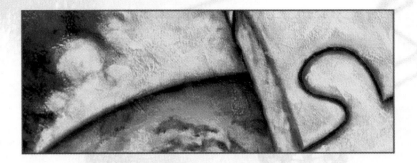

PART FIVE

Pricing

Pricing is a variable of the marketing mix that assumes widely different roles. It requires a considerable amount of science, as well as art, to manage. Part Five consists of two chapters on this critical element in the marketing mix. Chapter 12 examines the role of pricing in the marketing mix, as well as price determination in both theory and practice. Chapter 13 examines various pricing decisions that have to be made, as well as the overall management of this function.

CHAPTER 12

Price Determination

CHAPTER OBJECTIVES

1. To discuss the concept of pricing objectives and their use.
2. To review basic economic pricing principles and the concept of price elasticity.
3. To identify the practical problems involved in applying economics price theory concepts to actual pricing decisions.
4. To outline the major approaches to price setting.
5. To review break-even analysis and discuss its use in pricing decisions.
6. To introduce and show the benefits of the marketing approach to pricing.
7. To present a useful model for setting a price.

In 1994 a press report announced that Compaq Computer Corp was about to start yet another round of price-cutting on personal computers. The report described the strategy as follows:

> This time, Compaq won't be slashing prices, as it did two years previously, in order to survive. Instead, it will be bidding for dominance of the global computer industry.
>
> Once Compaq's new factory space in Texas, Scotland, Singapore, China, and Brazil is completed, the company will have both the capacity and the financial wherewithal to increase its already-leading 12.5 percent share of the PC market.
>
> Compaq isn't announcing price cuts but is planning to roll out a score of new computers. However, the chief financial officer admitted the company's gross profit margin, sales less the cost of goods, is a little high at 26.5 percent, and that they could live with margins as low as 23 percent. That spells "Price war" as Compaq continues its effort to become the top brand in PCs.
>
> Compaq's lead is evident to anyone who looks at income statements. The company's gross margin is more than triple those of smaller rivals like Dell Computer Corp., Gateway 2000 Inc., and Packard-Bell Electronics Inc. Presumably, Compaq's profit margin is far ahead of that of IBM Personal Computer Co., though that rival's results aren't disclosed separately from those of International Business Machines Corp.
>
> Compaq in a price-cutting mood signals trouble for a rival like AST Research, where chairman Safi Qureshey's strategy is to price slightly below Compaq and build market share in places where Compaq is weak, including Southeast Asia.[1]

Compaq's strategy is worth watching. After a number of years of producing a fine product, it ran into difficulties and used a price-cutting strategy to build sales and survive. Then, in anticipation of a much higher volume, it expanded manufacturing capacity greatly, and worked on lowering its costs per unit so that it would have enough profit margin to comfortably cut prices even more. Using price to generate business is a powerful tool, as long as others don't neutralize its effects with deeper cuts.

Pricing decisions can create opportunities or problems for a company. Obviously a decision to cut prices was the right one to help Compaq survive. Combined with other production and marketing decisions, the pending new round of price cutting looks like it could lead to greater sales and profitability.

INTRODUCTION

Part Four examined the first critical element of a firm's marketing mix: the determination of the goods and services to offer the target market. Part Five focusses on price, the second element of the marketing mix. Determination of profitable and justified prices is the result of pricing objectives and various approaches to setting prices, the topics of this chapter. The following chapter focusses on management of the pricing function and discusses pricing strategies, price–quality relationships, and both industrial pricing and the pricing of public services. The starting place for examining pricing strategy is to understand the meaning of the term *price*.

Price is *the value that a buyer exchanges for a good or service, the value of an item being what it can be exchanged for in the marketplace.* This implies that the value is ultimately determined by customers. In earlier times, the price of an acre of land might have been twenty bushels of wheat, three cattle, or a boat. Price is a measure of what one must exchange in order to obtain a desired good or service. When the barter process was abandoned in favour of a monetary system, price became the amount of money required to purchase an item. As David Schwartz has pointed out, contemporary society uses a number of terms to refer to price:

> Price is all around us. You pay *rent* for your apartment, *tuition* for your education, and a *fee* to your physician or dentist.
>
> The airline, railway, taxi, and bus companies charge you a *fare*; the local utilities call their price a *rate*; and the local bank charges you *interest* for the money you borrow.
>
> The price for taking your car on the ferry to Prince Edward Island or Vancouver Island is a *toll*, and the company that insures your car charges you a *premium*.
>
> Clubs or societies to which you belong may make a special *assessment* to pay unusual expenses. Your regular lawyer may ask for a *retainer* to cover her services.
>
> The "price" of an executive is a *salary*; the price of a salesperson may be a *commission*; and the price of a worker is a *wage*.
>
> Finally, although economists would disagree, many of us feel that *income taxes* are the price we pay for the privilege of making money.[2]

All products have some degree of **utility**, or *want-satisfying power*. While one individual might be willing to exchange the utility derived from a colour television for a vacation, another may not be willing to make that exchange. Prices are a mechanism that allows the consumer to make a decision. In contemporary society, of course, prices are translated into monetary terms. The consumer evaluates the utility derived from a range of possible purchases and then allocates his or her exchange power (in monetary terms) so as to maximize satisfaction. Pricing may be the most complicated aspect of the marketing manager's job. It is somewhat difficult to determine the price needed to realize a profit. But an even greater problem is that of determining a price that consumers will respond to positively and that can be maintained in a competitive environment.

price
The value that a buyer exchanges for a good or service. The value of an item is what it can be exchanged for in the marketplace.

utility
The want-satisfying power of a product or service.

Price is fundamental to many aspects of the economic system. Price often serves as a means of regulating economic activity. The employment of any or all of the four factors of production (land, labour, capital, and entrepreneurship) is dependent upon the price received by each.

For an individual firm, prices (along with the corresponding quantity that will be sold) represent the revenue to be received. Prices, therefore, influence a company's profit as well as its use of the factors of production. Early written accounts refer to attempts to develop a fair, or just, price. The "fair price" differs dramatically depending on one's perspective. If you are buying gasoline in Thunder Bay, you will have one set of criteria to judge whether the price is fair. If you are driving late at night on a deserted highway north of Lake Superior and the tank is nearly empty, another price perception emerges.

PRICE AND THE MARKETING MIX

Just as price is highly important in affecting economic activity, it is a central consideration in the development of a marketing mix. A key question when setting a price is, "What is the role of price in this marketing mix?" One marketing strategy will assign a major role to price as a means of attracting customers and sales. The discount food chain, Save-On Foods, is an example. Toward the other end of the spectrum, the marketing strategy of Lexus uses high price as a signal of the value of that fine car. In another marketing mix, price will play a much less important role. It can thus be seen that there are different possible *objectives* for price.

Low pricing plays a significant role in Swiss Chalet's marketing mix by establishing the chain's restaurants as places where customers receive value for their money. By offering easily prepared dishes that require a minimum of preparation and service in a casual setting, Swiss Chalet's low prices can be consistently maintained.

Pricing Objectives

Pricing objectives are a crucial part of a means–end chain from overall company objectives to specific pricing policies and procedures (see Figure 12.1). The goals of the firm and the marketing organization provide the basis for the development of pricing objectives, which must be clearly established before pricing policies and procedures are implemented.

A firm may have as its primary objective the goal of becoming the dominant supplier in the domestic market. Its marketing objective might then be to achieve maximum sales penetration in all sales regions. The related pricing goal would be sales maximization (through low prices). This means–end chain might lead to the adoption of a low-price policy implemented through providing the highest cash and trade discounts in the industry.

Pricing objectives vary from firm to firm. In an interesting U.S. study, marketers identified the primary and secondary pricing objectives of their companies. Meeting competitive prices was most often mentioned, but many marketers ranked two profitability-oriented objectives higher: a specified rate of return on investment and specified total profit levels. These two objectives ranked first and second as *primary* pricing objectives. The findings are shown in Table 12.1.

Pricing objectives can be classified into four major groups: (1) profitability objectives, (2) volume objectives, (3) competition-meeting objectives, and (4) prestige objectives. Profitability objectives include profit maximization and target return goals.

■ Figure 12.1 **The Role of Pricing Objectives in Contemporary Marketing**

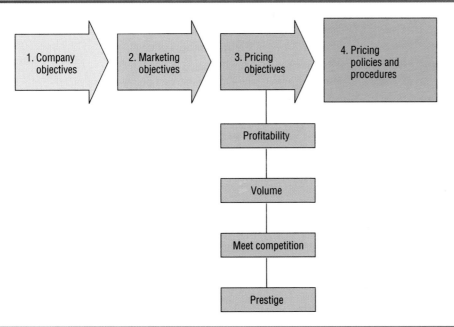

■ Table 12.1 **Primary and Secondary Pricing Objectives of Firms**

Pricing Objective	Percentage of Respondents Ranking the Items		
	As Primary Objectives	As Secondary Objectives	As Either Primary or Secondary Objectives
Meeting competitive price level	38.3	43.0	81.3
Specified rate of return on investment	60.9	17.2	78.1
Specified total profit level	60.2	17.2	77.4
Increased market share	31.3	42.2	73.5
Increased total profits above previous levels	34.4	37.5	71.9
Specified rate of return on sales	47.7	23.4	71.1
Retaining existing market share	31.3	35.9	67.2
Serving selected market segments	26.6	39.1	65.7
Creation of a readily identifiable image for the firm and/or its products	21.9	41.4	63.3
Specified market share	15.6	40.6	56.2
Other	5.5	—	5.5

Profitability Objectives

Businesses need to make profits in order to survive. How much profits? In classical economic theory, the traditional pricing objective has been to *maximize profits*. In terms of actual business practice, this means that profit maximization would be the basic objective of individual firms.

Profits, in turn, are a function of revenue and expenses:

$$\text{Profits} = \text{Total Revenues} - \text{Total Costs}$$

Revenue is determined by the selling price and the quantity sold:

$$\text{Total Revenue} = \text{Price} \times \text{Quantity Sold}$$

Price, therefore, should be increased up to the point where it causes a disproportionate decrease in the number of units sold. A 10 percent price increase that results in only an 8 percent cut in volume adds to the firm's revenue. However, a 10 percent hike that causes an 11 percent sales decline reduces total revenue.

profit maximization
The point where the addition to total revenue is just balanced by an increase in total cost.

This approach is referred to as *marginal analysis*. The point of **profit maximization** is where *the addition to total revenue is just balanced by an increase in total cost.* This is a valuable concept, which the reader should understand. Making it work, however, is not so easy. The basic problem centres on the difficulty of achieving this delicate balance between marginal revenue and marginal cost. As a result, relatively few firms actually achieve the objective of profit maximization. A significantly larger number prefer to direct their efforts toward goals that are more easily implemented and measured.

Consequently, target return objectives have become quite common in industry, particularly among the larger firms where public pressure may limit consideration of the profit maximization objective. Telephone and other utility companies are an example of this phenomenon. **Target return objectives** may be *either short-run or long-run goals and usually are stated as a percentage of sales or investment.* A company, for instance, may seek a 15 percent annual rate of return on investment or an 8 percent rate of return on sales. A specified return on investment was the most commonly reported pricing objective in Table 12.1.

Goals of this nature also serve as useful guidelines in evaluating corporate activity. One writer has aptly expressed it: "For management consciously accepting less than maximum profits, the target rate can provide a measure of the amount of restraint. For firms making very low profits, the target rate can serve as a standard for judging improvement."[3] Furthermore, they are more likely to result in a more stable and planned profit pattern for the company. This contrasts with a profit maximization approach, which can be very unstable.

Target return objectives offer several benefits to the marketer. As noted above, they serve as a means for evaluating performance. They also are designed to generate a "fair" profit, as judged by management, shareholders, and the general public as well. When using such target objectives, managements should avoid a short-term perspective. For example, if a product has contributed according to target for a time and now faces price competition, it still could be making a good contribution to overhead and should not be arbitrarily dropped.

Volume Objectives

Some writers argue that a better explanation of actual pricing behaviour is William J. Baumol's belief that firms attempt to **maximize sales** within a given profit constraint.[4] In other words, they set *a minimum floor at what they consider to be the lowest acceptable profit level and then seek to maximize sales* (subject to this profit constraint) in the belief that increased sales are more important to the long-run competitive picture. The company will continue to expand sales as long as its total profits do not drop below the minimum return acceptable to management.

Another volume-related pricing objective is the **market share objective** — that is, the goal is set *to control a specific portion of the market for the firm's product.* The company's specific goal can be to maintain or increase its share of a particular market. For example, a firm may desire to increase its 10 percent share of a particular market to 20 percent.[5] As Table 12.1 indicates, about two-thirds of all responding firms list retaining existing market share as either a primary or a secondary pricing objective.

Market share objectives can be critical to the achievement of other objectives. High sales, for example, may mean more profit. The extensive *Profit Impact of Market Strategies (PIMS)* project conducted by the Marketing Science Institute analyzed more than 2000 firms and revealed that two of the most important factors influencing profitability were product quality and a large market share. Market share appears to be the objective of Compaq, as discussed at the beginning of the chapter.

Meeting Competition as a Pricing Objective

Status quo objectives — *objectives based on the maintenance of stable prices* — are the basis of the pricing philosophy for many enterprises. This philosophy usually stems

target return objectives
Either short-run or long-run goals, usually stated as a percentage of sales or investment.

sales maximization
The pricing philosophy analyzed by economist William J. Baumol. Baumol believes that many firms attempt to maximize sales within a profit constraint.

market share objective
To control a specific portion of the market for the firm's product.

status quo objectives
Objectives based on the maintenance of stable prices.

from a desire to minimize competitive pricing action. The maintenance of stable prices allows the firm to concentrate its efforts on nonprice elements of the marketing mix, such as product improvement or promotion. Canada Packers deemphasized price competition and developed an advertising campaign emphasizing product features that differentiated its product, Tenderflake lard, from the competition. As a result, market share and profits increased significantly. The company was even able to raise prices gradually. Status quo objectives remain a significant factor in pricing.

Prestige Objectives

prestige objectives
The establishment of relatively high prices in order to develop and maintain an image of quality and exclusiveness.

Another category of pricing objectives unrelated to either profitability or sales volume is that of prestige objectives. **Prestige objectives** involve *the establishment of relatively high prices in order to develop and maintain an image of quality and exclusiveness.* Such objectives reflect marketers' recognition of the role of price in the creation of an overall image for the firm and its products and services. It appears that Birks and Holt Renfrew follow this strategy. Many luxury perfume manufacturers also use prestige pricing to suggest quality. And Rolls-Royce has opted for a higher-price image with its Cabriolet convertible model, priced at approximately $150 000.

PRICE DETERMINATION

There are three general approaches to determining price. One is price derivation, based on theoretical economic analysis. A second is the cost-plus approach, where the costs of producing the product are determined, and a margin of profit is added on. The third method is the marketing approach. The marketing approach is built

Acura is well known for its quality and luxury. In this advertisement, a car from Acura's TL Series is depicted with the creative passion of the Renaissance, an era in which great works of art were created. The resulting effect positions the car as a prestigious product that is itself an art form.

upon aspects of the economic-analysis and cost-plus methods, and adds an important marketing dimension to come up with a realistic price.

PRICE DETERMINATION IN ECONOMIC THEORY

Few businesses follow economic theory strictly in setting prices. Because of this, some students ask why we should bother with reviewing the economic approach to pricing. The reason is that *the concepts of economic price theory are essential to understand, and they apply to almost any pricing situation.* These concepts are important building blocks that help us understand what is going on in a particular pricing situation.

The microeconomic approach, or price theory, assumes a profit maximization objective and leads to the derivation of correct equilibrium prices in the marketplace. Price theory considers both supply and demand factors and thus is a more complete analysis than what is typically found in practice.

Demand refers to a schedule of the amounts of a firm's product or service that consumers will purchase at different prices during a specific period. *Supply* refers to a schedule of the amounts of a product or service that will be offered for sale at different prices during a specified time period. These schedules may vary for different types of market structures.

Market Structures

There are four types of market structures: pure competition, monopolistic competition, oligopoly, and monopoly. Very briefly, **pure competition** is *a market structure in which there is such a large number of buyers and sellers that no one of them has a significant influence on price.* Other characteristics of pure competition include a homogeneous product and ease of entry for sellers, and complete and instantaneous information.

This marketing structure is largely theoretical in contemporary society; however, some uncontrolled sectors of the agricultural commodity sector exhibit many of the characteristics of such a market, and provide the closest example of it.

Monopolistic competition is also *a market structure with a large number of buyers and sellers.* However, in this market there is *some degree of heterogeneity in good and/or service and usually geographical differentiation.* The existence of differentiation allows the marketer some degree of control over price. Most retail stores fall into this category, which partially explains why small retailers can exist with prices 5 to 10 percent higher than their larger competitors.

An **oligopoly** is *a market structure in which there are relatively few sellers.* Each seller may affect the market, but no one seller controls it. Examples are the automobile, steel, tobacco, and petroleum-refining industries. Because of high start-up costs, new competitors encounter significant entry barriers. **Oligopsony** is the other side of the coin: *a market in which there are only a few buyers.*

A **monopoly** is *a market structure with only one seller of a product with no close substitutes.* Anti-combines legislation has tended to eliminate all but *temporary* monopolies, such as those provided by patent protection, and *regulated* monopolies, such as the public utilities (telephone, electricity, gas). Regulated monopolies are granted by government in markets where competition would lead to an uneconomic duplication of services. In return for this monopoly, government regulates the monopoly rate of return through regulatory bodies such as the Canadian Transport Commission, the Canadian Radio-television and Telecommunications Commission, the

pure competition
A market structure in which there is such a large number of buyers and sellers that no one of them has a significant influence on price.

monopolistic competition
A market structure with a large number of buyers and sellers where heterogeneity in good and/or service and usually geographical differentiation allow the marketer some control over price.

oligopoly
A market structure in which there are relatively few sellers.

oligopsony
A market in which there are only a few buyers.

monopoly
A market structure with only one seller of a product with no close substitutes.

National Farm Products Marketing Council, and provincial public utility regulatory commissions.

Revenue, Cost, and Supply Curves

Within each of these market structures the elements of demand, costs, and supply must be considered. The demand side of price theory is concerned with *revenue curves*. *Average revenue* (AR) is obtained by dividing *total revenue* (TR) by the *quantity* (Q) associated with these revenues:

$$AR = \frac{TR}{Q}$$

The plotted average revenue line is actually the demand curve facing the firm. *Marginal revenue* (MR) is the change in total revenue (ΔTR) that results from selling an additional unit of output (ΔQ). This can be shown as

$$MR = \frac{\Delta TR}{\Delta Q}$$

In order to complete the analysis, the supply curves must be determined for each of these market situations. A firm's cost structure determines its supply curves. Let us examine each of the cost curves applicable to price determination.

average cost
Obtained by dividing total cost by the quantity associated with this cost.

Average cost (AC) is obtained by dividing total cost by the quantity (Q) associated with the total cost. *Total cost* (TC) is composed of both fixed and variable components. *Fixed costs* are those costs that do not vary with differences in output, while *variable costs* are those that change when the level of production is altered. Examples of fixed costs include executive compensation, depreciation, and insurance. Variable costs include raw materials and the wages paid to production workers.

average variable cost
The total variable cost divided by the related quantity.

marginal cost
The change in total cost that results from producing an additional unit of output.

Average variable cost (AVC) is simply the total variable cost (TVC) divided by the related quantity. Similarly, *average fixed cost* (AFC) is determined by dividing total fixed costs (TFC) by the related quantity. **Marginal cost** (MC) is the change in total cost (ΔTC) that results from producing an additional unit of output (ΔQ). Thus, it is similar to *marginal revenue*, which is the change in total revenue resulting from the production of an incremental unit. The point of profit maximization is where marginal costs are equal to marginal revenues.

These cost derivations are shown in the following formulas:

$$AC = \frac{TC}{Q} \qquad AFC = \frac{TFC}{Q}$$

$$AVC = \frac{TVC}{Q} \qquad MC = \frac{\Delta TC}{\Delta Q}$$

The resulting *cost curves* are shown in Figure 12.2. The marginal cost curve (MC) intersects the average variable cost curve (AVC) and average cost curve (AC) at their minimum points.

In the short run, a firm will continue to operate even if the price falls below AC, provided it remains above AVC. Why is this rational market behaviour? If the firm were to cease operations after the price fell below AC, it would still have some fixed costs, but *no revenue*. Any amount received above AVC can be used to cover fixed

■ Figure 12.2 **Cost Curves**

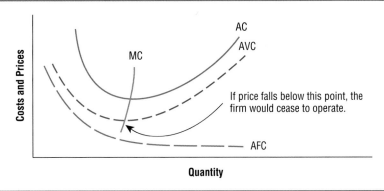

How, then, are prices set in each of the product market situations? Figure 12.3 shows how prices are determined in each of the four product markets. The point of profit maximization (MC = MR) sets the equilibrium output (Point A), which is extended to the AR line to set the equilibrium price (Point B). In the case of pure competition, AR = MR, so price is a predetermined variable in this product market.

costs. The firm is acting rationally by continuing to produce as long as price exceeds AVC since this is minimizing losses. If price falls below AVC, the firm would cease operations because continued operation would result in real losses from out-of-pocket costs per unit, with no control of fixed costs. The **supply curve**, therefore, is *the marginal cost curve above its intersection with AVC* since this is the area of rational pricing behaviour for the firm.

supply curve
The marginal cost curve above its intersection with average variable cost.

The Concept of Elasticity in Pricing Strategy

Although the intersection of demand and supply curves determines the equilibrium price for each of the market structures, the specific curves vary. To understand why, it is necessary to understand the concept of elasticity.[6]

Elasticity is *a measure of the responsiveness of purchasers and suppliers to changes in price.* The *price elasticity of demand* is the percentage change in the quantity of a product or service demanded, divided by the percentage change in its price. A 10 percent increase in the price of eggs that results in a 5 percent decrease in the quantity of eggs demanded yields a price elasticity of demand for eggs of 0.5.

elasticity
A measure of the responsiveness of purchasers and suppliers to changes in price.

Elasticity Terminology

Consider a case in which a 1 percent change in price causes more than a 1 percent change in the quantity supplied or demanded. Numerically, that means an elasticity greater than 1.0. When the elasticity of demand or supply is greater than 1.0, it is termed *elastic.*

If a 1 percent change in price results in less than a 1 percent change in quantity, a good's elasticity of supply or demand will be numerically less than 1.0 and is called *inelastic.* The demand for eggs in the example above is inelastic. There was a recent period when retail gasoline prices rose 50 percent, but gasoline sales fell by only about 8 percent.

■ Figure 12.3 **Price Determination in the Four Product Markets**

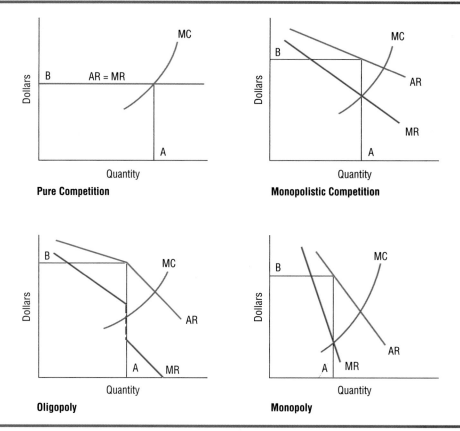

An extreme case occurs when the quantity supplied or demanded does not change at all when the price changes. Then the supply or demand is called *perfectly inelastic.*

The case in which a 1 percent change in price results in exactly a 1 percent change in quantity is called *unit* (or *unitary*) *elastic.*

Determinants of Elasticity

Why is the elasticity of supply or demand high for some goods and services and low for others? What constitutes the specific determinants of demand elasticity?[7]

One factor determining the elasticity of demand is the availability of substitutes. If a product or service has close substitutes, the demand tends to be elastic. The demand for olive oil, for instance, is more elastic than it would be if other salad oils were not available as substitutes. The demand for cars is less elastic than it would be if good public transportation was available everywhere. A related factor is the availability of more important complements. The demand for motor oil, for example, tends to be inelastic because it is a complement to the more important good, gasoline.

Elasticity of demand is also influenced by whether a product or service is a necessity or a luxury. For example, dining out is a luxury for most people. If restaurant prices increase, most people can respond by eating at home instead. By contrast, eggs and milk are considered necessities, so price changes have less effect on consumption, at least in the short run.

Elasticity is further influenced by the portion of a person's budget that is spent on a product or service. Matches, for example, are no longer really a necessity, and good substitutes exist. Nonetheless, the demand for matches is thought to be very inelastic because people spend so little on them that they hardly notice a price change. However, the demand for housing and transportation is not perfectly inelastic even though they are necessities. Both occupy a large part of people's budgets, so a change in price cannot be ignored.

Elasticity of demand is also affected by the time perspective under consideration. Demand is often less elastic in the short run than in the long run. Consider the demand for home heating fuel. In the short run, when the price goes up, people find it difficult to cut back on the quantity they use. They are accustomed to living at a certain temperature, dressing a certain way, and so forth. Given time, though, they may find ways to economize. They can better insulate their homes, form new habits of dressing more warmly, or even move to a warmer climate.

All the factors mentioned here are only tendencies, yet often the tendencies reinforce one another. The classic case of inelastic demand is salt, which has no good substitute, is a nutritional necessity, and uses a very small part of one's budget. Sometimes, though, the rules just do not seem to fit. Alcohol and tobacco, which are not necessities and do occupy a large share of some personal budgets, also are subject to notoriously inelastic demand.

Elasticity and Revenue

There is an important relationship between the elasticity of demand and the way that total revenue changes as the price of a good or service changes. Suppose Montreal wants to find a way to raise more money for its public transportation system. One possible fund-raising method is to change the transit fare, but should it be raised or lowered? The correct answer depends on the elasticity of demand for subway rides. A 10 percent decrease in fares is sure to attract more riders, but unless there is more than a 10 percent increase in riders, total revenue will fall. A 10 percent increase in fares will bring in more money per rider, but if more than 10 percent of the riders are lost, revenue will fall. A price cut will increase revenue only if demand is *elastic*, and a price increase will raise revenue only if demand is *inelastic*.

Practical Problems in Applying Price Theory

From the viewpoint of the marketer, price theory concepts are sometimes difficult to apply in practice. What are their practical limitations?

1. Many firms do not attempt to maximize profits. Economic analysis is subject to the same limitations as the assumptions upon which it is based — for example, the proposition that all firms attempt to maximize profits.
2. It is difficult to estimate demand curves. Modern accounting procedures provide the manager with a clear understanding of his or her cost structure. The

manager, therefore, can readily comprehend the supply side of the price equation. But it is difficult to estimate demand at various price levels. Demand curves must be based on market research estimates that are often not as exact as cost figures. Although the demand element can be identified, it is often difficult to measure in the real-world setting.

3. Inadequate training and communications hinder price theory in the real world. Many businesspeople lack the formal training in economics to be able to apply its concepts to their own pricing decisions. On the other hand, many economists remain essentially theorists devoting little interest or effort to real-world pricing situations. This dual problem significantly hinders the use of economic theory in actual pricing practice.[8]

In spite of these problems, it is very useful for pricing decision-makers to consider whether demand for their product is elastic or inelastic, what kind of market structure they are operating in, and other related theoretical matters.

COST-PLUS PRICE SETTING

For many firms, price determination tends to be based on some form of the cost-plus approach.

cost-plus pricing
Pricing technique using base cost figure per unit to which is added a markup to cover unassigned costs and to provide a profit.

Cost-plus pricing uses some *base cost figure per unit to which is added a markup to cover unassigned costs and to provide a profit.* The only real difference in the multitude of cost-plus techniques is the relative sophistication of the costing procedures employed. For example, the local clothing store may set prices by adding a 40 percent markup to the invoice price charged by the supplier. This markup is expected to cover all other expenses, as well as permit the owner to earn a reasonable return on the sale of the garments.

In contrast to this rather simple pricing mechanism, a large manufacturer may employ a pricing formula that requires a computer to handle the necessary calculations for a sophisticated costing procedure. But in the end, the formula still requires someone to make a decision about the markup. The clothing store and the large manufacturer may be vastly different with respect to the *cost* aspect, but they are remarkably similar when it comes to the *markup* side of the equation.

The above discussion demonstrates a major problem associated with cost-oriented pricing: *costs should not determine prices, since the proper function of cost in pricing is to determine the profit consequences of pricing alternatives.* That is, costs in the long run only determine the floor for the price. Unfortunately, this is not always understood by some companies.

Full-Cost Pricing

The two most common cost-oriented pricing procedures are the full-cost method and the incremental-cost method. *Full-cost pricing* uses all relevant variable costs in setting a product's price. In addition, it considers an allocation of the fixed costs that cannot be directly attributed to the production of the specific item being priced. Under the full-cost method, if job order 515 in a printing plant amounts to 0.000127 percent of the plant's total output, then 0.000127 percent of the firm's overhead expenses are allocated to this job. This approach, therefore, allows the pricer to recover all costs plus the amount added as a profit margin.

The full-cost approach has two basic deficiencies. First, there is no consideration of the demand for the item or its competition. Perhaps no one wants to pay the price that the firm has calculated. Second, any method of allocating overhead, or fixed expenses, is arbitrary and may be unrealistic. In manufacturing, overhead allocations are often tied to direct labour hours. In retailing, the mechanism is sometimes floor area in each profit centre. Regardless of the technique, it is difficult to show a cause-and-effect relationship between the allocated cost and most products.

Incremental-Cost Pricing

One way to overcome the arbitrary allocation of fixed expenses is by *incremental-cost pricing*, which attempts to use only those costs directly attributable to a specific output in setting prices. For example, consider a small manufacturer with the following income statement:

Sales (10 000 units at $10)		$100 000
Expenses		
Variable	$50 000	
Fixed	$40 000	$ 90 000
Net Profit		$ 10 000

Suppose that the firm is offered a contract for an additional 5000 units. Since the peak season is over, these items can be produced at the same average variable cost. Assume that the labour force would be idle otherwise. In order to get the contract, how low could the firm price its product?

Under the full-cost approach, the lowest price would be $9 each. This is obtained by dividing the $90 000 in expenses by an output of 10 000 units. The full-cost pricer would consider this a profitless situation. When pricing in this manner, there is a real problem with using full cost. This is set as a floor below which the price will not be allowed to fall. Instead, the type of costs should be understood. Then they can be viewed as somewhat flexible, and serve as a reference point to which flexible mark-ups are added.

The incremental-cost approach, on the other hand, would permit a price of anywhere from $5.01 upwards depending on the competition. If competition were strong, a price of $5.10 would be competitive. This price would be composed of the $5 variable cost related to each unit of production, plus a 10 cents per unit contribution to fixed expenses and overhead. With these conditions of sale, note the revised income statement:

Sales (10 000 at $10 plus 5 000 at $5.10)		$125 500
Expenses		
Variable (15 000 × $5)	$75 000	
Fixed	$40 000	$115 000
Net Profit		$ 10 500

Profits were increased under the incremental approach. Admittedly, the illustration is based on two assumptions: (1) the ability to isolate markets so that selling at the lower price would not affect the price received in other markets, and (2) the absence of certain legal restrictions on the firm. The example, however, does show that profits can sometimes be enhanced by using the incremental approach.

Limitations of Cost-Oriented Pricing

While the incremental method eliminates one of the problems associated with full-cost pricing, it fails to deal effectively with the basic malady: *cost-oriented pricing does not adequately account for product demand.*

The problem of estimating demand is as critical to these approaches as it is to classical price theory. To the marketer, the challenge is to find some way of introducing demand analysis into cost-plus pricing. A well-reasoned approach to pricing is, in effect, a comparison of the impact of a decision on total sales receipts, or revenue, and on total costs. It involves the increase or decrease in revenue and costs, not just of the product under consideration, but of the business enterprise as a whole.

MARKETING APPROACHES TO PRICING

Marketing is an eclectic discipline. It draws good ideas from many sources. A *marketing approach to pricing* is no exception. A marketing approach recognizes the numerous valuable concepts developed by economic theory. Especially valuable are the concepts of demand estimation and price elasticity. Cost accounting is also considered essential in pricing. Without a thorough understanding of costs, a firm's pricing policies can soon go awry.

A marketing approach to pricing adds the dimension of *consumer analysis* to the foregoing approaches. For example, this approach might accept that a profit margin of, say, 35 percent would be desirable for the firm. It also considers potential demand for the product, as well as price elasticity. It goes beyond these considerations, however. The marketing approach asks the question of *how potential consumers*

Nacan Products sells both unmodified starch (commodity starch) and modified specialty starches to papermakers and corrugators. Prices for unmodified starch are usually negotiated between supplier and customer, often in a competitive context. The pricing policy for specialty starches, however, takes into account that customers know that these products' special patented properties produce substantial savings in the manufacturing process. Nacan asks for — and readily gets — higher prices for these products.

would respond to such a price. Would this price cross some possible psychological threshold and be viewed as much higher than it really is? Or would the proposed price seem so low that it would negatively affect the product's image and sales? The astute marketer asks a host of other questions based on the unique perspective of consumer orientation.

In addition to considering the responses of various consumer segments, the marketing approach to pricing considers competitors individually, in addition to as a whole. In some cases, prior experience will have shown that a key competitor will likely respond in a certain way to any pricing moves. For example, car rental firms will have quite a good understanding of their competitors' likely response to any pricing change that they might make. Psychological thresholds of key competitors are also important.

From a marketing perspective, a product that is new to the world, as opposed to being merely new to the company, passes through distinctive stages in its life cycle. The appropriate pricing policy is likely to be different at each stage. Perhaps the most difficult task is establishing an initial price for the product. In later stages of the product life cycle, pricing is complicated enough, but at that point, strategic decisions hinge largely on decisions to meet or beat the competition in various ways.

A PRICING DECISION FLOW CHART

A good example of one marketing approach to pricing is G. David Hughes's pricing procedure for new products (see Figure 12.4). This procedure can be used for market entries that are new to the company as well. It adds a number of marketing considerations as well as taking into account many of the points considered in this chapter.[9]

Establish the range of acceptable prices. The first step is to establish a price range that is consistent with corporate values, objectives, and policies. The pricing policies of top executives who are risk takers may be different from those of risk averters. The range of prices will be predicated on the company's desire to establish a discount image or a quality image. Similarly, a decision to use a prestige channel of distribution will determine channel discount structures, which in turn will be reflected in a final price.

Set price for a planned target market. As with virtually all marketing mix decisions, the pricing process has to be developed with a specific target market in mind. Given some estimate of the demand curve for the target segment, the price strategist attempts to identify the price that will maximize sales or profits.

Estimate demand for the brand. This price is then positioned against competitive prices to determine expected market share. If this share is too small, the strategist will go back to the generic demand (i.e., primary demand, or those needs that can be met by a product category) and select a new price.

Estimate competitors' reactions. Once a price is selected that provides what seems to be an acceptable sales volume, the next task is to estimate how competitors will react. A very low price may cause a price war in an oligopoly. An exceptionally high price may attract lower-priced competition. If either of these responses would destroy the basic marketing strategy, the strategist must go back and select a new price.

Consider public policy implications. Unfavourable reactions from the public may take many forms. Provincial or federal authorities may look on a given price strategy in a monopoly-type situation as unconscionable and therefore subject to legislation or

■ Figure 12.4 **Pricing Decision Flow Chart**

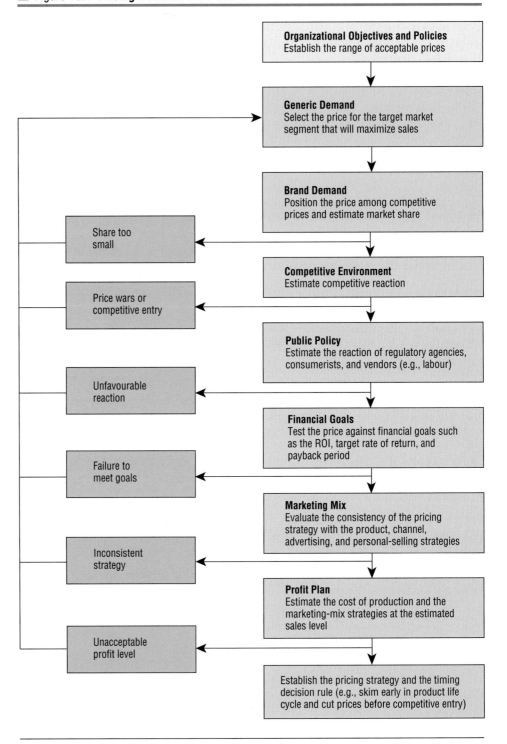

Source: Adapted from G. David Hughes, *Marketing Management: A Planning Approach* (Menlo Park, CA: Addison-Wesley, 1978), p. 325. Used by permission of the author.

regulation. Consumerists may regard a price as excessive and boycott all of the company's products. Labour unions may regard a price increase as an indication that the company can now afford to raise wages.

Test the price against financial goals. The next test is to see if the pricing strategy will meet financial goals such as return on investment (ROI), target rate of return on sales, or a payback period. Failure to meet financial goals sends the pricing strategist back to the generic-demand curve to select a new price for analysis. In actual practice, the strategist will probably have tested the price against the financial goals before proceeding to the positioning of the price among other brands, because rough calculations can be based on previous experience. In fact, it is desirable to make profit plans as early as the concept stage during new-product development. These plans can be continually updated as the product passes through the development stages.

Evaluate its congruence in the mix. The selected price must be evaluated in terms of the product, channel, advertising, and personal-selling strategies that will be used in the market segment in question. The role of price in the marketing mix should be specifically identified, and all elements of the mix must blend together. Any inconsistencies must be reconciled by altering the price or one of the other elements of the mix.

A low price is appropriate when the product category is at the mature stage in its cycle. A low price may also be appropriate when there is little promotion, the product is mass-produced, market coverage is intense, production is capital intensive, technological change is slow, the product is needed to complete the product line, few services are offered, the product is disposable, or the life cycle is short.

Develop a profit plan. The cost of production and the cost of the marketing-mix strategy at the estimated sales level provide inputs for the profit plan. An inadequate profit may send the strategist back to setting a new price or to reducing the cost of other elements in the marketing mix.

Finalize actual price and timing. The last stage in the process is to establish the final price. This is done in light of the preceding steps, but it also takes into specific consideration the actual prices of competing products. For example, the profit plan calculation might indicate a price a $71.87, but the final price offered to the market might be $69.95. This might be chosen for psychological reasons (it sounds less expensive), or to meet the prices of competitors. If a high-priced skimming strategy (described in Chapter 13) has been chosen, a timing decision should also be reached in order to be ready to cut prices when predetermined conditions occur.

Many procedures that are used to determine price are not this elaborate. The foregoing is one of a number of similar possible processes that may be employed.

Break-even Analysis: A Useful Tool in Pricing

Break-even analysis is *a means of determining the number of goods or services that must be sold at a given price in order to generate sufficient revenue to cover total costs.* Figure 12.5 shows the calculation of the break-even point graphically. The total cost curve includes both fixed and variable segments, and total fixed costs are represented by a horizontal shaded bar. Average variable cost is assumed to be constant per unit as it was in the example used for incremental pricing.

break-even analysis
A means of determining the number of goods or services that must be sold at a given price in order to generate sufficient revenue to cover total costs.

■ Figure 12.5 **Break-even Chart**

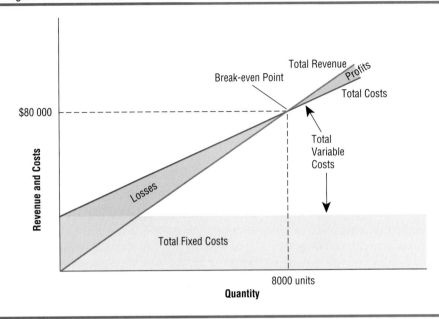

The break-even point is the point at which total revenue (TR) just equals total cost (TC). It can be found by using the following formulas:

$$\text{Break-even Point (in units)} = \frac{\text{Total Fixed Costs}}{\text{Per-unit Selling Price} - \text{Average Variable Cost}}$$

$$= \frac{\text{Total Fixed Costs}}{\text{Per-unit Contribution to Fixed Cost}}$$

$$\text{Break-even Point (in dollars)} = \frac{\text{Total Fixed Costs}}{1 - \dfrac{\text{Variable Cost per Unit}}{\text{Selling Price}}}$$

In our earlier example, a selling price of $10 and an average variable cost of $5 resulted in a per-unit contribution to fixed costs of $5. This figure can be divided into total fixed costs of $40 000 to obtain a break-even point of 8000 units, or $80 000 in total sales revenue:

$$\text{Break-even Point (in units)} = \frac{\$40\ 000}{\$10 - \$5} = \frac{\$40\ 000}{\$5} = 8000 \text{ units}$$

$$\text{Break-even Point (in dollars)} = \frac{\$40\ 000}{1 - \dfrac{\$5}{\$10}} = \frac{\$40\ 000}{0.5} = \$80\ 000$$

$$\text{Break-even Profit Point (in dollars)} = \frac{\$40\ 000 + 10\% \text{ of Sales (\$8000)}}{1 - \dfrac{\$5}{\$10}} = \frac{\$48\ 000}{0.5} = \$96\ 000$$

Break-even analysis is an effective tool for marketers in assessing the sales required to cover costs and achieve specified profit levels. It is easily understood by both marketing and nonmarketing executives and may assist in deciding whether required sales levels for a certain price are in fact realistic goals. Extending this analysis a bit further, a simple profit breakdown is also shown in the example. If a 10 percent profit on sales was desired, sales of $96 000 would be required. More data would be needed if a return on investment or some other measure was used as a profitability target.

However, break-even analysis is not without shortcomings. First, the model assumes that costs can be divided into fixed and variable categories. Some costs, such as salaries and advertising outlays, may be either fixed or variable depending on the particular situation. In addition, the model assumes that per-unit variable costs do not change at different levels of operation. However, these may vary as a result of quantity discounts, more efficient utilization of the workforce, or other economies resulting from increased levels of production and sales. Finally, the basic break-even model does not consider demand. It is a cost-based model and does not directly address the crucial question of whether consumers will actually purchase the product at the specified price and in the required quantities to break even or to generate profits. The challenge of the marketer is to modify break-even analysis and the other cost-oriented approaches to pricing in order to introduce demand analysis. Pricing must be examined from the buyer's perspective. Such decisions cannot made in a management vacuum in which only cost factors are considered.

The Dynamic Break-even Concept

In Figure 12.5, the break-even analysis was based on the assumption of a constant $10 retail price regardless of quantity. What happens when different retail prices are considered? **Dynamic break-even analysis** *combines the traditional break-even analysis model with an evaluation of consumer demand.*

Table 12.2 summarizes both the cost and the revenue aspects of a number of alternative retail prices. The cost data are based on the costs used earlier in the basic break-even model. The expected unit sales for each specified retail price are obtained from consumer research. The data in the first two columns of Table 12.2 represent a demand schedule by indicating the number of units consumers are expected to purchase at each of a series of retail prices. This data can be superimposed on a break-even chart in order to identify the range of feasible prices for consideration by the marketing decision-maker. This is shown in Figure 12.6.

As Figure 12.6 indicates, the range of profitable prices exists from a low of approximately $8 (TR$_4$) to a high of $12 (TR$_2$), with a price of $10 (TR$_3$) generating

dynamic break-even analysis
Combines the traditional break-even analysis model with an evaluation of consumer demand.

■ Table 12.2 **Revenue and Cost Data for Dynamic Break-even Analysis**

	Revenues			Costs		
Price	Quantity Demanded	Total Revenue	Total Fixed Costs	Total Variable Costs	Total Cost	**Total Profit (or Loss)**
$14	3 000	$ 42 000	$40 000	$ 15 000	$ 55 000	($13 000)
12	6 000	72 000	40 000	30 000	70 000	2 000
10	10 000	100 000	40 000	50 000	90 000	10 000
8	14 000	112 000	40 000	70 000	110 000	2 000
6	26 000	156 000	40 000	130 000	170 000	(14 000)

■ Figure 12.6 **Dynamic Break-even Chart Reflecting Costs and Consumer Demand**

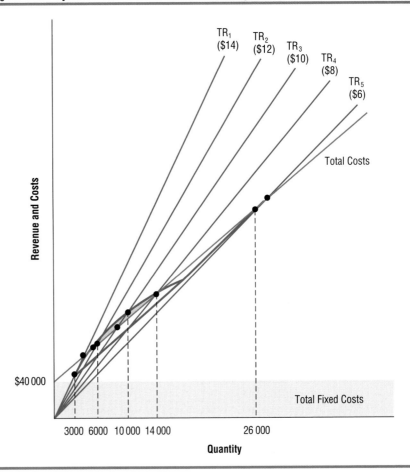

the greatest projected profits. Changing the retail price produces a new break-even point. At a relatively high $14 retail price, the break-even point is 4445 units; at a $10 retail price the break-even point is 8000 units; and at a $6 price, the break-even point is 30 000 units.

The contribution of dynamic break-even analysis is that it forces the pricing decision-maker to consider whether consumers are likely to purchase the required number of units of a good or service that will achieve the break-even point at a given price. The analysis demonstrates that a larger number of units sold does not necessarily produce added profits, since — other things being equal — lower prices are necessary to stimulate added sales. Consequently, careful consideration of both costs and consumer demand is necessary in determining the most appropriate price.

Working with Prices: Markups, Markdowns, and Turnover

In working with prices, marketers often must consider three basic concepts: markups, markdowns, and turnover. An ability to handle these is essential for many day-to-day marketing decisions.

MARKUPS

A **markup** is *the amount a producer or channel member adds to cost in order to determine the selling price.* It is typically stated as either a percentage of the selling price or of cost. The formulas used in calculating markup percentages are as follows:

$$\text{Markup Percentage on Selling Price} = \frac{\text{Amount Added to Cost (the Markup)}}{\text{Price}}$$

$$\text{Markup Percentage on Cost} = \frac{\text{Amount Added to Cost (the Markup)}}{\text{Cost}}$$

Consider an example from retailing. Suppose an item selling for $1.00 has an invoice cost of $0.60. The total markup is $0.40. The markup percentages would be calculated as follows:

$$\text{Markup Percentage on Selling Price} = \frac{\$0.40}{\$1.00} = 40\%$$

$$\text{Markup Percentage on Cost} = \frac{\$0.40}{\$0.60} = 67\%$$

To determine selling price when only cost and markup percentage on selling price are known, the following formula is used:

$$\text{Price} = \frac{\text{Cost in Dollars}}{100\% - \text{Markup Percentage on Selling Price}}$$

In the example cited above, price could be determined as $1.00:

$$\text{Price} = \frac{\$0.60}{100\% - 40\%} = \frac{0.60}{60\%} = \$1.00$$

Similarly, the markup percentage can be converted from one basis (selling price or cost) to the other by using the following formula:

$$\text{Markup Percentage on Selling Price} = \frac{\text{Markup Percentage on Cost}}{100\% + \text{Markup Percentage on Cost}}$$

$$\text{Markup Percentage on Cost} = \frac{\text{Markup Percentage on Selling Price}}{100\% - \text{Markup Percentage on Selling Price}}$$

Again, using the data from the example above, the following conversions can be made:

$$\text{Markup Percentage on Selling Price} = \frac{67\%}{100\% + 67\%} = \frac{67\%}{167\%} = 40\%$$

$$\text{Markup Percentage on Cost} = \frac{40\%}{100\% - 40\%} = \frac{40\%}{60\%} = 67\%$$

markup
The amount a producer or channel member adds to cost in order to determine the selling price.

MARKDOWNS

markdown
A reduction in the price of an item.

A related pricing issue that is particularly important to retailers is markdowns. Markups are based partially on executive judgements about the prices consumers are likely to pay for a given good or service. If buyers refuse to pay the price, however, the marketer must take a **markdown**, *a reduction in the price of the item.* For purposes of internal control and analysis, the markdown percentage is computed as follows:

$$\text{Markup Percentage} = \frac{\text{Markdown}}{\text{``Sale'' (New) Price}}$$

Suppose no one was willing to pay $1.00 for an item and the marketer decided to reduce the price to $0.75. The markdown percentage would be

$$\text{Markup Percentage} = \frac{\$0.25}{\$0.75} = 33\frac{1}{3}\%$$

From a customer's viewpoint, this is only a 25 percent reduction, which is known as the "off-retail percentage." This is the percentage that should be quoted in advertisements. Markdowns are also used for evaluative purposes. For instance, department managers or buyers in a large department store could be evaluated partially on the basis of the average markdown percentage on the product lines for which they are responsible.

TURNOVER

All too often, traditional markup and markdown percentages lead to competitive inertia within an industry. Standard percentages are too frequently applied to all items in a given category regardless of factors such as demand.

stock turnover
The number of times the average inventory is sold annually.

A method for avoiding competitive inertia is to use flexible markups that vary with **stock turnover** — *the number of times the average inventory is sold annually.* The figure can be calculated by one of the following formulas. When inventory is recorded at retail:

$$\text{Stock Turnover} = \frac{\text{Sales}}{\text{Average Inventory}}$$

When inventory is recorded at cost:

$$\text{Stock Turnover} = \frac{\text{Cost of Goods Sold}}{\text{Average Inventory}}$$

Store A, with $100 000 in sales and an average inventory of $20 000 (at retail), would have a stock turnover of 5. Store B, with $200 000 in sales, a 40 percent markup rate, and an average inventory of $30 000 (at cost), would have a stock turnover of 4.

Store A

$$\text{Stock Turnover} = \frac{\$100\,000}{\$20\,000} = 5$$

Store B

$200 000	Sales
− 80 000	Markup (40 percent)
$120 000	Cost of Goods Sold

$$\text{Stock Turnover} = \frac{\$120\,000}{\$30\,000} = 4$$

■ Table 12.3 **Relationship between Markup Percentage and Stock Turnover**

Stock Turnover Rate in Relation to the Industry Average	Markup Percentage in Relation to the Industry Average	Product Example
High	Low	Soft Drinks
Average	Average	Motor Oil
Low	High	Sports Cars

While most marketers recognize the importance of turnover, they often use it more as a measure of sales effectiveness than as a pricing tool. However, it can be particularly useful in setting markup percentages if some consideration is given to consumer demand.

Table 12.3 indicates the relationship between stock turnover and markup. Above-average turnover, such as for grocery products, is generally associated with relatively low markup percentages. On the other hand, higher markup percentages typically exist in such product lines as jewellery and furniture, where relatively lower annual stock turnover is common and inventory and overhead costs must be covered through higher margins.

This chapter has described the basic considerations for determining price. The next chapter continues the discussion and delves into issues concerning the managing of pricing.

■ KEY TERMS

price	monopolistic competition	elasticity
utility	oligopoly	cost-plus pricing
profit maximization	oligopsony	break-even analysis
target return objectives	monopoly	dynamic break-even
sales maximization	average cost	analysis
market share objective	average variable cost	markup
status quo objectives	marginal cost	markdown
prestige objectives	supply curve	stock turnover
pure competition		

■ INTERACTIVE SUMMARY AND DISCUSSION QUESTIONS

1. Pricing objectives must be set before a pricing decision. The four main pricing objectives are profitability, volume, meeting the competition, and prestige. Give one or two product examples for which each objective seems to apply.

2. The two main profitability objectives are profit maximization and target return objectives. Explain the advantages and disadvantages of each.

3. In the case of volume objectives, some firms attempt to maximize sales within a given profit constraint. Others use a market share objective. Explain the advantages and disadvantages of each.

4. Besides trying to make as much money as possible, what other advantages are there of prestige pricing? What are the disadvantages?

5. One approach to determining price is based on theoretical economic analysis, which uses the concepts of supply and demand. Using these concepts, show how price can be determined theoretically.

6. In the short run, a firm will continue to operate even if a price falls below average cost, provided it remains above average variable cost. Why is this rational market behaviour?

7. Elasticity of demand is a measure of the responsiveness of purchasers and suppliers to changes in price. Explain why it is extremely important to take elasticity of demand into consideration in setting prices.

8. Price theory is very useful in understanding many of the forces in the marketplace that should be considered in setting prices, but are quite difficult to apply in practice. Explain.

9. Cost-plus pricing uses some base cost figure per unit to which is added a markup to cover unassigned costs and to provide a profit. However, costs should not determine prices, since the proper function of cost in pricing is to determine the profit consequences of pricing alternatives. Explain.

10. Explain why incremental-cost pricing is a better procedure than full-cost pricing.

11. The marketing approach to pricing takes the price theory and cost-accounting approaches to prices into consideration, and adds a pragmatic use of consumer analysis as well as a strategic evaluation of likely competitor response. Your new boss asks you to write a short memo outlining an approach to pricing a new mountain bike. How might the marketing approach to pricing be applied? What are the broad necessary steps that you would recommend?

12. Break-even analysis is a means of determining the number of goods or services that must be sold at a given price in order to generate sufficient revenue to cover total costs. Calculate the break-even point in dollars and units for a product with a selling price of $25, related fixed costs of $126 000, and per-unit variable costs of $16.

CHAPTER 13

Managing the Pricing Function

1. To highlight the importance of establishing pricing policies before individual prices are set.
2. To examine the implications of skimming and penetration pricing strategies.
3. To describe how prices are quoted.
4. To explain negotiated prices and competitive bidding.
5. To explain the concept of transfer pricing.
6. To discuss pricing in the public sector.

"A diamond is forever." — a De Beers' advertisement

Taken literally, De Beers' slogan can't be contested. Made of pure crystallized carbon, a diamond will never deteriorate physically. This durability has imbued the gem with a mystique that dates back to antiquity.

Since 1934, De Beers has proven to be a powerful marketing machine that both inspires desire for the gem and controls its value and investment potential.

The romantic imperative of possessing eternal love is what the marketing of diamonds is all about. When the British–South African diamond monopoly De Beers Consolidated Mines Ltd. introduced its slogan back in 1938, its aim was to make the diamond engagement ring "a psychological necessity." It worked. Today more than 80 percent of engaged women in Canada sport diamond rings.

The power of De Beers' message was even more profound in Japan, where, for centuries, arranged marriages precluded the need for romantic symbols. In 1967, fewer than 5 percent of Japanese brides wore diamonds. That year, the cartel hired J. Walter Thompson to sell the diamond to the Japanese as a visible sign of progressive, luxurious, Western values; by the '80s, more than 60 percent of Japanese brides were wearing rocks.

The pricing of diamonds is remarkable. The De Beers organization controls more than 85 percent of the diamond market. The cartel has weathered revolutions and nationalizations without ever loosening its grip on exclusive rights to diamond deposits. It so rigidly controls prices that, according to a VP at the New York Diamond Exchange: "It makes OPEC look like a bunch of Girl Scouts."

Since 1934, when De Beers formed its London-based marketing arm, the Central Selling Organization, prices for rough, unpolished gems have never declined. If demand slumps, the cartel stockpiles.

"Show her she's the reason it's never been lonely at the top. A full carat or more. Halfway isn't your style. Every diamond is rare, and, like love, becomes more precious with time."

Despite that hint of long-term appreciation in its advertising, De Beers has always emphasized that diamonds should not be bought as a long-term investment. Spokesman Andrew Lamont offers a long list of reasons: "Each diamond is unique, so the price of each varies. Also, dealer markups can be exorbitant, the reliability of standard pricing is a problem and the resale market can be volatile."

It is true that the wholesale price of a flawless D one-carat diamond has risen to $17 000–19 000 today from $2 000–4 000 in 1971. But according to Salomon Brothers, average diamond prices rose only 7.5 percent over the past five years, 9.6 percent in the previous decade, and 9.9 percent over the past 20 years. "What people don't realize," says one jeweller, "is that you buy retail but sell wholesale, so the diamond has to appreciate at least 300 percent in some cases before you break even."[1]

The pricing of diamonds illustrates many pricing concepts: supply and demand, size of the organization, pricing policies, psychological pricing, the relationship between advertising and pricing, and the significance of retail markups in the market price. The management of the pricing variable is challenging because there are so many possible aspects to consider.

INTRODUCTION

The previous chapter introduced the concept of price and outlined the three main approaches to determining a price. Beyond this, however, there are many other pricing issues that the manager must understand. These include the setting of pricing policies, strategic decisions as to the level at which price should be set, and numerous day-to-day issues in pricing management. These will be the subject of this chapter.

PRICING POLICIES

pricing policy
A general guideline based on pricing objectives that is intended for use in specific pricing decisions.

price structure
An outline of the selling price and the various discounts offered to middlemen.

Pricing policies are important for the proper management of pricing. They provide the overall framework and consistency needed in pricing decisions. A **pricing policy** is *a general guideline based on pricing objectives that is intended for use in specific pricing decisions*. Pricing policies affect the **price structure**, which is *an outline of the selling price and the various discounts offered to middlemen*. Price structure decisions take the selected price policy as a given, and specify the discount structure details. Pricing policies have great strategic importance, particularly in relation to competitive considerations. They are the bases on which pricing decisions are made. Future Shop, for example, has a policy that says that it will never be undersold, and that if a customer buys from it and then finds a lower price, a portion of the price difference will be refunded.

Many businesses would be well advised to spend more managerial effort in establishing and periodically reviewing their pricing policies. Companies normally give a great deal of thought and planning to engineering, manufacturing, advertising, and sales promotion policies. It is essential that the same kind of careful study and planning be directed toward the formulation of price policies that will best serve the long-run objectives of the business.

International competition is another reason for establishing clearly formulated price policies. For example, in the retailing sector, the incursion of large U.S. low-price competitors has forced Canadian retailers to rethink quickly their pricing practices. Perhaps if Canadian retailers had been more conscious of the potential international competition, they might have established pricing policies and prices that would have made the Canadian market seem less attractive to foreign competitors.

Pricing policies provide a focus in dealing with varied competitive situations. The type of policy is dependent upon the environment within which the pricing decision must be made. The types of policies to be considered are skimming versus penetration pricing, price flexibility, relative price levels, price lining, and promotional prices. They should all be arrived at through an analysis of the role of pricing in the marketing mix as well as the use of a pricing procedure similar to those described in Chapter 12.

Skimming versus Penetration Pricing Policies

In pricing new products, the initial price that is quoted for an item may determine whether or not the product will eventually be accepted in the marketplace. The initial price also may affect the amount of competition that will emerge. Consider the options available to a company pricing a new product. They may price at the level of comparable products, very high, or very low. Figure 13.1 illustrates that the market is made up of different layers of potential customers with varying degrees of willingness and ability to pay depending on whether prices are higher or lower.

A **skimming pricing** policy chooses *a high entry price*. The name is derived from the expression "skimming the cream." The plan is to sell first to consumers who are willing to pay the highest price, then reduce the price (perhaps introduce a less fancy model) and market to the next level, and so on. One purpose of this strategy is to allow the firm to recover its development costs quickly. The assumption is that competition will eventually drive the price to a lower level, as was the case, for example, with compact discs.

A skimming policy, therefore, attempts to maximize the revenue received from the sale of a new product before the entry of competition. Ballpoint pens were introduced shortly after World War II at a price of about $20. Today, the best-selling ballpoint pens are priced at less than $1. Other examples of products that have been introduced using a skimming policy include television sets, Polaroid cameras, videocassette recorders, home computers, and pocket calculators. Subsequent

skimming pricing
Choosing a high entry price; to sell first to consumers who are willing to pay the highest price, then reduce the price.

■ **Some Marketers Set Their Prices above the Prevailing Market Price**

"All I need is one good customer."

Source: Reprinted from *The Saturday Evening Post*, © 1974.

■ Figure 13.1 **The Market for Product X at Various Price Levels**

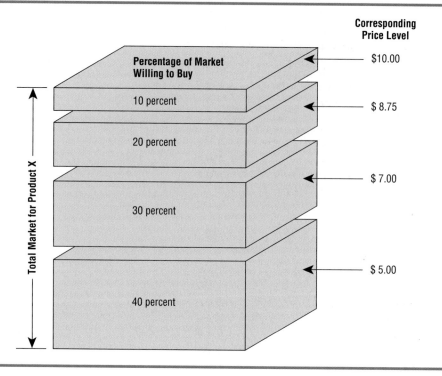

price reductions allowed the marketers of these products to appeal to additional market segments that are more price sensitive.

A skimming strategy permits the marketer to control demand in the introductory stages of the product's life cycle and to adjust its productive capacity to match demand. A danger of low initial price for a new product is that demand may outstrip the firm's production capacity, resulting in consumer and intermediary complaints and possibly permanent damage to the product's image. Excess demand occasionally results in poor-quality products as the firm strives to satisfy consumer desires with inadequate production facilities.

During the late growth and early maturity stages of the product life cycle, the price is reduced for two reasons: (1) the pressure of competition and (2) the desire to expand the product's market. Figure 13.1 shows that 10 percent of the market for Product X would buy the item at $10, while another 20 percent would buy at $8.75. Successive price declines will expand the firm's market as well as meet new competition.

A skimming policy has one chief disadvantage: it attracts competition. Potential competitors who see the innovating firms make large returns also enter the market. This forces the price even lower than it might have had to be using a different pricing policy under a sequential skimming procedure. However, if a firm has patent protection — as Polaroid had — or a proprietary ability to exclude competition, it may use a skimming policy for a relatively long period. Figure 13.2 indicates that 14.4 percent of the respondents in one pricing study used a skimming policy. Skimming also appears to be more common in industrial markets than in consumer markets.

Penetration pricing is the opposite policy in new-product pricing. It results in *an entry price for a product lower than what is estimated to be the long-term price.* The pricing

penetration pricing
An entry price for a product lower than what is estimated to be the long-term price.

■ Figure 13.2 **Use of New-Product Pricing Strategies**

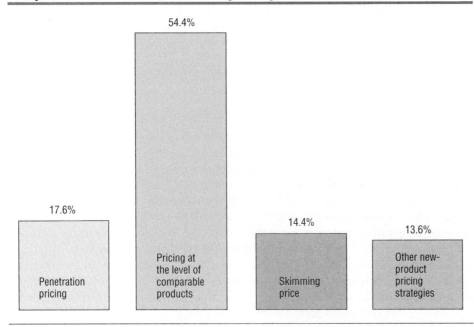

Source: Louis E. Boone and David L. Kurtz, *Pricing Objectives and Practices in American Industry: A Research Report.* All rights reserved.

study shown in Figure 13.2 suggests that penetration pricing is used more often in consumer markets. Soaps and toothpastes are often good examples of this kind of pricing. For instance, a new combined shampoo and conditioner could be introduced with a cents-off label to induce consumers to try it.

The premise is that an initially lower price will help secure market acceptance. Since the firm later intends to increase the price, brand popularity is crucial to the success of a penetration policy. One advantage of such a policy is that it discourages competition from entering, since the prevailing low price does not suggest the attractive returns associated with a skimming policy.

Penetration pricing is likely to be used in instances where demand for the new product or service is highly elastic and large numbers of consumers are highly price sensitive. It is also likely to be used in instances where large-scale operations and long production runs result in substantial reductions in production and marketing costs. Finally, penetration pricing may be appropriate in instances where the new product is likely to attract strong competitors when it is introduced. Such a strategy may allow it to reach the mass market quickly and capture a large share of the market before the entry of competitors. With penetration pricing, the marketers will likely forgo some profits, at least in the short run.

The key decision, of course, is when to move the price to its intended level. Consumers tend to resist price increases; therefore, correct timing is essential. The solution depends upon the degree of brand loyalty that has been achieved. Brand loyalty must be at the point where a price increase would not cause a disproportionate decrease in customers. A series of modest price changes, rather than a single large hike, also can retain customers. Often, firms will use cents-off deals to enter at a lower price. These can then be phased out more easily.

A firm may, of course, decide to use neither a skimming nor a penetration price. It may try to price a new product at the point where it is intended to sell in the long run. All three new-product pricing strategies are common, but it can be seen from Figure 13.2 that this last strategy was chosen in 54 percent of new-product pricing situations.

Price Flexibility

flexible pricing
A variable price policy.

Marketing executives must also determine company policy with respect to **flexible pricing**. Is the firm going to have just one price or pursue *a variable price policy* in the market? As a generalization, *one-price policies* characterize situations where mass selling is employed, and *variable pricing* is more common where individual bargaining typifies market transactions, for example, the purchase of a car.

A one-price policy is common in Canadian retailing since it facilitates mass merchandising. For the most part, once the price is set, the manager can direct his or her attention to other aspects of the marketing mix. Flexible prices, by contrast, are found more in wholesaling and industrial markets. This does not mean that price flexibility exists only in manufacturing industries. A study of the retail home appliance market concluded that people who had purchased identical products from the same dealer had often paid different prices for them. The primary reasons for the differences were customer knowledge and bargaining strength.[2]

While variable pricing has the advantage of flexibility in selling situations, it may result in conflict with the Combines Act provisions. It may also lead to retaliatory pricing on the part of competitors, and it is not well received by those who have paid the higher prices.

Relative Price Levels

Another important pricing policy decision concerns the relative price level. Are the firm's prices to be set above, below, or at the prevailing market price? In economic theory, this question would be answered by supply and demand analysis. However, from a practical viewpoint, marketing managers *administer* prices. In other words, they subjectively set the markup percentages to achieve the price level desired. The decision-maker must still develop a basic policy in regard to relative price levels. A fine clothing store, such as Harry Rosen, would probably have a policy of pricing at a level higher than most other clothing retailers.

Following the competition is one method of negating the price variable in marketing strategy, since it forces competition to concentrate on other factors. Some firms choose to price below or above competition. These decisions are usually based on a firm's cost structure, overall marketing strategy, and pricing objectives.

PRICING PRACTICES

Price Lining

price lining
The practice of marketing merchandise at a limited number of prices.

Most companies sell a varied line of products. An effective pricing strategy should consider the relationship among the firm's products rather than view each in isolation. Specifically, **price lining** is *the practice of marketing merchandise at a limited* *number of prices.* For example, a clothier might have a $195 line of men's suits and a $325 line. Price lining is used extensively in retail selling. It can be an advantage to both retailer and customer. Customers can choose the price range they wish to pay, then concentrate on all the other variables, such as colour, style, and material. The retailer can purchase and offer specific lines rather than a more generalized assortment.

Price lining requires that one identify the market segment or segments to which the firm is appealing. For example, a suitcase manufacturer may see its market not as all luggage, but as the "medium-priced, hard-side" portion of the luggage trade. The firm must decide how to *line* its product prices. A dress manufacturer might have lines priced at $89.95, $159.95, and $199.95. Price lining not only simplifies the administration of the pricing structure, but also alleviates the confusion of a situation in which all products are priced separately. Price lining is really a combined product/price strategy.

One problem with a price-line decision is that once it is made, retailers and manufacturers have difficulty in adjusting it. Rising costs, therefore, put the seller in the position of either changing the price lines, with the resulting confusion, or reducing costs by production adjustments, which opens the firm to the complaint that "XYZ Company's merchandise certainly isn't what it used to be!"

Promotional Prices

A **promotional price** is *a lower-than-normal price used as an ingredient in a firm's selling strategy.* In some cases promotional prices are recurrent, such as the annual shoe store sale: "Buy one pair of shoes, get the second for one cent." Or a new pizza restaurant may have an opening special to attract customers. In other situations, a firm may introduce a promotional model or brand to allow it to compete in another market.

Promotional pricing is often seen at the retail level. One type is **loss leaders**, *goods priced below cost to attract customers* who, the retailer hopes, will then buy other regularly priced merchandise. The use of loss leaders can be effective, and is a commonly used means of generating business.

> Probably one of the best innovators of this pricing method was Cal Mayne. He was one of the first men to systematically price specials and to evaluate their effect on gross margins and sales. Mayne increased sales substantially by featuring coffee, butter, and margarine at 10 percent below cost. Ten other demand items were priced competitively and at a loss when necessary to undersell competition. Still another group of so-called secondary demand items were priced in line with competition. Mayne based his pricing policy on the theory that a customer can only remember about 30 prices. Keep prices down on these items and the customer will stay with you.[3]

The ethical or moral implications of this practice are not being considered here. Some studies have indeed reported considerable price confusion on the part of consumers. One study of consumer price recall reported that average shoppers misquoted the price they last paid for coffee by over 12 percent, toothpaste by over 20 percent, and green beans by 24 percent. While some people hit the prices exactly, others missed by several hundred percent.[4] The use of loss leaders is common in several branches of retailing today.

Three potential pitfalls should be considered when one faces a promotional pricing decision:

promotional price
A lower-than-normal price used as an ingredient in a firm's selling strategy.

loss leader
Goods priced below cost to attract customers.

1. The Competition Act may prohibit some types of promotional pricing practices. (See Chapter 2.)
2. Some consumers are little influenced by price appeals, so promotional pricing will have little effect on them.[5]
3. Continuous use of an artificially low rate may result in its being accepted as customary for the product. Bic pens were introduced as a low-price product (with corresponding manufacturing costs). It would be extremely difficult to raise their prices significantly now.

Psychological Pricing

psychological pricing
The use of prices to suggest values of a product or attributes of a product/price offering.

Psychological pricing is *the use of prices to suggest values of a product or attributes of a product/price offering.* Prestige pricing, mentioned in Chapter 12, is one of many forms of psychological pricing.

The psychology of pricing can be complicated. Professor Lee Kreul has found through research that in restaurant newspaper advertisements for a meal costing less than $7, the price usually ends in 9 (e.g., $4.99). This implies a discount. For meals costing above $7, prices usually end in 5. Professor Kreul believes that as prices go up, the ending number changes because it takes more than one cent to create the discount illusion. Furthermore, people interested in paying more than $7 might think that a price ending in 9 suggests discounts, low quality, or hurried service.[6]

odd pricing
Prices are set ending in some amount just below the next rounded number.

Odd pricing is a good example of the application of psychological pricing. *Prices are set ending in some amount just below the next rounded number.* A price of $16.99 is assumed to be more appealing than $17 (supposedly because it is a lower figure).

Originally odd pricing was used to force clerks to make change, thus serving as a cash control device within the firm.[7] Now it has become a customary feature of contemporary price quotations. For instance, one discounter uses prices ending in 3 and 7 rather than 5, 8, or 9 because of a belief that customers regard price tags of $5.95, $6.98, and $7.99 as *regular* retail prices, while $5.97 and $6.93 are considered *discount* prices. Obviously, intuition and experience play a part in establishing an odd pricing policy.

The Price–Quality Concept

One of the most researched aspects of pricing is the relationship between price and the consumer's perception of the product's quality.[8] In the absence of other cues, price is an important factor in the consumer's perception of the product's quality.[9] The higher the price, the better the buyer believes the quality of the product to be. One study asked 400 people what terms they associated with the word *expensive*. Two-thirds of the replies were related to high quality, such as *best* and *superior*.[10] The relationship between price and perceived quality is a well-documented fact in contemporary marketing.

price limits
Limits within which product quality perception varies directly with price.

Probably the most useful concept in explaining price–quality relationships is the idea of **price limits**.[11] It is argued that consumers have *limits within which product quality perception varies directly with price*. A price below the lower limit is regarded as too cheap, while one above the higher limit means it is too expensive. Most consumers do tend to set an acceptable price range when purchasing goods and services. The range, of course, varies, depending on consumers' socio-economic characteristics and buying dispositions. Consumers, nonetheless, should be aware that

IKEA has made a name for itself as a purveyor of low-cost, well-designed furniture. But low prices mean low quality to many shoppers. To combat this perception, IKEA customers can literally see the quality and workmanship of its furniture being tested in IKEA stores. Tests such as these also help to extend the notion of quality to other low-cost products at IKEA and to the company's overall image. IKEA advertisements such as this one often group many low-cost items together, creating the impression that there are numerous good deals available.

price is not necessarily an indicator of quality. Alberta Consumer and Corporate Affairs summarized seven price–quality research studies, six covering *Consumer Reports* analyses of 932 products between 1940 and 1977, and one for 43 products tested by *Canadian Consumer* between 1973 and 1977. It found that while there was a positive relationship between price and quality, the correlation was low (Spearman rank correlation = .25). In addition, about 25 percent of products tested had a negative price–quality relation. That is, products ranked lower in performance had higher prices than products deemed superior by the Canadian and U.S. consumer testing organizations.[12]

Unit Pricing

Consumer advocates have often pointed out the difficulty of comparing consumer products that are available in different-size packages or containers. Is an 800 g can selling for 75 cents a better buy than two 450 g cans priced at 81 cents or another brand that sells at three 450 g cans for 89 cents? The critics argue that there should be a common way to price consumer products.

Unit pricing is a response to this problem. Under unit pricing, all prices are stated *in terms of some recognized unit of measurement (such as grams and litres) or a standard numerical count.* There has been considerable discussion about legislating mandatory unit pricing. The Consumers' Association of Canada has endorsed unit pricing, and many of the major food chains have adopted it.

The real question, of course, is whether unit pricing improves consumer decisions. One study found that the availability of unit prices resulted in consumer savings, and that retailers also benefited when unit pricing led to greater purchases of store brands. The study concluded that unit pricing was valuable to both buyer and

unit pricing
All prices are stated in terms of some recognized unit of measurement (such as grams and litres) or a standard numerical count.

seller and that it merited full-scale use.[13] Others have questioned the amount of use of unit pricing by consumers.

PRICE QUOTATIONS

How prices are quoted depends on many factors, such as cost structures, traditional practice in the particular industry, and the policies of individual firms. In this section, we shall examine the reasoning and methodology behind price quotations.

list price
The rate normally quoted to potential buyers.

The basis upon which most price structures are built is the **list price**, *the rate normally quoted to potential buyers*. List price is usually determined by one or a combination of the methods discussed in Chapter 12. The sticker prices on new cars are good examples. They show the list price for the basic model, then add the list price for the options that have been included.

Discounts, Allowances, and Rebates

market price
The amount that a consumer pays.

The amount that a consumer pays — the **market price** — may or may not be the same as the list price. In some cases, discounts or allowances reduce the list price. List price is often used as the starting point from which discounts that set the market price are derived. Discounts can be classified as cash, quantity, or trade.

cash discounts
Reductions in price that are given for prompt payment of a bill.

Cash discounts are those *reductions in price that are given for prompt payment of a bill.* They are probably the most commonly used variety. Cash discounts usually specify an exact time period, such as "2/10, net 30." This would mean that the bill is due within 30 days, but if it is paid in 10 days, the customer may subtract 2 percent from the amount due. Cash discounts have become a traditional pricing practice in many industries. They are legal provided that they are granted to all customers on the same terms. Such discounts were originally instituted to improve the liquidity position of sellers by reducing accounts receivable, lower bad-debt losses, and reduce the expenses associated with collecting bills. Whether these advantages outweigh the relatively high cost of capital involved in cash discounts depends on the seller's need for liquidity as well as alternative sources (and costs) of funds.

trade discounts
Payments to channel members or buyers for performing some marketing function normally required of the manufacturer.

Trade discounts, which are also called *functional discounts*, are *payments to channel members or buyers for performing some marketing function normally required of the manufacturer.* These are legitimate as long as all buyers in the same category, such as wholesalers and retailers, receive the same discount privilege. Trade discounts were initially based on the operating expenses of each trade category, but have now become more of a matter of custom in some industries. An example of a trade discount would be "40 percent, 10 percent off list price" for wholesalers. In other words, the wholesaler passes the 40 percent on to his or her customers (retailers) and keeps the 10 percent discount as payment for activities such as storing and transporting. The price to the wholesaler on a $100 000 order would be $54 000 ($100 000 less 40% = $60 000 less 10%). Note the sequence in which the discount calculations are made.

quantity discounts
Price reductions granted because of large purchases.

Quantity discounts are *price reductions granted because of large purchases.* These discounts are justified on the grounds that large-volume purchases reduce selling expenses and may shift a part of the storing, transporting, and financing functions to the buyer. Quantity discounts are lawful provided they are offered on the same basis to all customers.

Quantity discounts may be either noncumulative or cumulative. Noncumulative quantity discounts are one-time reductions in list price. For instance, a firm might

■ Table 13.1 **A Noncumulative Quantity Discount Schedule**

Units Purchased	Price
1	List price
2–5	List price less 10 percent
6–10	List price less 20 percent
Over 10	List price less 25 percent

offer the discount schedule in Table 13.1. Cumulative quantity discounts are reductions determined by purchases over a stated time period. Annual purchases of $25 000 might entitle the buyer to an 8 percent rebate, while purchases exceeding $50 000 would mean a 15 percent refund. These reductions are really patronage discounts since they tend to bind the customer to one source of supply.

Allowances are similar to discounts in that they are deductions from the price the purchaser must pay. The major categories of allowances are trade-ins and promotional allowances. **Trade-ins** are often used in the sale of durable goods such as cars. They permit a reduction without altering the basic list price by *deducting from the item's price an amount for the customer's old item that is being replaced.*

Promotional allowances are *extra discounts offered to retailers so that they will advertise the manufacturer along with the retailer.* They are attempts to integrate promotional strategy in the channel. For example, manufacturers often provide advertising and sales-support allowances for other channel members. Many manufacturers offer such allowances to retail dealers.

Rebates are *refunds by the seller of a portion of the purchase price.* They have been used most prominently by automobile manufacturers eager to move models during periods of slow sales. Manufacturers' rebates are sometimes used to stimulate sales of small appliances such as coffeemakers or hair dryers. Manufacturers' rebate coupons are placed in the retail outlets near the product being promoted.

Geographic Considerations

Geographic considerations are important in pricing when the shipment of heavy, bulky, low unit-cost materials is involved. Prices may be quoted with either the buyer or the seller paying all transportation charges or with some type of expense sharing.

A firm's competitiveness often depends on how it handles the costs of transportation. In the extreme case, where the cost of transportation is high compared with the value of the product (e.g., cement) the competitive limits of a firm's territory can easily be defined. In cases where product margins are high or transportation costs are low, market coverage can be extensive. Furthermore, the more differentiated the product, the easier it is for a company to pass along the costs of distribution in the price.

The seller has several alternatives in handling transportation costs. These are FOB plant, uniform delivered price, and zone pricing.

FOB plant or *FOB origin* pricing provides a price that does not include any shipping charges. *The buyer must pay all the freight charges.* The seller pays only the cost of loading the merchandise aboard the carrier selected by the buyer. The abbreviation FOB means *free on board*. Legal title and responsibility pass to the buyer once the purchase is loaded and a receipt is obtained from the representative of the common carrier.

trade-ins
Deductions from an item's price of an amount for the customer's old item that is being replaced.

promotional allowances
Extra discounts offered to retailers so that they will advertise the manufacturer along with the retailer.

rebates
Refunds by the seller of a portion of the purchase price.

FOB plant
The buyer must pay all the freight charges.

Prices may also be shown as FOB origin — freight allowed. *The seller permits the buyer to subtract transportation expenses from the bill.* The amount the seller receives varies with the freight charges charged against the invoice. This alternative, called **freight absorption**, is commonly used by firms with high fixed costs (who need to maintain high volume) because it permits a considerable expansion of their market, since a competitive price is quoted regardless of shipping expenses.

The same price (including transportation expenses) is quoted to all buyers when a **uniform delivered price** is the firm's policy. Such pricing is the exact opposite of FOB prices. This system is often compared with the pricing of a first-class letter, which is the same across the country. Hence, it is sometimes called *postage-stamp pricing*. The price that is quoted includes an *average* transportation charge per customer, which means that distant customers are actually paying a lesser share of selling costs while customers near the supply source pay what is known as *phantom freight* (the average transportation charge exceeds the actual cost of shipping).

In **zone pricing**, which is simply a modification of a uniform delivered pricing system, *the market is divided into different zones and a price is established within each.* Canadian parcel post rates depend on zone pricing. The primary advantage of this pricing policy is that it is easy to administer and enables the seller to be more competitive in distant markets. Figure 13.3 shows how a marketer in Winnipeg must divide its market into geographic segments. All customers in zone 1 would be charged $10 per unit of freight, while more distant customers would pay freight costs based on the zone in which they are located.

NEGOTIATED PRICES AND COMPETITIVE BIDDING

Many situations involving government and industrial procurement are not characterized by set prices, particularly for nonrecurring purchases such as a defence sys-

■ Figure 13.3 **Zone Pricing for a Winnipeg Firm**

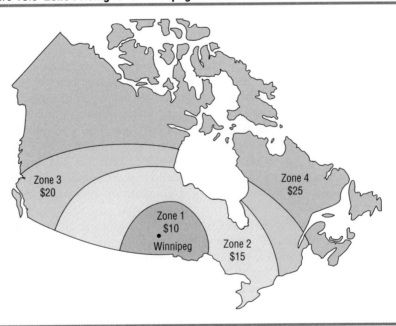

tem for the armed forces. Markets such as these are growing at a fast pace. Governmental units now spend nearly half of Canada's GDP!

Competitive bidding is *a process by which buyers request potential suppliers to make price quotations on a proposed purchase or contract.* **Specifications** give *a specific description of the needed item (or job)* that the government or industrial firm wishes to acquire. One of the most important tasks in modern purchasing management is to describe adequately what the organization seeks to buy. This generally requires the assistance of the firm's technical personnel, such as engineers, designers, and chemists.

Competitive bidding strategy should employ the concept of *expected net profit*, which can be stated as

$$\text{Expected Net Profit} = P\,(\text{Bid} - \text{Costs})$$

where P = the probability of the buyer accepting the bid.

Consider the following example. A firm is contemplating submitting a bid for a job that is estimated to cost $23 000. One executive has proposed a bid of $60 000; another, $50 000. It is estimated that there is a 40 percent chance of the buyer accepting bid 1 ($60 000) and a 60 percent chance of the buyer accepting bid 2 ($50 000). The expected net profit formula indicates that bid 2 would be best since its expected net profit is the higher of the two.

$$
\begin{aligned}
\text{Bid 1} \quad \text{ENP} &= 0.40\,(\$60\ 000 - \$23\ 000) \\
&= 0.40\,(\$37\ 000) \\
&= \$14\ 800
\end{aligned}
$$

$$
\begin{aligned}
\text{Bid 2} \quad \text{ENP} &= 0.60\,(\$50\ 000 - \$23\ 000) \\
&= 0.60\,(\$27\ 000) \\
&= \$16\ 200
\end{aligned}
$$

The most difficult task in applying this concept is estimating the likelihood that a certain bid will be accepted. But this is not a valid reason for failing to quantify one's estimate. Prior experience often provides the foundation for such estimates.

In some cases, industrial and governmental purchasers use **negotiated contracts** instead of inviting competitive bidding for a project. In these situations, *the terms of the contract are set through talks between the buyer and the seller.* Where there is only one available supplier, or where contracts require extensive research and development work, negotiated contracts are likely to be employed.

Some provincial and local governments permit their agencies to negotiate purchases under a certain limit, say $500 or $1000. This policy is an attempt to reduce costs since obtaining bids for relatively minor purchases is expensive and there is little prospect of large savings to the agency involved.

In times of inflation, the fear that inflation may have unknown effects on the economic viability of prices has become a major deterrent to companies bidding for or negotiating contracts that take some time to implement. One response has been to include an **escalator clause**[14] that *allows the seller to adjust the final price based on changes in the costs of the product's ingredients between the placement of the order and the completion of construction or delivery of the product.* Such clauses typically base the adjustment calculation on the cost-of-living index or a similar indicator. While an estimated one-third of all industrial marketers use escalator clauses in some of their bids, these are most commonly used with major projects involving long time periods and complex operations.

---

competitive bidding
A process by which buyers request potential suppliers to make price quotations on a proposed purchase or contract

specifications
A specific description of a needed item or job that the buyer wishes to acquire.

negotiated contract
The terms of the contract are set through talks between the buyer and the seller.

escalator clause
Allows the seller to adjust the final price based on changes in the costs of the product's ingredients between the placement of the order and the completion of construction or delivery of the product.

international pricing
Setting prices to be charged to buyers in other countries taking into consideration exchange risk, price escalation through multiplication of channels, and transportation.

exchange risk
The risk of negotiating a price in another nation's currency and finding upon delivery of the product that currency's value has dropped in relation to your country's currency.

price escalation
The increase in final price in a foreign market over a domestic price because of having to pay for the services of additional channel members in getting the product to that market.

International pricing takes all of the foregoing into consideration, as appropriate, but requires additional considerations: exchange risk, price escalation through multiplication of channels, and transportation.

Suppose, after looking at costs and exchange rates, you agree to sell your product for 3000 rubles to a company in Russia, and to deliver it in six months. You could lose a great deal of money if the value of the ruble should fall — say, by 25 percent. In this case, the buyer would pay the amount of rubles agreed to, but you would receive only 75 percent of the value you expected. This is known as **exchange risk**. One way of avoiding this risk is to negotiate the price to be paid in Canadian dollars, or some other stable currency. There are several other ways of compensating for this, which are beyond the scope of this book.

Selling internationally often requires additional channel members to handle the product in another country, resulting in **price escalation**. If customary margins are given to all channel members, the market price can escalate beyond what is acceptable to final customers. Thus the international marketer must rethink its expected markup and negotiate lower margins with channel members.

Shipping products overseas may be a significant additional cost for many products. As with price escalation, the international marketer cannot just simply add on the increased transportation costs. Innovative solutions to reducing transportation costs and a willingness to absorb some of these costs may be necessary in order to come up with a price that is acceptable in an international setting.

THE TRANSFER PRICING PROBLEM

transfer price
The price for sending goods from one company profit centre to another.

profit centre
Any part of the organization to which revenue and controllable costs can be assigned, such as a department.

One pricing problem peculiar to large-scale enterprises is that of determining an internal **transfer price** — that is, *the price for sending goods from one company profit centre to another.* As a company expands, it usually needs to decentralize management. Profit centres are then set up as a control device in the new decentralized operation. **Profit centres** are *any part of the organization to which revenue and controllable costs can be assigned, such as a department.*

In large companies, the centres can secure many of their resource requirements from within the corporate structure. The pricing problem becomes what rate Profit Centre A (maintenance department) should charge Profit Centre B (sales department) for the cleaning compound used on B's floors. Should the price be the same as it would be if A did the work for an outside party? Should B receive a discount? The answer to these questions depends on the philosophy of the firm involved.

The transfer pricing dilemma is an example of the variations that a firm's pricing policy must deal with. Consider the case of UDC-Europe, a Universal Data Corporation subsidiary that itself has ten subsidiaries. Each of the ten is organized on a geographic basis, and each is treated as a separate profit centre. Intercompany transfer prices are set at the annual budget meeting. Special situations, like unexpected volume, are handled through negotiations by the subsidiary managers. If complex tax problems arise, UDC-Europe's top management may set the transfer price.

PRICING IN THE PUBLIC SECTOR

The pricing of public services has also become an interesting, and sometimes controversial, aspect of contemporary marketing. A good example is the price of tuition for college and university students (see the accompanying box).

APPLYING THE CONCEPTS

Setting Tuition Fees

Thousands of university students camped in front of the parliament, chanted and sang, and generally complained about their current and future plight. They should have stayed home.

Theirs is among the weakest of all cases directed against the federal government by interest groups opposed to social-policy reform. Happily, many university students understand both what a good deal they are getting and why the country's doleful fiscal situation requires them to pay more.

In the last few years, fees have been rising. But these rises have brought fees back — in *real* terms — to their levels in the mid-to-late seventies. In other words, for more than 15 years fees rose less rapidly than inflation, and so declined in real terms.

Courtesy of the fiscal crisis of all governments, fees will continue rising. Protesting students fear that the federal government's social-policy reform, including income-contingent student loan programs, will force them still higher.

Some facts please. In Ontario universities, student tuition and other fees amount to about an average of $2,562 a year. Across the border, in the publicly financed system of New York State, student tuition and fees are $4,200 (Canadian). Consider the fees, expressed in Canadian dollars, in other publicly funded American state systems: Massachusetts, $7,629; Michigan, $7,137; Pennsylvania, $6,892; California (Berkeley), $5,792; Minnesota, $4,616. (Out-of-state residents pay a hefty premium ranging from $4,000 in New York to $10,000 in Michigan.)

So Canadian university students are contributing much less to their education than their American counterparts in publicly funded universities. But how much are Canadian students paying of their education?

Undergraduate fees across Canada cover only 10 to 17 percent of universities' total income. Higher education benefits not just those who receive it. Society gains from the acquisition and spread of knowledge, reasoning skills, research and a host of other advantages conferred by higher education. So society at large, through the tax system, should pick up a healthy chunk of the universities' expenses.

But students themselves benefit financially from this education. Their incomes after graduation are usually higher, and often much higher, than the incomes of those who do not attend university. At the height of the last recession, the unemployment rate for those with university degrees was one-third of the national rate.

Students have been getting a good deal. Rather than getting mad at governments, they should realize how they benefit themselves from public subsidies.

Source: Adapted from Jeffrey Simpson, "Students Should Stop Whining about Tuition Fees and Be Thankful," *The Globe and Mail* (November 17, 1994), p. A18. Used by permission of *The Globe and Mail.*

Do you agree with this analysis of the pricing of higher education? From a marketing perspective, how would you analyze the situation?

Traditionally, government services either were very low-cost or were priced using the full-cost approach: users paid all the costs associated with the service. In some cases there have been attempts to set prices using incremental or marginal pricing, which considers only those expenses specifically associated with a particular activity. However, it is often difficult to determine the costs that should be assigned to a particular activity or service. Governmental accounting problems are often more complex than those of private enterprise.

Another problem in pricing public services is that taxes act as an *indirect* price of a public service. Someone must decide the relative relationship between the direct and indirect prices of such a service. A shift toward indirect tax charges (where an income or earnings tax exists) is generally a movement toward charging on the *ability to pay* rather than on the *use* principle.

The pricing of any public service involves a basic policy decision as to whether the price is an instrument to recover costs or a technique for accomplishing some other social or civic objective. For example, public health services may be priced near zero so as to encourage their use. On the other hand, parking fines in some cities are high so as to discourage use of private cars in the central business district. Pricing decisions in the public sector are difficult because political and social considerations often outweigh the economic aspects. As governments have cut services and/or transferred them to the private sector, the pricing problem has been simplified somewhat as tax and public policy considerations have been largely eliminated.

■ KEY TERMS

pricing policy	list price	zone pricing
skimming pricing	market price	competitive bidding
penetration pricing	cash discount	specifications
flexible pricing	trade discount	negotiated contract
price lining	quantity discounts	escalator clause
promotional pricing	trade-in	international pricing
loss leader	promotional allowance	exchange risk
psychological pricing	rebate	price escalation
odd pricing	FOB plant	transfer price
price limits	freight absorption	profit centre
unit pricing	uniform delivered price	

■ INTERACTIVE SUMMARY AND DISCUSSION QUESTIONS

1. A pricing policy is a general guideline based on pricing objectives that is intended for use in specific pricing decisions. Pricing policies affect the price structure. Give an example of the price structure of a product you are familiar with. What is the likely pricing policy for that product?
2. Pricing policies provide focus in dealing with varied competitive situations. Explain why it is very important to have a pricing policy in such situations.
3. A skimming policy chooses a high entry price. Explain the reasons why a business might choose such a policy. What are the potential disadvantages?
4. Penetration pricing is the opposite policy to a skimming policy in new-product pricing. Explain the reasons why a business might choose penetration pricing. What are the potential disadvantages?
5. Penetration pricing is likely to be used in instances where demand for a new product or service is highly elastic and large number of consumers are highly price sensitive. Explain.

6. A business might set prices to be relatively higher than those of most competitors. Give an example of such a business and explain why this might be a good strategy.

7. Price lining is the practice of marketing merchandise at a limited number of prices. In what circumstances is such a practice desirable? Why?

8. Psychological pricing is the use of prices to suggest values of a product or attributes of a product/price offering. Make a list of as many different examples of psychological pricing as you can think of.

9. Behind a list price quotation is a number of other prices and price practices, such as market price, cash discounts, trade discounts, and quantity discounts. Explain each in relation to the list price.

10. Another set of terms related to geographic considerations are FOB plant, freight absorption, uniform delivered price, and zone pricing. Explain each term.

11. In international marketing, some important additional considerations that affect pricing are exchange risk, price escalation, and transportation. Explain how each of these can affect the final realized price.

12. Pricing in the public sector is complex because different objectives and motives are often involved. Describe how this applies in the pricing of postsecondary tuition.

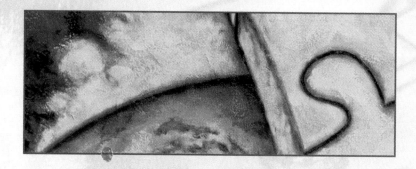

This section deals with the third element of the marketing mix, focussing on the activities and institutions involved in moving products and services to the firm's chosen target market. Chapter 14 introduces the basic concepts related to channels, as well as the related physical distribution. Chapters 15 and 16 analyze wholesalers and retailers, the marketing institutions that make up marketing channels.

CHAPTER 14

Channel and Distribution Strategy

CHAPTER OBJECTIVES

1. To discuss channel strategy as one of the elements of the marketing mix.
2. To relate channel strategy to the concept of total quality management.
3. To explain the role of distribution channels in marketing strategy.
4. To describe the various types of channels of distribution.
5. To outline the major strategy alternatives in using marketing channels.
6. To describe conflict and co-operation in the distribution channel.
7. To show how the physical distribution system contributes to the functioning of marketing channels.

Within two years, personal computers will be selling faster than television sets, predicts Benny Alagem, president and chief executive of white-hot Packard Bell Electronics Inc.

The 58-year-old company figures to have a big piece of that action, and if recent history is any indicator, it probably will. Mr. Alagem made these comments at the Canadian rollout of Packard Bell's all-in-one multimedia PCs, and the opening of the new Canadian manufacturing facility.

The new PCs move Packard Bell closer toward Mr. Alagem's view of a world in which every home has more than one personal computer and every computer serves as a number of appliances.

"We are positioning it as a centrepiece in the home," he said, "You have seven different appliances come into play in one unit." The seven appliances in Packard Bell's new Spectria are CD player, stereo, TV and video player, phone answering system, modem, fax, and personal computer.

The company does not compete by developing major new technologies. However, they do a remarkable job of pioneering little things that are specifically target marketed, such as pre-loaded software and toll-free technical support. Many of these have now become industry standards. The company has proven to be very adept at doing those things that are important in the purchasing decision. It concentrates on designing a product to meet a specific target market and helping to nurture that market. In addition, Packard Bell has positioned itself to be in the right place at the right time, selling products into the home market through mass market retail channels.

The company needs its new Canadian facilities — three times the size of its old space — just to keep up with Canadian sales growth (around 57 percent in 1994). Worldwide the privately held company had revenue of $1.25 billion (U.S.) in 1993, and approximately $2.3 billion in 1994.

In what to some must seem like a dream, the company has displaced International Business Machines in the upper ranks of PC vendors, behind only Compaq and Apple.

Mr. Alagem and his staff explain that the company has been around for a long time, but concentrating on the home market for PCs. The company concentrated on moving its product through mass merchandise retail stores.

"From the start, we envisioned that the consumer utilization of PCs was going to grow," Mr. Alagem said. "Our greatest attention was to the development of units that can be used at home, plug-and-play units that are easy to use but are not less sophisticated."

Since that time, Packard Bell has easily dominated in the retail market for PCs, but until recently wasn't saying much. A couple of years ago, when Compaq, Apple, and IBM decided to start pushing their machine in electronics shops and department stores, it looked like the writing was on the wall for comparatively tiny Packard Bell.

"People wondered if we would be forced out and we'd answer, humbly, that we would have to wait and see," said Mal Ransom, the company's vice-president of marketing.

What did happen, he said, was that the entry of the industry giants legitimized a marketing channel, which had previously been shunned as too unsophisticated for serious computer buyers.

"What happened is that the channel grew — not just grew, it exploded," Mr. Ransom said. Mr. Alagem added, "Our goals are not dictated by market share. Market share numbers for us are historical numbers, and it's good to look at them for a few minutes . . . Our major objective is to provide state-of-the-art technology that the consumer wants."[1]

It is clear that much of Packard Bell's success has been due to a strategic decision concerning the channel of distribution to be used for its product. The product is good, but not superior, to that of competitors. But the company had a clear vision of its target market, and how to reach this market.

INTRODUCTION

Marketing channels create time, place, and ownership utility in a direct way. Let's take the example of swimwear. Products for the coming spring and summer have already been produced in the months of December and January, and are en route to retail stores throughout the continent. Information from the marketing department has allowed swimwear manufacturers to identify preferences for new colours, styles, and fabrics and to produce products of the highest quality for each market. However, swimwear of even the highest quality will fail to generate adequate sales unless it is delivered to the right place (place utility), at the right time (time utility), and with appropriate legal requirements (ownership utility). Swimwear meeting consumers' quality expectations, available in the appropriate outlet the first warm day in April, accompanied by a sales receipt indicating ownership, will be able to provide buyers with form, time, place, and ownership utility — and a little later they'll slip it on, tiptoe across a sunny beach, and dip a pale toe into the chilly water.

A manufacturer of swimwear must therefore work out a clear channel strategy in order for the entire distribution process to work. Let us now consider basic channel strategy as the starting point for a discussion of the distribution function and its role in the marketing mix. Emphasis will be placed on the role of total quality management (*TQM*) in channel strategy. More North American organizations are learning that what they do prior to supplying the customer has a tremendous influence on performance, measured by cost or customer responsiveness. TQM takes the customer's needs and wants (as stated in the customer's own words) and seeks to preserve them as information is passed to process and manufacturing units. Products are produced that possess superior technical features and meet the needs and wants of customers.

This chapter covers such basic issues as the role and types of distribution channels, channel strategy and composition as a means of assuring total quality management, logistics functions performed within the marketing channel, and conflict and co-operation in the distribution channel.[2] Chapters 15 and 16 deal with wholesaling and retailing, the marketing institutions in the distribution channel. This section begins with a look at what marketers call distribution channels.

Carson luggage is made in Ottawa, Staedtler pens and erasers come from Germany, plywood is produced in British Columbia, and Timex watches are assembled in Toronto. All are sold throughout Canada. In each case, some method must be devised to bridge the gap between producer and consumer. Distribution channels provide the purchaser with a convenient means of obtaining the products that he or she wishes to buy. **Distribution channels** (also called marketing channels) are *the paths that goods — and title to these goods — follow from producer to consumer.*[3] Specifically, the term *channels* refers to the various marketing institutions and the interrelationships responsible for the flow of goods and services from producer to consumer or industrial user. Intermediaries are the marketing institutions in the distribution channel. A **marketing intermediary**, or middleman, is *a business firm operating between the producer and the consumer or industrial purchaser.* The term therefore *includes both wholesalers and retailers.*

Wholesaling is *the activities of intermediaries who sell to retailers, other wholesalers, and industrial users but not significant amounts to ultimate consumers.* The terms *jobber* and *distributor* are considered synonymous with wholesaler in this book.

Confusion can result from the practices of some firms that operate both wholesaling and retailing operations. Sporting goods stores, for example, often maintain a wholesaling operation in marketing a line of goods to high schools and colleges as well as operating retail stores. For the purpose of this book, we will treat such operations as two separate institutions.

A second source of confusion is the misleading practice of some retailers who claim to be wholesalers. Such stores may actually sell at wholesale prices and can validly claim to do so. However, *stores that sell products purchased by individuals for their own use and not for resale* are by definition **retailers**, not wholesalers.

distribution channels
The paths that goods — and title to these goods — follow from producer to consumer.

marketing intermediary
A business firm operating between the producer and the consumer or industrial purchaser.

wholesaling
The activities of intermediaries who sell to retailers, other wholesalers, and industrial users but not in significant amounts to ultimate consumers.

retailer
A store that sells products purchased by individuals for their own use and not for resale.

THE ROLE OF DISTRIBUTION CHANNELS IN MARKETING STRATEGY

Distribution channels play a key role in marketing strategy since they provide the means by which goods and services are conveyed from their producers to consumers and users. The importance of distribution channels can be explained in terms of the utility that is created and the functions that are performed.

The Functions Performed by Distribution Channels

The distribution channel performs several functions in the overall marketing system.[4] These include facilitating the exchange process, sorting to alleviate discrepancies in assortment, standardizing transactions, holding inventories, assisting in the search process, and transporting materials and finished products.[5]

FACILITATING THE EXCHANGE PROCESS

The evolution of distribution channels began with the exchange process described in Chapter 1. As market economies grew, the exchange process itself became complicated. With more producers and more potential buyers, intermediaries came into existence to facilitate transactions by cutting the number of marketplace contacts. For example, if ten orchards in the Okanagan valley each sell to six supermarket chains, there are a total of 60 transactions. If the producers set up and market their apples through a co-operative, the number of contacts declines to 16. This process is described in detail in Chapter 15.

SORTING TO ALLEVIATE DISCREPANCIES IN ASSORTMENT

Another essential function of the distribution channel is to adjust discrepancies in assortment. For economic reasons, a producer tends to maximize the quantity of a limited line of products, while the buyer needs a minimum quantity of a wide selection of alternatives. Thus, there is a discrepancy between what the producer has to offer and what the customers want. **Sorting** is *the process that alleviates discrepancies in assortment by re-allocating the outputs of various producers into assortments desired by individual purchasers.*

Figure 14.1 shows an example of the sorting process. First, an individual producer's output is divided into separate homogeneous categories such as the various types and grades of apples. These apples are then combined with the similar crops of other orchards, a process known as *accumulation*. These accumulations are broken down into smaller units or divisions, such as crates of apples. This is often called *breaking bulk* in marketing literature. Finally, an assortment is built for the

sorting
The process that alleviates discrepancies in assortment by re-allocating the outputs of various producers into assortments desired by individual purchasers.

Figure 14.1 **The Sorting Process**

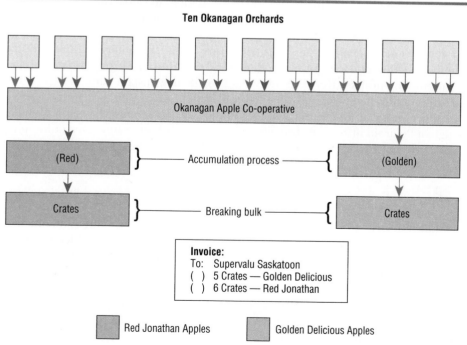

next level in the distribution channel. For example, the Okanagan co-operative might prepare an assortment of five crates of Golden Delicious and six crates of Red Jonathan apples for Supervalu supermarket in Saskatoon.

STANDARDIZING TRANSACTIONS

If each transaction in a complex market economy were subject to negotiation, the exchange process would be chaotic. Distribution channels standardize exchange transactions in terms of the product, such as the grading of apples into types and grades, and the transfer process itself. Order points, prices, payment terms, delivery schedules, and purchase lots tend to be standardized by distribution channel members. For example, supermarket buyers might have on-line communications links with the co-operative cited in Figure 14.1. Once a certain stock position is reached, more apples would automatically be ordered from either the co-operative's current output or its cold storage.

HOLDING INVENTORIES

Distribution channel members hold a minimum of inventories to take advantage of economies of scale in transporting and to provide a buffer for small changes in demand.

THE SEARCH PROCESS

Distribution channels also accommodate the search behaviour of both buyers and sellers. (Search behaviour was discussed earlier in Chapter 7). Buyers are searching for specific products and services to fill their needs, while sellers are attempting to find what consumers want. A college student looking for some Golden Delicious apples might go to the fruit section of Supervalu in Saskatoon. Similarly, the manager of that department would be able to provide the Okanagan co-operative with information about sales trends in his or her marketplace.

PHYSICALLY DISTRIBUTING PRODUCTS

Storing products in convenient locations for shipment to wholesale and retail establishments allows firms to embody time utility in the product. Place utility is created primarily by transporting the product. Customer satisfaction is heavily dependent on reliable movement of products to ensure their availability. Eastman Kodak Company committed a major marketing blunder in the late 1970s when it launched a multimillion-dollar advertising campaign for its new instant camera before adequate quantities had been delivered to retail outlets. Many would-be purchasers visited the stores and, when they discovered that the new camera was not available, bought a Polaroid instead. By providing consumers with time and place utility, physical distribution contributes to implementing the marketing concept.

TYPES OF DISTRIBUTION

Literally hundreds of marketing channels exist today; however, there is no one marketing channel that is superior to all others. The "best" channel for Electrolux vacuum cleaners may be direct from manufacturer to consumer through a sales force of 1000 men and women. The "best" channel for frozen french fries may be from food processor to agent intermediary to *merchant wholesaler* (a wholesaler who takes title) to supermarket to consumer. Instead of searching for a "best" channel for all products, the marketing manager must analyze alternative channels in the light of consumer needs and competitive restraints to determine the optimum channel or channels for the firm's products.[6]

Even when the proper channels have been chosen and established, the marketing manager's channel decisions are not ended. Channels, like so many of the other marketing variables, change, and today's ideal channel may prove obsolete in a few years.

For example, the typical channel for motor oil until the 1960s was from oil company to company-owned service stations, because most oil was put in cars there. But a significant number of oil purchases are now made by motorists in automotive supply stores, discount department stores, and even supermarkets, as today many motorists put in or change the motor oil themselves. Others use rapid oil-change specialty shops. And the channel for Shell, Esso, Texaco, Quaker State, and Castrol must change to reflect these changes in consumer buying patterns.

Figure 14.2 depicts the major channels available for marketers of consumer and industrial goods. In general, industrial products channels tend to be shorter than consumer goods channels because of geographic concentrations of industrial buyers, a relatively limited number of purchasers, and the absence of retailers from the chain. The term *retailer* refers to consumer goods purchases. Service channels also tend to be short because of the intangibility of services and the need to maintain personal relationships in the channel.

Direct Channel

The simplest, most direct marketing channel is not necessarily the best, as is indicated by the relatively small percentage of the dollar volume of sales that moves *directly from the producer to the consumer.* Less than 5 percent of all consumer goods are candidates for the producer-to-consumer channel. Dairies, Tupperware, Avon cosmetics, and numerous mail-order houses are examples of firms whose marketing moves directly from manufacturer to ultimate consumer.

Direct channels are much more important in the industrial goods market, where most major installations and accessory equipment — and many of the fabricated parts and raw materials — are marketed through *direct contacts between producer and user.*

All-Aboard Channel

Probably the longest channel is *from producer to agent to wholesaler to retailer to consumer.* Where products are produced by a large number of small companies, a unique intermediary appears to perform the basic function of bringing buyer and seller together — the agent, or broker. **Agents** are, in fact, *wholesaling intermediaries, but they differ from the typical wholesaler in that they do not take title to the goods.*

They merely represent the producer or the regular wholesaler (who does take title to the goods) in seeking a market for the producer's output or in locating a source of supply for the buyer. Say a canner of vegetables in Ontario has 6000 cases of string beans to sell. The firm informs the food brokers (agents) regularly used in various provinces of this fact. A broker in the Maritimes ascertains that the Maritime supermarket chain Sobey's will buy 800 cases. The broker takes the order, informs the canner, and, if the price is acceptable, the canner ships the order to Sobey's. The canner bills Sobey's and sends a commission cheque (approximately 3 percent of the sale price) to the food broker for the service of bringing buyer and seller together.

agent
A wholesaling intermediary who differs from the typical wholesaler in that the agent does not take title to the goods.

■ Figure 14.2 **Alternative Distribution Channels**

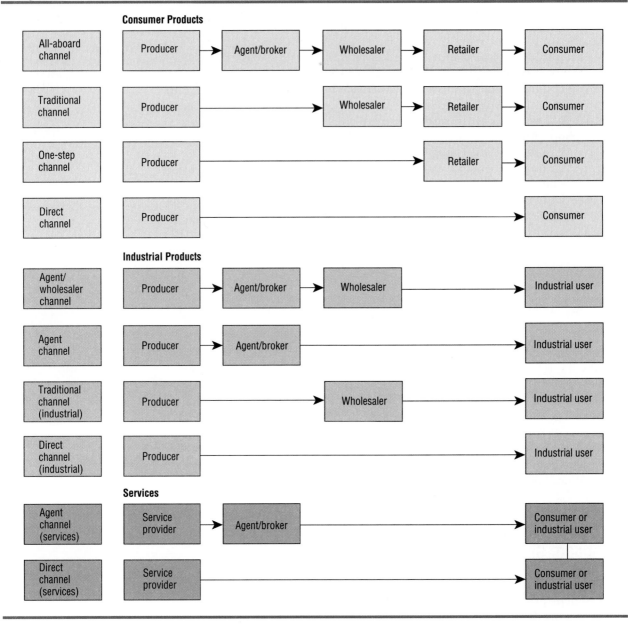

One-Step Channel

This channel is being used more and more, and in many instances it has taken the place of the traditional channel. When large retailers are involved, they are willing to take on many functions performed by the wholesaler — consequently, goods move *from producer to retailer to consumer.*

SAS Institute, a Canadian software company, markets directly to businesses looking for solutions to manage and handle information. SAS provides not only the software itself, but also support, consulting, and education services to its clients.

Traditional Channel (Consumer)

The traditional marketing channel for consumer goods is *from producer to wholesaler to retailer to user.* It is the method used by literally thousands of small manufacturers or companies producing limited lines of products and by as many or more small retailers. Small companies with limited financial resources use wholesalers as immediate sources of funds and as a marketing arm to reach the hundreds of retailers who will stock their products. Smaller retailers rely on wholesalers as *buying specialists* to ensure a balanced inventory of goods produced in various regions of the world.

The wholesaler's sales force is responsible for reaching the market with the producer's output. Many manufacturers also use sales representatives to call on the retailers to assist in merchandising the line. These representatives serve the manufacturer as sources of market information and influence, but will generally not make the sales transaction. If they initiate a sale, they give it to a wholesaler to complete.

Agent/Wholesaler Channel

Producer to agent to wholesaler to industrial user. Similar conditions often exist in the industrial market, where small producers often use a channel to market their offerings. The agent wholesaling intermediary, often called a manufacturer's representative or manufacturer's agent, serves as an independent sales force in contacting large, scattered wholesalers and some key industrial buyers. For example, a manufacturer of specialty industrial tapes might use agents to sell to industrial wholesalers and to encourage the wholesaler's sales force to push the product to industrial users.

Agent Channel

Where the unit sale is small, a **merchant wholesaler** must be used to cover the market economically. By maintaining regional inventories, merchant wholesalers can achieve transportation economies by stockpiling goods and making the final small shipment over a small distance. But where the unit sale is large and transportation costs account for a small percentage of the total product costs, the *producer to agent to industrial user* channel may be employed. The agent wholesaling intermediaries become, in effect, the company's sales force. For example, a producer of special castings might engage agents who are already calling on potential customers with other lines to represent it as well.

Traditional Channel (Industrial)

Similar characteristics in the industrial market often lead to the use of *wholesalers between the manufacturer and industrial purchaser*. The term **industrial distributor** is commonly used in the industrial market to refer to those wholesalers who take title to the goods they handle. These wholesalers are involved in the marketing of small accessory equipment and operating supplies, such as building supplies, office supplies, small hand tools, and office equipment.

Direct Channel (Services)

Distribution of services to both consumers and industrial users is usually simpler and more direct than for industrial and consumer goods. In part, this is due to the intangibility of services; the marketer of services does not often have to worry about storage, transportation, and inventory control. Shorter channels, often direct from service provider to consumer or industrial user, are typically used.

Many services can be performed only on a direct basis, and personal relationships between performers and users are very important. Consumers will remain clients of the same bank, automobile repair shop, or hair stylist as long as they are reasonably satisfied. Likewise, public accounting firms and attorneys are retained on a relatively permanent basis by industrial buyers.

Agent Channel (Services)

When *service providers use marketing intermediaries to reach consumers or industrial users*, these are usually *agents or brokers*. Common examples include insurance agents, securities brokers, travel agents, and entertainment agents.

For instance, travel and hotel packages are sometimes created by intermediaries and then marketed at the retail level by travel agents to both vacationers and firms wanting to offer employee incentive awards.

A Special Note on Channel Strategy for Consumer Services

A dominant reason for patronage of many consumer services, such as banks, motels, and auto rental agencies, is convenient location. It is absolutely essential that careful consideration be given to selecting the retail site. For example, banks locate branches in suburban shopping centres and malls. The installation of automated electronic tellers that enable customers to withdraw funds and to make deposits when a bank's offices are closed is a further example of attempts to provide convenience, as well as more efficient operations.

Multiple Channels

An increasingly common phenomenon is the use of more than one marketing channel for similar products. These *multiple channels* (or dual distribution) are used when the same product is marketed both to the ultimate consumer and to industrial users. Dial soap is distributed through the traditional grocery wholesaler to food stores to the consumer, but a second channel also exists, from the manufacturer to large retail chains and motels that buy direct from the manufacturer. Competition among retailers and other intermediaries striving to expand lines, profitability, and customer service has created these multiple channels.

In other cases, the same product is marketed through a variety of types of retail outlets. A basic product such as a paintbrush is carried in inventory by the traditional hardware store; it is also handled by such nontraditional retail outlets as auto accessory stores, building supply outlets, department stores, discount houses, mail-order houses, supermarkets, and variety stores. Each retail store may use a different marketing channel.

Firestone automobile tires are marketed

1. Directly to General Motors, where they serve as a fabricated part for new Chevrolets
2. Through Firestone stores, company-owned retail outlets
3. Through franchised Firestone outlets
4. From the factory to tire jobbers to retail gas stations

Each channel enables the manufacturer to serve a different market.

Reverse Channels

While the traditional concept of marketing channels involves movement of products and services from producer to consumer or industrial user, there is increasing interest in reverse channels. **Reverse channels** are *the paths goods follow from consumer to manufacturer or to marketing intermediaries.* These channels are normally seen in recycling. For example, metal, paper, or glass are sent back from user to manufacturer for reuse.

reverse channels
The paths goods follow from consumer to manufacturer or to marketing intermediaries.

Reverse channels increase in importance as raw materials become more expensive, and as additional laws are passed to control litter and the disposal of packaging materials such as soft-drink bottles. In order for recycling to succeed, four basic conditions must be satisfied:

1. A technology must be available that can efficiently process the material being recycled
2. A market must be available for the end product — the reclaimed material
3. A substantial and continuing quantity of secondary product (recycled aluminum, reclaimed steel from automobiles, recycled paper) must be available

4. A marketing system must be developed that can bridge the gap between suppliers of secondary products and end users on a profitable basis[7]

In some instances, the reverse channel consists of traditional marketing intermediaries. In the soft-drink industry, retailers and local bottlers perform these functions. In other cases, manufacturers take the initiative by establishing redemption centres. A concentrated attempt by the Reynolds Metals Company in one area permitted the company to recycle an amount of aluminum equivalent to 60 percent of the total containers marketed in the area. Other reverse-channel participants may include community groups, which organize "clean-up" days and develop systems for rechannelling paper products for recycling, and specialized organizations developed for waste disposal and recycling.

Reverse channels for product recalls and repairs Reverse channels are also used for product recalls and repairs. Ownership of some products (for example, tires) is registered so that proper notification can be sent if there is a product recall. In the case of automobile recalls, owners are advised to have the problem corrected at their dealership. Similarly, reverse channels have been used for repairs to some products. The warranty for a small appliance may specify that if repairs are needed in the first 90 days, the item should be returned to the dealer. After that period, the product should be returned to the factory. Such reverse channels are a vital element of product recalls and repair procedures.

Facilitating Agencies in the Distribution Channel

facilitating agency
An agency that provides specialized assistance for regular channel members (such as producers, wholesalers, and retailers) in moving products from producer to consumer.

A **facilitating agency** *provides specialized assistance for regular channel members (such as producers, wholesalers, and retailers) in moving products from producer to consumer.* Included in the definition of facilitating agencies are transportation companies, warehousing firms, financial institutions, insurance companies, and marketing research companies.

Through its Clean Earth Campaign, Canon collects and remanufactures empty toner cartridges from laser printers, photocopiers, and facsimile machines. Once a used cartridge is returned to Canon, it is disassembled. Reusable parts are remanufactured, and materials like plastic and aluminum are melted down and remoulded for use in new cartridges or for a variety of other products. In this way, Canon reverses the flow from manufacturer to consumer.

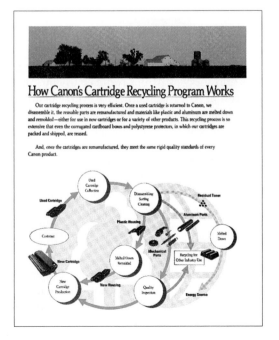

PHYSICAL DISTRIBUTION IN THE MARKETING CHANNEL

Physical distribution or logistics involves *a broad range of activities concerned with efficient movement of finished products from the source of raw materials to the production line and, ultimately, to the consumer.* Physical distribution activities include such crucial decision areas as customer service, inventory control, materials handling, protective packaging, order processing, transportation, warehouse site selection, and warehousing. Physical distribution is important to marketers because its activities represent roughly half of all marketing costs. A second — and equally important — aspect is the role physical distribution activities play in providing *customer service*. Robert Woodruff, former president of The Coca-Cola Company, emphasized the role of physical distribution in his firm's success when he stated that his organization's policy is to "put Coke within arm's length of desire."

physical distribution
A broad range of activities concerned with efficient movement of products from the source of raw materials to the production line and, ultimately, to the consumer.

Components of the Physical Distribution System

A system may be defined as an organized group of parts or components linked according to a plan to achieve specific objectives. The physical distribution system contains the following elements: customer service, transportation, inventory control, materials handling, and warehousing.

CUSTOMER SERVICE

What level of customer service should be provided? Customer service standards are the quality-of-service levels the firm's customers will receive. For example, a customer service standard of one firm might be that 60 percent of all orders will be shipped within 48 hours after they are received, 90 percent in 72 hours, and all orders within 96 hours. Setting the standards for customer service to be provided is an important marketing channel decision. Federal Express has a policy of answering the phone after the first ring.

TRANSPORTATION

How will the products be shipped, and by what carrier? The transportation system in Canada is a regulated industry, much like the phone and power industries. The federal and provincial governments perform both promotional and regulatory functions to maintain a viable Canadian transportation system. Transport Canada, a government agency within the federal bureaucracy, supports technological developments associated with the airways, waterways, and highways in Canada. Analogous agencies operate at the provincial level of government, although the scope and magnitude of their promotional support is significantly lower than that provided by the federal government. The Canadian Transport Commission (CTC), an agency of the federal government, is responsible for the air, rail, pipeline, and inland water components of the transportation industry. Each province has a transportation regulatory agency whose functions are equivalent to those of the CTC. In general, the purpose of government intervention in the transportation sector is to assure the development of a sound, efficient transportation infrastructure while protecting the public against abusive tactics.

Three legal forms of transportation carriers exist to provide linkages between the various channel members: common, contract, and private. **Common carriers** must "hold themselves out" to serve the general public for a fee. They must receive appropriate regulatory authority to perform transport service, and must adhere to

common carriers
Transportation carriers that provide service to the general public, and are subject to regulatory authority including fee setting.

guidelines and rules as to rate setting, mergers, application of accounting procedures, and financial dealings. Although common carriers perform transportation services between each of the marketing channel intermediaries, nonetheless they most frequently operate between manufacturers, wholesalers, and retailers moving goods of high value.

contract carriers
Transportation carriers that only serve customers they have contracts with. Contracts include rates to be charged.

Contract carriers do not offer their services to the public at large. Rather, they enter into contractual arrangements with select customers. All rates and charges are included in the contractual instrument along with additional terms and conditions associated with the provision of service. Although regulatory requirements for contract carriers are significantly less than for common carriers, rules and standards are in effect at both the federal and provincial levels of government to delineate the scope of their authority to perform transportation services. Contract carriers tend to operate between raw material suppliers and manufacturers, and between manufacturers, rather than between wholesalers, retailers, and final customers, since they tend to be commodity and final goods consolidators other than break-bulk operators.

Private carriers are not providers of transportation for a market fee. Instead they perform transportation services for a particular firm and may not solicit other transportation business. The test to determine whether a carrier is a private or a for-hire carrier is to ask whether the "primary business" is transportation or not. Legal status is dependent on the percentage of revenues accruing from transportation activities or the ratio of transportation to nontransportation-related assets. Owing to the exclusive nature of their operations, and the fact that transportation is incidental to the main operations of the firm, private carriers are not subject to economic regulation by either the federal or the provincial governments. They are, however, subject to federal and provincial safety regulations, as are others who use transportation facilities.

There are five major transportation alternatives, referred to as modes, that link the various channel intermediaries. These are *railways, trucking, water carriers, pipelines,* and *air freight.* Railways are the largest transporters (as measured by tonne-kilometres of freight) and are considered the most efficient mode in moving bulk commodities over long distances. They are readily available in most locations in North America, although line abandonment has reduced considerably the operating systems of the major rail carriers over the past three decades. Likewise, railways are quite flexible in that many different commodities, raw materials, liquids, grains, as well as finished goods can be safely and efficiently moved.

Trucking companies compete with railways in several product categories; however, where speed, flexibility, and frequency of service are important, motor carriers often outperform rail carriers. The truck shows its inherent advantage in moving high-valued goods short to intermediate distances. While the rate per tonne-kilometre is often greater for truck than for rail carrier, the service advantages provided by truck often more than compensate for the added expenditures. Furthermore, the variety of available trucking technologies provides the shipper with a broad array of options in transporting goods to market. No other mode rivals trucking in the range of transportation options.

Water carriers are much like rail carriers in that they tend to perform best in moving bulky low-valued commodities long distances. Whether along the inland waterway system, the Great Lakes, or in international commerce, water carriers tend to carry bulk cargoes at rather low speeds. They do possess the advantage in international commerce of moving freight of all kinds as no other mode can, given present technologies. Rates per tonne-kilometre tend to be lowest for this mode, reflecting in part the relatively low value per unit of weight of cargoes typically carried by water. The exception to this general case is the provision of container service for medium- to high-value goods. Container ships provide manufacturers the opportunity of extending market channels to locations that are quite distant from sourcing and producing sites. The presence of scale economies in production and distribution permit effective competition with local production.

Air freight is often referred to as "premium transportation" because of the high-cost–high-service nature of the mode. Speed is the single most important factor in the selection of air over other freight carriers, and the rate per tonne-kilometre tends to be among the highest of all modes. Cut flowers from southern U.S. growing fields, fresh seafood from Vancouver, and component parts urgently needed for a downed assembly line in Ontario are examples of the types of goods often moved by air freight carriers. In recent years, growth in demand for expedited small parcel and parcel post service has exploded, and companies like Emery Worldwide and Federal Express have developed as a response to this demand.

Pipeline transportation is the mode least likely to be used within a marketing channel except in specific industries such as oil extraction and refining, coal extraction, and in industries where raw commodities can be pulverized into small pellets or a powder, mixed with water, and transported in suspension.

INVENTORY CONTROL

How much inventory should be maintained at each location? Inventory control analysts have developed a number of techniques that aid the physical distribution manager in effectively controlling inventory costs. The most basic is the **EOQ (economic order quantity)** model. This technique emphasizes *a cost trade-off between two fundamental costs involved with inventory: inventory holding costs and order costs.* As Figure 14.3 indicates, these two cost items are then "traded off" to determine the optimum order quantity of each product.

No aspect of physical distribution strategy has experienced the changes brought by acceptance of the TQM philosophy as much as inventory practice and policy. Once it is recognized that significant resources are often tied up in inventory, it

EOQ (economic order quantity)
A model that emphasizes a cost trade-off between inventory holding costs and order costs.

■ Figure 14.3 **The EOQ Model**

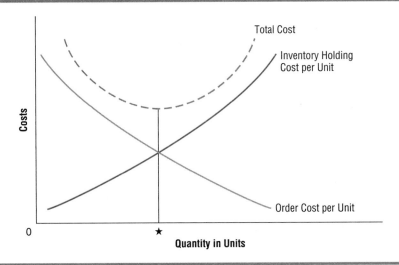

should come as no surprise that some of the new frontiers in distribution cost savings have accrued from minimizing inventory holding costs. The Japanese capitalized on this simple idea several decades ago with the implementation of **just-in-time (JIT)** inventory systems. The basic idea is to identify stocking levels that meet peak efficiency minimums and to trade off higher transportation expenditures for reduced inventory holding expenditures.

The concept can be visualized in the following illustration. Imagine a young couple entering an automobile dealership in Calgary. They have a vague idea of the features they would like to have in their dream car and have sought out the services of an informed representative to assist them in their purchase decision. The representative activates her computer and asks the young couple for the specific features they would like in their car: exterior and interior colours, fabric type, stereo system, wheel type, suspension, and so forth. As the couple discuss the various options, the representative enters the information into the computer. Once the features have all been selected, she pushes a button and a simulated version of the car with the designated features is superimposed on the colour monitor.

Assuming the couple agree on the features and a transaction occurs, the representative activates an order to the manufacturer, who contacts various component suppliers and assembly plants to ship parts for the car. An order is sent to the battery manufacturer, the stereo manufacturer, the engine manufacturer, and to all other component suppliers who contribute to the production of the ordered car. From the subassembly plants, the various components are produced and then shipped to the next unit in the manufacturing chain.

The important point is that inventories are not held in large amounts anywhere in the manufacturing or marketing channel. Instead, upon receiving the order, the subassembler produces the component and transports it in minimum efficient lot sizes to the next assembler in the channel. The JIT method results in significant reductions in inventory costs even though transportation costs may increase. Just as important as reducing inventory costs, however, are the gains accruing from reductions in set-up and changeover times in procedures and equipment modifications, in more rapid response to changes in market conditions, and in the increased awareness of total quality management by using the most recent technologies in producing component parts.

MATERIALS HANDLING

How do we develop efficient methods of handling products in the factory, warehouse, and transport terminals? All the activities associated with moving products among the manufacturer's plants, warehouses, wholesalers, retailers, and transportation company terminals are called materials handling. Two important innovations have developed — *combining as many packages as possible into one load* (**unitization**) and *combining several unitized loads* (**containerization**) — which have revolutionized the materials handling field. The materials handling system must be thoroughly coordinated in order that plants and warehouses that service the various channel intermediaries perform effectively.

WAREHOUSING

Where will the products be located? How many warehouses should be used? Warehouses lend themselves exceptionally well to automation, with the computer as the heart of the operation. *Distribution warehouses* are designed to assemble and then redistribute products, whereas **break-bulk warehouses** *receive consolidated shipments from a central distribution centre, and then distribute them in smaller shipments to individual customers in more limited areas.* Another type of warehouse, the *storage ware-*

house, stores products for moderate to long periods of time in an attempt to balance supply and demand for producers and purchasers.

These companies are interrelated, and decisions made in one area affect the relative efficiency of other areas. For this reason alone, an efficient physical distribution system must be implemented in order for a TQM strategy to function effectively.

The Objective of Physical Distribution

The objective of a firm's physical distribution system is to produce a specified level of customer service while minimizing the costs involved in physically moving and storing the products and raw materials from production or extraction locations to the point where the end product is ultimately purchased. To achieve this, the physical distribution manager makes use of three basic concepts: (1) the total cost approach, (2) the use of cost trade-offs, and (3) the avoidance of suboptimization.

The premise that all relevant factors in physically moving and storing products should be considered as a whole and not individually forms the basis of the *total-cost approach.* It is impossible to optimize each component of the physical distribution system. Thus, a firm may incur higher transportation costs and in so doing lower its inventory costs. The basic question to ask is whether the *cost trade-off* between the two physical distribution activities has resulted in an actual lowering of total physical distribution costs. To the extent that total distribution costs are higher after the substitution of more transportation for inventory resources, the distribution system is likely to be suboptimizing. *Avoidance of suboptimization* requires that the elements of the physical distribution system be employed in the proportions that generate the least total costs for a given level of customer service.

The integration of these three basic concepts forms what is commonly referred to as the *physical distribution concept.* The uniqueness of the physical distribution concept is not in the individual functions that are performed to assure customer satisfaction; rather, it stems from the integration of all of these functions into a unified whole.

In a way, the physical distribution concept is a movement/storage–oriented version of the *total quality management concept.* Whereas the physical distribution concept applies to activities and institutions within the channel that physically move material and information from point to point, the total quality management concept applies to *all* management activities involved in creating, moving, and marketing a product.

CHANNEL STRATEGY DECISIONS

Marketers face several channel strategy decisions. The selection of a specific distribution channel is the most basic of these, but the level of distribution intensity and the issue of vertical marketing systems must also be addressed.

Selection of a Distribution Channel

What is an appropriate marketing channel if you wish to sell bottled water to Japan? What makes a direct channel (manufacturer to consumer) best for the Fuller Brush Company? Why do operating supplies often go through both agents and merchant wholesalers before being purchased by the industrial firm? Why do some firms employ multiple channels for the same product? The firm must answer many such questions when it determines its choice of marketing channels. The choice is based on an analysis of the market, the product and the producer, and various competitive factors. Each is often of critical importance, and all are often interrelated.

MARKET FACTORS

A major determinant of channel structure is whether the product is intended for the consumer or the industrial market. Industrial purchasers usually prefer to deal directly with the manufacturer (except for supplies or small accessory items), but most consumers make their purchases from retail stores. Products sold to both industrial users and the consumer market usually require more than one channel.

The geographic location and the needs of the firm's potential market will also affect channel choice. Direct sales are possible where the firm's potential market is concentrated in a few regions. For example, industrial production tends to be concentrated in a relatively small geographic region, making direct contact possible. The small number of potential buyers also increases the feasibility of direct channels.

On the other hand, consumer goods are purchased by every household everywhere. Since consumers are numerous and geographically dispersed, and purchase a small volume at a given time, intermediaries must be employed to market products to them efficiently.

In Canada, population distribution is an extremely influential factor in channel decisions. For example, the markets for fishing nets are on the two coasts, with smaller markets on the Great Lakes, Lake Winnipeg, and a few other large lakes. The Rockies and the Canadian Shield effectively divide markets and strongly affect channels of distribution. Our relatively smaller and widely dispersed centres of population tend to result in less specialized wholesaling and retailing institutions than in the United States and other developed, heavily populated countries. This may limit the range of channel opportunities available to the marketing manager.

Order size will also affect the marketing channel decision. Manufacturers are likely to employ shorter, more direct channels in case where retail customers or industrial buyers place relatively small numbers of large orders. Retail chains often employ buying offices to negotiate directly with manufacturers for large-scale purchases. Wholesalers may be used to contact smaller retailers.

Shifts in consumer buying patterns also influence channel decisions. As newer retail forms such as Superstore, Costco, and Toys R Us have become more popular, manufacturers have had to shift their emphasis to distribute products through these channels as well.

Market factors and buyer expectations are equally important to consider in developing international distribution and channel structures. For example, many more channel intermediaries are typically involved in Japan. In the distribution of soap, for instance, the product goes from manufacturer to large wholesaler to smaller wholesaler to very small wholesaler, and finally to the retailer.

PRODUCT FACTORS

Product characteristics also play a role in determining optimum marketing channels. *Perishable products*, such as fresh produce and fruit, and fashion products with short life cycles, *typically move through relatively short channels* direct to the retailer or to the ultimate consumer. Old Dutch Potato Chips are distributed by company salespeople–truck drivers direct to the retail shelves. Each year, Hines & Smart Corporation ships over 2 million kg of live lobsters by air, in specially designed insulating containers, directly to restaurants and hotels throughout North America.

Complex products, such as custom-made installations or computer equipment, are typically sold direct from the manufacturer to the buyer. As a general rule, *the more standardized a product, the longer the channel will be.* Such items will usually be marketed by wholesalers. Also, products requiring regular service or specialized repair services usually avoid channels employing independent wholesalers. Automobiles are marketed through a franchised network of regular dealers whose employees receive regular training on how to service their cars properly.

Another generalization concerning marketing channels is that *the lower the unit value of the product, the longer the channel.* Convenience goods and industrial supplies with typically low unit prices are frequently marketed through relatively long channels. Installations and more expensive industrial and consumer goods go through shorter, more direct channels.

PRODUCER FACTORS

Companies with adequate resources — financial, marketing, and managerial — will be less compelled to use intermediaries in marketing their products. A financially strong manufacturer can hire its own sales force, warehouse its products, and grant credit to the retailer or consumer. A weaker firm relies on intermediaries for these services (although some large retail chains may purchase all of the manufacturer's output, making it possible to by-pass the independent wholesaler). Production-oriented firms may be forced to use the marketing expertise of intermediaries to replace the lack of finances and management in their organization. In the international marketplace, producers often rely on intermediaries because they know the market better, and it is usually cheaper than setting up a new distribution system.

A firm with a broad product line is better able to market its products directly to retailers or industrial users since its sales force can offer a variety of products to customers. Larger total sales allow the selling costs to be spread over a number of products and make direct sales more feasible. The single-product firm often discovers that direct selling is an unaffordable luxury.

The manufacturer's need for control over the product will also influence channel selection. If aggressive promotion for the firm's products at the retail level is desired, the manufacturer will choose the shortest available channel. For new products, the manufacturer may be forced to implement an introductory advertising campaign before independent wholesalers will handle the item.

COMPETITIVE FACTORS

Some firms are forced to develop unique marketing channels because of inadequate promotion of their products by independent intermediaries. Avon concentrated on house-to-house selling rather than being directly involved in the intense competition among similar lines of cosmetics in traditional channels. This radical departure from the traditional channel resulted in tremendous sales by the firm's thousands of neighbourhood salespeople. Similarly, Honeywell discovered that its home security system, Concept 70, was being inadequately marketed by the traditional, wholesaler-to-retailer channel and switched to a direct-to-home sales force.

Table 14.1 summarizes the factors affecting the choice of optimal marketing channels and shows the effect of each characteristic on the overall length of the channel.

Determining Distribution Intensity

Adequate market coverage for some products such as fine furniture could mean one dealer for each 50 000 people. On the other hand, Procter & Gamble defines

■ Table 14.1 **Factors Affecting Choice of Distribution Channels**

Factor	Channels Tend to Be Shorter When:
Market Factors	
Consumer market or industrial market	Users are in industrial market
Geographic location of target market	Customers are geographically concentrated
Customer service needs	Specialized knowledge, technical know-how, and regular service needs are present
Order size	Customer places relatively small number of large orders
Product Factors	
Perishability	Products are perishable, either because of fashion changes or physical perishability
Technical complexity of product	Products are highly technical
Unit value	Products have high unit value
Producer Factors	
Producer resources — financial, managerial, and marketing	Manufacturer possesses adequate resources to perform channel functions
Product line	Manufacturer has broad product line to spread distribution costs
Need for control over the channel	Manufacturer wishes to control the channel
Competitive Factors	
Need for promotion to channel members	Manufacturer feels that independent intermediaries are inadequately promoting products

adequate coverage for Crest toothpaste as almost every supermarket, discount store, drugstore, and variety store, plus many vending machines.

INTENSIVE DISTRIBUTION

intensive distribution
A form of distribution that attempts to provide saturation coverage of the potential market.

Producers of convenience goods who *attempt to provide saturation coverage of their potential markets* are the prime users of **intensive distribution**. Soft drinks, bread, candy, and chewing gum are available in convenient locations to enable purchasers to buy with a minimum of effort.

Bic pens can be purchased in thousands of retail outlets in Canada. TMX Watches of Canada Ltd. uses an intensive distribution strategy for its Timex watches. Consumers may buy a Timex in many jewellery stores, the traditional retail outlet for watches. In addition, they may find Timex in discount houses, variety stores, department stores, hardware stores, and drugstores.

Mass coverage and low unit prices make the use of wholesalers almost mandatory for such distribution. An important exception to this generalization are products sold and delivered on a direct-to-customer basis. For example, Avon operates direct to the consumer through a nationwide network of neighbourhood salespeople who purchase directly from the manufacturer, at 60 percent of the retail price, and service a limited area with cosmetics, toiletries, jewellery, and toys. Other examples are Tupperware, Mary Kay, and other "home party" companies.

It must be remembered that while a firm may wish for intensive distribution, the retailer or industrial distributor will carry only products that sell in enough volume to make a profit. If demand is low, the producer may have to settle for less than complete market coverage.

SELECTIVE DISTRIBUTION

As the name implies, **selective distribution** involves *the selection of a small number of retailers to handle the firm's product line.* This can work *if* consumers are willing to shop around for the product category. By limiting its retailers, the firm may reduce its total marketing costs, such as those for sales force and shipping, while establishing better working relationships within the channel. This practice may also be necessary to give the retailers an incentive (through having a product available to a limited number of sellers) to carry the product and promote it properly against many competing brands. Co-operative advertising (where the manufacturer pays a percentage of the retailer's advertising expenditures and the retailer prominently displays the firm's products) can be used to mutual benefit. Marginal retailers can be avoided. Where product service is important, dealer training and assistance is usually forthcoming from the manufacturer. Finally, price cutting is less likely since fewer dealers are handling the firm's line.

selective distribution
The selection of a small number of retailers to handle the firm's product line.

EXCLUSIVE DISTRIBUTION

When *manufacturers grant exclusive rights to a wholesaler or retailer to sell in a geographic region*, they are practising **exclusive distribution**, which is an extreme form of selective distribution. The best example of exclusive distribution is the automobile industry. For example, a city of 100 000 might have a single Toyota dealer or one Cadillac agency. Exclusive distribution arrangements are also found in the marketing of some major appliances and in fashion apparel. Powerful retailers may also negotiate to acquire exclusive distribution.

exclusive distribution
The granting of exclusive rights by manufacturers to a wholesaler or retailer to sell in a geographic region.

Some market coverage may be sacrificed through a policy of exclusive distribution, but this is often offset through the development and maintenance of an image of quality and prestige for the products, with more active attention by the retailer to promote them, and the reduced marketing costs associated with a small number of accounts. Producers and retailers co-operate closely in decisions concerning advertising and promotion, inventory to be carried by the retailers, and prices.

THE LEGAL PROBLEMS OF EXCLUSIVE DISTRIBUTION

The use of exclusive distribution presents a number of potential legal problems. Three problems areas exist: exclusive dealing, tied selling, and market restriction. Each will be examined briefly.

Exclusive dealing *prohibits a marketing intermediary* (either a *wholesaler or, more typically, a retailer) from handling competing products.* Through such a contract, the manufacturer is assured of total concentration on the firm's product line by the intermediaries. For example, an oil company may consider requiring all dealers to sign a contract agreeing to purchase all of their accessories from that company.

exclusive dealing
An arrangement whereby a supplier prohibits a marketing intermediary (either a wholesaler or, more typically, a retailer) from handling competing products.

The legal question is covered in Part IV of the Competition Act, which prohibits exclusive dealing by a major supplier if it is likely to

1. Impede entry into or expansion of a firm in the market
2. Impede introduction of a product into or expansion of sales of a product in the market
3. Have any other exclusionary effect in the market, with the result that competition is or is likely to be lessened substantially.[8]

tied selling
An arrangement whereby a supplier forces a dealer who wishes to handle a product to also carry other products from the supplier or to refrain from using or distributing someone else's product.

market restriction
An arrangement whereby suppliers restrict the geographic territories for each of their distributors.

A second problem area is **tied selling**. In this case, *a supplier forces a dealer who wishes to handle a product to also carry other products from the supplier or to refrain from using or distributing someone else's product.* Tied selling is controlled by the same provision as exclusive dealing.

The third legal issue of exclusive distribution is the use of **market restriction**. In this case, *suppliers restrict the geographic territories for each of their distributors.* The key issue is whether such restrictions substantially lessen competition. If so, the Restrictive Trade Practices Commission has power to order the prohibition of such practices. For example, a *horizontal territorial restriction*, where retailers or wholesalers agree to avoid competition in products from the same manufacturer, would likely be declared unlawful.

VERTICAL MARKETING SYSTEMS

There are some channel members, and even entire channels of distribution, that act quite independently. They have no formal long-term ties to others in the channel, but build relationships with buyers or sellers in an autonomous fashion.

vertical marketing system
A network of channel intermediaries organized and centrally managed to produce the maximum competitive impact.

More commonly, other intermediaries have found it desirable to form a **vertical marketing system**. A vertical marketing system (VMS) is *a network of channel intermediaries organized and centrally managed to produce the maximum competitive impact.* In such a system, the co-ordination of the various channel members can produce operating efficiencies, deep market penetration, and greater profits. Vertical marketing systems produce economies of scale through their size and elimination of duplicated services. There are three types of VMS: corporate, administered, and contractual. They are depicted in Table 14.2.

Corporate System

When there is single ownership of all stages of the marketing channel, a *corporate vertical marketing system* exists. Holiday Inn owns a furniture manufacturer and a carpet mill. Bata Shoes owns a retail chain of shoe stores. Many McDonald's food outlets are corporate-owned.

Administered System

Channel co-ordination is achieved through the exercise of economic and "political" power by a dominant channel member in an *administered vertical marketing system.* Canadian General Electric has a network of major appliance dealers who aggressively display and promote the line because of its strong reputation and brand. Although independently owned and operated, these dealers co-operate with the manufacturer because of the effective working relationships enjoyed over the years and the profits to be realized from selling the widely known, well-designed, broad range of merchandise.

Contractual System

The most significant form of vertical marketing is the *contractual vertical marketing system.* It accounts for nearly 40 percent of all retail sales. Instead of the common

■ Table 14.2 **Three Types of Vertical Marketing Systems**

Type of System	Description	Examples
Corporate	Channel owned and operated by a single organization	Bata Shoes Firestone Sherwin-Williams Singer McDonald's (partial)
Administered	Channel dominated by one powerful member that acts as channel captain	Kodak General Electric Corning Glass
Contractual	Channel co-ordinated through contractual agreements among channel members	**Wholesaler-Sponsored Voluntary Chain** IGA Canadian Tire Independent Druggists Alliance (IDA) Allied Hardware **Retail Co-operative** Associated Grocers **Franchise Systems** McDonald's (partial) Century 21 Real Estate AAMCO Transmissions Coca-Cola® bottlers Ford dealers

ownership of channel components that characterizes the corporate VMS or the relative power relationships of an administered system, the contractual VMS is characterized by formal agreements between channel members. In practice, there are three types of agreements: the wholesaler-sponsored voluntary chain, the retail co-operative, and the franchise.[9]

WHOLESALER-SPONSORED VOLUNTARY CHAIN

The wholesaler-sponsored voluntary chain represents an attempt by the independent wholesaler to preserve a market for the firm's products through the strengthening of the firm's retailer customers. In order to enable the independent retailers to compete with the chains, the wholesaler enters into a formal agreement with a group of retailers whereby the retailers agree to use a common name, standardize their facilities, and purchase the wholesaler's products. The wholesaler often develops a line of private brands to be stocked by the members of the voluntary chain. A common store name and similar inventories allow the retailers to achieve cost savings on advertising, since a single newspaper advertisement promotes all retailers in the trading area. IGA, with a membership of approximately 800 food stores, is a good example of a voluntary chain.

RETAIL CO-OPERATIVES

A second type of contractual VMS is the retail co-operative, which is established by a group of retailers who set up a wholesaling operation to compete better with the chains. A group of retailers purchase shares of stock in a wholesaling operation and agree to purchase a minimum percentage of their inventory from the firm. The members may also choose to use a common store name, such as Home Hardware, and develop their own private brands in order to carry out co-operative advertising.

Buying groups like wholesaler-sponsored chains and retail co-operatives are not a new phenomenon in the Canadian distribution industry. They date back at least 50 years, some having evolved from the co-operative movement of the early years of the century. Under the Competition Act, suppliers may charge different prices for different volumes of purchases, so long as these prices are available to all competing purchasers of articles of like quantity and quality. And suppliers have done so; it is common practice to offer volume rebates. Thus, buying groups improve the small retailers' bargaining position with their suppliers, thus increasing competition for their large rivals.

In some cases, buying groups have failed because of difficulties with organization and management. In others, the buying group concept has worked very well, with some groups now as large as the chains. The chains themselves have now formed their own buying groups. Recently, five of these large buying groups in the food industry represented some 14 000 stores and accounted for about 85 percent of all retail food sales in Canada. This development leads to the concern that while buying groups may improve the balance of market power in some areas, there is a possibility of abuse of power in others.[10]

FRANCHISING

franchise
An agreement whereby one firm (franchisee) agrees to meet the operating requirements of a successful business (franchisor) in return for the right to carry the name and products of the franchisor.

A third type of contractual VMS is the **franchise**. A franchise is *an agreement whereby one firm (franchisee) agrees to meet the operating requirements of a successful business (franchisor) in return for the right to carry the name and products of the franchisor*. The franchisee pays a predetermined royalty on sales to the franchisor. In addition, the franchisee typically receives a variety of marketing, management, technical, and financial services in exchange for a specified fee. Kentucky Fried Chicken started out by franchising its stores, but the company now has the resources to pay for and manage its own stores.

Although franchising attracted considerable interest beginning in the late 1960s, the concept actually began 100 years earlier when the Singer Company established franchised sewing-machine outlets. Early impetus for the franchising concept came after 1900 in the automobile industry.[11] The soft-drink industry is another example of franchising, but in this case the contractual arrangement is between the syrup manufacturer and the wholesaler-bottler.

The franchising form that created most of the excitement both in retailing and on Wall Street in the late 1960s was the retailer franchise system sponsored by the service firm. McDonald's Corporation is an excellent example of such a franchise operation. McDonald's brought together suppliers and a chain of hamburger outlets. It provided a proven system of retail operation (the operations manual for each outlet weighs over 1 kg) with a standardized product and ingenious promotional campaigns. This enabled lower prices to be offered to customers through the franchisor's purchasing power on meat, buns, potatoes, napkins, and other supplies. In return, the franchisee pays a fee for the use of the name (over $150 000 for McDonald's) and a percentage of gross sales. Other familiar examples include Hertz, Avis, Pizza Hut, and Weight Watchers.

Fast-food franchising has already proven itself in the international market. In Tokyo, London, Rome, Paris, and Moscow, McDonald's hamburgers are consumed daily. Kentucky Fried Chicken has opened nearly 500 restaurants in Canada and in such locations as Manila, Munich, Nice, Nairobi, Hong Kong, and Japan. In some countries, adjustments to the North American marketing plans have been made to

The Second Cup is a successful Canadian company that is best known for serving different types of coffee at its stores. It also sells fresh coffee beans. Well known as a quality franchise, businesspeople trying to start a small venture can buy a Second Cup store and have the security of its reputation. In turn, the franchisee is obligated to follow franchise regulations. This way, the franchisor can safeguard its reputation.

match local needs. Although their menu is rigidly standardized in Canada, McDonald's executives approved changes to the menu in outlets in France. Kentucky Fried Chicken replaced french fries with mashed potatoes to satisfy its Japanese customers.

Although many franchises are profitable, the infatuation with the franchising concept and the market performance of franchise stocks have lured dozens of new-comers into the market who have failed. Lacking experience and often with a well-known celebrity's name as their sole asset, many of these firms have disappeared almost as quickly as they entered the market.

The median investment for a franchise varies tremendously from one business area to another. A pet-sitting franchise might sell for as low as $9500, whereas a restaurant franchise will likely average over $250 000. The great bulk of the nation's franchises are in the "traditional" franchise areas such as auto dealers, service stations, and soft-drink bottlers. Figure 14.4 shows the proportion of sales accounted for by the various franchise categories.

Despite the many franchise opportunities available, there are few specific regulations with respect to the proper disclosure of information to prospective franchisees. It is worthwhile to evaluate the opportunity carefully before investing.

The foregoing discussion has shown that vertical marketing systems, whether in the form of corporate, administered, or contractual systems, have become a dominant factor in the consumer goods sector of the Canadian economy. Over 60 percent of the available market is currently in the hands of retail components of VMS.

LEADERSHIP AND CO-OPERATION IN THE CHANNEL

Leadership and co-operation in the marketing channel are necessary for the successful implementation of marketing strategy. Channel leadership is a function of one's power within the distribution channel, and the most powerful often becomes

■ Figure 14.4 **How Franchising Branches Out**

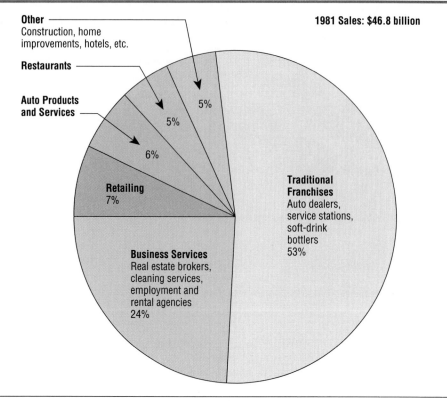

Source: Based on data from Statistics Canada, Merchandising and Services Division, 1982.

channel captain
The most dominant member of the distribution channel.

the dominant and controlling member of the channel — the **channel captain**. Historically, the role of channel captain belonged to the manufacturer or wholesaler, since retailers tended to be both small and locally oriented. However, retailers are increasingly taking on the role of channel captain as large retail chains assume traditional wholesaling functions and even dictate product design specifications to the manufacturer. For example, Loblaws Supermarkets in Canada has developed a line of products called President's Choice. Sainsbury's in Britain has its own lines of products as well.

Distribution channels must be organized and regarded as a systematic co-operative effort if operating efficiencies are to be achieved. In a sense, the forward-thinking organizations are those that form strategic alliances among channel members in order to take advantage of the competitive attributes each possesses. These alliances include direct channel participants as well as facilitating agencies such as transportation companies, legal organizations, and the like. No longer is it likely that completely independent channel players will dominate the competition in globally oriented industries. Organization and co-operation between independent entities within the channel is a must today.

Co-operation and mutual understanding based on enlightened self-interest are far from the reality of channel relations, according to numerous authors. Instead, many channel relationships are marked by intense rivalry and conflict.

Channel conflict can evolve from a number of sources. For example, a manufacturer of cough lozenges may have planned that its product display would be placed near the cash register to encourage impulse purchases. Many retailers might be unwilling to do this because of many other items taking up the same space. In other situations, a manufacturer might wish certain market information from retailers, but they may not be interested in co-operating. A wholesaler might find that it is being by-passed by a retailer that buys direct from a manufacturer. Manufacturers may wish to dictate the resale prices of their merchandise. These may be lower or higher than the prices that retailers feel are appropriate to their circumstances.

Channel relationships are dynamic. Just when channel procedures and relationships seem to be sorted out, a competitive action by some channel member upsets the balance, and a whole series of countermoves are triggered in order to adjust to the changing competitive situation. It is this continuing process that results in the evolution of new and improved channel forms to serve consumer needs.

The study of channels of distribution, and the changes that continually occur, can be fascinating. After this rather extensive overview of channel and distribution strategy, the next two chapters will look more closely at wholesaling and retailing, the two main components of the distribution channel.

channel conflict
Rivalry and conflict between channel members because of sometimes different objectives and needs.

■ KEY TERMS

distribution channels	physical distribution	selective distribution
marketing intermediary	common carriers	exclusive distribution
wholesaling	contract carriers	exclusive dealing
retailer	EOQ (economic order	tied selling
sorting	quantity)	market restriction
agent	JIT (just in time)	vertical marketing system
merchant wholesaler	unitization	franchise
industrial distributor	containerization	channel captain
reverse channels	break-bulk warehouse	channel conflict
facilitating agency	intensive distribution	

■ INTERACTIVE SUMMARY AND DISCUSSION QUESTIONS

1. The distribution channel performs several functions in the overall marketing system. These include facilitating the exchange process, sorting, standardizing transactions, holding inventories, assisting in the search process, and transporting. Provide an example of each function.

2. In the all-aboard channel, the product moves from producer to agent/broker to wholesaler to retailer to consumer. Describe how this works, and the names of intermediary companies, using some product you are familiar with.

3. An increasingly common phenomenon is the use of more than one marketing channel for similar products. In what ways could multiple channels produce channel conflict? Be specific.

4. The physical distribution system contains the following elements: customer service, transportation, inventory control, materials handling, and warehousing. Explain how the specification of customer service can affect each of the other elements.

5. Economic order quantity emphasizes a cost trade-off between two fundamental costs involved with inventory: inventory holding costs and order costs. Explain how EOQ works.

6. Show how the notion of a cost trade-off should be applied to the elements of the physical distribution system listed in question 4.

7. Distribution intensity for various products ranges from intensive to selective to exclusive. Which degree of distribution intensity is appropriate for each of the following?
   a. *Maclean's* magazine
   b. Caterpillar bulldozers
   c. Johnson outboard motors
   d. Dove soap
   e. Cuisinart food processors
   f. Kawasaki motorcycles
   g. Waterford crystal

8. Would your answers in question 7 change if your market target was China? If so, how?

9. A vertical marketing system (VMS) is a network of channel intermediaries organized and centrally managed to produce the maximum competitive impact. Distinguish among the following types of VMS: corporate, administered, and contractual.

10. A franchise is an agreement whereby one firm (franchisee) agrees to meet the operating requirements of another successful business (franchisor) in return for the right to carry the name and products of the franchisor. What advantages does franchising offer the small retailer?

11. Why would any manufacturer deliberately choose to limit market coverage through a policy of exclusive coverage?

12. Transportation alternatives can be categorized as common, contract, and private legal forms of transportation. In what circumstances would each be used?

CHAPTER 15

Wholesaling

CHAPTER OBJECTIVES

1. To provide an overview of the many types of wholesaling intermediaries and their functions.
2. To explain the issues involved in changing from the use of one channel intermediary type to a different system.
3. To identify the conditions under which a manufacturer is likely to assume wholesaling functions rather than use independents.
4. To distinguish between merchant wholesalers, and agents and brokers.
5. To identify the major types of merchant wholesalers and instances in which each type might be used.

When Hiroshi Tanami heard that his new Feathercraft folding kayak had arrived from Vancouver, he asked his boss for half a day off and rushed to the air cargo terminal to pick it up.

"As soon as I got back to our apartment, my wife and I opened the boxes and promptly started assembling it," Mr. Tanami said. "Although the assembled kayak occupies most of our living room and dining room space, we don't feel like disassembling it at all. My wife even says that she will invite her friends to show off the kayak, even though there may not be enough room for them to sit and relax."

In crowded Japan, folding kayaks are preferred by most buyers and easily outsell rigid models. Since Feathercraft made its first sale in Japan, this country has become the company's second largest market. Despite the impressive statistics, Feathercraft's experience in the Japanese market has been less than sterling. While volumes are high, profits are poor.

The problem is a familiar one. The multi-layered Japanese distribution system means a Feathercraft kayak can go through five middlemen before a paddler gets it out of a shop. Right now, Feathercraft sells Japan-bound kayaks to its agent Pacific Edge Canada, which sells them to affiliate Pacific Edge Japan. Pacific Edge Japan sells each kayak to Japan's A&F Corp., a camping equipment distributor, which then sells to a retailer. In many cases A&F sells the kayak to yet another distributor, which sells it to a retailer.

The result is that Feathercraft's entry-level "K-light" kayak (the best kayak on the market), which retails for $1 900 in Canada, sells in Japan for 278 000 yen or almost $3 900. The two-seater, top-of-the-line goes for 650 000 yen or about $9 100. "Right now, the kayaks are too expensive," said Takao Akatsu, president of A&F, Feathercraft's main distributor in Japan.

Feathercraft has decided to eliminate at least one of the members in the distribution channel. This will lower the price, and increase the margins for the remaining channel members. It is hoped that the lower prices will attract more customers and make the venture more profitable.[1]

It is clear that despite having an excellent product that suits the needs of the Japanese market, the distribution system has almost put the product out of reach of even affluent Japanese consumers. It takes more than a good product that serves the needs of the market to have a marketing success. In international business, the multiplication of channel layers can be a real problem.

INTRODUCTION

Wholesaling is the initial marketing institution in most channels of distribution from manufacturers to consumer or industrial user. Chapter 14 introduced the basic concepts of channel strategy, primarily from the manufacturer's viewpoint. We will now shift our attention to the institutions within the distribution channel.

Wholesaling intermediaries are a critical element of the marketing mixes of many products, but many intermediaries are also separate business entities with their own marketing mixes. A good starting point for the discussion is to look at the terminology used in wholesaling.

WHOLESALING FUNCTIONS

wholesalers
Wholesaling intemediaries who take title to the products they handle.

wholesaling intermediaries
Intermediaries who assume title, as well as agents and brokers who perform important wholesaling activities without taking title to the products.

Wholesaling involves the activities of people or firms who sell to retailers and other wholesalers or to industrial users, but not in significant amounts to ultimate consumers. The term **wholesaler** (or merchant wholesaler) is applied only to *those wholesaling intermediaries who take title to the products they handle.* **Wholesaling intermediaries** (or wholesaling middlemen) is a broader term that describes not only *intermediaries who assume title,* but also *agents and brokers who perform important wholesaling activities without taking title to the products.* Under this definition, then, a wholesaler is a *merchant intermediary.*

The route that goods follow on the way to the consumer or industrial user is actually a chain of marketing institutions — wholesalers and retailers. Only 3 percent of the dollar value of all goods sold to the ultimate consumer is purchased directly from the manufacturer. The bulk of all products sold passes through these marketing institutions.

An increasing number of consumer complaints about high prices is heard each year. The finger of guilt is often pointed at wholesalers and retailers, the intermediaries who allegedly drive prices up by taking "high profits." Discount stores often advertise that their prices are lower since they buy direct and eliminate the intermediaries and their profits. Chain stores often assume wholesaling functions and by-pass the independent wholesalers.

Are these complaints and claims valid? Are wholesaling intermediaries anachronisms doomed to a swift demise? Answers to these questions can be formulated by considering the functions and costs of these marketing intermediaries.

Wholesaling Intermediaries Provide a Variety of Services

A marketing institution will continue to exist only so long as it fulfils a need by performing a required service. Its death may be slow, but it is inevitable if other channel members discover that they can survive without it. Figure 15.1 examines a number of possible services provided by wholesaling intermediaries. It is important to note that numerous types of wholesaling intermediaries exist and that not all of them provide every service listed in Figure 15.1. Producers–suppliers and their customers, who rely on wholesaling intermediaries for distribution, select those intermediaries providing the desired combination of services.

The list of possible services provided by wholesaling intermediaries clearly indicates the provision of marketing utility — time, place, and ownership — by these intermediaries. The services also reflect the provision of the basic marketing functions of buying, selling, storing, transportation, risk taking, financing, and market information.

The critical marketing functions — transportation and convenient product storage, reduced costs of buying and selling through reduced contacts, market information, and financing — form the basis of evaluating the efficiency of any

■ Figure 15.1 **Possible Wholesaling Services for Customers and Producers–Suppliers**

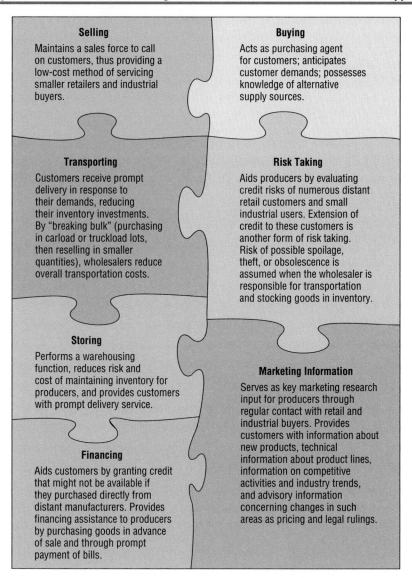

Selling
Maintains a sales force to call on customers, thus providing a low-cost method of servicing smaller retailers and industrial buyers.

Buying
Acts as purchasing agent for customers; anticipates customer demands; possesses knowledge of alternative supply sources.

Transporting
Customers receive prompt delivery in response to their demands, reducing their inventory investments. By "breaking bulk" (purchasing in carload or truckload lots, then reselling in smaller quantities), wholesalers reduce overall transportation costs.

Risk Taking
Aids producers by evaluating credit risks of numerous distant retail customers and small industrial users. Extension of credit to these customers is another form of risk taking. Risk of possible spoilage, theft, or obsolescence is assumed when the wholesaler is responsible for transportation and stocking goods in inventory.

Storing
Performs a warehousing function, reduces risk and cost of maintaining inventory for producers, and provides customers with prompt delivery service.

Marketing Information
Serves as key marketing research input for producers through regular contact with retail and industrial buyers. Provides customers with information about new products, technical information about product lines, information on competitive activities and industry trends, and advisory information concerning changes in such areas as pricing and legal rulings.

Financing
Aids customers by granting credit that might not be available if they purchased directly from distant manufacturers. Provides financing assistance to producers by purchasing goods in advance of sale and through prompt payment of bills.

marketing intermediary. The risk-taking function is present in each of the services provided by the wholesaling intermediary.

TRANSPORTATION AND PRODUCT STORAGE

Wholesalers transport and store products at locations that are convenient to customers. Manufacturers ship products from their warehouses to numerous wholesalers, who then ship smaller quantities to retail outlets that are convenient to the purchaser. A large number of wholesalers and most retailers assume the inventory function (and cost) for the manufacturer. The retailer benefits through the convenience afforded by local inventories, and the manufacturer's cash needs are reduced since the firm's products are sold directly to the wholesaler or retailer.

At the wholesale level, costs are reduced through making large purchases from the manufacturer. The wholesaler receives quantity discounts from the manufacturer — along with reduced transportation rates, since economical carload or truckload shipments are made to the wholesaler's warehouses. At the warehouse, the wholesaler breaks bulk into smaller quantities and ships to the retailer over a shorter distance than would be the case if the manufacturer filled the retailer's order directly from a central warehouse.

COST REDUCTIONS

Costs are often lowered when intermediaries are used, since the sales force of the retailer or wholesaler can represent many manufacturers to a single customer. As Figure 15.2 indicates, the number of transactions between manufacturers and their customers is markedly reduced through the introduction of an intermediary (a wholesaler or retailer). Reduced market contacts can lead to lowered marketing costs. When a wholesaling intermediary is added, the number of transactions in this illustration is reduced from sixteen to eight, thereby creating economies of scale by providing an assortment of goods with greater utility and at lower cost than without such an intermediary.

INFORMATION

Because of their central position between the manufacturer and retailers or industrial buyers, wholesalers serve as important information links. Wholesalers provide their retail customers with useful information about new products. They also supply manufacturers with information concerning market reception of their product offerings.

FINANCING

Wholesalers provide a financing function as well. Wholesalers often provide retailers with goods on credit. By purchasing goods on credit, retailers can minimize their cash investments in inventory and pay for most of their purchases as the goods are being sold. This allows them to benefit from the principle of *leverage*: a minimum investment inflates their return on investment. For example, a retailer with an investment of $1 million and profits of $100 000 will realize a return on investment (ROI) of 10 percent. But if the necessary invested capital can be reduced to $800 000 through credit from the wholesalers, and if the $100 000 profits can be maintained, the retailer's ROI increases to 12.5 percent.

Wholesalers of industrial goods provide similar services for the purchasers of their goods. In the steel industry, intermediaries called metal service centres currently market approximately one-fifth of the steel shipped by Canadian mills. Such a centre may stock as many as 6500 items for sale to many of the thousands of major metal users who buy their heavy-usage items in large quantities directly from the steel mills, but who turn to service centres for quick delivery of special orders and

■ Figure 15.2 **Achieving Transaction Economy with Wholesaling Intermediaries**

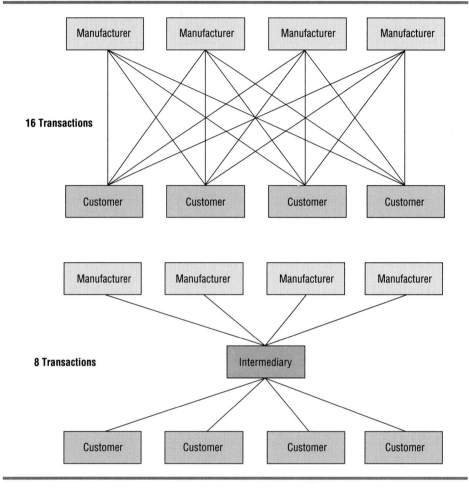

other items used in small quantities. While an order from the mills may take 90 days for delivery, a service centre can usually deliver within 24 to 48 hours. Such service reduces the investment needed in stock.

Who Should Perform Distribution Channel Functions?

While wholesaling intermediaries often perform a variety of valuable functions for their producer, retailer, and other wholesale clients, these functions could be performed by other channel members. Manufacturers may choose to by-pass independent wholesaling intermediaries by establishing networks of regional warehouses, maintaining large sales forces to provide market coverage, serving as sources of information for their retail customers, and assuming the financing function. In some instances, they may decide to push the responsibility for some of these functions through the channel on to the retailer or the ultimate purchaser. Large retailers who choose to perform their own wholesaling operations face the same choices.

A fundamental marketing principle is that marketing functions must be performed by some member of the channel; they may be shifted, but they cannot be eliminated. Either the larger retailers who by-pass the wholesaler and deal directly with the manufacturer will assume the functions previously performed by wholesaling intermediaries, or these functions will be performed by the manufacturer. Similarly, a manufacturer who deals directly with the ultimate consumer or with industrial buyers will assume the functions of storage, delivery, and market information previously performed by marketing intermediaries. Intermediaries themselves can be eliminated from the channel, but the channel functions must be performed by someone.

The potential gain for the manufacturer or retailer who might be considering by-passing wholesaling intermediaries can be estimated from the profit structure of the wholesaling industry. After-tax profitability runs about 1.7 percent on income, and 11.4 percent on equity.[2] These amounts could theoretically be saved *if* channel members performed the wholesale functions as efficiently as independent wholesaling intermediaries. Such savings could be used to reduce retail prices, to increase the profits of the manufacturer or retailers, or both. In general, profit levels are low. High turnover is therefore a necessity to provide adequate returns on investment.

TYPES OF WHOLESALING INTERMEDIARIES

As mentioned previously, various types of wholesaling intermediaries are present in different marketing channels. Some provide a wide range of services or handle a broad line of products, while others specialize in a single service, product, or industry. Table 15.1 classifies wholesaling intermediaries based on two characteristics: *ownership* (whether the wholesaling intermediary is independent, manufacturer-owned, or retailer-owned) and *title flows* (whether title passes from the manufacturer to the wholesaling intermediary or not). There are, in turn, three basic types of ownership: (1) independent wholesaling, which can involve either merchant wholesalers (who do take title to goods) or agents and brokers (who do not);[3] (2) manufacturer-owned sales branches and offices; and (3) retailer-owned co-operatives and buying offices.

Manufacturer-Owned Facilities

Increasing volumes of products are being marketed directly by manufacturers through company-owned facilities. There are several reasons for this trend: some products are perishable, some require complex installation or servicing, others need more aggressive promotion, still others are high-unit-value goods that the manufacturer wishes to control through the channel directly to the purchaser. Among the industries that have largely shifted from using independent wholesaling intermediaries to using company-owned channels are paper, paint, lumber, con-

■ Table 15.1 **Categorizing Wholesaling Intermediaries**

Classification Based on Ownership of the Intermediary
- Independent wholesaling intermediaries
- Manufacturer-owned sales branches and offices
- Retailer-owned co-operatives and buying offices

Classification Based on Title Flows
- Merchant wholesalers (take title)
- Agents and brokers (do not take title)

struction materials, piece goods, and apparel manufacturers.[4] More than 50 percent of all industrial goods are sold directly to users by the manufacturer, and slightly more than one-third of *all* products are marketed through manufacturer-owned channels.[5]

This does not mean that independent wholesalers are being squeezed out. Their numbers remain in the thousands, and their volume of trade in the billions of dollars.

SALES BRANCHES AND OFFICES

The basic distinction between sales branches and sales offices is that the **sales branch** of a company *carries inventory, and processes orders to customers from available stock.* The branch duplicates the storage function of the independent wholesaler and serves as an office for sales representatives in the territory. Sales branches are prevalent in the marketing of commercial machinery and equipment, petroleum products, motor vehicles, and chemicals.

sales branch
Manufacturer-owned facility that carries inventory and processes orders to customers from available stock.

A **sales office**, by contrast, *does not carry stock but serves as a regional office for the firm's sales personnel.* Maintaining sales offices in close proximity to the firm's customers helps reduce selling costs and improve customer service. The firm's listing in the local telephone directory and *Yellow Pages* may result in sales for the local representative. Many buyers prefer to deal with a local representative rather than take the time to write letters to distant suppliers.

sales office
Manufacturer-owned facility that does not carry stock but serves as a regional office for the firm's sales personnel.

Since warehouses represent a substantial investment in real estate, smaller manufacturers and even larger firms developing new sales territories may choose to use **public warehouses**. These are *independently owned storage facilities.* For a rental fee, the manufacturer may arrange to store its inventory in one of the nation's many public warehouses for shipment by the warehouse to customers in the area. The warehouse owner will break bulk (divide up a carload or truckload), package inventory into smaller quantities to fill orders, and even bill the purchaser for the manufacturer. The public warehouse can provide a financial service for the manufacturer, too, by issuing a warehouse receipt for the inventory. The receipt can then be used as collateral for a bank loan.

public warehouse
Independently owned storage facility.

OTHER OUTLETS FOR THE MANUFACTURER'S PRODUCTS

In addition to using a sales force and regionally distributed sales branches, manufacturers often market their products through trade fairs and exhibitions and merchandise marts. **Trade fairs** or trade exhibitions are *periodic shows at which manufacturers in a particular industry display their wares for visiting retail and wholesale buyers.* The Montreal toy show and the Toronto, Montreal, and Calgary furniture shows are annual events for both manufacturers and purchasers of toys and furniture.

trade fairs
Periodic shows at which manufacturers in a particular industry display their wares for visiting retail and wholesale buyers.

Trade fairs are very important in international marketing. Many companies get their first foothold in a foreign market by attending a trade show in the country of interest. Through the display of their products at international shows, the potential international marketer can often get a very good idea about the potential interest in their product from businesses that attend. Furthermore, such events often result in finding suitable distributors for the products in the new market.

A **merchandise mart** provides space for *permanent exhibitions at which manufacturers may rent showcases for their product offerings.* One of the largest is Place Bonaventure in Montreal, which is approximately a block square and several storeys high. Thousands of items are on display there. A retail buyer can compare the offerings of dozens of competing manufacturers and make many purchase decisions in a single visit to a trade fair or merchandise mart.

merchandise mart
Permanent exhibition at which manufacturers rent showcases for their product offerings.

Merchandise marts also provide a means for international buyers to quickly learn about the products of a region or country. In Taiwan, a gleaming, multi-storied World Trade Centre has space for trade fairs on the main floor. As well, it has several floors comprising hundreds of small glass-fronted rooms. Each one displays the products of a producer. The interested buyer can enter and find more information about the products, their prices, and their availability. Thus, instead of a Canadian buyer flying to Taipei and trying to wade through the Taiwanese *Yellow Pages* to find appropriate suppliers, he or she can just go to the World Trade Centre.

Independent Wholesaling Intermediaries

merchant wholesaler
A wholesaler who takes title to the products carried.

agents and brokers
Wholesaling intermediaries who may take possession of the products, but do not take title to them.

As has been mentioned earlier, there are many independent wholesaling intermediaries. Table 15.2 shows that they are flourishing. They perform vital functions in the marketing of goods and services, and their role and categorization should be understood clearly. These intermediaries may be divided into two categories: **merchant wholesalers**, who *take title to the products*, and **agents and brokers**, who *may take possession of the products, but do not take title to them*. Merchant wholesalers account for 86.6 percent of all sales handled by independent wholesalers. As Figure 15.3 indicates, they can be further classified as full- or limited-function wholesalers.

MERCHANT WHOLESALERS

Full-function merchant wholesalers provide a complete assortment of services for retailers or industrial purchasers. They are found in convenient locations, thus allowing their customers to make purchases on short notice. To minimize their customers' inventory requirements, they usually maintain a sales force that regularly calls on retailers, makes deliveries (sometimes), and extends credit to qualified buyers. In the industrial-goods market, the full-function merchant wholesaler (often called an *industrial distributor*) usually markets machinery, less-expensive accessory equipment, and supplies.

Full-function merchant wholesalers prevail in industries where retailers are small and carry large numbers of relatively inexpensive items, none of which is stocked in depth. The hardware, drug, and grocery industries have traditionally been serviced by them.

rack jobber
Wholesaler who provides the racks, stocks the merchandise, prices the goods, and makes regular visits to refill the shelves.

A unique type of service wholesaler emerged after World War II as supermarkets began to stock high-margin nonfood items. Since the supermarket manager possessed little knowledge of such products as toys, housewares, paperback books, records, and health and beauty items, the **rack jobber** provided the necessary

■ **Table 15.2 Wholesale Trade by Type of Operation, 1986 and 1992**

Type of Operation	Number of Establishments		Volume of Trade ($ billions)		Percentage of Volume of Trade	
	1986	1992	1986	1992	1986	1992
Merchant wholesalers	62 189	63 121	199.7	248.7	84.9	86.6
Agents and brokers	4 534	1 758	35.5	38.6	15.1	13.4
Total	**66 723**	**64 879**	**235.2**	**287.3**	**100.0**	**100.0**

Source: The 1986 data have been obtained from Statistics Canada, *Market Research Handbook*, 1990, Catalogue No. 63-224. The 1992 data have been obtained from Statistics Canada, *Wholesale Trade Statistics, Wholesale Merchants, Agents and Brokers*, Catalogue No. 63-226, as cited in *Market Research Handbook*, 1995, Catalogue No. 63-225, pp. 95, 96. Reproduced by permission of the Minister of Supply and Services Canada.

■ Figure 15.3 **Classification of Independent Wholesaling Intermediaries**

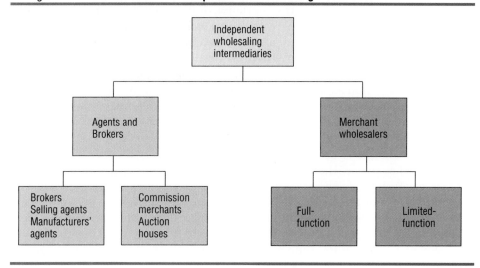

expertise. This wholesaler *provides the racks, stocks the merchandise, prices the goods, and makes regular visits to refill the shelves.* In essence, the rack jobber rents space from the retailer on a commission basis. Rack jobbers have expanded into drug, hardware, variety, and discount stores.

Since full-function merchant wholesalers perform a large number of services, their costs are sometimes as high as 20 percent of sales. Attempts to reduce the costs associated with dealing with the full-function wholesaler have led to the development of a number of *limited-function* intermediaries. Four types of limited-function merchant wholesalers are cash-and-carry wholesalers, truck wholesalers, drop shippers, and direct-response wholesalers.

Cash-and-carry wholesalers *perform most wholesaling functions except financing and delivery.* They first appeared on the marketing stage in the grocery industry during the Depression era of the 1930s. In an attempt to reduce costs, retailers drove to the wholesaler's warehouse, paid cash for their purchases, and made their own deliveries. By eliminating the delivery and financing functions, cash-and-carry wholesalers were able to reduce operating costs to approximately 9 percent of sales.

Although feasible in servicing small stores, such wholesalers have generally proven unworkable for the large-scale operation. The chain store manager is unwilling to perform the delivery function, and the cash-and-carry operation typically operates today as one department of a regular full-service wholesaler.

Truck wholesalers, or truck jobbers, *market products that require frequent replenishment.* One category is food items such as bread, potato chips, candy, and dairy products. They make regular deliveries to retail stores and simultaneously perform the sales, delivery, and collection functions. Another category is supply items for service stations and garages. The relatively high cost of operating a delivery truck and the low dollar volume per sale account for their relatively high operating costs of 15 percent. The truck wholesaler does, however, provide aggressive promotion for these product lines.

The **drop shipper** *takes orders from customers and places them with producers, who then ship directly to the customers.* Although drop shippers take title to the products, they never physically handle — or even see — the goods. Since they perform no storage or handling function, their operating costs are a relatively low 4 to 5 percent of sales.

cash-and-carry wholesaler
Limited-function merchant wholesaler who performs most wholesaling functions except financing and delivery.

truck wholesaler
Limited-function merchant wholesaler who markets products that require frequent replenishment.

drop shipper
Limited-function merchant wholesaler who takes orders from customers and places them with producers, who then ship directly to the customers.

Drop shippers operate in fields where the product is bulky and customers make purchases in carload lots. Since transportation and handling costs represent a substantial percentage of the total cost of such products as coal and lumber, drop shippers do not maintain an inventory and thereby eliminate the expenses of loading and unloading carload shipments. Their major service is in developing a complete assortment for customers. For example, drop shippers constitute a highly skilled group of sellers of lumber products from British Columbia. While the major forest-product firms, such as MacMillan-Bloedel and British Columbia Forest Products, have their in-house lumber traders, independent drop shippers compete head to head with them in selling the output of independent sawmills to eastern Canada and the United States.

direct-response wholesaler
Limited-function merchant wholesaler who relies on catalogues rather than on a sales force to contact retail, industrial, and institutional customers.

The **direct-response wholesaler** is a limited-function merchant wholesaler who *relies on catalogues rather than on a sales force to contact retail, industrial, and institutional customers.* Purchases are made by mail or telephone by relatively small customers in outlying areas. Mail-order operations are found in the hardware, cosmetics, jewellery, sporting goods, and specialty-food lines, as well as in general merchandise.

Table 15.3 compares the various types of merchant wholesalers in terms of the services they provide. Full-function merchant wholesalers and truck wholesalers are relatively high-cost intermediaries because of the number of services they perform, while cash-and-carry wholesalers, drop shippers, and direct-response wholesalers provide fewer services and thus have relatively low operating costs.

AGENTS AND BROKERS

A second group of independent wholesaling intermediaries — the agents and brokers — may or may not take possession of the products they handle, but they never take title to them. They normally perform fewer services than the merchant wholesalers and are typically involved in bringing together buyers and sellers. Agent wholesaling intermediaries may be classified into five categories — commission merchants, auction houses, brokers, selling agents, and manufacturers' agents.

commission merchant
An agent wholesaling intermediary who takes possession when the producer ships goods to a central market for sale.

Commission merchants predominate in the marketing of agricultural products. The **commission merchant** *takes possession when the producer ships goods to a central market for sale.* The commission merchant acts as the producer's agent and receives an agreed-upon fee when a sale is made. Since customers will inspect the products and prices may fluctuate, the commission merchant is given considerable latitude in making decisions. The owner of the goods may specify a minimum price, but the

■ Table 15.3 **Services Provided by Merchant Wholesalers**

Services	Full-Function Wholesalers	Limited-Function Wholesalers			
		Cash-and-Carry Wholesalers	Truck Wholesalers	Drop Shippers	Direct-response Wholesalers
Anticipates customer needs	Yes	Yes	Yes	No	Yes
Carries inventory	Yes	Yes	Yes	No	Yes
Delivers	Yes	No	Yes	No	Yes (by mail)
Provides market information	Yes	Rarely	Yes	Yes	No
Provides credit	Yes	No	No	Yes	Sometimes
Assumes ownership risk by taking title	Yes	Yes	Yes	Yes	Yes

commission merchant will sell them on a "best price" basis. The commission merchant deducts the appropriate fee from the price and the balance is remitted to the original seller.

A valuable service in such markets as used cars, livestock, antiques, works of art, fur, flowers, and fruit is performed by agent wholesaling intermediaries known as **auction houses**. They *bring buyers and sellers together in one location and allow potential buyers to inspect the merchandise before purchasing through a public bidding process.* A commission, often based on the sale price, is charged by the auction company for its services. Auction houses tend to specialize in merchandise categories such as agricultural products and art. Sotheby's is a world-famous auction house specializing in art and related products.

The task of **brokers** is to *bring buyers and sellers together.* They operate in industries characterized by a large number of small suppliers and purchasers — real estate, frozen foods, and used machinery, for example. They may represent either buyer or seller in a given transaction, but not both. The broker receives a fee from the client when the transaction is completed. The service performed is finding buyers or sellers and negotiating for exchange of title. The operating expense ratio for the broker, which may be as low as 2 percent, rises depending on the services performed.

Because brokers operate on a one-time basis for buyers or sellers, they cannot serve as an effective marketing channel for manufacturers seeking regular, continuing services. A manufacturer that seeks to develop a more permanent channel using agent wholesaling intermediaries must evaluate the services of either the selling agent or the manufacturers' agent.

For small, poorly financed, production-oriented manufacturers, the **selling agent** may prove an ideal marketing channel. These wholesaling intermediaries have even been referred to as independent marketing departments, since they are *responsible for the total marketing program for a firm's product line.* They typically have full authority over pricing decisions and promotional outlays, and they often provide financial assistance for the manufacturer. The manufacturer can concentrate on production and rely on the expertise of the selling agent for all marketing activities.

auction house
An agent wholesaling intermediary that brings buyers and sellers together in one location and allows potential buyers to inspect the merchandise before purchasing through a public bidding process.

broker
An agent wholesaling intermediary who brings buyers and sellers together; operates in industries with a large number of small suppliers and purchasers.

selling agent
An agent wholesaling intermediary who is responsible for the total marketing program for a firm's product line.

Sotheby's auctions are only one part of the services offered by the famous art auction house. Sotheby's provides experts who estimate the value of an art piece being considered for auction. These art experts also prepare catalogues for buyers who wish to know in advance what will be auctioned, and offer advice on buying to prospective purchasers.

Selling agents are common in the textile, coal, sulphur, and lumber industries. Their operating expenses average about 3 percent of sales.

Instead of a single selling agent, a manufacturer may use a number of manufacturers' agents. A **manufacturers' agent** is essentially *an independent salesperson who works for a number of manufacturers of related but noncompeting products* and receives a commission based on a specified percentage of sales. Manufacturers' agents can be thought of as an independent sales force. Although some commissions may be as high as 20 percent of sales, they usually average between 6 and 7 percent. Unlike the selling agent, who may be given exclusive world rights to *market* a manufacturer's product, the manufacturers' agent *sells* in a specified territory.[6]

Manufacturers' agents reduce their selling costs by spreading the cost per sales call over a number of different products. An agent in the plumbing supplies industry may represent a dozen different manufacturers.

Producers may use manufacturers' agents for several reasons. First, when they are developing new sales territories, the costs of adding new salespeople to "pioneer" new territories may be prohibitive. The agents, who are paid on a commission basis, can perform the sales function in the new territories at a much lower cost to the manufacturer.

Second, firms with unrelated lines may need to employ more than one channel. One line of products may be marketed through the company's sales force. A second, unrelated line might be marketed through independent manufacturers' agents. This is particularly common where the unrelated product line is a recent addition and the regular sales force has no experience with the products.

Finally, small firms with no existing sales force may turn to manufacturers' agents in order to have access to the market. A newly organized firm producing pencil sharpeners may use office equipment and supplies manufacturers' agents to reach retail outlets and industrial purchasers.

The importance of selling agents is not quite limited because many manufacturers desire better control of their marketing programs. However, the volume of sales handled by manufacturers' agents has increased substantially.

The various types of agents and brokers are compared in Table 15.4.

Retailer-Owned Facilities

Retailers have also assumed numerous wholesaling functions in attempts to reduce costs or to provide special services. Independent retailers have occasionally banded together to from buying groups in order to achieve cost savings through quantity purchases. Other groups of retailers have established retailer-owned wholesale facilities by forming a co-operative chain. Larger chain retailers often establish centralized buying offices to negotiate large-scale purchases directly with manufacturers for the members of the chain.

Independent Wholesaling Intermediaries — A Durable Marketing Institution

Many marketing observers of the 1920s felt that the end had come for the independent wholesaling intermediaries as chain stores grew in importance and attempted to by-pass them. From 1929 to 1939, the independents' sales volume dropped, but it has since increased again.

manufacturers' agent
An independent salesperson who works for a number of manufacturers of related but noncompeting products.

Table 15.4 Services Provided by Agents and Brokers

Services	Commission Merchants	Auction Houses	Brokers	Selling Agents	Manufacturers' Agents
Anticipates customer needs	Yes	Some	Some	Yes	Yes
Carries inventory	Yes	Yes	No	No	No
Delivers	Yes	No	No	No	Infrequently
Provides market information	Yes	Yes	Yes	Yes	Yes
Provides credit	Some	No	No	Some	No
Assumes ownership risk by taking title	No	No	No	No	No

A good example is Airwick Industries, a well-known manufacturer and marketer of household cleaners and deodorizers. Airwick's distribution network consisted entirely of independent wholesaling intermediaries. As often happens, growth in sales led the company to consider converting to company-owned distribution facilities. It gradually began converting the independents to company-owned distribution facilities. However, Airwick managers were unable to detect improved performance in the new situations. Thus they decided to close the sales offices and return to the use of independent distributors.

Table 15.2 shows how the relative numbers and shares of total independent wholesale trade volumes changed over two recent years. Independent wholesaling intermediaries are far from obsolete. Their continued importance is evidence of the ability of independent wholesaling intermediaries to adjust to changing conditions and changing needs. Their market size proves their ability to continue to fill a need in many marketing channels.

■ KEY TERMS

wholesalers	merchandise mart	direct-response
wholesaling	merchant wholesalers	wholesaler
intermediaries	agents and brokers	commission merchant
sales branch	rack jobber	auction house
sales office	cash-and-carry wholesaler	broker
public warehouse	truck wholesaler	selling agent
trade fairs	drop shipper	manufacturers' agent

■ INTERACTIVE SUMMARY AND DISCUSSION QUESTIONS

1. The term *wholesaler* is applied only to those wholesaling intermediaries who take title to the products they handle. The term *wholesaling intermediary* is a broader term that also includes others who perform important wholesaling activities. Differentiate among merchant wholesalers, agents, and brokers.

2. A marketing institution will continue to exist only so long as it fulfils a need by performing a required service. Does this mean that large retailers will gradually take over from wholesalers and put them out of business?

3. The number of actual transactions in an economic system comprised of manufacturers and customers can be *reduced* significantly by inserting one or more intermediaries between the manufacturer and the consumer. Explain.

4. Wholesaling intermediaries can be classified based on ownership of the intermediary and on title flows. Assuming that the independent wholesaling intermediary was the first type established in the "ownership" category, discuss the reasons why the other two types in that category might have emerged.

5. Match each of the products in the first column with the most appropriate wholesaling intermediary:

_____ Groceries	a. Drop shipper
_____ Potato chips	b. Truck wholesaler
_____ Coal	c. Auction house
_____ Grain	d. Manufacturers' agent
_____ Antiques	e. Full-function merchant wholesaler
	f. Commission merchant

6. Merchant wholesalers take title to products. Agents and brokers may take possession, but do not take title to products. Why is the operating-expense ratio of the merchant wholesaler higher than that of a typical agent or broker?

7. Comment on the following statement: Drop shippers are one type of merchant wholesaler who are good candidates for elimination. All they do is process orders. They don't even handle the goods.

8. The term *broker also* appears in the real-estate and securities fields. Are such brokers identical to the agent wholesaling intermediaries described in this chapter?

9. Trade fairs are periodic shows at which manufacturers in a particular industry may display their wares for visiting buyers. Explain how an international marketer of agricultural machinery might make use of such a trade fair.

10. A manufacturers' agent is essentially an independent salesperson who works on a commission basis for a number of manufacturers of related but noncompeting products. Under what circumstances would a company employ manufacturers' agents?

CHAPTER 16

Retailing

CHAPTER OBJECTIVES

1. To show the role played by retailing in the marketing mix.
2. To outline the decision framework for retailing.
3. To distinguish between limited-line retailers and general-merchandise retailers.
4. To identify and explain each of the five bases for categorizing retailers.
5. To identify the major types of mass merchandisers.
6. To outine the various types of nonstore retailing.
7. To distinguish between chain and independent retailers.
8. To contrast the three types of planned shopping centres.
9. To identify new trends in retailing.

Change is upon us — and it's fast, furious, and unforgiving. Nowhere is this more evident than in Canada's retail sector, where marketers try to understand buying behaviour and chart our future shopping patterns. Retailers who do not keep in touch with the trends in consumer buying patterns will find themselves at a serious disadvantage. The bankruptcy of Consumers Distributing in the fall of 1996 is a painful example of what happened when a proud Canadian company could not respond fast enough to changing technology and the onslaught of "big-box" retailers such as Wal-Mart and Future Shop.

During the early part of the 1990s, sales at Consumers remained relatively constant at about $600 million. The company even had an operating profit of $21.8 million in 1994. To the casual observer, Consumers seemed to be holding its own. But most retail experts and senior management at Consumers knew that the company had lost its competitive edge. It was at a crossroads, and the future of its business was at stake. One only had to observe the impact of its "pencil-and-paper" catalogue strategy on customer service. According to James McLeod, a merchandising analyst with Richardson Greenshields of Canada, a typical shopping excursion at Consumers for many meant flipping through a large catalogue, filling out an order form with a pencil, and standing in a long lineup — only to find out the desired item was out of stock. "Not only did you not get what you wanted, but it cost you time to find that out," said Mr. McLeod.

Two major competitive forces sounded a wake-up call in the Consumers marketing department. First, there was the onslaught of big-box retailing, with its high-volume/low-price strategy. Even Zellers had to rethink its "Where the Lowest Price Is the Law" strategy. Second, the "cybermall" revolution meant that almost any retailer, large or small, could now offer a catalogue electronically. The overnight popularity of armchair shopping meant that Consumers' archaic pencil-and-paper retail system had to go. Now customers could shop at home on CD-ROM catalogues, for example, and then simply "click in their order." No more walking, waiting, or phoning. Cybermalls were beginning to change the face of retailing worldwide.

Senior management at Consumers had to reinvent its customer service, distribution, and merchandising strategies. It had to decide whether to become a big-box retailer and/or a cybermall. But one thing was clear: the company had to move fast. A retail revolution was underway, and the competition was moving fast. The winners would be those retailers who could focus and service a growth niche.

Consumers' retail war plan was this: First, the company built and market-tested a new high-tech superstore in Toronto. This superstore concept was an ambitious attempt to shed Consumers' reputation for spotty service and out-of-stock problems. It featured an expanded product showroom and touch-screen computers that allowed customers to browse electronically for items and, eventually, pay for purchases with a credit card. Consumers invited retail experts to tour the Toronto prototype. Mr. McLeod had this to say: "It's quite a bit different than anything that I've seen them do in the past. It's almost like a marriage of some traditional retailing and merchandising techniques with the economics of their catalogue-showroom concept." It was reviews like this that led to an aggressive management plan to open 70 such stores by the end of 1998.

Next, Consumers initiated marketing tests for an electronic version of its catalogue. Using this interactive service, its customers would not have to leave the comfort of their homes. Within the next few years, Consumers had planned to create new shelves in cyberspace.

Unfortunately for Consumers, it just couldn't move fast enough. By the summer of 1996, the company asked for court protection from its creditors. It was $250 million in debt and needed some additional breathing space to implement its plan. But, by the fall of that year, it failed to convince its financial backers that it could compete in the new retail arena. An impatient group of four banks pulled the plug. Almost overnight, 3700 full- and part-time employees lost their jobs, and some 400 faithful trade suppliers were given little chance of getting any of their money back.[1]

The changes that Consumers was virtually forced into reflect the constant change that occurs in the retail world. Retailing represents one of marketing's most dynamic aspects. Retailers who do not keep in touch with the trends in the marketplace will find themselves trying to catch up with newly emerging companies.

Suppose you were the CEO of Consumers and you were given another chance to save the company, how would you reinvent Consumers Distributing to compete successfully in the new economy?

INTRODUCTION

In a very real sense, retailers *are* the marketing channel for most consumers, since consumers have little contact with manufacturers and almost none with the wholesaling intermediaries. The services provided — location, store hours, quality of salespeople, store layout, selection, and returns, among others — often figure even more importantly than the physical product in buying decisions.

Retailers are both customers and marketers in the channel. They market goods and services to ultimate consumers and also are the consumers for wholesalers and manufacturers. Because of their critical location in the channel, retailers may perform an important feedback role in obtaining information from customers and transmitting it to manufacturers and other channel members.

Retailing is the "last step of the marketing channel" for the consumer goods manufacturer. Whether the manufacturer has established a company-owned chain of retail stores or uses several of the thousands of retail stores in Canada, the success of the entire marketing strategy rides on the decisions of consumers in the retail store.

Retailing may be defined as *all the activities involved in the sale of goods and services to the ultimate consumer*. Retailing involves not only sales in retail stores, but also several forms of nonstore retailing. These include telephone and direct-response sales, automatic merchandising, and direct house-to-house solicitations by salespeople.

retailing
All the activities involved in the sale of goods and services to the ultimate consumer.

EVOLUTION OF RETAILING

Early retailing in Canada can be traced to the voyageurs, to the establishment of trading posts by the Hudson's Bay Company and others, and to pack peddlers who literally carried their wares to outlying settlements. After the trading post days, the Hudson's Bay and other retailers evolved into the institution known as the *general store*. The general store was stocked with general merchandise to meet the needs of a small community or rural area. Here customers could buy clothing, groceries, feed, seed, farm equipment, drugs, spectacles, and candy. The following account provides a good description of this early retail institution:

> The country store was in many respects a departmental store on a small scale, for a well-equipped store contained a little of everything. On one side were to be seen shelves well filled with groceries, crockery-ware, and a few patent medicines, such as blood purifiers, painkillers, and liniments; on the other side, a well assorted stock of dry goods, including prints, woolens, muslins, calico, cottons, etc. At the back, a lot of hardware, comprising nails, paints, oils, putty, glass, and garden tools, as well as an assortment of boots and shoes — from the tiny copper-toe to the farmer's big cowhide. In the back room, at the rear end of the store, were to be found barrels of sugar and New Orleans molasses, crates of eggs, and tubs of butter and lard. With this miscellaneous mixture — tea, coffee, dry goods, codfish, and boots and shoes — the odour of the country store was truly a composite one, and trying to the olfactory organs of the visitor. The country merchant was usually a man in good circumstances, for he was

obliged in most cases to give a year's credit, the farmers paying their bills in the fall of the year, after the "threshing" or the "killing"; their only source of revenue at any other time being from butter and eggs, which their wives took to the country store, usually once a week, and exchanged for store goods. Perhaps there was no more popular place of meeting than the country store.[2]

The basic needs that caused the general store to develop also doomed this institution to a limited existence. Since the general store owners attempted to satisfy the needs of customers for all types of "store-bought" goods, they carried a small assortment of each good. As the villages grew, the size of the market was large enough to support stores specializing in specific product lines, such as groceries, hardware, dry goods, and drugs. Most general stores either converted into more specialized limited-line stores or closed. But the general store did, and in some rural areas still does, fill a need for its customers. General stores are still operated profitably in less developed countries, where income levels cannot support more specialized retailers, and in a few isolated parts of Canada as well.

Innovation and Competition in Retailing

Retailing is an extremely competitive industry. A major determinant of success is to develop a *differential advantage* over competitors. Without a sustainable differential advantage, no retailer will last for long. Therefore, retailing is one of the most dynamic components of the economic system. As consumers, we see these changes occurring almost on a daily basis, yet we often do not think about the virtual warfare going on around us.

Retailing operations are remarkable illustrations of the marketing concept in operation. Retail innovations often develop as attempts to better satisfy particular consumer needs, or to make the enterprise more competitive.

As consumers' needs and lifestyles change, institutions emerge to meet this demand. The supermarket appeared in the early 1930s to meet consumer desires for lower prices. Its success was enhanced by the fact that cars and good roads were commonly available. Convenience food stores such as 7-Eleven today meet the need for readily available basic products at all hours. Superstores and membership and warehouse clubs such as Costco serve consumers who want low prices and are willing to travel significant distances, as well as give up services.

Large-format specialty stores such as Home Depot are a particularly potent competitor because they provide low prices and breadth and depth of merchandise, as well as services. Department stores provide a wide variety of other products and services to meet other customer needs. Vending machines, door-to-door retailers, and mail-order retailing offer buyers convenience. Planned shopping centres provide a balanced array of consumer goods and services and include ample parking for their customers.

MARKETING STRATEGY IN RETAILING

The retailer's decision-making process, like the producer's and wholesaler's, centres on the two fundamental steps of (1) analyzing, evaluating, and ultimately selecting a *target market*, and (2) developing a *marketing mix* designed to satisfy the chosen target market profitably. In other words, the retailer must develop a product offering to appeal to the chosen consumer group, set prices, and choose a location and method of distribution. Finally, the retailer has to develop a marketing communications strategy.[3]

The Target Market

Canada's 165 000 retail establishments are involved in developing specific marketing mixes to satisfy chosen market segments. Like other marketers, retailers must start by selecting the target market to which they wish to appeal. Marketing research is often used in this aspect of retail decision making. For example, retailers entering new countries, or even new markets in the same country, have been surprised that the target market of their home location apparently does not exist in the new location. Canadian Tire expanded to the larger U.S. market with the purchase of White Stores, Inc.,[4] but found U.S. market acceptance of virtual carbon copies of the successful Canadian stores so limited that the firm abandoned that market after significant losses. Marks and Spencer, one of Britain's most successful retailers, had similar difficulties when it entered the Canadian market. Marketing research can help a company adjust to a new environment faster.

Sometimes a retailer finds it necessary to shift target markets. For example, stores established to serve specialty markets, such as skiers or snowmobilers, have found that lack of snow or changes in consumer recreation habits have forced them to expand or change their offerings to serve more viable target markets. Market selection is as vital an aspect of retailers' marketing strategy as it is for any other marketer.[5]

The Marketing (Retail) Mix

The retail mix is a unique offering to the market based on decisions about goods and services, prices, location and distribution, and retail image and promotion.

Goods and Services Strategy

Retailers must also determine and evaluate their offerings with respect to the following:

1. General goods/service categories
2. Specific lines
3. Specific products
4. Inventory depth
5. Range of assortment

These decisions are determined by the size of the retailer, as well as whether the store tends to concentrate on convenience, shopping, or specialty goods. Other marketing factors can influence goods and/or service offerings. For instance, Toys R Us distinguishes itself by specializing and providing great breadth and depth of assortment at low prices.

Product strategy evolves to meet competition and changing consumer needs. The success of Loblaws' Superstores forced Safeway to develop its large Food For Less establishments. On a more limited scale, a decision by Kmart to provide a special area devoted to patio equipment would likely have to be matched by Zellers if the new Kmart section proved to be popular.

Retail Pricing Strategy

Pricing is another critical element of the retailing mix. The essential decisions concern relative price levels. Does the target market want service and high quality, high-priced merchandise (as offered by Holt Renfrew), or lower-priced items (like Zellers)? Price is such an important variable in the retail marketing mix that it continually drives the establishment of new types of retail operations, such as Costco. These will be discussed in more detail later.

Other pricing decisions concern markups, markdowns, loss leaders, odd pricing, and promotional pricing. The retailer is the channel member with direct responsibility for the prices paid by consumers. As Chapters 12 and 13 pointed out, the prices that are set play a major role in buyer perceptions of the retail market.

Location and Distribution Decisions

Real-estate professionals often say that there are three critical factors for establishing a retail establishment: "Location, location, location." A store must be in an appropriate location for the type and price of merchandise carried. Small service outlets such as dry cleaners have discovered that there is a difference between being on the "going to work" side of a busy street and the "going home" side. Other retailers have found success in small strip-type neighbourhood shopping centres that are close to where people live. These centres continue to flourish despite the advent of larger suburban community shopping centres.[6]

retail trade area analysis
Studies that assess the relative drawing power of alternative retail locations.

Retail trade area analysis refers to *studies that assess the relative drawing power of alternative retail locations*. For example, shoppers might be polled as to where they live, how they get to the stores they shop at, how long it takes, how often they shop, and the like. Similarly, the credit charges of an existing store might be plotted to show what its service area is.

law of retail gravitation
Principle that delineates the retail trade area of a potential site on the basis of distance between alternative locations and relative populations.

Another technique to use is the law of retail gravitation, sometimes called Reilly's law after its originator, William J. Reilly.[7] The **law of retail gravitation**, originally formulated in the 1920s, *delineates the retail trade area of a potential site on the basis of distance between alternative locations and relative populations*. The formula is

$$\frac{\text{Breaking point}}{\text{in km from A}} = \frac{\text{km between A and B}}{1 + \sqrt{\dfrac{\text{Population of B}}{\text{Population of A}}}}$$

Assume a retailer is considering locating a new outlet in Town A or Town B, which are located 60 km from each other. The population of A is 80 000 and the population of B is 20 000. One question that concerns the retailer is where people living in a small rural community located on the highway between the two towns 25 km from Town B are likely to shop.

According to the law of retail gravitation, these rural shoppers would most likely shop in Town A even though it is 10 km farther away than Town B. The retail trade area of A extends 40 km toward B, and the rural community is located only 35 km away.

$$\frac{\text{Breaking point}}{\text{in km from A}} = \frac{60}{1 + \sqrt{\dfrac{20\ 000}{80\ 000}}} = \frac{60}{1 + \sqrt{.25}} = \frac{60}{1.5} = 40$$

The formula can be applied inversely to find Town B's trade area, yielding a figure of 20 km, which falls 5 km short of the rural community:

$$\text{Breaking point in km from B} = \frac{60}{1 + \sqrt{\dfrac{80\ 000}{20\ 000}}} = \frac{60}{1 + \sqrt{4}} = \frac{60}{3} = 20 \text{ km}$$

The complete trade area for A or B could be found by similar calculations with other communities.

The application of this technique is limited in an area of urban sprawl, regional shopping centres, and consumers who measure distances in terms of travel time. As a result, a contemporary version of retail trade analysis has been offered by David Huff.

Huff's work is an interurban model that assesses the likelihood that a consumer will patronize a specific shopping centre. Trading areas are expressed in terms of a series of probability contours. The probability that a consumer will patronize a specific shopping centre is viewed as a function of centre size, travel time, and the type of merchandise sought.[8] Such models are more often used for structuring decision making than as a precise, predictive tool.

OTHER DISTRIBUTION DECISIONS

Retailers are faced with a variety of other distribution decisions, largely in order to ensure that adequate quantities of stock are available when consumers want to buy. The definition of "adequate" will vary with the service strategy of the retailer. In many traditional retail situations, since the cost of carrying inventory is high, a high-margin full-service retailer will likely have a greater depth and range of merchandise than a low-margin, limited-time, high-volume outlet. This generalization does not hold in the case of some large-format specialty stores, such as Office Depot.

Retail Image and Promotional Strategy

Retail image refers to *the consumer's perception of a store and of the shopping experience it provides.*[9] Promotional strategy is a key element in determining the store's image with the consumer. Another important element is the amenities provided by the retailer — the so-called atmospherics.

> **retail image**
> The consumer's perception of a store and of the shopping experience it provides.

Promoting a store with screaming headlines about fantastic once-in-a-lifetime sale prices creates a substantially different image from that using a subdued, tasteful illustration of obviously stylish, elegant clothing. Similarly, walking into a discount store redolent of caramel popcorn produces an image dramatically different from that of entering a beautifully carpeted boutique.

Regardless of how it is accomplished, the objective of retailer promotional strategy should be to align the consumer's perception of the store with other elements of the retailing mix: retail image should match the target market that is selected.

The Differentiation Triangle

Differentiation is a key factor in competitive strategy.[10] Retailers can differentiate themselves in many ways. However, three elements — price, location, and store atmosphere and service — are typically used to differentiate stores from competitors in the same strategic group. The **differentiation triangle** is shown in Figure 16.1.

> **differentiation triangle**
> Differentiation of a retail store from competitors in the same strategic group through price, location, store atmosphere, and/or service.

Changes in these elements do not transform a store from one type to another (e.g., a convenience store to a department store). Yet the way the elements are used

■ Figure 16.1 **Differentiation Triangle: Avenues for Differentiation Within Strategic Groups**

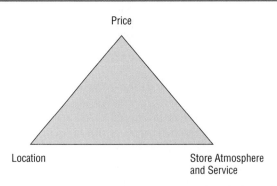

Source: Avijit Ghosh, *Retail Management*, 2nd ed. (Fort Worth, TX: Dryden, 1994), pp. 59–60. Reprinted by permission of the publisher.

is important since they give the customer reasons to choose one store over another. For example, location is very important, as we have already discussed.

Price is a powerful tool in the retail mix. It is not always the differentiating factor, but retailers must understand when it does play that role. In such a circumstance, retailers are finding that they cannot "play around" with discounting. Price cuts must be truly significant in order to compete with other retailers who have also chosen price as a means of differentiation.

Stores can also differentiate by improving store atmosphere and customer service. Unfortunately, many retailers have ignored this element's potential and allowed service quality to deteriorate in the pursuit of cost savings. As manufacturers and other service providers are learning to emphasize total quality in their products, retailers also need to re-evaluate the quality of their service.

CATEGORIZING RETAILERS

The nation's retailers come in a variety of forms. Since new types of retail operations continue to evolve in response to the changing demands of their markets, no universal classification has been devised. The following characteristics or bases can be used in categorizing them:

1. Shopping effort expended by customers
2. Services provided to customers
3. Product lines
4. Location of retail transactions
5. Form of ownership

Any retailing operation can be classified using each of these five bases. A 7-Eleven store may be classified as a convenience store (category 1), self-service (category 2), relatively narrow product lines (category 3), in-store retailing (category 4), and a member of a corporate chain (category 5). Figure 16.2 illustrates the bases for classifying retail operations.

■ Figure 16.2 **Bases for Classifying Retailers**

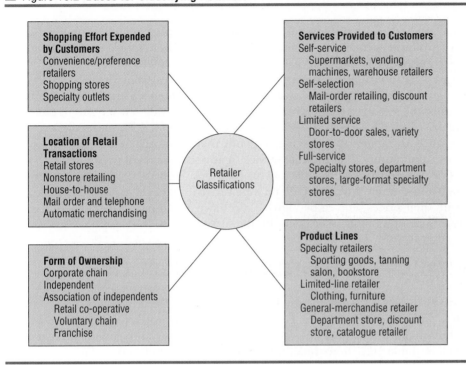

Shopping Effort Expended by Customers
Convenience/preference retailers
Shopping stores
Specialty outlets

Location of Retail Transactions
Retail stores
Nonstore retailing
House-to-house
Mail order and telephone
Automatic merchandising

Form of Ownership
Corporate chain
Independent
Association of independents
  Retail co-operative
  Voluntary chain
  Franchise

Retailer Classifications

Services Provided to Customers
Self-service
  Supermarkets, vending machines, warehouse retailers
Self-selection
  Mail-order retailing, discount retailers
Limited service
  Door-to-door sales, variety stores
Full-service
  Specialty stores, department stores, large-format specialty stores

Product Lines
Specialty retailers
  Sporting goods, tanning salon, bookstore
Limited-line retailer
  Clothing, furniture
General-merchandise retailer
  Department store, discount store, catalogue retailer

RETAILERS CLASSIFIED BY SHOPPING EFFORT

A classification of consumer goods based on consumer purchase patterns in securing a particular product or service was presented in Chapter 9. This system can be extended to retailers by considering the reasons consumers shop at a particular retail outlet. The result is a classification scheme in which retail outlets, like consumer goods, are categorized as convenience–preference, shopping, or specialty. The type of retail outlet has a significant influence on the marketing strategies the retailer should select. *Convenience–preference retailers* focus on convenient locations, long store hours, rapid checkout service, and adequate parking facilities. Small food stores, gasoline retailers, and some barber shops are included in this category.

Shopping stores typically include furniture stores, appliance retailers, clothing outlets, and sporting goods stores. Consumers will compare prices, assortments, and quality levels of competing outlets before making a purchase decision. Managers of shopping stores attempt to differentiate their outlets through advertising, window displays, in-store layouts, knowledgeable salespeople, and appropriate merchandise assortments.

Specialty retailers provide some combination of product lines, service, and reputation that results in consumers' willingness to expend considerable effort to shop there. Holt Renfrew and Birks have developed a sufficient degree of loyalty among many shoppers to be categorized as specialty retailers.

The foregoing categories are not absolute. The most exclusive specialty store carries handkerchiefs, and many supermarkets have gourmet good departments.

RETAILERS CLASSIFIED BY SERVICES PROVIDED

Some retailers seek a differential advantage by developing a unique combination of service offerings for the customers who compose their target market. Retailing operations may be classified according to the extent of the services they offer. Figure 16.3 indicates the spectrum of retailer services from virtually no services (self-service) to a full range of customer services (full-service retailers).

Since the self-service and self-selection retailers provide few services to their customers, retailer location and price are important factors. These retailers tend to specialize in staple and convenience goods that are purchased frequently by customers and require little product service or advice from retail personnel.

The full-service retail establishments focus more on fashion-oriented shopping goods and specialty items and offer a wide variety of services for their clientele. As a result, their prices tend to be higher than those of self-service retailers due to the higher operating costs associated with the services.

RETAILERS CLASSIFIED BY PRODUCT LINES

Perhaps the most commonly used method of categorizing retailers is to consider the product lines they handle. Grouping retailers by product lines produces three major categories: limited-line stores, specialty stores, and general-merchandise retailers. Table 16.1 shows retail trade for various types of outlets. From this it can be seen that Canadians spend the most on food and automobiles.

■ Figure 16.3 **Classification of Retailers on the Basis of Customer Service Levels**

Self-Service	Self-Selection	Limited-Service	Full-Service

Characteristics

Very few services	Restricted services	Limited variety	Wide variety of services
Price appeal	Price appeal	of service	Fashion merchandise
Staple goods	Staple goods	Less price appeal	Specialty merchandise
Convenience goods	Convenience goods	Shopping goods	

Examples

Warehouse retailing	Discount retailing	Door-to-door	Specialty stores
Supermarkets	Variety stores	Telephone sales	Department stores
Mail-order retailing	Mail-order retailing	Variety stores	
Automatic vending			

Source: Adapted from Larry D. Redinbaugh, *Retailing Management: A Planning Approach*, p. 12. Copyright © 1976 McGraw-Hill Book Company. Used by permission of McGraw-Hill, Inc.

■ Table 16.1 **Total Retail Sales by Trade Group, 1992 and 1993**

Trade Group	1992	1993	Percentage Change 1992/1993
	\$000 000		
All Stores — Total	**185 049.2**	**193 815.0**	**+4.7**
Supermarkets and grocery stores	45 444.8	47 695.8	+5.0
All other food stores	3 111.6	3 385.6	+8.8
Drugs and patent medicine stores	10 721.5	11 889.2	+10.9
Shoe stores	1 506.4	1 614.0	+7.1
Men's clothing stores	1 666.4	1 739.2	+4.4
Women's clothing stores	3 671.9	3 819.2	+4.0
Other clothing stores	3 904.0	4 264.1	+9.2
Household furniture and appliance stores	7 660.5	8 385.5	+9.5
Household furnishing stores	2 171.9	2 246.7	+3.4
Motor vehicle and recreational vehicle dealers	38 500.9	41 365.2	+7.4
Gasoline service stations	14 168.0	14 245.8	+0.5
Automotive parts, accessories, and services	10 288.2	10 871.0	+5.7
General merchandise stores	20 859.9	20 494.6	−1.8
Other semi-durable goods stores	6 416.0	6 658.1	+3.8
Other durable goods stores	4 935.1	5 207.0	+5.5
Other retail stores	10 021.9	9 934.2	−0.9

Source: Statistics Canada, *Market Research Handbook*, 1995, Catalogue No. 63-225, p. 75. Reproduced by permission of the Minister of Supply and Services Canada.

Limited-Line Retailers

A large assortment of a single line of products or a few related lines of products are offered in **limited-line stores**. Their development paralleled the growth of towns when the population grew sufficiently to support them. These operations include such retailers as furniture stores, hardware stores, grocery stores and supermarkets, appliance stores, and sporting goods stores. Examples of limited-line stores include Sherwin-Williams (paints), Leon's and House of Teak (furniture), Radio Shack (home electronics), Pegabo and Bata (shoes), Calculator World (electronic calculators), D'Allaird's (ready-to-wear), and Coles (books).

These retailers choose to cater to the needs of a specific target market — people who want to select from a complete line in purchasing a particular product. The marketing vice-president of a limited-line firm might summarize the limited-line retailer's strategy this way: "Eatons can show customers 3 types of tents, but we can show them 25."

THE SUPERMARKET

The supermarket concentrates mainly on a single line — groceries — but this line contains many different products.

A **supermarket** can be defined as *a large-scale, departmentalized retail store offering a large variety of food products* such as meats, produce, dairy products, canned goods, and frozen foods in addition to various nonfood items. It operates on a *self-service* basis and emphasizes price and adequate parking facilities. Supermarket customers typically shop once or twice a week and make fill-in purchases between each major shopping trip. Supermarkets account for 71.8 percent of food store sales in Canada.

limited-line store
Retailer that offers a large assortment of a single line of products or a few related lines of products.

supermarket
Large-scale, departmentalized retail store offering a large variety of food products.

Bookstores appeal to readers who want more than the current bestsellers or romances provided by department and drug stores. They know that a bookstore can offer consumers a choice of many different subjects as well as several choices on the same subject. Some bookstores even limit themselves to one subject. SWIPE, a bookstore in Toronto, specializes in books on advertising and design.

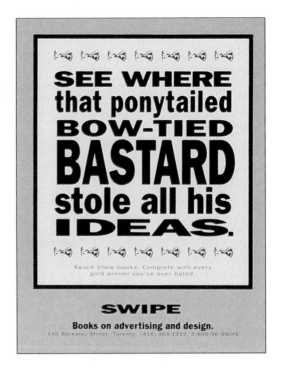

In recent years, supermarkets have become increasingly competitive. One Ontario supermarket attempted to increase its share of the market through a well-publicized price-cutting program. The ramifications were quickly felt in other areas of the country where branches of competing chains operate. Retaliation by other supermarkets was swift, and temporary price cuts ensued — as well as reductions in profits. Supermarket profits average only about 1 percent of sales after taxes. However, a high turnover of 20–26 times per year provides attractive returns on investment.

With a razor-thin profit margin, supermarkets compete through careful planning of retail displays in order to sell more merchandise per week and reduce the amount of investment in inventory. Product location is studied carefully in order to expose the consumer to as much merchandise as possible (and increase impulse purchases). In an attempt to fight the tendency of consumers to eat many of their meals outside the home, supermarkets have begun to feature their own delicatessens and bakeries and to devote a limited portion of their stores to nonfood items. Nonfood products such as toiletries, magazines, records, over-the-counter drugs, prescription pharmaceuticals, and small kitchen utensils are carried for two reasons: (1) consumers have displayed a willingness to buy such items in supermarkets and (2) supermarket managers like them because they have a higher profit margin than the food products. Nonfood sales have grown substantially as a percentage of supermarket sales.

The trend in this category is toward larger stores. Many of these, such as Loblaws' Superstores, carry a variety of other merchandise, such as clothing, hardware, and gift items.

Specialty Stores

specialty store
Retailer that handles only part of a single line of products.

A **specialty store** typically *handles only part of a single line of products*. However, this narrow line is stocked in considerable depth. Such stores include meat markets, shoe stores, bakeries, furriers, and luggage shops. Although some of these stores are operated by chains, most are run as independent small-scale operations. The specialty store is perhaps the greatest stronghold of the independent retailer, who can develop expertise in providing a very narrow line of products for his or her local market.

Specialty stores should not be confused with specialty goods, for the specialty store typically carries convenience and shopping goods. The label "specialty" comes from the practice of handling a specific, narrow line of merchandise.

General-Merchandise Retailers

DEPARTMENT STORES

The department store is actually a series of limited-line and specialty stores under one roof. A **department store**, by definition, is *a large retailer that handles a variety of merchandise* that includes apparel and accessories, home furnishings, cosmetics, housewares, and appliances. It serves the consumer by acting as a one-stop shopping centre for almost all personal and household items.

department store
Large retailer that handles a variety of merchandise.

A distinguishing feature of the department store is indicated by its name. The entire stock is *organized around departments* for the purposes of service, promotion, and control. A general merchandising manager is responsible for the entire store's product planning. Reporting to the merchandising manager are the buyers who manage each department. The buyers typically run the departments almost as independent businesses and are given considerable discretion in merchandising and layout decisions. Acceptance of the retailing axiom that "well-purchased goods are half sold" is indicated in the department manager's title of *buyer*. The buyers, particularly those in charge of high-fashion departments, spend a considerable portion of their time making decisions concerning the inventory to be carried in their departments.

The department store has been the symbol of retailing since the turn of the century. It started in Canada with Timothy Eaton in 1869, when he purchased the 4 m wide dry-goods store and stock of William Jennings for $6500. Eaton established a one-price cash policy (instead of bargaining and paying in produce), and formulated the famous "goods satisfactory or money refunded" guarantee. By 1929, half the retail sales in Canada were made at Eaton's.[11]

Today, almost every urban area in Canada has one or more department stores associated with its downtown area and its major shopping areas. Department stores have had a major impact in many cities. For example, as recently as 1969, Eaton's received 40 percent of every retail dollar (except groceries) in Winnipeg.[12]

The impact of department stores on urban life is not confined to Canada. Such stores are, of course, widespread in the United States. European shoppers associate London with Harrod's and Paris with Au Printemps. Australians associate Melbourne and Sydney with Myers/Cole.

Department stores are known for offering their customers a wide variety of services such as charge accounts, delivery, gift wrapping, and liberal return privileges. In addition, approximately 50 percent of their employees and some 40 percent of their floor space are devoted to nonselling activities. As a result, department stores have relatively high operating costs, averaging between 45 and 60 percent of sales.

Department stores have faced intense competition in the past 30 years. Their relatively high operating costs make them vulnerable to such new retailing innovations as discount stores, catalogue merchandisers, and hypermarkets (discussed later in this section). In addition, department stores are typically located in downtown business districts and experience the problems associated with limited parking, traffic congestion, and urban migration to the suburbs.

Department stores have displayed a willingness to adapt to competition and changing consumer desires. Reducing prices through lowering service levels has been one notable response by some department stores. Also, department stores have followed the movement of the population to the suburbs by opening major branches in outlying shopping centres. Canadian department stores have led other retailers in maintaining a vital and dynamic downtown through modernizing their stores, extending store hours, emphasizing attracting the trade of tourists and people attending conventions, and focussing on the residents of the central cities.

VARIETY STORES

variety store
Retailer that offers an extensive range and assortment of low-priced merchandise.

Retailers that *offer an extensive range and assortment of low-priced merchandise* are called **variety stores**. Two examples are Woolworth and Stedmans. Most of the products carried by these stores are quite basic. Consumers seldom have strong preferences for particular brands. Thus stores can carry a limited range in each product line without losing potential customers. The nation's variety stores account for only about 0.64 percent of all retail sales. Variety stores have steadily declined in popularity. Many have evolved into or have been replaced by other retailing categories such as discounting.

MASS MERCHANDISERS

mass merchandiser
Retailer that concentrates on high turnover of items, emphasizes lower prices than department stores, and offers reduced services.

Mass merchandisers are direct competitors of department stores. **Mass merchandisers** *concentrate on high turnover of items, emphasize lower prices than department stores, and offer reduced services.* Typically, they give considerable attention to small appliances, hardware, automotive products, and sporting goods in addition to apparel.

Major types of mass merchandisers are discount houses, hypermarkets, and catalogue retailers.

DISCOUNT HOUSES

discount house
Retailer that, in exchange for reduced prices, does not offer such traditional retail services as credit, sales assistance by clerks, and delivery.

The birth of the modern **discount house** came at the end of World War II when a New York operation named Masters discovered that a very large number of customers were willing to shop at a store that *did not offer such traditional retail services as credit, sales assistance by clerks, and delivery, in exchange for reduced prices.* Within a very brief period, retailers throughout the country followed the Masters formula and either changed over from their traditional operations or opened new stores dedicated to discounting. At first the discount stores were primarily involved with the sale of appliances, but they have spread into furniture, soft goods, drugs, and even food.

The new discounters operated large stores, advertised heavily, and emphasized low prices on well-known brands. And consumers, who had become accustomed to self-service by shopping at supermarkets, responded in great numbers to this retailing innovation. Conventional retailers such as Kresge and Woolworth joined the discounting practice by opening their own Kmart and Woolco stores.

As the discount houses move into new product areas, a noticeable increase in the number of services offered as well as a corresponding decrease in the discount margin is evident. Carpeted floors are beginning to appear in discounters' stores, credit is increasingly available, and many discounters are even quietly dropping the term *discount* from their name. Even though they still offer fewer services, their operating costs are increasing as they become similar to the traditional department stores (which have adopted some of the discount stores' practices).

As these trends have continued, and other retailers have adjusted their offerings to compete with them, the original competitive threat of the discount phenomenon has waned. However, the purchase of the aging Woolco operations by American discount chain Wal-Mart has renewed the competitive challenge. Wal-Mart generates differential price advantage through great purchasing power and efficiencies in distribution. In addition to low prices, it competes by offering extra services. Zellers, Kmart, and Canadian Tire are three major retailers that are being especially challenged by Wal-Mart.

Two new formats have evolved in the discount store category.[13] These are *membership and warehouse clubs* and *large-format specialty stores*. An example of a **membership and warehouse club** is Costco. *Customers must purchase a membership card* (about $35) *before they can enter the store*. The stores are often located in an industrial subdivision, and are constructed like warehouses, with steel walls and roofs and cement floors. They range in size between 9000 and 12 000 m². Customers vie with fork-lift trucks in the aisles, as all merchandise is stored on tall metal shelving.

One of each item is displayed, and the price is marked on a card on the shelf. Large-size packaging, in most instances, requires the buyer to purchase a supply that will last several months. There is no service, and prices are low enough that many small businesses are seen buying merchandise for resale. These warehouses are having a sizable impact on the retail market, as well as on the market share of traditional retailers.

The new threat to existing retailers is the development of very large specialty retailers. **Large-format specialty stores** can be of similar size to warehouse clubs. They are known as *category killers*. The characteristics of these stores give some reasons for this name:

1. They are very large, and specialize in one type of merchandise. Each store has a huge variety to choose from.
2. They use low-cost warehouse-type building structures.
3. They sell a very large volume of merchandise at very low prices. The average gross margin is approximately 8 percent.
4. Their average sales per square metre are $4300 — about twice as much as traditional retailers.
5. These new retailers offer a great deal of service. For example, consider Lewiscraft's large new hobby and craft store located north of Toronto. It looks like a warehouse, has a huge selection of craft items, and even offers "how-to" arts and crafts and hobby classes taught by professionals. Home Depot has a large staff of trained professionals to give advice to do-it-yourselfers.
6. These category killers locate in a free-standing suburban location. This gives them 35 to 50 percent lower location costs than in the downtown area. Other costs are often much less than in more congested retail areas.

Another example of a large-format specialty store is Chapters, a bookstore stacked with 100 000 different types of books. Included is live children's entertainment and a cappuccino bar with a reading room. Yet another example is Petsmart, a pet supply store of 1800 m². This is about ten times larger than typical stores. It carries 6500 products to keep animals happy, healthy, and fashionable.

Because of their size, and the warehouse-type facility, these two types of retailers are also known as *big box retailers*. The development of these two types of discount operations is a classic example of retailers seeking a differential advantage. In the case of the category killers, they are very strong on at least two aspects of the differential triangle: price and service. Consumers have ready access to virtually anything they want in a particular category without shopping around — and likely at a lower price. Selection plus service at a low price is a hard combination for traditional retailers to beat.

In Edmonton, Toronto, and other cities, groupings of two or more large-format retailers in the same area are forming **power nodes**. These have a large drawing power and are pulling consumers away from traditional shopping areas.

membership and warehouse clubs
Very large, warehouse-type retail stores that offer low prices because of their no-frill format and paid membership requirement.

large-format specialty stores
Large warehouse-type retail stores that specialize in selling a great variety of one category of merchandise at very low prices.

power node
Groupings of two or more large-format retailers resulting in large customer drawing power.

Established retailers are scrambling to compete. Canadian Tire, for example, is increasing the size of its stores and adopting a warehouse format. It has also announced new lower prices.

Hypermarkets **Hypermarkets** are giant *mass merchandisers that operate on a low-price, self-service basis and carry lines of soft goods, hard goods, and groceries.* Hypermarkets are sometimes called superstores, although this latter term has also been used to describe a variety of large retail operations.[14] The *hypermarché,* or hypermarket, began in France and has since spread to a limited degree to Canada and the United States. The Hypermarché Laval outside Montreal was the first to open and had 19 500 m² of selling space (eleven to fifteen times the size of the average supermarket) and 40 checkouts. A typical hypermarket is like a shopping centre in a single store. It sells food, hardware, soft goods, building materials, auto supplies, appliances, and prescription drugs, and has a restaurant, a beauty salon, a barber shop, a bank branch, and a bakery. Many of these superstores are currently in operation throughout the world. It appears that they are more popular in Europe than in North America. This is likely because North America already had many large, well-developed shopping centres before the hypermarket concept arrived.

> **hypermarket**
> Mass merchandiser that operates on a low-price, self-service basis and carries lines of soft goods, hard goods, and groceries.

Catalogue retailers **Catalogue retailers** *mail catalogues to their customers and operate from a showroom* displaying samples of their products. Orders are filled from a back-room warehouse. Price is an important factor for catalogue store customers, and low prices are made possible by few services, storage of most of the inventory in the warehouse, reduced shoplifting losses, and handling of products that are unlikely to become obsolete such as luggage, small appliances, gift items, sporting equipment, toys, and jewellery. The largest catalogue retailer in Canada is Consumers Distributing. (Mail-order catalogue retailing is discussed later in this chapter.)

> **catalogue retailer**
> Retailer that mails catalogues to its customers and operates from a showroom displaying samples of its products.

RETAILERS CLASSIFIED BY LOCATION OF RETAIL TRANSACTION

A fourth method of categorizing retailers is by determining whether the transaction takes place in a store. While the overwhelming majority of retail sales occur in retail stores, nonstore retailing is important for many products. Nonstore retailing includes direct house-to-house sales, mail-order retailing, and automatic merchandising machines. These kinds of sales account for about 1.7 percent of all retail sales.

House-to-House Retailing

One of the oldest marketing channels was built around *direct contact between the retailer–seller and the customer at the home of the customer* — **house-to-house retailing**. It provides convenience for the consumer and allows the manufacturer to control the firm's marketing channel. House-to-house retailing is a minor part of the retailing picture, with less than 1 percent of all retail sales.

> **house-to-house retailer**
> Retailer that sells products by direct contact between the retailer–seller and the customer at the home of the customer.

House-to-house retailing is conducted by a number of different merchandisers. Manufacturers of such products as bakery and dairy products and newspapers use this channel. Firms whose products require emphasis on personal selling and product demonstrations may also use it. Such products and services include, for example, cosmetics (Avon), vacuum cleaners (Electrolux), household brushes (Fuller Brush Company), encyclopedias (World Book), and insurance.

Some firms — such as Tupperware and Stanley Home Products — use a variation called *party-plan selling* where a customer gives a party and invites several neighbours and friends. During the party, a company representative makes a presentation of the product, and the host or hostess receives a commission based on the amount of products sold.

The house-to-house method of retailing would appear to be a low-cost method of distribution. No plush retail facilities are required, no investment in inventory is necessary, and most house-to-house salespeople operate on a commission basis. In fact, this method is an extremely high-cost approach to distribution. Often the distribution cost of a product marketed through retail stores is half that of the same product retailed house-to-house. High travel costs, the problems involved in recruiting and training a huge sales force that generally has a high turnover, nonproductive calls, several layers of commissions, and the limited number of contracts per day result in high operating expenses.

MULTILEVEL MARKETING

Another version of house-to-house retailing is **multilevel marketing**. This type of marketing depends heavily on the *personal influence network* of consumers and "positive thinking" techniques. Many different products are sold, from burglar alarms to cosmetics and "wellness" products such as vitamins and meal supplements. Examples of such companies are Amway and Shaklee.

The system depends on a network of people.[15] As many as possible are recruited to sell the products to friends, family, and acquaintances. In return, the salesperson, or "independent distributor," gets a commission. But the real money comes in when the salesperson recruits others who become distributors.

In return for bringing in new people — known in the business as "down-lines" — the recruiter receives a cut of all of their sales. If these new people also recruit, they get a cut of that too. Commissions can travel five or six layers up the network of distributors, depending on the company's policy. A key to making the system work is to keep all involved highly motivated. Consequently, a regular series of local and district motivational meetings are a standard requirement.

Critics say multilevel marketers flog a deck of dreams that is stacked against the people who buy it. But supporters see it as an entrepreneurial opportunity that is open to anyone and requires little start-up capital.

Federal regulations require multilevel marketers to disclose realistic earnings forecasts for distributors. For example, Interior Design Nutritional, a spinoff of Nu Skin International, reports that 70 percent of participants earn an annual average of $2000. This is not much. New candidates are recruited on the basis of the opportunity of earning much more.

About 750 000 Canadians are involved full- or part-time in one or more of the 300 to 400 multilevel marketing companies starting up, progressing or fizzling out in this country at any given time, according to federal government figures. Although 70 percent of these companies collapse before they are eight months old, it is a multibillion-dollar industry that spans the continent and is rapidly going global. The Better Business Bureau receives between 5000 and 7000 industry-related complaints every year. Most are from people who have stockpiled product they purchased in an effort to keep their sales quotas up, and then could not unload it. Others paid substantial fees to become distributors only to find the job was not the paved road to prosperity they were led to expect.

multilevel marketing
The development of a network among consumers to sell and deliver from one level of consumers to another using social obligation, personal influence, and motivational techniques.

Mail-Order Retailing

mail-order merchandiser
Retailer that offers its customers
the option of placing merchandise
orders by mail, by telephone, or by
visiting the mail-order desk of a
retail store.

The customers of **mail-order merchandisers** can *place merchandise orders by mail, by telephone, or by visiting the mail-order desk of a retail store.* Goods are then shipped to the customer's home or to the local retail store.

Many department stores and specialty stores issue catalogues to seek telephone and mail-order sales and to promote in-store purchases of items featured in the catalogues. Among typical department stores, telephone and mail-generated orders account for 15 percent of total volume during the Christmas season.

Mail-order selling began in Canada in 1894 when Eaton's distributed a slim 32-page booklet to rural visitors at the Canadian National Exhibition in Toronto. That first catalogue contained only a few items, mostly clothing and farm supplies. Simpsons soon followed, and mail-order retailing became an important source of products in isolated Canadian settlements.

Even though mail-order sales represent only a small percentage of all retail sales, it is an important channel for many consumers who desire convenience and a large selection of colours and sizes.

With the demise of the Eaton's catalogue sales operations in 1976, apparently due to a failure to introduce effective cost and inventory control measures, Sears became the one major mail-order catalogue marketer left in Canada. Sales have been strong. Sears now has nearly 1300 catalogue sales offices across Canada and produces eleven catalogues a year, with a combined distribution of 45 million.[16]

Mail-order houses offer a wide range of products — from novelty items (Regal Gifts) to sporting equipment (S.I.R.). The growing number of women who work outside the home, increasing time pressures, and a decline in customer service in some department stores augur well for catalogue sales.

Automatic Merchandising

Automatic vending machines — the true robot stores — are a good way to purchase a wide range of convenience goods. These machines accounted for over $424.5 million in sales in Canada.[17] Approximately 213 000 vending machines are currently in operation throughout the country.

While automatic merchandising is important in the retailing of some products, it represents less than 1 percent of all retail sales. Its future growth is limited by such factors as the cost of machines and the necessity for regular maintenance and repair. However, with the possibility of credit card readers in these machines, a wide variety of additional, more expensive products can be sold.

Automatically vended products are confined to convenience goods that are standardized in size and weight, with a high rate of turnover. Prices for some products purchased in vending machines are higher than store prices for the same products.

RETAILERS CLASSIFIED BY FORM OF OWNERSHIP

The fifth method of classifying retailers is by ownership. The two major types are corporate chain stores and independent retailers. In addition, independent retailers may join a wholesaler-sponsored voluntary chain, band together to form a retail co-operative, or enter into a franchise arrangement through contractual agreements with a manufacturer, wholesaler, or service organization. Each type has its special characteristics.

Chain Stores

Chain stores are *groups of retail stores that are centrally owned and managed and that handle the same lines of products.* The concept of chain stores is certainly not new; the Mitsui chain was operating in Japan in the 1600s. Woodwards, Zellers, The Bay, and Reitman's have operated in Canada for many years.

The major advantage possessed by chain operations over independent retailers is economies of scale. Volume purchases through a central buying office allow such chains as Provigo and Wal-Mart to obtain lower prices than independents. Since a chain such as Provigo has hundreds of retail stores, specialists in layout, sales training, and accounting systems may be used to increase efficiency. Advertising can also be effectively used. An advertisement in a national magazine for Eaton's promotes every Eaton's store in Canada.

Chains (excluding food stores) account for approximately one-third of all retail stores, and their dollar volume of sales amounts to 42 percent of all retail sales. At present, chains dominate four fields: department stores, variety stores, shoe stores, and food stores.[18]

Many of the larger chains in Canada have expanded their operations to the rest of the world. Sears now has branch stores in Spain, Mexico, and several countries in South America. Safeway operates supermarkets in Germany, the United Kingdom, and Australia. Bowring's has expanded internationally, as has Marks & Spencer. Direct retailers such as Avon and Tupperware have sales representatives in Europe, South America, and Southeast Asia.

chain stores
Groups of retail stores that are centrally owned and managed and that handle the same lines of products.

Independent Retailers

Independents have attempted to compete with chains in a number of ways. Some independents were unable to do so efficiently and went out of business. Others have joined retail co-operatives, wholesaler-sponsored voluntary chains, or franchise operations. Still others have remained in business by exploiting their advantages of flexibility in operation and knowledge of local market conditions. The independents continue to represent a major part of Canadian retailing.

SHOPPING CENTRES

Planned Shopping Centres

A pronounced shift of retail trade away from the traditional downtown retailing districts and toward suburban shopping centres developed after 1950. A **planned shopping centre** is a *group of retail stores planned, co-ordinated, and marketed as a unit to shoppers in a particular geographic trade area.* These centres followed population shifts to the suburbs and focussed on correcting many of the problems involved in shopping in the downtown business districts. Ample parking and locations aways from the downtown traffic congestion appeal to the suburban shopper. Additional hours for shopping during the evenings and on weekends facilitate family shopping.

planned shopping centre
Group of retail stores planned, co-ordinated, and marketed as a unit to shoppers in a particular geographic trade area.

TYPES OF SHOPPING CENTRES
There are three types of planned shopping centres. The smallest and most common is the *neighbourhood shopping centre*, which most often comprises a supermarket

APPLYING THE CONCEPTS

Using Loyalty Marketing to Keep Customers

Loyalty marketing is the process of providing incentives to customers so that they will want to return again and again. Such activities are sometimes called "continuity programs." The development of a loyalty-marketing program is more important for those companies or industries in a commodity-like business, where there is less ability to differentiate by product. Customer loyalty today equals the best sale price.

Airlines started the continuity programs. Their objectives was to attract and maintain their principal customer, the business traveller, using frequent-flyer programs. These programs have become so important to the airlines, due to the loyalty factors, repeat business, and the marketing value of the frequent-flyer list, that they can't afford to drop them.

One of the most outstanding loyalty programs is the Zellers Club Z program. Zellers developed the first on-line frequent-buyer system (points are given with purchases) in North America. The initial objectives of Club Z included specific financial targets for market penetration, customer shopping frequency, incremental purchase, and new customers. Not only were these targets exceeded, but the program continues to outperform expectations.

Another goal was to increase the frequency of purchase of everyday consumables. Zellers wanted to find a way to drive up sales of such things as shampoo or toothpaste rather than having to "give them away" in order to get customers back into the store.

On an individual customer basis, Zellers wanted to build frequency per customer and spending per customer. The Club Z program enabled the company to delineate a specific day in the week, hour in the day, or department in the store where it could give double points. For example, the fashion department gave double points on Valentine's Day.

Club Z also provides a database so that Zellers knows exactly where Club Z members live and how much they spend. Zellers can thus identify profiles of individuals who are good consumers, and target them. Loyalty programs like this one enable to firm to add an important degree of differentiation to its offerings that truly builds loyalty.

Source: Excerpted from a presentation by Arthur Smith, former executive vice-president of Zellers, in *Marketing Magazine* (January 22, 1990), p. 20. Reprinted with permission.

Is this a useful strategy in the light of the competition from mass merchandise discounters such as Wal-Mart?

and a group of smaller stores such as a drugstore, a laundry and dry cleaner, a small appliance store, and perhaps a beauty shop and barbershop. Such centres provide convenient shopping for perhaps 5000 to 15 000 shoppers who live within a few minutes' commuting time of the centre. These centres typically contain five to fifteen stores whose product mix is usually confined to convenience goods and some shopping goods.

Community shopping centres typically serve 20 000 to 100 000 people in a trade area extending a few kilometres in each direction. These centres are likely to contain 15 to 50 retail stores, with a branch of a local department store or a large variety store as the primary tenant. In addition to the stores found in a neighbourhood centre, the community centre is likely to have additional stores featuring shopping goods, some professional offices, and a branch of a bank.

The largest planned centre is the *regional shopping centre*, a giant shopping district of at least 30 000 m² of shopping space, usually built around one or more major department stores and containing as many as 300 smaller stores. In order to be successful, regional centres must be located in areas where at least 150 000 people reside within 30 minutes' driving time of the centre. Characteristically, they are temperature-controlled, enclosed facilities. The regional centres provide the widest product mixes and the greatest depth of each line.

Such a centre is the West Edmonton Mall, located in Jasper Place, a suburb of Edmonton. Said to be the largest shopping centre in the world, the West Edmonton Mall is located in a densely populated area and is easily accessible to both cars and pedestrians. Catering to a range of suburban clientele, the stores at this mall offer a variety of quality merchandise to their customers. Because of its unique features, such as an amusement park, wave pool, skating rink, and hotel, this mall also counts on tourist traffic.

Planned shopping centres account for approximately 40 percent of all retail sales in Canada. Their growth has slowed in recent years, however, as the most lucrative locations are occupied and the market for such centres appears to have been saturated in many regions. Recent trends have developed toward the building of smaller centres in smaller cities and towns.

SCRAMBLED MERCHANDISING

A characteristic of retailing is the steady deterioration of clear-cut delineations of retailer types. Anyone who has attempted to fill a prescription recently has been exposed to the concept of **scrambled merchandising** — *the retail practice of carrying dissimilar lines to generate added sales volume.* The large mass-merchandising drugstore carries not only prescription and proprietary drugs, but also gifts, hardware, housewares, records, magazines, grocery products, garden supplies, even small appliances. Gasoline retailers sell bread and milk; supermarkets carry antifreeze, televisions, cameras, and stereo equipment.

scrambled merchandising
The retail practice of carrying dissimilar lines to generate added sales volume.

Scrambled merchandising was born out of retailers' willingness to add dissimilar merchandise lines in order to offer additional high-profit lines, as well as to satisfy consumer demands for one-stop shopping. It complicates manufacturers' channel decisions because attempts to maintain or increase a firm's market share mean, in most instances, that the firm will have to develop multiple channels to reach the diverse retailers handling its products.

THE WHEEL-OF-RETAILING HYPOTHESIS

M.P. McNair attempted to explain the patterns of change in retailing through what has been termed the **wheel of retailing**. According to this hypothesis, *new types of retailers gain a competitive foothold by offering lower prices to their customers through the reduction or elimination of services.* Once they are established, however, they evolve by adding more services, and their prices gradually rise. Then they become vulnerable to a new low-price retailer who enters with minimum services — and the wheel turns.

wheel of retailing
Hypothesized process of change in retailing, which suggests that new types of retailers gain a competitive foothold by offering lower prices through the reduction or elimination of services; but once established, they add more services and their prices gradually rise, so that they then become vulnerable to a new low-price retailer with minimum services — and the wheel turns.

Most of the major developments in retailing appear to fit the wheel pattern. Early department stores, chain stores, supermarkets, and discount stores all emphasized limited service and low prices. In most instances, price levels have gradually increased as services have been added.

There have been some exceptions, however. Suburban shopping centres, convenience food stores, and vending machines were not developed on a foundation of low-price appeals. However, the wheel pattern has been present often enough in the past that it should serve as a general indicator of future developments in retailing.

RETAILING THROUGH THE INTERNET

The Internet has become not only an information source and a means of communication, but also an important business tool. Retailing is one area that can be greatly facilitated through its use. For example, Bolen's Books in Victoria set up a home page for the purposes of retailing its line of books. Within a year of starting to retail on the Internet, they had covered the costs of setting up and running the system. They now receive orders from around the world. Blaney's Travel agency publishes special travel deals on the Internet in order to generate new clients. It offers its travel services to anyone logging onto its home page. These are but two examples of the thousands of firms retailing through the Internet. The applications are only limited by the creativity of the company.

teleshopping
The selection and electronic purchase of merchandise that has been displayed on a computer.

An important trend that may soon become quite prevalent is **teleshopping**. Teleshopping involves *the selection and electronic purchase of merchandise that has been displayed on computers.*[19]

Computers are found in virtually every business and in a large number of homes. The number of home computers is growing rapidly and it is expected that within a short time most homes will have one. Bill Gates, CEO of Microsoft, and others in the industry have predicted that as these homes get hooked up to digital information links, it will be only a matter of time before the computer, telephone, television, and on-line information services converge into a single system for handling all home entertainment, education, information, and communication needs.

If you want to watch a movie, play a computer game, buy the latest music recording by your favourite artist, or get hold of some new software, you will just dial in to the information highway over the phone line and download whatever product or service you want, charging the cost to a debit or credit card.

The ultimate mix of computer technology, consumerism, and television, however, would come with use of the shopping channel, where consumers could design "virtual shopping malls" in which they were the only customers. These would work by having the consumer designate which shops he or she would like to frequent (from either an on-screen or published catalogue) — the system would then respond by displaying a video game–style representation of a mall with shop fronts. The consumer would then use the handheld controller to "walk through" the custom-designed on-screen malls, stopping at the shops whose goods he or she might be interested in buying.

The on-screen shop fronts, when entered, would be replaced with an on-screen catalogue of the goods available in that shop. By pointing at the picture of any item, consumers will be able to get detailed information on it, including price, warranty details, and estimated delivery times.

Will such a system really happen? A sceptic would say that predictions of computer retailing have been made for over 30 years. The theme is the same — only the format of the implementation varies. On the other hand, we are much closer to the interactive link described above. It will happen, so a more relevant question remains: how many people will use such a system?

There are several inhibiting factors. First, many people wish to inspect products personally. The tangible aspects of touch, smell, and sight will remain important for

Duthie Books
Virtual Bookstore
(Vancouver, BC, Canada)

Explore Duthie Books' online database of 50,000 titles in 150 subject areas and order directly from our Web pages. Read the latest digital issue of our quarterly journal of reviews, *The Reader*, and keep up on the latest in the book world in our News section. You can find out more about Duthie Books and our six locations in Vancouver, BC, Canada by contacting our Virtual Bookstore:
e-mail: info@duthiebooks.bc.ca
Our address on the World Wide Web:
http://www.wimsey.com/~duthie/

Book lovers no longer need to leave home to shop for books, providing they have access to the Internet. Customers of the Duthie Books Virtual Bookstore can browse through the title database, read reviews of forthcoming titles, and place orders using the on-line ordering form. On-line customers have been enthusiastic about Duthie's new service.

many products. Second, many people prefer the experience of going out to shop. Third, personal service will remain important for some products. Finally, people may be unwilling to wait for delivery of products.

Teleshopping via an interactive system is likely to be most effective for products where look, feel, smell, and personal service are not important in the purchase decision.

This chapter has described some aspects of the many faces of retailing. As this is the end of the marketing channel that handles millions of products and services, there is a vast array of retailers that can be categorized in several different ways. A basic characteristic of retailing is change. New retail forms are continually emerging. Existing retailers gradually adjust to meet the new competition. If they cannot adjust, they disappear.

■ KEY TERMS

retailing	variety store	catalogue retailer
retail trade area analysis	mass merchandiser	house-to-house retailer
law of retail gravitation	discount house	multilevel marketing
retail image	membership and	mail-order merchandiser
differentiation triangle	warehouse club	chain stores
limited-line store	large-format specialty	planned shopping centre
supermarket	store	scrambled merchandising
specialty store	power node	wheel of retailing
department store	hypermarket	teleshopping

■ INTERACTIVE SUMMARY AND DISCUSSION QUESTIONS

1. The retailer's decision process centres on analyzing and selecting a target market and developing a marketing (or retailing) mix designed to satisfy that market. Compare and contrast the marketing mix with the retailing mix.
2. The law of retail gravitation (Reilly's law) delineates the retail trade area of a potential site on the basis of distance between alternative locations and relative

populations. Assume that a large-format specialty retailer is considering opening an outlet in Town A, population 144 000. The retailing firm wants to know how far its trade area would extend toward Town B (population 16 000), 72 km away. Apply the law of retail gravitation to the retailer's problem. What other factors should be taken into consideration in this location decision?

3. The differentiation triangle has the following elements: price, location, and store atmosphere and service. Explain the importance of this triangle in considering a retailer's competitive options.

4. There are three types of retailers if classified by shopping effort: convenience–preference stores, shopping stores, and specialty retailers. In which of these types would the following products likely fit?
   a. Kodak film
   b. *Foundations of Marketing* textbook
   c. Computer paper
   d. Fax machine
   e. Leather slippers
   f. Cartier watch
   g. Picture framing

5. Some general-merchandise retailers include department stores, variety stores, mass merchandisers, and discount houses. If you were marketing a new line of perfume, which of these outlets would you choose to use first? Why?

6. Large-format specialty stores can be of similar size to warehouse clubs. They are known as category killers. Explain why.

7. There are relatively few large warehouse and membership clubs in each community, yet the significance of this type of retail operation to retail competition in general is great. How can this be?

8. Multilevel marketing has several distributor levels, makes use of a personal influence network, and promises great rewards to those who work hard. What is your evaluation of these promised rewards?

9. Chain stores are groups of retail stores that are centrally owned and managed and that handle the same lines of products. Illustrate how the chain store concept results in powerful competition.

10. The wheel-of-retailing hypothesis postulates that new types of retailers gain a competitive advantage by offering lower prices to their customers through reduction of services. Gradually they add services and increase prices, opening the door to new low-cost retailers entering the market. List several examples of the wheel of retailing in operation. Can you list examples that do not conform to this hypothesis?

11. Teleshopping appears to be a real possibility as the information highway develops. What is your assessment of the future of teleshopping?

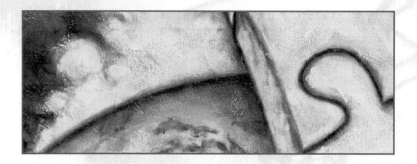

PART SEVEN

Marketing Communications

CHAPTER 17
Marketing Communications Strategy

CHAPTER 18
Marketing Communications Applications: Advertising, Publicity, Sales Promotion, and Personal Selling

Probably the most visible component of marketing is advertising. This is just one component of the mix of variables used by the marketer to communicate with current and potential customers. Marketers are often quick to express opinions about marketing communications, but in reality, marketing communications strategy is quite complex. Part Seven concludes with a chapter dealing with some of the basic concepts of applying marketing communications.

CHAPTER 17

Marketing Communications Strategy

CHAPTER OBJECTIVES

1. To provide a theoretical model of the communications process; to show how various marketing communications must conform to this model in order to be effective.
2. To explain the concept of the marketing communications mix.
3. To show the marketing communications mix as part of the marketing mix.
4. To contrast pulling and pushing marketing communications strategies.
5. To discuss the appropriateness of different types of marketing communications objectives.
6. To explain the concept of a marketing communications budget.
7. To discuss the appropriateness of different types of marketing communications budgets.
8. To consider marketing communications in the light of some public criticisms.

Traffic reporters referred to it simply as a visual distraction. They were partly right. Commuters slowed down and rubber-necked. Some abandoned their cars at the shoulder to get out and watch.

A massive multicoloured blimp, the latest gimmick from the marketing grab-bag of British band Pink Floyd, had touched down at Buttonville Airport just north of Toronto.

The band wasn't there. But the blimp was: 20 metres high and 60 metres long, decorated with gaudy artwork that would do a New York subway train proud. Inside, Pink Floyd music wafted through the spacious gondola under the $6.7-million (U.S.) airship.

The band wasn't to play for another two months. However, the blimp criss-crossed the continent several months ahead, hawking the band. And in Miami, where Pink Floyd started its tour, it served as a light show in the sky.

The Pink Floyd Airship comes courtesy of Airship International Ltd. of Orlando, Florida. They have four blimps, each of which rents for between $300 000 and $400 000 (U.S.) a month.

Basically, the blimp is a flying bill-board. And as Scott Bennett of Airship International points out, they are showcased during huge sporting events such as the Commonwealth games — and are visible during the event, not during commercial breaks when TV viewers head for the bathroom or the kitchen.

There is this intangible: blimp love.

"I've had people come out and cry. As soon as you take off, they start crying," pilot Corky Belanger said. "I've had women almost delirious with excitement. And I'm talking about grown women now. It's something they've wanted to do all their life. I don't know what it is about blimps that fascinate people. I really don't. They fascinate me and I've been doing it for 20 years."[1]

An attention-getting device, used in a creative way to transmit a message — that is the essence of marketing communications. And the variations that people think up are endless. This is what makes marketing communications one of the most interesting and exciting elements of the marketing mix.

INTRODUCTION

You have come up with a wonderful product. You have determined the market segment that it would serve, appraised customer needs, analyzed competitors' offerings, and defined a positioning strategy. How then should its advantages be communicated to the target audience?

A vast array of communication alternatives are available. How about direct mail (is it really "junk," as some people claim?), or celebrity advertising? Perhaps the main communication message should be carried by salespeople. But that might cost too much. On the other hand, why waste money by not spending enough on marketing communications? How much *is* "enough"?

These few questions just scratch the surface of the many issues involved in developing and implementing a marketing communications strategy. It is an exhilarating and creative process that requires tough thinking and a very systematic approach. This chapter and the next will introduce the domain of marketing communications.

Marketing communications, the fourth variable in the marketing mix, is defined as *all activities and messages that inform, persuade, and influence the consumer in making a purchase decision.* Figure 17.1 depicts the relationship between a firm's marketing communications strategy and the other elements of the overall marketing plan.

marketing communications
All activities and messages that inform, persuade, and influence the consumer in making a purchase decision.

The marketing manager sets the goals and objectives of the firm's communications approach in accordance with overall organizational objectives and the goals of the marketing organization. Then, based on these goals, the various elements of marketing communications — advertising, personal selling, sales promotion, publicity, and public relations — are formulated in a co-ordinated plan. This plan, in turn, becomes an integral part of the total marketing strategy for reaching selected

■ Figure 17.1 **Integrating the Marketing Communications Plan into the Total Marketing Mix**

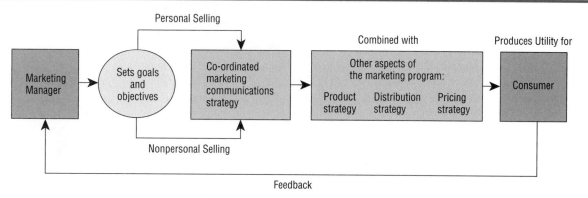

consumer segments. Finally, the feedback mechanism, in such forms as marketing research and field reports, closes the system by identifying any deviations from the plan and by suggesting modifications or improvements.

THE COMMUNICATIONS PROCESS

Figure 17.2 shows a generalized communications process using terminology borrowed from radio and telecommunications.[2] The sender is the *source* of the communications system, since he or she seeks to convey a *message* (a communication of information or advice or a request) to a *receiver* (the recipient of the communication). The message must accomplish three tasks in order to be effective:

1. It must *gain the attention* of the receiver.
2. It must *be understood* by both the receiver and the sender.
3. It must *stimulate* the needs of the receiver and *suggest* an appropriate method of satisfying these needs.[3]

The message must be *encoded,* or translated into understandable terms, and transmitted through a communications medium. *Decoding* is the receiver's interpretation of the message. The receiver's response, known as *feedback,* completes the system. Throughout the process, *noise* can interfere with the transmission of the message and reduce its effectiveness.

In Figure 17.3, the marketing communications process is applied to promotional strategy. The marketing manager is the sender in the system. The message is encoded in the form of sales presentations, advertisements, displays, or publicity releases. The *transfer mechanism* for delivering the message may be a salesperson, the advertising media, or a public relations channel.

■ Figure 17.2 **A Generalized Communications Process**

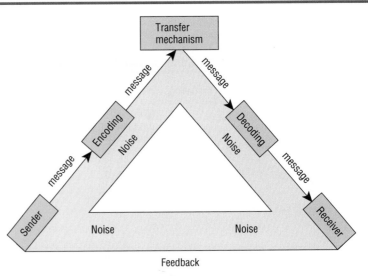

■ Figure 17.3 **The Process of Marketing Communications**

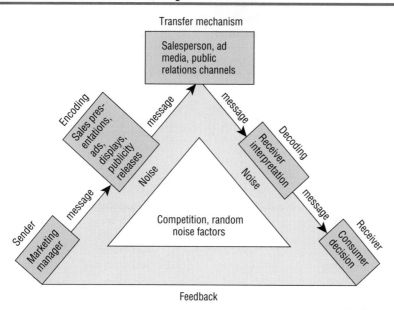

The *decoding* step involves the consumer's interpretation of the sender's message. This is the most troublesome aspect of marketing communications, since consumers often do not interpret a promotional message in the same way as does its sender. Because receivers are likely to decode messages based on their own frames of reference or individual experiences, the sender must be careful to ensure that the message is properly encoded to match the target audience.

Feedback is the receiver's response to the message. It may take the form of attitude change, purchase, or nonpurchase. In some instances, a firm may use marketing communications to create a favourable attitude toward its new products or services. Such attitude changes may result in future purchases. In other instances, the objective of the communication is to stimulate consumer purchases. Such purchases indicate positive responses to the firm, its product/service offerings, its distribution channels, its prices, and its promotion. Even nonpurchases can serve as feedback to the sender. They may result from ineffective communication in that the message was not believed, not remembered, or failed to persuade the receiver that the firm's products or services are superior to its competitors. Feedback can be obtained from field sales reports and such techniques as marketing research studies.

Noise represents interference at some stage in the communications process. It may result from such factors as competitive promotional messages being transmitted over the same communications channel, misinterpretation of a sales presentation or an advertising message, receipt of the promotional message by the wrong person, or random noise factors, such as people conversing — or leaving the room — during a television commercial.

Table 17.1 illustrates the steps in the communications process with three examples of promotional messages. Although the types of promotion vary from a highly personalized sales presentation to such nonpersonal promotion as two-for-one coupons and television advertising, each form of promotion goes through each stage in the communications model.

■ Table 17.1 **Examples of Marketing Communications**

Type of Promotion	Sender	Encoding	Transfer Mechanism	Decoding by Receiver	Feedback
Personal selling	Sharp Business Products	Sales presentation on new model office copier	Sharp sales representative	Office manager and employees in local firm discuss Sharp sales presentation and those of competing suppliers	Order placed for the Sharp copier
Two-for-one coupon (sales promotion)	Wendy's Hamburgers	Wendy's marketing department and advertising agency	Coupon insert to weekend newspaper	Newspaper reader sees coupon for hamburger and saves it	Hamburgers purchased by consumers using the coupon
Television advertising	Walt Disney Enterprises	Advertisement for a new family-entertainment animated movie is developed by Disney's advertising agency	Network television during programs with high percentage of viewers under 12 years old	Children see ad and ask their parents to take them to movie; parents see ad and decide to take children	Movie ticket purchased

THE MARKETING COMMUNICATIONS MIX

marketing communications mix
The blend of personal selling and nonpersonal communications (including advertising, sales promotion, and public relations) by marketers in an attempt to accomplish information and persuasion objectives.

Similar to the marketing mix, in planning marketing communications, numerous variables must be considered and blended together. The marketing communications mix is a subset of the marketing mix. The **marketing communications mix** is a blend of *personal selling and nonpersonal communications (including advertising, sales promotion, and public relations) by marketers in an attempt to accomplish information and persuasion objectives.* Figure 17.4 illustrates this relationship.

Personal selling and advertising are the most significant elements of the mix, since they usually account for the bulk of a firm's marketing communications expenditures. A discussion of each of these elements is presented in Chapter 18. Here only a brief definition will be given in order to set the framework for the overall discussion of marketing communications.

Personal Selling

personal selling
A seller's promotional presentation conducted on a person-to-person basis with the buyer.

Personal selling may be defined as *a seller's promotional presentation conducted on a person-to-person basis with the buyer.* It is a direct face-to-face form of promotion. Personal

■ Figure 17.4 **The Marketing and Marketing Communications Mixes**

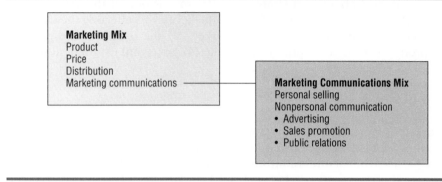

selling was also the original form of promotion. Today it is estimated that 600 000 people in Canada are engaged in this activity.

Nonpersonal Communication

Nonpersonal communication is divided into advertising, sales promotion, and public relations. Advertising is usually regarded as the most important of these forms.

Advertising may be defined as *paid nonpersonal communication through various media by business firms, nonprofit organizations, and individuals who are in some way identified with the advertising message and who hope to inform or persuade members of a particular audience.*[4] It involves the mass media, such as newspapers, television, radio, magazines, and billboards. Business realizes the tremendous potential of this form of communication, and advertising has become increasingly important in marketing. Mass consumption makes advertising particularly appropriate for products that rely on sending the same message to large audiences.

Sales promotion includes *"those marketing activities, other than personal selling, mass media advertising, and publicity, that stimulate consumer purchasing and dealer effectiveness,* such as displays, shows and expositions, demonstrations, and various nonrecurrent selling efforts not in the ordinary routine."*[5] Sales promotion is usually practised together with other forms of advertising to emphasize, assist, supplement, or otherwise support the objectives of the promotional program. It is growing in importance.

Public relations is *a firm's effort to create favourable attention and word-of-mouth* among various publics — including the organization's customers, suppliers, shareholders, and employees; the government; the general public; and the society in which the organization operates. Public relations programs can be either formal or informal. Every organization, whether or not it has a formalized, organized program, must be concerned about its public relations.

FACTORS AFFECTING USE OF MARKETING COMMUNICATIONS MIX ELEMENTS

How can a marketer know which of the retailing mix elements to use? Precise quantitative measures to determine the effectiveness of each component of the

advertising
Paid nonpersonal communication through various media by business firms, nonprofit organizations, and individuals who are in some way identified with the advertising message and who hope to inform or persuade members of a particular audience.

sales promotion
Those marketing activities, other than personal selling, mass media advertising, and publicity, that stimulate consumer purchasing and dealer effectiveness.

public relations
A firm's effort to create favourable attention and word-of-mouth.

communications mix in a given market segment are not generally available. Thus, choosing a proper mix of communications elements is one of the most difficult tasks facing the marketing manager. Some of the key factors affecting the choice of mix elements are (1) the nature of the market, (2) the nature of the product, (3) the product's stage in the product life cycle, (4) price, and (5) funds available.

Nature of the Market

The marketer's target audience has a major impact on what type of retail mix elements will work best. In cases where there is a limited number of buyers (as, for example, with a manufacturer of printing presses), personal selling may prove highly effective. However, markets characterized by a large number of potential customers scattered over a large geographic area may make the cost of contact by personal salespeople prohibitive; in such instances, marketers may make extensive use of advertising (as, for example, is done for Kodak film).

The type of customer also affects the marketing communications mix. A target market made up of industrial purchasers or retail and wholesale buyers is more likely to require personal selling than one consisting of ultimate consumers. Also, because the value of their purchases is significant, it is economically feasible to use personal selling.

Nature of the Product

A second important factor in determining an effective marketing communications mix is the product itself. Highly standardized products with minimal servicing requirements are less likely to depend on personal selling than are higher-priced custom products that are technically complex and require servicing. Consumer goods are more likely to rely heavily on advertising than are industrial goods.

Within each product category, marketing communications mixes vary. For instance, installations typically involve a heavy reliance on personal selling as compared with the marketing of operating supplies. Convenience goods rely heavily on manufacturer advertising, and personal selling plays only a small role.

On the other hand, personal selling is often more important in the marketing of shopping goods, and both personal selling and nonpersonal selling are important in the marketing of specialty goods. Finally, personal selling is likely to be more important in the marketing of products characterized by trade-ins.

Stage in the Product Life Cycle

The marketing communications mix must also be tailored to the stage in the product life cycle. In the introductory stage, heavy emphasis is placed on personal selling to inform the marketplace of the merits of the new product and to gain distribution. Salespeople contact marketing intermediaries to secure interest and commitment to handle the new product. Trade shows and exhibitions are frequently used to inform and educate prospective dealers and ultimate consumers. Any advertising at this stage is largely informative, and sales promotional techniques, such as samples and cents-off coupons, are designed to influence consumer attitudes and stimulate initial purchases.

As the product moves into the growth and maturity stages, advertising becomes more important in attempting to persuade consumers to make purchases. Personal-selling efforts continue to be directed at intermediaries in an attempt to expand distribution. As more competitors enter the marketplace, advertising stresses product differences in an attempt to persuade consumers to purchase the firm's brand. Reminder advertisements begin to appear in the maturity and early decline stages.

Price

The price of the product is a fourth factor in the choice of marketing communications mix elements. Advertising is a dominant mix component for low-unit-value products due to the high costs per contact involved in personal selling. The cost of an industrial sales call, for example, has been estimated at nearly $230.[6] As a result, it has become unprofitable to promote lower-value products through personal selling. Advertising, by contrast, permits a low promotional expenditure per sales unit since it reaches mass audiences. For low-value consumer products, such as chewing gum, colas, and snack foods, advertising is the only feasible means of promotion.

Funds Available

A very real barrier to implementing any marketing communications strategy is the size of the budget. If a 30-second television commercial costs a packaged-goods company $100 000 to shoot, and one showing nationally during a special event costs $6000 or more, television advertising is costly. Even though the message is received by millions of viewers and the cost per contact is relatively low, such an expenditure for just one showing would exceed the entire promotional budget of thousands of firms.

For many new or smaller firms, the cost of national mass advertising is prohibitive, so they are forced to seek less-expensive, and possibly less-efficient, methods. One common approach involves using smaller, local media. Neighbourhood retailers may not be able to advertise in metropolitan newspapers or on local radio and television stations; apart from personal selling, therefore, their limited promotional budgets may be allocated to an eye-catching sign, one of the most valuable promotional devices available to small retailers, or local circulation of handbills.

Table 17.2 summarizes the factors that influence the determination of marketing communications mix elements for a marketing program.

MARKETING COMMUNICATIONS STRATEGY — PULL OR PUSH?

Broadly speaking, there are two marketing communications policies that may be employed: a pulling strategy and a pushing strategy. A **pulling strategy** is *a promotional effort by the seller to stimulate final-user demand, which then exerts pressure on the distribution channel.* The plan is to build consumer demand for the product by means of advertising so that channel members will have to stock the product to meet that demand. If a manufacturer's advertising efforts result in shoppers' requesting the retailer to stock an item, they will usually succeed in getting that item on the retailer's shelves, since most retailers want to stimulate repeat purchases by satisfied customers.

pulling strategy
A promotional effort by the seller to stimulate final-user demand, which then exerts pressure on the distribution channel.

■ Table 17.2 **Factors Influencing the Marketing Communications Mix**

| | Emphasis on | |
Factor	Personal Selling	Advertising
Nature of the Market		
Number of buyers	Limited number	Large number
Geographic concentration	Concentrated	Dispersed
Type of customer	Industrial purchaser	Ultimate consumer
Nature of the Product		
Complexity	Custom-made, complex	Standardized
Service requirements	Considerable	Minimal
Type of good	Industrial	Consumer
Use of trade-ins	Trade-ins common	Trade-ins uncommon
Stage in the Product Life Cycle	Introductory and early growth stages	Latter part of growth stage and maturity and early decline stages
Price	High unit value	Low unit value
Funds Available	Affects all decisions in the mix	

A pulling strategy may be required to motivate marketing intermediaries to handle a product when they already stock a large number of competing products. When a manufacturer decides to use a pulling strategy, personal selling is often largely limited to contacting intermediaries, providing requested information about the product, and taking orders. Advertising and sales promotion are the most commonly used marketing communications elements in a pulling strategy.

pushing strategy
The promotion of the product first to the members of the marketing channel, who then participate in its promotion to the final user.

By contrast, a **pushing strategy** relies more heavily on personal selling. Here, the objective is *the promotion of the product first to the members of the marketing channel, who then participate in its promotion to the final user.* This can be done through personal-selling efforts by the firm's sales force, co-operative advertising allowances, trade discounts, and other dealer supports. Such a strategy is designed to produce marketing success for the firm's products by motivating representatives of wholesalers and/or retailers to spend a disproportionate amount of time and effort in promoting these products to customers.

While these are presented as alternative policies, it is unlikely that very many companies will depend entirely on either strategy. In most cases, marketers employ a mixture of the two.

Timing

In situations where both advertising and personal selling are used, timing is another factor to consider in the development of a marketing communications strategy. Figure 17.5 shows the relative importance of advertising and selling in different periods of the purchase process. During the pretransactional period (before the actual sale), advertising has been found to be more important than personal selling. It is often argued that one of the primary advantages of a successful advertising

■ Figure 17.5 **Relative Importance of Advertising and Selling**

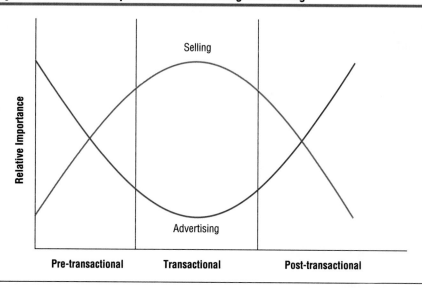

Source: Harold C. Cash and W.J.E. Crissy, "The Salesman's Role in Marketing," *The Psychology of Selling*, Vol. 12 (New York: Personnel Development Associates).

program is that it sensitizes prospects to the product, and it assists the salesperson in approaching the prospect. Personal selling becomes more important than advertising during the transactional phase of the process. In most situations, personal selling is the actual mechanism of closing the sale. In the posttransactional stage, advertising regains primacy in the communication effort. It serves as an affirmation of the customer's decision to buy a particular good or service, as well as a reminder of the product's favourable qualities, characteristics, and performance.

MARKETING COMMUNICATIONS OBJECTIVES

"Set clear objectives" is an axiom of good business. However, management has always found that determining exactly what it expects marketing communications to achieve is a perplexing problem. In most cases, it is too simplistic to expect a direct correlation between advertising and sales results. Generally, strategy for this mix element should be oriented toward achieving clearly stated, measurable communications objectives.

The specific objective must vary with the situation. However, the following can be considered objectives of marketing communications: (1) to provide information, (2) to increase demand, (3) to differentiate the product, (4) to accentuate the value of the product, (5) to stabilize sales, and (6) in a limited number of situations, to produce sales.

Providing Information

The traditional function of marketing communications was to inform the market about the availability of a particular product. Indeed, a large part of modern marketing communications effort is still directed at providing product information to potential customers. An example of this is the typical university or college extension course program advertisement appearing in the newspaper. Its content emphasizes informative features, such as the availability of different courses. Southam Business Information has employed an interesting idea in advertising to potential business advertisers. It shows the back of a station wagon covered with bumper stickers, then makes the point: "To communicate effectively, deal with one idea at a time." By doing this, it educates potential advertisers, as well as showing how Southam can help.

The informative function often requires repeated customer exposures. For instance, "in a . . . study concerning customer acceptance of a new durable good, it was found that . . . at least several months were required after introduction (and accompanying promotion) before consumers became generally aware of the item and somewhat familiar with its characteristics."[7]

Stimulating Demand

The primary objective of most marketing communications efforts is to increase the demand for a specific brand of product or service. This can be shown by using the familiar demand curves of basic economics (see Figure 17.6). Successful promotion can shift demand from schedule 1 to schedule 2, which means that greater quantities can be sold at each possible price level. Cadbury Schweppes Powell accomplished this with its "Thick" bars, in a campaign that brought the chocolate bars to a position among the top five brands in the Canadian market.[8]

Differentiating the Product

Product differentiation is often an objective of the firm's marketing communications efforts. Homogeneous demand, represented by the horizontal line in Figure 17.7,

■ Figure 17.6 **Promotion Can Help Marketers Achieve Demand Objectives**

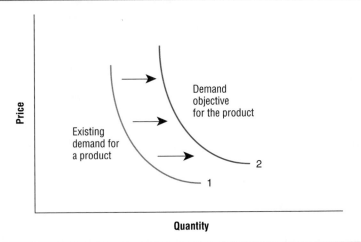

■ Figure 17.7 **Product Differentiation**

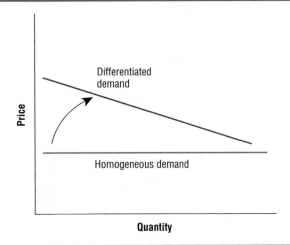

means that consumers regard the firm's output as no different from that of its competitors. In such cases, the individual firm has no control over such marketing variables as price. A differentiated demand schedule, in contrast, permits more flexibility in marketing strategy, such as price changes.

For example, McCain's, a producer of frozen vegetables, advertises the dependable high quality and good taste of its products. This differentiates these products from others. Consequently, some consumers wanting these attributes are willing to pay a higher price for McCain's than they would for other brands. Similarly, the high quality and distinctiveness of Cross pens are advertised, resulting in Cross's ability to ask for and obtain a price 100 times that of some disposable pens. With the exception of commodities, most products have some degree of differentiation, resulting in a downward-sloping demand curve. The angle of the slope varies somewhat according to the degree of product differentiation.

Accentuating the Value of the Product

Marketing communications can point out important features of a product to buyers, thereby accentuating the value of the product. The good or service might then be able to command a higher price in the marketplace. For example, status-oriented advertising may allow some retail clothing stores to command higher prices than others. The demand curve facing a prestige store may be less responsive to price differences than that of a competitor without a quality reputation. The responsiveness to price differences is shown in Figure 17.8.

Stabilizing Sales

A company's sales are not uniform throughout the year. Fluctuations can occur for cyclical, seasonal, or other reasons. Reducing these variations is often an objective of the firm's marketing communications strategy. Lee E. Preston elaborates:

Energizer uses the Pink Bunny and the line "It keeps on going and going and ...." to differentiate its product from those of competitors. A new battery company based in Mississauga, Ontario, also tapped into animated commercials in a campaign to differentiate its product — a rechargeable alkaline battery. The company, Pure Energy Battery Corporation, claims that the battery is superior to the regular ones sold by Duracell and Eveready. Although the product is priced higher, Pure Energy is confident that consumers will buy its battery because, in the long run, it will save them money and it is environmentally friendly.

Advertising that is focused on such attitudinal goals as "brand loyalty" and such specific sales goals as "increasing repeat purchases" is essentially aimed at stabilizing demand. The prominence of such goals in the current literature and in advertising planning discussions suggests that stabilizing demand and insulating the market position of an individual firm and product against unfavourable developments is, in fact, one of the most important purposes of promotional activity at the present time.[9]

Producing Sales

In a limited number of situations, marketing communications are the direct cause of a sale. One example would be a direct-mail campaign offering a product for sale. If consumers respond with orders, the cause-and-effect relationship between the message and the response is clear. Newspaper advertising offering various items on sale can also bring a flow of purchasers. Note that producing sales is only one of the legitimate expectations for marketing communications, and is not considered the predominant one.

BUDGETING FOR MARKETING COMMUNICATIONS EFFORTS

Marketing communications budgets can differ not only in amount but also in composition. Industrial firms generally invest a larger proportion of their budgets in

■ Figure 17.8 **Promotion Can Accentuate the Value of the Product**

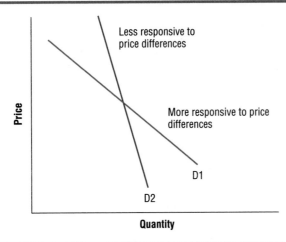

personal selling than in advertising, while the reverse is usually true of most producers of consumer goods.

A simple model showing the productivity of marketing communications expenditures is shown in Figure 17.9. In terms of sales revenue, initial expenditures on marketing communications usually result in increasing returns. There appear to be some economies associated with larger expenditures. These economies result from such factors as the cumulative effects of repeated communications and repeat sales.

Evidence suggests that sales initially lag behind advertising for structural reasons (filling up the retail shelves, low initial production, lack of buyer knowledge). This produces a threshold effect, where there are no sales but lots of initial investment in advertising. A second phase might produce returns (sales) proportional to a given marketing communications expenditure; this would be the most predictable range.

Finally, the area of diminishing returns is reached when an increase in marketing communications expenditure does not produce a proportional increase in sales.

How Much Should Be Spent on Marketing Communications?

Theoretically, the optimal method of determining how much to spend on marketing communications (known as a marketing communications budget) is to expand it until the cost of each additional increment equals the additional incremental revenue received. In other words, the most effective allocation procedure is to increase expenditures until each dollar of expense is matched by an additional dollar of profit (see Figure 17.9). This procedure — called *marginal analysis* — results in the maximization of the input's productivity. The difficulty arises in identifying this optimal point. In practice, doing so is virtually impossible.

The common methods of determining a marketing communications budget are by percentage of sales, fixed sum per unit, meeting competition, and task-objective method.

Percentage of sales is a very common (but dangerous) way of allocating budgets. The percentage can be based on either past (for example, previous-year) or forecasted (current-year) sales. While the simplicity of this plan is appealing, it is not an effective way of achieving the basic communications objectives. Arbitrary percent-

■ Figure 17.9 **Marketing Communications Sales Curve**

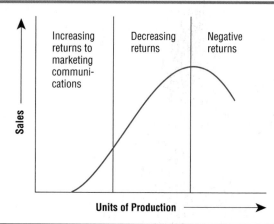

Source: Adapted from John C. Narver and Ronald Savitt, *The Marketing Economy: An Analytical Approach*, p. 294. Copyright © 1971 by Holt, Rinehart and Winston, Inc. Used by permission of the authors.

age allocations (whether applied to historical or future sales figures) fail to allow the required flexibility. Furthermore, such reasoning is circular, for the advertising allocation is made to depend on sales, rather than vice versa, as it should be. Consider, for example, the implications of a decline in sales.

The *fixed sum per unit* approach differs from percentage of sales in only one respect: it applies a predetermined allocation to each sales or production unit. This also can be set on either a historical or a forecasted basis. Producers of high-value consumer durable goods, such as cars, often use this budgeting method.

Another traditional approach is simply to match competitors' outlays — in other words, *meet competition* — on either an absolute or a relative basis. However, this kind of approach usually leads to a status quo situation at best, with each company retaining its market share. Meeting the competition's budget does not necessarily relate to the objectives of promotion and, therefore, seems inappropriate for most contemporary marketing programs.

task-objective method
A sequential approach to allocating marketing communications budgets that involves two steps: (1) defining the realistic communication goals the firm wants the marketing communications mix to accomplish; and (2) determining the amount and type of marketing communications activity required to accomplish each of these objectives.

The **task-objective method** of developing a marketing communications budget is *based on a sound evaluation of the firm's communications objectives*, and is thus better attuned to modern marketing practices. It involves two sequential steps:

1. The organization must *define the realistic communication goals* the firm wants the marketing communications mix to accomplish — for example, a 25 percent increase in brand awareness, or a 10 percent rise in consumers who realize that the product has certain specific differentiating features. The key is to specify quantitatively the objectives to be accomplished. They then become an integral part of the marketing communications plan.
2. The organization, on the basis of experience and expert advice, must *determine the amount and type of marketing communications activity required to accomplish each of these objectives*. The communications activities thus identified, and costed out, determine the firm's budget.

A crucial assumption underlies the task-objective approach: that the productivity of marketing communications expenditures is measurable. That is why the objectives must be carefully chosen, quantified, and co-ordinated with the rest of the marketing mix. Generally, an objective like "We wish to achieve a 5 percent increase in sales" is an ill-conceived marketing objective, because a sale is the culmination of the effects of *all* elements of the marketing mix. A more appropriate advertising objective might be "To make 30 percent of the target market aware of the facilities available at our health spa."

MEASURING THE EFFECTIVENESS OF MARKETING COMMUNICATIONS

It is widely recognized that part of a firm's marketing communications effort is ineffective. John Wanamaker, a successful nineteenth-century retailer, once observed, "I know half the money I spend on advertising is wasted; but I can never find out which half."

Measuring the effectiveness of marketing communications is an extremely important research question, particularly among advertisers. Studies aimed at this measurement objective face several major obstacles, among them the difficulty of isolating the effect of the marketing communications variable.

Most marketers would prefer to use a **direct-sales results test** to measure the effectiveness of marketing communications. Such a test attempts to *ascertain for each dollar of promotional outlay the corresponding increase in revenue.* The primary difficulty involves controlling the other variables that operate in the marketplace. A $1.5 million advertising campaign may be followed by an increase in sales of $20 million. However, this shift may have more to do with a sudden price hike by the firm's leading competitor than with the advertising expenditure. Therefore, advertisers are turning to establishing and assessing achievable, measurable objectives.

direct-sales results test
A test that attempts to ascertain for each dollar of promotional outlay the corresponding increase in revenue.

With the increasing sophistication of marketing analysts, analytical techniques, and computer-based marketing information systems, banks of historical data on marketing communications expenditures and their effects are being subjected to ever more scrutiny. More and more is being learned about measuring and evaluating the effects of marketing communications activity. While the technical literature in marketing reveals much of what is happening in this critical area, firms are reluctant to release much of this information. Not only do they wish to keep their proprietary information about how the market works to themselves for competitive reasons, but they do not want competitors knowing the methods and decision routines used in planning marketing communications activity.

Other methods of assessing marketing communications effectiveness include inquiries about the product, about changes in attitudes toward the product, and about improvements in public knowledge and awareness. One indicator of probable advertising effectiveness would be the elasticity or sensitivity of sales to marketing communications based on historical data concerning price, sales volume, and advertising expenditures.

It is difficult for the marketer to conduct research in a controlled environment like that which can be set up in other disciplines. The difficulty of isolating the effects of marketing communications causes many to abandon all attempts at measurement. Others, however, turn to indirect evaluation. These researchers concentrate on quantifiable factors, such as recall (how much is remembered about specific products or advertisements) and readership (the size and composition of the audience). But it remains difficult to relate these variables to sales. Does extensive ad readership actually lead to increased sales? Another problem is the high cost of research. To assess the effectiveness of marketing communications expenditures correctly may require a significant investment.

THE VALUE OF MARKETING COMMUNICATIONS

Various aspects of marketing communications have often been the target of criticism. A selection of these would include the following:

- "Advertising contributes nothing to society."
- "Most advertisements and sales presentations insult my intelligence."
- "Promotion 'forces' consumers to buy products they cannot afford and do not need."
- "Advertising and selling are economic wastes."
- "Salespeople and advertisers are usually unethical."

Consumers, public officials, and marketers agree that all too often many of these complaints are true.[10] Some salespeople do use unethical sales tactics. Some product advertising is directed at consumer groups that can least afford to purchase the particular item. Many television commercials are banal and annoying.

While such components of the marketing communications mix as advertising can certainly be criticized on many counts, it is important to remember that marketing communications play a crucial role in modern society. This point is best

■ Marketing Communications Is an Essential Part of the Mix

**"I'm sorry we couldn't convince you, but as someone once said—
'doing business without advertising is like winking at a girl in the dark. You
know what you're doing, but nobody else does!' "**

Source: *Marketing Magazine* (April 10, 1989), p. 4.

explained by looking at the importance of marketing communications on the business, economic, and social levels.

Business and Nonprofit Enterprise Importance

Marketing communications is essential for both profit and nonprofit organizations, both large and small. The long-term rise in outlays for advertising and other communications elements is well documented and certainly attests to management's faith in this element of the marketing communications mix. It is difficult to conceive of an enterprise that does not attempt to promote its goods or services in some manner or another. Most modern institutions simply cannot survive in the long run without communicating with their market.

Nonbusiness enterprises also recognize the importance of this variable. The Canadian government is now the largest advertiser in Canada, promoting many programs and concepts. Religious organizations too have acknowledged the importance of promoting what they do. Even labour organizations have used marketing communications channels to make their viewpoints known to the public at large. In fact, advertising now plays a larger role in the functioning of nonprofit organizations than ever before.

Economic Importance

Advertising has assumed a degree of economic importance, if for no other reason than that it is an activity that employs thousands of people. More importantly, however, effective advertising has allowed society to derive the benefits of learning about new products and new ways of doing things. This can set many economic activities into motion.

Marketing communications strategies that increase the number of units sold permit economies in the production process, thereby lowering the production costs assigned to each unit of output. Lower consumer prices then allow these products to become available to more people. Similarly, advertising subsidizes the informational content of newspapers and the broadcast media. In short, advertising pays for many of the enjoyable entertainment and educational aspects of contemporary life, as well as lowering product costs.

Social Importance

Criticisms such as "Most advertising messages are tasteless" and "Advertising contributes nothing to society" forget the foregoing economic facts. Furthermore, they ignore the fact that there is no commonly accepted set of standards or priorities existing within our social framework. We live in a varied economy characterized by consumer segments with differing needs, wants, and aspirations. What is tasteless to one group may be quite informative to another. Advertising is faced with an "averaging" problem that escapes many of its critics. The one generally accepted standard in a market society is freedom of choice for the consumer. Consumer buying decisions will eventually determine what is acceptable practice in the marketplace.

Advertising has become an important factor in the campaigns to achieve such socially oriented objectives as stopping smoking and promoting family planning, physical fitness, the elimination of drug abuse, and the support of countless benev-

Grand & Toy's commitment to its own Code of Environmental Conduct involves recycling and reducing in its own offices and making environmentally friendly products available to its customers. Advertising ensures that Grand & Toy customers are made aware of the recycled Grand & Toy products.

olent causes. Advertising performs an informative and educational task that makes it extremely important in the functioning of modern society. As with everything else in life, it is how one uses advertising, not advertising itself, that can be criticized.

■ KEY TERMS

marketing communications	personal selling	pulling strategy
marketing communications mix	advertising	pushing strategy
	sales promotion	task-objective method
	public relations	direct-sales results test

■ INTERACTIVE SUMMARY AND DISCUSSION QUESTIONS

1. A generalized model of the communications process includes the following elements: sender, encoding, transfer mechanism, decoding, and receiver. Using this model, explain how a sales presentation could be structured to make it work better. Using this model, show how a sales presentation could become ineffective.

2. The marketing communications mix comprises the following elements: personal selling and nonpersonal communication (which comprises advertising, sales promotion, and public relations). Using Xerox copiers as an example, propose a realistic communications mix, and show how it should blend with the rest of the marketing mix.

3. The factors that influence the use of marketing communications mix elements are the nature of the market, the nature of the product, the product's stage in the product life cycle, price, and funds available. If CD players are in the late

growth stage of the product life cycle, what would be an appropriate type of advertising message for a CD player manufacturer?

4. A pulling strategy is a promotional effort by the seller to stimulate final-user demand, which then exerts pressure on the distribution channel. A pushing strategy is the promotion of the product first to the members of the marketing channel, who then participate in its promotion to the final user. Would you use a pushing strategy for introducing a new line of drinks that would compete with products such as Clearly Canadian? Explain.

5. Six different types of objectives are the focus of different marketing communications strategies: (1) to provide information, (2) to increase demand, (3) to differentiate the product, (4) to accentuate the value of the product, (5) to stabilize sales, and (6) to produce sales. Give examples of situations in which each type of objective would be appropriate.

6. Explain the effects of advertising being used to shift the demand curve to the right.

7. The common methods of determining the amount of money to be spent on marketing communications are percentage of sales, fixed sum per unit, meeting competition, and task-objective method. Discuss the pros and cons of the percentage-of-sales method.

8. A new store featuring specialty music geared for the 35–45 age group is about to open. Describe exactly how the store could establish a communications budget using the task-objective method.

9. Marketing communications is sometimes maligned. However, three categories of contributions are made by this part of the marketing mix: business importance, economic importance, and social importance. Defend the proposition that marketing communications offers a significant social contribution.

CHAPTER 18

Marketing Communications Applications: Advertising, Publicity, Sales Promotion, and Personal Selling

CHAPTER OBJECTIVES

1. To identify the categories of advertisements.
2. To introduce the main advertising media.
3. To describe the process of creating an advertisement.
4. To explain publicity and its functions.
5. To discuss sales promotion and its various elements.
6. To classify the three basic types of selling.
7. To outline the seven steps in the sales process.
8. To specify the functions of sales management.

The Car Care Report opens with Colleen Richter explaining how she worked her way up the ladder at Midas Canada Inc., taking courses on repairing mufflers, brakes, and steering.

With upbeat music in the background and fast-paced shots of cars, the 10-minute television program also features a "Tech Talk" segment with auto journalist Julie Wilkinson expounding on the ins and outs of front-end suspension.

The show winds up with testimonials from Midas auto technicians about company training courses and a toll-free telephone number to receive up to $100 in coupons. "Trust your car to Midas," the voice-over says.

Welcome to the world of infomercials, Canadian style — a soft-sell version of advertising dressed up in a documentary format.

Midas is believed to be the first advertiser in Canada to produce infomercials for daytime viewing on a Canadian network, CTV. That's because the traditional 30-minute infomercial is restricted to running between midnight and 6 A.M. according to regulations set down by the Canadian Radio-television and Telecommunications Commission.

However, Midas found a way to bend the rules but still stay within them. It bought up all 10 minutes of network time allotted in every hour for advertising on CTV's Canada AM Weekend (the remaining 2 minutes of ad time permitted in an hour is slotted for local stations) and is airing 26 different infomercials.

"We've got a story to tell and it's difficult to tell it in 15- or 30-second commercials," says Richard Miller, director of advertising and promotion for Midas in Agincourt, Ontario. Midas wants to communicate that it does more than just fix mufflers, he says. It also wants to provide general advice to car owners because research indicates they are frustrated and uncomfortable with repair shops.

"The infomercial business in the United States is probably one of the hottest mediums going in advertising," he adds. "Canada's just catching up." Indeed some advertising officials north of the border are hankering after the opportunity to show infomercials.

In February, Ford of Canada and National Ford & Mercury Dealers Association launched a multimillion-dollar national campaign with 30 minute infomercials between midnight and 6 A.M. on Canadian stations. They show a leasing expert explaining to a woman the advantages of leasing vehicles.

The Canadian Direct Marketing Association is urging the CRTC to loosen its regulations. The association estimates a potential $645-million market in Canada for infomercials and home shopping, and backs bids for specialty channels to broadcast such material. Canadians, it estimates, already buy $100 million a year in goods and services touted in U.S. infomercials.

The rising popularity of various forms of televised home shopping, including direct response infomercials (with toll-free numbers) and home shopping clubs signal profound changes not only in viewing patterns, but in the medium itself.

"The television is being transformed from a passive to an interactive device which can immediately and conveniently satisfy consumer wants."[1]

INTRODUCTION

Marketing communications efforts constantly change and evolve. Midas has used regular advertising for years, but the company's need to communicate in an expanded way led to this new format. As we saw in Chapter 17, marketing communications consists of both personal and nonpersonal elements. The range of marketing communications options is extensive. This chapter will discuss the rapidly developing areas of publicity and sales promotion in addition to advertising and personal selling.

ADVERTISING

If you sought to be the next prime minister of Canada, you would need to communicate with every possible voting Canadian. If you had invented a new calculator and went into business to sell it, your chances of success would be slim without informing and persuading students and business of your calculator's usefulness. In both these situations you would discover, as have countless others, that you would need to use advertising to communicate to buyers or voters. In the previous chapter, advertising was defined as paid nonpersonal communication through various media by business firms, nonprofit organizations, and individuals who are in some way identified with the advertising message and who hope to inform or persuade members of a particular audience.

Today's widespread markets make advertising an important part of business. Since the end of World War II, advertising and related expenditures have risen faster than have gross domestic product and most other economic indicators. Furthermore, about 85 000 people are employed in advertising, according to Statistics Canada.[2]

Three advertisers — General Motors of Canada, Procter & Gamble, and The Thomson Group — spent more than $70 million each for advertising in 1993. Table 18.1 ranks the top advertisers in Canada. It is particularly noteworthy that governments, both federal and provincial, are such a major force in Canadian advertising. The government is still one of the nation's largest advertising spenders in spite of having cut its total spending by almost half since 1988. Total 1990 advertising media expenditures were about $10.2 billion. This means that about $392 is spent on advertising each year for every person in Canada.[3]

Advertising expenditures as a proportion of sales vary among industries and companies. Cosmetics companies are often cited as an example of firms that spend a high percentage of their funds on advertising and promotion. Management consultants Schonfeld & Associates studied more than 4000 firms and calculated their average advertising expenditures as a percentage of both sales and gross profit margin. Estimates for selected industries are given in Figure 18.1. Wide differences exist among industries. Advertising spending can range from 0.2 percent (as is the case with iron and steel foundries) to more than 7 percent of sales (as in the soap and detergent industry).

Some form of advertising aimed at boosting product sales has probably existed since the development of the exchange process.[4] Most early advertising was vocal. Criers and hawkers sold various products, made public announcements, and chanted advertising slogans like this one (now familiar to many as a nursery rhyme):

One-a-penny, two-a-penny, hot-cross buns
One-a-penny, two for tuppence, hot-cross buns

Signs were also used in early advertising. Most were symbolic and used to identify products and services. In Rome, a goat signified a dairy; a mule driving a mill, a bakery; a boy being whipped, a school.

Later, the development of the printing press greatly expanded advertising's capability. A 1710 advertisement in the *Spectator* billed one tooth powder as "the Incomparable Powder for cleaning of Teeth, which has given great satisfaction to most of the Nobility and Gentry in England."

Until 1990, professionals such as doctors and dentists were restricted in the amount of advertising they could do. In June 1990, the Supreme Court of Canada

▉ Table 18.1 **The Top 10 Advertisers in Canada, 1993**

Rank	Name	Revenue (thousands of dollars)
1	General Motors of Canada	113 048.4
2	Procter & Gamble	84 499.5
3	The Thomson Group	70 159.3
4	BCE	53 972.9
5	John Labatt Ltd.	50 036.0
6	Eaton's of Canada	47 135.9
7	Sears Canada	46 582.1
8	Government of Canada	43 928.7
9	The Molson Companies	42 873.6
10	Chrysler Canada	41 171.5

Source: A.C. Nielsen. Reprinted by permission.

■ Figure 18.1 **Estimates of Average Advertising to Sales in 10 Industries**

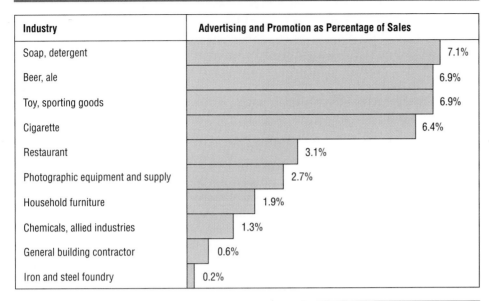

Industry	Advertising and Promotion as Percentage of Sales
Soap, detergent	7.1%
Beer, ale	6.9%
Toy, sporting goods	6.9%
Cigarette	6.4%
Restaurant	3.1%
Photographic equipment and supply	2.7%
Household furniture	1.9%
Chemicals, allied industries	1.3%
General building contractor	0.6%
Iron and steel foundry	0.2%

Source: Schonfeld & Associates, Inc., Chicago. Survey conducted in 1982.

struck down prohibitions on advertising by the Royal College of Dental Surgeons of Ontario as a violation of freedom of expression. This means that not only dentists but other professionals, such as lawyers, accountants, and architects, are free to advertise their services. Thus, consumers should be more fully informed about available services, as they are for other products.

One identifying feature of advertising in the last half of the twentieth century is its concern for researching the markets that it attempts to reach. Originally, advertising research dealt primarily with media selection and the product. Then, advertisers became increasingly concerned with aiming their messages more specifically through determining the appropriate *demographics* (such characteristics as the age, gender, and income level of potential buyers). Now, understanding consumer behaviour has become an important aspect of advertising strategy. As discussed in Chapter 3, psychographics can be useful in describing potential markets for advertising appeals. Increased knowledge of such factors as lifestyle and personal attitudes has led to improved advertising decisions.

The emergence of the marketing concept, with its emphasis on a company-wide consumer orientation, saw advertising take on an expanded role as marketing communications assumed greater importance in business. Advertising provides an efficient, inexpensive, and fast method of reaching the much-sought-after consumer. Its extensive use now rivals that of personal selling. Advertising has become a key ingredient in the effective implementation of the marketing concept.

ADVERTISING PLANNING

Advertising planning begins with effective research. Research results allow management to make strategic decisions, which are then translated into tactical execution —

budgeting, copywriting, scheduling, and the like. Finally, there must be some feedback mechanism for measuring the effectiveness of the advertising. The elements of advertising planning are shown in Figure 18.2.

There is a real need for following a sequential process in advertising decisions. Novice advertisers are often guilty of being overly concerned with the technical aspects of advertisement construction, while ignoring the more basic steps such as market analysis. The type of advertisement that is employed in any particular situation is related largely to the planning phase of this process.

POSITIONING

The concept of positioning was introduced in Chapter 4. It involves developing a marketing strategy aimed at a particular segment of the market in order to achieve a desired position vis-à-vis the competition in the mind of the prospective buyer. Advertising is the most important component in the marketing mix for positioning a product. A variety of positioning strategies is available to the advertiser:

■ Figure 18.2 **Elements of Advertising Planning**

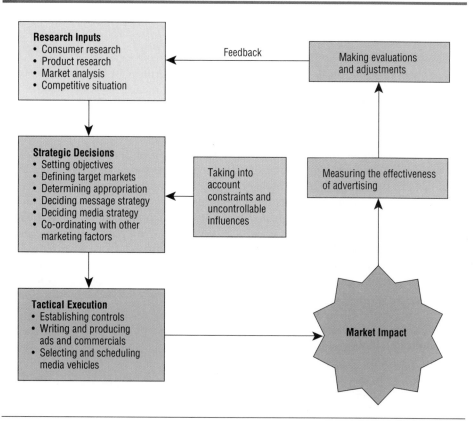

Source: Adapted from S. Watson Dunn and Arnold M. Barban, *Advertising: Its Role in Modern Marketing,* 5th ed. (Hinsdale, IL: Dryden, 1982), p. 202. Used by permission of the publisher.

1. By attributes (Crest is a cavity fighter.)
2. By price/quality (Sears is a value store.)
3. By competitor ("Avis is only number two in rent-a-cars, so why go with us? We try harder.")
4. By application (Gatorade is for quick, healthful energy after exercise and other forms of physical exertion.)
5. By product user (Mercedes-Benz cars are for discriminating executives.)
6. By product class (Carnation Instant Breakfast is a breakfast food.)[5]

CATEGORIES OF ADVERTISEMENTS

Essentially, there are two basic types of advertisements: product and institutional. The former type can be subdivided into informative, persuasive, and reminder-oriented categories.

Product advertising deals with the *nonpersonal selling of a particular good or service.* It is the type we normally think of when the subject of advertising comes up. **Institutional advertising**, by contrast, is concerned with *promoting a concept, idea, or philosophy, or the good will of an industry, company, or organization.* It is often closely related to the public relations function of the enterprise.

product advertising
Nonpersonal selling of a particular good or service.

institutional advertising
Promoting a concept, idea, or philosophy, or the good will of an industry, company, or organization.

Informative Product Advertising

All advertising seeks to influence the audience, as does any type of communication. **Informative product advertising** *seeks to develop demand through presenting factual information on the attributes of the product or service.* For example, an advertisement for a new type of photocopier would attempt to persuade through citing the various unique product and/or service features of that copier. Informative product advertising tends to be used in promoting new products, since a major requirement in such cases is to announce availability and characteristics that will satisfy needs. Thus it is often seen in the introductory stages of the product life cycle.

informative product advertising
Advertising that seeks to develop demand through presenting factual information on the attributes of a product or service.

Persuasive Product Advertising

In **persuasive product advertising**, *the emphasis is on using words and/or images to try to create an image for a product and to influence attitudes about it.* In contrast to informative product advertising, this type of advertising contains little objective information. Coca-Cola® and Pepsi use persuasive techniques in their lifestyle advertisements featuring a group of happy people enjoying the product. Persuasive advertising is generally used more after the introductory stage of the product life cycle.

persuasive product advertising
Advertising that emphasizes using words and/or images to try to create an image for a product and to influence attitudes about it.

Reminder-Oriented Product Advertising

The goal of **reminder-oriented product advertising** is *to reinforce previous promotional activity by keeping the product's or service's name in front of the public.* It is used in the maturity period as well as throughout the decline phase of the product life cycle. An example of a reminder-oriented slogan is Coca-Cola's® well-known "You can't

reminder-oriented product advertising
Advertising whose goal is to reinforce previous promotional activity by keeping the product's or service's name in front of the public.

beat the real thing." Figure 18.3 illustrates the general relationship between the type of advertising and the stage of the life cycle.

Institutional Advertising

As mentioned earlier, institutional advertising seeks to increase public knowledge of a concept, idea, philosophy, industry, or company. In the early 1980s, the oil industry was experiencing a degree of unfavourable publicity. One firm's communications director said, "We decided we had a story to tell."[6] Consequently, the company tripled its corporate advertising budget to $3 million and undertook an extensive program to educate the public about the company's contributions to society. Other firms, such as Volkswagen, have continuously advertised their innovativeness and reliability.

MEDIA SELECTION

One of the interesting phenomena in the world of recorded music is the small but significant group of consumers who prefer vinyl records to CDs. They argue that the music on vinyl is "warmer" and not as "antiseptic" as on CDs. Suppose you want to advertise to these people. A mass television campaign might reach them, but you would waste your message on most of the audience. The proper approach would be to find an advertising medium that would be more focussed on that group.

One of the most important decisions in developing an advertising strategy is media selection. A mistake at this point can cost a company literally millions of dollars in ineffectual advertising. Media strategy must achieve the communications goals mentioned earlier.

Research should identify the target market, determine its size and characteristics, and then match the target with the audience and effectiveness of the available media. The objective is to achieve adequate media coverage without advertising

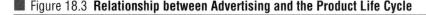

■ Figure 18.3 **Relationship between Advertising and the Product Life Cycle**

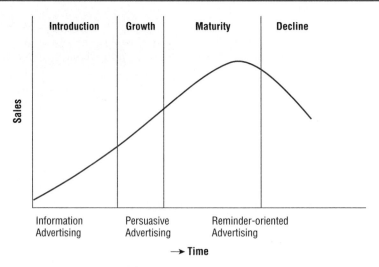

Cola-Cola® is perhaps the most well-known soft drink in the world. The company's aggressive marketing campaigns often include catchy reminder-oriented slogans that are remembered long after they have been replaced. Slogans like "Coke is it!" "You can't beat the real thing," and, most recently, "Always Coca-Cola®" are heard repeatedly in jingles and have made the product a household name.

beyond the identifiable limits of the potential market. Finally, alternative costs are compared to determine the best possible media purchase.

There are numerous types of advertising media, and the characteristics of some of the more important ones will be considered here.[7] The advantages and disadvantages of each are shown in Table 18.2.

Newspapers

About 26 percent of Canada's total advertising revenues, the largest share received by any of the media, is spent on advertising in newspapers (including weekend supplements).[8] The primary advantages of newspapers are flexibility (advertising can be varied from one locality to the next), community prestige (newspapers have a deep impact on the community), intense coverage (in most places about nine out of ten homes can be reached by a single newspaper), and reader control of exposure to the advertising message (unlike audiences of electronic media, readers can refer back to newspapers). The disadvantages are a short lifespan, hasty reading (the typical reader spends only 20 to 30 minutes on the newspaper), and poor reproduction.

Magazines

Magazines are divided into such diverse categories as consumer magazines, farm and business publications, and directories. They account for about 12 percent of all advertising. The primary advantages of magazine advertising are selectivity of target markets, quality reproduction, long life, the prestige associated with some magazines, and the extra services offered by many publications. Canadian consumer

Institutional advertising can increase the public's awareness of a company while contributing to society. The Pepsi Foundation's goal is to educate teens on the topic of substance abuse. It also raises funds to support national and grassroots drug and alcohol programs. Advertisements such as this shows consumers that Pepsi is not simply a soft-drink manufacturer but a company made up of people who care about society and want to make it a better place.

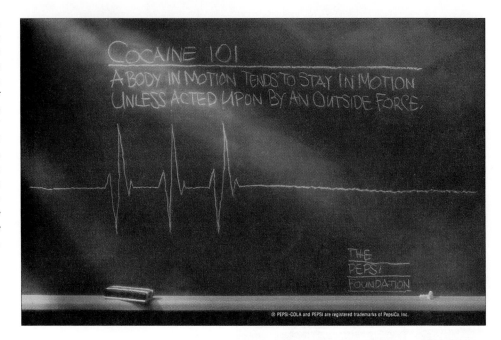

magazines have pioneered many controlled distribution techniques. Our postal code system, with its six-digit forward sortation area (FSA) and local delivery unit (LDU), can be linked with census data at the enumeration area (EA) level to produce well-defined circulation clusters based on demographics, life cycles, or other interest–activity profiles.[9] The primary disadvantage is that magazines lack the flexibility of newspapers, radio, and television.

Television

Television is the second-largest advertising medium. It now accounts for about 14 percent of total advertising volume. Television advertising can be divided into three categories: network, national spot, and local spot. The Canadian Broadcasting Corporation, the Canadian Television Network, and Global Television are the three national networks. Network advertising usually accounts for over two-thirds of the total television advertising expenditures. A national "spot" refers to non-network broadcasting used by a general advertiser (for example, Black & Decker might choose to place an advertisement in several cities across the country, without buying time from a total television network.) Local spots, primarily used by retailers, consist of locally developed and sponsored commercials. Television advertising offers the following advantages: impact, mass coverage, repetition, flexibility, and prestige. Its disadvantages include the temporary nature of the message, high costs, high mortality rates for commercials, some evidence of public distrust, and lack of selectivity.

Radio

Advertisers using the medium of radio can also be classified as network or local advertisers. Radio accounts for about 7 percent of total advertising volume. The

■ Table 18.2 **Advantages and Disadvantages of the Various Advertising Media**

Media	Advantages	Disadvantages
Newspapers	Flexibility Community prestige Intense coverage Reader control of exposure Co-ordination with national advertising Merchandising service	Short lifespan Hasty reading Poor reproduction
Magazines	Selectivity Quality reproduction Long life Prestige associated with some magazines Extra services	Lack of flexibility

Television	Great impact
	Mass coverage
	Repetition
	Flexibility
	Prestige
		Temporary nature of
		   message
		High cost
		High mortality rate for
		   commercials
		Evidence of public distrust
		Lack of selectivity

Radio	Immediacy
	Low cost
	Practical audience
	   selection
	Mobility
		Fragmentation
		Temporary nature of
		   message
		Little research information

Outdoor
Advertising
	Quick communication of
	   simple ideas
	Repetition
	Ability to promote products
	   available for sale nearby
		Brevity of the message
		Public concern over aesthetics

Direct Mail	Selectivity Intense coverage Speed Flexibility of format Complete information Personalization	High cost per person Dependence on quality of mailing list Consumer resistance

Source: Adapted from S. Watson Dunn and Arnold M. Barban, *Advertising: Its Role in Modern Marketing*, 5th ed. (Hinsdale, IL: Dryden, 1982), pp. 513–77. Used by permission of the publisher.

advantages of radio advertising are immediacy (studies show that most people regard radio as the best source for up-to-date news); low cost; flexibility; practical, low-cost audience selection; and mobility (radio is an extremely mobile broadcast medium). Radio's disadvantages include fragmentation (for instance, Montreal has about 19 AM and FM station), the unavailability of the advertising message for future reference, and less available research information than for television.

Direct Mail

Sales letters, postcards, leaflets, folders, broadsides (which are larger than folders), booklets, catalogues, and house organs (periodical publications issued by an organization) are all forms of direct-mail advertising. The advantages of direct mail include selectivity, intensive coverage, speed, format flexibility, complete information, and the personalization of each mailing piece. Direct-mail purchasers also tend to be consistent buyers by mail.[10] A disadvantage of direct mail is its high cost per reader. Direct-mail advertising also depends on the quality of the mailing list.[11] Often those unfamiliar with the efficacy of direct mail condemn it all as "junk mail." They are very surprised to find that many people respond positively to such advertising. In fact, marketing research surveys consistently show a majority who say they prefer to receive it. Effectively used, direct mail is a successful and lucrative marketing tool.

Outdoor Advertising

Outdoor advertising such as billboards can be a highly effective way of catching people's attention. While television and radio audiences often switch channels during commercials, research shows that people reread 100 percent of a poster. This Hostess Potato Chips billboard, designed by BBDO Canada, effectively uses humour and vibrant colours to attract passers-by.

Posters (commonly called billboards), painted bulletins or displays (such as those that appear on building walls), and electric spectaculars (large, illuminated — sometimes animated — signs and displays) make up outdoor advertising. Accounting for 6 percent of advertising volume, this form of advertising has the advantages of quick communication of simple ideas, repetition, and the ability to promote products that are available for sale nearby. Outdoor advertising is particularly effective in metropolitan and other high-traffic areas. Disadvantages of the medium are the brevity of its message and public concern over aesthetics; however, a simple message can be extremely powerful.

ORGANIZING THE ADVERTISING FUNCTION

While the ultimate responsibility for advertising decisions often rests with top marketing management, the organization of the advertising function varies among companies. A producer of a technical industrial product may be served by a one-person operation primarily concerned with writing copy for trade publications. A consumer-goods company, on the other hand, may have a large department staffed with advertising specialists.

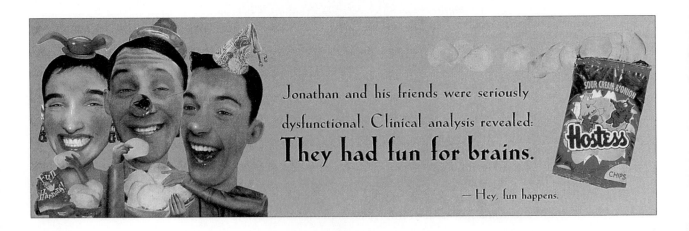

The advertising function is usually organized as a staff department reporting to the vice-president (or director) of marketing. The *director of advertising* is an executive position heading the functional activity of advertising. The individual filling this slot should not only be a skilled and experienced advertiser, but also be able to communicate effectively within the organization. The success of a firm's promotional strategy depends on the advertising director's willingness and ability to communicate both vertically and horizontally. The major tasks typically organized under advertising include advertising research, art, copywriting, media analysis, and, in some cases, sales promotion.

Advertising Agencies

Many advertisers also make use of an independent advertising agency. The **advertising agency** is *a marketing specialist firm that assists the advertiser in planning and preparing its advertisements.* There are several reasons why advertisers use an agency for at least a portion of their advertising. Agencies are typically staffed with highly qualified specialists who provide a degree of creativity and objectivity that is difficult to maintain in a corporate advertising department. In some cases using an agency reduces the cost of advertising, since the agency does not require many of the fixed expenses associated with internal advertising departments. Effective use of an advertising agency requires a close relationship between advertiser and agency.

advertising agency
A marketing specialist firm that assists the advertiser in planning and preparing its advertisements.

CREATING AN ADVERTISEMENT

The final step in the advertising process is developing and preparing an advertisement, which should flow logically from the promotional theme selected. This step should thus be a complementary part of the marketing mix, with its role in total marketing strategy carefully determined. In addition, major factors to consider when preparing an advertisement are its creativity, its continuity with past advertisements, and possibly its association with other company products.

What should an advertisement accomplish? Regardless of the exact appeal that is chosen, an ad should (1) gain attention and interest, (2) inform and/or persuade, and (3) eventually lead to buying action.

Gaining attention should be productive. That is, the reason for gaining consumers' attention should be to instil some recall of the product. Consider the case of the Gillette Company, which had a chimpanzee shave a man's face in a commercial. After tests in two cities, one Gillette man observed, "Lots of people remembered the chimp, but hardly anyone remembered our product. There was fantastic interest in the monkey, but no payoff for Gillette."[12] The advertisement gained the audience's attention, but it failed to lead to buying action. An ad that fails to gain and hold the receiver's attention is ineffectual.

Information and persuasion is the second factor to consider when creating an advertisement. For example, insurance advertisements typically specify the features of the policy and may use testimonials in attempting to persuade prospects.

Stimulating buying action is often difficult, however, since an advertisement cannot actually close a sale. Nevertheless, if the first steps have been accomplished, the advertising has likely been well worthwhile. Too many advertisers fail to suggest how the receiver of the message can buy the product if he or she so desires.

Retail Advertising

Retail advertising is the advertising done by stores that sell goods or services directly to consumers. Retail advertising accounts for a sizable portion of total advertising expenditures. Supermarkets advertise weekly specials, restaurants and fast-food chains promote the quality of their products, and lawyers advertise such services as handling accident claims.

There is great variability in the quality of retail advertising. Some, like McDonald's, is created by professionals, and generally follows the procedures described previously. Other retail advertising, like much local automobile dealer advertising, appears to be slapped together by rank amateurs. Because retail advertising is frequently prepared without the benefit of professional advertising experience or adequate research, there appears to be considerable scope for improving the effectiveness of such advertising.

One aspect of advertising that involves a retailer/manufacturer relationship is **co-operative advertising**. This involves *the sharing of advertising costs between the retailer and the manufacturer.* For example, Canada Packers may pay 50 percent of the cost of a 50 cm² area of a supermarket chain's weekly newspaper ad that features one or more of Canada Packers' products.

Co-operative advertising benefits both retailer and manufacturer. From the retailer's viewpoint, it permits a store to secure additional advertising that it would not otherwise have. The manufacturer benefits from having retailers share in advertising costs. In addition, if the retailer has invested in the advertisement, it will not only carry the manufacturer's product but also try to be sure of having enough in stock to satisfy demand.

co-operative advertising
The sharing of advertising costs between the retailer and the manufacturer.

THE ADVERTISING CAMPAIGN

When a company develops a marketing communications strategy, it often does not restrict its plan to advertising alone. Just as a military campaign combines many elements in a strategic effort to meet objectives, the elements of the communications mix are similarly blended to provide maximum consumer impact. The opening of a Brettons store in downtown Toronto gives an example.

To announce the opening of its new store, Brettons used many media, including magazines, subway posters, billboards, radio, newspapers, direct mail, and public relations. Toronto issues of *Flare* and *Maclean's* included special sections with a mix of ads and "advertorial" (an advertisement set up to look like an editorial). Local radio stations were used first for "teaser" ads (designed to stimulate interest, but not reveal the sponsor), and then for "launch" (opening) ads. In addition, a direct mailing went to 200 000 households. Furthermore, Brettons launched a national charge-card campaign, with 700 000 delivered through a combination of postal drops and the Toronto editions of *Flare* and *Maclean's*. The first 15 000 new card-holders in Toronto were offered a year's free subscription to *Flare*.[13]

MESSAGE THEMES

Advertising messages are delivered using many classic techniques. The structure of the message; the use of various appeals, such as humour, sex, and fear; and the use of comparative advertising are examples.

Structure

Since readers tend to skim advertising, a number of subheadings that summarize the entire message are usually an advantage. Because of many competing stimuli, it is necessary to attract the audience's attention. Bold headlines, colour, sound effects, louder sound during a television commercial, and unusual images are only a few of the methods used by advertisers.

Use of Humour, Sex, and Fear

Most people say they love humour in advertising, and many think that all advertisements should use this technique. Unfortunately, with advertising, it is not that simple. Even advertising humour classics, such as those developed for Alka Seltzer a few years ago, failed. Humour must not detract from the central message the advertiser wishes to deliver. Also, many attempts at humour in advertising are not that funny. The bottom line in advertising is to communicate the advertiser's message.

In order to gain attention, some advertisers use sexual images. It is now believed that unless such images are used in a setting that is natural to the product, this approach does not help. Furthermore, society is becoming resistant to advertisers who are seen to be exploiting women in their advertising. For example, women's groups have objected to the brewing industry about their thinly disguised sex/lifestyle ads. A classic longitudinal study of the effects of erotic content on brand recall showed that as erotic content increases, the probability of people correctly recalling the associated brand decreases.[14]

Fear is another technique used in advertising. Advertisers sometimes appeal to people's fear of social stigma in their ads for deodorants, breath sweeteners, and dandruff treatments. Antidrinking advertisements showing powerful images of fatal car crashes have been created to limit drinking by young people. Life insurance companies sometimes use the fear of dying, or of leaving loved ones uncared for, in their advertising appeals. Research has shown that fear appeals can be effective unless the appeal is so strong that individuals psychologically repress the message because it disturbs them too much.

Comparative Advertising

Comparative advertising *makes direct promotional comparisons with competitive brands.* The strategy is best employed by firms that do not lead the market.

Companies used to be afraid to mention the name of their competitor's product because that was thought to be a "free" reminder about that product, sometimes going to ridiculous lengths. For example, a salesperson speaking about a product in comparison with well-known competition could say only "that other product" or use some other euphemism. Everyone listening immediately substituted the competing brand for the euphemism.

This is seen both in personal selling and in advertising. Many advertisers are now choosing to compare their products directly with those of competitors. The comparison can sometimes take the form of an attack on the competition.

Comparative advertising can be challenged in the courts, as was the case when Robin Hood Multifoods compared a pie crust made with its shortening to one made with Maple Leaf Foods Inc. Tenderflake and Gainsborough lard. The court

comparative advertising
Advertising that makes direct promotional comparisons with competitive brands.

After twenty years of clinical research, Bristol-Myers Squibb believed it had evidence to show that Excedrin was superior in its ability to relieve headache pain. The company took its claims to the Canadian Health Protection Branch, which granted it the right to make a name-brand comparison with competing brand Tylenol. Through television and print ads, Bristol-Myers Squibb hopes to position Excedrin as a better alternative to the more well-known brand.

ordered Robin Hood to pull its ads because they would "have the effect of diminishing Maple Leaf's reputation and lead to a loss of good will as well. They tend to create the impression that . . . [Maple Leaf's] product will be a misshapen pie and not a normal pie."[15]

Advertisers sometimes get carried away using the comparative approach. During the 1993 federal election campaign, the Conservatives used an advertisement emphasizing Jean Chrétien's partially paralyzed mouth. The outcry among all Canadians caused the ad to be pulled after only one day.

Marketers who contemplate using comparative advertising should take precautions to ensure that they can substantiate their claims, because such advertising has the potential of producing lawsuits. From a long-run perspective, advertisers need to decide whether a more solid product and company image can be created by a message devoted to communicating about and positioning a product in its own right, or by comparing the product with others.

These are a few examples of the many technical issues in creating advertising messages. Message creation is serious business — thousands of messages are wasted every day because advertisers use worn-out phrases and unimaginative messages. The famous advertiser William Bernbach put it well when he said,

> *You must crash through the wall*
>
> What brand of vanity or indifference leads us to believe that we can . . . sit alongside world-shaking events and even be noticed? Our reader is confronted daily with history-making news. The papers are filled with sensationalism. . . . With this deafening roar of frightening conflict beating about his ears, how do we expect him to hear our advertising story? How are we going to pierce this wall around him? . . . And if we pierce this wall, how are we going to get through that second wall, an almost impenetrable wall of competition crying its wares?
>
> Only a message with a tremendous vitality carried in a dramatic graphic treatment will ever reach your consumer. What's the use of saying all the right things in the world

if nobody's going to read them? And believe me, nobody's going to read them if they are not done with freshness, originality and imagination.[16]

Table 18.3 provides a summary of important points made by Bernbach concerning advertising messages.

ASSESSING THE EFFECTIVENESS OF AN ADVERTISEMENT

For many firms, advertising represents a major expenditure, so it is imperative to determine whether a campaign is accomplishing its promotional objectives. Determining advertising's effectiveness, however, is one of the most difficult undertakings in marketing. It consists of two primary elements — pretesting and post-testing.

Pretesting

Pretesting is *the assessment of an advertisement's effectiveness before it is actually used*. It includes a variety of evaluative methods. For example, to test magazine advertisements, the ad agency Batten, Barton, Durstine & Osborn cuts ads out of advance copies of magazines and then "strips in" the ads it wants to test. Interviewers later check the impact of the advertisements on the readers who receive free copies of the revised magazine. Many other techniques are used for pretesting advertising.

pretesting
The assessment of an advertisement's effectiveness before it is actually used.

Post-testing

Post-testing is *the assessment of advertising copy after it has been used*. Pretesting is generally a more desirable testing method than post-testing because of its potential cost savings. But post-testing can be helpful in planning future advertisements and in making adjustments to current advertising programs.

post-testing
The assessment of advertising copy after it has been used.

■ Table 18.3 **Important Points about Advertising Messages**

1. Crash through the wall! Not to be different is virtually suicide.

2. Impressions outweigh numbers.
   • Nobody counts the number of ads you show, they just remember the impressions you make.
   • Make your ad so provocative, so artful, that it is many times more effective than your competitors'.

3. Create personality.
   • Differentiate your ad from the competition's, and produce individuality.

4. Don't waste the reader's time.
   • Don't just get attention with an easy, irrelevant gimmick. Make sure the attention-getting element stems from your product.

5. Make your ads memorable.

APPLYING THE CONCEPTS

Are the Concepts Being Properly Applied?

You may have noticed that the automongers at General Motors have launched (to borrow a durable Madison Avenue verb) a massive media campaign with the catchline "Genuine Chevrolet."

The advertising masterminds must have anticipated a few quizzically raised eyebrows, because in full-page ads this week the large-type catchline was immediately following by the question, "What is Genuine Chevrolet?"

And this was the answer: "It's not a slogan. It's not just a theme. It's a commitment to a new way of life at Chevrolet."

I don't know about you, but I found this response just a trifle unenlightening. In fact, it raised at least two more questions which the Chevy people neglected either to ask or answer: (1) Has somebody been hawking cheap, imitation Chevvies at those street-corner stands, along with ersatz Rolexes and mock Gucci bags? (2) If "Genuine Chevrolet" means "a commitment to a new way of life at Chevrolet," has the company itself been flogging something other than the genuine article (not to be confused with "the real thing," which is another product — and another enigma — altogether)?

The advertising people had plenty of alternatives, and they were all carefully considered. I know this, because Word Play obtained a partial transcript of a meeting of the Ongoing Ad Hoc Strategic Thrust Task Group of the advertising firm of Blah, Blurb, Bafflegab and Bletherskite (not its genuine name). Here it is:

BRAD: *Okay, basically we seem to be in agreement that* unvarnished, unadulterated, dyed-in-the-wool, honest-to-God *and* the real McCoy *Chevrolet won't work. How about* Authentic Chevrolet?

CHAD: Authentic's *a good solid word, no question. But it makes me think of some old document, like a manuscript, or the Dead Sea Scrolls, or a Brian Mulroney doodle. Is that the image we want for today's Chevrolet? We might just as well go for* indubitable *or* veritable *or* forsooth. *Why not* "Chevrolet Per Se"? *At least it rhymes.*

THAD: *Chad's got a point, Brad. We need a word that's very nineties. Not too flashy, not too slick. Respectable, but not ancient. Something decent, honest, sincere, sort of middle-of-the-infobahn. Something genuine.*

AHMAD: *Hey! Gen-yoo-wine! Got a nice ring to it. Kinda reminds you of generous, gentle, genial, genius and genesis. Not to mention — heh, heh —* Gen-eral Motors.

BRAD: *I think I can sense a lot of support here for* genuine. *It's a fine word — a word that has stood the test of time. It worked for our spiritual forefathers, the much-maligned and misunderstood snake-oil salesmen. It worked for the beer company that successfully marketed "genuine-draft" beer in bottles . . .*

CHAD: *But isn't bottled draft beer a genuine oxymoron? Don't you think we've used* genuine *in so many artificial, contradictory, spurious, counterfeit, phony contexts that it's now utterly devoid of meaning? Like* unique, improved, recommended by *and* much, much more? *Aren't we just going for* genuine *because it looks and sounds good, even though it means zilch?*

BRAD: *You catch on fast, Chad.*

Source: Robertson Cochrane, " 'Genuine' Is Genuinely Meaningless," *The Globe and Mail* (July 9, 1994), p. D6. Reprinted by permission of the author.

What would William Bernbach, quoted previously in this chapter, say about this? What do you say?

In one of the most popular post-tests, the *Starch Readership Report,* interviewers ask people who have read selected magazines whether they have read various ads in them. A copy of one of the magazines is used as an interviewing aid, and each interviewer starts at a different point in the magazine. For larger ads, respondents are also asked about specifics such as headlines and copy. All readership or recognition tests assume that future sales are related to advertising readership.

Regardless of the exact method used, marketers must realize that pretesting and post-testing are expensive and must, therefore, plan to use them as effectively as possible.

DIRECT MARKETING

Marketers have increasingly used various advertising media to make a selling offer directly to the target market. The results of these direct marketing efforts have been so impressive that this practice has grown steadily. **Direct marketing** is *an interactive system of marketing that uses one or more advertising media to effect a measurable response and/or transaction at any location.*[17]

Two distinguishing words are *measurable response.* Direct marketing uses various media such as catalogues, direct mail, magazines, television, radio, and newspapers to make a specific offer. The purpose of this offer is to elicit a direct positive response (usually, an order). This contrasts with general advertising for the purpose of creating an image, or communicating for some other purpose.

Direct marketing anticipates a relatively immediate response (sale) that can be measured against the marketing effort put forth. For example, a television offer of a special CD set would encourage buyers to phone an 800 number or write in to order it and charge it to their credit card. If the campaign costs $70 000 and orders

direct marketing
An interactive system of marketing that uses one or more advertising media to effect a measurable response and/or transaction at any location.

Direct mail has very little time to catch the attention of the recipient before it is tossed, but the words "free snow removal" are guaranteed to intrigue winter-weary Canadians. Motivated by the offer of something free and beneficial, most recipients opened this award-winning brochure and read the copy. The offer was for 30 days of free cable service with a reduced installation charge, which eliminated the TV "snow" on up to 43 channels. The success of this direct-mail campaign indicates that recipients thought this offer was a good deal, even if they still had to shovel snow.

amount to $200 000, the marketer can take other costs into consideration and readily calculate whether or not the direct marketing effort was profitable. Similarly, Tilley Endurables elicits direct orders for its Tilley hat and other casual clothing in *The Globe and Mail*, along with a number of other direct marketers. Some comparisons between direct marketing and general advertising are shown in Table 18.4.

Much direct marketing is done through direct mail. Computerization has made this medium extremely versatile, and direct mail can be very focussed. For example, you receive a personalized letter inviting you to a mutual funds seminar. Another arrives announcing a special concert featuring the music you like. These letters were aimed directly at you because you subscribe to a financial magazine or order CDs regularly from a club by mail.

Information about potential mail recipients is so important that an industry has evolved to collect and rent databases. These not only provide names and addresses, but also past purchase behaviour.[18] List houses, or list brokers, specialize in collecting lists and keeping them up-to-date. A direct marketer must find the right combination of lists to use. This may be done by going directly to the list rental division of major publications or organizations, or to a broker specializing in the selection of lists. About 2000 lists are for rent in Canada.

Lists from many sources are combined and duplicate names are removed. Rental for lists generally costs 5 or 6 cents a name. Those who rent their lists usually insist on approving samples of the material that will be mailed. The renter agrees to one use per rental.

Mailing lists never enter the possession of the renter. Rather, the provider sends a computer tape or disks via the broker to one of several businesses that specialize in combining computer lists and generating labels, envelopes, and customized letters.

■ Table 18.4 **Comparison of Direct Marketing and General Advertising**

Direct Marketing	General Advertising
Selling to individuals. Customers are often identifiable by name, address, and purchase behaviour.	Mass selling. Buyers identified as broad groups sharing common demographic and psychographic characteristics.
Products have added value or service. Distribution is important product benefit.	Product benefits do not always include convenient distribution channels.
The medium is the marketplace.	Retail outlet is the marketplace.
Marketer controls product until delivery.	Marketer may lose control as product enters distribution channel.
Advertising used to motivate an immediate order or inquiry.	Advertising used for cumulative effect over time to build image, awareness, loyalty, benefit recall. Purchase action deferred.
Repetition used within ad.	Repetition used over time.
Consumers feel high perceived risk — product bought unseen. Recourse is distant.	Consumers feel less risk — have direct contact with the product and direct recourse.

Source: Bob Stone, *Successful Direct Marketing Methods*, 5th ed. (Lincolnwood, IL: NTC Publishing Group, 1994).

It is at this stage that duplicates and those on various "do-not-mail" lists are removed. Labels and materials then move on to a mailing house, which stuffs the envelopes and puts them in the mail.

The range of products offered by direct marketing is large, ranging from computers (sold by Dell) to tax preparation to pest control and many other services. But not everyone prefers to buy directly from manufacturers — many consumers enjoy shopping and browsing in person.

A problem with direct marketing is that consumers have difficulty avoiding and ignoring it, so there is a fair amount of animosity toward its continuous flow. In addition, privacy sometimes becomes an issue. This writer recently received a letter that said, "You have more than 15 000 frequent-flyer air mile points. You can increase them by accepting our offer." How did the direct marketer know how many points I had? Why did the airline company release this information? Direct marketers may learn about consumer purchase behaviour from the list categories they purchase, but should be careful not to make consumers feel that their privacy has been compromised.

Direct marketing continues to be used successfully in new applications and has become an important part of marketing. The main threat to its long-term viability is negative public reaction to the intrusiveness of this medium. At the moment, despite a rather small and vocal consumer group that opposes direct marketing, it does not appear that legislation prohibiting it will soon appear.

PUBLICITY

A key factor in marketing is to gain awareness. This is also one of the main objectives of advertising. Awareness and interest sometimes can also be generated through publicity. **Publicity** is *the generation of awareness about a product beyond regular advertising methods.* Generally, publicity is much less costly than advertising because it depends on some characteristic, activity, or event to make it "newsworthy" and stimulate media attention. In North America, over 100 000 media editors[19] are constantly searching for news and public interest stories, including stories about interesting new products, new product uses, and new services.

Coleco's publicity campaign for its Cabbage Patch dolls is a classic example of the power of publicity.[20] Planned almost a year before, the campaign was orchestrated with the advertising and promotion campaign to peak in December 1983. The ultimate sales response was overwhelming.

Publicity is also generated by attention-getting activities. Kellogg uses a larger-than-life mascot of Tony the Tiger for appearances at public venues. "Kids go nuts — they love the characters," says Carol Reader, product manager for children's cereals at Kellogg. "This is a very inoffensive way to remind people about a product."[21]

Publicity has a number of advantages and disadvantages. One advantage is its greater credibility because the information is perceived to be offered by an unbiased source. Another advantage is that coverage often occurs with great speed, which is further enhanced by word-of-mouth. The public interest generated can often be considerably greater than could be created with an advertising campaign. If an editor thinks your message is newsworthy and runs it, others are likely to pick it up, and terrific momentum can occur.

The disadvantage of publicity is that it is out of the control of the marketer. There is little control over execution or timing. Thus, it is not possible to count on

publicity
The generation of awareness about a product beyond regular advertising methods.

the fact that there will be *any* publicity at all, what actually will be said about the product, or when this might happen. Another problem is that even if the story is run, the marketer cannot be sure what will be said. Furthermore, each medium is likely to try covering the topic from a different angle. Photos and videotapes provide some control because they cannot be so readily edited.

The process of gaining publicity is a delicate one. It requires good relationships with the media. The marketing company's publicist prepares a kit with a writeup, or press release, on the product and any other relevant materials such as pictures, videotapes, and other background information. The objective is to present the message as conveniently as possible without removing the possibility for the media to create their own angle on the story. Some media will publish the press release as it is, while others never do so because they view it as advertising. Many times, marketers will provide a spokesperson that the media can build the story around.

Publicity can also be generated through publicity stunts or giving the product away to celebrities. Tilley advertises that its sports clothing is worn by Sir Edmund Hillary, the first man to climb Mt. Everest. Products are often given away to charities or to be won as contest prizes. In the case of some products, such as cars and computer software, the product is lent to media specialists on the topic so that they can try it and write about it.

The media are very aware of the publicity objectives of marketers, and they are sensitive to being manipulated. Therefore, they are usually very careful about promoting performance superiority claims. Thus, independent test performance results should be supplied to them if available.

Publicity and public relations management are closely associated, but there are some distinct differences. **Public relations management** is "*the management function that evaluates public attitudes, identifies the policies and procedures of an organization with the public interest, and executes a program of action (and communication) to earn public understanding and acceptance.*"[22] Public relations is usually more focussed on overall company image than on a particular product.

Furthermore, as the definition implies, it is a business function that *monitors* public attitudes. Thus it is *proactive* rather than *reactive*. After assessing the public's attitude and perceptions about the company, the public relations manager communicates with management to bring about any necessary organizational change, and then communicates this to the public through advertising and the publicity methods already discussed. Public relations is also used to soften negative publicity that might arise from possible faults in company performance that could affect consumers' willingness to buy the company's products.

public relations management
The management function that evaluates public attitudes, identifies the policies and procedures of an organization with the public interest, and executes a program of action (and communication) to earn public understanding and acceptance.

Celebrity Marketing and Role Model Marketing

Wayne Gretzky is a well-known hockey player whose name is associated with several different products. Many companies believe that **celebrity marketing** — *having celebrities lend their name and influence to the promotion of a product* — is worth the cost of paying the celebrity for his or her endorsement of the product. These marketers feel that there will be a positive association between the public acceptance of the celebrity and the acceptance of their product.

While the risk is perhaps not too great, if the celebrity falls out of favour, the company will have to try to quickly dissociate itself from that person. This happened to Hertz when O.J. Simpson was accused of murdering his ex-wife.

Celebrity marketing can be expensive. Nora beverages of Mirabel, Quebec, uses role model marketing instead. **Role model marketing** *associates a product with the posi-*

celebrity marketing
Having celebrities lend their name and influence to the promotion of a product.

role model marketing
Marketing technique that associates a product with the positive perception of a type of individual or a role.

tive perception of a type of individual or a role. Nora sells its Naya brand bottled water in almost 3000 vending machines across North America. In one campaign, it placed 40 machines along Los Angeles County beaches — an unusual locale for the units. The company also donated $185 000 to help operate these beaches. In exchange, the company was allowed to advertise on lifeguard stands ("Naya — made when the world was still pure") and put its logo on the time and temperature blackboards. The role model association here is with 150 healthy-looking lifeguards. Lifeguards are held in high esteem — they take care of their bodies and it is assumed that they are concerned about nutrition.[23] As the cost of celebrity marketing increases and the availability of suitable celebrities decreases, role model marketing is a useful alternative.

SALES PROMOTION

Sales promotion is another type of nonpersonal selling. It does not have as high a profile as some other marketing communications activities, but is extremely important. As advertising media become more cluttered with competing messages, marketers are turning to an increased use of sales promotion. A study of marketing communications expenses of Canadian packaged goods companies showed that sales promotion accounted for about half as much as advertising expenditures.[24] As we learned in Chapter 17, sales promotion may be defined as those marketing activities that focus specifically on stimulating consumer purchasing at the point of sale, and improving dealer effectiveness. It includes such activities as point-of-purchase advertising; specialty advertising; samples, coupons, and premiums; loyalty points; deals; rebates; and contests. More than one of these options may be used in a single promotional strategy, but probably no promotional strategy has ever used all the options in a single program. While they are not mutually exclusive, sales promotion methods are generally employed on a selective basis.

Sales promotion techniques may be used by all members of a marketing channel — manufacturers, wholesalers, and retailers — and are typically targeted at specific markets. For example, a manufacturer such as Texize Corporation might combine trial sample mailings of a new spot remover to consumers with a sales contest for wholesalers and retailers who handle the new product. In both instances, the sales promotion techniques are designed to supplement and extend the other elements of the firm's promotional mix.

Point-of-Purchase Advertising

Displays and demonstrations that seek to promote the product at a time and place closely associated with the actual decision to buy are called **point-of-purchase advertising**. The in-store promotion of consumer goods is a common example. Such advertising can be extremely useful in carrying forward a theme developed in another element of promotional strategy. A life-sized display of a celebrity used in television advertising, for instance, can become a realistic in-store display. Displays also serve as an effective attention-getter and reminder.

point-of-purchase advertising
Displays and demonstrations that seek to promote the product at a time and place closely associated with the actual decision to buy.

Specialty Advertising

Specialty advertising is a *sales promotion medium that utilizes useful articles to carry the advertiser's name, address, and advertising message* to reach target customers.[25] The

specialty advertising
Sales promotion medium that utilizes useful articles to carry the advertiser's name, address, and advertising message.

origin of specialty advertising has been traced to the Middle Ages, when wooden pegs bearing the names of artisans "were given to prospects to be driven into their walls and to serve as a convenient place upon which to hang armour."[26]

Examples of contemporary advertising specialties carrying a firm's name include calendars, pencils, pens, paperweights, matchbooks, personalized business gifts of modest value, pocket diaries, shopping bags, memo pads, balloons, measuring sticks, key rings, glasses, and hundreds of other items.

Samples, Coupons, Premiums, Deals, Rebates, and Loyalty Programs

The distribution of samples, coupons, and premiums is probably the best-known sales promotion technique. *Sampling* involves free distribution of an item in an attempt to obtain consumer acceptance. This may be done on a door-to-door basis, by mail, through demonstrations, or as an insertion into packages containing other products. Sampling is especially useful in promoting new products.

Coupons offer a discount, usually some specified price reduction, from the next purchase of a product. Coupons are readily redeemable with retailers, who also receive an additional handling fee. Mail, magazine, newspaper, package insertion, and in-store displays are standard methods of distributing coupons.[27]

Premiums, bonus items given free with the purchase of another product, have proven effective in getting consumers to try a new product or a different brand.[28] Service stations, for example, use glassware, ice scrapers, and beach balls to convince noncustomers to try their brand. Premiums are also used to encourage response to direct-marketing offers. The value of premium giveaways runs into millions of dollars each year.

Deals to consumers are price reductions designed to encourage trial of a product or to counteract a competitor's promotion. Deals are also commonly used to encourage retailers to stock enough merchandise. For example, Old Dutch might offer retailers one free case of potato chips with every dozen purchased. The retailers then benefit from selling this "100 percent profit" case of chips. The manufacturer also gains because the deal has encouraged retailers to stock lots of product. Deals are short-term in nature.

Rebates have several uses. In some cases, they are used to encourage consumers to purchase. For example, Kodak offered a $4 rebate to consumers who purchased a package of five films. The consumer was required to mail in a form and proof of purchase. Rebates are also used to induce channel member loyalty to a manufacturer. A carpet manufacturer keeps track of the number of metres of carpeting sold by a retailer during the year, and provides a rebate of 25, 35, or 40 cents per metre depending on whether the retailer sold up to one of three preset targets.

loyalty program
A program that gives rewards such as points or free air miles with each purchase in order to stimulate repeat business.

Loyalty programs stimulate repeat purchases. Similar in concept to rebates, some businesses assign points, based on value, to every purchase. The points are automatically posted by computer after each purchase. After a customer has accumulated a certain number of points, they may be used to purchase products. Zellers Club Z points are an outstanding example. Club Z now has 7.9 million members and an incredible reach of 65 percent of all Canadian households.[29] The introduction of Club Z points was a major factor in making Zellers one of the leading retailers in the country. Airline companies such as Canadian and Air Canada have also created a great deal of loyalty with their frequent-flyer air-mile programs.

Contests

Firms may sponsor contests to attract additional customers, offering substantial cash or merchandise prizes to call attention to their products. A company might consider employing a specialist in developing this type of sales promotion because of the variety and complexity of schemes available.

Trade Shows

A small machinist company in central Manitoba invented a machine to hold, dispense, and measure heavy rolls of carpeting. This was an excellent product with worldwide potential. How should this firm, having little marketing experience, no sales force, and no international experience, distribute its product? A series of trade shows was the answer. This resulted in sales and interested dealerships in several different countries.

A **trade show** is *an organized exhibition of products based on a central theme.* The theme might be Canadian manufactured products, agricultural products, or toys, for example. The trade show is held in a centre that is accessible to buyers and runs for a specified number of days. Each exhibiter rents display space and has personnel available to answer questions. Trade shows are organized by trade associations, businesses, and governments (to promote products in another country). For example, the Canadian government organizes an annual trade show of Canadian agricultural machinery in Dubbo, Australia. It also organizes the rental of enough space for several Canadian companies that might be interested in joining to form a Canadian presence at other trade shows.

trade show
An organized exhibition of products based on a central theme.

PERSONAL SELLING

Personal selling was defined in Chapter 17 as a seller's promotional presentation conducted on a person-to-person basis with the buyer. Selling is an inherent function of any business enterprise. Accounting, engineering, personnel management, and other organizational activities are useless unless the firm's product can be sold to someone. Thousands of sales employees bear witness to the importance of selling in the Canadian economy. While advertising expenses in the average firm may represent from 1 to 3 percent of total sales, selling expenses are likely to equal 10 to 15 percent of sales. In many firms, personal selling is the single largest marketing expense.

As Chapter 17 pointed out, personal selling is likely to be the primary component of a firm's marketing communications mix when customers are concentrated geographically; when orders are large; when the products or services are expensive, technically complex, and require special handling; when trade-ins are involved; when channels are short; and when the number of potential customers is relatively small.

In instances where personal selling is the primary component of a firm's marketing mix, advertising may be used in a support role to assist the salespeople. Much of Avon's advertising is aimed at assisting the neighbourhood salesperson by strengthening the image of Avon, its products, and its salespeople. Table 18.5 summarizes the factors affecting personal selling's importance in the overall marketing communications mix.

■ Table 18.5 **Factors Affecting the Importance of Personal Selling in the Promotional Mix**

	Personal Selling Is Likely to Be More Important When:	**Advertising Is Likely to Be More Important When:**
Consumer is	geographically concentrated, relatively small numbers	geographically dispersed, relatively large numbers
Product is	expensive, technically complex, custom-made, special handling required, trade-ins frequently involved	inexpensive, simple to understand, standardized, no special handling, no trade-ins
Price is	relatively high	relatively low
Channels are	relatively short	relatively long

CATEGORIES OF SELLING

The sales job has evolved into a professional occupation. Today's salesperson is more concerned with helping customers select the correct product to meet their needs than with simply selling whatever is available. Modern professional salespeople advise and assist customers in their purchase decisions. Where repeat purchases are common, the salesperson must be certain that the buyer's purchases are in his or her best interest, or else no future sales will be made. The interests of the seller are tied to those of the buyer.

Not all sales activities are alike. While all sales activities assist the customer in some manner, the exact tasks that are performed vary from one position to another. Three basic types of selling can be identified: (1) order processing, (2) creative selling, and (3) missionary sales.

Most sales jobs do not fall into any single category. Instead, we often find salespeople performing all three types of selling to a certain extent. A sales engineer for a computer firm may be doing 50 percent missionary sales, 45 percent creative selling, and 5 percent order processing. In other words, most sales jobs require their incumbents to engage in a variety of sales activities. However, most selling jobs are classified on the basis of the primary selling task that is performed. We shall examine each of these categories.

Order Processing

order processing
Selling at the wholesale and retail levels; involves identifying customer needs, pointing out these needs to the customer, and completing the order.

Order processing is most often typified by selling at the wholesale and retail levels. Salespeople who handle this task must do the following:

1. *Identify customer needs:* For instance, a soft-drink route salesperson determines that a store that normally carries inventory of 40 cases has only 7 cases left in stock.
2. *Point out the needs to the customer:* The route salesperson informs the store manager of the inventory situation.

3. *Complete (or write up) the order:* The store manager acknowledges the situation; the driver unloads 33 cases; the manager signs the delivery slip.

Order processing is part of most selling jobs and becomes the primary task whereby needs can be readily identified and then acknowledged by the customer. Selling life insurance usually requires more than simple order processing. However, one insurance company reported that during a period of civil unrest in Belfast, Northern Ireland, one of its representatives, Danny McNaughton, sold 208 new personal-accident income-protection policies in a week. McNaughton averaged one sale every twelve minutes of his working day.[30] Apparently, the need for insurance was readily recognized in Belfast.

Creative Selling

When a considerable degree of analytical decision making on the part of the consumer is involved in purchasing a product, the salesperson must skilfully solicit an order from a prospect. To do so, creative selling techniques must be used. New products often require a high degree of **creative selling**. The seller *must make the buyer see the worth of the item.* Creative selling may be the most demanding of the three selling tasks.

creative selling
Selling that involves making the buyer see the worth of the item.

Missionary Selling

Missionary selling is an indirect type of selling; people *sell the good will of a firm and provide customers with technical or operational assistance.* For example, a toiletries company salesperson may call on retailers to look after special promotions and overall stock movement, although a wholesaler is used to take orders and deliver merchandise. In more recent times, technical and operational assistance, such as that provided by a systems specialist, have also become a critical part of missionary selling.

missionary selling
Selling that emphasizes selling the firm's good will and providing customers with technical or operational assistance.

CHARACTERISTICS OF SUCCESSFUL SALESPEOPLE

The saying "Salespeople are born, not made" is untrue. Most people have some degree of sales ability. Each of us is called upon to sell others our ideas, philosophy, or personality at some time. However, some individuals adapt to selling more easily than others. Selling is not an easy job; it involves a great deal of hard work. Many college and university graduates find it to be an extremely rewarding and challenging career.

Effective salespeople are self-motivated individuals who are well prepared to meet the demands of the competitive marketplace. The continuing pressure to solve buyers' problems requires that salespeople develop good work habits and exhibit considerable initiative.

Successful sales representatives are not only self-starters, they are also knowledgeable businesspeople. Salespeople are also in the peculiar position of having their knowledge tested almost continually, so sales success is often a function of how well a salesperson can handle questions. Salespeople must know their company, their products, their competition, their customers, and themselves. They must also be able to analyze customer needs and fit them with products and services that satisfy those requirements.

THE SALES PROCESS

The sales process involves seven steps. While the terminology may vary, most authorities agree on the following sequence:

1. Prospecting and qualifying
2. Approach
3. Presentation
4. Demonstration
5. Handling objections
6. Closing
7. Follow-up

Prospecting and Qualifying

prospecting
Identifying potential customers.

Prospecting — *identifying potential customers* — is difficult work that often involves many hours of diligent effort. Prospects may come from many sources: previous customers, friends and neighbours, other vendors, nonsales employees in the firm, suppliers, and social and professional contacts. New sales personnel often find prospecting frustrating, since there is usually no immediate payoff. But without prospecting, there are no future sales. Prospecting is a continuous process because there will always be a loss of some customers over time, a loss that must be compensated for by the emergence of new customers or the discovery of potential customers who have never been contacted. Many sales management experts consider prospecting to be the very essence of the sales process.

qualifying
Determining that the prospect is really a potential customer.

Qualifying — *determining that the prospect is really a potential customer* — is another important sales task. Not all prospects are qualified to become customers. Qualified customers are people with both the money and the authority to make purchase decisions.[31] A person with an annual income of $25 000 may wish to own a $100 000 house, but this person's ability to actually become a customer must be questioned.

Approach

approach
The initial contact between the salesperson and the prospective customer.

Once the salesperson has identified a qualified prospect, he or she collects all available information relative to the potential buyer and plans an **approach** — *the initial contact between the salesperson and the prospective customer*. All approaches should be based on comprehensive research. The salesperson should find out as much as possible about the prospect and the environment in which the prospect operates.

Presentation

presentation
The act of giving the sales message to a prospective customer.

When the salesperson *gives the sales message to a prospective customer*, he or she makes a **presentation**. The seller describes the product's major features, points out its strengths, and concludes by citing illustrative successes.[32] The seller's objective is to talk about the product or service in terms that are meaningful to the buyer — that is, to discuss benefits rather than technical specifications. Thus, the presentation is

APPLYING THE CONCEPTS

The Real Job of Selling

The term *salesperson* all too often conjures up unpleasant visions. But the tasks of the modern salesperson are so different and so complex. Take, for example, the case of Louis J. Manara, a superb salesperson employed by American Cyanamid. The changes that have occurred in Manara's job were depicted in a *Fortune* article as follows:

> When Manara began selling chemicals for Cyanamid, the job was relatively straightforward. The salesman was assigned a territory and dispatched to tap every possible customer. He was told little about his division's goals, nothing about the profitability of his bag of products. His marching orders were uncomplicated: sell all you can, as fast as you can.
>
> But in the past decade the salesperson's job has become vastly more complex — so much so that a number of executives believe a new job title is required. "Salesman is just too narrow a word," says one marketing manager. Gordon Sterling, Manara's division president, pinpoints the basic change. "Ten years ago, it was sales, sales, sales," he says. "Now we tell our salespeople: don't just sell — we need information. What do our customers need? What is the competition doing? What sort of financial package do we need to win the order?"
>
> Probing for market intelligence is not the only new duty. Manara is also expected to mediate disputes between Cyanamid's credit department, newly vigilant in these times of costly money, and slow-paying customers. He has to sort out customer complaints concerning Cyanamid products. He must keep abreast of fast changes in both government regulations and world chemical markets.
>
> In brief, the sales representative's job requires applying informed management skills to solving customers' problems.

Source: Hugh D. Menzies, "The New Life of a Salesman," *Fortune* (August 11, 1980), p. 173. © 1980 Time Inc. All rights reserved. Reprinted with permission.

What do you think has led to this change in the selling job?

the stage where the salesperson relates product features to customer needs. The presentation should be clear and concise, and should emphasize the positive.

Demonstration

Demonstration can play a critical role in a sales presentation. A demonstration ride in a new automobile allows the prospect to become involved in the presentation. It awakens customer interest in a way no amount of verbal presentation can. Demonstrations supplement, support, and reinforce what the sales representative has already told the prospect. The key to a good demonstration is planning. A unique demonstration is more likely to gain a customer's attention than a "usual" sales presentation. But such a demonstration must be well planned and executed if a favourable impression is to be made. One cannot overemphasize the need for the salesperson to check and recheck all aspects of the demonstration before delivering it.

Handling Objections

A vital part of selling involves handling objections. It is reasonable to expect a customer to say, "Well, I really should check with my family," or "Perhaps I'll stop back next week," or "I like everything except the colour." A good salesperson, however, should use each objection as a cue to provide additional information to the prospect. In most cases, an objection such as "I don't like the bucket seats" is really the prospect's way of asking what other choices or product features are available. A customer's question reveals an interest in the product. It allows the seller an opportunity to expand a presentation by providing additional information.

Closing

closing
The act of asking the prospect for an order.

The moment of truth in selling is the **closing**, for this is when the salesperson *asks the prospect for an order*. A sales representative should not hesitate during the closing. If he or she has made an effective presentation, based on applying the product to the customer's needs, the closing should be the natural conclusion.

A surprising number of salespeople have a hard time actually asking for an order. But to be effective, they must overcome this difficulty.

Follow-up

follow-up
The postsales activities that often determine whether a person will become a repeat customer.

The *postsales activities that often determine whether a person will become a repeat customer* constitute the sales **follow-up**. To the maximum extent possible, sales representatives should contact their customers to find out if they are satisfied with their purchases. This step allows the salesperson to psychologically reinforce the buyer's original decision to buy. It gives the seller an opportunity, in addition to correcting any sources of discontent with the purchase, to secure important market information and to make additional sales. Automobile dealers often keep elaborate records on their previous customers. This allows them to remind individuals when they might be due for a new car. One successful travel agency never fails to telephone customers on their return from a trip. Proper follow-up is a logical part of the selling sequence.

Managing the Sales Effort

sales management
Securing, maintaining, motivating, supervising, evaluating, and controlling the field sales force.

The selling function is made effective through **sales management**, which is defined as *securing, maintaining, motivating, supervising, evaluating, and controlling the field sales force*. The sales manager is the link between the firm and the marketplace through the sales force. The sales manager has a challenging task that involves interpreting and implementing company strategy through a diverse group of sales representatives. Similarly, since the sales force also represents the customer, the sales manager is required to represent customers' and sales representatives' needs and concerns to senior management.

The sales manager performs seven basic managerial functions: (1) recruitment and selection, (2) training, (3) organization, (4) supervision, (5) motivation, (6) compensation, and (7) evaluation and control. Each of these is an elaborate and demanding task; unfortunately, describing them in detail is beyond the scope of this book. There are many books on sales management that an interested reader can refer to.

■ KEY TERMS

product advertising
institutional advertising
informative product
   advertising
persuasive product
   advertising
reminder-oriented
   product advertising
advertising agency
co-operative advertising
comparative advertising
pretesting

post-testing
direct marketing
publicity
public relations
   management
celebrity marketing
role model marketing
point-of-purchase
   advertising
specialty advertising
loyalty program
trade show

order processing
creative selling
missionary selling
prospecting
qualifying
approach
presentation
closing
follow-up
sales management

■ INTERACTIVE SUMMARY AND DISCUSSION QUESTIONS

1. Advertising expenditures as a proportion of sales vary among different industries and companies because of the different role that advertising plays in the different marketing mixes. Rank the following industries in terms of proportionate advertising expenditures (1 = lowest proportion), and then explain your reasoning.
   _____ Soap/detergent
   _____ Chemicals
   _____ Restaurant
2. Advertising is the most important component in the marketing mix for positioning a product. An object can be positioned by attributes, price/quality, competitor, application, product user, and product class. Give an example of each.
3. There are four basic types of advertising: informative product advertising, persuasive product advertising, reminder-oriented product advertising, and institutional advertising. What type of advertising would you recommend for Ford Motor Company? For Compaq computers? For Mohawk gas? Explain your reasoning.
4. Television is the second-largest advertising medium. Television advertising can be divided into three categories: network, national spot, and local spot. When would each be used, and who would be the likely users?
5. "The final step in the advertising process is the development and preparation of an advertisement." Outline the earlier steps.
6. Co-operative advertising involves the sharing of advertising costs between the retailer and the manufacturer. Develop an argument favouring *or* opposing the use of co-operative advertising by a marketer who is currently preparing an advertising plan. Make any assumptions that are necessary.
7. Comparative advertising makes direct promotional comparisons with competitive brands. Suggest a list of conditions under which a company should consider using comparative advertising.

8. The famous advertiser William Bernbach said about advertising, "You must crash through the wall." Explain and elaborate the meaning of this statement.

9. Direct marketing is an interactive system of marketing that uses one or more advertising media to effect a measurable response or transaction at any location. Compare and contrast this with general advertising.

10. Publicity is generating awareness about a product beyond regular advertising methods. Discuss the advantages and limitations of using publicity.

11. Develop a plan for a publicity campaign for a newly opened dry cleaner in a strip mall near a residential neighbourhood.

12. Celebrity marketing is the process of engaging celebrities to lend their names and influence in promoting a product. Role model marketing associates a product with the positive perception of a type of individual or role. Give an example of a role model marketing campaign.

13. Sales promotion includes such activities as point-of-purchase advertising; specialty advertising; samples, coupons, premiums, deals, rebates, loyalty programs, and contests. Sales promotion seems to be growing at the expense of advertising. How can this be?

14. The three basic types of selling are order processing, creative selling, and missionary selling. Give an example of each.

15. The expression "Salespeople are born, not made" is untrue. Explain why.

16. The sales process involves seven steps: prospecting and qualifying, approach, presentation, demonstration, handling objections, closing, and follow-up. Distinguish between the sales process and a sales call.

PART EIGHT

Additional Marketing Management Considerations

Thus far, this book has dealt with the fundamental components of marketing. The reader may see the coverage as having been extensive, but there are many other important aspects of marketing. The chapters in this final section introduce three of them. Chapter 19 discusses the application of marketing in the international environment. Chapter 20 illustrates that marketing can be applied to not-for-profit organizations such as charities, religious groups, associations, and government organizations.

The final chapter reiterates a theme introduced in Chapter 1: the focus of marketing planning and implementation should be the consumer. Today's competitive environment requires that the management and implementation of every facet of the marketing program must go far beyond "adequate." A fervent commitment to total customer satisfaction is a requirement for long-term success, and the company's progress toward this goal must be carefully monitored.

CHAPTER 19

Global Marketing

CHAPTER OBJECTIVES

1. To introduce some of the fundamental concepts that underlie international business.
2. To identify aspects of marketing strategy that are of importance in the global marketplace.
3. To outline the environment for international business.
4. To consider the marketing mix in the light of competition in a global environment.
5. To illustrate the importance of trading blocs.
6. To outline various approaches to global marketing taken by companies.

Glegg Water Conditioning Inc.'s equipment can make water so pure you shouldn't drink it. If you tried, it would soon be drawing particles from the lining of your stomach.

As unappetizing as that sounds, such pure water is the steady diet of factories around the world making everything from computer chips to insulin, and more of them each year are buying purification systems from privately owned Glegg in Guelph, Ontario.

Started in 1978 by a 26-year-old with $15 000, the company's annual sales have steadily climbed to an estimated $53 million this year. More than 96 percent of them are outside of Canada. "We've never focused on the Canadian market," founding company president Robert Glegg says, "Never."

Instead, Glegg has treated the United States and Canada as one market, and in a deliberate fashion established itself as a leader in supplying equipment to several sectors such as semiconductor manufacturing and power generation.

"Some of the major competitors that Glegg has down here just had unique problems and have created opportunities for Robert's shark-like tendencies to clean their clock, which he has," says Harold Novick, a New Jersey-based consultant who has advised Glegg on its sales network and once ran one of its U.S. competitors in the early 1980s.

Glegg hasn't been afraid to look overseas either. Of 1993 sales, 10 percent were in Latin America and 5 percent in Asia. The company's goal is to make 70 percent of its sales in off-shore markets. "We need volume, and there's only so much volume domestically."

Ordinarily tap water may be fine for human consumption, but minerals and other contaminants in it can eventually gum up boiler works or make pharmaceuticals lethal. For such customers as computer-chip makers, Glegg's systems reduce impurities in water to levels as low as 20 parts per trillion.

Water purified to that extent becomes a solution so low in concentration — in a sense, empty — that it will try to draw compounds from anything it touches in order to reach an equilibrium with its environment.

Glegg has built its international sales on a network of independent manufacturing representative organizations, which now number 42. The reps work entirely on commission and Glegg is usually one of a handful of compatible companies they represent in a specific geographic area such as a U.S. state. The reps, which aim to sell to a specific industry and area over the long term, provide Glegg with local contacts and a thorough understanding of area businesses, but at no cost if a sale isn't made.

Glegg backs up that network with eight salaried sales executives who are spread across North America and Europe. The company also relies on its executives travelling extensively to meet customers face to face.

"From our perspective, you have to be there," says Mark Huehnergard, Glegg's vice-president and general manager of its high-purity business group.

The international market has provided the opportunity for Glegg to be successful, and to grow. The company has benefited because it quickly understood the many possibilities that are available. It accepted the risks of going international, and is now reaping the rewards.[1]

INTRODUCTION

International trade is vital to a nation and its business for several reasons. International business expands the market for a country's or firm's products and thus makes possible further production and distribution economies. An added benefit to an exporting firm with global trade experience is that it can compete more effectively with foreign competitors who enter this market at a later date. Furthermore, international involvement will be the only way many firms can survive in the competitive world marketplace. Global marketing can also mean more jobs at home. It is estimated that some 30 000 to 40 000 new jobs are supported by every billion export dollars.

Some Canadian companies are heavily dependent on their ability to sell their products abroad. For manufacturers like General Motors, MacMillan Bloedel, Alberta and Southern Gas, and others, the majority of sales dollars come from customers in other countries. Many smaller companies have also discovered the value of selling into international markets. Indeed, some companies, like high-tech Seastar Optics of Sidney, BC, would find it difficult to survive without international sales. For such companies, the Canadian market may not even be large enough for their specialized products.

Business is now international. Whether you are a farmer, a small local retailer, a wholesaler, or one of the established Canadian telephone companies, you will be affected by global competition. International goods, services, and competitors are found in virtually every aspect of the Canadian (and every other country's) economy. In the development of business strategy, this international dimension must be as carefully considered as the domestic environment.

Some 2 million Canadians — 1 in 5 of the labour market — work in areas directly or indirectly related to export trade. Thus, there is a good chance that every single Canadian has a close connection with export trade through family or friends. Thirty cents of every dollar of our gross national product (GNP) comes from our exports.

Our exports pay for the things we import to meet our high standard of living expectations — our morning orange juice, fresh vegetables in winter, wool and cotton clothes, TV sets, some cars, and some computers. On another level, exports also pay for the interest and dividends on foreign investment, for the deficit on tourism, for access to foreign technologies, and for the borrowing that different levels of government use to finance our economic development.[2]

In other words, foreign trade is important to Canada from both the *exporting* and the *importing* viewpoints. International trade is more important to the economy of some countries than others. Countries such as the United Kingdom, Belgium, the Scandinavian countries, and New Zealand are heavily dependent on international trade. On the other hand, although the United States is both the largest exporter and the largest importer in the world, its exports account for only about 7.7 percent of its gross national product. Compare this to the percentages for Belgium (46 percent) and West Germany (23 percent). Canadian exports account for about 30 percent of our GNP. Canada's leading trading partners are shown in Table 19.1. The United States is clearly our chief trading partner, supplying about 70.7 percent of our imports and buying about 77.6 percent of our exports.

There are both similarities and differences between international and domestic marketing. This chapter examines characteristics of the global marketplace, environmental influences on marketing, and the development of an international marketing mix.

MEASURING A COUNTRY'S INTERNATIONAL TRADE ACTIVITY

Since imports and exports are important contributors to a country's economic welfare, governments and other organizations are concerned about the status of various components of international marketing. The concepts of balance of trade and balance of payments are a good starting point for understanding international business.

■ Table 19.1 **Growth in Exports and Imports of Canada's Major Trading Partners, January–August 1994/95[1]**

	Export Value		Import Value	
	% Change Jan–Aug/94 to Jan–Aug/95	$ Million Jan–Aug/95	% Change Jan–Aug/94 to Jan–Aug/95	$ Million Jan–Aug/95
United States	+18.3	133 620	+15.8	111 887
Japan	+25.0	7 806	+11.6	5 961
European Union	+39.2	9 702	+30.3	13 930
Other OECD Countries[2]	−3.2	2 417	+28.3	5 422
All other countries	+32.9	12 652	+3.9	13 794
Total	**+20.3**	**166 197**	**+16.1**	**150 994**

[1] Seasonally adjusted.

[2] Includes Australia, Iceland, Mexico, New Zealand, Norway, Switzerland, and Turkey.

Source: Statistics Canada, *The Daily* (October 18, 1995), Catalogue No. 11-001E, p. 4. Reproduced by permission of the Minister of Supply and Services Canada.

Balance of Trade

A nation's **balance of trade** is determined by *the relationship between a country's exports and its imports*. A favourable balance of trade (trade surplus) occurs when the value of a nation's exports exceeds its imports. This means that, other things being equal, new money would come into the country's economic system via the sales abroad of the country's products. An unfavourable balance of trade (trade deficit), by contrast, results when imports exceed exports. The net money flow then would be outward, other things being equal. On the whole, Canada has maintained a favourable balance of trade (see Figure 19.1).

balance of trade
The relationship between a country's exports and its imports.

Balance of Payments

A country's balance of trade plays a vital role in determining its **balance of payments**, *the flow of money into or out of a country*. However, other factors are also important. A favourable balance of payments indicates that there is a net money inflow; an unfavourable balance of payments means that there is a net money outflow from the country.

The balance of payments is also affected by such factors as tourism, interest on foreign borrowings, military expenditures abroad, investment abroad, and foreign aid. A money outflow caused by these factors may exceed the money inflow from a favourable balance of trade and leave a nation with an unfavourable balance of payments.

balance of payments
The flow of money into or out of a country.

■ Figure 19.1 **Canada's Exports, Imports, and Trade Balance***

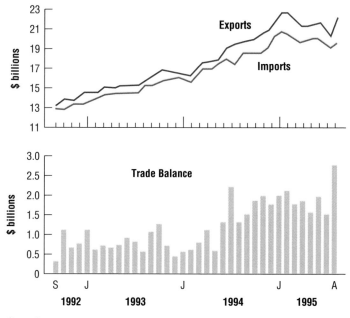

* Seasonally adjusted.

Source: Statistics Canada, *The Daily* (October 18, 1995), Catalogue No. 11-001E. Reproduced by permission of the Minister of Supply and Services Canada.

In recent years, Canada has had an unfavourable balance of payments, even when the nation had a favourable balance of trade. Foreign travel and interest on foreign borrowings have contributed to this situation.

Exchange Rate Adjustments

exchange rate
The rate at which a nation's currency can be exchanged for other currencies or gold.

When the real value of a currency is out of line with international currencies in terms of relative buying power, the **exchange rate**, *the rate at which a nation's currency can be exchanged for other currencies or gold*, may change. (See the discussion of the hamburger standard in the accompanying box for an unusual but practical example.) Some countries try to fix the exchange rate. In Canada we have a floating rate. Fluctuations in the exchange rate have a significant impact on both the balance of trade and the balance of payments. Because of this, government policy may lead to efforts to stem significant fluctuations by buying or selling foreign — that is, U.S. — currency.

devaluation
Situation in which a nation reduces the value of its currency in relation to gold or some other currency.

Devaluation occurs *when a nation reduces the value of its currency in relation to gold or some other currency.* Devaluation of the dollar has the effect of making Canadian

---

APPLYING THE CONCEPTS

A Practical Measure of the Rate of Exchange: *The Economist*'s "Hamburger Standard"

It is time to update our McDonald's hamburger standard. We launched it three years ago as a ready reckoner of whether currencies are at their correct exchange rates. Big-Mac watchers rely on the theory of purchasing-power parity (PPP), which argues that in the long run the exchange rate between two currencies is "in equilibrium" (i.e., at PPP) when it equalizes the prices of a basket of similar goods and services in both countries.

Our basket is just a Big Mac. The burger's virtue is that it is produced locally with little change in recipe in 50 countries. So international-distribution costs are not the distorting factor which they would be if we used, say, the price of [*The Economist*] in different countries, as a few readers have suggested.

However, we have made one change. A year ago our estimates of the dollar's Mac-PPPs were based on the New York price of a hamburger. We have now found that the price of a Big Mac varies much more in America than within other countries. The recommended American price before tax is $1.55; in central Manhattan our correspondent had to fork out a top-of-the-range $2.48 ($2.29 before tax). So this time we have used the average post-tax price in four American cities — $2.02.

In Tokyo a Big Mac costs ¥370. Dividing this by the dollar price yields a Mac-PPP of $1 = ¥183, compared with a current exchange rate of ¥133. In other words, the dollar is undervalued by 27 percent. The dollar is also 11 percent undervalued against the D-mark, which has a Mac-PPP of DM2.13, but it is almost spot on against sterling. This in turn implies that the pound's PPP against the D-mark is DM3.44 — i.e., its actual rate is 7 percent too low. British manufacturers thus have little need to squeal. Mr. Nigel Lawson, the chancellor of the exchequer, can safety aim for a stronger pound. In contrast to sterling, most of the EMS currencies, like the French franc and the lira, look overvalued against the D-mark.

(continued)

Big MacCurrencies

Currency	Hamburger Prices* in Local Currency	Implied PPP** of the Dollar	Actual Exchange Rate 11/04/89	% Over (+) or Under (−) Valuation of the Dollar
Australia	A $2.10	1.04	1.24	+19
Belgium	BFr 90	45	39.5	−12
Britain	£1.26	0.62	0.59	−5
Canada	C $2.15	1.06	1.19	+13
Denmark	DKr 24.75	12.3	7.33	−40
France	FFr 17.70	8.76	6.37	−27
Holland	FL 5.10	2.52	2.13	−15
Hong Kong	Hk $7.60	3.76	7.78	+107
Ireland	IR £1.30	0.64	0.71	+11
Italy	Lire 3300	1634	1382	−15
Japan	¥370	183	133	−27
Singapore	S $2.80	1.39	1.96	+41
South Korea	Won 2400	1188	666	−44
Spain	Ptas 280	139	117	−16
Sweden	SKr 21	10.4	6.41	−38
United States***	$2.02	—	—	—
West Germany	DM 4.30	2.13	1.89	−11
Yugoslavia	Dinar 7000	3465	9001	+160

* Prices may vary between branches
** Purchasing-power parity: foreign price divided by dollar price
*** Average of New York, Chicago, San Francisco, and Atlanta

Source: McDonald's.

The currencies of Hongkong and Singapore still look too cheap against the dollar — one reason that America's trade deficit remains huge. But Mac-PPPs do not support Washington's call for South Korea to continue to upvalue its currency. The dollar appears to be 44 percent undervalued against the won. Indeed, Seoul has the dearest Big Macs in our sample. American Big-Mac watchers should focus their attention closer to home: Big Macs are 12 percent dearer in the United States than in its leading trade partner, Canada — i.e., the American dollar needs to fall against the Canadian one.

Source: "The Hamburger Standard," *The Economist* (April 15, 1989), p. 86. © 1989 The Economist Newspaper Ltd. Reprinted with permission.

products less expensive abroad and trips to Canada cheaper for foreign visitors. On the other hand, imports are more expensive. As a result, cross-border shopping becomes much less attractive. **Revaluation**, a less typical case, occurs *when a country adjusts the value of its currency upward*. Either of these actions may force firms to modify their world marketing strategies. In the mid-1990s, the Canadian dollar lost value compared with most major world currencies.

revaluation
Situation in which a country adjusts the value of its currency upward.

GLOBAL MARKETING: SOME BASIC CONCEPTS

The Pacific island republic of Nauru has only a few thousand people but has one of the richest deposits of phosphate in the world. Australia has vast grazing lands, while Hong Kong's 4.1 million people are crowded into a small area that has become one of the most urbanized territories in the world. Hong Kong is a world trader in its own right as well as a source of foreign exchange for the People's Republic of China through its handling many of China's goods. Kuwait has rich oil fields but few other industries or resources. Should these countries try to diversify their product base in order to increase their self-sufficiency?

These situations lead to arguments that nations are usually better off if they specialize in certain products or marketing activities. By doing what they do best, nations are able to exchange the products not needed domestically for foreign-made goods that are needed. Nauru could attempt to develop a tourist trade, but it has opted for specializing in phosphate mining. This allows a higher standard of living than would be possible through diversified business enterprises.

On the other hand, if "specialization" means selling nonrenewable resources, a country could find itself without a specialty and have a devastating balance of trade when these resources diminish. For example, Canada has quite a high volume of trade with Japan and maintains a positive balance of trade with that country. The problem for Canada is that it sells Japan mostly raw materials (coal, wood, pulp, softwood lumber, precious metals, fish, and wheat) while importing manufactured goods (cars, computers, telecommunications equipment, and photographic products). The challenge is to expand exports of finished goods that create more jobs at home.

Specialization by countries sometimes produces odd situations. A classic example occurred when Britain's Conservative Party issued T-shirts with the party slogan "Put Britain First." Later, it was discovered that the T-shirts were made in Portugal.[3] Similarly, a number of "Buy Canadian" stickers can be found on the rear bumpers of Subarus and Toyotas.

An understanding of the concepts of absolute and comparative advantage is important to the study of global trade. These concepts explain why all countries can benefit from trade. A nation has an **absolute advantage** in the marketing of a product if it *is the sole producer of or can produce the product for less than anyone else.* Since few nations are sole producers and economic conditions rapidly alter production costs, examples of absolute advantage are rare.

The concept of **comparative advantage**, although a bit complicated, explains why it is beneficial for all nations to trade with one another. Comparative advantage is a *relative* concept. In *comparison with* Nation B, what goods should Nation A trade?

Nation A should produce and trade those products that it can *produce more efficiently per unit of output than it can produce other products.* Thus, if Nation A produces three products, it should concentrate on producing the product that it does so most efficiently.

Nation A should also buy products that it might produce, but less efficiently, from Nation B. It should do this *even if* it could produce them more efficiently than Nation B. In total, its outputs will be maximized by concentrating on its most efficiently produced product.

Nation B has a comparative advantage in the product that it trades to Nation A because it is the one that Nation B is most efficient at producing. Trade can be beneficial to both countries regardless of absolute costs. Nations will usually produce and export those goods in which they have the greatest comparative advantage (or

absolute advantage
Advantage said to be held by a nation that is the sole producer of a product or that can produce a product for less than anyone else.

comparative advantage
Advantage said to be held by a nation that can produce a given product more efficiently per unit of output than it can produce other products.

least comparative disadvantage) and import those items in which they have the least comparative advantage (or the greatest comparative disadvantage).

Table 19.2 suggests how the comparative advantage concept works for Canada. The export commodities tend to be those in which there is a comparative advantage over the trading partners. Being an industrialized nation with ample natural resources, Canada tends to export manufactured items, such as cars and machinery, and natural resources, such as grain, wood, and ores. By contrast, countries with lower-cost labour tend to specialize in products that require a significant labour content, such as textiles, shoes, and clothing.

Of course, there are also noneconomic reasons for not specializing in certain items. Some countries refuse to specialize their productive efforts because they want to be self-sufficient. The Communist nations typically followed this pattern, to their disadvantage and downfall. It gradually became clear that it is impossible for a country to be fully self-sufficient. Trade is necessary. Still other nations adopt the self-sufficiency viewpoint only for certain commodities that they regard as important to their long-run development. Canada, for instance, has taken steps to reduce its dependence on foreign oil.

COMPETING IN THE INTERNATIONAL MARKET

While some Canadian firms have never ventured outside their own domestic market, others have discovered the challenges as well as the payoffs of marketing abroad. In some ways, marketing in Malaysia is very similar to marketing in Canada. That is, the marketing *principles* discussed in this book apply everywhere. However, the economic environment and culture often result in significant differences in the *implementation* of a marketing plan.

Market size, for example, means different things in different countries. Mexico has a population three and a half times as large as Canada's. However, its potential market for many products is quite small since the per capita income is only about $2100, compared with Canada's $13 000. Consequently, a marketer of a prestige

■ Table 19.2 **Leading Commodities in Canadian Foreign Trade**

Principal Commodity Grouping[1]	Exports ($ millions)	Imports ($ millions)
Agricultural and fishing products	12 620	9 000
Energy products	15 673	5 671
Forestry products	25 602	1 409
Industrial goods and materials	31 820	30 385
Machinery and equipment	33 810	49 739
Automotive products	41 871	34 263
Other consumer goods	4 551	17 236
Special transactions trade[2]	6 809	3 587

[1] Figures not adjusted to balance of payment basis.

[2] Mainly, these are low-valued transactions, value of repairs to equipment, and goods returned to country of origin.

Source: Statistics Canada, *The Daily* (October 18, 1995), Catalogue No. 11-001E, p. 4. Reproduced by permission of the Minister of Supply and Services Canada.

product might not be too interested in the mass market in Mexico. Nevertheless, there could well be a very profitable market niche of well-to-do customers.

Buyer Behaviour

There are many influences on buyer behaviour. Some of these, as was discussed in Chapter 2, represent various components of the external environment. In international marketing, the culture of the country is a key factor. Such cultural factors influence not only buyers, but also all business relationships.

The cultural nuances cannot be underestimated. In Japan, for instance, it is wiser not to say "no" when asked a question. When a Japanese client asks if it is possible to modify a particular product, it might be better to say "I'll think about it" or "Let me get back to you in a few days." Marketers must be careful that their marketing strategies comply with local customs, tastes, and buying practices.

Long-term relationships are very important. When, for example, Northern Telecom became the first non-Japanese telephone-equipment supplier to make a major sale to Nippon Telegraph and Telephone with a $250-million seven-year deal, it was the culmination of a four-year marketing effort. Much of this effort was "trust-building" work. The company president alone made eleven trips to Japan within a space of six months.

Economic and Societal Factors

International marketing is also affected and influenced by economic and societal factors. The economic status of some countries makes them less (or more) likely candidates for international business expansion. Nations with lower per capita income cannot afford the technical equipment necessary in an industrialized society, so they may be poor markets for expensive industrial machinery but good markets for agricultural hand tools. Wealthier countries can prove to be prime markets for the products of many Canadian industries, particularly those involved with consumer goods and advanced industrial products.

Many products have failed abroad simply because the producing firm tried to use the same marketing strategy that was successful at home. Consider an advertising strategy based primarily on the use of print media that features testimonials. Such a campaign would offer dim prospects in a less-developed nation with a high degree of illiteracy.

North American products do not always meet the needs of foreign consumers. Some products of North American automobile manufacturers have traditionally been rejected by European drivers, who complain of poor handling, high fuel consumption, and poor styling. Since an understanding of local, economic, and societal variables is not obvious to one who is used to the Canadian situation, international marketers must carefully monitor these factors in all of the markets in which they operate.

Trade Restrictions

tariff
A tax levied against products imported from abroad.

Assorted trade restrictions also affect world trade. These restrictions are most commonly expressed through tariffs. A **tariff** is *a tax levied against products imported from* *abroad.* Some tariffs are based on a set tax per unit. Others are figured on the value of the imported product. Tariffs may be classified as either revenue or protective tariffs. *Revenue tariffs* are designed to raise funds for the government. Most of the revenue of the Canadian government in the early years of Confederation came from this source. *Protective tariffs* are designed to raise the retail price of imported goods to that of similar domestic products or higher. In the past, it was believed that a country should protect its infant industries by using tariffs to keep out foreign-made products. Some foreign goods would still enter, but the addition of a high tariff payment would make the domestic products competitive. Protective tariffs are usually higher than revenue tariffs. Different interest groups argue about whether or not tariffs should be raised to protect employment and profits in domestic Canadian industry. It is debatable whether, in the long run, such a goal is obtainable through tariff protection.

The **General Agreement on Tariffs and Trade (GATT)** is *an international trade agreement to gradually lower tariffs.* GATT has sponsored eight major tariff negotiations that have reduced the overall level of tariffs by over 33 percent throughout the world. It also established systems for resolving trade disputes between countries. The latest series, the Uruguay Round, was the most difficult one in which to reach agreement. The results, however, have led to another round of tariff reductions.

There are other forms of trade restrictions. An **import quota** *sets limits on the amount of products that may be imported in a certain category.* One country may use unofficial quotas to limit imports. When Canadian hog farmers began to take over the U.S. Midwest market, U.S. officials "discovered" that Canadian meat might have certain additives that might be "harmful" and, therefore, restricted imports. The objective of import quotas is to protect local industry and employment and preserve foreign exchange. The ultimate form of a quota is an **embargo**, *a complete ban on importing a particular product.*

Foreign trade can also be regulated by exchange control through a central bank or government agency. **Exchange control** means that *firms gaining foreign exchange by exporting must sell their foreign exchange to the central bank or agency, and importers must buy foreign exchange from the same organization.* The exchange control authority can then allocate, expand, or restrict foreign exchange according to existing national policy.

Dumping — A Marketing Problem

In a battle between shoe manufacturers and retailers, Revenue Canada sided with Canadian manufacturers and imposed dumping charges on imported women's footwear from low-cost overseas producers. It was expected that between $22 million and $41 million in dumping charges would be imposed. Importers, including retailers, contend that most of the new charges will be passed on to consumers through price increases of up to 30 percent. Canadian shoe manufacturers argued that this estimate was much exaggerated.

The term **dumping** is applied to situations in which *products are sold at significantly lower prices in a foreign market than in a nation's own domestic market.* If foreign goods sell in Canada for substantially lower prices than Canadian products, the likely consequence is a loss of jobs here. National Revenue, Canada Customs and Excise Branch, investigates alleged cases of dumping. If there is a preliminary determination of dumping, the Deputy Minister submits the finding to the Anti-Dumping Tribunal. The tribunal must make an inquiry within 90 days and issue a finding as to

GATT (General Agreement on Tariffs and Trade)
An international trade agreement to gradually lower tariffs.

import quota
A limit set on the amount of products that may be imported in a certain category.

embargo
A complete ban on importing a particular product.

exchange control
Requirement that firms gaining foreign exchange by exporting must sell their foreign exchange to the central bank or agency, and importers must buy foreign exchange from the same organization.

dumping
Practice of selling products at significantly lower prices in a foreign market than a nation's own domestic market.

whether dumping is causing or likely to cause national injury to the production in Canada of like goods. This may lead to the imposition of anti-dumping duties by Customs and Excise. The tariff charge is designed to protect Canadian business and employment by raising the product's price up to what it sells for in its home market.

Some critics have argued that fear of the dumping procedure and its tariff causes many foreign markets to keep their export prices higher than would normally be the case. The result, it is argued, is higher prices for the Canadian consumer. It is likely that dumping will remain a controversial topic in international trade for some time.

Since the new Uruguay Round of GATT was finalized, there have been fears that reduced tariffs will lead to more frequent claims of dumping. These claims might be used instead of tariffs to protect domestic industries that are suffering from international competition. The new GATT treaty tried to impose more restrictions on the use of the anti-dumping mechanisms, but some observers believe that these will not be effective.[4] A new organization, the **World Trade Organization (WTO)**, will encompass the GATT structure and set rules governing trade.

World Trade Organization (WTO)
An institution established to set rules and govern world trade based on the provisions of GATT.

Political and Legal Factors

In doing business in another country, the international marketer may find that the political environment there requires some modifications in the ways of doing business. For example, China is a socialist, centrally planned economy. Companies wishing to do business there must obtain permission from several layers of government. Doing business in another country means that a company is a guest in that country. Success requires recognition of the political priorities of the host.

International relations can also affect business activities. For example, during the apartheid years in South Africa, the Canadian government, as well as others, would not allow its country's firms to do business in that country. Similarly, a trade embargo was established against the Serbs in Bosnia.

Each country has evolved a legal system that reflects the values of its culture. As in Canada, most countries have many laws that control the way business is done. For example, Malaysia has laws against cigarette advertising, but the cigarette companies have found a way around these laws by adding other products, such as clothing, to their line. Then they prominently advertise brand names such as Marlborough, ostensibly to promote the other products. A different set of rules can be found in Canada, where a third of a cigarette package must be in black and white, with the words "Smoking can kill you" printed on it.

Canadians marketing food products in the United States find that the requirements for stating the contents are different and more strict than in Canada. All commercials in the United Kingdom and Australia must be cleared in advance. In the Netherlands, ads for candy must also show a toothbrush. Some nations have **local content laws** that *specify the portion of a product that must come from domestic sources.* This may force a manufacturer to ship a product unassembled and to have the assembly done in the host country. These examples suggest that managers involved in international marketing must be well versed in legislation affecting their specific industry.

local content laws
Laws specifying the portion of a product that must come from domestic sources.

The legal environment for Canadian firms operating abroad can be divided into three dimensions:

1. Canadian law
2. International law
3. Legal requirements of host nations

CANADIAN LAW

International business is subject to various trade regulations, tax laws, and import/export requirements. One significant provision in the Competition Act exempted from anticombines laws groups of Canadian firms acting together to develop foreign markets. An example is the cartel of Canadian uranium producers, which was designed to increase prices received in international markets. The intent of allowing this is to give Canadian industry economic power equal to that possessed by foreign cartels. A **cartel** is *the monopolistic organization of a group of firms.* Companies operating under this provision must not reduce competition within Canada and must not use "unfair methods of competition." It is hard to say whether companies can co-operate internationally and remain competitive without collusion in the domestic market. Canadian law also restricts the export of certain strategic goods, such as military hardware, to certain countries.

cartel
The monopolistic organization of a group of firms.

INTERNATIONAL LAW

International law can be found in the treaties, conventions, and agreements that exist among nations. Canada has many **friendship, commerce, and navigation (FCN) treaties**. These treaties *address many aspects of commercial relations with other countries,* such as the right to conduct business in the treaty partner's domestic market, and *constitute international law.*

Other international agreements concern international standards for various products, patents, trademarks, reciprocal tax treaties, export control, international air travel, and international communications. For example, the leading nations of the world established the International Monetary Fund, which facilitates foreign exchange transactions among nations to conduct international trade.

friendship, commerce, and navigation (FCN) treaties
Treaties that address many aspects of commercial relations with other countries; such treaties constitute international law.

LAWS OF THE HOST NATION

The legal requirements of host nations affect foreign marketers. For example, some nations limit foreign ownership in their business sectors. Global marketers obey the laws and regulations of the countries within which they operate.

CANADIAN GOVERNMENT ASSISTANCE TO EXPORTERS

Exporting is of great importance to a country. It creates jobs and helps bring about a positive balance of trade, thus making the entire economy more prosperous. Consequently, governments have active programs to help companies become more active in the global marketplace. Provincial governments provide information and guidance to businesses and even set up foreign trade offices in major markets such as Japan, Hong Kong, and Britain.

The Canadian government has trade officers in every embassy and consulate around the world. These people seek out opportunities for Canadian goods and services and send this information back to Canada. They also help Canadian businesspeople make the right contacts when travelling abroad. Furthermore, trade officers may arrange trade shows that demonstrate Canadian products. For example, in Australia, a large Canadian agricultural equipment show is held in Dubbo, a big agricultural town.

In Canada, External Affairs and International Trade Canada has trade officers in many major cities; these individuals facilitate export planning by Canadian firms and connect them with the overseas consulates. Their offices are also good sources of secondary data concerning exporting and various countries.

Moreover, through these same offices the Canadian government administers various travel support programs in the form of loans to firms needing to go to a foreign market to initiate trade. If the venture is successful, the loan must be paid back.

The Export Development Corporation (EDC) is a Canadian Crown corporation that provides financial services to Canadian exporters and foreign buyers in order to facilitate and develop export trade.[5] It does this through a wide range of insurance, guarantee, and loan services not normally provided by the private sector.

EDC services are provided for Canadian exporters who are offering competitive products in terms of price, quality, delivery and service, to help them compete internationally. Exporters in other countries have access to similar support facilities from their governments.

Canadian firms of any size can insure their export sales against nonpayment by foreign buyers. EDC facilitates this by (normally) assuming 90 percent of the commercial and political risks involving insolvency or default by the buyer, as well as blockage of funds in a foreign country. EDC will also make long-term loans to foreign buyers of Canadian capital goods and services. Funds are paid directly to Canadian suppliers on behalf of the borrower, in effect providing the exporters with cash sales. EDC policy is to achieve maximum private-sector involvement in export financing; it therefore provides 100 percent guarantees to banks and financial institutions to facilitate the exporters' banking arrangements.

THE MARKETING MIX IN THE GLOBAL SETTING

A fundamental marketing principle is that the marketing mix must be designed to meet the needs of the target market. This holds whether the marketing is done in Canada or a foreign market. Thus, depending on the international situation, some marketing elements may be relatively unchanged, whereas others require significant modification.

Some products seem to be "global" products, and virtually the same marketing mix can be used everywhere. Examples are Levi jeans, Coca-Cola®, Rolex watches, and most industrial products. In these cases, a universal comprehension of the product exists or has been developed through international media, or there are common behaviour patterns between countries. A computer is not "culture-bound," whereas a food item, or the place and method of serving it, could be very much an acquired preference moulded by culture. For example, many Germans accustomed to heavy, dark bread might find Canadian mass-produced bread unappetizing.

Adaptation is required for many products — and for managerial styles. Let us consider a few examples of adaptations to the marketing mix.

Product Decisions

Customer expectations define quality and value, and those expectations are not always the same as they are in Canada. Northern Telecom learned that lesson after it sold its SL-1 telephone answering and switching system to a large Japanese department store. Among the features of the product is one called "music on hold." Both Japanese and North American customers are familiar with this. However, familiarity

Kellogg is the world's most successful cereal company, having over half of the world's market share. Kellogg has recently opened plants in Latvia, India, and China, hoping to win millions of converts from traditional breakfasts to a North American–style breakfast.

and expectations are two very different things. The Japanese *expect* to hear music under all circumstances while waiting to be connected. The SL-1 gave them music while they waited to be connected to a particular department, but if that call was transferred to somebody else, no music would play. As a result, the Japanese callers assumed they had been disconnected and hung up. Rather than trying to reshape the listening habits of 130 million Japanese, the company redesigned its equipment to meet Japanese expectations.

Government-established product standards often differ among countries. Host-country standards obviously must be met. For example, a Canadian marketer of packaged food products must meet specific nutritional label information requirements. Similarly, electrical products must meet varying codes from country to country. Germany, for example, has very rigid requirements for products such as fax machines that are connected to the telephone system. Thus, well-known brands accepted in Canada are not allowed in Germany.

Pricing Decisions

When exporting, a cost-plus approach to pricing can quickly destroy potential opportunities. This is because more intermediaries are often required. If all these intermediaries take a standard markup based on a percentage of the cost they pay, the resulting price escalation can be so large that the product is priced out of the foreign market. This problem can be avoided by reconsidering the internal costing system, as well as whether the standard markups are necessary in this situation.

Because exchange rates fluctuate, marketers must be careful to consider whether the price that they are asking for will be enough at the time of delivery. The currency of the deal might devalue, thus possibly wiping out all profits. Because of this, a stable commonly traded currency such as U.S. dollars may be chosen as the currency of payment.

If a country has limited foreign exchange reserves, it may not be able to afford to pay for a product in foreign currency. It is sometimes necessary to think about payment in different terms. For example, Northern Telecom will sometimes agree to accept payment in kind from customers. "Deals often hinge on how willing companies are to set aside more cherished commercial practices and accept payment in the form of copper, sugar cane, bamboo, rice, or even a boatload of figs," says Alan Lytle, Northern Telecom's vice-president of marketing.

Marketing Communications

In Canada, sales representatives sometimes try to develop rapport with a client by asking about his or her family. In Saudi Arabia, this could be taken as an insult. Advertising messages also vary from country to country. In France, sexually explicit advertising is more common than in Canada, and the British tend to use more humour.

Because communication is so entwined with culture, the subtle nuances that make messages acceptable or unacceptable should be, at least, monitored by a local communicator before use. Preferably, local communicators should develop the message so that it accords with pre-established company strategy.

Distribution Decisions

Distribution is one of the major problems in developing a marketing plan for a foreign market. This is especially true if exporting. The logistics of moving products are often very complicated. Fortunately, service firms called freight forwarders specialize in distribution and can be counted on to help solve the physical distribution problem. Obviously, both the service provided and the transportation add to the cost structure and must be reflected in the price or compensated for by reducing in other costs.

Another problem is deciding which are the proper channels of distribution to use. The system may be quite different from what the Canadian marketer is accustomed to. In some countries, it may be difficult to find the necessary wholesaling intermediaries. In Japan, the opposite is true: channels of distribution normally consist of many layers of wholesalers who sell the product to others of their kind, who finally sell it to the retailer. As in the domestic market, the marketer has to solve the problem of how to persuade the channels to carry and promote the product.

From the foregoing discussion, it is clear that the marketing mix is likely to require some adaptation before success in the foreign market can be achieved. An attitude of openness and flexibility is essential. Alan Lytle, vice-president of highly successful Northern Telecom, cogently gives the reasons for success in the global market:

> If there's one word that sums up the core features of marketing . . . especially internationally, that word would be "accommodation."

Companies who desire international success must be willing to accommodate their products and marketing strategies to the needs of the customer and the attitudes and business practices of the country they're operating in, no matter how demanding they may be.

If that means having to make major and costly product modifications to meet the technical requirements and customer expectations, so be it.

If it means investing years of time and money in order to build trust and establish a presence to win that first contract, then that too has got to be done.

If it means applying a sensitive understanding of cultural behaviour, such as learning the language, then that must be done as well.

And if it means fashioning an appealing financed co-operative marketing package that maximizes the benefits of the products you sell, that must be done.

Only by embracing these kinds of value-charged initiatives can you hope to surmount the complex barriers and challenges of international marketing. Companies who do will find themselves well on the way to global competitive success. Companies who don't will sadly discover their respective customers won't care or give a fig for their work.[6]

COMPANY APPROACHES TO GLOBAL MARKETING

A variety of approaches to global marketing can be seen. Some firms do not get involved at all. Others export occasionally when an order happens to arrive from overseas or possibly when they have some excess product. Both of these could be classified as "not-committed approaches."

Among firms committed to international business, Warren Keegan has identified four different approaches to involvement in international business: ethnocentric, polycentric, regiocentric, and geocentric.[7]

A company that is **ethnocentric** *assumes that its way of doing business in its home market is the proper way to operate, and it tries to replicate this in foreign markets.* As the previous discussion has shown, such an inflexible approach is likely to severely inhibit the effectiveness of a firm's efforts in another country.

The opposite of the ethnocentric approach is the **polycentric** approach. Companies that are polycentric *assume that every country is different and that a specific marketing approach should be developed for each separate country.* This attitude certainly overcomes the inflexibility of ethnocentricity. For many firms, being insightful enough to see the pitfalls of the ethnocentric approach and being willing to adapt have become the foundation of success and are cause for some pride. Such an approach can be more costly, however, because the marketing must be custom-tailored to each individual country.

As business has become more global in its orientation, managers have found that it is not always necessary to develop a separate plan for each country. A **regiocentric** approach *recognizes that countries with similar cultures and economic conditions can be served with a similar marketing mix.* As has been mentioned earlier, in the case of some products it is possible to take a **geocentric** approach. This means *developing a marketing mix that meets the needs of target consumers in all markets.* Note that this is different from an ethnocentric approach. Depending on circumstances, polycentric, regiocentric, and geocentric strategies can each be appropriate.

A related issue centres on how to serve foreign markets. Should a firm try to do so by exporting only? Or should it take the risk of setting up a manufacturing operation in another country? A firm might also reduce risk by setting up a joint venture with a local company in the market of interest, but that would reduce the control it has over the venture. The exploration of such questions is beyond the scope of this book.

ethnocentric company
Firm that assumes that its way of doing business in its home market is the proper way to operate, and tries to replicate this in foreign markets.

polycentric company
Firm that assumes that every country is different and that a specific marketing approach should be developed for each separate country.

regiocentric company
Firm that recognizes that countries with similar cultures and economic conditions can be served with a similar marketing mix.

geocentric company
Firm that develops a marketing mix that meets the needs of target consumers in all markets.

INTEGRATION OF WORLD MARKETS

One country would find it difficult to product all the goods and services it needed, so international trade occurs. Nevertheless, every country tends to jealously protect its own producers and markets. This results in a maze of laws, tariffs, and restrictions that need to be overcome by trading firms.

GATT has been a significant influence in lowering tariffs and some restrictions. However, some countries decide to go further and make agreements to open their borders for trading with one another. The North American Free Trade Agreement among Canada, the United States, and Mexico is an example of this. Even though inter-country trade was very large, each country agreed that it would be to the advantage of all to simplify the process.

Different types of arrangements are used to achieve greater economic integration. The simplest approach is a **free trade area**, *within which participants agree to free trade of goods among themselves.* Normally such agreements are phased in over a period of time in order to allow companies in both countries to adjust.

A **customs union** *establishes a free trade area, plus a uniform tariff for trade with non-member nations.* The European Community (EC), comprising Belgium, Britain, Denmark, France, Germany, Greece, Ireland, Italy, Luxembourg, Portugal, The Netherlands, and Spain is the best example of a customs union.

In 1992, these nations went beyond a customs union and formed a more integrated **economic union**. Such an agreement *establishes a free flow not only of goods, but also of people, capital, and services.* Even an individual country's control of the value of its own currency and social programs have been given up to some degree. The European Union (EU) has resulted in a trading bloc that is unparalleled in history. It now constitutes a giant single market of nearly 400 million consumers. The rest of

free trade area
Area established by agreement among two or more nations within which participants agree to free trade of goods among themselves.

customs union
Agreement among two or more nations that establishes a free trade area, plus a uniform tariff for trade with nonmember nations.

economic union
Agreement among two or more nations that establishes a free flow not only of goods, but also of people, capital, and services.

■ **World Markets Are Becoming More Integrated**

Source: PA Graphics. Reprinted by permission of Arnoldo DeAlmeida.

the world watches it with fascination and some nervousness. Some nations worry that the EU could turn into Fortress Europe, slamming the door on trade with its members.

The **North American Free Trade Agreement (NAFTA)** started with the **Canada–U.S. Free Trade Agreement (FTA)**. It reinforced the long-term trading relationship between Canada and the United States. Each country has traditionally been the other's biggest customer. NAFTA includes Mexico and builds on the trading and other relationships between the three countries (see Figure 19.2 and Table 19.3).

In the world marketplace, the United States has been the target of many trading countries. This has resulted in serious negative trade balances for the United States. Gradually that country began to put significant restrictions on trade, restrictions that threatened Canadian business as well. In addition, the States arbitrarily made judgements about whether Canadian firms were trading "fairly." The potential of further restrictions and arbitrary decisions encouraged Canada to negotiate the Free Trade Agreement that had been under discussion.

Under the agreement, tariffs on certain goods were eliminated as of January 1, 1989, the commencement date. All tariffs are scheduled to be gradually eliminated according to a timetable over a ten-year period. Companies can now bid on government procurement projects worth $25 000 (U.S.) or more in other countries. This now gives companies in each country access to government business through NAFTA. A Trade Commission was created to supervise the agreement. As well, a dispute settlement mechanism and panels of individuals to settle disputes were established.

This agreement has brought hardships to some industries as companies settle their operations in one country or another. On the other hand, it presents great opportunities to others who seek them out. The concept is now well enough accepted by the three member nations that further expansion is being undertaken. Chile will be the fourth member of NAFTA, and other South American countries will be added as they develop economically and politically.

North American Free Trade Agreement (NAFTA)
The agreement establishing a free trade area among Canada, the United States, and Mexico that followed the FTA.

Free Trade Agreement (FTA)
The agreement establishing a free trade area between Canada and the United States that preceded NAFTA.

■ Figure 19.2 **How Entrepreneurs Feel about NAFTA**

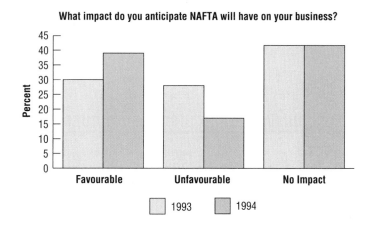

Source: Arthur Andersen Enterprise Group Survey of Entrepreneurs, *The Financial Post* (June 11, 1994), p. 15. Reprinted with permission.

■ Table 19.3 **How the NAFTA Three Compare, 1992**

	Canada	United States	Mexico
Population (millions)	27	255	90
Population growth (%)	1.5	1.1	1.9
Area (millions sq. km)	10	9.4	2
Literacy rate (%)	95	95	89
GDP (US $ billions)	570	5 951	334
Per capita GDP (US $)	20 727	23 382	3728
Exports (US $ billions)	133	440	28
Imports (US $ billions)	125	536	48
Current account balance (US $ billions)	−23	−66	−22
Inflation (%)	2	3	15

Source: The Royal Bank of Canada, *EconoBrief*, Vol. 4, No. 1 (January 10, 1994), p. 1. Reprinted with permission.

The evolution of the European Community and NAFTA have made other nations, such as Japan and other Asian countries, somewhat concerned about the possible negative effects of trading blocs on those on the outside. Asia Pacific countries have formed a working group called the Asia Pacific Economic Council (APEC) to consider economic matters. Canada and the United States are members. It is too soon to tell whether this will develop into a trading bloc as well.

The global marketplace is dynamic and exciting. It is now clear that the growth of most firms will depend on some involvement in foreign marketing. The movement toward globalization of business is accelerating, and this will create many opportunities for the student of marketing who wants to be part of the world marketplace.

■ KEY TERMS

balance of trade	import quota	regiocentric company
balance of payments	embargo	geocentric company
exchange rate	exchange control	free trade area
devaluation	dumping	customs union
revaluation	local content laws	economic union
absolute advantage	cartel	NAFTA
comparative advantage	FCN treaties	FTA
tariff	ethnocentric company	
GATT	polycentric company	

■ INTERACTIVE SUMMARY AND DISCUSSION QUESTIONS

1. Global business is one of the most important economic activities for Canada. Why is it important to Canadian firms? To the Canadian economy?
2. A nation's balance of trade is determined by the relationship between its exports and its imports. If a nation exports more than it imports, how can it have a negative balance of *payments*?
3. Is the marketing mix in the global context likely to be different from that in the domestic context?

4. Devaluation occurs when a nation reduces the value of its currency in relation to gold or some other currency. Explain how devaluation is likely to affect trade.

5. The concept of comparative advantage explains why it is beneficial for all nations to trade with one another. Comparative advantage is a *relative* concept. In *comparison with* Nation B, what goods should Nation A trade?

6. GATT is an international trade agreement to gradually lower tariffs among countries. Why are nations are striving to do this?

7. Dumping is a situation in which products are sold at significantly lower prices in a foreign market than in a nation's own domestic market. If countries are seeking to lower tariffs, and therefore prices, isn't dumping a good thing?

8. The legal environment for Canadian firms operating abroad can be divided into three dimensions: Canadian law, international law, and the legal requirements of host nations. What do Canadian law and international law have to do with business a Canadian company conducts in another country?

9. The concept of the marketing mix applies in international marketing just as it does in domestic marketing. However, marketing in a foreign country might not be the same as in Canada, even for the same product. Explain.

10. Four different approaches to involvement in international business are ethnocentric, polycentric, regiocentric, and geocentric. Explain each of these approaches.

11. World markets are being drawn together through various treaties among nations. Three significant types of trading arrangements have emerged: free trade area, customs union, and economic union. Differentiate among the three.

12. Trade restrictions such as import quotas and embargoes may be employed to restrict or to stimulate international marketing activities. How might a country do each of these, and what would be the effect?

13. Comment on the following statement: "It is sometimes dangerous for a firm to attempt to export its marketing strategy."

14. Give an example — hypothetical or actual — of a firm with the following approach to international marketing. How would the marketing mix compare with that used in the home market?
    a. Exporting in response to external demand
    b. Ethnocentric approach
    c. Polycentric approach
    d. Regiocentric approach
    e. Geocentric approach

15. The following business opportunity was listed in *CandExport*:[7]

    > Singapore — a services and supplies company wishes to import *water treatment products for the pharmaceutical, food and beverages industries.* Contact Randy Yang, Marketing Manager Jelen Supplies and Services, Singapore. Tel. _____; Fax _____; Telex _____.

    Assume that you work for a company that supplies such products. Outline the possible opportunities that such a venture might bring to your firm, and then list the possible problems. What steps should be taken to fully follow up on this advertisement?

16. Assume that you market a product in Canada on which there is a 20 percent U.S. tariff and a 25 percent Canadian tariff for products coming from the United States. In two years the product will be tariff-free under the terms of NAFTA. What are the challenges and opportunities of such a change? What should your company do in anticipation of the change?

CHAPTER 20

Not-for-Profit Marketing

CHAPTER OBJECTIVES

1. To outline the primary characteristics of nonprofit organizations that distinguish them from profit-seeking organizations.
2. To show that marketing applies to nonprofit organizations in the same way as it does to businesses.
3. To identify the main categories of marketing in nonprofit settings.
4. To examine the application of the marketing mix in nonprofit settings.

Long-term sponsorship commitments that allow performing arts groups to plan years ahead are getting harder to find. Too many companies, worried about their own survival, want to review their donation policies annually.

But Power Corporation of Canada has demonstrated sustained support to the performing arts in Montreal. It is not afraid to look ahead, committing to five years of funding for Festival Mozart Plus of the Orchestre Symphonique de Montréal.

The Orchestre Symphonique de Montréal nominated Power for the Sustained Support award, citing the 14 years Power has supported Festival Mozart Plus. In 1990, the firm entered an agreement for five more years of funding, says Eada Rubinger, director of sponsorship for the orchestra.

This long-term commitment has allowed the orchestra to book sought-after soloists, such as Louis Lortie, Sarah Chang, and Cecilia Bartoli, whose schedules are filled years in advance, she says.

Power Corporation's sponsorship is exceptional partly because it seems to be based on a conviction by its principals, the Desmarais family, that culture must flourish in the community, Rubinger says.

Power Financial Corporation subsidiaries, such as Great West Life Assurance Corp. and Investors Group Inc., have also become sponsors. Power is the holding company for a group of financial services resources and communications firms.[1]

This type of support is critical to organizations such as the Orchestre Symphonique de Montréal. In order to achieve this support, nonprofit organizations must market themselves to two different target markets. First, there is a need to develop a marketing plan with respect to the public target market. Second, the organization must market its activities, and its mission, to sponsoring organizations such as Power Corporation.

Clearly, the Orchestre Symphonique de Montréal has been successful on both counts. In addition to the support from Power Corporation, the OSM draws sellout crowds to its Festival Mozart Plus, performs a full season of over 100 concerts, and continues to record, building a discography that numbers more than 65 titles.

INTRODUCTION

Too often, people look at the *advertising* done by nonprofit organizations (NPOs)[2] and equate it with marketing. By now, the reader will realize that marketing is much more than advertising or selling. Marketing involves the application of the entire marketing mix in accordance with a well-planned marketing strategy.

For example, consider the Heart and Stroke Foundation. Its products are heart disease education and research. There are two target markets for this organization: potential donors and those who need to be educated. Because of this, the Foundation should have two highly interrelated marketing strategies. Both education and research are in accord with people's needs for health information and medical care, but if support for the Foundation's efforts is to continue, the public must perceive the Foundation's products to be valuable.

Potential donor segments must be identified in order to appeal to the various motivations in the population. For those who have heart disease, fear of the disease might be a motivation. Others may simply recognize that this is a worthy cause. Corporate donors may have less obvious motivations to which the Foundation should appeal. Marketing research may be necessary to develop a complete picture of the factors that would create a favourable response to an appeal for funds.

Marketing research may also be needed in order to learn how best to communicate current findings and advice concerning heart disease and to distribute appeal literature.

Another task for the Foundation is to find, manage, and motivate the thousands of volunteers who collect funds for its work. This process has some similarities to sales management in a profit organization but is broader in scope, especially since the motivation of volunteers is different from that of paid employees.

Above all, proper marketing planning will greatly improve the direction and effectiveness of this nonprofit organization. Not only has the Heart and Stroke Foundation discovered the benefits of this approach, but many other nonprofit organizations have also successfully applied marketing thinking to their efforts.

In Chapter 1, marketing was defined as the process of planning and executing the conception, pricing, promotion, and distribution of ideas, goods, and services to create exchanges that satisfy individual and organizational objectives. Although much of the text up to now has concentrated on organizations that operate for profit, the activities of the Heart and Stroke Foundation are as representative of modern marketing activities as are the marketing programs of IBM, Wendy's, and Canada Packers. Our definition of marketing is sufficiently comprehensive to encompass nonprofit as well as profit-seeking organizations.

A substantial portion of our economy is composed of **nonprofit organizations (NPOs)** — *those whose primary objective is something other than returning a profit to their owners.* An estimated one out of every ten service workers and one of six professionals are employed in the nonprofit sector. The nonprofit sector includes thousands of religious organizations, human service organizations, museums, libraries, colleges and universities, symphony orchestras and other music organizations, and organizations such as government agencies, political parties, and labour unions.

Nonprofit organizations can be found in both public and private sectors of society. In the public sector, federal, provincial, and local governmental units and agencies whose revenues are derived from tax collection have service objectives not keyed to profitability targets. One part of External Affairs and International Trade

nonprofit organization (NPO)
Organization whose primary objective is something other than returning a profit to its owners.

Canada, for instance, provides services that facilitate exports of Canadian products. A provincial department of natural resources regulates conservation and environmental programs. The local animal control officer enforces ordinances that protect both people and animals.

Some public-sector agencies may be given revenue or behaviour goals. An urban-transit system might be expected to pay a great deal of its costs out of revenues, for example. But society does not expect these units to routinely produce a surplus that is returned to taxpayers.

The private sector offers an even more diverse array of nonprofit settings. Art institutes, churches, labour unions, private schools, the United Way, the Rotary Club, and the local country club all serve as examples of private-sector, nonprofit organizations. The diversity of these settings suggests how pervasive organizational objectives other than profitability really are in a modern economy.

The market offering of the nonprofit organization is frequently more nebulous than the tangible goods or service provisions of profit-seeking firms. Table 20.1 lists social issues and ideas, ranging from family planning to the use of motorcycle helmets, that represent the offerings made by some nonprofit organizations to their publics.

The diversity of these issues suggests the size of the nonprofit sector and the marketing activities involved in accomplishing their objectives. As will be discussed in the next section, they are different from their profit-seeking counterparts in a number of ways.

CHARACTERISTICS OF NONPROFIT ORGANIZATIONS

Nonprofit organizations have a special set of characteristics that affect their marketing activities. Like the profit-oriented service offerings discussed in Chapter 11,

■ Table 20.1 **Social Issues Marketed by Nonprofit Organizations**

Abortion rights	Fire prevention	911 (emergency number)
Affirmative action	Fluoridation	Nonsmokers' rights
Alcoholism control	Forest fire prevention	Nuclear energy
Birth defects	Foster parenthood	Physical fitness
Blood	Fraternal organizations	Police, support of
Blue laws	Free enterprise	Pollution control
Buy Canadian goods	Freedom of the press	Population control
Cancer research	French immersion	Prison reform
Capital punishment	Gay rights	Religion
CARE packages	Housing co-operatives	Right to life
Carpooling	Legalized gambling	Save the whales
Child abuse	Literacy	Seatbelt use
Child adoption	Littering prevention	Solar energy
Consumer co-operatives	Mass transportation	STD hotline
Crime prevention	Mental health	Suicide hotline
Drunk driving	Metric system	Tax reform
Energy conservation	Military recruiting	UNICEF
Euthanasia	Motorcycle helmets	United Way
Family planning	Museums	

Source: Most of these issues are listed in Seymour H. Fine, *The Marketing of Ideas and Social Issues* (New York: Praeger, 1981), pp. 13–14. Copyright © 1981 by Praeger Publishers, New York. Reprinted by permission of Greenwood Publishing Group, Inc., Westport, CT.

APPLYING THE CONCEPTS

Applying Marketing Principles to Nonprofit Challenges

Canada's registered charities are scrambling to find new ways to live with a long-term drop in revenue expected in the balance of the 1990s.

"We must not just be clever at raising funds in the future," says Linda Mollenhauer, president of the Toronto-based Canadian Centre for Philanthropy. "We are going to have to re-map the entire charitable sector and then think hard about how we are going to fund it."

Re-mapping the sector — which includes hospitals, universities and churches — has already begun. Charities with parallel objectives are giving up their proud independence and merging. Others are ruthlessly cutting costs.

"The charity sector is in terrible trouble," Mollenhauer says. Canada's charities get more than half — 56% — of their revenue from government and only 11% from individuals and companies. "Government contributions have dropped and will continue to drop."

The lion's share (58%) of the $86 billion raised for charities went to hospitals and teaching institutions. But half of Canada's federally registered charities report revenues of less than $50,000 a year.

Source: Excerpted from Philip Mathias, "Redefining Philanthropy," *The Financial Post* (July 9, 1994), p. 4. Reprinted by permission of *The Financial Post*.

What could the application of sound marketing principles do to help various charities out of their financial dilemma?

---

the product offered by a nonprofit organization is often intangible. A hospital's diagnostic services exhibit marketing problems similar to those inherent in marketing a life insurance policy.

A second feature of nonprofit organizations is that *they must deal with multiple publics.* As Professor Philip Kotler points outs,

> Nonprofit organizations normally have at least two major publics to work with from a marketing point of view: their clients and their funders. The former pose the problem of *resource allocation* and the latter, the problem of *resource attraction*. Besides these two publics, many other publics surround the nonprofit organization and call for marketing programs. Thus a college can direct marketing programs toward prospective students, current students, parents of students, alumni, faculty, staff, local business firms, and local government agencies. It turns out the business organizations also deal with a multitude of publics but their tendency is to think about marketing only in connection with one of these publics, namely their customers.[3]

A customer or service user *may have less influence than a customer of a profit-seeking (or for-profit) firm.* A government employee may be far more concerned with the opinion of a member of the Cabinet than with that of a service user. Furthermore, nonprofit organizations often possess some degree of monopoly power in a given geographical area. As an individual, a person might object to the local United Way's inclusion of a crisis centre among its beneficial agencies, but as a contributor who accepts the merits of the United Way appeal, this same person recognizes that a portion of total contributions will go to the agency in question.

Another problem involves *the resource contributor, such as a legislator or a financial backer, who interferes with the marketing program*. It is easy to imagine a political candidate harassed by financial supporters who want to replace an unpopular campaign manager (the primary marketing position in a political campaign.)

Perhaps the most commonly noted feature of the nonprofit organization is its lack of a **bottom line**, which refers to *the overall-profitability measure of performance*. That is, nonprofit organizations have goals other than profit. While a nonprofit organization may attempt to maximize its return from a specific service, less measurable goals such as service level standards are the usual substitute for an overall evaluation. The net result is that it is often difficult to set marketing objectives that are in line with overall organizational goals.

Another characteristic is the *lack of a single clear organizational structure*. Nonprofit organizations often refer to constituencies that they serve, but these are often considerably less exact than, for example, the shareholders of a profit-oriented corporation. Nonprofit organizations often have multiple organizational structures. A hospital might have an administrative structure, a professional organization consisting of medical personnel, and a volunteer organization that dominates the board of trustees. These people may sometimes work at cross-purposes and not be totally in line with the marketing strategy that has been devised.[4]

A final characteristic of the nonprofit sector is that it is sometimes inefficient. Often two or more NPOs work toward the same "cause." For example, there may be several affirmative-action groups. Religious organizations, many with very similar objectives, abound and overlap. This could be seen as a duplication or multiplication of efforts. Clearly, however, there is competition in many cases, and the competition is not only to win a larger portion of the client target market. In fundraising, for example, the same types of NPOs sometimes compete for donor support. In addition, competition for personnel, such as fundraisers, also occurs.

While the above factors may also characterize some profit-oriented organizations, they are certainly prevalent in nonprofit settings. These characteristics affect the implementation of marketing efforts in such organizations and must be considered in the development of an overall strategy.

TYPES OF NONPROFIT MARKETING

Although nonprofit organizations are at least as varied as profit-seeking organizations, it is possible to categorize them based on the type of marketing each requires. The three major types of marketing among NPOs are person marketing, idea marketing, and organization marketing.

Person Marketing

Person marketing refers to *efforts designed to cultivate the attention, interest, and preference of a target market toward a person*.[5] This type of marketing is typically employed by political candidates and celebrities.

Leadership campaigns for political parties are good examples of person marketing. Serious contenders conduct research into the various voter segments and develop strategies to reach them. Similarly, in a profit-seeking setting, various musicians are carefully marketed to subsegments of the total market. The marketing mix for marketing Anne Murray is different from that for k.d. lang.

---

bottom line
The overall-profitability measure of performance.

person marketing
Efforts designed to cultivate the attention, interest, and preference of a target market toward a person.

Idea Marketing

The second type of nonprofit marketing deals with causes and social issues rather than an individual. **Idea marketing** refers to *the identification and marketing of a cause to chosen consumer segments.*[6] A highly visible marketing mix element frequently associated with idea marketing is the use of *advocacy advertising*, discussed in Chapter 18. The importance of wearing sunscreen is an idea currently being marketed in several countries. Antismoking marketing programs have been so successful that many people have quit smoking, and legislation has been passed that forbids smoking in public places.

idea marketing
The identification and marketing of a cause to chosen consumer segments.

Organization Marketing

The third type of nonprofit marketing, **organization marketing**, *attempts to influence others to accept the goals of, receive the services of, or contribute in some way to an organization.* Included in this category are *mutual benefit* organizations, such as churches, labour unions, and political parties; *service* organizations, such as colleges, universities, hospitals, and museums; and *government* organizations, such as military services, police and fire departments, the post office, and local communities.[7]

organization marketing
Attempts to influence others to accept the goals of, receive the services of, or contribute in some way to an organization.

UNDERSTANDING OF MARKETING BY NONPROFIT ORGANIZATIONS

Nonprofit organizations often have too limited an understanding of marketing. In many cases, marketing is taken to mean simply marketing communications. The development of well-thought-out marketing strategy, as well as consideration of other components of the marketing mix — product development, distribution, and pricing strategies — have too often been largely ignored. Marketing, considered and practised merely as aggressive promotion, is a short-lived, surface-level solution for a variety of organizational problems and objectives. For instance, one university decided to "adopt marketing" and thought it was doing so by planning to release balloons containing scholarship offers. And a "marketing planning" conference for a private school consisted mainly of developing new slogans for advertisements.

Professor Seymour H. Fine conducted a survey of nonprofit organizations to assess the degree of marketing sophistication present. His findings, illustrated in Table 20.2, revealed that many respondents were unaware of, or at least reluctant to admit to, the presence of marketing efforts in their organizations.

Nonprofit organizations need to take the time to develop a comprehensive marketing approach. One university, for example, conducted a comprehensive marketing audit that designated strong and weak areas in its product mix (program offerings). It was then possible to develop strategies after the basic parameters of market, resources, and mission had been identified and analyzed.

IMPORTANCE OF MARKETING TO NONPROFIT ORGANIZATIONS

Marketing as a recognized function is a late arrival to the management of nonprofit organizations. The practices of improved accounting, financial control, personnel

■ Table 20.2 **Responses of Selected Nonprofit Organization Representatives**

Nonprofit Organization	Response to the Question "Do you have a marketing department or equivalent?"
Public health service official	"Marketing fluoridation is not a function of government — promotion and public awareness is."
Administrator of regional women's rights group	"We have never thought of ourselves as marketing a product. We have people who are assigned equal pay for work of equal value as their 'item.' "
Group crusading for the rights of the left-handed	"Don't understand the term [marketing]; we do lobbying, letter writing to appropriate government and commercial concerns."
A national centre for the prevention of child abuse	"We disseminate information without the marketing connotation. Besides, demand is too great to justify marketing."
Recruiting officer	"Not applicable."

Source: Adapted from Seymour H. Fine, *The Marketing of Ideas and Social Issues* (New York: Praeger, 1981), p. 53. Copyright © 1981 by Praeger Publishers, New York. Used by permission of Greenwood Publishing Group, Inc., Westport, CT.

selection, and strategic planning were all implemented before formal marketing planning. Nevertheless, nonprofit organizations have begun to accept marketing enthusiastically. For example, university administrators attend seminars and conferences to learn how better to market their own institutions.

Marketing's rise in the nonprofit sector could not be continued without a successful track record. While it is often more difficult to measure results in nonprofit settings, marketing can already point to examples of success. The Church of the Nazarene in Canada, for instance, has used a telemarketing campaign called "Phones for You" to develop a target clientele interested in supporting the start of new churches. And one art gallery's marketing analysis resulted in defining two distinct market segments it should serve. Marketing is increasingly an accepted part of the operational environment of successful nonprofit organizations. Table 20.3 presents a hypothetical job description for a marketing director at a college or university.

DEVELOPING A MARKETING STRATEGY

The need for comprehensive marketing planning and control rather than a mere increase in marketing communications expenditures has already been noted. Substantial opportunities exist for effective, innovative strategies since there has been little previous marketing effort in most nonprofit settings.

Marketing Research

Many decisions in nonprofit settings (as well as in business) are based on little, if any, research. For example, numerous Canadian art galleries arbitrarily establish programs and schedules with little or no reference to audience marketing research.

APPLYING THE CONCEPTS

Barriers to Overcome in Managing Nonprofits

- If there's something wrong in the not-for-profit sector, it's almost certain you won't hear about it from the people who work there. You're more likely to get the story when it hits the papers, which is usually after it is too late. It often turns out staff knew there was a problem but nothing was done.
- The executive director of a non-profit group must successfully juggle the demands — often conflicting — of his or her board, employees, clients and financial contributors. On top of that, the director must manage public relations, human resources, fund raising and administration. This person has to wear so many hats because these organizations are typically very small, sometimes with fewer than 10 employees.
- One of the biggest problems in the not-for-profit sector is the lack of a bottom line, the ultimate benchmark for private-sector accomplishment. "It's hard to measure what you're working toward," says one expert. He added that even good leaders sometimes can't handle the complexities of social-justice agendas.
- "When the organization is values-driven, there are often competing visions of the right way to go. The atmosphere is often most fractious where complex issues such as race or gender are involved." "All it takes is two people agreeing [on a different approach] and you've got a clique." "It's not up front; it's all done through whispers in the hallways."
- The issue of accountability is a constant problem.

Source: Excerpted from Chris Howard, "Office Politics," *The Globe and Mail* (November 29, 1994), p. A22. Reprinted by permission of the author.

How does all this relate to the application of marketing planning and practices in the nonprofit organization?

Adequate marketing research can be extremely important in a variety of nonprofit settings. Resident opinion surveys in some cities have proven valuable to public officials.[8] The analysis of projected population trends has led school boards to build new schools and to phase out others.

Product Strategy

Nonprofit organizations face the same product decisions as profit-seeking firms. They must choose a product, service, person, idea, or social issue to be offered to their target market. They must decide whether to offer a single product or a mix of related products. They must make product identification decisions. The fact that the United Way symbol and the Red Cross trademark are as familiar as McDonald's golden arches or the Shell logo illustrates the similarity in the use of product identification methods.

A common failure among nonprofit organizations is assuming that heavy promotional efforts can overcome a poor product strategy or marketing mix. For

■ Table 20.3 **Job Description: Director of Marketing for a University**

Position Title: Director of Marketing

Reports to: A vice-president designated by the president

Scope: University-wide

Position Concept: The director of marketing is responsible for providing marketing guidance and services to university officers, school deans, department chairpersons, and other agents of the university.

Functions: The director of marketing will
1. Contribute a marketing perspective to the deliberations of the top administration in its planning of the university's future
2. Prepare data that might be needed by any officer of the university on a particular market's size, segments, trends, and behavioural dynamics
3. Conduct studies of the needs, perceptions, preferences, and satisfactions of particular markets
4. Assist in the planning, promotion, and launching of new programs
5. Assist in the development of communication and promotion campaigns and materials
6. Analyze and advise on pricing questions
7. Appraise the workability of new academic proposals from a marketing point of view
8. Advise on new student recruitment
9. Advise on current student satisfaction
10. Advise on university fundraising

Responsibilities: The director of marketing will
1. Contact individual officers and small groups at the university to explain services and to solicit problems
2. Rank the various requests for services according to their long-run impact, cost-saving potential, time requirements, ease of accomplishment, cost, and urgency
3. Select projects of high priority and set accomplishment goals for the year
4. Prepare a budget request to support the anticipated work
5. Prepare an annual report on the main accomplishments of the office

Major Liaisons: The director of marketing will
1. Relate most closely with president's office, admissions office, development office, planning office, and public relations department
2. Relate secondarily with the deans of various schools and chairpersons of various departments

Source: Philip Kotler, "Strategies for Introducing Marketing into Nonprofit Organizations," *Journal of Marketing* (January 1979), p. 42. Reprinted by permission of the American Marketing Association.

example, some liberal arts colleges tried to use promotion to overcome their product mix deficiencies when students became increasingly career-oriented. Successful institutions adjust their product offerings to reflect customer demand.

Pricing Strategy

Pricing is typically a very important element of the marketing mix for nonprofit organizations. Pricing strategy can be used to accomplish a variety of organizational goals in nonprofit settings. These include

She's 46. And She's Looking For A Future In The Bottom Of A Bottle.

Help Street Haven help others.
Please give generously. Call **1-800-263-2595**.

SL ShareLife

*Helping the whole community
through Catholic agencies*

Sharelife is a nonprofit agency that raises funds to help people who may otherwise not receive support. The agency's marketing must address several purposes. People must first be made aware of the problems in our society, and those problems must be presented in such a way that people will feel sympathetic. A call for action in the form of giving to an agency whose purpose is to help is the final purpose of such advertising.

1. *Profit maximization.* While nonprofit organizations by definition do not cite profitability as a primary goal, there are numerous instances in which they do try to maximize their return on a single event or a series of events. The $1000-a-plate political fundraiser is an example.

2. *Cost recovery.* Some nonprofit organizations attempt to recover only the actual cost of operating the unit. Mass transit, colleges, and airports are common examples. The amount of recovered costs is often dictated by tradition, competition, or public opinion.

3. *Providing market incentives.* Other nonprofit groups follow a penetration pricing policy or offer a free service to encourage increased usage of the product or service. Winnipeg's bus system policy of free fares on special "Dash" buses in the downtown area reduces traffic congestion, encourages retail sales, and minimizes the effort required to use downtown public services.

4. *Market suppression.* Price is sometimes used to discourage consumption. In other words, high prices are used to accomplish social objectives and are not directly related to the costs of providing the product or service. Illustrations of suppression include tobacco and alcohol taxes, parking fines, tolls, and gasoline excise taxes.[9]

Distribution Strategy

Distribution channels for nonprofit organizations tend to be short, simple, and direct. If intermediaries are present in the channel, they are usually agents, such as an independent ticket agency or a specialist in fundraising.

Nonprofit organizations often fail to exercise caution in planning and executing the distribution strategy. For example, organizers of recycling centres sometimes complain about lack of public interest when their real problem is an inconvenient location or lack of adequate drop-off points. In a number of cities, this problem has been solved by dropping blue boxes off at people's homes. By contrast, some public agencies, like health and social welfare departments, have set up branches in neighbourhood shopping centres to be more accessible to their clientele. Nonprofit marketers must carefully evaluate the available distribution options if they are to be successful in delivering their products or in serving their intended consumers.

Marketing Communications Strategy

It is common to see or hear advertisements from nonprofit organizations such as educational institutions, churches, and public service organizations.

Marketing communications are affected by a variety of factors including relative involvement in the nonprofit setting, pricing, and perceived benefits.[10] But overall, marketing communications are seen by many nonprofit managers as the primary solution to their marketing problems. As noted earlier, this view is often naïve, but it does not diminish the importance of this mix element in a nonprofit setting.

Marketing an idea takes just as much marketing knowledge as marketing a product. Preaching solely about the health problems caused by cigarettes is not an effective way to reach young people — talking about the ramifications on their love lives is. This message was reproduced on large transit posters and placed in bus shelters, thus effectively reaching its target audience.

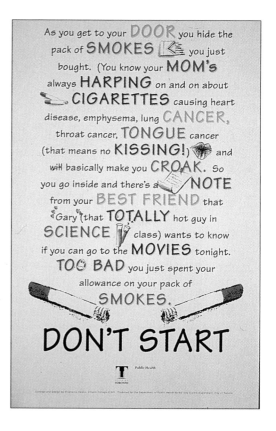

All types of marketing communications elements have been used. The Canadian Forces has used television advertising to attract recruits. Fundraising for some support groups for the handicapped is done through personal selling over the telephone. Volunteers are an essential part of the marketing program for many nonprofit organizations. They are used to "sell" (canvass) by phone or in person. Such individuals pose a significant "sales management" problem. With a paid sales force, it is easy to demand certain behaviour on the part of sales personnel or to provide various financial incentives to affect their behaviour. Similar methods are not as readily available with volunteers. Other stimulation and incentives, such as public recognition or receptions, are used as substitutes. Even so, it is unlikely that the same effects can be achieved.

Advertising is a desirable marketing communications option. However, because the cost of media is high, fund-raising drives often rely on publicity and public relations efforts, such as appearances on TV talk shows, to promote their product. Charitable groups have used badges, paper flowers, and other specialty advertising items to identify donors or contributions and to promote their particular cause. Marketing communications will remain a key ingredient of most nonprofit organizations' marketing plans.

THE FUTURE OF NONPROFIT MARKETING

While marketing has gained increasing acceptance in the nonprofit sector of society, it is still viewed with suspicion by some of the people involved. The heavy emphasis on marketing communications is one reason. Marketing efforts in nonprofit organizations often lack the sophistication and integration found in the marketing of profit-oriented industries. Marketing is too often seen as the "quick-fix" solution to a more basic problem. To combat this, nonprofit marketers must market their own discipline in a realistic and socially responsible manner. The client must be helped to understand the opportunities, benefits, behaviour modifications, and commitment involved in adopting the marketing concept in a nonprofit setting.

■ KEY TERMS

nonprofit organization (NPO)	bottom line	idea marketing
	person marketing	organization marketing

■ INTERACTIVE SUMMARY AND DISCUSSION QUESTIONS

1. A nonprofit organization is one whose primary objective is something other than returning a profit to its owners. Give an example of other core objectives that such organizations could have.
2. Listed below are the special characteristics of nonprofit organizations. Explain how each might affect the way nonprofit organizations practise marketing.
   a. Often intangible product
   b. Often dealing with multiple publics
   c. Customer may have less influence than a customer of a profit-seeking organization
   d. Lack of a bottom line
   e. Lack of a single clear organizational structure
   f. Inefficient operation

3. Three types of marketing among NPOs are person marketing, idea marketing, and organization marketing. For which of these would the application of marketing principles be the most difficult? Explain.

4. The marketing mix is just as applicable to not-for-profit marketing as it is to for-profit marketing. Would there be any differences in applying the marketing mix in the case of not-for-profit marketing? Use examples to explain your answer.

5. Market suppression, or deterring demand, is sometimes practised in nonprofit marketing. Give examples of this. Which of the elements of the marketing mix would most likely be applicable in accomplishing market suppression?

6. Cite several examples of circumstances in which penetration pricing might be practised by public utilities.

7. How would you assess the marketing performance of the following?
   a. Your college or university
   b. Canadian Postal Workers Union
   c. Planned Parenthood
   d. The re-election committee of a local politician

8. Outline the marketing program of your college or university. Make any reasonable assumptions necessary. Where are the major strengths and weaknesses of the current program? What recommendations would you make for improving it?

9. Compare distribution and marketing communications strategies of nonprofit organizations with those used by profit-seeking enterprises.

10. Why might there be a greater tendency for a nonprofit organization to define marketing inaccurately?

CHAPTER 21

Total Customer Satisfaction in Marketing

CHAPTER OBJECTIVES

1. To show the importance of establishing a process of reviewing the results of the marketing effort.
2. To review the importance of striving for total customer satisfaction in marketing planning.
3. To relate the concept of control to the marketing planning process.
4. To outline the steps involved in a marketing effectiveness audit.
5. To explain the concept of benchmarking and its application in producing customer satisfaction and company competitiveness.
6. To evaluate some aspects of the impact of marketing on society.

Dressed in his dark overcoat, Nicholas Samson looks like any other affluent urban Christmas shopper on a quest for silk lingerie or the latest electronic gizmo. But last week, Samson, a professional "mystery shopper," was on the prowl for customer service rather than gifts, when he visited a photography store in a suburban Toronto mall. Samson headed to the camera counter and waited behind a row of customers already being served. His gaze lingered on three young female salesclerks giggling together at an adjacent counter. They ignored him. Although the company's service standard calls for customers to be greeted within 30 seconds of entering the store, almost two minutes had passed since Samson arrived. Just then, a salesclerk appeared and capably answered Samson's detailed inquiries about cameras. The clerk was knowledgeable, helpful, and pleasant — which, a few minutes later, sitting on a bench in the mall, Samson duly noted as he filled out a multi-point report card on the store's performance. The grade: 80 out of a possible 100. "On the whole, I thought it was pretty good service," said Samson. "But I'm still kind of ticked off about those girls ignoring us."

Mystery shopping is an established retail technique that is gaining a new urgency as Canadian retailers face aggressive, new competition from such sleek U.S. retail giants as The Gap and Wal-Mart Stores Inc. Eaton's department stores, which have been using mystery shopping for decades, try to "shop" all their sales employees at least once a year. Glenn Quarrington, Eaton's vice-president of human resources, says that mystery shopping is a good way to measure service quality. "And what gets measured," adds Quarrington, "gets done."

There are other ways to monitor customer service levels. Alan Goddard, vice-president of corporate affairs at Canadian Tire Corp. Ltd., says that, in addition to mystery shoppers, the chain plans to introduce a new direct response system. Computer terminals will be installed in stores, and customers will be encouraged to answer service questionnaires. "We're not looking for people to tell us how satisfied they are," says Goddard, "we want to hear the complaints."

Regardless of the method, the real issue is constantly upgrading customer service. "The hard part is to go the step beyond," says Quarrington, "and figure out what we can do to distinguish ourselves by finding genuine service opportunities."[1]

This retailing example is only one illustration of the growing significance placed by leading firms from many industries on seeking to provide total customer satisfaction. Other firms will ignore the trend at their peril.

INTRODUCTION

This book has been about finding and serving customers profitably. In discussing the issue, we have developed an understanding of the many elements involved in the marketing planning process. As shown in Table 21.1, the final aspect of the marketing planning process is *control* — *determining whether the objective of achieving consumer satisfaction has been met.*

The criterion for assessing success in this area should be more than *satisfaction* — it must be *total* customer satisfaction. Total customer satisfaction means that a good or service totally conforms to the customer's requirements. For example, when asked by a waiter, "How was your meal?" how many times have you said, "Fine," even though you were not really satisfied? Our objective must be to create "raving fans" if we are to assume a position of leadership in the market in which we have chosen to compete. Only by systematically reviewing the outcome of the process can improvements be made in the marketing plan.

Consider the following scenario:

"How is your company performing?" William Brand asked. "Sales and profits are up," the president replied. "In fact, our financial people tell me this year we will have one of our best 'bottom lines' ever!"

■ Table 21.1 **The Marketing Planning Process**

I. Situation Analysis: Where Are We Now?
 A. Historical background
 B. Consumer analysis
 • Who are the customers we are trying to serve?
 • What market segments exist?
 • How many consumers are there?
 • How much do they buy and why?
 C. Competitive analysis

II. Marketing Objectives: Where Do We Want to Go?
 A. Sales objectives
 B. Profit objectives

III. Strategy: How Can We Get There?
 A. Product/service decisions
 B. Pricing decisions
 C. Distribution decisions
 D. Communication decisions
 E. Financial considerations
 F. Control aspects

Source: Adapted from Thomas O'Connor, Stephen K. Keiser, Robert E. Stevens, and Lynn J. Loudenback, *Contemporary Marketing*, 6th ed., Study Guide (Fort Worth, TX: Dryden, 1989), p. 482.

Mr. Brand was reviewing with the president the recent accomplishments of a manufacturer of computer components as they prepared to set the stage for planning the company's strategy for next year.

"Today's financial results measure the outcomes of strategic initiatives taken in the past. Are you monitoring the critical factors which will create success in the future?" Brand challenged.

"What do you mean? Aren't strong financial controls the proper measuring tools to monitor business performance?" the president said, somewhat taken aback.

Financial measures, used alone, are like driving a car while watching the rearview mirror. They tell a company where it has been. A manager also needs a forward-looking view toward building success in the areas that lead to a long-run competitive advantage. The key success factors include product quality, after-sale service, corporate flexibility, and employee innovativeness.[2]

In a recent study of the marketing planning practices of the top 500 Canadian firms, this author found that only 57.8 percent of firms developed a written marketing plan. Furthermore, only 25.4 percent included a post-mortem of the past year's results in their current marketing plan. How could such performance lead to total customer satisfaction?

THE VALUE VISION

Most managers have been taught to manage *activity* rather than *value*. Strategic plans for production, sales, and administration of business units are often focussed on short-term gross volume improvements rather than on long-term value-building. These plans reward on the basis of quantity rather than value added. This skews performance toward activity and short-term gain.[3]

The vision of an organization should be to *add value* for customers and employees. Without a clear understanding of value, all marketing activity is in danger of falling into the activity trap. *Activity is the process by which value is created.* Value should be the heart of organizational purpose.

What is value? **Value** is a subjective term, and is defined by the customer. Each customer defines it somewhat differently. It is too simplistic to say that value is synonymous with customer satisfaction. Value is *part of customer expectations.* These are often complex and sometimes hidden, and they change. Expectations are a combination of cost, time, quantity, quality, and human factors.

Pepsi-Cola is an example of a company that diligently seeks out customer values. It surveyed 10 000 customers to develop sixteen priorities for its total quality effort. For example, it found that customers wanted improved deliveries. Two years later, it followed up with a survey of 2000 customers to see how it was doing.

Johnson & Johnson's McNeil Consumer Products subsidiary, which manufactures the Tylenol product line, found that it had become too inwardly focussed. It set up a special booth in its plant for workers who previously had had no opportunity to interact with customers. In this booth, they can now hear queries and complaints from the outside world that come in on an 800 line.[4]

If a company wants to build value, it has to recognize that value starts with the customer. However, there is a problem in simply asking customers what they want. They often cannot define their wants clearly. There are two main reasons for this. First, when technology is involved, laypeople are unqualified to judge a product, and to specify what they want. Second, the customer is focussed on his or her problem, not on the supplier's good or service. The supplier is only a means to helping customers reach their goals.

value
A subjective term that is defined by the customer; part of customer expectations, which are a combination of cost, time, quantity, quality, and human factors.

In spite of this, the marketer must find out which values to offer. Some key questions to ask customers: "What are you trying to achieve?" "What other forces are at work on you?" "What are your problems and opportunities?" "Who is pressuring you?"

The Value-Adding Chain

Building value is a function of a five-link chain, as shown in Figure 21.1. This chain links the corporate vision and its human and material assets to the customer's requirements. Any weak link in the value-adding chain breaks the bond between the business and the customer.

The *culture* of the organization must be right. Cultural factors spur people to design systems that fit the culture. When a corporation's vision and culture are out of sync, a fatal flaw is exposed and the organization experiences problems. For example, when Jan Carlzon took over the ailing Linjeflyg airline in Sweden, he started by calling all employees into an empty airplane hangar and asking them for their ideas and help in resurrecting the airline. The result was that Linjeflyg changed from offering high-priced travel that only businesses could afford to offering real travel value to a great number of other customers by dramatically lowering prices. This vision brought about a great change in the culture of the organization. Within two years, the company was profitable.

Systems form the second link in the value-adding chain. They direct employee and management behaviour in the desired direction. Systems are inherently powerful — like a river, they flow along taking everything in their path in one direction. However, like rivers, some systems are lazy, winding, uncertain, and slow. Other rivers are more direct, deep, and strong. When these are flowing in the right direction, they establish a force of tremendously effective power in the marketplace.

The integration of culture and systems affects *performance*, or employee behaviour. This performance produces operating *results*, such as quality, productivity, and service outcomes. The final link, *value*, achieves customer satisfaction and competi-

■ Figure 21.1 **The Value-Adding Chain**

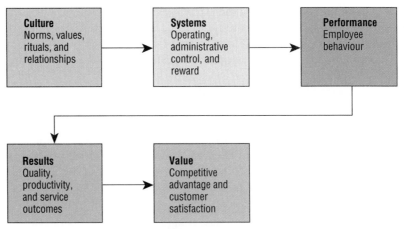

Source: Adapted from Jac Fitz-enz, *Benchmarking Staff Performance: How Staff Departments Can Enhance Their Value to the Customer* (San Francisco: Jossey-Bass Inc., Publishers, 1993), p. 16. Reprinted by permission of the publisher.

tive advantage. Every link in the chain should be observed for its impact on customer value.

QUALITY OR VALUE?

Quality is an overworked management term that is used to describe too many things. Quality is just one type of outcome from operations. The other two are productivity and service. Organizations do not survive and prosper because they provide quality. Collectively, quality, productivity, and service should comprise value.

BENCHMARKING

The core issue of the marketing plan is how to add value. One way of achieving this is through benchmarking. The computer industry has used the term *benchmarking* for many years to compare the characteristics of computers. A standard software program is run on each computer being tested, and various aspects of their performance are measured. The best performance on each characteristic becomes the standard, or benchmark, against which all others are compared.

The concept of *comparison with the best* is much better than merely setting objectives. It is of little value for one company to set an objective for its computer to increase the number of calculations per second from 500 to 700 when the benchmark rate for another computer is 1100. The only way to be competitive is to meet or beat the benchmark. The Japanese have a word for this concept — *dantotsu* — which means striving to be "the best of the best."

Benchmarking is *the comparison of performance with industry best practices.* It is now applied to organizational performance, such as marketing programs. The advantages of using benchmarking are that managers are forced to seek out the best practices in the external environment, and must strive to incorporate these best practices in company marketing planning.

benchmarking
The comparison of performance with industry best practices.

There are four fundamental requirements for using benchmarking as a tool to provide value to customers:[5]

1. *Know your operation.* It is fundamental for a company to develop a good understanding of the strengths and weaknesses of its internal operation.
2. *Know the industry leaders and competitors.* Only a comparison with the best practices of leaders and competitors will provide the correct benchmarks to strive for. In addition, knowing their key strengths and weaknesses will lead to good decisions for differentiating products.
3. *Incorporate the best.* As a company finds out the strengths in others, it should not hesitate to learn from them, and copy, modify, or incorporate these strengths into its own operation.
4. *Develop superiority.* As the company's marketing planning and implementation respond by meeting and improving upon the benchmarks set by others, it will be on the right track for providing total customer satisfaction in marketing. Being the best of the best in dimensions that consumers value brings an organization closest to the goal of providing total customer satisfaction.

The Benchmarking Process

Benchmarking comprises five stages: *planning, analysis, integration, action,* and *maturity.* Within these stages there are ten distinct steps.

PLANNING

The process starts with *identifying what is to be benchmarked*. For example, if consumers value competent, friendly service, this should be measured. Other examples might be excellent after-sale service, clear and interesting advertising, or high-quality products.

Identifying leading companies and competitors is the next step. These are the companies that are now doing the best job on these characteristics. Careful attention should be paid to international competitors, as the leaders need to set the standard no matter where they are found. Note that some companies might be better on some benchmark characteristics than others. Therefore, the comparison could be with more than one firm.

Collecting data includes using sound marketing research methodology and the many marketing research techniques. At this stage, it is important to derive quantifiable goals as well as to search out and document the best industry practices.

ANALYSIS

performance gap
The difference between the company's performance and that of the best of the best.

The next step is *determining the current performance gap*. The **performance gap** is *the difference between the company's performance and that of the best of the best*. This gap can be positive, negative, or nonexistent. Is the benchmarking partner better? Why is it better? By how much? How can its practices be incorporated or adapted for implementation?

Step 6 of the benchmarking process is *projecting future performance levels*. It is also important to project whether current performance, for the benchmark partner as well, is improving or not. Such projections might show a narrowing of the gap or that the gap will be even wider in the competitor's favour in two to five years.

INTEGRATION

Once the findings are established, it is critical to *communicate the benchmark findings and gain acceptance from the rest of the organization*. The organization must have faith in the methodology, and understand and accept the findings, if change is to occur.

Following this, *functional goals must be established*. This is a critical part of the process, as it involves converting benchmark findings into a statement of operational principles. To make the necessary changes, the organization must subscribe to these principles. They will be the criteria upon which the organization will focus in order to provide the value that will lead to customer satisfaction.

ACTION

Implementing these principles involves *developing action plans, implementing specific actions and monitoring progress*, and *recalibrating benchmarks*. Recalibration is necessary over time as the external environment is constantly changing.

MATURITY

Maturity is reached when the plans have been implemented, and a position of leadership has occurred in each of the benchmarked conditions. This is the necessary process that will lead to total customer satisfaction. The benchmark process steps are shown in Table 21.2.

A graphic way of showing how a benchmarking exercise can help a company find where it is positioned is shown in the performance gap chart in Figure 21.2. This shows that the company's historic performance in providing marketing information in comparison with a benchmark competitor is poor, and is likely to get worse if it doesn't adjust.

■ Table 21.2 **The Benchmarking Process**

Planning
1. Identify what is to be benchmarked.
2. Identify comparative companies.
3. Determine data collection method and collect data.

Analysis
4. Determine current "performance gap."
5. Project future performance levels.

Integration
6. Communicate benchmark findings and gain acceptance.
7. Establish functional goals.

Action
8. Develop action plans.
9. Implement specific actions and monitor progress.
10. Recalibrate benchmarks.

Maturity
- Leadership position attained.
- Practices fully integrated into processes.

Source: Robert C. Camp, *Benchmarking: The Search for Industry Best Practices That Lead to Superior Performance* (Milwaukee: ASQC Quality Press, 1989), p. 17.

A similar analysis can be done for each of the salient characteristics that contribute to total value, as perceived by the customer. For example, Pepsi-Cola could undertake such an analysis for each of its sixteen priorities.

WHAT IS CUSTOMER SATISFACTION?

In choosing the value elements to benchmark, marketers need to concentrate on relevant measures that bear on whether or not customer satisfaction has been achieved. What is customer satisfaction, really? Here are some answers given by managers:[6]

- "You have to start with the definition of customer satisfaction and quality from the customer perspective. Do the diagnostic work. What are the key factors that drive the customer on the good or service?"
- "The customer doesn't care about your system. The customer cares about satisfaction; having problems handled."
- "The customer doesn't care how you track his order. What the customer thinks is, 'I need the answer as to what the status of my shipment is, within the hour.' They don't care about how you execute, only that you do. They care about the *results*."

There is a common thread in the above responses: customer satisfaction comes down to the ability to better serve your customers. As the managers' comments imply, organizations have to get beyond the lip-service paid to satisfaction. One way they are doing this is by going into the marketplace and measuring satisfaction regularly.

■ Figure 21.2 **Performance Gap Chart**

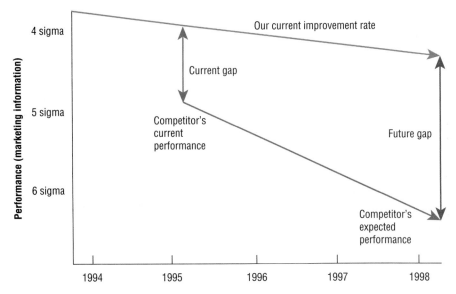

Note: A sigma is one standard deviation from the mean.

Source: Jac Fitz-enz, *Benchmarking Staff Peformance: How Staff Departments Can Enhance Their Value to the Customer* (San Francisco: Jossey-Bass Inc., Publishers, 1993), p. 31. Reprinted by permission of the publisher.

While most companies try to differentiate themselves by providing a succession of new product features, Hewlett-Packard is a company that has chosen not to rely solely on product features to create differentiation. Its European division decided to use customer satisfaction as an additional explicit method of differentiation. Its stated goal is to keep customers forever, and the company has created a new position called "customer satisfaction executive" to help ensure that it achieves this goal.

H-P has also established a customer satisfaction program. The three components of the program are customer feedback input, customer satisfaction surveys, and total quality control. The company carefully monitors and documents customers' gripes as well as compliments. H-P has recognized that it should not always focus on the negative comments but explicitly consider the positive feedback that is received as well. The company administers worldwide "relationship" surveys every 18 months. These focus on asking how satisfied the customer is with the company as a whole, and how H-P rates against its competition. As well, some product questions are asked. By collecting this information on a regular basis, the company can evaluate whether it is making progress in its goal of providing customer satisfaction from year to year. The third aspect of the customer satisfaction program is a program of total quality control in production and service. With such a comprehensive program, it is not surprising that the worldwide relationship surveys show a steady improvement in customer satisfaction.[7]

Many companies are still behind in the trend toward making customer service number one. They haven't quite realized that customer service is a critically important marketing tool.

Customer satisfaction must be defined from an external, customer-based viewpoint. Marketing executives must lead their organizations to a better understand-

ing of customer satisfaction defined in customer terms. Products may be perfectly manufactured, but they will fail if they do not meet market requirements.

For example, when informed consumers see ads proclaiming high-quality service provided by an airline, they are likely to think, "Why waste the money on hype when I can't get through on the phone to make an inquiry?" Furthermore, staff who see the ads will say, "Why put all that money into marketing and nothing into providing us with the means of improving the quality of customer treatment?"

Reassuring the public that the company cares and provides high-quality service is a sound way to build a customer base and profitability, but only if such claims are undeniably true. Total customer satisfaction must be a constant byword of managing every facet of the marketing program. **Total customer satisfaction** means that *a good or service totally conforms to the customer's requirements*. This, of course, cannot be done without an active program of monitoring customer satisfaction.

total customer satisfaction
A situation where a good or service totally conforms to the customer's requirements.

Taking Total Customer Satisfaction from Slogan to Substance

To take total customer satisfaction from slogan to substance, management should follow these guidelines:

1. Identify customer segments and the characteristics that they consider most important for the good or service.
2. Identify specific requirements for each target market.
3. Translate resolved customer requirements into objectives and specifications for the marketing plan.

APPLYING THE CONCEPTS

Is Total Customer Satisfaction in Retailing a Myth?

The only place I can find service in Canada is in the dictionary — but the dictionary definition is wrong.

I go to The Bay in search of service, defined in the *Penguin Canadian Dictionary* as the function or occupation of being helpful or useful. I stand under the huge sign that says SERVICE. Nothing happens, nobody appears. I expand my search. I go to Eaton's. I stand under the sign that says SERVICE. Nothing happens. No one appears. The only thing that standing under the sign serves to do is to try my patience.

The usual quest for service goes something like this. I enter the store. There is nobody in sight. I can hear my voice echo through the store. *HHeelloo, ddooees aannyy bbooddyy wwoork hheerree?* You usually have to search for someone to help you. Finding a salesperson represents phase one of your quest. The next step is finding the product you want. You secure the help of a salesperson. You ask for comparative product information. Which product is better and why? Often the salesperson knows little more than you do.

Getting service over the phone is a whole other source of frustration. It goes something like this: "Hello, I have a problem with . . ." You explain the problem. "I'm sorry," the person responds, "I'll transfer you to someone who can help you . . ." Click, the line disconnects. Now you've really got a problem: rage.

What irks people even more than the shortage of service is the abundance of *attitude.* We understand that stores are short of staff, but when we do encounter a sales clerk it's not uncommon to get the "Whadya want, don't bug me" attitude. What ever happened to service with a smile?

Forget the smile for a minute, try just getting a salesperson to acknowledge you. Many salespeople are adept at ignoring customers. They don't come up to you and offer their assistance. In some stores, stocking shelves seems to be a higher priority. A friend of mine related an all-too-familiar story. She went to pay for clothing at one of the big department stores downtown. The cashier was on the phone and in the midst of conversation. My friend waited, simultaneously becoming apprised of the cashier's evening plans. Then the cashier said to the person on the phone, "Just a second," and she turned to my friend. "Do you want that?" My friend nodded. The cashier proceeded to ring in the sale and arrange her upcoming weekend.

With our increasingly global economy, free trade and lowered tariff barriers, Canada must improve its service to stay competitive. Perhaps we need to redefine service in Canada. The Ontario government defines medically underserviced areas as Kenora, Parry Sound and Thunder Bay, to name a few. I hasten to point out that as Canadians we're all underserviced.

Source: Excerpted from Joanne Milner, "Forget the Smile — Whatever Happened to Service?!?" *The Globe and Mail* (November 9, 1994), p. A24. Reprinted by permission of the author.

Do you agree with Joanne Milner's observations and conclusions? What issues should be considered in balancing service and costs?

4. Identify the steps in the implementation process.
5. Determine the capability of the process to meet the requirements.
6. Select measurements for critical process steps.
7. Implement the program — fulfil customer values relating to the good or service. This must be the overriding goal for the organization in every department.

▇ Showing the Customer How Much You Care

"Congratulations Mr. Harkins,
you're our 1 millionth CUSTOMER!"

Source: PA Graphics. Reprinted by permission of Arnoldo DeAlmeida.

Every service must be measured against the same standard, and every employee should be working toward 100 percent satisfaction of each value attribute.

- Communicate these goals and standards to all employees, whether or not they communicate with the public. The best salespeople cannot make a company popular and profitable if other aspects of the organization are inefficient or error-prone.
- Train all employees in a voluntary, co-operative atmosphere. It is woefully inadequate for a vice-president or chief executive officer to announce that "all employees should do their best" without universal training in what that means and how to achieve it.
- Give rewards, financial and otherwise, to those employees whose involvement leads to improvements in customer satisfaction and real cost savings.

8. Evaluate the results of the process and identify steps for improvements.

Figure 21.3 gives an example of a quality service client survey used by the Royal Bank.

Flexibility: Serving Customers Better

Leading companies have created new possibilities for customers by providing more choices and better response times. They have accomplished this by pushing their operations to perform much more flexibly. Instead of running a production line to produce one specific product for a week, companies are organizing to change production from one product to another within hours. The purpose is to maximize the flexibility of the whole company's response to demand.[8]

For example, product life cycles for low-end computers are measured within months these days, so flexible production lines allow the company to guard against running short of a hot model or overproducing one whose sales have slowed.

Figure 21.3 **Sample Quality Service Client Survey**

ROYAL BANK

QUALITY SERVICE SURVEY

Your Opinion Counts!

INSTRUCTIONS

Given your experiences over the past year with the Royal Bank branch you deal with most often, circle the number which best describes your opinion on the importance of each service aspect and your satisfaction with each service aspect. Please complete all questions that are applicable to you.

Ce questionnaire est également publié en français.

HOW IMPORTANT IS IT? — EXTREMELY UNIMPORTANT 0 1 2 3 4 5 6 7 8 9 10 EXTREMELY IMPORTANT

HOW SATISFIED ARE YOU? — EXTREMELY DISSATISFIED 0 1 2 3 4 5 6 7 8 9 10 EXTREMELY SATISFIED / NOT APPLICABLE X

SERVICE ASPECTS

- Branch hours are convenient to me
- I can conduct my banking without being overheard by others
- There are always enough tellers available to handle the volume of customers
- Automated banking machines have the range of services and information I need
- I always feel like I am welcome at my branch
- The branch is designed in a way that I always know where to go
- The level of service is consistent between branches
- I receive my chequing account statement on time every month
- There is always someone available to look after me when I need help
- Branch staff skillfully handle unusual banking situations

QUALITY SERVICE SURVEY

HOW IMPORTANT IS IT? — EXTREMELY UNIMPORTANT 0 1 2 3 4 5 6 7 8 9 10 EXTREMELY IMPORTANT

HOW SATISFIED ARE YOU? — EXTREMELY DISSATISFIED 0 1 2 3 4 5 6 7 8 9 10 EXTREMELY SATISFIED / NOT APPLICABLE X

SERVICE ASPECTS

- Everyone in the branch works to serve customers when the branch is busy
- Branch staff make me feel like my business is appreciated
- Branch staff help to make my banking easy and save me time
- Branch staff handle my transactions without assistance
- Branch staff make my banking hassle-free
- Branch staff take direct responsibility for resolving problems
- Branch staff always treat me with respect
- Branch staff always look for ways to serve me better
- Branch staff work hard at making sure my transactions are completed quickly
- Branch staff are helpful when I have a question
- Branch staff have an excellent knowledge of all products, fees, and services
- Branch staff explain all product or service options in full without my asking
- Telephone enquiries are responded to quickly
- Branch staff have the experience necessary to handle my banking needs
- Branch staff always contact me when it's time to renew my investments, loans, or mortgages
- Account entries and transactions are handled accurately
- Bank errors are corrected quickly the first time
- If I have a banking problem or enquiry, I only have to "tell my story once"
- An automated banking machine is always working when I go to use it
- I do not have to wait long at an automated banking machine
- The products and services I receive are good value for the money

(continued)

Figure 21.3 (continued)

QUALITY SERVICE SURVEY

Please rate Royal Bank's service overall, taking into account all aspects of the way the bank serves you. Please circle the one number which best describes your opinion.

Extremely Poor   Extremely Good

0   1   2   3   4   5   6   7   8   9   10

On average, how often do you conduct your Royal Bank banking through:
Please circle the appropriate number in each column.

	a Royal Bank banking machine	another Bank's banking machine	a Royal Bank Teller
Every day	1	1	1
4 - 6 times per week	2	2	2
2 - 3 times per week	3	3	3
Once a week	4	4	4
Every 2 - 3 weeks	5	5	5
Once a month	6	6	6
Every 2 -3 months	7	7	7
Less often	8	8	8
Never	9	9	9

Of your last 10 Royal Bank transactions, how many would be done through:

a Royal Bank teller _____
a Royal Bank banking machine _____
another financial institution's banking machine _____
10 (MUST ADD TO TEN)

Please indicate below which financial institution is your **main** one, that is the financial institution where you have most of your products and services, **and** which **others** you deal with:

	MAIN (Circle one choice only)	OTHERS (Circle as many as applicable)
Bank of Montreal	1	1
Canada Trust	2	2
C.I.B.C.	3	3
National Bank	4	4
Royal Bank	5	5
Royal Trust	6	6
Scotiabank	7	7
Toronto Dominion	8	8
Any Other Trust	9	9
Any Caisse Populaire	10	10
Any Credit Union	11	11
Any Stock/Discount Brokerage	12	12
Alberta Treasury	13	13
Any Others	14	14

In the past year, has the staff at your Royal Bank branch:
Please circle the appropriate number in each column.

	YES	NO
Discussed your overall financial situation with you?	1	2
If so, were you provided with specific recommendations?	1	2

QUALITY SERVICE SURVEY

In the **past year**, did you move any of your products or services **to another financial institution?**
If so, which products or services?

	Yes 1	No 2

In the **next year**, would you be likely to:
Please circle the appropriate number in each column.

	NOT AT ALL LIKELY	NOT VERY LIKELY	SOMEWHAT LIKELY	VERY LIKELY	EXTREMELY LIKELY
Acquire additional products or services from Royal Bank? Why is that?	1	2	3	4	5

If you deal exclusively with Royal Bank, please go to the next question.

	NOT AT ALL LIKELY	NOT VERY LIKELY	SOMEWHAT LIKELY	VERY LIKELY	EXTREMELY LIKELY
Move your products or services with other financial institutions **to Royal Bank?** If so, which products or services?	1	2	3	4	5
Move any of your Royal Bank accounts and services **to another financial institution?** If so, which products or services?	1	2	3	4	5
Recommend Royal Bank to relatives and friends?	1	2	3	4	5

We are working hard to improve customer service during the busy times at your Royal Bank branch. Please help us to identify what is **most** important to you when the branch is busy by ranking each of the activities listed below from the most important to least important. Give the most important item a "1" and the second most important a "2" and so on, in the space provided.

RANK

Other employees assist tellers with the line-up _____

Staff work with a sense of urgency _____

An employee offers customers in the line-up a demonstration on using the banking machine or account updater, where available, to help ease the line-up _____

While waiting there is an opportunity to review/read current brochures of interest _____

While waiting there is an opportunity to view an informative video on products and services _____

Tellers train clients who have not completed their forms, how to complete them properly, so they will not slow the line-up in the future _____

Staff do not take time to identify additional banking requirements customers may have _____

Separate tellers or areas serve certain customer groups such as seniors, VIP customers, handicapped customers _____

Form 5/94 (9999999991)

Source: Royal Bank of Canada, Retail Banking Quality Service Survey, May 1994. Reprinted by permission of the Royal Bank of Canada.

Kao Corp., Japan's biggest soap and cosmetics company, has developed incredible flexibility in distribution. The company and its wholly owned wholesalers can deliver goods within 24 hours to any of 280 000 shops, whose average order is for just seven items.

The key is a sophisticated information system. Brand managers see daily sales, stock, and production figures. Within a day, they can learn whether a competitor is running a sale. This network virtually eliminates the lag between an event in the market (e.g., Mrs. Takada buys a bar of soap) and the arrival of the news at the company.

A flexible factory is useless if a company doesn't know what is selling, and it doesn't help to know the market cold if the company can't react to it back at the plant. Building flexibility into an organization enables a firm to add value for customers in several ways. It can provide enhanced product features for specific market segments, lower product prices, rapid change of the product mix, introduction of many new products, and excellent customer response time. Thus, incorporating flexibility into production and marketing can greatly enhance customer satisfaction, and make such organizations extremely competitive in the marketplace.

ASSESSING OTHER ASPECTS OF MARKETING PERFORMANCE: THE MARKETING AUDIT

As an aid in determining where an organization stands with respect to providing total quality to its customers, Philip Kotler has devised an auditing system to measure marketing effectiveness. This *marketing audit* is based on five variables: consumer philosophy, integrated marketing organization, adequate marketing information, strategic orientation, and operational efficiency. These activities are defined as follows:[9]

1. *Customer philosophy.* Does management acknowledge the primacy of the marketplace and of customer needs and wants in shaping company plans and operations?
2. *Integrated marketing organization.* Is the organization staffed so that it will be able to carry out marketing analysis, planning, and implementation and control?
3. *Adequate marketing information.* Does management receive the kind and quality of information needed to conduct effective marketing?
4. *Strategic orientation.* Does marketing management generate innovative strategies and plans for long-run growth and profitability?
5. *Operational efficiency.* Are marketing plans implemented in a cost-effective manner, and are the results monitored for rapid corrective action?

Table 21.3 presents a suggested marketing effectiveness audit and a scoring system for assessing overall effectiveness.

ETHICS IN MARKETING: AN IMPORTANT COMPONENT OF QUALITY MARKETING MANAGEMENT

Marketing planning is based on an understanding of the consumer and the environment. The output of this process is a stream of goods and services designed to

■ Table 21.3 **The Marketing Effectiveness Audit**

Customer Philosophy

A. Does management recognize the importance of designing the company to serve the needs and wants of chosen markets?

0 ☐ Management primarily thinks in terms of selling current and new products to whomever will buy them.

1 ☐ Management thinks in terms of serving a wide range of markets and needs with equal effectiveness.

2 ☐ Management thinks in terms of serving the needs and wants of well-defined markets chosen for their long-run growth and profit potential for the company.

B. Does management develop different offerings and marketing plans for different segments of the market?

0 ☐ No.

1 ☐ Somewhat.

2 ☐ To a good extent.

C. Does management take a whole marketing system view (suppliers, channels, competitors, customers, environment) in planning its business?

0 ☐ No. Management concentrates on selling and servicing its immediate customers.

1 ☐ Somewhat. Management takes a long view of its channels, although the bulk of its effort goes to selling and servicing the immediate customers.

2 ☐ Yes. Management takes a whole marketing system view, recognizing the threats and opportunities created for the company by changes in any part of the system.

Integrated Marketing Organization

D. Is there high-level marketing integration and control of the major marketing functions?

0 ☐ No. Sales and other marketing functions are not integrated at the top and there is some unproductive conflict.

1 ☐ Somewhat. There is formal integration and control of the major marketing functions but less than satisfactory co-ordination and co-operation.

2 ☐ Yes. The major marketing functions are effectively integrated.

E. Does marketing management work well with management in research, manufacturing, purchasing, physical distribution, and finance?

0 ☐ No. There are complaints that marketing is unreasonable in the demands and costs it places on other departments.

1 ☐ Somewhat. The relations are amicable although each department pretty much acts to serve its own power interest.

2 ☐ Yes. The departments co-operate effectively and resolve issues in the best interest of the company as a whole.

F. How well organized is the new-product development process?

0 ☐ The system is ill-defined and poorly handled.

1 ☐ The system formally exists but lacks sophistication.

2 ☐ The system is well structured and professionally staffed.

Adequate Marketing Information

G. When were the latest marketing research studies of customers, buying influences, channels, and competitors conducted?

0 ☐ Several years ago.

1 ☐ A few years ago.

2 ☐ Recently.

H. How well does management know the sales potential and profitability of different market segments, customers, territories, products, channels, and order sizes?

0 ☐ Not at all.

1 ☐ Somewhat.

2 ☐ Very well.

I. What effort is expended to measure the cost-effectiveness of different marketing expenditures?

0 ☐ Little or no effort.

1 ☐ Some effort.

2 ☐ Substantial effort.

Strategic Orientation

J. What is the extent of formal marketing planning?

0 ☐ Management does little or no formal marketing planning.

1 ☐ Management develops an annual marketing plan.

2 ☐ Management develops a detailed annual marketing plan and a careful long-range plan that is updated annually.

K. What is the quality of the current marketing strategy?

0 ☐ The current strategy is not clear.

1 ☐ The current strategy is clear and represents a continuation of traditional strategy.

2 ☐ The current strategy is clear, innovative, data-based, and well reasoned.

(continued)

■ Table 21.3 (continued)

L. What is the extent of contingency thinking and planning?

0 ☐ Management does little or no contingency thinking.

1 ☐ Management does some contingency thinking, although little formal contingency planning.

2 ☐ Management formally identifies the most important contingencies and develops contingency plans.

Operational Efficiency

M. How well is the marketing thinking at the top communicated and implemented down the line?

0 ☐ Poorly.

1 ☐ Fairly well.

2 ☐ Successfully.

N. Is management doing an effective job with the marketing resources?

0 ☐ No. The marketing resources are inadequate for the job to be done.

1 ☐ Somewhat. The marketing resources are adequate, but they are not employed optimally.

2 ☐ Yes. The marketing resources are adequate and are deployed efficiently.

O. Does management show a good capacity to react quickly and effectively to on-the-spot developments?

0 ☐ No. Sales and market information is not very current and management reaction time is slow.

1 ☐ Somewhat. Management receives fairly up-to-date sales and market information; management reaction time varies.

2 ☐ Yes. Management has installed systems yielding highly current information and fast reaction time.

Total Score

Rating Marketing Effectiveness

The auditing outline can be used in this way. The auditor collects information as it bears on the 15 questions. The appropriate answer is checked for each question. The scores are added — the total will be somewhere between 0 and 30. The following scale shows the equivalent in marketing effectiveness:

0–5	None
6–10	Poor
11–15	Fair
16–20	Good
21–25	Very good
26–30	Superior

To illustrate, 15 senior managers in a large building materials company were recently invited to rate their company using the auditing instrument in this exhibit. The resulting overall marketing effectiveness scores ranged from a low of 6 to a high of 15. The median score was 11, with three-fourths of the scores between 9 and 13. Therefore, most of the managers thought their company was at best "fair" at marketing. Several divisions were also rated. Their median scores ranged from a low of 3 to a high of 19. The higher scoring divisions tended to have higher profitability. However, some of the lower scoring divisions were also profitable. An examination of the latter showed that these divisions were in industries where their competition also operated at a low level of marketing effectiveness. The managers feared that these divisions would be vulnerable as soon as competition began to learn to market more successfully.

An interesting question to speculate on is the distribution of median marketing effectiveness scores for *Fortune* "500" companies. My suspicion is that very few companies in that roster would score above 20 ("very good" or "superior") in marketing effectiveness.

Source: Philip Kotler, "From Sales Obsession to Marketing Effectiveness," *Harvard Business Review* (November–December 1977), pp. 70–71. Copyright © 1977 by the President and Fellows of Harvard College. All rights reserved.

serve the needs of the consumer and to return a profit to the company. In this process, marketing plays a significant role in society.

Historically, some marketers have neglected the social issues involved in their activities and have operated on the edge of accepted societal standards of propriety and honesty. Various regulations and licence requirements have been enacted to limit certain marketing practices. Gradually, society has decided that it is not willing to tolerate questionable business behaviour. Thus, society now expects that marketers will act in a socially responsible manner.

Social responsibility is *the marketer's acceptance of the obligation to consider profit, consumer satisfaction, and the well-being of society as being of equal value in evaluating the performance of the firm*. It is the recognition that marketers must be concerned with the qualitative measures of consumer and social benefits as well as with the quantitative measures of sales, revenue, and profits by which marketing performance has traditionally been measured.

Marketing ethics are *the marketer's standards of conduct and moral values*. Ethics involve the decision to do what is morally right. People develop standards of ethical behaviour based on their own systems of values. Their "individual ethics" help them deal with the various ethical questions in their personal lives. However, when they are in a work situation, a serious conflict may materialize. Individual ethics may differ from the "organizational ethics" of the employer.

Such conflict may be resolved to some degree by adherence to professional ethical standards. These standards could be based on a concept of professionalism that transcends both organizational and individual ethics. It depends on the existence of a professional peer group that can exercise collective sanctions on a marketer's professional behaviour. The professional association to which most marketers belong is the American Marketing Association. It has published a Marketing Code of Ethics, as shown in Table 21.4.

One thing is clear, however: just as total customer satisfaction expectations are growing for the products marketed, the same standards are expected of the ethical decisions made by marketers. It is recommended that students of marketing think through and develop quality standards of ethical behaviour *before* they are faced with the inevitable ethical dilemmas they will confront in the day-to-day practice of marketing. Such a stance will result in more honourable marketing practices — and a better world.

social responsibility
The marketer's acceptance of the obligation to consider profit, consumer satisfaction, and the well-being of society as being of equal value in evaluating the performance of the firm.

marketing ethics
The marketer's standards of conduct and moral values.

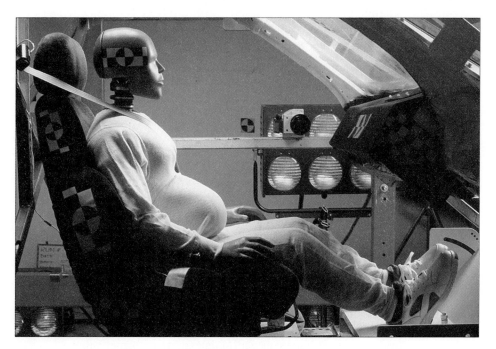

Social responsibility is an important part of General Motors' philosophy. In 1994, GM developed the world's first "pregnant" crash test dummy to help study the effects of vehicle crashes on pregnant women. A television commercial on the crash test dummy "with a special glow" was aired to make consumers aware of the new innovation and to further demonstrate GM's commitment to developing safety standards that meet the needs of all drivers and passengers.

■ Table 21.4 **A Marketing Code of Ethics**

As a member of the American Marketing Association, I recognize the significance of my professional conduct and my responsibilities to society and to the other members of my profession:

1. By acknowledging my accountability to society as a whole as well as to the organization for which I work.

2. By pledging my efforts to assure that all presentation of goods, services, and concepts be made honestly and clearly.

3. By striving to improve marketing knowledge and practice in order to better serve society.

4. By supporting free consumer choice in circumstances that are legal and are consistent with generally accepted community standards.

5. By pledging to use the highest professional standards in my work and in competitive activity.

6. By acknowledging the right of the American Marketing Association, through established procedure, to withdraw my membership if I am found to be in violation of ethical standards of professional conduct.

Source: American Marketing Association, *Constitution and Bylaws*, rev. ed. (Chicago: American Marketing Association, 1977), p. 20. Reprinted by permission of the American Marketing Association.

THE CHALLENGES OF MARKETING

Marketing is one of the most interesting disciplines. The process of applying marketing thinking in competitive situations could hardly be more challenging. A career in marketing requires great sensitivity to the many variables that must be taken into consideration. Continued success demands the highest levels of creativity on the part of the marketer. And since conditions, people, and the environment are constantly changing, a career in marketing will rarely be boring! The fact that many company presidents began their careers in marketing attests to the breadth of business understanding developed through the profession of marketing.

■ KEY TERMS

value	performance gap	social responsibility
benchmarking	total customer satisfaction	marketing ethics

■ INTERACTIVE SUMMARY AND DISCUSSION QUESTIONS

1. Financial results measure the outcomes of strategic initiatives taken in the past. A manager also needs a forward-looking view toward building success in the future. Explain how an emphasis on total customer satisfaction can assist in directing the company's activities.

2. Activity is the process by which value is created. Why are managers often programmed to manage activity rather than value?

3. Value should be the focus of marketing activity. However, value is a subjective term, and is defined by the customer. How, then, can a marketing program that tries to provide total customer satisfaction determine customer values?

4. Building value is a function of a five-link chain composed of culture, systems, performance, and results, which lead to the provision of value. Explain how this chain works.

5. Total quality is a popular management goal, but value is more fundamental. Explain.

6. Benchmarking is the comparison of performance with industry best practices. The concept of "comparison with the best" provides better standards for control of a marketing plan than setting objectives. Give an example to illustrate this concept.

7. There are four fundamental requirements in using benchmarking as a tool to provide value to customers: know your operation, know the industry leaders and competitors, incorporate the best practices, and develop superiority. Using a small business that you are familiar with as an example, explain how these requirements might be explained or applied in terms of that business.

8. The performance gap is the difference between a company's performance and that of the best of the best. Why is it important not only to determine the current performance gap, but to project the future gap as well?

9. Review the benchmarking process in Table 21.2. Apply it to two or three marketing features of a local bookstore.

10. An emphasis on flexibility is a competitive thrust that can provide significant customer value. Explain how this necessarily involves most aspects of the organization.

11. A marketing audit is based on five variables: customer philosophy, integrated marketing organization, adequate marketing information, strategic orientation, and operational efficiency. Outline the probable steps in a marketing audit for a local dry-cleaning company.

12. Social responsibility is the marketer's acceptance of the obligation to consider profit, consumer satisfaction, and the well-being of society as being of equal value in evaluating the performance of the firm. Henry Ford II has argued that in a competitive market system, a firm cannot afford to meet the expense of environmental improvements unless competitors are also legally required to follow the same standards. Discuss.

13. In detail, describe how the total customer satisfaction concept could be applied to the marketing management system of a company you are familiar with.

Notes

Chapter 1

1. Peter F. Drucker, *The Practice of Management* (New York: Harper and Row, 1954), p. 37.
2. Adapted from M. Kubr, ed., *Management Consulting: A Guide to the Profession* (Geneva: International Labour Organization, 1977), p. 189.
3. Richard P. Bagozzi, "Marketing as an Organized Behavioral System of Exchange," *Journal of Marketing* (October 1974), p. 77. Further work by Bagozzi on this subject appears in "Marketing as Exchange," *Journal of Marketing* (October 1975), pp. 32–39, and in "Marketing as Exchange: A Theory of Transactions in the Marketplace," *American Behavioral Scientist* (March–April 1978), pp. 535–36.
4. Bagozzi, "Marketing as an Organized Behavioral System," p. 77.
5. Wroe Alderson, *Marketing Behavior and Executive Action* (Homewood, IL: Irwin, 1962), p. 292.
6. T.G. Povey, "Spotting the Salesman Who Has What It Takes," *Nation's Business* (July 1972), p. 70.
7. Alexander Hlam and Charles D. Schewe, *The Portable MBA in Marketing* (New York: John Wiley & Sons, 1992), p. 12.
8. "AMA Board Approves New Marketing Definition," *Marketing News* (March 1, 1985), p. 1.
9. Many discussions of this topic have suggested that marketing passed through a series of "eras": product, sales, and market orientations. However, Ronald A. Fullerton shows that there is little historical support for the concept of progression through various eras in his article "How Modern Is Modern Marketing? Marketing's Evolution and the Myth of the 'Production Era,'" *Journal of Marketing* (January 1988), pp. 108–25.
10. Henceforth, the term "product" will apply to both goods and services, except as otherwise noted. The marketing principles that apply to products normally apply to services as well.
11. Theodore Levitt, *Innovations in Marketing* (New York: McGraw-Hill, 1962), p. 7.
12. The following discussion is based on Benson P. Shapiro, "What the Hell Is 'Market Oriented'?" *Harvard Business Review* (November–December 1988), pp. 120–22.
13. Mansour Javidan and John Rigby, *Marketing*, Proceedings of the Annual Conference of the Administrative Sciences Association of Canada, Vol. 11, Part 3, pp. 147–56.
14. "AMA Board Approves New Marketing Definition," p. 1.

Chapter 2

1. Excerpted from Patricia Lush, "Scott's British Arm Shuns Firms Cutting in Clayoquot," *The Globe and Mail* (March 1, 1994), p. B5. Reprinted by permission of *The Globe and Mail*.
2. John Kohut, "Competition Body Charges NutraSweet with Monopolizing Canadian Market," *The Globe and Mail* (June 2, 1989).
3. Adapted from Drew Fagan, "Tribunal Sours NutraSweet's Success," *The Globe and Mail* (October 5, 1990).
4. Consumer and Corporate Affairs, *Misleading Advertising Bulletin* (January–March 1986), p. 7.
5. James Walker and Alan D. Gray, "$1 Million Ad Fine Signal to Retailers," *The Financial Times* 72:6 (July 1983), p. 14.
6. Consumer and Corporate Affairs, personal communication.
7. Consumer and Corporate Affairs, *Misleading Advertising Bulletin* (July–September 1986), p. 11
8. Many economists argue that society is capable of preventing future depressions through intelligent use of various economic policies. Thus, a recession is followed by a period of recovery.
9. The concept of environmental forecasting is examined in T.F. Mastri, "Environmental Forecasting," *Fairleigh Dickinson University Business Review* (Winter 1973), pp. 3–10.
10. Interesting articles related to this topic include Philip Kotler and Sidney J. Levy, "Demarketing, Yes, Demarketing," *Harvard Business Review* (November–December 1971), pp. 74–80; David W. Cravens, "Marketing Management in an Era of Shortages," *Business Horizons* (February 1974), pp. 79–85; A.B. Blankenship and John H. Holmes, "Will Shortages Bankrupt the Marketing Concept?" *MSU Business Topics* (Spring 1974), pp. 13–18; Philip Kotler, "Marketing During Periods of Shortages," *Journal of Marketing* (July 1974), pp. 20–29; Zohrab S. Demirdjian, "The Role of Marketing in an Economy of Affluence and Shortages," *Business and Society* (Spring 1975), pp. 15–21; Nessim Hanna, A.H. Kizilbash, and Albert Smart, "Marketing Strategy Under Conditions of Economic Scarcity," *Journal of Marketing* (January 1975), pp. 63–67; Sunier C. Aggarwal, "Prepare for Continual Materials Shortages," *Harvard Business Review*

(May–June 1982), pp. 6–10; Joseph Deutsch, "Effects of a Public Advertising Campaign on Consumer Behavior in a Demarketing Situation," *International Journal of Research in Marketing* 2:4 (1985), pp. 287–90; and Guprit S. Kindra, "Demarketing Inappropriate Health Care Consumption," *Journal of Health Care Marketing* 15:2 (Summer 1995), pp. 10–14.

11. David Thompson, "Rising to the Challenge," *Marketing Magazine* (May 2, 1983), p. 13.

12. Adapted from Andrew Van Velzen, "Secular Society Gave Couple Their Niche: The Wedding Business," *The Globe and Mail* (August 14, 1989), p. C1.

Chapter 3

1. Excerpted from Scott Haggett, "Rotisserie Chicken: Eateries' Golden Egg," *The Financial Post* (June 4, 1994), p. 53. Reprinted by permission of *The Financial Post*.

2. See Scott M. Smith and Leland L. Beik, "Market Segmentation for Fund Raisers," *Journal of the Academy of Marketing Science* (Summer 1982), pp. 208–16.

3. This section relies heavily on Harry H. Hiller, *Canadian Society: A Sociological Analysis* (Scarborough, ON: Prentice-Hall, 1976), pp. 13–37.

4. T.R. Weir, "Population Changes in Canada, 1867–1967," *Canadian Geographer* 2:4 (1967), p. 198.

5. Larry H. Long, "On Measuring Geographic Mobility," *Journal of the American Statistical Association* (September 1970).

6. Kenneth Runyon, *Consumer Behavior* (Columbus, OH: Merrill, 1980), p. 35.

7. These examples are from an earlier life-cycle study — see William D. Wells and George Gubar, "Life Cycle Concept in Marketing Research," *Journal of Marketing Research* (November 1966), p. 362; see also Frederick W. Derrick and Alane K. Lehfeld, "The Family Life Cycle: An Alternative Approach," *Journal of Consumer Research* (September 1980), pp. 214–17; Robin A. Douthitt, "Family Composition, Parental Time, and Market Goods: Life Cycle Trade-Offs," *Journal of Consumer Affairs* 24:1 (Summer 1990), pp. 110–33; Rob Lawson, "Patterns of Tourist Expenditure and Types of Vacation Across the Family Life Cycle," *Journal of Travel Research* 29:4 (Spring 1991), pp. 12–18; and Fabian Linden, "Welcome to the Middle Ages," *Across the Board* 28:7 (July–August 1991), pp. 9–10.

8. Based on Statistics Canada, *Family Income: Census Families, 1986 Census*, Catalogue No. 93-117; and *Income Distribution by Size in Canada, 1994*, Catalogue No. 13-207, p. 88.

9. Statistics Canada, *Changes in Income in Canada, 1970–1980*, Catalogue No. 99-941.

10. This section is adapted from John Chaplin "Pigeonholes for Consumers," *Marketing Magazine* (October 16, 1989), p. 28.

11. John J. Burnett, "Psychographic and Demographic Characteristics of Blood Donors," *Journal of Consumer Research* (June 1981), pp. 62–86; Mary Ann Lederhaus and Ronald J. Adams, "A Psychographic Profile of the Cosmopolitan Consumers," in *Proceedings of the Southwestern Marketing Association*, eds. Robert H. Ross, Frederic B. Kraft, and Charles H. David (Wichita, KS: Southwestern Marketing Assoc., 1981), pp. 142–45; J. Paul Merenski, "Psychographics: Valid by Definition and Reliable by Technique," *Developments in Marketing Science*, ed. Venkatakrishna V. Bellur (Miami Beach: Academy of Marketing Science, 1981), pp. 161–66; Jack A. Lesser, "The Generalizability of Psychographic Market Segments Across Geographic Locations," *Journal of Marketing* 50:1 (January 1986), pp. 18–27; "Psychographics Help Marketers Find and Serve New Market Segments: Scenario for Setting Psychographics to Work," *Marketing News* 21:9 (April 24, 1987), pp. 4–5; and Rebecca Piirto, "Clothes with Attitude," *American Demographics* 12:10 (October 1990), pp. 10, 52, 54.

12. Daniel Yankelovich, "New Criteria for Market Segmentation," *Harvard Business Review* (March–April 1964), pp. 83–90.

13. See Russell I. Haley, "Benefit Segmentation: A Decision-Oriented Research Tool," *Journal of Marketing* (July 1968), pp. 30–35.

Chapter 4

1. Excerpted from Elizabeth Renzetti, "It's the Revenge of the 'Vinyl People,'" *The Globe and Mail* (November 12, 1994), p. C3. Reprinted by permission of *The Globe and Mail*.

2. This section is based on materials written by J.D. Forbes, University of British Columbia.

3. "Small Clothes Are Selling Big," *Business Week* (November 16, 1981), pp. 152, 156.

4. Philip Kotler and Ravi Singh, "Basic Marketing Strategy for Winning Your Marketing War," *Marketing Times* (November–December 1981), pp. 23–24.

5. A similar analysis is suggested in Robert M. Fulmer, *The New Marketing* (New York: Macmillan, 1976), pp. 34–37; Philip Kotler, *Marketing Management: Analysis, Planning, Implementation, and Control*, 7th ed. (Englewood Cliffs, NJ: Prentice-Hall, 1991), pp. 263–86; E. Jerome McCarthy and William D. Perreault, *Basic Marketing: A Global Managerial Approach*, 11th ed. (Homewood, IL: Irwin, 1993), pp. 81–104; and Roger Brooksbank, "The Anatomy of Marketing Positioning Strategy," *Marketing Intelligence and Planning* 12:4 (1994), pp. 10–14.

6. "Properly Applied Psychographics Add Marketing Luster," *Marketing News* (November 12, 1982), p. 10.

7. Victoria Burrus, "A Burning Ambition," *The Globe and Mail* (August 8, 1994), p. B4.

Chapter 5

1. Excerpted from Rod McQueen, "Fast Forward to the New Economy," *The Financial Post* (July 9, 1994), p. 7. Reprinted by permission of *The Financial Post*.

2. Official definition of the American Marketing Association.

3. John A. Gonder, "Marketing Research in Canada," in *Cases and Readings in Marketing*, ed. R.H. Rotenberg (Toronto: Holt, Rinehart and Winston, 1974), p. 221.

4. Bertram Schoner and Kenneth P. Uhl, *Marketing Research: Information Systems and Decision Making* (New York: Wiley, 1975), p. 199.

5. Wide Area Telephone Service is a telephone company service that allows a business firm to make unlimited long-distance calls for a fixed rate per region.

6. *Wall Street Journal* (June 28, 1972).

7. See Fred D. Reynolds and Deborah K. Johnson, "Validity of Focus-Group Findings," *Journal of Advertising Research* (June 1978), pp. 21–24; and Bobby J. Calder, "Focus Groups and the Nature of Qualitative Marketing Research," *Journal of Marketing Research* (August 1977), pp. 353–64.

8. This discussion follows William G. Zikmund, *Exploring Marketing Research*, 4th ed. (Hinsdale, IL: The Dryden Press, 1982), pp. 450–77. See also William G. Zikmund, *Business Research Methods* (Chicago: The Dryden Press, 1991), pp. 329–54.

9. A useful article on sampling is Henry Assael and John Keon, "Nonsampling vs. Sampling Errors in Survey Research," *Journal of Marketing* (Spring 1982), pp. 114–23.

10. "Marketing Intelligence Systems: A DEW Line for Marketing Men," *Business Management* (January 1966), p. 32.

11. "Marketing Management and the Computer," *Sales Management* (August 20, 1965), pp. 49–60; see also Leon Winer, "Putting the Computer to Work in Marketing," *Pittsburgh Business Review* (November–December 1972), pp. 1–5ff; and "Computer-Assisted Marketing," *Small Business Reports* 14:5 (May 1989), pp. 76–78.

Chapter 6

1. Excerpted from Keith Damsell, "McDonald's, Harvey's in Food Fight," *The Globe and Mail* (June 13, 1994), p. B1. Reprinted by permission of the author.

2. A.J. Rowe, R.O. Mason, K.E. Dickel, and N.H. Snyder, *Strategic Management: A Methodological Approach* (Reading, MA: Addison-Wesley, 1989), p. 9.

3. Theodore Levitt, "Marketing and Corporate Purpose," in *Changing Strategies in a New Economy*, eds. Jules Backman and John A. Czepiel (Indianapolis: Bobbs-Merrill, 1977), p. 29.

4. For a more detailed discussion, see Yoram Wind and Thomas S. Robertson, "Marketing Strategy: New Directions for Theory and Research," *Journal of Marketing* (Spring 1983), pp. 12–15.

5. George S. Day and Robin Wensley, "Assessing Advantage: A Framework for Diagnosing Competitive Superiority," *Journal of Marketing* (Summer 1983), p. 82.

6. The following section is adapted from Wind and Robertson, "Marketing Strategy," pp. 16–22.

7. Alfred R. Oxenfeld and William L. Moore, "Customer or Competitor: Which Guideline for Marketing?" *Management Review* (August 1978), pp. 43–48.

8. Robert H. Hayes and William J. Abernathy, "Managing Our Emotional Way to Economic Decline," *Harvard Business Review* (July–August 1980), pp. 67–87.

9. Benson P. Shapiro, "Getting Things Done," *Harvard Business Review* (September–October, 1985), p. 28.

10. Dick Berry, *Marketing News* (December 24, 1990), p. 10.

11. Peter Chandler, "Strategic Thinking," *Business Victoria* (May 1994), p. 7.

Chapter 7

1. Adapted from Randall Scotland, "Nintendo, Sega Prepare for Showdown," *The Financial Post* (April 9, 1994), p. S26. Used by permission of *The Financial Post*.

2. This definition is adapted from James F. Engel, Roger D. Blackwell, and Paul W. Miniard, *Consumer Behavior*, 7th ed. (Hinsdale, IL: The Dryden Press, 1993), p. 4.

3. See Kurt Lewin, *Field Theory in Social Science* (New York: Harper and Row, 1964), p. 25; see also C. Glenn Walters, "Consumer Behavior: An Appraisal," *Journal of the Academy of Marketing Science* (Fall 1979), pp. 237–84.

4. A.H. Maslow, *Motivation and Personality* (New York: Harper and Row, 1954), pp. 370–96.

5. A.H. Maslow, *Motivation and Personality*, p. 382; see also George Brooker, "The Self-Actualizing Socially Conscious Consumer," *Journal of Consumer Research* (September 1976), pp. 107–12; and James Rada Jr., "What Makes Buyers Buy?" *American Salesman* 40:2 (February 1995), pp. 16–19.

6. E.E. Lawlor and J.L. Suttle, "A Causal Correlational Test of the Need Hierarchy Concept," *Organizational Behaviour and Human Performance* 3 (1968), pp. 12–35; see also Jerry L. Gray and Frederick A. Starke, *Organizational Behavior: Concepts and Applications*, 3rd ed. (Columbus, OH: Merrill, 1988), pp. 25–29; and James L. Gibson, John M. Ivancevich, and James H. Donnelly Jr., *Organizations: Behavior, Structure, Processes*, 7th ed. (Homewood, IL: Irwin, 1991), pp. 102–5.

7. George Katona, *The Powerful Consumer* (New York: McGraw-Hill, 1960), p. 132; see also Engel, Blackwell, and Miniard, *Consumer Behavior*, 6th ed., pp. 490–91.

8. Stuart Henderson Britt, "How Weber's Law Can Be Applied to Marketing," *Business Horizons* (February 1975), pp. 21–29.

9. John Brooks, "The Little Ad That Isn't There," *Consumer Reports* (January 1958), pp. 7–10; see also Del Hawkins, "The Effects of Subliminal Stimulation on Drive Level and Brand Preference," *Journal of Marketing Research* (August 1970), pp. 322–26; and Kathryn T. Theus, "Subliminal Advertising and the Psychology of Processing Unconscious Stimuli: A Review of Research," *Psychology and Marketing* 11:3 (May–June 1994), pp. 271–90.

10. See James H. Myers and William H. Reynolds, *Consumer Behaviour and Marketing Management* (Boston: Houghton Mifflin, 1967), p. 14.

11. Richard P. Barthol and Michael J. Goldstein, "Psychology and the Invisible Sell," *California Management Review* (Winter 1959), p. 34.

12. One researcher reports that some overt behaviour in pathologically prone individuals can be influenced if they appeal to the appropriate unconscious wish: see Jack Saegert, "Another Look at Subliminal Perception," *Journal of Advertising Research* (February 1979), pp. 55–57.

13. George S. Day, "Using Attitude Change Measures to Evaluate New Product Introductions," *Journal of Marketing Research* (November 1970), pp. 474–82; see also Stephen J. Miller, Michael B. Mazis, and Peter L. Wright, "The Influence of Brand Ambiguity on Brand Attitude Development," *Journal of Marketing Research* (November 1971), pp. 455–59; Frank Schuhmann, "Consumer Cognitive Systems: A Study of the Relationship Between Consumer Attitudes and Values," *Idaho Business and Economic Journal* (January 1975), pp. 1–15; Kent B. Monroe, "The Influence of Price Differences and Brand Familiarity on Brand Preferences," *Journal of Consumer Research* (June 1976), pp. 42–49; and Jeanne Lebsack, "Recognize the Signals Before Making Your Pitch," *Life Association News* 85:3 (March 1990), pp. 113, 115.

14. Learning is perhaps the most thoroughly researched field in psychology, and several learning theories have been developed. For a discussion of these theories, see Engel, Blackwell, and Miniard, *Consumer Behavior*, 7th ed., pp. 425–55.

15. This section is based on Michael L. Rothschild and William C. Gaidis, "Behavioral Learning Theory: Its Relevance to Marketing and Promotion," *Journal of Marketing* (Spring 1981), pp. 70–78.

16. John Koten, "For Kellogg, the Hardest Part is Getting People Out of Bed," *Wall Street Journal* (May 27, 1982), p. 27.

17. "Learning How to Please the Baffling Japanese," *Fortune* (October 5, 1981), p. 122.

18. Adapted from Engel, Blackwell, and Miniard, *Consumer Behavior*, 6th ed., p. 63.

19. This is noted in Engel, Blackwell, and Miniard, *Consumer Behavior*, 6th ed., p. 64.

20. Edward T. Hall, "The Silent Language in Overseas Business," *Harvard Business Review* (May–June 1960), p. 89.

21. Patricia L. Layman, "In Any Language, the Beauty Business Spells Success," *Chemical Week* (September 17, 1975), p. 26.

22. See Jean-Charles Chebat and George Hénault, "The Cultural Behavior of Canadian Consumers," in *Cases and Readings in Marketing*, ed. R.H. Rotenberg (Toronto: Holt, Rinehart and Winston, 1974), pp. 176–80 [this material also appeared in *Revue Commerce*, September 1971]; see also M. Brisebois, "Industrial Advertising and Marketing in Quebec," *The Marketer* (Spring–Summer 1966), p. 11; Annamma Joy, "Ethnicity as a Factor Influencing Use of Financial Services," *International Journal of Bank Marketing* 9:4 (1991), pp. 10–16; "What Quebec Wants," *Sales and Marketing Manager* 32: 7 (July 1991), pp. 16, 18; and Brian Dunn, "Nationalism in Advertising: Dead or Alive?" *Advertising Age* 64:49 (November 22, 1993), p. SS18.

23. Gail Chaisson, "The French Market Today," *Marketing Magazine* (June 1, 1981), pp. 11, 14.

24. Eleine Saint-Jacques and Bruce Mallen, "The French Market Under the Microscope," *Marketing Magazine* (May 11, 1981), p. 10.

25. Royal Commission on Bilingualism and Biculturalism.

26. Based on Jan Morin and Michel Ostiguy, "View from the Top," *Marketing Magazine* (June 1, 1981), p. 28.

27. M. Cloutier, "Marketing in Quebec," Industrial Marketing Research Association Conference, Toronto, March 1978.

28. Del I. Hawkins, Kenneth A. Coney, and Roger J. Best, *Consumer Behavior: Implications for Marketing Strategy*, 5th ed. (Homewood, IL: Irwin, 1992), pp. 137–38. The quotation is adapted from S.E. Asch, "Effects of Group Pressure upon the Modification and Distortion of Judgments," in *Readings in Social Psychology*, eds. E.E. MacCoby et al. (New York: Holt, Rinehart and Winston, 1958), pp. 174–83.

29. © "Lifestyles" is a trademark of Compusearch Micromarketing Data and Systems. Reprinted by permission of Compusearch Micromarketing Data and Sytems, 1995.

30. See Danny N. Bellenger and Elizabeth C. Hirschman, "Identifying Opinion Leaders by Self-Report," in *Contemporary Marketing Thought*, eds. Barnett A. Greenberg and Danny N. Bellenger (Chicago: American Marketing Association, 1977), pp. 341–44.

31. Engel, Blackwell, and Miniard, *Consumer Behavior*, 6th ed., pp. 176–82; see also Wilson Brown, "The Family and Consumer Decision Making," *Journal of the Academy of Marketing Science* (Fall 1979), pp. 335–43; Gary L. Sullivan, "The Family Purchase Decision Process: A Cross-Cultural Review and Framework for Research," *Southwest Journal of Business and Economics* 6:1 (Fall 1988), pp. 43–63; Erich Kirchler, "Spouses' Joint Purchase Decisions: Determinants of Influence Tactics for Muddling Through the Process," *Journal of Economic Psychology* 14:2 (June 1993), pp. 405–38; and John B. Ford, "Perception of Marital Roles in Purchase Decision Processes: A Cross-Cultural Study," *Journal of the Academy of Marketing Science* 23:2 (Spring 1995), pp. 120–31.

32. "Business Shifts Its Sales Pitch for Women," *U.S. News and World Report* (July 9, 1981), p. 46; Margaret LeRoux, "Exec Claims Most Ads to Women Miss the Mark,"

Advertising Age (May 21, 1979), p. 24; Ann Cooper, "Meeting Ms. Right," *Adweek* 36:44 (October 30, 1995), pp. 23–26; and Hallie Mummert, "Reaching Out to Women," *Target Marketing* 18:8 (August 1995), pp. 33–38.

33. George J. Szybillo, Arlene K. Sosanie, and Aaron Tenebein, "Should Children Be Seen but Not Heard?" *Journal of Advertising Research* (December 1977), pp. 7–13.

34. Lester Rand, *The Rand Youth Poll*, 1981.

35. See J.P. Liefeld, "Problem Recognition," in *Consumer Decision-Making: An Annotated Bibliography* (Ottawa: Consumer and Corporate Affairs, 1979).

36. B.M. Campbell, "The Existence of Evoked Set and Determinants of Its Magnitude in Brand Choice Behavior," in *Buyer Behavior: Theoretical and Empirical Foundations*, eds. John A. Howard and Lonnie Ostrom (New York: Knopf, 1973), pp. 243–44.

37. Engel, Blackwell, and Miniard, *Consumer Behavior*, 6th ed., p. 479.

38. For a thorough discussion of purchase location, see David L. Loudon and Albert J. Della Bitta, *Consumer Behavior: Concepts and Applications*, 3rd ed. (New York: McGraw-Hill, 1988), pp. 631–51.

39. Leon Festinger, *A Theory of Cognitive Dissonance* (Stanford, CA: Stanford University Press, 1962), p. 3.

40. See Robert J. Connole, James D. Benson, and Inder P. Khera, "Cognitive Dissonance Among Innovators," *Journal of the Academy of Marketing Science* (Winter 1977), pp. 9–20; David R. Lambert, Ronald J. Dornoff, and Jerome B. Kernan, "The Industrial Buyer and the Postchoice Evaluation Process," *Journal of Marketing Research* (May 1977), pp. 246–51; and William H. Cummings and M. Venkatesan, "Cognitive Dissonance and Consumer Behavior: A Review of the Evidence," *Journal of Marketing Research* (August 1976), pp. 303–8.

41. These categories were originally suggested in John A. Howard, *Marketing Management Analysis and Planning* (Homewood, IL: Irwin, 1963); the discussion here is based on Donald R. Lehmann, William L. Moore, and Terry Elrod, "The Development of Distinct Choice Process Segments over Time: A Stochastic Modelling Approach," *Journal of Marketing* (Spring 1982), pp. 48–50.

Chapter 8

1. Adapted from Daniel Stoffman, "Bombardier's Billion-Dollar Space Race," *Canadian Business* (June 1994), pp. 90–101. Used by permission of the author.

2. The development of the new type of pole and the problems involved in its adoption are described in Arch G. Woodside, "Marketing Anatomy of Buying Process Can Help Improve Industrial Strategy," *Marketing News* (May 1, 1981), Section 2, p. 11.

3. These are suggested in Patrick J. Robinson, Charles W. Farris, and Yoram Wind, *Industrial Buying and Creative Marketing* (Boston: Allyn and Bacon, 1967), Chapter 1. The discussion here follows Michael D. Hutt and Thomas W. Speh, *Business Marketing Management: A Strategic View of Industrial and Organizational Markets*, 5th ed. (Fort Worth, TX: The Dryden Press, 1995), pp. 70–77.

4. This section is based on Hutt and Speh, *Business Marketing Management*, 5th ed., pp. 104–12.

5. An interesting discussion of influences is found in Robert J. Thomas, "Correlates of Interpersonal Purchase Influence in Organizations," *Journal of Consumer Research* (September 1982), pp. 171–82. See also Robert E. Krapfel, Jr., "An Extended Influence Model of Organizational Buyer Behavior," *Journal of Business Research* (June 1982), pp. 147–57; Daniel H. McQuiston, "Novelty, Complexity, and Importance as Casual Determinants of Industrial Buyer Behavior," *Journal of Marketing* 53:2 (April 1989), pp. 66–79; and Tony L. Henthorne, "How Organizational Buyers Reduce Risk," *Industrial Marketing Management* 22:1 (February 1993), pp. 41–48.

6. This section is based on Manoj K. Agarwal, Philip C. Burger, and Alladi Venkatesh, "Industrial Consumer Behavior: Toward An Improved Model," in *Developments in Marketing Science*, eds. Venkatakrishna V. Bellur et al. (Miami Beach: Academy of Marketing Science, 1981), pp. 69–73.

7. These price cuts are described in Thomas F. O'Boyle, "Price Cutting Being Forced on Suppliers," *Wall Street Journal* (May 14, 1982).

8. The history and current status of reciprocal agreements are summarized in E. Robert Finney, "Reciprocity: Gone but Not Forgotten," *Journal of Marketing* (January 1978), pp. 54–59; see also William J. Kehoe and Byron D. Hewett, "Reciprocity and Reverse Reciprocity: A Literature Review and Research Design," in *Proceedings of the Southern Marketing Association*, eds. Robert S. Franz, Robert M. Hopkins, and Al Toma (New Orleans: November 1978), pp. 481–83; and Monroe M. Bird, "Reverse Reciprocity: A New Twist to Industrial Buyers," *Atlanta Economic Review* (January–February 1976), pp. 11–13.

9. Adapted from *How to Do Business with the Department of Supply and Services* (Ottawa: Supply and Services, 1980), pp. 1–11.

10. Based on "Out of the Maze," *Sales and Marketing Management* (April 9, 1979), pp. 44–52.

Chapter 9

1. Excerpted from Donald MacIntyre, "Clock Ticking Away for Seiko," *Bloomberg Business News*, as reprinted in *The Financial Post* (June 25, 1994), p. 55. Reprinted with permission.

2. A good summary of the product life cycle is contained in George S. Day, "The Product Life Cycle: Analysis and Applications Issues," *Journal of Marketing* (Fall 1981),

pp. 60–67; see also Gerald J. Tellis and C. Merle Crawford, "An Evolutionary Approach to Product Growth Theory," *Journal of Marketing* (Fall 1981), pp. 125–32.

3. This section relies on George S. Day, "The Product Life Cycle," pp. 60–65.

4. Ben M. Enis, Raymond LaGrace, and Arthur E. Prell, "Extending the Product Life Cycle," *Business Horizons* (June 1977), pp. 45–56.

5. William Qualls, Richard W. Olshavsky, and Ronald E. Michaels, "Shortening the PLC: An Empirical Test," *Journal of Marketing* (Fall 1981), pp. 76–80.

6. Fashion cycles are discussed in Raymond A. Marquardt, James C. Makens, and Robert G. Roe, *Retail Management: Satisfaction of Consumer Needs*, 3rd ed. (Hinsdale, IL: The Dryden Press, 1983), pp. 98–99; see also George B. Sproles, "Analyzing Fashion Life Cycles: Principles and Perspectives," *Journal of Marketing* (Fall 1981), pp. 116–24; and Richard Reed, "Fashion Life Cycles and Extension Theory," *European Journal of Marketing* 21:3 (1987), pp. 52–62.

7. Enis, LaGrace, and Prell, "Extending the Product Life Cycle."

8. Bill Abrams, "Warring Toothpaste Makers Spend Millions Luring Buyers to Slightly Altered Products," *Wall Street Journal* (September 9, 1981).

9. Gail Bronson, "Baby Food It Is, but Gerber Wants Teen-Agers to Think of It as Dessert," *Wall Street Journal* (July 17, 1981).

10. Karger, "5 Ways to Find New Use: Re-evaluate Your Old Products," p. 18.

11. Everett M. Rogers, *Diffusion of Innovations*, 4th ed. (New York: Free Press, 1995), pp. 243–51.

12. James Colemand, Elihu Katz, and Herbert Menzel, "The Diffusion of an Innovation among Physicians," *Sociometry* (December 1957), pp. 253–70.

13. Bryce Ryan and Neal Gross, "The Diffusion of Hybrid Seed Corn in Two Iowa Communities," *Rural Sociology* (March 1943), pp. 15–24.

14. Joseph Barry Mason and Danny Bellenger, "Analyzing High-Fashion Acceptance," *Journal of Retailing* (Winter 1974), pp. 79–88.

15. See James F. Engel, Robert J. Kegerries, and Roger D. Blackwell, "Word-of-Mouth Communication by the Innovator," *Journal of Marketing* (July 1969), pp. 15–19.

16. For a discussion of characteristics of first adopters, see William E. Bell, "Consumer Innovators: A Unique Market for Newness," in *Toward Scientific Marketing*, ed. Stephen A. Greyser (Chicago: American Marketing Association, 1964), pp. 89–95; see also Louis E. Boone, "The Search for the Consumer Innovator," *Journal of Business* (April 1970), pp. 135–40; David W. Cravens, James C. Cotham, and James R. Felix, "Identifying Innovator and Non-Innovator Firms," *Journal of Business Research* (April 1971), pp. 45–51; Lyman E. Ostland, "Identifying Early Buyers," *Journal of Advertising Research*

(April 1972), pp. 29–34; Robert A. Peterson, "Diffusion and Adoption of a Consumer Durable," *Marquette Business Review* (Spring 1974), pp. 1–4; Steven A. Baumgarten, "The Innovative Communicator in the Diffusion Process," *Journal of Marketing Research* (February 1975), pp. 12–18; Laurence P. Feldman and Gary M. Armstrong, "Identifying Buyers of a Major Automobile Innovation," *Journal of Marketing* (January 1975), pp. 47–53; Robert T. Green and Eric Langeard, "A Cross-National Comparison of Consumer Habits and Innovator Characteristics," *Journal of Marketing* (July 1975), pp. 34–41; and Frank Alpert, "Innovator Buying Behavior Over Time: The Innovator Buying Cycle and the Cumulative Effects of Innovations," *Journal of Product and Brand Management* 3:2 (1994), pp. 50–62.

17. Ronald Marks and Eugene Hughes, "Profiling the Consumer Innovator," in *Evolving Marketing Thought for 1980*, eds. John H. Summey and Ronald D. Taylor (New Orleans: Southern Marketing Association, 1980), pp. 115–18; Elizabeth Hirschman, "Innovativeness, Novelty Seeking and Consumer Creativity," *Journal of Consumer Research* (December 1980), pp. 283–95; and Richard W. Olshavsky, "Time and the Rate of Adoption of Innovations," *Journal of Consumer Research* (March 1980), pp. 425–28.

18. For a more thorough discussion of the speed of the adoption process, see Everett M. Rogers, *Division of Innovations*, 4th ed.

19. See Raymond A. Bauer, "Consumer Behavior as Risk Taking," in *Dynamic Marketing for a Changing World*, ed. Robert S. Hancock (Chicago: American Marketing Association, 1960), pp. 389–98; see also James R. Bettman, "Perceived Risk and Its Components: A Model and Empirical Test," *Journal of Marketing Research* (May 1973), pp. 184–90; Arch G. Woodside, "Informal Group Influence in Risk Taking," *Journal of Marketing Research* (May 1972), pp. 223–25; Robert D. Hisrich, Ronald J. Dornoff, and Jerome B. Kernan, "Perceived Risk in Store Selection," *Journal of Marketing Research* (November 1972), pp. 435–39; and James W. Taylor, "The Role of Risk in Consumer Behavior," *Journal of Marketing* (April 1974), pp. 54–60.

20. This discussion relies on Patrick E. Murphy and Ben M. Enis, "Classifying Products Strategically," *Journal of Marketing* (July 1986), pp. 24–42. Note that these authors argue that their classification system can be applied equally well to industrial products.

Chapter 10

1. Excerpted from "Odd Couples on Store Shelves," *The Globe and Mail* (July 7, 1994), p. B4. Reprinted by permission of *The Globe and Mail*.

2. Bill Abrams, "Despite Mixed Record, Firms Still Pushing for New Products," *Wall Street Journal* (November 12, 1981).

3. Abrams, "Despite Mixed Record," p. 25.

4. "The Money-Guzzling Genius of Biotechnology," *The Economist* (May 13, 1989), p. 69.

5. David S. Hopkins, *New Product Winners and Losers* (New York: Conference Board, 1980); see also "Booz Allen Looks at New Products' Role," *Wall Street Journal* (March 26, 1981).

6. Abrams, "Despite Mixed Record," p. 25.

7. This list is adapted from Roger Calantone and Robert G. Cooper, "New Product Scenarios: Prospects for Success," *Journal of Marketing* (Spring 1981), p. 49.

8. Robert G. Cooper, "The Myth of the Better Mousetrap: What Makes a New Product a Success?" *Business Quarterly* (Spring 1981), pp. 71, 72.

9. Abrams, "Despite Mixed Record," p. 25.

10. Reported in Ann M. Morrison, "The General Mills Brand of Manager," *Fortune* (January 12, 1981), pp. 99–107; another interesting discussion appears in "Brand Management System Is Best, but Refinements Needed," *Marketing News* (July 9, 1982), p. 12.

11. Jacob M. Duker and Michael V. Laric, "The Product Manager: No Longer on Trial," in *The Changing Marketing Environment: New Theories and Applications*, eds. Kenneth Bernhardt et al. (Chicago: American Marketing Association, 1981), pp. 93–96; and Peter S. Howsam and G. David Hughes, "Product Management System Suffers from Insufficient Experience, Poor Communication," *Marketing News* (June 26, 1981), p. 8.

12. Adapted from John R. Rockwell and Marc C. Particelli, "New Product Strategy: How the Pros Do It," *Industrial Marketing* (May 1982), p. 50.

13. For an excellent treatment of the product development process, see Robert D. Hisrich and Michael P. Peters, *Marketing Decisions for New and Mature Products: Planning, Development, and Control* (Columbus, OH: C.E. Merrill, 1984); Richard T. Hise, *Product/Service Strategy* (New York: Mason/Charter Publishers, 1977); A. Edward Spitz, *Product Planning*, 2nd ed. (New York: Mason/Charter, 1977); and Chester R. Wasson, *Dynamic Competitive Strategy and Product Life Cycles* (Austin, TX: Austin Press, 1978).

14. Rockwell and Particelli, "New Product Strategy," p. 50.

15. Quoted in Mary McCabe English, "Marketers: Better than a Coin Flip," *Advertising Age* (February 9, 1981), p. S-15. Copyright 1981 by Crain Communications, Inc.

16. Dylan Landis, "Durable Goods for a Test?" *Advertising Age* (February 9, 1981), pp. S-18, S-19.

17. Committee on Definitions, *Marketing Definitions: A Glossary of Marketing Terms* (Chicago: American Marketing Association, 1960), pp. 9–10.

18. "A Worldwide Brand for Nissan," *Business Week* (August 24, 1981), p. 104.

19. The question of brand choice is pursued in such articles as J. Morgan Jones and Fred S. Ziefryden, "An Approach for Assessing Demographic and Price Influences on Brand Purchase Behavior," *Journal of Marketing* (Winter 1981), pp. 36–46.

20. *Business Week* (February 20, 1960), p. 71.

21. Meir Statman and Tyzoon T. Tyebjee, "Trademarks, Patents, and Innovation in the Ethical Drug Industry," *Journal of Marketing* (Summer 1981), pp. 71–81.

22. Bill Abrams, "Brand Loyalty Rises Slightly, but Increase Could Be Fluke," *Wall Street Journal* (February 7, 1982).

23. Frances Phillips, "Private Label Appliances Vie with National Brands," *The Financial Post* (August 13, 1983).

24. Frances Phillips, "New Packaging Looks Are Making Some Products Winners," *The Financial Post* (June 4, 1983).

25. *Market Research Facts and Trends* (November–December 1989), p. 1.

26. "Packaging Linked to Ad's Effect," *Advertising Age* (May 3, 1982), p. 63.

27. Bill Abrams and David P. Garino, "Package Design Gains Stature as Visual Competition Grows," *Wall Street Journal* (August 6, 1981).

28. Robert Ball, "Warm Milk Wakes Up the Packaging Industry," *Fortune* (August 7, 1982), pp. 78–82.

29. Patricia Lush, "Tide's In, Plastic's Out in Environmentally Safer Pouches," *The Globe and Mail* (September 6, 1989).

Chapter 11

1. Excerpted from Philip Fine, "Teddies, Gorillas, Diapers on the Go," *The Globe and Mail* (April 12, 1994), p. C5. Reprinted by permission of the author.

2. The author thanks Anthony Leung for research performed and ideas presented for this chapter.

3. Edward Greenspon, "Services Industries Driving Growth, GATT Report Says," *The Globe and Mail* (September 15, 1989).

4. L. Berry, "Services Marketing Is Different," in *Marketing Management and Strategy: A Reader*, eds. P. Kotler and K.K. Cox (Englewood Cliffs, NJ: Prentice-Hall, 1988), p. 278.

5. A. Rushton and D. Carson, "The Marketing of Services: Managing the Intangibles," *European Journal of Marketing* (1989), p. 31.

6. J. Bateson, "Do We Need Services Marketing?" in *Marketing Management and Strategy*, eds. Kotler and Cox, pp. 278–86.

7. Valarie A. Zeithaml, A. Parasuraman, and Leonard L. Berry, "Problems and Strategies in Services Marketing," *Journal of Marketing* (Spring 1985), p. 33.

8. Theodore Levitt, "The Industrialization of Service," *Harvard Business Review* (September–October 1976), pp. 63–74.

9. L. Berry, "Services Marketing Is Different," p. 281.

10. L. Berry, "Services Marketing Is Different," p. 281.

11. G.L. Shostack, "Breaking Free from Product Marketing," *Journal of Marketing* (April 1977), pp. 73–80.

12. L. Berry, "Services Marketing Is Different," p. 281; and A. Rushton and D. Carson, "The Marketing of Services," p. 31.

Chapter 12

1. Excerpted from David Zielenziger, "Compaq Launches New Price War Round," *Bloomberg Business News*, as reprinted in *The Financial Post* (July 23, 1994), p. 54. Reprinted with permission.

2. Adapted from David J. Schwartz, *Marketing Today*, copyright © 1981 by Harcourt Brace Jovanovich, Inc.

3. Robert A. Lynn, *Price Policies and Marketing Management* (Homewood, IL: Irwin, 1967), p. 99; see also Stuart U. Rich, "Firms in Some Industries Should Use Both Target Return and Marginal Cost Pricing," *Marketing News* (June 25, 1982), Section 2, p. 11.

4. See William J. Baumol, "On the Theory of Oligopoly," *Economica* (August 1958), pp. 187–98; see also William J. Baumol, *Business Behavior, Value, and Growth* (New York: Harcourt Brace and World, 1967).

5. An interesting discussion appears in Carl R. Frear and John E. Swan, "Marketing Managers' Motivation to Revise Their Market Share Goals: An Expectancy Theory Analysis," in *Southwestern Marketing Proceedings*, eds. Robert H. Ross, Frederic B. Kraft, and Charles H. Davis (Wichita, KS: 1981), pp. 13–16; see also William Brand, "Pricing Strategies for Profit," *Sales and Marketing Management in Canada* 27:11 (December 1986), pp. 30–31.

6. This section is adapted from Edwin G. Dolan, *Basic Economics* (Toronto: Holt, Rinehart, and Winston, 1984), pp. 57–58; and Ross D. Eckert and Richard H. Leftwich, *Price System and Resource Allocation*, 10th ed. (Chicago: The Dryden Press, 1988), pp. 55–58.

7. For a discussion of the application of price elasticity to a consumer service, see Steven J. Skinner, Terry L. Childers, and Wesley H. Jones, "Consumer Responsiveness to Price Differentials: A Case for Insurance Industry Deregulation," *Journal of Business Research* (December 1981), pp. 381–96.

8. Some problems of using economic models in practice are discussed in Kent B. Monroe and Albert J. Della Bitta, "Models of Pricing Decisions," *Journal of Marketing Research* (August 1978), pp. 413–28; see also Robert J. Dolan and Abel P. Jeuland, "Experience Curves and Dynamic Models: Implications for Optional Pricing Strategies," *Journal of Marketing* (Winter 1981), pp. 52–62.

9. This section has been adapted from G. David Hughes, *Marketing Management: A Planning Approach* (Menlo Park, CA: Addison-Wesley, 1978), pp. 324–26.

Chapter 13

1. Excerpted from Anne Kingston, "De Beers' Dazzling Marketing Machine," *Financial Times of Canada* (March 27–April 2, 1989), p. 27. Reprinted by permission of the author.

2. Walter J. Primeaux, Jr., "The Effect of Consumer Knowledge and Bargaining Strength on Final Selling Price: A Case Study," *Journal of Business* (October 1970), pp. 419–26; another excellent article is James R. Krum, "Variable Pricing as a Promotional Tool," *Atlanta Economic Review* (November–December, 1977), pp. 47–50.

3. Bernie Faust et al., "Effective Retail Pricing Policy," *Purdue Retailer* (Lafayette, IN: Agricultural Economics, 1963), p. 2.

4. Karl A. Shilliff, "Determinants of Consumer Price Sensitivity for Selected Supermarket Products: An Empirical Investigation," *Akron Business and Economic Review* (Spring 1975), pp. 26–32.

5. John F. Willenborg and Robert E. Pitts, "Perceived Situational Effects on Price Sensitivity," *Journal of Business Research* (March 1977), pp. 27–38.

6. Jack C. Horn, "The High-Class Nickel Discount," *Psychology Today* (September 1982).

7. See David M. Georgoff, "Price Illusion and the Effect of Odd–Even Retail Pricing," *Southern Journal of Business* (April 1969), pp. 95–103; see also Dik W. Twedt, "Does the '9 Fixation in Retailing Really Promote Sales?" *Journal of Marketing* (October 1965) pp. 54–55; Benson P. Shapiro, "The Psychology of Pricing," *Harvard Business Review* (July–August 1968), pp. 14–16; David M. Georgoff, *Odd–Even Retail Price Endings: Their Effects on Value Determination, Product Perception, and Buying Propensities* (East Lansing, MI: Michigan State University, 1972); and JoAnn Carmin, "Pricing Strategies for Menus: Magic or Myth?" *Cornell Hotel and Restaurant Administration Quarterly* 31:3 (November 1990), pp. 44–50.

8. See, for instance, I. Robert Andrews and Enzo R. Valenzi, "The Relationship between Price and Blind-Rated Quality for Margarines and Butter," *Journal of Marketing Research* (August 1970), pp. 393–95; Robert A. Peterson, "The Price–Perceived Quality Relationship: Experimental Evidence," *Journal of Marketing Research* (November 1970), pp. 525–28; David M. Gardner, "An Experimental Investigation of the Price/Quality Relationship," *Journal of Retailing* (Fall 1970), pp. 25–41; Arthur G. Bedelan, "Consumer Perception as an Indicator of Product Quality," *MSU Business Topics* (Summer 1971), pp. 59–65; and R.S. Mason, "Price and Product Quality Assessment," *European Journal of Marketing* (Spring 1974), pp. 29–41.

9. J. Douglass McConnell, "An Experimental Examination of the Price–Quality Relationship," *Journal of Business* (October 1968), pp. 439–44; see also J. Douglass McDonnell, "The Alphabet and Price as Independent Variables: A Note on the Price–Quality Question," *Journal of Business* (October 1970), pp. 448–51; Jerry B. Gotlieb, "Effects of Price Advertisements on Perceived Quality and Purchase Intentions," *Journal of Business Research* 22:3 (May 1991), pp. 195–210; and William B. Dodds, "Effects of Price, Brand, and Store Information on Buyers' Product Evaluations," *Journal of Marketing Research* 28:3 (August 1991), pp. 307–19.

10. James H. Myers and William H. Reynolds, *Consumer Behavior and Marketing Management* (Boston: Houghton-Mifflin, 1967), p. 47.

11. See Kent B. Monroe and M. Venkatesan, "The Concepts of Price Limits and Psychophysical Measurement: A Laboratory Experiment," in *Marketing Involvement in Society and the Economy*, ed. Philip R. McDonald (Cincinnati: American Marketing Association, 1969), pp. 345–51.

12. *Market Spotlight* (Edmonton: Alberta Consumer and Corporate Affairs, March 1979).

13. J. Edward Russo, "The Value of Unit Price Information," *Journal of Marketing Research* (May 1977), pp. 193–201.

14. See Mary Louise Hatten, "Don't Get Caught with Your Prices Down: Pricing in Inflationary Times," *Business Horizons* (March–April 1982), pp. 23–28.

Chapter 14

1. Excerpted from Geoffrey Rowan, "Packard Bell at Right Place and Right Time," *The Globe and Mail* (September 21, 1994), p. B5. Reprinted by permission of *The Globe and Mail*.

2. The contribution of Professor Ed Bruning to this chapter is gratefully acknowledged.

3. Committee on Definitions, *Marketing Definitions: A Glossary of Marketing Terms* (Chicago: American Marketing Association, 1960), p. 10; some authors limit the definition to the route taken by the *title* to the goods, but this definition also includes agent wholesaling intermediaries who do not take title but who do serve as an important component of many channels.

4. This section is adapted from Louis W. Stern and Adel I. El-Ansary, *Marketing Channels*, 3rd ed. (Englewood Cliffs, NJ: Prentice-Hall, 1989), pp. 7–12.

5. The first five functions were developed in Wroe Alderson, "Factors Governing the Development of Marketing Channels," in *Marketing Channels for Manufactured Products*, ed. Richard M. Clewitt (Homewood, IL: Irwin, 1954), pp. 5–22.

6. Wilke English, Dale M. Lewison, and M. Wayne DeLozier, "Evolution in Channel Management: What Will Be Next?" in *Proceedings of the Southwestern Marketing Association*, eds. Robert H. Ross, Frederic B. Kraft, and Charles H. Davis (Wichita, KS: 1981), pp. 78–81.

7. Donald A. Fuller, "Aluminum Beverage Container Recycling in Florida: A Commentary," *Atlanta Economic Review* (January–February 1977), p. 41.

8. Combines Investigation Act, Part IV.1, 31.4, 1976.

9. See Michael Etgar, "Differences in the Use of Manufacturer Power in Conventional and Contractual Channels," *Journal of Retailing* (Winter 1978), pp. 49–62.

10. Adapted from Lawson A.W. Hunter, "Buying Groups," *Agriculture Canada: Food Market Commentary* 5:4, p. 15.

11. Thomas G. Marx, "Distribution Efficiency in Franchising," *MSU Business Topics* (Winter 1980), p. 5.

Chapter 15

1. Excerpted from Alan Freeman, "B.C.'s Feathercraft Kayaks Making Waves in Japan," *The Globe and Mail* (July 25, 1994), pp. B1, B2. Reprinted by permission of *The Globe and Mail*.

2. Industry, Science and Technology Canada, *Wholesale Trade Industry Profile* (Ottawa: 1988), p. 7.

3. An interesting discussion of types of wholesaling appears in J. Howard Westing, "Wholesale Indifference," *The Courier* (Spring 1982), pp. 3, 8.

4. James R. Moore and Kendell A. Adams, "Functional Wholesaler Sales Trends and Analysis," in *Combined Proceedings*, ed. Edward M. Mazze (Chicago: American Marketing Association, 1976), pp. 402–5.

5. Louis P. Bucklin, *Competition and Evolution in the Distributive Trades* (Englewood Cliffs, NJ: Prentice-Hall, 1972), p. 214.

6. For a profile of the typical manufacturers' agent, see Stanley D. Sibley and Roy K. Teas, "Agent Marketing Channel Intermediaries' Perceptions of Marketing Channel Performance," in *Proceedings of the Southern Marketing Association*, eds. Robert S. Franz et al. (New Orleans: 1978), pp. 336–39.

Chapter 16

1. Adapted from John Heinzl, "Consumers Stores Go Super," *The Globe and Mail* (October 5, 1994), p. B1. Used by permission of *The Globe and Mail*.

2. "Canuck," *Pen Pictures of Early Pioneer Life in Upper Canada* (Toronto: Coles, 1972), pp. 80–82.

3. Interesting discussions include Sak Onkvisit and John J. Shaw, "Modifying the Retail Classification System for More Timely Marketing Strategies," *Journal of the Academy of Marketing Science* (Fall 1981), pp. 436–53; and Bobby C. Vaught, L. Lyn Judd, and Jack M. Starling, "The Perceived Importance of Retailing Strategies and Their Relationships to Four Indexes of Retailing Success," in *Progress in Marketing: Theory and Practice*, eds. Ronald D. Taylor, John J. Bennen, and John H. Summey (Carbondale, IL: Southern Marketing Association, 1981), pp. 25–28.

4. Frances Phillips, "Canadian Tire Finds Texas Trail a Bit Bumpy," *The Financial Post* (March 26, 1983).

5. A good discussion appears in Mary Carolyn Harrison and Alvin C. Burns, "A Case for Departmentalizing Target Market Strategy in Department Stores," in *Progress in Marketing: Theory and Practice*, eds. Taylor, Bennen, and Summey, pp. 21–24.

6. Clayton Sinclair, "The New Priorities for Shopping Centres," *The Financial Times of Canada* (March 21, 1983).

7. The following discussion of Reilly and Huff's work is adapted from Joseph Barry Mason and Morris Lehman Mayer, *Modern Retailing: Theory and Practice*, 5th ed. (Homewood, IL: BPI/Irwin, 1990), pp. 679–81.

8. Huff's work is described in David Hugg, "A Probabilistic Analysis of Consumer Spatial Behavior," in *Emerging*

Concepts in Marketing, ed. William S. Decker (Chicago: American Marketing Association, 1972), pp. 443–61; shopping centre trade areas are also discussed in Edward Blair, "Sampling Issues in Trade Area Maps Drawn from Shopper Surveys," *Journal of Marketing* (Winter 1983), pp. 98–106.

9. Retail images are discussed in a variety of articles, for example, Pradeep K. Korgaonbar and Kamal M. El Sheshai, "Assessing Retail Competition with Multidimensional Scaling," *Business* (April–June 1982), pp. 30–33; Jack K. Kasulis and Robert F. Lush, "Validating the Retail Store Image Concept," *Journal of the Academy of Marketing Science* (Fall 1981), pp. 419–35; and Julie Baker, "The Influence of Store Environment on Quality Inferences and Store Image," *Journal of the Academy of Marketing Science* 22: 4 (Fall 1994), pp. 328–39.

10. This section is based on Anjit Ghosh, *Retail Management*, 2nd ed. (Fort Worth, TX: The Dryden Press, 1994), pp. 59–60.

11. See Ian Brown, "The Empire that Timothy Built," *The Financial Post Magazine* (May 1978), pp. 16–47.

12. Ian Brown, "The Empire that Timothy Built," p. 20.

13. Some of this section is based on Ken Jones, Wendy Evans, and Christine Smith, "New Formats in the Canadian Retail Economy," paper presented at the Retailing and Services Conference, Lake Louise, Alberta (May 7–10, 1994).

14. Superstores are discussed in Myron Gable and Ronald D. Michman, "Superstores — Revolutionizing Distribution," *Business* (March–April 1981), pp. 14–18.

15. This section is based on Tamsen Tilson, "Multilevel Marketing Sells Costly Dreams," *The Globe and Mail* (October 6, 1994).

16. Quoted by Mr. Knox, a Sears executive in Toronto.

17. Statistics Canada, *Vending Machine Operators*, 1988, Catalogue No. 63-213.

18. Statistics Canada, *Market Research Handbook*, 1990, Catalogue No. 63-224.

19. This section is based on Geof Wheelwright, "Even CD-ROMs Could Be History when Information Highway Opens," *The Financial Post Special Report* (October 15, 1994), p. C2.

Chapter 17

1. Excerpted from "A Crazy Thing Called Blimp Love," *The Globe and Mail* (May 4, 1994), p. A 15. Reprinted by permission of *The Globe and Mail*.

2. Similar communications processes are suggested in David K. Berlo, *The Process of Communications* (New York: Holt, Rinehart and Winston, 1960), pp. 23–38; and Thomas S. Robertson, *Innovative Behavior and Communication* (New York: Holt, Rinehart and Winston, 1971), p. 122; see also Claude Shannon and Warren Weaver, *The Mathematical Theory of Communication* (Urbana, IL: University of Illinois Press, 1978), p. 7; and

Wilbur Schramm, "The Nature of Communication Between Humans," in *The Process and Effects of Mass Communication*, rev. ed. (Urbana, IL: University of Illinois Press, 1971), pp. 3–53.

3. Wilbur Schramm, "The Nature of Communication Between Humans," pp. 3–53.

4. S. Watson Dunn and Arnold M. Barban, *Advertising: Its Role in Modern Marketing*, 7th ed. (Chicago: Dryden Press, 1990), p. 9.

5. Committee on Definitions, *Marketing Definitions: A Glossary of Marketing Terms* (Chicago: American Marketing Association, 1960), p. 20.

6. "Cost Analysis #2070," *Research Report* (New Orleans, LA: Trade Show Bureau, August 1988), p. 2.

7. Terrence V. O'Brien, "Psychologists Take a New Look at Today's Consumer," *Arizona Review* (August–September 1970), p. 2.

8. "Cadbury Gets Back in the Thick of the Action," *Marketing Magazine* (June 1, 1981), p. 1.

9. Lee E. Preston, *Markets and Marketing: An Orientation* (Glenview, IL: Scott, Foresman, 1970), p. 198. Copyright © by Scott, Foresman and Company.

10. See J. Edward Russo, Barbara L. Metcalf, and Debra Stephens, "Identifying Misleading Advertising," *Journal of Consumer Research* (September 1981), pp. 119–31.

Chapter 18

1. Excerpted from Marina Strauss, "Infomercials Get Midas Touch," *The Globe and Mail* (March 10, 1994), p. B4. Reprinted by permission of *The Globe and Mail*.

2. *A Report on Advertising Revenues in Canada* (Toronto: Maclean-Hunter Research Bureau, 1978), p. 3.

3. Francis Phillips, "Bring Back the Good Old Days," *The Financial Post 500* (Summer 1984), p. 200.

4. This section follows in part the discussion in S. Watson Dunn and Arnold M. Barban, *Advertising: Its Role in Modern Marketing*, 7th ed. (Chicago: The Dryden Press, 1990), pp. 16–19.

5. David A. Aaker and J. Gary Shansby, "Positioning Your Product," *Business Horizons* (May–June 1982), p. 62; see also Jack Trout and Al Ries, "Positioning: Ten Years Later," *Industrial Marketing* (July 1979), pp. 32–44; Kenneth G. Hardy, "The Power of Positioning Your Product Lines," *Business Quarterly* 51:3 (November 1986), pp. 90–92; and "Product Positioning: A Crucial Marketing Strategy," *Small Business Report* 13:4 (April 1988), pp. 18–22.

6. "Gulf to Tell a $3-Million Story," *Marketing Magazine* (May 25, 1981), p. 1; see also G.H.G. McDougall, "Comparative Advertising in Canada: Practices and Consumer Relations," *Canadian Marketer* (1978), pp. 14–20.

7. The discussion of various advertising media is adapted from material in Dunn and Barban, *Advertising: Its Role in Modern Marketing*, 7th ed., pp. 176–84.

8. The 1990 advertising volume percentages for the four major media (newspaper, television, magazines, and radio) are estimated by *Advertising Revenues in Canada* as reported by Martin Mehr, "Ad Revenues Projected to Top $10 Billion," *Marketing Magazine* (June 4, 1990).

9. Leonard Kubas, "Magazines Need It Razor Sharp," *Marketing Magazine* (April 6, 1987), p. 24.

10. Patrick Dunne, "Some Demographic Characteristics of Direct Mail Purchasers," *Baylor Business Studies* (July 1975), pp. 67–72.

11. Mailing lists are discussed in Jeffrey A. Tannenbaum, "Mailing List Brokers Sell More than Names to Their Many Clients," *Wall Street Journal* (February 19, 1974).

12. William M. Carley, "Gillette Co. Struggles as Its Rivals Slice at Fat Profit Margin," *Wall Street Journal* (February 2, 1972), p. 1.

13. Adapted from "Brettons Launch," *Marketing Magazine* (September 25, 1990), p. 4.

14. Ralph B. Weller, C. Richard Roberts, and Colin Neuhaus, "A Longitudinal Study of the Effect of Erotic Content upon Advertising Brand Recall," *Current Issues and Research in Advertising* (1979), pp. 145–61.

15. Marina Strauss, "Ontario Judge Rules Pie Crust Ads Are Half-Baked," *The Globe and Mail* (October 14, 1994), p. B1.

16. Excerpted from William Bernbach, address to Western Region Annual Meeting, American Association of Advertising Agencies (Pebble Beach, CA: November 13, 1965).

17. Bob Stone, *Successful Direct Marketing Methods*, 5th ed. (Lincolnwood, IL: NTC Business Books, 1994), p. 5.

18. This section draws from Jim Steinhart, "Their Aim Is True," *The Globe and Mail* (February 15, 1994).

19. Peter R. Dickson, *Marketing Management* (Fort Worth, TX: The Dryden Press, 1994), p. 457.

20. Jerry Adler, "Oh, You Beautiful Dolls!" *Newsweek* (December 12, 1983), pp. 78–81; Lynn Langway, "Harvesting the Cabbage," *Newsweek* (December 12, 1983), pp. 81–85; and Peter R. Dickson, *Marketing Management*, pp. 457–58.

21. Johanna Powell, "Mascot Maker Finds Success Is Little More than Child's Play," *The Financial Post* (September 11, 1989).

22. Raymond Simon, *Public Relations, Concept and Practices*, 2nd ed. (Columbus, OH: Grid Publishing, 1980), p. 8.

23. Marina Strauss, "Vending Machines Get the Picture," *The Globe and Mail* (August 18, 1994), p. B6.

24. Ken Riddel, "New Study Shows Sales Promotion Spending May Be Inflated," *Marketing Magazine* (April 23, 1990), pp. 1, 3.

25. This definition is adapted from "How to Play Championship Specialty Advertising" (Chicago: Specialty Advertising Association, 1978).

26. Walter A. Gaw, *Specialty Advertising* (Chicago: Specialty Advertising Association, 1970), p. 7.

27. See David J. Reibstein and Phyllis A. Traver, "Factors Affecting Coupon Redemption Rates," *Journal of Marketing* (Fall 1982), pp. 102–13.

28. See, for example, Carl-Magnus Seipel, "Premiums: Forgotten by Theory," *Journal of Marketing* (April 1971), pp. 26–34.

29. Maurice Simms, "Retailers Pin Hope on Marketing Skill," *The Globe and Mail* (February 15, 1994), p. B28.

30. Reported in "Sell, Sell, Sell," *Wall Street Journal* (September 14, 1971).

31. For an analysis of problems involved in identifying specific decision-makers in an industrial setting, see Thomas V. Bonoma, "Major Sales: Who *Really* Does the Buying?" *Harvard Business Review* (May–June 1982), pp. 111–19.

32. For an interesting discussion of promotional appeals, see Walter Gross, "Rational and Nonrational Appeals in Selling to Businessmen," *Georgia Business* (February 1970), pp. 1–3.

Chapter 19

1. Excerpted from Casey Mahood, "Glegg Makes a Splash Abroad," *The Globe and Mail* (April 12, 1994), pp. B1, B2. Reprinted by permission of *The Globe and Mail*.

2. Canada, *Export Trade Month Information Kit*, October 1983.

3. *The Age* (October 4, 1974), p. 1.

4. Oxford Analytica, "New GATT Rules Fail to Police Protectionism," *The Globe and Mail* (September 19, 1994), p. B1.

5. Adapted from *The Financial Post* (May 3, 1980).

6. "Northern Telecom: Mastering the International Market," *Business to Business Marketing* 94:13 (March 27, 1989), p. B12.

7. Warren Keegan, *Global Marketing Management* (New York: McGraw-Hill, 1989), pp. 31–33.

Chapter 20

1. Adapted from Susan Noakes, "Montreal Arts Powered by Corporate Support," *The Financial Post* (June 25, 1994), p. S19. Reprinted by permission of *The Financial Post*.

2. Also referred to as "not-for-profit" organizations; we will use the two terms interchangeably in this chapter.

3. Philip Kotler, *Marketing for Nonprofit Organizations* (Englewood Cliffs, NJ: Prentice-Hall, 1982), p. 9.

4. These differences and others are outlined in Harvey W. Wallender, III, "Managing Not-for-Profit Enterprises," *Academy of Management Review* (January 1978), p. 26; Cecily Cannon Selby, "Better Performance for 'Non-profits,'" *Harvard Business Review* (September–October 1978), pp. 93–95; see also John M. Gwin, "Constituent Analysis: A Paradigm for Marketing Effectiveness in the Not-for-Profit Organization," *European Journal of*

Marketing 24:7 (1990), pp. 43–48; and Katherine Gallagher, "Coping with Success: New Challenges for Nonprofit Marketing," *Sloan Management Review* 33:1 (Fall 1991), pp. 27–42.

5. Kotler, *Marketing for Nonprofit Organizations*, p. 482.

6. An excellent discussion of idea marketing appears in Jagdish N. Sheth and Gary L. Frazier, "A Model of Strategy Mix Choice for Planned Social Change," *Journal of Marketing* (Winter 1982), pp. 15–26.

7. David J. Rachman and Elaine Romano, *Modern Marketing* (Hinsdale, IL: The Dryden Press, 1980), p. 576; the delineation of person, idea, and organization marketing is proposed by Professors Rachman and Romano.

8. James M. Stearns, John R. Kerr, and Robert R. McGrath, "Advances of Marketing for Functional Public Policy Adminstration," in *Proceedings of the Southern Marketing Association*, eds. Robert S. Franz, Robert M. Hopkins, and Alfred G. Toma (Atlanta, GA: November 1979), pp. 140–43.

9. This section is based on Philip Kotler, *Marketing for Nonprofit Organizations*, pp. 306–9; see also Chris T. Allen, "Self-Perception Based Strategies for Stimulating Energy Conservation," *Journal of Consumer Research* (March 1982), pp. 381–90.

10. Michael L. Rothschild, "Marketing Communications in Nonbusiness Situations or Why It's So Hard to Sell Brotherhood Like Soap," *Journal of Marketing* (Spring 1979), pp. 11–20.

Chapter 21

1. Excerpted from Brenda Dalglish, "Snoops in the Shops," *Maclean's* (December 19, 1994), pp. 28, 29. Reprinted by permission of Maclean-Hunter Ltd.

2. Adapted from William A. Brand, "Use the Right Measures to Track Marketing Performance," *Sales and Marketing Management in Canada* (February 1988), p. 33.

3. This section is based on Jac Fitz-enz, *Benchmarking Staff Performance* (San Francisco: Jossy-Bass Publisher, 1993), pp. 8–17.

4. Rahul Jacob, "TQM, More than a Dying Fad?" *Fortune* (October 18, 1993), p. 67.

5. Based on Robert C. Camp, *Benchmarking: The Search for Industry Best Practices that Lead to Superior Performance* (Milwaukee: ASQC Quality Press, 1989), p. 4.

6. Adapted from Howard Schlossberg, "Customer Satisfaction Serves and Preserves," *Marketing News* (May 28, 1990), p. 8.

7. This section is based on Charlotte Klopp and John Sterlicchi, "Customer Satisfaction Just Catching on in Europe," *Marketing News* (May 28, 1990), p. 5.

8. This section is based on Thomas Stewart, "Brace for Japan's New Strategy," *Fortune* (September 21, 1992), pp. 63–68.

9. Philip Kotler, "From Sales Obsession to Marketing Effectiveness," *Harvard Business Review* (November–December 1977), pp. 67–75. The list of definitions is reprinted from p. 72. Copyright © 1977 by the President and Fellows of Harvard College; all rights reserved.

Glossary

absolute advantage Advantage said to be held by a nation that is the sole producer of a product or that can produce a product for less than anyone else.

accelerator principle The disproportionate impact that changes in consumer demand have on industrial market demand.

accessory equipment Second-level capital items that are used in the production of products and services but are usually less expensive and shorter-lived than installations.

adoption process A series of stages consumers go through, from learning of a new product to trying it and deciding to purchase it regularly or to reject it.

advertising Paid nonpersonal communication through various media by business firms, nonprofit organizations, and individuals who are in some way identified with the advertising message and who hope to inform or persuade members of a particular audience.

advertising agency A marketing specialist firm that assists the advertiser in planning and preparing its advertisements.

agent A wholesaling intermediary who differs from the typical wholesaler in that the agent does not take title to the goods.

agents and brokers Wholesaling intermediaries who may take possession of the products, but do not take title to them.

AIO statements Statements about activities, interests, and opinions that are used in developing psychographic profiles.

approach The initial contact between the salesperson and the prospective customer.

Asch phenomenon The impact that groups and group norms can exhibit on individual behaviour.

aspirational group A type of reference group with which individuals desire to associate.

attitudes A person's enduring favourable or unfavourable evaluations of some object or idea.

auction house An agent wholesaling intermediary that brings buyers and sellers together in one location and allows potential buyers to inspect the merchandise before purchasing through a public bidding process.

average cost Obtained by dividing total cost by the quantity associated with this cost.

average variable cost The total variable cost divided by the related quantity.

balance of payments The flow of money into or out of a country.

balance of trade The relationship between a country's exports and its imports.

benchmarking The comparison of performance with industry best practices.

bids Price quotations from potential suppliers.

bottom line The overall-profitability measure of performance.

brand A name, term, sign, symbols, or design (or some combination thereof) used to identify the products of one firm and to differentiate them from competitive offerings.

brand extension The decision to use a popular brand name for a new product entry in an unrelated product category.

brand insistence The ultimate stage of brand loyalty; occurs when consumers will accept no alternatives and will search extensively for the product.

brand name Words, letters, or symbols that make up a name used to identify and distinguish the firm's offerings from those of its competitors.

brand preference The second stage of brand loyalty; situation in which, based on previous experience, consumers will choose a product rather than one of its competitors — if it is available.

brand recognition The first stage of brand loyalty; situation in which a firm has developed enough publicity for a brand that its name is familiar to consumers.

break-bulk warehouse One that receives consolidated shipments from a central distribution centre, and then distributes them in smaller shipments to individual customers in more limited areas.

break-even analysis A means of determining the number of goods or services that must be sold at a given price in order to generate sufficient revenue to cover total costs.

broker An agent wholesaling intermediary who brings buyers and sellers together; operates in industries with a large number of small suppliers and purchasers.

buying centre Everyone who participates in some fashion in an industrial buying action.

cannibalizing Situation involving one product taking sales from another offering in a product line.

capital items Long-lived business assets that must be depreciated over time.

cartel The monopolistic organization of a group of firms.

cash-and-carry wholesaler Limited-function merchant wholesaler who performs most wholesaling functions except financing and delivery.

cash discounts Reductions in price that are given for prompt payment of a bill.

catalogue retailer Retailer that mails catalogues to its customers and operates from a showroom displaying samples of its products.

celebrity marketing Having celebrities lend their name and influence to the promotion of a product.

census A collection of marketing data from all possible sources.

chain stores Groups of retail stores that are centrally owned and managed and that handle the same lines of products.

channel captain The most dominant member of the distribution channel.

channel conflict Rivalry and conflict between channel members because of sometimes different objectives and needs.

closing The act of asking the prospect for an order.

cluster sample A probability sample that is generated by randomly choosing one or more areas or population clusters and then surveying all members in the chosen cluster(s).

cognitive dissonance The postpurchase anxiety that occurs when there exists a discrepancy between a person's knowledge and beliefs (cognitions).

commission merchant An agent wholesaling intermediary who takes possession when the producer ships goods to a central market for sale.

common carriers Transportation carriers that provide service to the general public, and are subject to regulatory authority including fee setting.

communication Personal selling, advertising, sales promotion, and publicity.

comparative advantage Advantage said to be held by a nation that can produce a given product more efficiently per unit of output than it can produce other products.

comparative advertising Advertising that makes direct promotional comparisons with competitive brands.

competitive bidding A process by which buyers request potential suppliers to make price quotations on a proposed purchase or contract.

competitive environment The interactive process that occurs in the marketplace in which competing organizations seek to satisfy markets.

component parts and materials Finished industrial goods that actually become part of the final product.

concept testing A marketing research project that attempts to measure consumer attitudes and perceptions relevant to a new-product idea.

consumer behaviour The activities of individuals in obtaining, using, and disposing of goods and services,

including the decision processes that precede and follow these actions.

consumer goods Those products and services purchased by the ultimate consumer for personal use.

consumer innovators The first purchasers — those who buy a product at the beginning of its life cycle.

containerization Combining several unitized loads.

contract carriers Transportation carriers that only serve customers they have contracts with. Contracts include rates to be charged.

convenience products Products that are lowest in terms of both effort and risk.

convenience sample A nonprobability sample based on the selection of readily available respondents.

co-operative advertising The sharing of advertising costs between the retailer and the manufacturer.

corporate strategy The overall purpose and direction of the organization that is established in the light of the challenges and opportunities found in the environment, as well as available organizational resources.

cost-plus pricing Pricing technique using base cost figure per unit to which is added a markup to cover unassigned costs and to provide a profit.

creative selling Selling that involves making the buyer see the worth of the item.

credence qualities Qualities for which, even after purchasing, the buyer must simply trust that the supplier has performed the correct service.

cue Any object existing in the environment that determines the nature of the response to a drive.

culture The complex of values, ideas, attitudes, institutions, and other meaningful symbols created by people that shape human behaviour, and the artifacts of that behaviour, transmitted from one generation to the next.

customs union Agreement among two or more nations that establishes a free trade area, plus a uniform tariff for trade with nonmember nations.

demand variability In the industrial market, the impact of derived demand on the demand for interrelated products used in producing consumer goods.

demarketing The process of cutting consumer demand for a product, because the demand exceeds the level that can reasonably be supplied by the firm or because doing so will create a more favourable corporate image.

department store Large retailer that handles a variety of merchandise.

depreciation The accounting concept of charging a portion of the cost of a capital item against the company's annual revenue for purposes of determining its net income.

derived demand In the industrial market, demand for an industrial product derived from (or linked to) demand for a consumer good.

devaluation Situation in which a nation reduces the value of its currency in relation to gold or some other currency.

differentiation triangle Differentiation of a retail store from competitors in the same strategic group through price, location, store atmosphere, and/or service.

diffusion process The filtering and acceptance of new products and services by the members of a community or social system.

direct marketing An interactive system of marketing that uses one or more advertising media to effect a measurable response and/or transaction at any location.

direct-response wholesaler Limited-function merchant wholesaler who relies on catalogues rather than on a sales force to contact retail, industrial, and institutional customers.

direct-sales results test A test that attempts to ascertain for each dollar of promotional outlay the corresponding increase in revenue.

disassociative group A type of reference group with which an individual does not want to be identified.

discount house Retailer that, in exchange for reduced prices, does not offer such traditional retail services as credit, sales assistance by clerks, and delivery.

distribution The selection and management of marketing channels and the physical distribution of goods.

distribution channels The paths that goods — and title to these goods —follow from producer to consumer.

drive Any strong stimulus that impels action.

drop shipper Limited-function merchant wholesaler who takes orders from customers and places them with producers, who then ship directly to the customers.

dumping Practice of selling products at significantly lower prices in a foreign market than in a nation's own domestic market.

dynamic break-even analysis Combines the traditional break-even analysis model with an evaluation of consumer demand.

economic environment The factors in a region or country that affect the production, distribution, and consumption of its wealth. Key elements are monetary resources, inflation, employment, and productive capacity.

economic union Agreement among two or more nations that establishes a free flow not only of goods, but also of people, capital, and services.

elasticity A measure of the responsiveness of purchasers and suppliers to changes in price.

embargo A complete ban on importing a particular product.

Engel's Laws As family income increases, (1) a smaller percentage goes for food, (2) the percentage spent on housing and household operations and clothing will remain constant, and (3) the percentage spent on other items will increase.

EOQ (economic order quantity) A model that emphasizes a cost trade-off between inventory holding costs and order costs.

escalator clause Allows the seller to adjust the final price based on changes in the costs of the product's

ingredients between the placement of the order and the completion of construction or delivery of the product.

ethnocentric company Firm that assumes that its way of doing business in its home market is the proper way to operate, and tries to replicate this in foreign markets.

evaluative criteria Features the consumer considers in making a choice among alternatives.

evoked set The number of brands that a consumer actually considers in making a purchase decision.

exchange control Requirement that firms gaining foreign exchange by exporting must sell their foreign exchange to the central bank or agency, and importers must buy foreign exchange from the same organization.

exchange process The means by which two or more parties give something of value to one another to satisfy felt needs.

exchange rate The rate at which a nation's currency can be exchanged for other currencies or gold.

exchange risk The risk of negotiating a price in another nation's currency and finding upon delivery of the product that currency's value has dropped in relation to your country's currency.

exclusive dealing An arrangement whereby a supplier prohibits a marketing intermediary (either a wholesaler or, more typically, a retailer) from handling competing products.

exclusive distribution The granting of exclusive rights by manufacturers to a wholesaler or retailer to sell in a geographic region.

expense items Products and services that are used within a short period of time.

experience qualities Characteristics of products that can be assessed mainly through using them.

exploratory research Learning about the problem area and beginning to focus on specific areas of study by discussing the problem with informed sources within the firm (a process often called *situation analysis*) and with knowledgeable others outside the firm (the *informal investigation*).

facilitating agency An agency that provides specialized assistance for regular channel members (such as producers, wholesalers, and retailers) in moving products from producer to consumer.

fads Fashions with abbreviated life cycles.

family brand Brand name used for several related products.

family life cycle The process of family formation, development, and dissolution.

fashions Currently popular products that tend to follow recurring life cycles.

fiscal policy The receipts and expenditures of government.

flexible pricing A variable price policy.

FOB plant The buyer must pay all the freight charges.

follow-up The postsales activities that often determine whether a person will become a repeat customer.

franchise An agreement whereby one firm (franchisee) agrees to meet the operating requirements of a successful business (franchisor) in return for the right to carry the name and products of the franchisor.

Free Trade Agreement (FTA) The agreement establishing a free trade area between Canada and the United States that preceded NAFTA.

free trade area Area established by agreement among two or more nations within which participants agree to free trade of goods among themselves.

freight absorption The seller permits the buyer to subtract transportation expenses from the bill.

friendship, commerce, and navigation (FCN) treaties Treaties that address many aspects of commercial relations with other countries; such treaties constitute international law.

GATT (General Agreement on Tariffs and Trade) An international trade agreement to gradually lower tariffs.

generic name A brand name over which the original owner has lost exclusive claim because all offerings in the associated class of products have become generally known by the brand name (usually that of the first or leading brand in that product class).

generic products Food and household staples characterized by plain labels, little or no advertising, and no brand names.

geocentric company Firm that develops a marketing mix that meets the needs of target consumers in all markets.

Hazardous Products Act A major piece of legislation that consolidated previous legislation and set significant new standards for product safety; defines a hazardous product as any product that is included in a list (called a schedule) compiled by Consumer and Corporate Affairs Canada or Health and Welfare Canada.

high-involvement products Products for which the purchaser is highly involved in making the purchase decision.

house-to-house retailer Retailer that sells products by direct contact between the retailer–seller and the customer at the home of the customer.

hypermarket Mass merchandiser that operates on a low-price, self-service basis and carries lines of soft goods, hard goods, and groceries.

hypothesis A tentative explanation about the relationship between variables as a starting point for further testing.

idea marketing The identification and marketing of a cause to chosen consumer segments.

import quota A limit set on the amount of products that may be imported in a certain category.

individual brand Brand that is known by its own brand name rather than by the name of the company producing it or an umbrella name covering similar items.

individual offering Single product within a product line.

industrial distributor A wholesaler who operates in the industrial goods market and typically handles small accessory equipment and operating supplies.

industrial goods Those products purchased to be used, either directly or indirectly, in the production of other goods or for resale.

industrial market Individuals and organizations that acquire goods and services to be used, directly or indirectly, in the production of other goods and services or to be resold.

inflation A rising price level resulting in reduced purchasing power for the consumer.

informative product advertising Advertising that seeks to develop demand through presenting factual information on the attributes of a product or service.

inseparability A characteristic of services in which the product is produced and consumed simultaneously.

installations Major capital assets that are used to produce products and services.

institutional advertising Promoting a concept, idea, or philosophy, or the good will of an industry, company, or organization.

intangible attributes Those attributes that cannot be experienced by the physical senses.

intensive distribution A form of distribution that attempts to provide saturation coverage of the potential market.

internal marketing A marketing effort aimed at those who provide the service so that they will feel better about their task and therefore produce a better product.

international pricing Setting prices to be charged to buyers in other countries taking into consideration exchange risk, price escalation through multiplication of channels, and transportation.

inventory adjustments In the industrial market, changes in the amounts of materials a manufacturer keeps on hand.

JIT (just in time) An approach to minimizing inventory costs through identifying minimal inventory stocking levels and arranging with suppliers to replenish stocks just in time to be used in production.

joint demand In the industrial market, demand for an industrial product that is related to the demand for other industrial goods.

judgement sample A nonprobability sample of people with a specific attribute.

label The part of a package that contains (1) the brand name or symbol, (2) the name and address of the manufacturer or distributor, (3) information about product composition and size, and (4) information about recommended uses of the product.

large-format specialty stores Large warehouse-type retail stores that specialize in selling a great variety of one category of merchandise at very low prices.

law of retail gravitation Principle that delineates the retail trade area of a potential site on the basis of distance between alternative locations and relative populations.

learning Changes in knowledge, attitudes, and/or behaviour, as a result of experience.

lifestyle The mode of living.

limited-line store Retailer that offers a large assortment of a single line of products or a few related lines of products.

line extension The development of individual offerings that appeal to different market segments but are closely related to the existing product line.

list price The rate normally quoted to potential buyers.

local content laws Laws specifying the portion of a product that must come from domestic sources.

loss leader Goods priced below cost to attract customers.

low-involvement products Products with little significance, either materially or emotionally, which a consumer may purchase first and evaluation later (while using them).

loyalty program A program that gives rewards such as points or free air miles with each purchase in order to stimulate repeat business.

mail-order merchandiser Retailer that offers its customers the option of placing merchandise orders by mail, by telephone, or by visiting the mail-order desk of a retail store.

manufacturers' agent An independent salesperson who works for a number of manufacturers of related but noncompeting products.

marginal cost The change in total cost that results from producing an additional unit of output.

markdown A reduction in the price of an item.

market Requires not only people and willingness to buy, but also purchasing power and the authority to buy.

market development strategy Finding new markets for existing products.

market orientation Paying careful attention to understanding customer needs and objectives, then making the business serve the interests of the customer rather than trying to make the customer buy what the business wants to produce.

market price The amount that a consumer pays.

market restriction An arrangement whereby suppliers restrict the geographic territories for each of their distributors.

market segmentation Grouping people according to their similarity in one or more dimensions related to interests in a particular product category.

market share objective To control a specific portion of the market for the firm's product.

marketing The process of planning and executing the conception, pricing, promotion, and distribution of ideas, goods, and services to create exchanges that satisfy individual and organizational objectives.

marketing channels The steps or handling organizations that a good or service goes through from producer to consumer.

marketing communications All activities and messages that inform, persuade, and influence the consumer in making a purchase decision.

marketing communications mix The blend of personal selling and nonpersonal communications (including advertising, sales promotion, and public relations) by marketers in an attempt to accomplish information and persuasion objectives.

marketing concept An organization-wide focus on providing chosen groups of customers with products that bring optimal satisfaction so as to achieve long-run profits.

marketing ethics The marketer's standards of conduct and moral values.

marketing functions Buying, selling, transporting, storing, grading, financing, risk taking, and information collection and dissemination.

marketing information system A set of routine procedures to continuously collect, monitor, and present internal and external information on company performance and opportunities in the marketplace.

marketing intermediary A business firm operating between the producer and the consumer or industrial purchaser.

marketing mix The blending of the four elements of marketing to satisfy chosen consumer segments.

marketing plan A program of activities that lead to the accomplishment of the marketing strategy.

marketing research The systematic gathering, recording, and analyzing of data about problems relating to the marketing of goods and services.

marketing strategy A strategy that focusses on developing a unique long-run competitive position in the market by assessing consumer needs and the firm's potential for gaining competitive advantage.

markup The amount a producer or channel member adds to cost in order to determine the selling price.

mass merchandiser Retailer that concentrates on high turnover of items, emphasizes lower prices than department stores, and offers reduced services.

membership and warehouse clubs Very large, warehouse-type retail stores that offer low prices because of their no-frill format and paid membership requirement.

membership group A type of reference group to which individuals actually belong, as with, say, a country club.

merchandise mart Permanent exhibition at which manufacturers rent showcases for their product offerings.

merchant wholesaler A wholesaler who takes title to the products carried.

microculture A subgroup with its own distinguishing modes of behaviour.

missionary selling Selling that emphasizes selling the firm's good will and providing customers with technical or operational assistance.

modified rebuy A situation in which purchasers are willing to re-evaluate their available options.

monetary policy The manipulation of the money supply and market rates of interest.

monopolistic competition A market structure with a large number of buyers and sellers where heterogeneity in good and/or service and usually geographical differentiation allow the marketer some control over price.

monopoly A market structure with only one seller of a product with no close substitutes.

motive An inner state that directs us toward the goal of satisfying a felt need.

MRO items Industrial supplies, so called because they can be categorized as maintenance items, repair items, and operating supplies.

multilevel marketing The development of a network among consumers to sell and deliver from one level of consumers to another using social obligation, personal influence, and motivational techniques.

multi-offer strategy The attempt to satisfy several segments of the market very well with specialized products and unique marketing programs aimed at each segment.

national brand (manufacturer's brand) A brand promoted and distributed by a manufacturer.

need The perceived difference between the current state and a desired state.

negotiated contract The terms of the contract are set through talks between the buyer and the seller.

new task buying First-time or unique purchase situations that require considerable effort on the part of the decision-makers.

nonprobability sample A sample chosen in an arbitrary fashion so that each member of the population does not have a representative chance of being selected.

nonprofit organization (NPO) Organization whose primary objective is something other than returning a profit to its owners.

North American Free Trade Agreement (NAFTA) The agreement establishing a free trade area among Canada, the United States, and Mexico that followed the FTA.

odd pricing Prices are set ending in some amount just below the next rounded number.

oligopoly A market structure in which there are relatively few sellers.

oligopsony A market in which there are only a few buyers.

opinion leaders Trend setters; individuals who are more likely to purchase new products early and to serve as information sources for others in a given group.

order processing Selling at the wholesale and retail levels; involves identifying customer needs, pointing out these needs to the customer, and completing the order.

organization marketing Attempts to influence others to accept the goals of, receive the services of, or contribute in some way to an organization.

penetration pricing An entry price for a product lower than what is estimated to be the long-term price.

perception The meaning that each person attributes to incoming stimuli received through the five senses.

perceptual screen The filter through which messages must pass.

performance gap The difference between the company's performance and that of the best of the best.

person marketing Efforts designed to cultivate the attention, interest, and preference of a target market toward a person.

personal selling A seller's promotional presentation conducted on a person-to-person basis with the buyer.

persuasive product advertising Advertising that emphasizes using words and/or images to try to create an image for a product and to influence attitudes about it.

physical distribution A broad range of activities concerned with efficient movement of products from the source of raw materials to the production line and, ultimately, to the consumer.

planned shopping centre Group of retail stores planned, co-ordinated, and marketed as a unit to shoppers in a particular geographic trade area.

point-of-purchase advertising Displays and demonstrations that seek to promote the product at a time and place closely associated with the actual decision to buy.

political and legal climate The laws and interpretation of laws that require firms to operate under competitive conditions and to protect consumer rights.

polycentric company Firm that assumes that every country is different and that a specific marketing approach should be developed for each separate country.

population or **universe** The total group that the researcher wants to study.

positioning Shaping the product and developing a marketing program in such a way that the product is perceived to be (and actually is) different from competitors' products.

post-testing The assessment of advertising copy after it has been used.

power node Groupings of two or more large-format retailers resulting in large customer drawing power.

preference products Products that are slightly higher on the effort dimension and much higher on risk than convenience products.

presentation The act of giving the sales message to a prospective customer.

prestige objectives The establishment of relatively high prices in order to develop and maintain an image of quality and exclusiveness.

pretesting The assessment of an advertisement's effectiveness before it is actually used.

price The value that a buyer exchanges for a good or service. The value of an item is what it can be exchanged for in the marketplace.

price escalation The increase in final price in a foreign market over a domestic price because of having to pay for the services of additional channel members in getting the product to that market.

price limits Limits within which product quality perception varies directly with price.

price lining The practice of marketing merchandise at a limited number of prices.

price structure An outline of the selling price and the various discounts offered to middlemen.

pricing The methods of setting competitive, profitable, and justified prices.

pricing policy A general guideline based on pricing objectives that is intended for use in specific pricing decisions.

primary data Data being collected for the first time.

private brand A brand promoted and distributed by a wholesaler or retailer.

probability sample A sample in which every member of the population has a known chance of being selected.

producers Those who transform goods and services through production into other goods and services.

product A total bundle of physical, service, and symbolic characteristics designed to produce consumer want satisfaction.

product advertising Nonpersonal selling of a particular good or service.

product development strategy Introducing new products into identifiable or established markets.

product diversification strategy The development of new products for new markets.

product improvement strategy A modification in existing products.

product life cycle A product's progress through introduction, growth, maturity, and decline stages.

product line A series of related products.

product management Decisions about what kind of product is needed, its uses, package design, branding, trademarks, warranties, guarantees, product life cycles, and new-product development.

product managers (brand managers) Individuals assigned one product or product line and given responsibility for determining its objectives and marketing strategies.

product mix The assortment of product lines and individual offerings available from a marketer.

product orientation A focus on the product itself rather than the consumer's needs.

profit centre Any part of the organization to which revenue and controllable costs can be assigned, such as a department.

profit maximization The point where the addition to total revenue is just balanced by an increase in total cost.

promotional allowances Extra discounts offered to retailers so that they will advertise the manufacturer along with the retailer.

promotional price A lower-than-normal price used as an ingredient in a firm's selling strategy.

prospecting Identifying potential customers.

psychographics The use of psychological attributes, lifestyles, and attitudes in determining the behavioural profiles of different consumers.

psychological pricing The use of pricing to suggest values of a product or attributes of a product/price offering.

public relations A firm's effort to create favourable attention and word-of-mouth.

public relations management The management function that evaluates public attitudes, identifies the policies and procedures of an organization with the public interest, and executes a program of action (and communication) to earn public understanding and acceptance.

public warehouse Independently owned storage facility.

publicity The generation of awareness about a product beyond regular advertising methods.

pulling strategy A promotional effort by the seller to stimulate final-user demand, which then exerts pressure on the distribution channel.

pure competition A market structure in which there is such a large number of buyers and sellers that no one of them has a significant influence on price.

pushing strategy The promotion of the product first to the members of the marketing channel, who then participate in its promotion to the final user.

qualifying Determining that the prospect is really a potential customer.

quantity discounts Price reductions granted because of large purchases.

quota sample A nonprobability sample that is divided so that different segments or groups are represented in the total sample.

rack jobber Wholesaler who provides the racks, stocks the merchandise, prices the goods, and makes regular visits to refill the shelves.

raw materials Farm products (such as cattle, wool, eggs, milk, pigs, and canola) and natural products (such as coal, copper, iron ore, and lumber).

rebates Refunds by the seller of a portion of the purchase price.

reciprocity The extension of purchasing preference to suppliers who are also customers.

reference group A group whose value structures and standards influence a person's behaviour.

regiocentric company Firm that recognizes that countries with similar cultures and economic conditions can be served with a similar marketing mix.

reinforcement The reduction in drive that results from a proper response.

reminder-oriented product advertising Advertising whose goal is to reinforce previous promotional activity by keeping the product's or service's name in front of the public.

research design A series of advance decisions that, taken together, make up a master plan or model for conducting the investigation.

response The individual's reaction to the cues and drives.

retail image The consumer's perception of a store and of the shopping experience it provides.

retail trade area analysis Studies that assess the relative drawing power of alternative retail locations.

retailer A store that sells products purchased by individuals for their own use and not for resale.

retailing All the activities involved in the sale of goods and services to the ultimate consumer.

revaluation Situation in which a country adjusts the value of its currency upward.

reverse channels The paths goods follow from consumer to manufacturer or to marketing intermediaries.

role The rights and duties expected of an individual in a group by other members of the group.

role model marketing Marketing technique that associates a product with the positive perception of a type of individual or a role.

sales branch Manufacturer-owned facility that carries inventory and processes orders to customers from available stock.

sales management Securing, maintaining, motivating, supervising, evaluating, and controlling the field sales force.

sales maximization The pricing philosophy analyzed by economist William J. Baumol. Baumol believes that many firms attempt to maximize sales within a profit constraint.

sales office Manufacturer-owned facility that does not carry stock but serves as a regional office for the firm's sales personnel.

sales orientation Focussing on developing a strong sales force to convince consumers to buy whatever the firm produces.

sales promotion Those marketing activities, other than personal selling, mass media advertising, and publicity, that stimulate consumer purchasing and dealer effectiveness.

scrambled merchandising The retail practice of carrying dissimilar lines to generate added sales volume.

search qualities Physical qualities that enable products to be examined and compared. This eases the task of choosing between them.

secondary data Previously published matter.

selective distribution The selection of a small number of retailers to handle the firm's product line.

selling agent An agent wholesaling intermediary who is responsible for the total marketing program for a firm's product line.

service A product without physical characteristics; a bundle of performance and symbolic attributes designed to produce consumer want satisfaction.

shaping The process of applying a series of rewards and reinforcement so that more complex behaviour can evolve over time.

shopping products Products that are usually purchased only after the consumer has compared competing products.

simple random sample A probability sample in which every item in the relevant universe has an equal opportunity of being selected.

single-offer strategy The attempt to satisfy a large or a small market with one product and a single marketing program.

skimming pricing Choosing a high entry price; to sell first to consumers who are willing to pay the highest price, then reduce the price.

social class The relatively permanent divisions in a society into which individuals or families are categorized based on prestige and community status.

social responsibility The marketer's acceptance of the obligation to consider profit, consumer satisfaction, and the well-being of society as being of equal value in evaluating the performance of the firm.

socio-cultural environment The mosaic of societal and cultural components that are relevant to the organization's business decisions.

sorting The process that alleviates discrepancies in assortment by re-allocating the outputs of various producers into assortments desired by individual purchasers.

specialty advertising Sales promotion medium that utilizes useful articles to carry the advertiser's name, address, and advertising message.

specialty products Products that are highest in both effort and risk, due to some unique characteristics that cause the buyer to prize that particular brand.

specialty store Retailer that handles only part of a single line of products.

specifications Specific descriptions of needed items for prospective bidders.

SSWDs Single, separated, widowed, or divorced people.

stagflation High unemployment and a rising price level at the same time.

Standard Industrial Classification (SIC) codes A series of industrial classifications developed by the federal government for use in collecting detailed statistics for each industry.

status Relative position in a group.

status quo objectives Objectives based on the maintenance of stable prices.

stock turnover The number of times the average inventory is sold annually.

straight rebuy A recurring purchase decision involving an item that has performed satisfactorily and is therefore purchased again by a customer.

subliminal perception A subconscious level of awareness.

supermarket Large-scale, departmentalized retail store offering a large variety of food products.

supplies Regular expense items necessary in the daily operation of a firm, but not part of its final product.

supply curve The marginal cost curve above its intersection with average variable cost.

SWOT analysis A method used for analyzing a firm's chances for success in a market under the headings of *strengths, weaknesses, opportunities,* and *threats.*

systematic sample A probability sample that takes every nth item on a list, after a random start.

tangible attributes Those attributes that can be experienced by the physical senses, such as sight, touch, and smell.

target market A market segment that a company chooses to serve.

target market decision analysis The evaluation of potential market segments.

target return objectives Either short-run or long-run goals, usually stated as a percentage of sales or investment.

tariff A tax levied against products imported from abroad.

task-objective method A sequential approach to allocating marketing communications budgets that involves two steps: (1) defining the realistic communication goals the firm wants the marketing communications mix to accomplish; and (2) determining the amount and type of marketing communications activity required to accomplish each of these objectives.

technological environment The applications of knowledge based on scientific discoveries, inventions, and innovations.

teleshopping The selection and electronic purchase of merchandise that has been displayed on a computer.

test marketing The selection of areas considered reasonably typical of the total market, and introducing a new product to these areas with a total marketing campaign to determine consumer response before marketing the product nationally.

tied selling An arrangement whereby a supplier forces a dealer who wishes to handle a product to also carry other products from the supplier or to refrain from using or distributing someone else's product.

total customer satisfaction A situation where a good or service totally conforms to the customer's requirements.

trade discounts Payments to channel members or buyers for performing some marketing function normally required of the manufacturer.

trade fairs Periodic shows at which manufacturers in a particular industry display their wares for visiting retail and wholesale buyers.

trade industries Organizations, such as retailers and wholesalers, that purchase for resale to others.

trade show An organized exhibition of products based on a central theme.

trade-ins Deductions from an item's price of an amount for the customer's old item that is being replaced.

trademark A brand that has been given legal protection and has been granted solely to its owner.

transfer price The price for sending goods from one company profit centre to another.

truck wholesaler Limited-function merchant wholesaler who markets products that require frequent replenishment.

uniform delivered price The same price (including transportation expenses) that is quoted to all buyers.

unit pricing All prices are stated in terms of some recognized unit of measurement (such as grams and litres) or a standard numerical count.

unitization Combining as many packages as possible into one load.

Universal Product Code A code readable by optical scanners that can print the name of the item and the price on the cash register receipt.

utility The want-satisfying power of a product or service.

value A subjective term that is defined by the customer; part of customer expectations, which are a combination of cost, time, quantity, quality, and human factors.

value added The increase in value of input material when transformed into semi-finished or finished goods.

variety store Retailer that offers an extensive range and assortment of low-priced merchandise.

venture-team concept An organizational strategy for developing new products through combining the management resources of marketing, technology, capital, and management enterprise.

vertical marketing system A network of channel intermediaries organized and centrally managed to produce the maximum competitive impact.

warranty A guarantee to the buyer that the supplier will replace a defective product (or part of a product) or refund its purchase price during a specified period of time.

Weber's Law The higher the initial intensity of a stimulus, the greater the amount of the change in intensity that is necessary in order for a difference to be noticed.

wheel of retailing Hypothesized process of change in retailing, which suggests that new types of retailers gain a competitive foothold by offering lower prices through the reduction or elimination of services; but once established, they add more services and their prices gradually rise, so that they then become vulnerable to a new low-price retailer with minimum services — and the wheel turns.

wholesalers Wholesaling intermediaries who take title to the products they handle.

wholesaling The activities of intermediaries who sell to retailers, other wholesalers, and industrial users but not in significant amounts to ultimate consumers.

wholesaling intermediaries Intermediaries who assume title, as well as agents and brokers who perform important wholesaling activities without taking title to the products.

World Trade Organization (WTO) An institution established to set rules and govern world trade based on the provisions of GATT.

zone pricing The market is divided into different zones and a price is established within each.

Photo Credits

Name and Company Index

Subject Index

READER REPLY CARD

We are interested in your reaction to *Foundations of Marketing*, Sixth Canadian Edition, by M. Dale Beckman, David L. Kurtz, and Louis E. Boone. You can help us to improve this book in future editions by completing this questionnaire.

1. What was your reason for using this book?

❑ university course ❑ continuing education course ❑ personal interest

❑ college course ❑ professional development ❑ other _____

2. If you are a student, please identify your school and the course in which you used this book.

3. Which chapters or parts of this book did you use? Which did you omit?

4. What did you like best about this book?

5. What did you like least about this book?

6. Please identify any topics you think should be added to future editions.

7. Please add any comments or suggestions.

8. May we contact you for further information?

Name: _____

Address: _____

_____

Phone: _____

(fold here and tape shut)

MAIL ➤ POSTE

Canada Post Corporation / Société canadienne des postes

Postage paid
If mailed in Canada

Port payé
si posté au Canada

Business Reply

Réponse d'affaires

0116870399   01

0116870399-M8Z4X6-BR01

Heather McWhinney
Director of Product Development, College Division
HARCOURT BRACE & COMPANY, CANADA
55 HORNER AVENUE
TORONTO, ONTARIO
M8Z 9Z9